RITUALS OF PROSECUTION

The Roman Inquisition and the Prosecution of Philo-Protestants in Sixteenth-Century Italy

JANE K. WICKERSHAM

Rituals of Prosecution

The Roman Inquisition and the Prosecution of Philo-Protestants in Sixteenth-Century Italy

UNIVERSITY OF TORONTO PRESS
Toronto Buffalo London

Toronto Buffalo London
www.utppublishing.com

ISBN 978-1-4426-4500-4

Toronto Italian Studies

Library and Archives Canada Cataloguing in Publication

Wickersham, Jane K., 1971–
Rituals of prosecution : the Roman inquistion and the prosecution of philo-Protestants in sixteenth-century Italy / Jane K. Wickersham.

Includes bibliographical references and index.
ISBN 978-1-4426-4500-4

1. Inquisition – Italy – History – 16th century. 2. Protestants – Italy – History – 16th century. 3. Prosecution – Italy – History – 16th century. 4. Heresy – Italy – History – 16th century. 5. Trials (Heresy) – Italy – History – 16th century. 6. Civil procedure – Italy – History – 16th century. 7. Courts – Italy – History – 16th century. 8. Italy – Church history – 16th century. I. Title.

BX1723.W42 2012 272′.2094509031 C2012-902242-X

This book has been published with the aid of a grant from the University of Oklahoma.

University of Toronto Press acknowledges the financial assistance to its publishing program of the Canada Council for the Arts and the Ontario Arts Council.

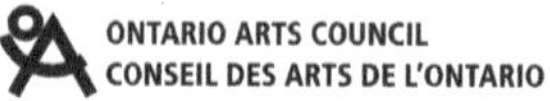

University of Toronto Press acknowledges the financial assistance to its publishing program of the Canada Book Fund.

Contents

Acknowledgments

'Were there Protestants in Italy?' That question, innocently asked of me the summer between my first and second year of graduate school, prompted my interest in researching this topic. My initial answer was, 'I don't know,' and I have many people to thank for their assistance, advice, and support as I have travelled the intellectual journey that has resulted in this book.

The Department of History at Indiana University gave me an encouraging intellectual community during my years as a graduate student, and generously funded my education and dissertation research. My adviser, Arthur Field, and my dissertation committee, Wietse De Boer, Constance Furey, and James C. Riley, proved to be careful readers and challenging questioners, who enriched my intellectual development. I also thank James M. Diehl and the late William B. Cohen for their conversation, humour, and priceless counsel. Michael Grossman, the former editor of the *American Historical Review*, and his editorial staff at the time were committed to providing their graduate assistants with valuable professional experience and advice. Roark Atkinson, Jason Crouthamel, Grace Coolidge, Janine Larmon Peterson, and Mara Lazda have all affected this project's outcome in many ways, both then and now.

Working with Carla Zecher in the Center for Renaissance Studies at the Newberry Library was an invaluable experience. She and Jim Grossman generously provide material, moral, and intellectual support to young scholars beginning their careers. Within that fantastic intellectual community, Diana Maury Robin quickly became a great friend and mentor to whom I owe much.

I am grateful to the University of Oklahoma's Research Council and the College of Arts and Sciences for generously supporting my research and this book's publication. My colleagues in the Department of History have proven to be an incredibly welcoming group. Their collective support has been priceless, but in particular, I thank my department chair, Robert Griswold, for his unfailing encouragement. Jose R. Canoy, Roberta Magnusson, Judith S. Lewis, and Melissa Stockdale all read parts of the manuscript, and I thank them for their help and thoughtful comments.

Thomas S. Mayer, Christopher Black, and Massimo Firpo patiently read this manuscript, gave extensive advice, and saved me from some rather humbling mistakes. At the University of Toronto Press, Ron Schoeffel has gently and kindly guided me along the path to publication, and Anne Laughlin, the managing editor, has guided me through the printing process equally kindly, with the able assistance of Harold Otto, the copy-editor. I also would like to thank the anonymous readers of the manuscript, to whom I will always be grateful for their sharp eyes, thought-provoking comments, and useful suggestions.

The research for this book was conducted in multiple stages over several years, and I have to thank the administration and staff of many archives and libraries for their help and patience with my spoken Italian: Archivio di Stato di Modena; Archivio di Stato di Siena; the Archivio di Stato di Venezia; Archivio Segreto Vaticano; Biblioteca Apostolica Vaticana; Biblioteca comunale dell'Archiginnasio Bologna; Biblioteca Nazionale Firenze; Biblioteca della Fondazione Querini Stampalia Venezia; I Tatti Renaissance Library; and the Trinity College Library Dublin.

Finally, my mother and father, Ellen and Peter Wickersham, always have encouraged me in every endeavour; I owe my love of reading and history to them and can never thank them enough. I also thank my sister (and best friend) Karen for her constant encouragement and my brother Pete, his wife Katya, their children Nick, Abby, and Tommy, and my aunt Ann for cheering me on. At long last, you get to see the end result!

RITUALS OF PROSECUTION

The Roman Inquisition and the Prosecution of Philo-Protestants in Sixteenth-Century Italy

Introduction

> Thus we can see that such a multitude of ceremonies in the mass is a kind of Judaism, manifestly contrary to Christianity. I do not intend to disapprove ceremonies which contribute to decency and public order and increase reverence for the sacrament, provided they are sober and suitable.[1]
>
> John Calvin, 'Short Treatise on the Lord's Supper'

During the Reformation, Christian rites and ritual practices fundamentally changed for many in Western Europe. Protestant theologians created new ritual practices in accord with their doctrines because they were not just a matter of 'mere practice' but inextricably related to any doctrinal conceptualization of the faith.[2] Justification by faith alone did not mean by doctrine alone. Catholic theologians were equally determined to maintain and amplify traditional Catholic practice both to reinvigorate the Church and to ward off heretical incursions into those geographic areas that remained Catholic. While Protestants and Catholics all referred to each other scathingly as heretics, on all sides of the confessional divide, theology was not just a question of establishing correct doctrinal belief, but also one of establishing correct religious practices that would inform, instruct, and edify. Such 'ceremonies,' or ritual practices, were intrinsic to religion itself. But what the Protestants considered to be more pure forms of ritual practice intrinsic to their doctrines, the Catholic Church considered to be intrinsic to the very definition of heresy and schism. Thus, the Roman Inquisition would be recreated in 1542 to prosecute it.

Catholic ritual practice, as it stood on the eve of the Reformation, was rich in its diversity. Mass, Catholicism's main ceremony of worship, often was performed daily by a mulitude of priests in urban areas and attended by the laity; but most lay people took communion once a year at Easter, preceded by their annual confession. The liturgical calendar, furthermore, structured cycles of feasts and celebrations. It began with the First Sunday of Advent in late November or early December, then celebrated Christmas and Epiphany in late December and early January, and held ritual celebrations in February and March immediately before Ash Wednesday, Lent and Easter in spring, followed by the Ascension (40 days after Easter), Pentecost (50 days after Easter), and Corpus Christi (eleven days after Pentecost), All Saints' on 1 November, and finally ending with a new Advent. The other Catholic sacraments – baptism, confirmation, marriage, holy orders, and extreme unction – marked the transformative moments of life, from birth to reaching adulthood to death.

Beyond liturgy and sacraments there were an abundance of para-liturgical ritual practices. Such practices were informed by religious doctrine and related to the Catholic liturgical calendar; but they were more informal in that they could be performed according to lay initiative. The accompaniment or leadership of priests was optional, although clergy often participated. These para-liturgical ritual practices could encompass a wide variety of personal devotions, from reading books of hours to praying the rosary; they could also be collective religious devotions, such as urban areas' devotions to patron saints or the annual Easter pageants in which entire communities would re-enact Christ's crucifixion, descent into Hell, and resurrection.[3]

Protestant theologians would take issue with all of these Catholic ritual practices, the para-liturgical as well as the liturgical. Theologians north of the Alps, as they developed and codified the ritual practices of their rapidly emerging denominations, would alter the sacramental structure by reducing the number to two; alter many of the ways in which the liturgical calendar was celebrated; and attempt to completely stop their congregants from utilizing the majority of Catholic para-liturgical practices. But those same Protestant thelogians, of course, could not agree among themselves as to what should replace them; in the latter part of the sixteenth century religious division went far beyond a dualistic divide between Catholic and Protestant, although many in the Catholic Church preferred just such a conceptual dichotomy at the time. The Protestant theologians north of the Alps, as they developed their nascent denominations, disagreed among themselves as to what constituted appropriate religious ceremonies or ritual practices, precisely because they often disagreed among themselves as to the doctrines informing and structuring them. In fact, the conflicts among the Reformers can be described, at least in part, as originating in how each of them evaluated older Catholic liturgical and para-liturgical practices. Which Catholic ritual practices were legitimate, and which were not? What legitimate meanings could be ascribed to them? Which should be kept, even if in radically altered form? Which should be done away with completely? Each new Protestant belief system answered these questions at least a little bit differently, and all of these new religious beliefs and practices developed with what was, as it was perceived at the time, almost blinding speed.

The nature of religious heterodoxy in sixteenth-century Italian lands only added to this complexity. Many heterodox believers in Italian lands read the printed works of northern European Reformers. But those same heterodox often also listened to preachers native to the Italian states, who developed their own distinctive doctrines that were not necessarily identical to the ideas of any one northern European Reformer. Finally, many philo-Protestants developed their own distinctive approaches to the reform of doctrine and ritual practice through conversation and debate as well as through reading. The Catholic Church ultimately deemed all of these idiosyncratic, eclectic, and indigenous beliefs heterodox, in addition to the doctrines espoused by northern European Reformers. The Roman Inquisition would prosecute such believers alongside those who explicitly identified themselves with one of the northern European confessions and steadfastly utilize the term 'Lutheran' to describe them all.

The religious landcape in latter sixteenth-century Italy was very broad and complex indeed. That the heterodox, regardless of their own particular doctrinal formulations, tended to deviate from what they considered to be the erroneous ritual practices of Catholicism formed important commonalities among all of the heterodox. That the institution reorganized to prosecute the heterodox, the Roman Inquisition, categorically refused to use any terms of differentiation to recognize that complexity is significant. Inquisitors prosecuting them in the mid-to-late sixteenth century focused on ritual practice as a way to gain evidence useful to prosecution. Philo-Protestants in Italian states consistently and regularly argued about or vigorously protested Catholic ritual practices with others and often avoided the ones they felt were illegitimate, pollutive, and harmful to faith. The more dedicated heterodox believers created their own alternative religious communities in order to practise their faith in ways they considered valid and meaningful. And even if some philo-Protestants were inclined to attend Catholic Mass in the hope of avoiding prosecution, they often continued to proselytize elsewhere by critiquing that very institution and Catholic ritual practices in what they hoped would be more discreet ways – behaviour that could be called quasi-Nicodemite.

This book, therefore, examines how the Roman Inquisition defined the relationship between doctrine and ritual practice, and utilized that very relationship to find evidence with which to prosecute philo-Protestants. The Roman Inquisition was the primary means of attempting to maintain orthodoxy forcibly and, as such, was an integral part of the Catholic Church's overall efforts to promote confessional solidarity and identity in Counter-Reformation Italy. This construction of distinct religious identities in the wake of the Reformation, which historians have come to call confessionalization, reached its fullest extent in the later sixteenth and early seventeenth centuries as the Catholic Church, along with its new Protestant counterparts, defined, advanced, and inculcated religious belief and practice through catechisms, sermons, and liturgy. Historians have also noted how all churches, both Catholic and Protestant, attempted to formulate methods of disciplining the religious community: the Roman Inquisition was one such method.[4]

The Roman Inquisition's task was punishing and correcting heretics – defined as those who held heretical beliefs and refused to recant them when caught. The principles of defining heretics, and the legal principles of prosecuting them, however, had been developed and articulated in inquisition manuals over centuries. The authors of those manuals, furthermore, theoretically framed the parameters of correct prosecution legally; and consistently they used the phrase 'word or deed' to describe ideal evidentiary standards. The heretic whose heresy remained only in the mind committed a secret sin left to God to punish. Such a one was the true Nicodemite who attended Catholic services while believing in heresy mentally. Heretical beliefs, externally manifested in word or deed, became public crimes against God and community that required public punishment.[5] In its theoretical conceptualization, then, inquisitorial prosecution was concerned with the relationship between idea and action; it punished actions, but religious belief caused those actions. The wider Catholic community would be protected from public heretical crimes, while the individual heretic also would be given the opportunity to save his or her soul through inquisitorial correction.

As manual authors also recognized, in theory the means of prosecution began within the wider Catholic community, in the form of two witnesses who could testify as to the heretical 'words and deeds' of a prospective defendant. But that defendant would be interrogated in order to produce a confession of wrongdoing. As Francisco Peña asserted, 'because [since] the crime of heresy is devised in the mind and lies hidden in the spirit, commonly it cannot be proved otherwise than through the criminal's own confession.'[6] This confession had to be accompanied by remorse and a willingness to be corrected, thereby preserving both the Catholic community and the defendants' souls.

The one thing that could destroy the efficacy of the entire inquisitorial *processo* (or 'process,' as the legal procedure was known at the time) for both individual heretic and the wider Catholic community, was lies. The possibility of lying heretics, faked penitence, and false confessions could never be eliminated entirely, but much of the advice dispensed in inquisition manuals concerning the interrogation of defendants was aimed at minimizing the possibility. For that reason, the authors considered evidence relating to ritual practice to be crucial. A person's engagement with ritual practice – whether continuing to attend Catholic services, avoiding them, arguing with others about them, or engaging in heterodox ritual practices – could serve to indicate the degree of danger the individual posed to the wider Catholic community. Furthermore, such a theoretical approach to prosecution was firmly grounded within the historical development of the inquisition as a legal system. Inquisition manuals, therefore, provide an opportunity to examine the inquisitorial process as it developed historically. New experiences with heresy in the sixteenth century were evaluated according to the inquisition's traditional way of interpreting the role ritual practice had played in identifying and prosecuting heresies in the past.

A comparison of the contents of inquisition manuals to the transcripts of inquisition processes suggests that it was the adaptation of past experience and procedures, updated to fit the varied religious landscape of mid-sixteenth century Italian lands, which allowed the Roman inquisitors to approach preserving what they considered to be the health of Catholicism. But there was a time differential between theory and practice. That the manuals produced in the later sixteenth century lagged behind both the Protestant Reformation and the Roman Inquisition's reorganization in 1542, however, has engendered questions concerning their usefulness to historians. Did they accurately reflect earlier inquisitorial legal practices? By comparing late sixteenth- and early seventeenth-century manuals to inquisition processes held beginning in the mid-sixteenth century, this book seeks to demonstrate that the later manuals, in fact, were reasonably accurate, and reflected how earlier inquisitors had functioned, because both the manual authors and earlier inquisitors dealt with essentially the same legal procedure in theory and in practice – one which emphasized the value of ritual practice as a barometer of religious belief.

This perspective is especially appropriate given that so much of the inquisitorial *processo* was itself a ritualized experience as it was conducted in reality.[7] Most notably, the defendants' experiences before the tribunal followed established patterns and rhythms, and long-established ritualized language described the entire event. At the end of those processes, for example, those who admitted their wrongdoing were sentenced for their spiritual crimes as guilty of being lightly or vehemently suspect in heresy, or guilty of formal heresy. Penitent defendants, therefore, can be referred to as 'suspects in heresy' or as 'convicted suspects' at the ends of their processes. Manual authors, however, also used terms such as 'suspect' or 'suspicion' to describe people, and the evidence they generated to bring about processes, according to the sentence such people should receive at conviction. For clarity the subjects of inquisitorial investigation initiated from evidence will be referred to as 'suspected heretics.'

That descriptive language would reach the public's ears when convicted suspects had to read abjurations, or formal admissions of their enumerated crimes. Convicted suspects also had to perform penance in public. Such ritual punishment (and penance) occurred as much for the purpose of edifying and instructing the orthodox as for reconciling the formerly heterodox and ensuring their continued participation in Catholic ritual practices. The true heretics, of course, were those unwilling to confess, thereby refusing the correction of the Catholic Church. They also offered a public, ritualized lesson to the Catholic community by suffering a public execution at the stake.

The *processo* itself, although conducted in secret, was just as ritualized in language and formulation as the public aspects. Inquisitorial procedure was the product of the Catholic Church's past encounters with heresy, the basic theoretical principles of which had become codified in canon law in the thirteenth century. Those principles were subsequently expanded and modified through the medium of legal commentaries, glosses, and practical manuals over centuries of activity. Medieval inquisitions had been founded in the early thirteenth century as a means of combating heresies of the time, beginning with the Cathar heresy in northern Italy and southern France, and following them the Waldensians. Each individual inquisitorial tribunal was staffed by Dominican, and sometimes Franciscan, friars whom the pope appointed directly to employ the *inquisitio*. Originally a feature of Roman Law, the *inquisitio* properly referred to the judicial process employed to investigate certain crimes. It meant that a judge investigated the crime and controlled any resulting process from beginning to end, as opposed to a judicial process in which the accusation was brought by one citizen against another, with the judge acting as an arbiter between the two. The *inquisitor* brought any civil or criminal charges that resulted from the investigation on his own authority; the participation of an accuser was therefore unnecessary. As churchmen, however, inquisitors required the assistance of the secular arm to arrest, imprison, torture, and execute, thereby avoiding the inquisitors being involved actively in inflicting physical punishment.[8]

After having dealt with Cathar and Waldensian heresy, inquisitors in Italian states continued to function and mostly focused on dealing with witchcraft. By the end of the fifteenth century, inquisitors in Italian lands often served long terms but only dealt with a few cases a year. The Spanish Inquisition, founded in 1478 by Pope Sixtus IV's bull, soon thereafter was organized to be an integrated and permanent institution; its first task was prosecuting *conversos* and *moriscos*, Christians of Jewish and Muslim origin respectively. The bull, however, gave the Spanish crown, in 1478 Ferdinand of Aragon and Isabella of Castile, the right to appoint Dominican inquisitors in their lands. The Spanish Inquisition would therefore remain jurisdictionally separate from the Roman Inquisition and its inquisitors appointed by the Spanish crown.[9]

In 1542, Pope Paul III restructured inquisition tribunals in north-central Italy with his bull *Licet ab initio* in which the existing medieval tribunals were reorganized and expressly given the task of prosecuting philo-Protestants. He created the *Sacra Congregatio romanae et universalis Inquisitionis seu Sancti Officii* (the Congregation of the Roman and Universal Inquisition or Holy Office) as an administration that, in theory, would see to the religious orthodoxy of all Christendom in the wake of the Protestant Reformation. Pope Paul III initially appointed eight cardinals to a council, who acted as general inquisitors and were the supreme judges concerning questions of faith and orthodoxy. The Congregation of Cardinals was expanded to fifteen in 1555 by Pope

Paul IV, who regularly met with it personally, as was his right (although not every pope would do so). These cardinals had the power to delegate their papally derived authority in matters of orthodoxy to other ecclesiastical judges, the inquisitors assigned to a particular city or diocese, and often operated independently from the papacy, to the point of pursuing agendas with which the pope disagreed.[10] Pope Paul III therefore created a hierarchical structure in which local tribunals ideally were subordinated to one central court in Rome led by cardinals, although under varying degrees of papal oversight.

On the Italian peninsula, however, in areas politically controlled by the Spanish, that theory often failed to translate to reality. The Spanish crown ruled Naples through the appointment of viceroys from 1504 until the early eighteenth century. King Philip II (r. 1556–1598), however, was reluctant to allow Roman inquisitors appointed by the pope; and the papacy was equally reluctant to allow Philip to expand the Spanish Inquisition's jurisdiction and authority. Various solutions to the stalemate occurred, including the Roman Holy Office appointing individual *commissari* ('commisaries') to the viceroyalty; delegating the power of investigation to episcopal courts, usually managed by the bishops' vicars; appointing special vicars to travel through designated areas; and designating a selection of Jesuits to manage investigative activities. It was not uncommon for secular royal judges to cooperate with some of these efforts. But by the 1580s, the situation had stabilized; the Congregation of Cardinals in Rome operated with, and through, bishops' courts to prosecute heresy.

The Spanish ruled Milan from 1525 until the early eighteenth century, and there was juridsictional conflict there as well. During the 1540s state governors prosecuted heresy in the face of heterodox sympathy among some churchmen. By the 1550s, individual inquisitors and episcopal vicars, including Michele Ghislieri (the future Pope Pius V), found their attempts to perform their duties stymied by local civil goverments and chapters of cathedral canons, among others. By the 1566, with Philip II's two attempts to implement a Spanish tribunal having been foiled, Archbishop Carlo Borromeo coordinated the activities of inquisitors in Lombardy, although often in conflict with the congregation in Rome and individual inquisitors, particularly concerning cases of witchcraft. The political contentiousness affected inquisitorial efficacy.[11] Finally, the Roman Inquisition generally did not operate in northern Europe, because monarchs such as Francis I and Charles V often preferred to make their own arrangements concerning heresy.

Therefore, in reality the Roman Inquisition operated in most of the city-states in central and northern Italy, the governments of which had to take account of the papacy as both a political and religious institution. The Roman Inquisition's tribunals, however, utilized most of the same procedures employed by medieval and Spanish tribunals. Given that the Roman Inquisition was in 1542 being revived and significantly expanded after a period of relative inactivity, it is not surprising that legal manuals devoted to explaining inquisitorial activities that had developed in past centuries and other geographic locations were also revived and republished.[12] Inquisition manuals had developed in the High Middle Ages (the earliest, the *Processus inquisitionis,* was composed perhaps in 1248 or 1249), concurrent with medieval inquisitions' efforts to deal with the heresies of their time. From the late-thirteenth century onward, however, they expanded dramatically to include procedural guidelines, defining and categorizing different types of heresy, advice concerning interrogation techniques, and descriptions of doctrinal errors that bordered on being works of Catholic apology. In composing these manuals, inquisitorial authors drew on the material stored in their archives, their own experiences, and the vast Catholic corpus of polemical literature stretching back to the early Church.[13] They also came to include the foundational bulls and laws of the institution, as codified in canon law, and the glosses produced by legal experts concerning the constituent parts of the canons, including succeeding generations of *Glossae Ordinariae.*[14] Finally, authors of inquisitors' manuals cited the material contained in other inquisition manuals.

These manuals, in some ways, rendered explications about heterodox ideas safe. Their readers were immediately provided with Catholic antidotes to heterodox ideas and practices. Furthermore, fixing heterodox ideas in manuals meant that the heretics' own works could be destroyed (possible, and indeed often accomplished, in the centuries before the printing press), since inquisitors could consult their own manuals instead of the heretical originals.[15] In addition, manual authors in the sixteenth and seventeenth centuries most likely presented this information in an inherently negative light for a reason. With the invention of the printing press and subsequent development of a lay market for printed books, it was simply not possible to ensure that these manuals would not reach the hands of the literate public beyond professional jurists, although the lay and non-professional audience for legal tomes written in Latin was presumably quite limited.

Antoine Dondaine has proposed the best-known classification of inquisitorial manuals, a static schema based upon his examination of early medieval manuals from the thirteenth century. He distinguished between five distinct types: official texts concerning ecclesiastical jurisdiction and civil authority; consultations written by jurists and members of the ecclesiastical hierarchy; formularies concerning procedure; manuals of practicing inquisitors; and treatises that discussed the doctrines and practices of heretics. As Andrea Errera has pointed out, however, inquisition manuals underwent continuous evolution over the course of centuries. But by the fourteenth century, in at least one case, and among later sixteenth-century authors more generally, the trend was to combine all of these topics into a single manual. Nicholas Eymeric's *Directorium Inquisitorum*, originally written in the fourteenth century and edited for sixteenth-century use by Francisco Peña, for example, contained the relevant canons, their ordinary glosses, formularies, and extensive descriptions of appropriate procedural norms from both time periods. Peña even retained Eymeric's equally extensive doctrinal descriptions of all heresies from the ancient period to the fourteenth century.

By the time authors and editors began producing manuals suited to the reorganized Roman Inquisition, in the last quarter of the sixteenth century, they already had a body of literature expressing a clear sense of history and precedents from which to draw their ideas concerning the definition and prosecution of heresy. Heresy, as it was defined theologically, originally had appeared alongside descriptions of correct legal norms in earlier manuals, but beginning in the later sixteenth century the balance between theology and law in re-edited and new manuals had been adapted to focus on law despite retaining the earlier theological explanations.[16] Historians have pointed out that sixteenth-century tribunals often kept manuals among their papers and records. There was no 'standard' manual, however, nor is it possible to state definitively if inquisitors utilized them daily.

Finally, when the Roman Inquisition chose to deviate from earlier traditions of inquisitorial practice, as it did in a few notable instances, the manuals cited those earlier precedents and provided rationalizations to justify doing so. For example, Roman Inquisition tribunals, unlike their Spanish counterparts, did not confiscate defendants' property permanently for its own use, although temporary confiscations for the duration of processes brought some income. But tribunals in north-central Italy regularly returned property to the repentant (the repentant constituting the vast majority of processes); the property of the minority who were recalcitrant, however, did contribute to tribunals' funding, sometimes for the long term as real estate rented out. Overall funding of the Roman tribunals, however, tended to be unreliable and fell short covering all expenses.[17]

Although variations in legal procedure across time and space were duly noted, variations in heresies were often portrayed as regurgitations of past heresies. That sixteenth-century inquisitors, and later manual authors steadfastly referred to all Reform theologies as 'Lutheranism,' probably served both their authors, and the Catholic Church, propagandistically.[18] Historians now recognize the Protestant Reformation as a distinctively new event theologically, ritually, politically, and culturally, to name but a few significant avenues that have been investigated in modern historical research. But the authors of manuals had a vested interest in representing the religious controversies of their time in the exact opposite light. Propagandistically, a focus on ritual allowed them to claim that the new and rapidly multiplying Protestant sects (not to mention the sheer variety of beliefs and practices among Italians) were not at all 'new.' These heresies, according to many manual authors, were merely new forms of older heresies that the Catholic Church had dealt with and defeated in its past. For example, by focusing on the specific act of baptizing a Christian who had already been baptized once before, authors of manuals in the later sixteenth century were able to claim that the Anabaptists of their own time were merely repeating the earlier mistakes of the Donatist sect of late Antiquity. The theological and historical context of each groups' use of rebaptism was not the point; that the Church had encountered it before, condemned it, and successfully eliminated it, was.[19] In this, manual authors continued the battles between Protestant and Catholic propagandists at the beginning of the Reformation to lay claim to the Ancient Church and the Church Fathers as sources of authority and legitimacy. Both sides attempted to argue that they most resembled the true Ancient Church, and their opponents the ancient heresies, as when Melanchthon charged Catholics with 'Pelagian' heresy.[20]

But recognizing the importance of ritual practice served pratical purposes as well. Heterodox activities, or 'rites and ceremonies,' were readily noticeable and produced appropriate 'points of entry' to begin processes. Some ritual practices of different Protestant denominations were visually similar; and both the heterodox in Italian lands and Protestants north of the Alps tended to object to Catholic sacraments, liturgy, and para-liturgical ritual practices, regardless of their particular doctrinal perspective in so doing. The broad focus on ritual practice, including seemingly minor traditional practices such as refusing to fast during Lent, allowed inquisitors to identify suspected heretics.[21] Inquisitors in the mid-to-late sixteenth century in Italian lands utilized such actions and protests as evidence to prosecute philo-Protestants; examining the reality of those legal processes is one of this book's tasks.

Both sixteenth-century inquisitors and later sixteenth- and seventeenth-century manual authors shared a firm grounding in a legal system that encouraged placing prosecutorial importance upon ritual practice. Later authors expressed a hierarchy of what kinds of evidence (or 'indications,' as they termed it, provided by witness testimony) indicated varying degrees of suspicion of guilt, from which an investigation and process could begin. Statements made in conversation, according to these authors, were too unstable. Conversations, and the words utilized during them, could be misinterpreted, misheard, misconstrued, and manipulated – or at least those who uttered them would try to claim such as a defence. As many manual authors bluntly declared, it was the nature of heretics to lie. What philo-Protestants did, in terms of protesting or criticizing Catholic 'rites and ceremonies,' or embracing alternatives, according to inquisitorial standards of proof, was a more certain form of evidence from which to elicit a confession. As manual authors put it, anyone who participated in heretical rites and ceremonies, or consistently avoided Catholic ones, could hardly be unaware of the significance of such actions. It is another of this book's tasks, therefore, to examine how manual authors evaluated ritual practice, or 'rites and ceremonies,' as legal evidence, method of discovery, and piece of propaganda, within the overall process of defining heresy and prosecuting it and to compare those legal principles to the reality of earlier trials.

I examine four important manuals written to address the particular legal and theoretical context of the Roman Inquisition's earlier activities. One of these manuals was the most popular one of the later sixteenth century, although it had been written originally in the fourteenth century. Nicholas Eymeric (c. 1320–1399), a Dominican theologian, papal chaplain, and inquisitor general of Aragon, completed his manuscript of *Directorium Inquisitorum* in 1376; it was first printed in 1500 with subsequent printings in 1503 and 1536. Eymeric's career was rather contentious; born in Catalonia, he joined the Dominicans in 1334, and completed his theological studies in Paris by 1352. He taught at the

Dominican convent in Barcelona until he became the inquisitor general of Aragon from 1357 to 1360. He continued to participate in inquisitorial activity after 1365, but he was expelled from the realm by Peter IV of Aragon in 1375 for his tactless conduct concerning his inquisitorial duties. He was recalled by King John I in 1388, only to be exiled again by that monarch in 1393 for his offensive behaviour while conducting his duties, especially his role in prosecuting the followers of Raymond Lull and St Vincent Ferrer, both of whom he considered to be theological deviants and prominently featured in his manual. Allowed to return to his native Gerona in 1396, he died there in 1399.[22]

Another Spanish Dominican, Francisco Peña, employed in the Curia at the papal court in Rome, completely re-edited and expanded the work, which was printed for the first time in Rome in 1578. Peña's commentaries concerning Eymeric's original text emphasized the Church's traditions, long-standing arguments for Church and papal authority, and historicized the norms of inquisition procedure from its origins to his own day. Peña, born at Villaroja around 1540, completed his doctorate in theology at the University of Valencia. Thereafter, he spent most of his life on the Italian peninsula, first by moving to the Spanish College in Bologna and earning his doctorate *in utroque iure* (both canon and civil law). It was during this period that Peña developed his interest in inquisitorial law, developing a relationship with Bologna's inquisitor Antonio Balducci, who gave Peña access to the tribunal's archives. He arrived in Rome during the pontificate of Gergory XIII as legal counsel to the Spanish delegation just as the inquisition trial of Bartolomé Carranza, the archbishop of Toledo, was transferred from Spain to Rome in 1567, along with the Spanish judge in charge of the process, Diego Simancas. The entire process was quite contentious, and often is portrayed as a battle between the Spanish and Italian tribunals as to which possessed the better inquisitorial style. Peña also would serve on the committee that reviewed and printed a definitive edition of canon law at the behest of Gregory XIII. He served as the auditor for the Crown of Aragon from 1588 to 1604, and as dean of the Rota from 1604 until his death in 1612. Peña, despite his professional duties, managed to be a prolific editor of inquisitorial texts; among others, he edited and put into print the texts of Ambrogio Vignati, Paolo Grillandi, Juan de Rojas, Jean Gerson, and Bernard of Como. In Venice in 1584 he published an edition combining the work of Vignati, Palacios Rubios, Grillandi, Rategno, and Rojas, along with his own commentary, entitled *De Iudiciis Criminalibus S. Inquisitionis*; soon after he published an edition of Zanchino Ugolini's work, as it had been edited by his contemporary, Camillo Campeggi, inquisitor general of Ferrara and Modena, with his own commentary and additional material drawn from Simancas.

All of those works were cited in Peña's most definitive edition of the *Directorium Inquisitorum*. Peña utilized the 1503 printed edition of Eymeric's work, corrected against four manuscript versions, two of which came from the Biblioteca Apostolica and the Bologna tribunal's archives. Structurally, Peña divided the manual into three sections. The first part consisted of seventy-five pages explaining the true faith, mainly drawn from other texts and glosses of canon law. Peña only made twenty-six comments concerning the material in this section of the manual, and it mainly served to establish correct doctrine and the Church's authority to prosecute heresy. The second part was devoted to topics concerning inquisitorial authority and procedure, selected for the most part from canon law sources, and a series of fifty-eight *quaestionum*, or questions, regarding correct practices. To Eymeric's original work Peña added eighty-three glosses, which were more extensive than those of the first part of the manual. The third part provided an explanation of inquisitorial procedure in practice: how to call witnesses, arrest defendants, take testimony, and other procedural issues. Eymeric wrote 131 questions, and Peña 180 glosses to address those questions. Besides the 1578 edition, there were three more editions printed in Rome, in 1585, 1587, and 1597, in addition to two Venetian editions produced in 1591 and 1607. Peña expanded his comments beginning with the 1585 edition; the 1587 edition is considered to be definitive, and was reprinted three times in 1595. It was one of the most widely known manuals of its kind, and was considered the most comprehensive manual for inquisitors in the late sixteenth and early seventeenth centuries. It came to be used as the primary source for most subsquent manuals. It stands, therefore, as the most important manual of its day. [23]

The author of the *Tractatus de haeresi*, Propsero Farinacci was, in contrast, an Italian and for much of his life a layman; he did not receive the first tonsure until 1594 in order to accept a canonical benefice at St John Lateran. Probably educated in both canon and civil law at Perugia by 1566, he was a brilliant jurist, writing a five-volume work which comprehensively covered all legal procedure, of which the *Tractatus* was the fifth and last, from 1581 to 1614; all five volumes would become standard legal reading for the next two centuries. Yet he also was completely unprincipled and impetuous; he quite famously lost an eye in a fight. Farinacci first came to prominence under the patronage of Cardinal Marco Sittico d'Altemps by defending the cardinal's 'nephew' against charges of rape in 1585; he also defended Beatrice Cenci and her relations by marriage, who were charged with parricide. These cases made his reputation, and he was supported by several cardinals and popes during his career. He held a variety of positions in the papal bureaucracy, including working for Camillo Borghese in the Camera Apostolica; as Pope Paul V, Borghese appointed Farinacci procurator general of the fiscal in 1606. Farinacci would find himself fired from that office in 1611 for abusing his position. Among other irregularities, Farinacci trumped up charges against the marchese of Riano, Paolo Emilio Cesi, in order to recover the 1,000 scudi he had lost to Cesi in a game of craps. Farinacci's (mostly) successful career, furthermore, progressed despite his multiple arrests, as in 1584 for throwing an arquebus off the Ponte Sisto rather than be caught bearing arms illegally, among other incidents. Most notoriously, he was charged with sodomy in 1595. The sixteen-year old boy who had accused Farinacci later withdrew his accusation – under torture.

His legal publications were well respected, even if Farinacci himself was not. All five volumes were printed for the first time in 1616, two years before his death. The fifth volume, the *Tractatus*, was organized according to eighteen *quaestionibus*, each divided into multiple *regulis*, in which Farinacci would posit general rules. Each of the *regulae*, however, would be modified by *ampilationibus* and *limitationibus* ('amplifications' and 'limitations') explaining a multitude of qualifications and limitations, in which Farinacci would quote every major legal opinion on the subject at hand and not a few minor ones. The work, therefore, was designed to explicitly note concordance or disagreement, which is extremely useful in identifying contentious or problematic points of inquisitorial procedure across centuries of scholarship.[24] Farinacci also practiced secular law, and therefore demonstrated how inquisitorial and secular legal practice converged or diverged; an examination of his manual therefore contributes a broader perspective concerning norms of inquisitorial practice.

The two other manuals examined here were both produced in the early seventeenth century by men who had worked for inquisition tribunals; their perspectives, as authors who also applied these principles in practice, are valuable indeed. Cesare Carena's *Tractatus de Officio Sanctissimae Inquisitionis*, first published in 1636, and Eliseo Masini's *Sacro Arsenale* of 1621 were both much shorter than those of Peña and

Farinacci. Masini wrote the bulk of his work in Italian rather than Latin, although some Latin passages remained. Carena's manual consisted of nineteen *titulorum,* which were then subdivided into thematic points of explanation numbering anywhere from five to over twenty. The nineteen titles were divided into three parts – the first addressing the inquisition's right to jurisdiction in matters concerning the faith, the second defining heresies and crimes against the faith, and the third detailing inquisitorial procedure. His biography is rather sparse, deriving only from references he made about himself in his works. A native of Cremona, he earned an MA in theology at Padua in 1613 and a degree in jurisprudence at Pavia in 1619. Upon his return to Cremona, he became an auditor for Cardinal Pietro Campori, bishop of Cremona, and was appointed consultor to the Holy Office in Cremona (1626) and, finally, procurator fiscal for the tribunal in 1627. He also published Francisco Peña's manuscript concerning inquisitorial procedure, entitled *Introductio seu praxis inquisitorum,* which had circulated widely at local inquisition tribunals. Together with Masini's *Sacro Arsenale,* Carena's *Tractatus* was the most widely diffused manual of the first half of the seventeenth century.[25]

Masini's manual and the *Directorium Inquisitorum* remain the manuals most often consulted by modern scholars. Masini's career was an exercise in the varieties of practical experiences as an inquisitor, which no doubt affected the contents of his manual. After Masini entered the Dominican order in 1584, his career was advanced by the patronage of Agostino Galamini, the inquisitor of Brescia (1592) and Genoa (1597–1600). When Galamini became a commissary for the congregation in Rome in 1604, Masini accompanied him. Masini, through Galamini's influence, became inquisitor of Ancona in 1607 and Mantua beginning in 1608; from 1609 until his death in 1627 he was inquisitor of Genoa. In Genoa, he oversaw at least twenty-eight public abjurations for heresy. But Masini also was disciplined twice by the congregation in Rome for procedural errors, perhaps placing him in a unique position to advise other potential inquisitors when he wrote his manual later in his career.

Masini, in addition to writing mostly in the vernacular – the first inquisition manual in Italian – structured the work in two very accessible parts. In the first, he discussed inquisitorial procedure, beginning with the nature of inquisitorial authority and who would be subject to it and ending with the appropriate formulas to use when absolving penitent convicts of excommunication. In between, he explained the basic variations of processes, in conversational style, including sample formularies as templates for his readers. In the second part, Masini wrote pithy pieces of advice in what resembles modern-day bullet-point format. Masini no longer cited his authorities, as Peña, Farinacci, and Carena had. But he did utilize other works; his chapter concerning witchcraft relied heavily upon the uncredited *Instructio pro formandis processibus in causis strigum*.[26]

Masini's work, along with Carena's *Tractatus*, represent the adaptation of inquisitorial tradition to the cumulative experiences of dealing with a multi-confessional Europe. For example, when explaining the proper procedure for torture, Masini stated that it was possible to absolve a criminal who survived two torture sessions while continuing to deny the 'first confession.' He said that this could happen if the criminal had been 'tortured enough,' and if the proof was not 'very urgent.' Otherwise, the criminal should be sent to a third round of torture. [27] The issue of how many times a recalcitrant defendant could be tortured before being let go had been contested hotly within the pages of Peña's and Farinacci's works; by Masini's time, a rationale had been worked out to reconcile both judicial perspectives. Inquisitorial procedure operated according to circumscribed boundaries, but within those parameters there was some room to maneuver or to employ different interpretations of prosecutorial principles. Individual inquisitors could choose to be either more lenient or more severe; they also increasingly responded to the requirements of those further up the hierarchy in Rome. [28]

My first chapter situates the book within the broader scope of ritual studies and addresses how heterodoxy came to develop in Italian lands in the early sixteenth century, from sources both domestic and foreign. It seeks to establish what constituted Catholic ritual practice and the ways in which a variety of heterodox would seek to change it. In the next two chapters I examine the nature of ritual practice as evidence and how manual authors established the criteria by which it could be used to begin a process. In Chapter 2 I illustrate how manual authors had adapted the Catholic Church's past encounters with heresy to the new context of the Protestant Reformation by the late sixteenth century, particularly regarding how inquisition manuals, canon law, and Catholic traditions analysed the role ritual practice played in defining and categorizing heresy. Manual authors achieved that adaptation by formulating a hierarchy of actions they considered to be indicative of commitment to heterodox doctrines.

In Chapter 3 I consider the polemical literature of Protestant Reformers, both Italian and northern European, concerning Catholic ritual practice, and the concomitant issues related to ritual, especially the impact they believed it would ostensibly have on the faith of philo-Protestants living in Catholic lands. I also examine the inquisition's rules about witnesses, since it was through the testimony of witnesses that inquisitors could gather enough evidence to begin prosecution. Finally, I compare the later recommendations of inquisition manuals to earlier process records from the mid-sixteenth century to demonstrate a concordance between the two, if not firmly establish a definitive path of transmission.

In this chapter, and all subsequent chapters, the *processi* were selected for the legal principles they exemplify. For example, in 'Word and Deed: Indications of Suspicion,' I examine the discovery of potential heretics, from the inquisitors' and witnesses' points of view in mid-to-late sixteenth-century processes. I also utilize the testimony of witnesses to investigate the importance of proselytizing, or evangelical activity, to philo-Protestants in Italy, and the ways in which their attitudes toward Catholic ritual practice, or engagement in heterodox alternatives, contributed to their prosecutions.

It should be noted that notaries were instructed to record testimony of both witnesses and defendants in the vernacular exactly as it was spoken. Unfortunately, this was not always the case – answers recorded in the third or second person, or partially in Latin, do make appearances. As other scholars have noted, what was recorded during a process was dependent upon the notaries and their methods, which could be varied indeed. Some processes' records examined by other researchers show signs of having been reworked from notes, while other surviving records were copies of originals. Some records (although none used here) indicate that what was recorded was not everything that was said. Other records, including some used in this work, were highly detailed, to the point of recording the physical reaction and attitude of the person being questioned, for example. Despite flawed record-keeping, however, the records nevertheless reveal, in many cases, genuine voices of witnesses and defendants.[29] Finally, the testimony was also not always grammatically correct by modern standards, or even the standards of the time. Yet those grammatical flaws represent the fact that many of those who came before tribunals were sixteenth-century 'everymen,' who were dealing with a very intimidating and possibly dangerous set of circumstances. Therefore, for the sake of authenticity I have chosen to leave the original grammatical flaws intact, and the idiosyncrasies of notaries will be noted where applicable.

The remaining chapters examine how ritual played an important role within *processi*. Among the many other forms of evidence, ritual practice was one piece of the total puzzle inquisitors were charged with solving. But manual authors, and inquisitors, working a few decades apart, of course, made it clear, in practice and in theory, that they hoped evidence relating to ritual practice could be used to gauge or interpret other types of evidence. In Chapter 4 I examine two representative sample defendants who recanted and reconciled themselves to the Church in Modena in 1555. The chapter also discusses the criteria by which inquisitors decided to employ mercy in their treatment of defendants. In particular, the speed of confession, represented by Giovanni Terrazzano's process, and pleas of ignorance, relevant to Claudio da Roteglia's, might incline inquisitors to accept defendants' characterization of themselves in the best, and most Catholic, light possible.

In Chapter 5, I examine three *processi* of suspected heretics who attempted to defend themselves much more aggressively, even confrontationally. In the processes of Prospero, a *capeler*, and Battista Amai della Bambine, that confrontation was literal; the tribunal in Venice, prosecuting them in 1572, arranged for the two poor artisans to confront each other in person in the hopes of extracting full confessions from them both after several rounds of questioning proved less than satisfactory. Bartolomeo Nelli, thanks to the activities of his lawyer, almost succeeded in convincing the tribunal that his heresies were not all that serious – until his conscience dictated that he attempt to stand firm in his faith. The tactics he and his lawyer, Lucarini, employed to mount a defence before the tribunal in Siena in 1559–1560 reveal the limits and potential pitfalls of procedure. Zuane (Giovanni) Finetti's case is, admittedly, somewhat singular – he successfully defended himself against false accusations and was declared innocent by the Venetian tribunal in 1566–1567. The charges his accusers chose to falsify, however, reveal much about popular perceptions of philo-Protestant heresy at the time; and Finetti's defence reveals how tribunals could use defendants' records of ritual practice as key pieces of evidence. Each case is representative of a range of possible permutations in inquisitorial procedure, both in the tactics used by inquisitors and the individual 'qualities' of suspected heretics and their efforts to defend themselves.

Torture would only be used against the very small group of defendants (less than 5 percent) who refused to confess. There could be two permutations to the refusal to confess; an accused could deny both 'words and deeds' and any intent, or confess to having said and done what the witnessses reported, but deny any heretical intent in so doing and saying. Any denial of either the evidence or heretical intent would result in the employment of torture in an attempt to elicit confessions. The *processi* selected for examination in Chapter 6, therefore, are not necessarily representative of the majority of any tribunal's caseload, but they do demonstrate the outer limits of inquisition as a legal procedure. These processes also demonstrate why torture, as the option of last resort, was thought to be necessary to maintain the integrity of the procedure as a whole. Pietro Curioni (prosecuted in Modena in 1568), Zuanbattista Sambeni (Venice in 1568–1569), and Girolamo (Hieronimo), a shoemaker in Udine (1543–1544), all were led into torture chambers because the respective tribunals suspected they were lying and seeking to conceal what had to be revealed in order to neutralize the threat to the broader Catholic community.

In Chapter 7, however, I discuss the reason that inquisitors considered confessions and reconciliation to the Church their success stories, and executions their failures. The inquisitor's task was not only to uncover heresy and investigate it, but also to shepherd the heterodox back into the orthodox community.[30] Inquisitors accomplished this through the penances they assigned to those sentenced as guilty but willing to confess to heretical error. For example, one defendant, sentenced to the galleys, was instructed to pray the Hail Mary (a prayer Protestants decried as insufficiently Biblical) several times a day, ensuring his rehabilitation as a Catholic even as he rowed for his punishment.

In this way, inquisitors pulled the heterodox back into the orthodox community; those convicted of heterodoxy performed the very actions they had avoided, protested, and criticized, and that often had signaled their heterodox identity in the first place. Manual authors stated that such penance served to expiate the public sin of heresy, but there is reason to think that these later manual authors, and mid-sixteenth-century inquisitors, hoped for a reform (for lack of a better word) of belief as well. Philo-Protestants sentenced to such rehabilitative acts would find themselves participating in those very ceremonies of the Catholic Church that non-Catholics widely considered a pollutant to philo-Protestant faith. Abjured and sentenced suspects in heresy might very well have viewed their penances as adversely affecting their faith; for inquisitors, requiring convicted suspects in heresy to perform Catholic religious rites and practices might very well have been appropriate penance indeed.

The prosecution of heterodoxy in Italian lands, therefore, took place within the boundaries of appropriate inquisitorial practice, developed according to the legal norms of canon law over centuries. But the prosecution of heresy was as much a function of theology as law; of necessity, the authors of inquisitorial manuals had to interpret philo-Protestant ideas and practices in terms appropriate for the prosecution of it. By utilizing ritual as a means of investigation, prosecution, and rehabilitation, the Roman Inquisition maintained, defended, and perhaps even improved the unity and community of Catholicism in north-central Italy.

Chapter One

Philo-Protestantism in Italian Lands: Beliefs and Practices

Alessandro del Fornari's religious narrative is indicative of how the mid-sixteenth century's religious controversies played out in an urban envirnoment among average people. He had already spent June of 1568 in Modena's city prison because he had hit his wife with a shoemaking tool during an argument. But while there, Fornari apparently preferred to discuss topics of a religious nature – he had told his fellow prisoners that purgatory did not exist, causing quite the commotion in the cells. One of the other prisoners, called Florio, had countered that it did. When Fornari had repeatedly insisted that the Catholic Church was wrong about purgatory, Florio had threatened to report Fornari to the brothers at San Domenico because he deserved 'the fire.' Alessandro shot back that Florio deserved to stay in prison because he could not pay his debts. Thus the argument ended. Florio, though, made good on his threat; he, along with Cristoforo da San Martino, Tommaso, and Bartolomeo gave testimony about Fornari to Modena's Dominican inquisitors, housed in their convent of San Domenico.[1]

Modena's Holy Office found this more than enough evidence to open a process against Fornari. In addition, another witness, Diana (Florio's wife), testified that Fornari was publicly known as a 'Lutheran' because he ate meat on Fridays and Saturdays, blasphemed against the Holy Mother and the saints, and had once yelled 'God, God, traitor!' to an image of Christ.[2] Once the tribunal in Modena began the process in March of 1568, exactly how Fornari had come to their attention became clear. Fra Niccolò da Finale took testimony from Florio, who said that he had told Fra Domenico da Imola about Fornari in the cathedral (after paying off his debts, one presumes), since Fornari was obviously a 'Lutheran.' In addition to purgatory, Fornari had argued about the cult of the saints and the use of images in worship with his fellow prisoners. After they had been released Fornari had come to Florio's house and broken a crucifix in anger and yelled '*Dio traditore!*' (apparently their association extended past their prison days despite their religious arguments).[3]

On 31 March, Alessandro was brought into the tribunal to answer questions. After he promised to tell the truth, the inquisitor asked Fornari if he went to confession, to which Fornari replied that he had gone to sacramental confession with a priest and had always believed it was necessary. Fornari then proceeded to confess all of his errors. He believed it was permissible to eat meat anytime; that papal indulgences held no validity; and that there was no purgatory in the next life. He had learned these errors, he claimed, from the heterodox preaching of Bartolomeo della Pergola about twenty-five years before. Pergola, a Minorite friar, nevertheless had preached such heresies in Modena in 1544. When the tribunal asked if he had any prohibited books, Fornari replied that he did not because he could neither read nor write. He also denied having any accomplices in heresy. The following day, 1 April, Fornari confessed to the above errors. A note included on the last page of his trial said that he was sentenced to house arrest.[4] By 1568, such a sentence was not the worst the tribunal could have imposed, since being held under house arrest would allow Fornari to continue practicing his profession. It was an important concession to make for a shoemaker expected to support a family, but it still allowed the convicted suspect Fornari to come into contact with friends, neighbours, and customers.

Fornari's process illustrates the complexities of inquisitorial prosecution, and exemplifies the difficult decisions inquisitors had to make. When brought before Fra Niccolò, Fornari admitted to holding some heterodox beliefs, and attempting to pass those beliefs onto others through discussion in prison. Additionally, he had practiced his beliefs by refusing to fast during Lent and engaging in iconoclasm. He had learned his hetereodox beliefs in the mid-1540s from the mouth of a Minorite friar, who had been the traditional Lenten preacher chosen to educate the Catholic Modenese community as to the meaning of Christ's Passion and sacrifice for humanity in the weeks before Easter. Bartolomeo della Pergola had preached heresy instead, to the pleasure of some in the town and the outrage of others at the time. Fornari had found at least some of his preaching amenable and remembered it for twenty-five years.

Yet, before the tribunal Fornari had maintained that he remained within the bounds of the Catholic faith and practices, mainly through asserting that he practiced the Catholic sacrament of confession – especially since yearly confession and communion at Easter had been required by the Catholic Church since 1215. Was Fornari simply eclectic in his religious beliefs and practices, which many theologians at the time would have interpreted as contradictory, such as attending sacramental confession yearly and denying the existence of purgatory? Or was he a quasi-Nicodemite – a convinced philo-Protestant who continued to attend Catholic ritual practices as 'cover' while proselytizing philo-Protestant beliefs elsewhere? Or could Fornari simply have not realized that what the Minorite friar had preached was not good Catholic doctrine until the inquisitor of San Domenico pointed out that fact to him?

Given the variety of religious opinions on the Italian peninsula at the time, and the way in which those opinions were evangelized, all three interpretations were possible. Italian philo-Protestants, as has long been recognized in historical scholarship, defied neat and easy classification in the sixteenth century. Less recognized are the ways in which such diversity presented a prosecutorial problem for the Roman Inquisition. I argue that the inquisition solved that problem through investigating ritual practice at the time; this later became the focus of the late sixteenth- and early seventeenth-century's inquisitorial manuals' explication of the 'new' heresies. Although it is impossible to definitively chart a means of transmission, both manual authors and inquisitors dealt with the same inquisitorial procedure derived from canon law. Recognizing the importance of matters relating to ritual practice, grounded in the historical development of inquisitorial practice as it would be expressed by manual authors, proved useful in identifying suspected heretics and provided a solid foundation of evidence well-suited to prosecution. In practice in the mid-sixteenth century, philo-Protestants in Italian states, regardless of their particular doctrinal perspective, produced a range of responses to Catholic ritual practices. Theoretically, manual authors noted the uses to which evidence relating to ritual practice could be put in their late sixteenth- and early seventeenth-century manuals.

To demonstrate why ritual practice was a useful unifying factor in approaching the prosecution of philo-Protestants, in practice and later in theory, in this chapter I examine three key historiographic contexts. First, I examine the full diversity of philo-Protestant beliefs in Italian lands to explain the exact nature of the crisis with which the inquisition had to grapple. This chapter also examines the nature and ubiquity of Catholic ritual practice – public, communal, and private – to illustrate exactly those ritual practices to which philo-Protestants often would respond by avoidance and protest. Finally, the chapter examines how Catholics' and Protestants' differing theologies began to affect ritual practice and religion as it was experienced on a daily basis, thus becoming the theological sources of Italian philo-Protestant responses to Catholic ritual practice. Examining the historiography of those three contexts places the Roman Inquisition's activities, and perspective concerning ritual practice, within the larger context of Catholic reform and the Counter-Reformation.

Reform and Ritual Practice: Historiographic Perspectives

Those two terms – 'Catholic reform,' and 'Counter-Reformation' – have been the subject of much historiographic debate within successive phases of scholarship, and deservedly so. Catholic reform was an important focus for many in the Catholic Church long before Martin Luther's initial protest in 1517 and continued to be important throughout the sixteenth century. Prior to the Reformation, the need for a church reform of some kind increasingly had been recognized as a necessity in Italian lands as well as north of the Alps, and by both laypeople and clerics alike. The Fifth Lateran Council, for example, held from 1512 to1517, had recognized the financial abuses and absenteeism of the Church leadership, which often had consequences concerning the Church's ability to effectively minister to the laity; religious orders, such as the Franciscan Observants, had recognized a need to return to autsterity and to minister to the laity through their role as confessors; and Savonarola attempted reform in Florence, where the Dominican friar used his prophetic sermons to call for political and moral renewal against the secular and avaricious papacy of Pope Alexander VI, which led to his fiery execution for heresy in 1498.[5] Catholic reform, furthermore, continued to influence and inform the Catholic Church's ecclesiastical structures and theological emphases throughout the sixteenth century, including the structure of the Roman Inquisition. As William Hudon has put it when describing the career of the sixteenth-century Italian prelate Marcello Cervini (Pope Marcellus II, 1555), 'he sought to move the institution forward by – at least in part – looking backward.'[6]

While it is important to recognize the broader currents of Catholic reform, which predated the Reformation, there were significant ways in which the Catholic Church's actions after 1517 were a response to the new conditions the Reformation presented. There were institutions within the early modern Catholic Church that were created specifically to 'counter' the development of Reformation doctrines north of the Alps and heterodoxy in Italian lands, the Roman Inquisition chief among them.[7] Therefore I do not think it inappropriate to refer to the Counter-Reformation within the pages of this book, given its subject and analytical goals.

Heterodoxy in Italian lands, as also has long been recognized historiographically, in some ways predated the northern Protestant Reformation as well. Federico Chabod has identified currents of heterodox belief native to Italian lands, as has Delio Cantimori. Both scholars were interested in distinguishing distinctly 'Italian' concepts of heterodox belief from those of northern Europeans, and identifying those members of the Roman hierarchy who, they proposed, subsequently became sympathetic to Luther's ideas.[8]

Such independent doctrinal development, and their subsequent branding as heterodox, was important to the historiographical framework for some scholars, especially Benedetto Croce and Cantimori. In the view of those scholars, there were those in the Church hierarchy sympathetic to, but not identical with, northern European Reformers, who attempted to maintain one Church in Western Europe through negotiation and compromise with Reformers north of the Alps. This historiographic school of thought, furthermore, posited the dominance of these irenic ecclesiastics, called *spirituali,* until the perceived failure of negotiation caused a backlash against them, led by the *intransigenti* who had favoured aggressive repression from the first. This interpretive schematic of a sharp turn and sudden break in the early 1540s – from discussion and negotiation to repression – although elegant in its dichotomies, has been disrupted definitively by generations of scholarship. Scholars such as Eric Cochrane, among others, have taken issue with the concept that post-1540s repression had held back 'Italian' development through inhibiting cultural and intellectual production after the high point achieved during the Renaissance; he also pointed out that many deemed *intransigenti* knew and worked with *spirituali,* and vice-versa.[9] As William Hudon has noted, 'the outmoded generalizations that divided early modern Italian prelates into warring camps of *spirituali* versus *intransigenti* always sounded like the good guys against the bad guys [. . .],' but the distinctions between those of a more or less irenic frame of mind were not quite that sharp; nor did the refounding of the Roman Inquisition in 1542 represent a sharp break and immediate turn towards harsh repression.[10]

According to that dichotomous schema, the Roman Inquisition was recreated after the failure of the Colloquy of Ratisbon in 1541 (Rogensburg), which had been called to negotiate a doctrinal settlement between Catholics and Lutherans. Cardinal Gasparo Contarini had chaired the meeting held between Catholic theologians, such as Johann Eck and Johannes Gropper, and their Protestant counterparts, such as Martin Bucer and Melanchthon. Although the colloquy has often been portrayed as a naïve attempt on the part of the *spirituali* to integrate Lutheranism into the structure of the Catholic Church, recent scholarship, especially that of Elisabeth Gleason, has emphasized that churchmen, such as Contarini, first and foremost emphasized the unity of the Church through papal obedience. Although Contarini had come to a theological position resembling justification by faith alone as early as 1511, and throughout the colloquy was determined not to allow disputes over word choice to keep Protestants and Catholics apart, he also thought that his attitude of irenic cooperation might serve to 'shame' the Lutherans into listening. Ultimately the colloquy broke down over differing interpretations of the Eucharist after producing a statement of 'double justification,' or justification through both faith and works, which both Paul III and Protestant Reformers refused to ratify precisely because it was so vaguely worded. Eucharist, and the Catholic belief of transubstantiation, or the literal presence of Christ as body and blood after the consecration of the bread and wine, was non-negotiable for Contarini no matter how irenic his attitude.[11]

Much of the historiography regarding the *spirituali* also has priveleged discussion of doctrine – orthodox or heterodox, northern European or Italian – and largely overlooked how changes in doctrine led to, and were inseparable from, changes in ritual practice. There is reason to focus on doctrine, of course. The beginning of the Reformation as an event has been tied, historiographically, to Martin Luther's doctrinal formulation of justification by faith alone. But the occasion for Luther to express that doctrine came about because of the sale of indulgences. When Luther protested their sale in Germanic territory by posting his *Ninety-Five Theses* for academic debate at the University of Wittenberg in 1517, it was at first not necessarily apparent that it would lead to the splintering of western Christendom and the founding of new denominations of Christianity, complete with new ritual practices expressing what Reformers considered to be correct doctrine. Pope Leo X had authorized the sale of indulgences to support the reconstruction of St Peter's Basilica in Rome; Leo also allowed Albrecht Hohenzollern to become the archbishop of Mainz, one of the seven electors of the Holy Roman Emperor, while he continued to hold the see of Halberstadt and archbishopric of Magdeburg.

Indulgences, and the principle of paying for them, were theologically valid in the eyes of the Catholic Church's economy of salvation as it stood in the late medieval period. Justification and salvation were equally a product of faith and the performance of good works. Good works, furthermore, for the Catholic Church, were inextricably bound up with the sacrament of confession. Sacramental confession to a priest in this time had three constituent parts: genuine contrition on the part of the sinner; the act of confessing those sins to the priest; and reception of absolution, and penance, usually in the form of performing good works. Indulgences allowed contrite Christians to forgo the performance of penance in exchange for payments, conceived of as donations to worthy Church causes, such as rebuilding St Peter's Basilica. The good works of the living, furthermore, could aid the souls of the dead in purgatory in which the flawed but faithful could continue their spiritual purification before their final union with God.

At the time many Catholics protested the sale of induglences as a scandal but did not question the necessity of confession as a sacrament and good works as penance – both ritual practices to which indulgences were linked. But Martin Luther protested the doctrine itself; he believed that good works were of no justificatory use for either the living or the dead, although he would always emphasize good works as a necessary product of faith and mark of good Christian brotherhood and charity.[12] Justification by faith alone became the cornerstone of his theology, and it was the principle that all subsequent Protestant Reformers would share. Luther initially was condemned by Catholic authorities on the grounds that he questioned papal authority to issue indulgences. But it was Luther's insistence that indulgences, and ultimately purgatory, were not present in the New Testament that proved to be the source of the separation from the Catholic Church.[13]

Luther also came to believe that the Bible, rather than the traditions of the Catholic Church, was the final arbiter of religious faith and practice – he therefore tore down the Catholic Church's sacramental practices as well. Luther reduced the number of sacraments to two, baptism and the Eucharist, and redefined the meaning of both. He denied transubstantiation and considered baptism to be only the sign of justification through God's gift of unmerited grace.[14] Luther restructured his church, and his vision of the sacraments and ritual practice, along with his doctrine.

In their assessment of the *spirituali*, scholars such as Eva-Maria Jung and José C. Nieto have focused on how they first came to a parallel version of justification by faith alone, gathered together under the leadership of Juan de Valdés in Naples in the 1530s.[15] More recent scholarship also has described how the group coalesced in Naples, and came to include high-ranking prelates, including the apostolic protonotary Pietro Carnesecchi, the Capuchin general and popular preacher Bernardino Ochino (before 1534, an observant Franciscan), and Pietro Martire (Peter Martyr) Vermigli, a member of the Augustinian Canons Regular. Laypeople also participated, including the *literati* Marcantonio Flaminio, Mario Galeota (son of the lord of Monasterace), and noblewomen such as Giulia Gonzaga, countess of Fondi, Isabella Bresegna, wife of the Spanish governor of Piacenza, and Vittoria Colonna, marquise of Pescara. Through friendship, culture, and common interest the group came to include Cardinal Giovanni Morone, bishop of Modena, Cardinal Gasparo Contarini, and Cardinal Reginald Pole, cousin of Henry VIII.[16]

The reinstitution of the Roman Inquisition in 1542 caused more of a gradual build-up of increasing pressure on leading *spirituali* rather than a sharp and immediate turning point. While it is true that Bernardino Ochino and Pietro Martire Vermigli fled north in 1542 other *spirituali*, such as Isabella Bresegna, did not emigrate until the late 1550s and many of them never emigrated at all. Cardinal Morone was not prosecuted until the pontificate of Paul IV (1555–1559); and Pietro Carnesecchi not executed until his second trial in 1566–1567 because, after Giulia Gonzaga's death in 1566, their extensive correspondence (some of it in code) concerning their religious beliefs was confiscated by the Roman Inquisition. Morone would be absolved and later preside over the final session of the Council of Trent. Mario Galeota, a lifelong follower of Valdés who oversaw the translation and publication of Valdés's works, would survive several prosecutions. His first investigation had been conducted at the request of the Spanish viceroy in Naples in 1548, but Pedro Alvarez de Toledo refused to proceed against Galeota and others because he was worried that it would provoke a revolt. Galeota's second and third prosecutions had occurred beginning in 1554 and 1564, respectively. The archbishop of Naples had begun an investigation in 1553, only to have it stall out. But Paul IV insisted on its resumption after his election to the papacy in 1555; Galeota was in a prison in Rome from 1556 to 1559. After Paul IV's death, Pope Pius IV (Giovanni Angelo Medici) absolved Galeota, but he was prosecuted again in 1564, with his abjuration and sentence finally completed in June of 1567 (after he had been tortured).[17]

The *spirituali* also have been portrayed as indifferent to ritual practice. Valdés, in his first religious work, *Dialogue on Christian Doctrine* (1529), explicitly denied the need for sacramental confession once a year (or at all) and also criticized the Catholic Church's command to fast during Lent and at other crucial periods in the religious calendar. By the time Valdés completed *The Christian Alphabet*, in 1536, he had become more circumspect and, according to Daniel Crews, 'largely ignored the Church's structure' in his work; although he advised Giulia Gonzaga, the dialogue's other participant, to attend Mass regularly, he also expressed his opinion that confession to God was required, while confession to a priest was 'voluntary' – if the Church required it, perhaps voluntary compliance was not a bad idea.[18]

Scholars have recognized Erasmus of Rotterdam, in his vision of Catholic reform, was not enamoured with ritual practice. Erasmus was the most famous humanist scholar of his day, and thus appealed to the humanist-educated in Italy. He was equally well known for his broad critique of the early modern Catholic Church as a whole. Erasmus advocated interior piety, study of Scripture, and imitation of Christ as appropriate approaches to Catholic belief and practice. More pertinent to the subject of ritual practice, in many of his works published just prior to the Reformation, according to James D. Tracy, he completely excoriated what he thought were the excesses of Catholic ritual practices, ridiculing some practitioners as ignorant and unlearned concerning the basic doctrines of Christianity.

Erasmus's disparagement of some ritual practices was related to his particular view of Christianity and appropriate Christian practice, and firmly grounded in his critique of monasticism, humanist learning, and aestheticism. For Erasmus, contemporary monastic life focused too much on ceremony at the expense of true Christian living since monks practiced what he deemed superstitious rituals instead of practicing charity, for example. Erasmus thought the laity's adoption of monastic ritual practices in secular life – such as utilizing books of hours for devotion – misdirected lay piety. Erasmus advocated reform through returning to the true meaning of Scripture, preached among the laity, which would come from studying the Gospel in its most pure form. It was for this reason that Eramsus published his New Testament, in which the Latin text was corrected against the Greek. Furthermore, his scriptural interpretations make Erasmus's criticisms of what he called empty rituals and superstitions clear, although he would attempt to assert that Catholic ritual practices could be used profitably by the more ignorant members of society.[19] Many who read Erasmus agreed that Catholics needed the structure of ritual practice to maintain and inculcate faith regardless of what they may have thought of the rest of Erasmus's pronouncements concerning empty ritual, as we shall see below.

When examining Eramus's influence in Italian lands, Silvana Seidel Menchi has continued to emphasize his importance to the development of Italian heterodoxy more broadly in society, perhaps in spite of his own intentions, and with good reason. Those who read Erasmus's works often moved on to read Luther's works. Erasmus often became the 'gateway' to more heterodox religious opinions, especially Lutheran or Reformed positions.

But Erasmus's opinions concerning circumspect behaviour and his relative flexibility about Catholic tradition in many ways would remain quite singular in this period, although he clearly influenced other elite thinkers like Valdés. For example, Erasmus believed that it was permissible to refrain from stating one's views if such views would cause offence, but few who joined the Reform movement would agree with him, and Erasmus's pre-1517 publication record already had done the damage, offending as well as inspiring.[20] After the Reformation began, Erasmus always mantained that he did not object to ritual practices as long as those who performed them became aware of their spiritual meaning. He also never joined the side of the Reformation, affirming the efficacy of good works and, in his most famous exchange with Luther, defending the free will of Christians. But for many in Italian lands, Eramsus was increasingly seen as a Lutheran – what Eramsus made fun of, but ultimately reaffirmed in theory, if not in abusive practice, would be characterized by Protestant Reformers as pollutive and forbidden. The Index of 1559 banned his books, and inquisitors prosecuted anyone who expressed Erasmian opinions or acted in such a way as to indicate agreement with them.[21]

Finally, the *spirituali*, past their shared belief in emphasizing the necessity of God's grace to attain salvation, otherwise could differ widely in other respects, both in doctrine and in attempting various mechanisms to encourage reform, including emphasizing matters of ritual practice.[22] Eric Cochrane has noted that Vittoria Colonna was an important supporter of the Capuchins, for example and pointed out the importance of diocesan reform to many who associated with *spirituali* on occasion, such as Gian Matteo Giberti.[23] Ercole Gonzaga, the humanist-educated reforming bishop of Mantua, ensured that students in his seminary served as acolytes at Mass, went to confession once a month, and recited the Pater Noster, Ave Maria, and Credo three times daily. Gonzaga also promoted liturgical reform at the cathedral, staunchly defending Church traditions as edifying for both cathedral canons and laypeople. Gonzaga generally is not accounted as one of the full-fledged *spirituali*, but at one point in his life he was a friend of Gasparo Contarini, among others.[24] Hudon, in his examination of the prelate Marcello Cervini, has emphasized that many ecclesiastics working within the mid-sixteenth-century Catholic Church embraced the same goals, and has portrayed their differences of opinion in precisely how to achieve those goals as more finely tuned shades of gray among those supportive of reform in the Church, rather than concentrating on stark black-and-white analyses. Cervini, for example, although he served under Gian Pietro Carafa as one of the cardinals responsible for overseeing the Roman Inquisition, was also close friends with Gasparo Contarini and Reginald Pole for a time.

Even those churchmen directly involved in prosecuting heresy were not always quite so 'intransigent.' Cervini, according to Hudon, in carrying out his various duties as bishop, inquisitorial supervisor, legate, and cardinal used either more lenient or more stringent tactics as he saw fit depending on the situation.[25] And as Silvana Seidel Menchi has suggested, even after the refounding of the Roman Inquisition in 1542, inquisitors employed at local tribunals often negotiated with the subjects of their investigation more leniently, if they so chose. Fra Marino Venier, *il zotto*, employed carefully worded statements of doctrine to encourage confessions from some of those brought before his tribunal in Venice in the early 1550s, although Fra Marino would later be prosecuted himself in the 1560s.[26] Although at no point could coercion or repression not be considered a part of the Roman Inquisition's repetoire, there were noticable periods of more leniency as compared those of greater repression; during the papacies of Paul IV (Gian Pietro Carafa, r. 1555–1559) and Pius V (Michele Ghislieri, another former inquisitor general, r. 1566–1572) the local tribunals were encouraged to be more zealous and Paul IV initiated the trial proceedings against Cardinal Giovanni Morone, among others.[27] The inquisitorial system as a whole was designed to be flexible, either in the hands of the hierarchy or the individual inquisitor, and capable of ministering more leniently or punishing more harshly. Even 'intransigent' inquisitors could be merciful in judgment if they felt it was warranted.

Reform(s) in Italian Lands

The Roman Inquisition had to deal with an incredibly diverse religious landscape, although prelates and inquisitors resolutely referred to all heterodox as *luterani,* or 'Lutherans.' Italians, like the *spirituali,* often developed their religious ideas independently; just as often, Italians considered, discussed, and debated religious ideas from north of the Alps. Protestant doctrines first made their way south of the Alps through printed books, not surprisingly. The first to appear were Martin Luther's works in the late 1520s and early 1530s. Luther's *Open Letter to the Christian Nobility of the German Nation,* first published in 1520, was translated into Italian in 1533 with emendations specifically aimed at reaching an Italian audience and was read widely by those literate in the vernacular in the various Italian states. By 1525, an anthology of Luther's writings appeared in Italian states, anonymously translated; six editions were published, three under Luther's name, and three under Erasmus's. The edition avoided polemical arguments against the Catholic Church, but stated Luther's doctrinal position of justification by faith alone and encouraged a Christocentric piety.[28]

It was Melanchthon's *Loci communes rerum theologicarum,* however, translated into beautiful Italian and appearing sometime between 1530 and 1534, which systematized and summarized Reform theology and made a significant impact in Italian lands. Melanchthon, Luther's closest friend and ally in Wittenberg, appealed to humanist circles, especially admirers of Erasmus, since he realized that the humanist method of investigating the earliest sources of Christianity, most importantly Scripture itself, in their original languages was useful to the goals of constructing what he considered to be both correct doctrine and purifying a church corrupted by medieval scholasticism. The work was blatantly polemical, expressing Melanchthon's opinion of the abject state of the Catholic Church and papacy. Melanchthon's work reached Venice, Rome, Modena, Lucca, and Siena, and was also found in Florence and Naples.[29] While the work provided a clear exposition of justification by faith alone as a theological concept, it had much to say about the nature of good works. Melanchthon explicitly condemned the role of good works in salvation; in fact, that was the starting point for what he thought was an exposition of true evangelical doctrine. He placed his reference to the 'new Pelagians' in the Catholic Church at the beginning of the work's third chapter. The ancient Church had condemned Pelagius's idea that human nature could produce good works in and of itself as heretical in the early fifth century; a thousand years later the Catholic Church still maintained that, while good works contributed to salvation, they could not be performed without God aiding human nature in overcoming original sin. Melanchthon held that since human beings were continuously mired in a state of sin, they simply could not earn salvation through the performance of works at all – works flowed from faith, a gift from God.[30] His discussion of justification and faith began by disparaging the Catholic theology of works as too Pelagian – for many Catholic authors, and many of Melanchthon's readers, that was the pertinent point.

Although Roman Inquisition process records from the period before the 1550s are not abundant, those that are available reveal the wide circulation of Protestant texts: authors in addition to Luther and Melanchthon included Martin Bucer, Ulrich Zwingli, John Calvin, and Urbanus Rhegius. In particular, Zwingli, his successor in Zurich Heinrich Bullinger, and John Calvin, as the pre-eminent shapers of Swiss Reform theology, would present interpretations of the Eucharist different from those of Luther and Melanchthon, and wrote extensively concerning predestination, a doctrine Luther refused to elaborate, bringing more religious diversity to the attention of readers north and south of the Alps.[31] In the 1540s heterodox or Protestant literature written by Italian exiles living north of the Alps began to appear in Italy, from such authors as Bernardino Ochino, Pietro Martire Vermigli, Giulio della Rovere, Camillo Renato, and Pier Paolo Vergerio. Most of these works continued to circulate after the Roman Inquisition's reorganization and even after the first published papal Index of Prohibited Books of 1558–1559 because of book smuggling networks and the subterfuge of pseudonyms or total anonymity on title pages.[32]

Furthermore, by the 1530s, literature directed to a more popular Italian reading audience became available alongside the materials produced for a 'highbrow' audience. Three of the most important works that appeared in the Italian states in the 1530s were *Dottrina Vecchia e Dottrina Nuova*, the *Sommario della Sacra Scrittura*, and the *Beneficio di Cristo*, the last work symbolic of the merging of native Italian heterodox and northern Reform ideas.[33] The *Beneficio di Cristo* was one of the most influential religious works in this time and was well received on all levels of society. The work contains ideas that can be traced to Martin Luther, John Calvin, Melanchthon, and Juan de Valdés.[34] Tommaso Bozza, in fact, has asserted that the book contains paraphrasings of passages from Calvin's *Institutes of the Christian Religion*.[35] The work was unorthodox when compared to Tridentine reform ideals. Fra Benedetto da Mantova, who wrote the work, and Marcantonio Flaminio, the work's editor, emphasized reforming the individual based on personal experience and a return to biblical sources.

The doctrinal content was clearly heterodox because the book promoted justification by faith alone. It condemned a reliance on works for salvation, but declared that good works were inseparable from true faith. The work did, however, make passing mention of what works, performed through faith, were acceptable to God; they were not those of the 'false Christians who drag everything down to the level of carnal life.' Those that possessed a justifying and living faith would 'endeavor to lead a holy and spiritual life [...]';[36] imitation of Christ, one can infer, did not include votives to saints. The central theme of the book was the benefit of Christ's death to the individual Christian, hence the title. This book demonstrates the doctrinal ambiguity of the sixteenth century's first decades, since it described a reformed religion that had much in common with the Protestant Reformers but did not explicitly criticize or condemn the Catholic Church as an institution. The work was placed on the Index of 1559 and banned, but similar to the *Dottrina Vecchia e Dottrina Nuova* and the *Sommario della Sacra Scrittura*, the *Beneficio* remained popular into the 1560s and 1570s, and inquisitors repeatedly found it in their searches of houses and bookshops.[37]

Crucially, Antonio Brucioli's Italian translation of the New Testament gave those literate in the vernacular access to Scripture, which according to all Protestant Reformers was the sole source of faith and correct ritual practices. Brucioli's New Testament was reprinted many times between 1540 and 1546, and Brucioli directly aimed his translation at the lower social strata, although many who possessed a degree of literary culture read it as well. The use to which it could be put, however, was de-emphasized within the work itself. The edition's readers were obviously encouraged to read the Bible for themselves – another common link between all Protestant groups – but, of course, it did not explicitly describe Protestant doctrines. [38]

As yet another permutation of Christian belief and practices, Anabaptist writings began to appear in Italian lands in the late 1540s and 1550s, but lay preaching and proselytizing had been ongoing since the mid-1520s. Anabaptists accepted the principle of justification by faith alone, and the sacrament of the Eucharist; but they thought the sacrament of baptism should be undertaken consciously by adults rather than performed on passive infants. Anabaptism spread first in those areas closest to Switzerland and Southern Germany, where Anabaptist beliefs had originated, mainly the south Tyrol and in areas within the Venetian *terraferma* empire. We do not know the names of individual Anabaptists in these areas until the 1530s, however; Antonio *marangone* ('carpenter') was one of the first to express Anabaptist ideas in public in 1532.[39]

Camillo Renato, one of the more prominent Italian Anabaptist theologians and originally a Franciscan friar, embraced believer's baptism after having participated in reform currents in Ferrara; he then fled to Rhaetia to escape the inquisition. Ruled by the Swiss Confederation, Rhaetia and the Valtellina provided Italian Anabaptists with a safe haven from which to proselytize in northern Italian lands, since the Swiss Confederation allowed each town in these areas to determine its own religious affiliation. The proselytizers were often shadowy figures; even now, one of the most active is known merely as 'Il Tiziano,' who baptized and organized conventicles in Padua and Florence. It was Il Tiziano who had converted Pietro Manelfi, whose return to Catholicism and subsequent inquisitorial abjuration in 1551 gave Venetian inquisitors, and later historians, much of their information concerning the spread of Anabaptism in northern Italy, including a detailed description of the Anabaptist synod held in Venice in 1550. It was at this synod that Italian Anabaptists' tendency to emphasize the humanity of Christ and reject his divine nature became startlingly clear.[40] The denial of Christ's divine nature also may be attributable to Juan de Valdés's influence in Naples; he had *converso* ancestors. His followers Geronimo Busale, a Benedictine abbot, and the Cistercians Lorenzo Tizziano and Giovanni Laureto, all came to occupy leadership positions in Italian Anabaptist circles, and all at least doubted Christ's divinity. Laureto eventually emigrated to Thessalonika, where he declined to join the local Anabaptist conventicle in favour of converting to Sephardic Judaism.[41] As John Martin has emphasized, the more radical confessions, because they emphasized voluntary conversion and organization, lent themselves well to creating secret conventicles. The members of these conventicles in Italian lands also could be quite eclectic in their selection of beliefs, and did not conform always to one particular confession of faith, magisterial or radical, in its entirety.[42]

The spread of Anabaptism in Italian lands highlights the other, and unfortunately for modern historians more ephemeral, ways in which the reform-minded could popularize the full variety of heterodox ideas among all people, illiterate and literate, and among all social stations – preaching and discussion. Complementary and reciprocal to the spread of books, sermons spread the message, both magisterial and more radical. Preachers also did not have to do much in the way of subterfuge until the 1530s, when prelates became cognizant of the phenomenon of 'wolves in sheep's clothing.' In addition to Bernardino Ochino, preachers such as Agostino da Fivizzano, Andrea Ghetti da Volterra, Giulio della Rovere, Agostino Museo da Treviso, Ambrogio da Milano, and Agostino Mainardi spread the word, literally. Many of the preachers came from the Augustinian order and were among the first to adhere to Luther's teachings for that reason. In two books of *Prediche* containing Giulio della Rovere's sermons given immediately before his arrest in Venice in 1541 and following his escape from prison in February 1543, the Augustinian monk concentrated on *sola scriptura, sola gratia,* and *sola fide,* while avoiding overt statements against the Catholic Church.[43] These preachers went on to have varied careers; some fled to the Italian-speaking Swiss territories that fell outside the jurisdiction of the Roman Inquisition; others stayed and continued to preach, and found themselves in front of inquisitorial judges repeatedly; and some desisted completely when the situation became too dangerous.[44]

Preaching had the intended effect of spreading heterodox doctrines to a variety of people, at least in urban centres. In Bologna, for example, reform ideas circulated relatively easily because it was such an important theological centre, possessing one of the most important faculties of theology in Europe.[45] Bologna was also one of the cities where reform-minded clerics and laymen met and discussed the issues important to them. The ecclesiastics among them preached on a regular basis, too. Pier Paolo Vergerio stayed in Bologna in the early 1540s both in the Augustinian convent of San Giacomo, where he met Giulio da Milano, the preacher, and at San Francesco, where Vergerio stayed with Giovanni Buzio, another preacher of reform ideas. Both of these convents, and San Salvatore, became known as 'schools of heresy' in Bologna.[46]

The Catholic hierarchy, yet again defying the *spirituali/intransigenti* dichotomy, understood very well that preaching of this kind, as an incitement to rebel against Catholic discipline spiritually or temporally, was dangerous precisely because it could reach a wide audience including illiterates. The Master of the Sacred Palace in the 1530s, Tommaso Badia, confronted Agostino Mainardi by saying that difficult doctrines like predestination, the topic of an offending sermon, should not be sent out into the public arena, because the majority of the public were 'idiots' in the ecclesiastical hierarchy's opinion – without any formal theological training, clerical status, or knowledge of Latin.[47] Gasparo Contarini was the Venetian cardinal who had participated in the Colloquy of Ratisbon in 1541, and who had come to his own understanding of justification sympathetic to that of the Protestants in 1511; yet he also wrote a letter to Lattanzio Tolomei in which he stressed that concepts such as predestination, long a topic of discussion among Catholic theologians, should not be preached to the public because such a message was potentially politically subversive and could mislead the faith of the more uneducated.[48]

By the 1550s the printed material available to Italians interested in heterodox ideas had become more polemical in nature. Ritual practices common to early modern Catholicism – the cult of the saints, the sacrifice of the Mass, religious pilgrimage, indulgences, and concern for souls in purgatory – were condemned with ever-increasing contempt. This was mirrored by the organization of like-minded heterodox into conventicles and the development of self-conscious heterodox and philo-Protestant identities. The followers of Reform began to form conventicles for the purpose of worshipping outside the Catholic Church and attempting to proselytize others, often encouraged by those who had fled north, particularly Pietro Martire Vermigli and Pier Paolo Vergerio.[49]

One main reason for the increasingly strident criticism of the Catholic Church and the formation of secret conventicles lay in disagreements among new Reform sects north of the Alps concerning how to structure ritual practices in concordance with doctrine. Reformers, both magisterial and radical, approached restructuring the Eucharist and ritual practices by scrutinizing what they considered to be the proper biblical foundations of such practices and considering the effects they would have on their congregants and followers. Many aspects of Catholic ritual practice came to be seen as pollutants, temptations, and corrupters of faith – with each version of Protestant faith positing a different interpretation as to which ritual practices were licit, mirroring their theologians' differences of doctrinal opinion. Ritual practices became the primary agent of both Reform and confessionalization, or the process of clearly defining the doctrines and practices of different Protestant churches, which would then be imparted to all the members of those churches as a coherent religious culture and identity. In the process, all versions of Protestant faith permanently changed the structure and tone of what had been a vivid and varied Catholic ritual life.

Catholic Ritual Practice and the Protestant Critique

The ritual life Protestant denominations sought to change was both individual and communal, and above all publicly pervasive. Reform theologians produced multifarious protests against Catholic ritual practices, therefore, which would have daily practical effects that could not be avoided by those aware of the conflict. Studying the ritual practices of Catholicism in its own right, and as a frame for the Reformation, is crucial in establishing the nature of the religious environment in which the Reformation would arrive.

Richard Trexler, for one, has focused on how religious ritual practices structured Italian urban life in his seminal *Public Life in Renaissance Florence* (1980), although exploring the ritual conflicts of the Reformation was not his major concern. Trexler was intent on demonstrating that humanist Renaissance Florence was very much Christian in everyday life, and that 'conditions in the traditional European city were conducive to intense public ritual behavior, [and] that ritual was in fact at the core of the city's identity,' not 'simply a tribal or village phenomenon.' In the process he has described the ways in which ritual practice contributed to a sense of community identity immediately before the Reformation period.[50] In describing the interaction between civic and religious ritual practices, Trexler also has illuminated the ways in which sacred space, and ritual practices, came to be located and performed in the urban environment. Churches were, of course, among the most sacred locations, as the site of the Mass, religious devotion, and relics of saints. In his examination, quoting the noted Renaissance preacher Bernardino of Siena, Trexler emphasized the importance of the consecrated host – the body of Christ was present in the church – and the performance of the Mass, in which the priest effected Christ's literal presence through the consecration. Images and relics, including the host, when stationary in the church, served as objects of individual and group devotion.

As Trexler has noted, however, these objects of devotion were not always stationary in a church. During the feast of Corpus Christi, for example, the consecrated host was paraded through Florence accompanied by important religious and political figures. Relics and images also could be carried in procession; the image of Mary, Our Lady of Impruneta, was brought forth from the suburb of Impruneta and so taken through Florence when the city suffered weather-related crises. And Florentines celebrated the feasts of saints important to the city, particularly Zenobi and Joseph; in fact, the city government appointed feast organizers and enforcers, whose job it was to ensure that worship devoted to the saint proceeded with honour and decorum, and that the city's population did not violate the ban on working on such days.[51]

Trexler has also pointed out that young Florentines would be taught appropriate physical behaviour when engaging in personal or civic religious devotions. As Bernardino of Siena put it, if one should display respect for pope and emperor by removing one's hat, how could showing reverence for the Corpus Christi in the same way not be appropriate? To counter such irreverence as business negotiations being conducted in churches, boys playing in the aisles, and candles being sold, Bernardino instructed those who listened to his sermons to recite the appropriate prayer when entering a church, genuflect and bow one's head (with hat removed), make signs of the cross and genuflect at the appropriate times during Mass (especially when the names of Christ and the Virgin Mary were heard), and recite another prayer when sprinkled with holy water at the end of Mass.[52] These ritual practices would apply to public processions to a certain extent; and according to Trexler, such processions and use of images was more common than many of the Catholic sacraments. Confession to a priest usually occurred once a year for lay people, except for the extremely devout. Baptism, confirmation, marriage, and extreme unction only occurred when required; but processions happened several times a year, as did feasts dedicated to saints. Finally, for Trexler, private devotion to images was 'the training ground for larger public effusions,' for example, as when the sick had religious images brought to their sickbeds.[53]

Trexler's focus on the civic environment has been influential in subsequent historiography. Studies of the rural religious situation in fifteenth-, sixteenth-, and seventeenth-century Italian states also demonstrate the importance of ritual practice as a point of continuity in defining Catholic orthodoxy. As David Gentilcore has explained, examining the Terra d'Otranto, the organized forms of the 'ritual complex' including liturgy, the sacraments and sacramentals, and para-liturgical practices, existed alongside more informal, quasi-magical practices, both of which remained untouched by the post-Tridentine Church in rural southern Italy. In the process, Gentilcore points out that the sacramental rites authorized by the *Rituale Romanum*, commissioned by Pope Gregory XIII in 1575 and completed in 1584 included ceremonies for blessing water, houses, crops, and marriage beds alongside palms, candles, and sacred images – all ritual practices intended to be well suited to a rural agrarian community. Even in an area as yet untouched by Tridentine reform, the clergy encouraged the use of rosaries, prayers, the use of sacred images in houses, alongside palm branches and holy water, as a means of practicing faith and accessing divine protection.[54]

Continuing to investigate urban religious practice, several historians have found confraternities a subject of research that demonstrates the relationship between 'local religion, the universal Catholic Church, and civic government.' Studies concerning confraternities have proven particularly fruitful since the lay brother- and sisterhoods were an important vehicle of expressing civic pride. Brian Pullan has examined the 'civic Catholicism' of Venetian confraternities; John Henderson has explicated the foundation and expansion of Florence's confraternal organizations; Nicholas Terpstra has studied the role of confraternal charitable groups in Bologna; and David M. D'Andrea has studied how Trevisan confraternities expressed both civic pride and political relationships with the Venetian government. Finally, all of these confraternal organizations made processions in public many times a year and employed religious images and relics to do so; for example, the confraternity in Treviso, the Battuti, held 112 processions in 1467.[55]

Those sacramental activities were precisely the ones that some confraternity members interested in Reform doctrines might begin to object to, as Michelle Fontaine has demonstrated. In Modena, the confraternity of Santa Maria dei Battuti engaged in ritual meals, attended Masses for the dead, participated in members' funeral processions, made it a point to go to confession and take communion several times a year, and engaged in flagellation as a community. But beginning in 1497, the confraternity was split into two groups; the smaller 'strict' branch still practiced self-flagellation, while the larger branch only engaged in other ritual practices and charitable activities. Furthermore, in the 1530s and 1540s, some members of the larger branch began to withdraw from the confraternity's sacramental life by neglecting their duty to attend confession and communion. Of those members who began to withdraw, some would find themselves prosecuted for heresy, including Francesco Grillenzoni and Filippo Valentini. It was the loss of the confraternity's hospital, the object of their charitable activities, which brought the brothers back to behaving as a unified Catholic body participating in communal religious practice, according to Fontaine, but at that point the Battuti had a reputation of being in need of orthodox reform.[56] In this case, it was the confraternity's communal ritual practices that drew attention to those who were no longer quite so orthodox in their beliefs.

Ritual Catholicism, in fact, could unify any given group in civic solidarity as well as orthodox piety, but it also could reveal broad secular divisions. According to Edward Muir images, especially those of the Virgin Mary, were deployed deliberately in urban space to encourage reverential and decorous public behaviour in general, whether the devotions to the images were organized by a confraternity or governing body or not. In Udine, for example, the local government unsuccessfully attempted to reduce street violence by placing images in each quarter of the city and officially encouraging neighbourhood cults. In Venice, the images were just as often placed, and reverenced, by the neighbourhood spontaneously. Muir also has noted that 'the sacred presented itself in temporal cycles' within urban space, following the liturgical cycle along with fixed feasts dedicated to important local saints. There were, by one count, 406 fixed images of the Virgin in Venice, but some images were mobile, as was the consecrated Eucharist and 'the devout conveyed reverence through a demonstration that one had been properly socialized.'[57] Although governments and church officials could attempt to dominate how these sacred ritual practices were performed, in some cities, such as Naples and Udine, public ritual often served to reflect and magnify societal conflict instead of portraying the unity of the political community.[58]

The street corner Virgins of Venice were just one of the examples of informal ritual practice, enmeshed within parochial and civic politics and pride found in that city's urban landscape. Muir also has studied extensively the formal, structured ritual practices sponsored by Venice's oligarchic republican government in the sixteenth century. As Muir puts it, 'civic ritual' was a 'peculiar hybrid of liturgical and ceremonial elements,' meant to signify political and social relations within the city as well as Venice's special relationships with saints and, ultimately, God. For Venetians, their reputation as extremely pious was well deserved; in that city, patriotism and demonstrations of piety were inextricably interwoven. [59]

Venice celebrated the same religious festivals common to the Catholic liturgical calendar, but structured them in such a way as to reflect, and it was hoped integrate, disparate social and political elements (as Trexler has discovered in Florence). The annual celebration of Corpus Christi, for example, occurred all over Europe; but in Venice it was celebrated with processions in San Marco, the *piazza* ('square') that contained both the basilica that was home to the relics of the city's patron saint, Mark, and the seat of the Venetian secular government. It began when the government's elected head of state, the doge, entered the basilica and confessed to the patriarch of Venice. He then took his seat and, alongside city officials and magistrates, observed the procession. The procession included members of the major and minor confraternities in the city, the regular and secular clergy, with the patriarch bearing the consecrated host; the Venetian state's senators were each accompanied by a pilgrim bound for the Holy Land. Some organizations provided tableaux for the edification of those watching the procession. The procession contained nearly every corporate organization in Venice and, as Muir states, 'associated the regime with the support of pilgrimages.'[60]

Muir describes the Catholic liturgical calendar as two cycles of events; the first, from All Saints' Day on 1 November until Corpus Christi in May or June contained most of the holy dates associated with Christ and the Virgin, such as Christmas, Easter, and the Annunciation. In the second part of the calendar from summer into autumn, however, feasts devoted to more localized saints could develop. In Venice, the most important ritual processions involved the relics of St Mark – one on June 25 was dedicated to the miraculous discovery of those relics in the midst of rebuilding the basilica, and the other was held on his day in the liturgical calendar, April 25. Venice also held important celebrations dedicated to St George and St Nicholas, patron saint of fishermen and mariners. Finally, some acts of God, such as plague, required response; in 1575–1576 the Venetian senate commanded all religious houses to pray continuously, held frequent processions, and passed legislation declaring that, if delivered from plague, they would finance a church and annual communal procession. The procession to the Church of the Redeemer still takes place in July.[61]

Additionally, Muir has postulated that the Reformation in Europe was a period crucial for ritual theory. While rites had always been an important part of medieval Catholicism, according to Muir, the term 'ritual' was first applied in the pejorative sense of calling what another Christian sect did 'mere ritual' (mostly Protestants accusing Catholics). Muir has attributed this development to a fundamental shift in 'the understanding between human behavior and meaning.' Catholic rituals made something 'present,' as when transubstantiation occurred during the Eucharist, and the bread and wine were transformed into the literal body and blood of Christ. Since the body of Christ became literally 'present' in the church viewing the Mass was a good work, which could contribute to the viewer's own justification or that of a soul being purified in purgatory. According to Muir, Protestants in general developed a new, representational view of ritual practices that constructed them as 'an aspect of language that communicated meaning. The Eucharist reminded believers of Christ's sacrifice rather than offering up his actual physical body.'[62]

Natalie Zemon Davis has argued that the Protestants of Lyon reshaped ritual practice, particularly as enacted in urban space. When the town's Catholics moved through urban space with the sacred, such as carrying the consecrated host on Corpus Christi or in the processions of confraternities, they sought to unite all of the important geographical parts of the city and sanctify them. The Protestants, in contrast, moved through urban space singing Psalms along streets that 'were not sacred routes, but avenues of expression of the believer's faith [...].' The Calvinists effectively 'cut the tie between sacred and place [...]' and also restructured 'sacred time,' since the Calvinist liturgical year was much more simplified than the Catholic. In Catholic Lyon, the most intense times of ritual practice occurred in late December and early January, Lent, Easter, May and June, and August. According to Davis, the Calvinists had debated the necessity of declaring any sacred times at all; Sundays were merely a convenient agreed-on day for the good order of the Calvinist Church. The only ritual focus lay in the four times a year the Calvinist Church celebrated the Lord's Supper.[63]

Davis's work concerning open religious conflict between Catholic and Reformed in Lyon during the French Wars of Religion highlights that doctrine and appropriate ritual practice were not separate entities from the perspective of sixteenth-century theologians and believers. Martin Luther tackled the question of modelling 'true' religious practices alongside his doctrinal development for most of his career. Initially, in his original critique of Catholicism, Luther had taken issue with many of these ritual practices. His original protest against indulgences had led to his endorsement of two sacraments in his church: baptism and the Eucharist. The other five Catholic sacraments – holy orders, confession to a priest, confirmation, extreme unction, and marriage – he condemned as invalid because they were not clearly mandated in the Bible, in his considered theological opinion, as necessary to salvation.

Luther therefore decided that other ritual practices were not necessary to salvation as well. The use of images in worship; rich decoration of the altar on which the Eucharist would be blessed by the priest; the gold and silver plate used to hold the bread and wine; the adoration of saints' images, and prayers for their help and aid; none of these practices, for Luther, were biblically mandated as necessary for worship or justification by faith. Luther condemned the Catholic Mass as a farce perpetrated by a corrupt and wicked papacy, although Luther maintained Christ's real presence in the Eucharist in consubstantiation.[64]

When Luther engaged in polemics with Catholic authors and theologians, he portrayed such ritual practices as completely unnecessary and even argued for their deconstruction, particularly early in his career. When arguing against his first Reformed opponents, the Zwinglians in Zurich and Andreas Karlstadt in Wittenberg, however, Luther moderated his position. While he argued that images should not be used in an idolatrous manner and blindly adored as if they were the equal of God or Christ, capable of delivering divine aid to the believer in and of themselves, Luther also stated that he was not opposed to retaining images in churches, or rich altar vessels, or the trappings of Catholicism. Luther tore down some aspects of Catholic ritual life, but ultimately he left others intact as things 'indifferent,' which could be used well or badly depending on the correct faith and attitude of the believer. Luther advocated the continued use of old Catholic altars as long as the celebrant faced the congregation, and even endorsed the use of altarpieces depicting sacred images as instructive to the illiterate.[65]

As a result, many Lutheran churches, in a purely physical sense, continued to resemble Roman Catholic ones; while visual, and what Susan Karant-Nunn has described as psychological, continuity concerning the Eucharist was preserved, the doctrine and the ritual practices of the sacramentals were not. Carlos Eire has noted that Luther's attitude toward ritual practices, and the use of objects during them, developed as a response to Andreas Karlstadt's opposition to them, and his attempts to purify Wittenberg of sacred images while Luther was still living at Wartburg castle in 1521 and 1522. Karlstadt, originally a follower and supporter of Luther, developed his own theology concerning popular religious practices. He argued that images and popular rituals held back the faith of Christians and kept their faith from fully developing; they were a corruption of true Christian faith. He attempted to forcibly remove images from Wittenberg and performed a Eucharistic ceremony, in which he wore secular clothing, used plain vessels, and faced his congregation. It was these actions that brought Luther back to Wittenberg from Wartburg on the complaints of other followers, such as Melanchthon, and his protector Elector Frederick of Saxony, who thought that Karlstadt went too far. As Susan Karant-Nunn has maintained, Lutheranism, and all Protestant denominations, eliminated the need for church decoration and sacramentals by eliminating 'tangible, perceptible points of prior contact between the human and the divine,' but many Lutheran churches still contained these objects, not as necessary, but as a concession to the 'weaker brethren' who were still comforted by images of the divine. [66]

Lutheran theologians, and Lutheran churches, alone would maintain this position in the sixteenth century. Ulrich Zwingli in Zurich was the first to enact a Reform in which iconoclasm, or the destruction of sacred images and the firm prohibition of the ritual practices associated with sacred images, was central to its definition and success. In this branch of the Swiss Reformed tradition, his break with Catholic ritual practice was inspired by Erasmus; in Zwingli's capacity as Catholic preacher to pilgrims at Einsiedeln, he had read Erasmus's works and imbibed the Dutch humanist's aversion for outward, uninformed, and empty piety. But for Zwingli, his prohibition of such practices came from his interpretation of Scripture – the cult of the saints was not Christian. For Zwingli, any ritual practice not expressly authorized or prescribed in the Bible was prohibited completely for Christians. In two of his works, Zwingli insisted that the whole point of Christian belief was to place God at the centre of both faith and worship. Given man's corrupted nature, any worship not dedicated solely to God was false. Idolatry was the result of humanity, in its inherent imperfection, placing more value in created things rather than the purely spiritual.[67] Zwingli also broke with Luther concerning the correct interpretation of the Eucharist; Zwingli interpreted it as a memorial of Christ's sacrifice that served to fortify the faith of the participants, while Luther insisted on Christ's real presence in some fashion.[68]

Another prominent Reformed theologian, John Calvin, who began implementing his vision of Reform belief and practice in Geneva in the late 1530s and early 1540s, largely agreed with Zwingli concerning images and Catholicism's ritual practices. Calvin's written work explicitly borrowed Erasmus's sarcasm from *The Praise of Folly*; the Genevan Reformer decried continuing Catholic ritual practices in scathing terms. The theological core of his attacks – that nothing concerning God's divinity can be transferred, either to saint or image – had much in common with his Reformed predecessors, but Calvin was more expansive concerning its application. According to Carlos Eire, Calvin went beyond denouncing idolatry because he saw a definite relationship between the spiritual and the temporal. That relationship was, to use Eire's terminology, transcendent; proper ritual practice connected humanity and God. Therefore all ritual practices not laid down by God in the Bible were a corruptive agent and offensive to God. Humanity, because of its inherently sinful state, had to maintain constant discipline rather than backslide into superstitious Catholic practices.[69] Participation in Catholic ritual practices, either the Mass or the cult of the saints, was for Calvin a means of corrupting the pure faith of true Christians. The very existence of images, and their presence wherever worship of God occurred, was inherently idolatrous even without any deliberate intent on the part of the worshipper. The Catholic sacrifice of the Mass also was idolatrous, since it called for Catholics to adore hosts and wine that, according to Calvin, in no way contained the bodily presence of Christ.[70]

The magisterial Reform churches of Luther, Zwingli, and Calvin strongly criticized Catholic ritual practices – but they were called 'magisterial' because their doctrines and practices were implemented as state-approved denominational churches in Saxony, Zurich, Geneva, and elsewhere by university-educated theologians. The Anabaptists, in their theologies and doctrines, expressed an even more uncompromising dichotomy between themselves and the material world, church and state both. All Anabaptist sects advocated the baptism of believers – conscious, believing adults, fully aware of human sin and repentance, who chose regeneration and salvation through baptism. Their infant baptisms, performed when they were unaware of faith, were therefore completely invalid. Anabaptists envisioned their churches as separate from the unregenerate world, which included both state governments and state-supported churches. Instead, their churches were what they considered to be voluntary associations of the truly faithful. Anabaptists were a separatist, underground, and persecuted movement because of their strong stance against secular authority. They also were often pacifist, and they refused to participate in state-sponsored churches that required the participation of the entire secular community, although individual Anabaptist groups could espouse significantly divergent theological doctrines.[71]

Protestant opinion concerning Catholic ritual practices occupied a continuum. Luther thought some ritual practices *adiaphora* ('things indifferent'), or not necessary to practice but permitted. Other Reformers explicitly forbade many traditional Catholic practices in the most powerful terms. But some kind of critique of traditional Catholic practice was a common element in all of the Reformers' work and inextricable from each new denomination's theological principles. It was also the central theme of the most scathing condemnations of Catholicism, in both serious theological works and the more popular vehicles of pamphlets and broadsides. Preaching against ritual 'superstitions' and the images used while performing them inspired iconoclastic riots. Such sensational, and ferocious, critiques of Catholic ritual culture sent out a shockwave that still affected how inquisitors' manual authors evaluated the dangers of the Protestant menace in the late sixteenth and early seventeenth centuries.

Contemporaneously with such violent iconoclasm north of the Alps, in the 1550s and 1560s on the Italian peninsula discussions of ritual practice and its meaning intensified as different Protestant confessions sought to sharpen and clarify their doctrinal and ritual principles. As noted above, during this time conventicles of committed heterodox in Italian lands developed; these small groups of people gathered in private houses and workshops to read and discuss ideas and even, in some areas, to hold philo-Protestant services. These conventicles grew alongside more broadly evangelical ones, and even the members of Anabaptist conventicles or believers in more radical doctrines were often eclectic in their selection of particular beliefs and practices. [72] The proliferation of heterodox religious expression in a variety of forms reflected the Italian states' political, geographic, and economic fragmentation, and often mutual conflict, at the time. Significant differences existed between areas as distinct as Milan and the Trentino-Aldige, right on the border with Swiss and German areas eventually won over to various forms of the new religion.[73] In the midst of this diversity, inquisitors were concerned with constructing a relatively stable standard of prosecution that accounted for all of these variations; the term 'Lutheran' is indicative of how inquisitors viewed the variations among Protestant sects as all of a piece. Those variations were there, but the priority lay in finding a way to prosecute them all. Although manuals trailed behind inquisitorial action temporally, their authors shared that perspective.

It was also precisely during the 1550s and 1560s that the Counter-Reformation Catholic Church as a whole began to re-emphasize and reinvigorate these ritual practices as a means of educating the laity and inculcating a stronger sense of what it meant to be Catholic. Confraternities, for example, while they had existed long before the Counter-Reformation, continued to be a source of piety and social service. The activities of those institutions, along with other continued practices such as pilgrimage, like those made to the Marian shrine at Loreto throughout the early modern period, gesture to, as Hudon has put it, the 'popularity of post-Tridentine devotional life.' And while the Roman Inquisition did consist of a clerical elite, as did the Church hierarchy as a whole, it did not 'somehow st[and] outside of Western culture,' either in its recognition of ritual practice as integral to doctrine and religion or in its solicitation of witnesses to violations of ritual practice.[74]

In that nexus of religious activity, ritual practice played an important polemical role, at once both unifying and divisive. For example, John Frymire has recently examined the work of Mattheus Tympe, in which the northern-European Catholic priest and author, writing in the early seventeenth century, described ceremonial practices as the most effective means to 'define, maintain, and strengthen what remained of the Catholic community.'[75] Agostino Steuco, Paul III's papal librarian and a delegate to the Council of Trent, had begun to argue, as early as the 1530s while living in Venice, 'that sacred rites, processions, and relics rendered men pious and filled with a sense of religious awe.' According to Ronald Delph, Steuco thought that the sacred should permeate everyday life to preserve the Catholic faith in the midst of its troubles in the sixteenth century.[76]

A strong emphasis on ritual practice, particularly at the community level, was used to counteract religious dissent. As Michelle Fontaine has described, Egidio Foscarari (discussed extensively in Chapter 4) in 1550 became the resident bishop of Modena, a town of about 18,000 in north-central Italy, subject to the dukes of Ferrara. Religious heterodoxy had been common in Modena on all levels of society since the 1530s, even emerging in public arguments over the choice of a Lenten preacher in 1541. The Modenese had become well known in Italian lands as 'heretics' when Foscarari arrived and, through public ritual processions, 'silenced, at least publicly, the voice of heterodox dissent.'[77] According to Fontaine, Foscarari knew well that he had been sent to Modena to eliminate heresy, but saw that elimination within a broader context of implementing reform through his presence in the cathedral. Foscarari led processions, especially in response to crises such as drought and regularly said Mass on the major feast days. The Modenese responded by turning out in large numbers to attend these revitalized community ritual practices, which had noticeably lower attendance before Foscarari's arrival.[78]

Absences from Mass; failing to raise a hat as the bishop proceeded through the city with the body of Christ on the feast of Corpus Christi; debating whether or not one could utilize an image in private devotion; or, like Alessandro Fornari, yelling at a sacred image in a friend's house; all of these engagements with, or critiques of, ritual practices indicated belief in heresy to inquisitors, and to those friends, neighbours, and associates who witnessed such behavior or overheard those conversations. A focus on ritual practice also had the advantage of including all possible permutations of Protestant, evangelical, Anabaptist, or eclectic belief systems since all their practitioners, in some way and on some level, thought Catholic practices incorrect and sought to avoid, critique, or change them. Finally, the principle of focusing on ritual practice as a significant indicator of heretical belief had been a part of inquisitorial prosecution since its inception in the thirteenth century. What ritual practices, or avoidance thereof, inquisition authors and inquisitors working for the Roman Inquistion thought were significant to prosecution is key; those practices, and the source of the inquisition's emphasis on ritual practice, is the subject of the next chapter.

Chapter Two

'He may be a patron and receiver of heretics': Adapting the Principles of Prosecution

Inquisitorial Precedent

In February of 1567, Riccardo Perucolo, a *pintore* (painter) in Conegliano, a town within Venice's mainland empire, caught the interest of religious officials for the second time. In 1549, he had confessed to heretical crimes and received penance as punishment. In 1567, Camillo Speziari, the chancellor and vicar for the bishop of Ceneda in the Veneto, and Daniele Sbarato, a Franciscan friar who assisted the vicar, once again gathered evidence against Riccardo. They began by interviewing Matteo, the curate of San Martino's parish where Riccardo lived. Matteo could not give the tribunal in Conegliano much that was specific in the way of information: Riccardo had a bad reputation when it came to faith, especially since he had been prosecuted before. His wife's and his children's beliefs were also somewhat suspect, although Matteo could not remember exactly what they had said or done to merit such a reputation. Finally, Riccardo himself did not go to vespers or Mass very often, but the parish priests there had to admit that he confessed and took communion once a year. But in a further notation, taken down in August of 1567, the inquisitor and vicar noted that with the existing evidence they could arrest and charge Riccardo as a *fautor* (favourer) and *receptor* (receiver) of heretics, since he had helped 'Alessandro Augustini' flee Conegliano to join the Anabaptists in Moravia.[1]

That information had come courtesy of the inquisitor general of Venice, the Dominican Valerio Faenzi, who also sent along additional evidence. Riccardo was associated with someone who had been a conduit for forbidden religious books; therefore he was a notorious heretic, 'infect[ing] the poor and the innocent souls of children.' All parties, therefore, were exhorted to proceed with the case.[2] Riccardo, however, had fled the jurisdiction, with help from his own children. On 12 February 1568, the Venetian tribunal informed inquisitor Sbarato that the escaped Riccardo indeed could be condemned as a relapsed and impenitent heretic and turned over to the secular arm for execution if ever caught, 'in compliance with the disposition of the sacred canons,' or the precepts of canon law. They also confirmed that any extra expense necessary for Riccardo's recapture would be money well spent. One of the Venetian tribunal's deputies, the author of the letter, confirmed that the tribunal in Conegliano should prioritize the expedition of Riccardo's sentence *in absentia,* and after a bit of time had passed, should arrest Riccardo's children and proceed against those *complici,* or accomplices, accordingly. By the day the letter was sent, Riccardo and his two sons already had been caught by a handful of soldiers on the road to Germany. Riccardo was executed as a relapsed heretic on 22 February 1568.[3]

Riccardo's process, and the language utilized to describe his children's activities on his behalf, highlights the ways in which 'the sacred canons,' or the principles of canon law concerning heresy, were adapted to different temporal, cultural, and religious circumstances. The principles that guided the tribunals both in Venice and Conegliano were based on canon law; but by the sixteenth century, the terms 'favourer' or 'promotor' (*fautor*) and 'receiver' or 'shelterer' (*receptor*) were almost archaic and usually not utilized by inquisition staff in their correspondence – the Venetian tribunal responded using the more general term 'accomplices' (*complices*). Any guess as to why the vicar and Franciscan did so would be purely speculative, but it is possible that they found it necessary to read up on canon law and inquisitorial procedure to deal with the case. The staff in Conegliano could have found that language utilized in the canons relevant to heresy in the *Corpus iuris canonici,* widely available in print; but they also could have found those canons, along with the governing norms of the *inquisitio* procedure ('questioning'), within the pages of inquisition manuals.

The terms *fautor* (favourer) and *receptor* (receiver), which denoted people who helped heretics but were not necessarily heretics themselves, for example, can be found in Innocent III's decretal *Vergentis in senium* of 1199. In 1231 Innocent III's successor Gregory IX stated again the prosecutorial principle utilized against Riccardo – those who helped heretics could be condemned as if they were heretics, even without conclusive proof of heretical belief.[4] The legitimacy of doing so, however, would be questioned by Francisco Peña, the sixteenth-century editor of Nicholas Eymeric's fourteenth-century manual, the *Directorium Inquisitorum*.[5] Authors of these manuals, and those who glossed or edited them, presented the theoretical principles of inquisitorial prosecution to their readers. In the later sixteenth century these authors utilized canon law, glosses, lay legal manuals, works of theology, and other inquisition manuals to demonstrate not only the procedural rules, but also the way in which those rules had developed from canon law.

New manuals, or editions of older ones like Peña's edition of Eymeric's, became common in the latter half of the sixteenth century because the Catholic Church had a new set of heresies to confront and deal with to ensure the survival of the Church. The authors of these manuals, however, often asserted that the heresies they confronted were anything but new. Just as the theologians of the various Protestant sects claimed to be the true inheritors of the Ancient Church as a means of constructing legitimacy, inquisitorial authors emphasized that both sixteenth-century heresies, and the techniques developed to prosecute them, were anything but 'new.'[6]

Nevertheless the manuals demonstrate that a process of adaptation was necessary; the lack of originality in various Protestant doctrines might have been important to assert in polemics, but the Protestant Reformation, in reality, took place within a social, political, and cultural context that was very different from the Catholic Church's past encounters with heresy. The ways in which the inquisitorial literary tradition reflects this process of adaptation demonstrate what members of the Catholic hierarchy thought were the actions and words that could prove initial suspicion of heretical belief, and the relative importance of each as evidence. This chapter argues that inquisitorial authors, particularly Francisco Peña, Prospero Farinacci, and Cesare Carena, emphasized the importance of ritual practices in prosecuting a variety of philo-Protestant beliefs in the sixteenth century. To do so, they had to apply the principles of prosecution developed in the thirteenth century to philo-Protestant beliefs and ritual practices as they had developed a few decades earlier in the sixteenth century. In the adaptive process, these authors had to recognize, implicitly, the cultural and religious changes that had occurred, including the printing press and the Reformation's impact in urban centres, while simultaneously grounding their awareness and interpretation of what constituted 'Protestantism' within Catholic tradition and long-held principles of inquisitorial prosecution. Through their analysis of philo-Protestant protests against Catholic ritual practice, rendering it an important part of defining heresy, inquisition manual authors contributed to the confessionalization process. Devation from public ritual conformity had become a key piece of evidence in inquisition processes of the mid-to-late sixteenth century; the importance of such evidence also was later preserved within the pages of inquisition manuals. But in order to understand the process of adaptation, one has to examine the rules and traditions that were being adapted; this chapter, therefore, examines the canonical origins of the *inquisitio* and the heresies to which it was applied, in order to fully define and illustrate that adaptive process.

Canonical Literature

Canon law had developed as a normative legal code throughout the Middle Ages. It had begun in the twelfth century with Gratian's work, the *Concordantia discordantium canonum* (commonly called the *Decretum*); Gratian initially intended the work to be a textbook, so that church lawyers and students could have access to a standard text of sacred canons for study. Additionally, Gratian had claimed to reconcile and harmonize 'discordant' canons by juxtaposing those contradictions and achieving a concordance through dialectical reasoning. He thereby erected a coherent set of legal principles for the Church that, together with the civil law (*Corpus iuris civilis*), could serve society as an overarching legal structure for Western Christendom, the *ius commune* (common law). Gratian referred to the civil law rarely in his work; civil law was based on study of the Institutes, the Digest, the Codex, and the Novels, all compilations of Roman civil law produced in the first centuries CE and collected together in the 530s by the Emperor Justinian. But Gratian maintained that if canon law had no established solution to a particular question of legal theory or practice, an answer could be sought in Roman civil law. Thus, as R.H. Helmholz has put it, much of Roman civil law was subsequently 'canonized' by commentators and jurists. Finally, in principle Gratian maintained in his work that canon law only dealt with external acts subject to justice in this world.

After Gratian died (c. 1160) there were later additions to manuscripts of the *Decretum*, mostly put in place before about 1170. More references to the Justinian Code and Digest were added, along with the sections entitled *De poenitentia* and *De consecratione* ('On penitence' and 'On consecration'), which dealt with subjects of a more explicitly theological nature. Other passages were attributed to his student Paucapalea and therefore are called *paleae* (or 'chaff'). By the middle of the twelfth century, what had been a textbook was considered to be a legally based 'rule of life' for Christendom. As R. H. Helmholz has described it, however, there was 'no cleavage that could be called fundamental' between civil law and canon law; although the two were taught through separate faculties at universities, there were more theoretical similarities than differences, and many jurists trained in both.[7]

The Catholic Church added to Gratian's work throughout the Middle Ages. Pope Gregory IX instructed Raymond of Peñafort to collect papal judicial decisions subsequent to Gratian's formulation of the *Decretum*, known as the *Liber Extra* (promulgated 1234), partly as a response to the phenomenon of fake decretals circulating through Europe. The work contained papal decretals issued by Innocent III (d. 1216) and Honorius III (d. 1227), as well as those papal decretals collected by private jurists Bernard of Pavia (d. 1213), John of Wales (compiled c. 1216), and Johannes Teutonicus (d. 1245). It was Bernard of Pavia who established the chapter structure utilized by subsequent collections: *iudex, iudicium, clerus, connubia,* and *crimen* ('judge'; 'process'; 'clergy'; 'marriage'; 'crime'). Four later collections of papal decretals would also be considered normative collections: the *Liber Sextus,* produced under the aegis of Boniface VIII in 1298, the *Clementinae,* produced during the papacy of Clement V in 1317, and some of the laws of Pope John XXII and Sixtus IV, both compiled by Jean Chappuis and known as the *Extravagantes Johannis XXII* and *Extravagantes Communes,* respectively. After 1500, the entire collection came to be referred to as the official *Corpus iuris canonici;* and it was Pope Gregory XIII who had a legal commission review all the canons and print the collection in 1582 as the *Corpus iuris canonici* of the Catholic Church. Francisco Peña, the editor of Eymeric's inquisition manual, served on that commission.

Alongside the development of canon law throughout the Middle Ages, a large body of legal literature developed to explain the meaning of the canons to students, scholars, and practising lawyers, leading modern scholars to distinguish between decretists and decretalists. Decretists, such as Peñafort, wrote decretals on behalf of a pope. But soon after the compilation of the *Decretum,* glosses developed to enhance understanding and meaning, initially in response to questions that arose in classrooms at universities as the subject was being taught. Those who commented on, interpreted, or examined the decretals in glosses were decretalists. The first to be called the *Glossa Ordinaria,* or standard gloss for legal study, was composed by Accursius (1228), but other standard glosses included those of Karolus de Tocco (1215), Jacobus Columbi (about 1240), Johannes Teutonicus (about 1216), Bartholomew of Brescia's revision of Teutonicus (between 1238 and 1245), Bernard of Parma (about 1245), and Giovanni d'Andrea (about 1300).

Each author glossed only a selection of canons which had proven tricky to interpret in his career either as scholar or as practitioner. The gloss consisted of an interlinear note clarifying the meaning of particular words, and passages discussing the meaning of the text itself. Subsequent juridical experts then would write their own interpretations of both canon and gloss, in manuscript form before the end of the fifteenth century and thereafter in print. The glosses were largely incomprehensible without reference to the original decretal being explicated. In a similar way, the commentaries written to expound on the meaning of the canonical texts also could not be understood without reference to the original. Hostiensis's work, the *Lectura* concerning the Gregorian decretals, followed the decretals' order exactly, and his comments assume almost verbatim knowledge of the original; so did Giovanni d'Andrea's *Novella commentaria,* concerning both the *Decretum* and the *Liber Sextus*. Both authors most likely produced these commentaries and gloss apparatuses (*lectura*) by compiling the collective experience of years teaching in the classroom. The practice continued past the 'golden age' of decretists and decretalists, usually seen as coming to a close around 1375, into the early modern period; for example, the most important fifteenth-century commentary was that of Niccolò dei Tedeschi, also called Panormitanus (d. 1453). Over decades and centuries of work, commentators and jurists came to refer to the *communis opinio,* ('common opinion') concerning the appropriate interpretations of canons.

Decretalists from the mid-twelfth century onward also wrote *summae* concerning the growing *Corpus iuris canonici*; these were shorter and comprehensive summaries of canon law, which followed the order of the canons exactly but could be understood independently of the canons themselves. The most important *summa* of the *Decretum* during the latter twelfth century was Huguccio's. By the thirteenth century, canonists wrote *summae* concerning both the *Decretum* and the *Liber Extra,* the most important of which was that of Hostiensis. Another type of summary was the *ordines iudicarii* ('order of judgment'), which spelled out the technical aspects of legal procedure in courtrooms; a good example is William Durantis's *Speculum iudicale* (c. 1271) concerning canonical legal procedure.[8]

Finally, there were treatises concerning specialized subjects – including inquisition manuals, which drew on and utilized all of the above sources. Produced consistently from the beginnings of inquisitorial prosecution from the thirteenth century to the sixteenth and seventeenth centuries, manuals could vary widely as to structure, form, and contents. The first examples often simply gave templates of the necessary records to be kept, such as abjurations. From the thirteenth century onward, however, they expanded continually in length to include procedural guidelines, defining and categorizing different types of heresy, advice concerning interrogation techniques, and descriptions of doctrinal errors that bordered on being works of Catholic apology. In composing these manuals, their authors drew on the material stored in their archives, their own experiences, and the vast Catholic corpus of polemical literature stretching back to the early church, in addition to the legal literature described above. By the fourteenth century in at least one case, and among sixteenth-century authors more generally, the trend was to combine all of these topics into a single manual, including the texts of the applicable canon laws and citing the relevant legal opinions of canonists by abbreviated name and title.[9]

Canon Law and Inquisition: Defining Heresy

The principles underlying inquisitorial prosecution had been enshrined in canon law in the late twelfth and early thirteenth centuries. It was Pope Lucius III who had first decreed in the bull *Ad abolendam* (1184) that heretics, and their believers (*credentes*), favourers, and defenders (*defensores*) would be excommunicated from the church and turned over to the secular arm for punishment. Innocent III, in the decretal *Vergentis in senium* (1199), applied secular laws concerning treason (from the *Corpus iuris civilis*, or Roman civil law) to heresy and also decreed that convicted heretics could have their property confiscated and heirs disinherited; when Holy Roman Emperor Frederick II incorporated Innocent III's canons into the *ius commune* of the Holy Roman Empire, punishment for unrepentant heretics was declared to be death by burning, which then became normative for all of Western Europe. The gloss for Gregory IX's *Excommunicamus* explained why such penalties could be applied to those who unrepentantly helped heretics as well as to unrepentant heretics; those who learn, but do not teach, heresy and those who support heretics, although they may not yet believe, should be punished as heretics because they further the cause of heresy. He also had shifted responsibility for prosecuting heretics from bishops to specially appointed Dominican inquisitors beginning in 1227 and 1231. All of these decretals were included in the *Liber Extra,* and subsequently were summarized, commented on, analysed, and plumbed for meaning.[10]

In the effort to relate the broad principles of canon law to specific inquisitorial procedures necessary for the prosecution of heresy, Nicholas Eymeric, in his fourteenth-century *Directorium Inquisitorum,* already had an extensive variety of literature concerning canon law, the prosecution of heresy, and the very definition of heresy to draw on in the composition of his manual. That would be even more true for Francsico Peña in the later sixteenth century when he updated, expanded, and commented on Eymeric's work. In that sense, inquisition manuals served as a record of a continual effort over centuries to explain how theoretical principles of the *inquisitio* ideally *should* be employed.

The second part of Eymeric's manual, and Peña's commentaries, demonstrated those techniques of scholarship and explication. In that part of the *Directorum Inquisitorum,* Eymeric first reprinted the canons and glosses relevant to heresy. But then he discussed fifty-eight questions, the answers to which would define heresy thoroughly, which he considered to be fundamental to the office of inquisitor. To do so he cast a wide net concerning the sources he used, and gave both a general definition of heresy and an exhaustive list of specific iterations of it. To define the term 'heresy' in its broadest sense, he quoted Isidore of Seville concerning the Greek etymology of the word to introduce the subject: it meant choice. Those who chose to adhere to false doctrines, or errors, creating divisions within the unity of the Church, were heretics.

Peña's adaptations in his commentaries are representative of his critical technique in explicating Eymeric's text. He also consulted a wide range of sources, both temporally and geographically, in order to synthesize a general principle, or 'common opinion' that was mostly in rough agreement with Eymeric's original text, long a technique of legal study both canon and civil. In the process, Peña adapted his analysis of what constituted philo-Protestantism as it had developed earlier in the sixteenth century to the even earlier precedents of canon law and church traditions concerning prosecution. For example, concerning the origin and definition of the term 'heresy,' Peña emphasized that the word had existed before the advent of Christianity; ancient philosophers, such as the Stoics and Epicureans, had used the term in the context of making a choice but without any negative connotations, unlike the Christian usage of the word. Peña also noted that there were alternative theories as to the word's etymology; a minority of canonists thought the word derived from *eremite*, or hermit. Those reasoned that just as hermits separated themselves from society to live in the desert or the forest, heretics separated themselves from the Church community. Peña described the minority opinion for those of his readers who might have seen it elsewhere, but stressed the 'common opinion' of the majority. [11]

As Peña's commentaries further revealed, each Catholic author who had dealt with heresy across the centuries had produced his own definition of heresy, each slightly different from his predecessors. Peña therefore referred to five representative Catholic authors to explain Eymeric's definition. Three Spaniards – Guido Terrena, a fourteenth-century Carmelite, both prior general of his order and later a bishop; Tomás de Torquemada (1420–1498), a Dominican and the first inquisitor general of Castile and Aragon; and the Franciscan Alfonso de Castro (1495–1558), confessor to Charles V and Philip II – agreed concerning the voluntary and intellectual nature of heretical errors, but Torquemada added that the errant person had to be a baptized Christian, and Castro, alone of all authors, emphasized that such errors had to be manifest in enunciations or propositions. Peña also consulted non-Spanish sources, however. The German Conrad Bruns (Konrad Braun, c. 1495–1563), a lay jurist and Catholic controversialist in Vienna, emphasized pertinacious refusal to recant in his definition of heresy. The Dutchman Albert Pighius (1490–1542), theologian to three popes, archdeacon of St John's in Utrecht, participant in the Colloquy of Ratisbon and polemical author, strongly asserted that heresy was a crime of faith in which an individual elected to separate from the community of the Catholic Church.[12] The variations among these definitions can be attributed to the particular contexts of their formation; Torquemada, for example, was dealing with *conversos* in Spain (the Christians of Jewish descent accused of returning to Judaism), whereas Pighius's primary goal in 1538 was to denounce Henry VIII's separation from the Roman Church.[13] Taken together, this definition emphasized three critical areas: belief, refusal of correction, and separation from Catholic ritual practice.

Heresy as a defined concept, however, became a bit more complex in the third question of the fifty-eight. According to Eymeric, while all heresies were errors, not all errors were heresies. Of the two, non-heretical errors were far more common, which in theory could present inquisitors with a rather interesting problem. For Eymeric, in principle, the majority of people espousing religious errors were not properly called heretics. Religious errors were different from heresy, according to Peña's commentary, in that errors did not necessarily attack the Catholic faith – defendants could attempt to claim that they were merely in error, with no intent to commit heresy, so the distinction was an important one. Peña also referred his readers to the bull promulgated at the Council of Constance (1414–1418) during Martin V's papacy, which deemed some of Wycliff's and Hus's ideas errors, and some heretical errors, as an example.[14]

For many of his fifty-eight questions, Eymeric ensured that his readers would know the difference between heresy and error by listing all known heresies, from the ancient period to his own time. He utilized about ninety pages of his text to do so, and organized his definitions according to author, source, and type. Circumcellions, Arians, Donatists, Pelagians, Nestorians, and other heretics contemporaneous to the Church Fathers all received their (admittedly shorter) explanations alongside, for Eymeric, the more recent heresies of the Cathars, Waldensians, Beghards, and Beguines. Any reader consulting Eymeric's manual would know each and every permutation, despite Augustine's assertion that all heresies essentially repeated themselves in every age.

Given that sixty years had passed between Luther's protest and Peña's edition of the *Directorium Inquisitorum*, Peña's commentaries contain very little description concerning specific Protestant doctrines – about which Peña was anything but apologetic. In fact, he markedly praised Eymeric for refraining from detailing every single heretical belief or proposition, apparently oblivious to the obvious contradiction. In Peña's view, several esteemed doctors of the Church already had attempted to catalogue every version and permutation of heresy; such a task was quite laborious, and perhaps even be impossible to accomplish. Therefore, in Peña's considered view, general principles were more useful to inquisitors when faced with a multifarious array of heretical errors.[15]

Peña's laudatory comments concerning his brevity notwithstanding, after defining heresy comprehensively Eymeric then turned to the question of who could be called a heretic properly and truly. For Eymeric the complete heretic embodied two distinct criteria. First, he or she began by erring in the mind or intellect and, second, he or she held those errors voluntarily and with pertinacity, the second of which Konrad Braun, for one, had included in his definition of heresy. Only one who refused to repent could be convicted as a 'heretic.'[16] Eymeric's definition of a true heretic, derived from Aquinas's *Summa Theologiae,* therefore differed very little from Peña's more expansive treatment of heresy as a term earlier in the commentaries. While many theologians would describe heresy as the error itself, and the heretic as the one who held it and refused correction, in practice it was impossible to separate the heretical person from the error, since error itself was essentially an act of the will and intellect. Finally, Eymeric explained that there were only three sources of such heretical errors: deviation from the articles of faith, deviation from sacred Scripture, and deviation from anything the Church determined to be necessary to the faith.[17]

Eymeric then classified the term 'heretic' according to another binary scheme, which implicitly began to deal with the prospect of prosecuting them and also implicitly referenced the phenomenon Protestant theologians would scathingly call Nicodemism. First, Eymeric explained, some heretics were manifest, while others were secret. Manifest heretics revealed themselves by openly preaching their errors in public, or professing their errors in general. A state of manifest heresy also could be established through legal processes; those who were found guilty of their errors or who confessed to their errors in inquisitorial courts were manifest heretics. Secret heretics, however, while they held heretical errors in their thoughts, did not reveal them through their 'words or deeds,' in public or in private. This form of Nicodemism, or feigning Catholic belief through attendance at ritual practices despite believing differently in the mind, could not be prosecuted because it remained purely on the level of thought.[18] Peña thought it unnecessary to expand such a definition, since it had been established in canon law, specifically by *De verborum significatione* in the *Liber Extra,* although subsequent legal luminaries, such as Hostiensis and Panormitanus, and all canonists generally also treated the topic extensively.[19] Eymeric, writing in the fourteenth century, did not utilize the term 'Nicodemite' and neither did Peña – the phrase was popularized by John Calvin, despite his dissatisfaction with it. Eymeric, who died over a century before Calvin became active, utilized the term 'secret heretic' as did Peña.

Concerning those heretics who revealed themselves outwardly in some manifest way, *in verbo vel facto* ('in word or deed'), Eymeric classified them according to another binary scheme: affirmative or negative heretics. Eymeric defined affirmative heretics according to the exact same criteria as that of manifest heretics above, and heretics in general.

Negative heretics were those who continued to insist that they were good Catholics, despite the presence of legitimate proof – two credible witness testimonies. The category of 'the negative heretic,' in fact, exemplified how manual authors felt it necessary to include every bit of the Catholic Church's past legal decisions. As Richard M. Fraher has explained, Innocent II (d. 1143) had stated in principle that individual judges could consider a crime so 'notorious' either through the public *fama* ('reputation'), legitimate testimony, or both, that a conviction theoretically could occur even without a confession. The defendant who refused to confess would be forced to undergo a purgative oath; meaning that he or she would swear that he or she had not committed the crime supported by the official oaths of a certain number of fellow *compurgatores*, or members of the community also willing to swear that he or she had not committed the crime. But if the purgation was unsuccessful (i.e., *compuragtores* willing to come forward and so swear could not be found or the defendant simply refused), then the judge was empowered to impose punishment as if conviction had taken place – in theory, for heretical crimes, the death sentence was possible. As Fraher has noted, the principle was originally applied to cases of clerical concubinage but was later expanded to include heresy.[20] The principle stood as a part of church history; therefore Eymeric and Peña both explained it to their readers, even though such an end to an inquisition process must have been rare. In fact, this legal construct was, in some ways, a bit contradictory to other norms of inquisitorial procedure for heretics. In principle a defendant who never confessed to any of the evidence that had generated suspicion, even under torture, could be considered to have 'overcome' the evidence and be let go. In theory, manual authors thought that situation would occur when the initial proof was less conclusive.[21] In practice, standards of proof and the release of those who refused to confess under torture would be within the purview of the tribunal, most likely in consultation with the Congregation of Cardinals in Rome.

It was the heretic who still claimed to be Catholic despite evidence to the contrary, however, who potentially exemplified a form of quasi-Nicodemism. This heretic had propagated heresy, either through 'words' or 'deeds,' but when confronted with proof (usually in the form of witness testimony) denied it, and perhaps even proffered proof of Catholic ritual practice to counter the accusations. In that sense, negative heretics attempted to feign Catholicism when brought before the court. Both these definitions of manifest heretic – affirmative and negative – considered any word or action to be public, regardless of physical location. Whether the incidents that indicated suspicion of heresy took place in church, in the piazza, or within the four walls of a home, any utterance or action that could be construed as heretical was a public offence subject to inquisitorial prosecution.[22] True 'secrecy' only existed within the mind, and 'privacy,' for the inquisition, meant an absence of witnesses willing to testify.

Peña, however, in his comment concerning Eymeric's thirty-fourth question, utilized the opportunity to describe what exactly constituted proof of suspicion of heresy for his readers. In so doing, he focused almost exclusively on the 'deeds' that would indicate a heretic, affirmative or negative. He assured his readers that inquisitors could truly know heretics from their deeds as well as their words. Facts, or heretical deeds, most definitely were a way in which people indicated suspicion of erroneous interior faith.[23] Peña briefly mentioned one exceptional circumstance in which the heretical act itself would not reflect a corresponding heretical intent – if a person performed heretical acts out of fear or constraint, a theme he dealt with elsewhere in his commentaries concerning Eymeric's text – but otherwise Peña thought that heretical deeds performed of one's own will were definitive markers of violent suspicion of heresy at the very least, perhaps even *haeresis infamatus* ('infamous heresy').[24]

Giving his readers a few examples, Peña discussed several categories of heretical acts that would indicate suspicion of heretical belief to inquisitors. Peña proffered receiving the *consolamentum* at death ('the consolation'), the Cathar ritual practice meant to free the soul from its fleshly prison and allow reunion with God, as his first example of an act from which violent suspicion of heresy could be deduced.[25] Other such practices, which simply could not be interpreted as having any possible motivation other than heresy, included adoring demons; genuflecting before idols; exhibiting reverence for heretics; accepting communion according to heretical rites; and circumcision.[26] Peña admitted that it ought to be 'diligently observed' that presuming heresy from such acts was something of a 'legal fiction': suppositions of fact taken to be true by the court. As such, evidence to the contrary could be admitted in any inquisition proceeding. But as Peña warned his readers, such protestations against any heretical intent, when made concerning the adoration of demons or engaging in 'faithless rites,' should not be admitted to the court without extensive consideration. Who truly would believe such acts could have been perpetrated willingly without any heretical intent?

Peña allowed that any person who confessed to the heretical acts, but was found not to have any clear heretical intent, should be abjured as lightly or vehemently suspect in heresy and assigned salutary penance as punishment. But he also thought that proof of such a lack of heretical intent was difficult to produce; in theory, torture of the accused should be utilized to definitively settle the question of intent. And if the defendant in question was was unable to convince inquisitors that there was not any corresponding heretical intent, then he or she should be declared a formal heretic and given the greatest punishment, according to Peña [27]

Participation in heretical rites, therefore, was strong proof from which inquisitors could deduce suspicion of heresy. Peña also recognized a second category of public acts, from which heretical intent could not be deduced as strongly. People who visited heretics, or gave them money, or defended their persons, and other similar acts, Peña pointed out, might very well be performing these acts out of familial love and not because of any definitive heretical belief, although heretical belief very well might be present.[28] Riccardo's children, for example, who had broken him out of prison, might not be heretical believers but simply exemplars of filial piety of a sort. Or, conversely, they could be their father's co-religionists as well as his children, who simply had not been caught in heresy yet.

In his analysis, Peña was following long-established traditions in the development of the theory of inquisitorial prosecution – acts that pertained to ritual practice were almost certainly indicators of heretical belief, while those acts that helped support heretics physically were not so easily classified. In fact, Peña's entire list of heretical actions that were sure indicators of mental error was drawn from the Catholic Church's encounters with past heresies. The consolation and exhibiting reverence for heretics were examples drawn from the Catholic Church's dealings with Cathar heresy in the twelfth and thirteenth centuries; the reference to taking communion from heretics would be the only one that could be construed as applicable to prosecuting philo-Protestants, and was most likely first applied to the Waldensians, also originating in the late twelfth and thirteenth centuries, both of which are discussed below. Witches were considered to be heretical because they violated their baptismal vows to God by forswearing them to make a pact with the Devil, and therefore were subject to inquisitorial prosecution. Circumcision signalled apostasy, either on the part of *conversos* still attempting to practise Judaism (the reason for the creation of the Spanish Inquisition in 1478, but not unheard of in the Italian states), or those who converted to Judaism or Islam as adults, particularly those captured and enslaved in the Ottoman Empire.[29] These heretical acts, according to Peña, were emblematic of how the practice of religion was just as important as doctrinal belief, and therefore also important to inquisitorial prosecution. Acts that related to ritual practice established suspicion of heresy at the very least, both to inquisitors and to members of the Catholic community, who would often be called to serve as witnesses. But not all acts were to be equally valued as clear indicators of suspicious intent, and any heterodox act, or possible visible proof of suspicion, was evaluated in terms of its usefulness to inquisitorial prosecution according to principles established during the Catholic Church's history of prosecuting heresy.

Peña's transmission, and modification, of these principles became a standard part of subsequent inquisition manuals. Prospero Farinacci, in his *Tractatus de haeresi*, first published in 1616, also began the work by defining heresy in the first chapter and utilized Thomas Aquinas and Hostiensis as sources who, according to Farinacci, described heresy as a division or separation from the Catholic faith. He also cited much more recent sources, such as Umberto Locati, an early sixteenth-century Dominican inquisitor, who Farinacci described as defining heresy to be a deviation from the Christian faith, and the Catholic religion (or rites). Locati, in his *Opus quod iudiciale inquisitorum* (1568), did not use that language exactly, but he wrote that those who held different ways of thinking other than the common opinion had constructed heresies and sects.[30] When citing Eymeric explicitly, Farinacci limited himself to Eymeric's first question: heresies were words that introduced division. He also referred to Peña's commentaries briefly summarizing the arguments described above. Heretics, for Farinacci, separated themselves from community of the Catholic faithful, from which understanding of and belief in heresy could be presumed.[31] But if those definitions were not to his readers' liking, he cited other authors as well. For example, according to Farinacci it was Luis de Pàramo, a late sixteenth-century Spanish inquisitor in Sicily, who had emphasized that heretics refused the correction of the Church.[32] Farinacci defined heresy in much the same way as Eymeric and Peña, but utilized a broader array of sources, and framed his definition in a way that reflected the establishment of different sects in northern Europe as a result of the Reformation.

When it came to explaining exactly how such separation might play out in ritual practices, and describing the heretical doctrines of which they could be manifestations, Farinacci firmly followed Peña's example in declining to be specific. Farinacci admitted that heresy could be committed in many forms and that there were many different 'kinds' of errors.[33] There were so many different kinds of heresy, in fact, that any attempt to explain them all in his chapter, or even his entire manual, would excessively bore his readers. He therefore referred those readers still curious to a variety of sources, beginning with John XXII's 1318 edict, *Gloriosam*, which primarily focused on the errors of the Fraticelli. Martin V's 1418 edict dealt with the errors of Wycliff and Hus, while Leo X's *Exsurge Domine* in 1520 condemned Martin Luther's errors. Farinacci also thought that further knowledge of heretical sects could be sought in other inquisition manuals, including the *Repertorium Inquisitorum*, and, interestingly, Peña's edition of Eymeric. Farinacci commented to his readers that it was not his purpose to describe all different kinds of intellectual errors; his task was to explain how to investigate and punish them.[34]

Farinacci also firmly followed Peña's preservation of Eymeric's propensity for binary categories. For Farinacci, there were heresiarchs and their followers. Heresiarchs not only believed heretical errors, they invented them; but heresiarchs also could teach errors to others or publicly defend errors.[35] Concerning heretics who were neither originators, nor teachers, but followers, Farinacci imitated Eymeric (and many others) in establishing the dichotomy between affirmative and negative heretics. Farinacci cited Arnaldo Albertini, a sixteenth-century inquisitor in Sicily, particularly when it came to describing the punishment to be visited on negative heretics. Since negative heretics were convicted through words and deeds that clearly established a state of heresy, without a doubt, they should therefore be turned over to the secular arm for execution as impenitent heretics, since they refused to confess to the obvious heretical intent behind their words and actions (if the canonical purgation process utterly failed, one presumes).[36]

Having declined to list heresies and heretical acts specifically, Farinacci instead listed the essentials of Catholicism, the deviation from which would incur suspicion of heresy. To accomplish this he began with Martin V's edict of 1418, which stated that heretics proper thought badly of the Catholic Church's sacraments or believed differently than the articles of faith. Farinacci also acknowledged that many other works both before and after the Council of Constance asserted much the same thing, including the papal bull *Ad abolendam* and just about every inquisition manual ever produced. He officially listed the seven sacraments for those of his readers who may not have been familiar with them. He also defined the articles of faith as the Apostles' Creed and any requirements made by the pope or a council.[37] Furthermore, heretics, according to Farinacci, were prone to knowing Scripture well and presuming to expound or interpret it differently from the Catholic Church – here Farinacci's most important and extensive source was the Council of Trent, but he cited earlier sources as well, including the Council of Constance.[38] Anyone who believed or thought differently from these norms could be considered heretical; in all of this, Farinacci placed deviation from Catholic sacraments at the top of his list.

Farinacci, finally, explained that there was some disagreement among his different sources. In his effort to be completely comprehensive Farinacci, in effect, revealed that authors who had written about heresy, prosecution, and the appropriate interpretation of canon law over the centuries had disputed the proper understanding of certain points. In this particular case, Farinacci noted a minority opinion concerning exactly who could be considered heretics proper. Some doctors of the Church, according to Farinacci, had argued that people who merely deviated from only some of the articles of faith could only be considered heretics in a broader sense. Heretics proper not only believed errors but taught them to others. Farinacci noted that this was not the commonly held opinion; the majority of authors thought that heresiarchs were definitely heretics, but so were those who followed them and believed those false doctrines, even if they never actively sought to teach them to others.[39]

Heretical Precedent: Concept and Terminology

In recounting this debate concerning the relative importance of leading heretical movements or participating as followers, Farinacci was referring, if obliquely, to the same issues that both Eymeric and Peña raised when discussing the Catholic Church's past encounters with heresy. All these authors were alluding to the language used to describe the heresy against which the process of *inquisitio* had first been employed: the Cathars. The traces of the influence of this initial experience shaped how varying levels of heresy were categorized, and how to recognize heretical ritual practices or protests against Catholic ritual practices that could indicate suspicion of heresy.

Of the medieval heresies, the Catholic Church considered Catharism to be the most seriously threatening.[40] Medieval Catholic authors often declared Cathars to be the direct descendants of the Manicheans, the radical dualists described by Augustine, himself a former member of the sect. Historical evidence has not uncovered any direct connection between the Manicheans and the Cathars, and whether or not there was some degree of contact with the Bogomils, a radical dualist sect located in what was then the Byzantine Empire and now Bulgaria, is still a matter of some controversy among historians. The Council of Rheims (1157), for example, deemed the Cathars 'Manicheans,' because of Augustine's works on heresy, which still circulated in the Middle Ages.[41] The sect, or more properly from the modern historical point of view, sects of Cathars were established in southern France, most likely through the port of Marseilles, and in northern and central Italy by the twelfth century. Catharism was established in southern France at least by the 1150s; French Cathars most likely had proselytized northern Italian lands by 1165.[42] The inquisitorial tribunals founded to prosecute them beginning in 1227 were certainly effective, but the Catholic Church required the aid of secular authorities in both areas. In France this took the form of the Albigensian Crusade, which preceded inquisitorial activity in the area; Innocent III approved the use of military power, largely carried out by northern French minor nobles with King Philip Augustus's approval, against Count Raymond VI of Toulouse, who had been quite lenient toward Cathars in an effort to solidify his political power over his land holdings. In Italian communes, the cooperation of secular authorities was secured through Innocent III's use of the decretal *Vergentis in senium*, Gregory IX's appointment of inquisitors, negotiations with individual communal governments, and the incorporation of canon laws concerning heresy into the law code of the Holy Roman Empire. Since inquisition tribunals, as canonical courts, could not arrest, torture, or punish, the cooperation of the secular arm, whether gained through war, negotiation, or canonical sanctions like excommunication or interdict, was crucial.[43]

There were variations in doctrine among different Cathar sects in France and Italy, but most of them shared a core belief system that embraced several doctrinal positions and ritual practices. Most Cathar sects believed that earthly reality was created or dominated by Lucifer, a fallen angel or God's 'evil son.' All of creation was inherently evil and only by escaping creation could the soul trapped in evil flesh return to God. This could only occur through the Cathar believer receiving the *consolamentum*, or 'the consolation,' during which the postulant had the New Testament placed on his or her forehead, a baptism by fire or spirit, not evil water made of matter. This was the pre-eminent ritual that Peña still named as an example of clear proof of suspicion of heresy over three hundred years after Catharism had ceased to exist. Those who received this rite lived in a state of ascetic perfection, refusing to engage in anything related to human sexuality or sexual reproduction of any kind, including refusing to eat foods that were the product of sex or played a role in sexual reproduction. The Cathar 'perfect,' the sect's elite priesthood, who could be either male or female, ate neither meat, nor eggs, nor milk, subsisting entirely on grains, fruits, vegetables, and fish (born of water, not of sex, as it was believed, thanks to Aristotelian scientific models).[44]

These foods and other necessities of life often were provided by the non-perfect members of the sect, called *credentes*, or 'believers,' who lived in the world, married, had children, ate meat, and received the consolation on their deathbeds, which Catholic authors often characterized as corresponding to communion instead of baptism. These believers supported the Cathar perfect in the material sense, providing them with food, money, and a place to stay as they traveled among the Cathar faithful. The believers, and also defenders and protectors, would perform the *melioramentum*, an 'honouring' in which the believers would kneel and greet the perfect; Peña described this as 'adoring' heretics, in much the same way Catholics knelt before the consecrated host, as had Eymeric.[45] Thus there was a clear two-tiered system, from the perspective of Catholic polemicists, of teachers and spreaders of heresy (the perfect), and their followers (or believers).

Networks of believers and the perfect they supported relied heavily on family and kinship ties, initially a serious problem for the Catholic Church when it came to prosecution.[46] Therefore in 1199 Innocent III's bull *Vergentis in senium* was designed to punish defenders, receivers, patrons, and believers of heretics. Those found supporting heretics would be subject to such punishments as deprivation of office and inheritance rights, as well as confiscation of possessions, although the Fourth Lateran Council in 1215 reversed the decision concerning inheritance and added excommunication as a form of punishment. Innocent III justified such punitive, not rehabilitative, punishments through an analogy to the crime of lèse-majesté in Roman civil law. If those penalties could apply to those who plotted treason against a secular emperor, then why should they not apply to those guilty of treason against God and the true faith?[47]

It was Innocent III's successor, Gregory IX who, after detecting Cathars in Rome in 1231, provided new punishments for believers and other supporters of heretics; they could be judged as if they were heretics (the perfect) and punished with death. It was also Gregory IX who in 1227 and 1231 gave Dominican friars, among some other religious, commissions to operate as 'inquirers' into heresy. Inquisitors prosecuted the perfect, but they also prosecuted their followers and supporters, utilizing that terminology to do so. In Jacques Fournier's register of sentences, the terms *credentes* ('believers'), *fautores* ('favourers'), *defensores* ('defenders'), and *receptores* ('receivers') were utilized extensively.[48] The perfect received, and then gave believers, the consolation; *credentes*, or believers, believed the heresies taught by the perfect, asked to receive the consolation at death, and performed the *melioramentum*, or 'honouring' heretics, as Peña emphasized in his commentaries. These ritual practices were considered to surely indicate suspicion of heretical belief because they constituted definitive proof of participation in a heretical sect.

Those that supported heretics materially could be punished as if they were heretics, but that decision addressed a practical problem, not a theological one; assessing heretical intent from such support activities was much more uncertain. When Eymeric wrote the *Directorium Inquisitorum* in the fourteenth century, he again employed neat binary categories based on one general principle to clarify the issue. Believers who performed the *melioramentum* before the perfect were definitely suspect in heresy. Concerning the other three categories of supporters, Eymeric recognized that they could either have helped the heretics without necessarily believing in the heresies, or could have helped because they shared those beliefs. By the sixteenth century, when Peña wrote his commentaries concerning these issues, the terms 'favourers,' 'receivers,' 'defenders,' and 'believers' were rarely used in processes. Peña, however, left the chapters devoted to explaining these concepts intact, because the chapters demonstrated how actions were to be categorized theoretically, especially with an eye towards explaining what constituted a heretical ritual practice, what did not, and most importantly, why.

Raymond of Peñafort, for example, addressed that same issue when he had participated in the Council of Tarragona in 1242. That council and four others – the Councils of Narbonne (1243), Béziers (1246), Valence (1248), and Albi (1254) – sought to broaden the principles of inquisitorial prosecution as laid down in canonical bulls. Peñafort, in addition to becoming a general of the Dominican order and bishop, also had complied the *Liber Extra* on behalf of Gregory IX by 1234.

At Tarragona in 1242, for Peñafort, the heretics in question were the *Insabbatatos*, a term for the Waldensians, since their priests wore sandals as a mark of office; the term apparently relates to the French *sabot* ('shoes'). In his work, he applied and expanded the terminology developed from experiences prosecuting Cathars to describe Waldensians.[49]

Waldo of Lyon, the founder of the Waldensians, was not deemed heretical early in his career. A rich merchant, he gave up his material possessions to embrace the apostolic life of preaching and poverty in the late twelfth century. For example, he opened a soup kitchen in 1176 in Lyon in response to widespread famine. Good Catholic charitable activities aside, however, Waldo promoted self-instruction in doctrine through reading Scripture in translation. After commissioning vernacular translations and reading the Gospels for himself, he became intent on preaching publicly, as did his followers, reportedly both male and female. It was his insistence on preaching that eventually brought him into conflict with the papacy, although he was supported initially by the Bishop of Lyon Guichard. At the Third Lateran Council in 1179 at Rome, Pope Alexander III approved the apostolic vow of poverty but condemned Waldo and his followers' understanding of key doctrines such as the nature of Christ. Bishop Guichard's successor, Jean Bellesmain, banned the Waldensians from preaching and exiled them from Lyon. Lucius III's bull *Ad abolendam,* promulgated in 1184, attempted to invigorate bishops' ability to deal with heresy, by requiring them to visit parishes known for heresy once or twice a year in part to deal with Waldensianism as well as Catharism. The sect, or sects, quicly spread along the Rhine and Moselle, in Alsace, and to Trier, Mainz, and Strasbourg. A similar group existed along the Danube, but any connection with the Waldensians is unknown.[50]

In order to describe how to punish Waldensian heretics, Peñafort quite logically defined different categories of culpability for his readers first. Heretics persisted in their errors, and the *Insabbatati*'s main error, according to the bishop, was their refusal to obey ecclesiastical and secular power. His description of *credentes haereticorum*, or 'believers of heretics,' was similarly brief, stating only that they said words similar to heretics – the originators and teachers of heresy.[51] Peñafort described the ritual practices of followers as well; Waldensians knelt to listen to preaching, or called the Waldensian priests 'good men.' *Receptores*, or 'receivers,' welcomed the priests into their homes or some other location, two or more times, so they and other members of the sect could hear preaching. *Defensores*, or 'defenders,' were those who defended heretics in 'word or deed,' thereby inhibiting the ability of inquisitors to perform their duties. *Fautores*, or 'favourers,' could perform all of the above actions that supported heretics, but they also gave counsel, help, or favour to heretics.[52]

When Peñafort tackled how to judge and punish these actions, the issue of intent and knowledge were foremost in his logic. He rhetorically asked his readers: If, when confronted with those who hid heretics, or listened to them, or spoke with them, or thought them good men, could those helpers of heretics be judged to believe in the errors as well? Peñafort answered in the negative. Such proof would indicate vehement suspicion of belief, but it could not definitively establish the knowledge of, or belief in, heresy. There was one exception: if the collaborator was literate or wise, then ignorance of meaning was not even a theoretical possibility. The literate, according to Peñafort, should have known of their guests' heretical identity, and therefore could be assumed to have known it. The non-literate, however, might well have mistaken their guests for good Catholics, or even been deliberately misled, Peñafort seems to imply. He therefore instructed that inquisitors should use discretion concerning ordinary followers of heretics, advising that their punishments could be moderated according to circumstances. But when it came to *perfecti haeretici*, or 'perfect heretics,' to quote another of Peñafort's Catharisms (whom Farinacci would have called heresiarchs) and those followers who relapsed after a prior abjuration, the bishop advised perpetual incarceration as punishment. Even if they were willing to abjure and receive absolution from excommunication, their souls had to be saved without risking the souls of others, since relapsed followers had stubbornly clung to heresy although they had known better, because of their first processes.[53]

Peñafort was not the only medieval author to utilize Cathar terminology to describe Waldensian beliefs and practices, particularly as canonical texts, sample formulae of procedure, and definitions of different heresies came to be collected in instructional inquisitorial manuals – particularly that of Bernard Gui, notably an inquisitor at Toulouse in 1307. The first three parts concerning procedure in Gui's *Practica* were drawn from his own experiences and records; the fourth part, containing collections of papal bulls and the canons of councils, came from an anonymous Italian tract on the same subject, but Gui substantially reworked the text and made substantial additions. The fifth part contained Gui's descriptions of Cathars, 'Waldenses', the pseudo-Apostles, Beguins, Jews, and sorcerers, including descriptions of 'the way of life and the practices [. . .]' of the sects.[54] Despite the fact that the Waldensians evolved from quite different circumstances than the Cathars, the structure of preaching and ministry adopted by the sect lent itself to such a fusion in interpretation. As Peñafort and Gui both recognized, the Waldensians originated from within Catholicism; after the sect's papal condemnation, they needed to operate as an underground religious movement. As such, their methods of ministering to the faithful came to resemble the Cathars', even if their theology did not.

Scholars have debated whether or not one can refer to a single form of Waldensianism. The group split early on, thanks to the intervention of Durand of Osca who sought to bring them back within the boundaries of papal obedience, although that effort failed in the long run. There were variations between groups in different geographic areas; and how the sect defined itself and its doctrines evolved through the fourteenth and fifteenth centuries. In general, however, there was a core group of beliefs. The Waldensian priesthood required study of Scripture, followed by vows of poverty and celibacy. They wandered, in their sandals, or *sabots*, recruiting followers, called *amici*, or friends, who remained 'in the world' and supported them through alms. In addition to support, those who followed the Waldensian preachers in terms of belief participated in the study of Scripture, usually held in private houses, as well as a ritual meal held once a year on Holy Thursday, which medieval manual authors thought roughly approximated communion. Most Waldensian groups also came to deny purgatory and prayers for the dead, a fact that would be seized on by Reformation-era Catholic polemicists.[55]

That was especially the case because the Waldensian movement, unlike the Cathars, continued to exist, mostly in remote Alpine valleys in the Piedmont and in Calabria, until the Reformation. When some Waldensians paid visits to Reform theologians Oecolampadius and Martin Bucer, they were chided for upholding some 'Catholic' beliefs like celibacy of the priesthood. But in 1532, the Waldensian brothers attended a synod held at Chanforan where they met with Reformer Guillaume Farel. By 1555, the former Waldensians had formed Calvinist churches in San Lorenzo, Serre di Angrogna, Torre Pellice, and in other locations. The senate at Turin repeatedly severely criticized this and prosecutions were undertaken, but ultimately the former Waldensians were dealt with through military force, both in Piedmont and Calabria, in addition to prosecutions and the persuasive powers of the Jesuits. The other pre-Reformation heresies still in existence in the sixteenth century were the Hussites and Taborites in Bohemia; while those churches never joined a new Protestant denominations, Luther quite clearly at the Diet of Worms in 1521, and in subsequent publications, proclaimed himself at the very least sympathetic to Jan Hus and his followers. In 1575 the Lutheran, Hussite, and Bohemian Brethren churches agreed on a common confession, the *Confessio Bohemica*.[56] That the Waldensians effectively joined the Calvinist church, and the Hussites officially defined doctrinal beliefs in concord with Lutherans, must have reinforced the perception, for authors and Catholic churchmen like Peña, that there was not really anything 'new' concerning heresy in the sixteenth century.

When Eymeric wrote the *Directorium Inquisitorum* in the fourteenth century, he attempted to employ neat dualistic subsets to describe each category of supporters, based on that general principle of knowledge, so as to address the qualms Peñafort and others expressed concerning the prosecution of both perfect and supporters. Eymeric defined believers in heretics as consisting of two types: those who believe in heretics and those who believe in their errors and heresies. Both types could be proven guilty of being suspect in heresy either in words or in deeds. Believers could be expected to publicly preach and defend the errors of heretics, which could be established by the testimony of witnesses. But believers in heresy could establish their identity through their acts as well, and therefore would be seen (and Eymeric claimed he was 'using their words') adoring heretics (performing the *melioramentum*), and exhibiting reverence for them through their customs.[57] Eymeric also thought that the believers would receive the consolation, which he described as their 'communion.' Believers also listened to sermons, but frequently, not just once or twice. Eymeric also pointed out that those who served heretics, brought them money, and visited them could be considered believers in heresy, but that proof was less clear – they could also not be believers.[58]

Peña in his sixteenth-century commentaries concerning Eymeric's work was even further removed temporally from the Cathar example; he therefore had to consult two other sources to contextualize Eymeric's explanations, and utilized those sources to adapt those principles to the sixteenth century, despite his claims that the meaning of Eymeric's text was obvious. The two sources he found were an unnamed 'very old' writing and the work of Petrus de Palud, both in the collection of the Biblioteca Apostolica at that time. The unnamed manuscript described believers as those who held the beliefs, but did not embrace 'the mode of life,' by which the anonymous author most likely meant that believers did not behave or live as the perfect did. Palud (d. 1342), a Dominican theologian and Patriarch of Jerusalem who wrote prominent works against the Fraticelli in the early fourteenth century, proved familiar with Cathar heresies as well. He described those who held that the heretics were good men or had good faith as implicated in heresy, but not explicitly heretics (explicit heretics being, one assumes, the perfect).[59] This was probably one of the sources of the minority opinion Farinacci mentioned, but dismissed, which had considered followers of heresy as heretics only in the broadest sense.

Peña also required a third text from the Biblioteca Apostolica to explain the ritual practices in which believers participated, such as Eymeric's reference to the *melioramentum*. The text recorded the canons of the councils of Avignon and Narbonne, two of the most important councils for defining heresy and how to prosecute it. Of the two councils, according to Peña, that of Narbonne explained the practices characteristic of believers more extensively, but Peña briefly summarized both for his readers.[60] He quoted passages in which the consolation and the laying on of hands, professing honours for heretics, the use of the New Testament in ritual practices, serving heretics, and imploring heretics for their prayers, all hallmarks of Cathar believers' behaviour toward the perfect, were mentioned.

The Council of Narbonne, however, also had taken note of Waldensian beliefs; those at the council thought that in this sect, heretical believers praised the Waldensian version of communion or excused it. Believers in Waldensian heresy also praised their *barbes*, or clergy (so named for their beards, which they wore in imitation of the apostles), gave their confessions to them, called them friends of God and holy men, received them in their houses, ate with them, and gave them goods. The council also quoted the Second Letter of John (2 John 1) which warned against associating with heretics. Finally the council had asserted that those truly ignorant of the fact that Waldensians were heretics were not to be prosecuted or damned with the same ferocity. Peña ended his quotation from the Council of Narbonne by explaining to his readers that while these comments applied to the heresies of another time, such principles could be adapted easily to the sixteenth century if the conditions, rites, and ceremonies of several contemporary heresies were observed.[61]

Peña maintained, in this section, that while it might be easier to recognize a believer from statements made in public praising heretics, it was really the engagement in ritual practice that explicitly established a clear reason for one to be considered a suspected heretic – and obliquely referred to a variety of Nicodemism in the process.[62] For Peña, it was the act of attending 'heretical sermons' that demonstrated the principle. In order to be considered a believer by the inquisition, one had to hear those sermons more than once or twice. According to Peña, it was his contemporary, the Dominican inquisitor of Pavia, Ferrara, and Modena in much of the 1550s and 1560s, Camillo Campeggi, who had put it best in his own commentary concerning the fourteenth-century inquisition manual written by the Bolognese jurist Zanchino Ugolini. For Campeggi it simply was not prudent to easily presume heretical beliefs from only one or two acts of attending sermons. Adapting the principle to his own time (much as Campeggi did in his work) Peña expressed the opinion that those Catholics who had lived in the lands of heretics (Protestant countries), or those Catholics who lived in Catholic countries but attended secret conventicles once or twice, should not be judged guilty of believing in heresy. But if the person in question attended secret conventicles many, many times, then there was definitely suspicion of believing in heresy.[63] By the time Peña wrote these passages in his commentary, the fact that Italian philo-Protestants had begun to form secret convencticles to discuss Scripture and even practise what they considered to be 'pure' ritual practices a few decades earlier was commonly known, as will be discussed in the next chapter. It was also true that some philo-Protestants, or those sympathetic to Protestant doctrines, might continue to put in appearances at Catholic Mass, or at least part of the service, to imply or 'feign' continued commitment to Catholicism while also practising their new-found faith quietly, in what they hoped was 'private' space and discreetly.[64] Even if philo-Protestants continued to attend Catholic ritual practices as a cover (or not completely avoiding them), their attendance at alternative religious rituals would demonstrate their commitment to heresy.

To further emphasize the point Peña, as had Eymeric, referred to the Bible.[65] Eymeric cited the parable of two sons in Matthew 21:28; he and Peña both interpreted this passage to mean that, while words may be more easily said and heard, deeds were a better indication of conscience. In the parable, which Peña related to his readers, one son initially refused to obey his father and work in the vineyards, but changed his mind and went to work later, while the other son told he father he would go and then did not.[66] In the commentary, Peña duly noted that this text meant that actions clearly supersede words in Christ's judgment. Thus, verbal evidence, snatches of conversations, statements that heretics were 'good men' (which in Cathar parlance meant they were the perfect, or effectively priests, a point that seems to have been lost on both Eymeric and Peña) were not necessarily conclusive. Those who spoke favourably of heretics might be believers, and therefore were 'not without suspicion' either; they could be purged or abjured either lightly or vehemently, as the verbal evidence and assumed eventual confession warranted.[67]

Those who supported heretics materially, according to Eymeric were not automatically considered suspect in heresy. Continuing his dichotomous classification, receivers of heretics consisted of two kinds: those who knowingly sheltered heretics in their private homes, and those who had no idea their guests were not good Catholics but duplicitous heretics. The second had no serious intent of helping heretics, and therefore only those who knowingly and frequently received heretics into their homes were true 'receivers.' They could also be considered believers, if they knew of and agreed with their houseguests' heretical errors.[68]

Peña once again adapted the principle, and updated it to apply to a sixteenth-century context. In fact, Peña argued that a receiver could only prove complete ignorance of his or her visitors' heretical state with great difficulty in his Tridentine era. According to Peña, since most heretics were publicly known and notorious in any given area, there could not be any question as to whether anyone could be ignorant of the facts – since Peñafort's time, being ignorant of heresy and heretics had become much harder to prove. For Peñafort, only the illiterate could claim ignorance convincingly; for Peña, almost no one could claim ignorance of the religious controversies of his day, or deny knowledge of notorious heretics in the neighbourhood. This may well have been Peña's implicit recognition of the role of the printing press, especially in Europe's urban centres, in creating what constituted a widely known and much-discussed 'mass media' event on all levels of society. But for Peña, if the heretic in question was really infamous in the neighbourhood (quite possibly due to openly proselytizing and possession of print media) then inquisitors could presume that anyone, regardless of their status as 'literate' or not, cleric or lay person, should have known about their status as heretics, and was therefore an intentional receiver.[69] It is true that, in processes held in the mid-to-late sixteenth century, these terms were rarely if ever applied in practice. But Peña's insistence that, in the mid-to-late sixteenth century, ignorance of heresy was virtually impossible very well might explain why those terms were no longer used in processes, even though Peña dutifully respected inquisitorial traditions of prosecution and explained them for his readers in theory. Conceptually, Peña's rejection of ignorance as a plausible excuse in his day and age would play a significant role in how he evaluated philo-Protestant ritual practices, and philo-Protestant objections to Catholic ritual practice, as proof of heresy.

When describing the binary categorization of defenders, knowledge was again the key component for Eymeric. Defenders could defend both heretics and their heresies, or defend 'the person who erred' but not the errors. Defenders who defended the heretics as, well, people, and not the errors they espoused were not to be considered heretics.[70] In other words, Eymeric recognized that familial loyalty, or close friendship, might lie behind the 'defence,' not belief that the heretic was right. But Eymeric explicitly did not rule out prosecution or punishment for even that category of defenders, since they would be punished for furthering the cause of heresy, if not believing in it. To this, Peña added a list of the ways in which heretics might be defended: with, or without, arms; by warning them to flee; defending them 'in court'; or by verbally defending them outside the court. Peña noted that the original canons of Innocent IV and Clement IV only dealt with military or armed defence, but explained that the definition had been broadened since that time to include verbal defences as well.[71]

Prospero Farinacci's descriptions of believers, defenders, favourers, and receivers in his early seventeenth-century *Tractatus* were removed even further from their medieval origins. As a result, he tended to blend the terms in his accounts, but nevertheless maintained the customary emphasis on knowledge and intent when evaluating their constitutive actions. Farinacci also, in his explanations of these terms, demonstrated further refinements in adapting these concepts to philo-Protestant beliefs and ritual practices. Publishing in 1616, it is quite possible that Farinacci's work reflects more fully how late sixteenth- and early seventeenth-century inquisition tribunals had shifted their prosecutorial outlook to adjust to a multi-denominational Christian world.

Farinacci, following Giovanni Lorenzo Anania, author of sixteenth-century works concerning heresy and witchcraft, simply adapted the categories of believers and perfect to his earlier definitions of heretics and heresiarchs. Believers were the followers of heresiarchs, such as Martin Luther, who were the inventors of the errors. Farinacci prided himself on comprehensive works, and he therefore noted Peña's definition, originally drawn from the 'ancient manuscript,' which defined believers in heresy as those who believed but did not live the life (as perfect), among other variant definitions. But Farinacci ultimately opined that no definition was 'more pleasing' to him than that of his near-contemporary Cardinal Toletus (Francisco de Toledo, d. 1596, at one time a Jesuit theologian of the Collegio Romano), who defined believers as heretics because they knowingly held beliefs which were contrary to those of the Roman Catholic Church, even if those errors were not of their own invention. Such believers could take one of three forms: they could explicitly believe particular points of heresy; they could assert that they believed whatever some heresiarch, such as John Calvin, believed; or they could praise heretics as 'good and laudable men.'[72] Farinacci stopped short of referring to John Calvin as a 'perfect,' but the imprint of how the medieval Church evaluated Cathar heresy was very much present, even if adapted.

When it came time to explain how believers could reveal themselves through deeds as well as words the Cathar precedent came even more strongly to the fore. Farinacci quoted many authors, from Giovanni Calderini's *De haereticis (1571)* to the *Repertorium Inquisitorum* and Peña's commentaries, all of which described believers in heresy as those that wanted the consolation performed at their deaths. He also instructed his readers not to prosecute those who called for the consolation due to insanity. More relevant to the late sixteenth and early seventeenth centuries, Farinacci also described those who went to heretical sermons more than once or twice as believers in heresy as well.[73]

Ignorance of the heretical state of a person, however, still was possible according to Farinacci. In his chapter concerning favourers, he conflated what had been clearly defined and separate methods of support in earlier inquisitorial literature. He quoted the original definition of favourers accurately as he found it in several sources; but he also quoted Giovanni Lorenzo Anania as having written that all of those who defended heretics were to be called 'favourers.' Finally, Farinacci also called those who praised heretics 'receivers,' but only if they were completely aware of the objects of their praise's status as heretics, since those who erroneously thought them to be good Christians were not guilty of any heretical crime. [74]

Farinacci also listed five ways in which inquisitors could recognize favourers, which he drew from Peña's commentaries. Peña's own source was Ivonetus, whose work was again found in the Biblioteca Apostolica. Ivonetus, despite his 'rough and unstylish' words as Farinacci put it, still gave good advice. Ivonetus directed readers to recognize favourers not from their words, but 'from their nature,' which Peña had termed 'signs.'[75] A favourer could be recognized as someone who visited a captive heretic, murmured with him, and brought him food; someone who lamented a heretic's capture or death; someone who said a heretic was unjustly condemned; someone who looked on 'persecutors' of heretics with 'bitter faces' or 'tortured eyes'; and, finally, those who stole heretics' bones or ashes under the cover of night.[76] None of these actions were conclusively heretical, since they did not incorporate any clearly heretical ritual practice or statement of belief – other motivations, such as affection for the deceased, were possible.

This did not mean that unbelieving favourers should not be punished for their actions, if suspicions were proven true during the investigation and process. But the question of how to do so, or even if one should do so, had apparently been quite contentious in the wake of Gregory IX's decision in 1231. Some authors thought that receivers of heretics who did so only out of familial love should not be punished with excommunication (which could lead to the death penalty). Other authors, such as the celebrated Spanish author of inquisition manuals, Diego de Simancas, as well as Locati, Camillo Campeggi, and Peña, emphasized that those who received heretics but were not heretical believers themselves should be punished, just 'more gently' than those who were actually heretics.[77] Farinacci asserted that this latter recommendation was the more common opinion among the community of doctors. But one of the most respected lay jurists with degrees in both canon and civil law, Tiberio Deciani, was the strongest voice against imposing the same punishments for both heretics and their receivers, since the act of receiving a heretic did not necessarily indicate any 'consent' to heretical beliefs. Farinacci, ultimately, did not clearly come down on either side of the argument. Instead, he merely advised his readers that any punishment of receivers was 'arbitrary' and 'extraordinary,' meaning it occurred at the discretion of the inquisitor.[78]

The various disagreements over this issue also remained in the work of Cesare Carena, who had been appointed procurator fiscal and consultor for the Roman Inquisition's tribunal in Cremona by Urban VIII. He published his *Tractatus* in 1636; although even further removed from the medieval Cathar precedent he still dutifully described these terms for his readers. Like Farinacci, he conflated the terms favourers and receivers. And, like Farinacci, when he examined the question of whether or not to prosecute and punish those who protected heretics as people, without intending to protect their errors or heresy, Carena noted that previous authors had disagreed about the subject. According to Carena, most authors thought that true receivers took in heretics specifically 'on account of their heresy'; those who were ignorant of heresy should not be prosecuted. In Carena's characterization of the issue, prosecuting favourers despite their lack of intent to 'favour' heretics was a minority opinion and one he did not recommend. Concerning the particular question of prosecuting family members who were aware of their relatives' heresies, Carena bluntly asserted: 'Still, this is a controversy.' He nevertheless insisted that family members were to be punished, albeit 'more gently,' and added that the degree of punishment should also match the degree of consanguinity, gradually increasing the further one branched out on the family tree.[79] The prosecution of Riccardo's children, therefore, was controversial from the perspectives of both Farinacci and Carena. Peña, however, writing within a decade or two of Riccardo's process in 1567, portrayed such prosecutions as uncontroversial but recommended more lenient punishment.

All of these inquisitorial authors, therefore, were establishing a hierarchy of ritual practices and other activities in support of heretics that could, or could not, reflect the presence of serious heretical belief among those that performed them. Practices such as the consolation, displaying reverence toward the perfect, attending a communion service performed by heretical leaders, or attending heretical sermons multiple times could definitively establish strong suspicion of heretical belief. Actions that merely supported heretics might be indicative of heretical intentions, in theory, but they also might not be. Each author acknowledged that it was possible, in theory, for favourers, receivers, and defenders to be ignorant of the heretical beliefs supported by the person they aided. But for Peña, by the 1570s and 1580s the plausibility of such assertions was thin indeed; in his considered opinion, everyone knew about the religious controversies that had begun and developed in the sixteenth century, and no one could claim to be ignorant of philo-Protestants.

Broad Principles: Deviations from Orthodox Ritual Practice

When explaining the finer details of canons of the thirteenth-century Council of Narbonne and Council of Avignon, as those canons pertained to the distinction between ritual practices and support activities of Cathars and Waldensians, Francisco Peña had firmly maintained that such principles could be adapted to the heretical sects of his own day.[80] In fact, all the later sixteenth- and seventeenth-century inquisition manual authors did exactly that to some extent. To achieve that adaptation, Peña, Farinacci, and Carena all took the same factors into account when assessing the signification of ritual practices: action, intent, and the plausibility of ignorance. These authors, however, were just as likely to discuss what philo-Protestants in Italian lands did not do, or would not do, as they were to describe the things that heretics did do. Inquisitorial authors emphasized that privately held communion ceremonies or rebaptism of adults were the two most important alternative rituals that would signal a separate heretical conventicle and establish more than enough suspicion of heresy to begin a prosecution.[81] Gathering to read Scripture, and effectively preach, also was recognized as a sacral activity.[82] But manual authors markedly noted avoidance of Catholic ritual practices, critique of Catholic ritual activities, and violent actions such as iconoclasm, all of which had developed over the course of the Reformation, as almost certainly signalling heretical intent and not just lax religious practice or indifference. It was through emphasizing conformity to traditional practice of the Catholic faith as evidence of orthodoxy that the Roman Inquisition embraced the same perspective as churchmen who implemented Tridentine reform efforts and attempted to reinforce the public perception of religious unity in the community.

How the authors of these manuals came by this perception of philo-Protestant behaviour is more difficult to determine. Whether or not inquisitorial authors read Protestant literature, tracts, and polemical works cannot really be proven, and in fact is unlikely. Reading Catholic polemical works concerning Protestant ideas, beliefs, and religious practices, however, is more likely; Alfonso de Castro, a Spanish Franciscan in the service of Philip II of Spain, for example, mentioned to his readers in one of his works, *Adversus omnes haereses*, that Johann Faber had written a large book against the Anabaptists should they wish to know more about the sect.[83] Recent historical scholarship, furthermore, has examined the centrality of Catholic ritual practice to polemical works written against Protestants as well as the role of public community ritual practice in bolstering Catholicism during the Counter-Reformation.[84] What the authors of these manuals discussed in their works was a traditional evaluation of the importance of ritual practice to defining orthodox Catholicism and identifying orthodox Catholics; avoidance of and critiques of Catholic ritual practice were duly noted for their potential to signal heretical belief.

As Cesare Carena would note in his chapters devoted to explaining the heretical signs that would apply in post-Reformation Europe, the strongest indication of suspicion of heresy was skipping the annual confession and communion as the minimum for the laity instituted by the Fourth Lateran Council in 1215 as a means of identifying potential Cathars. Carena, in Chapter 17 of his *Tractatus*, entitled 'The various crimes observed by the Holy Office,' described those who avoided the annual required confession and communion as definitively heretical. Enforcement of that annual obligation was not comprehensive in the medieval period, though, and while the post-Tridentine church did a better job of enforcement in some areas, improvement was spotty, most likely, and dependent on the local bishop's inclinations.[85] That might be why Carena noted that one aspect of this proof of heresy remained controversial among his sources: Could inquisitors prosecute someone for refusing to confess and receive communion just once, or did the person have to indicate heretical intent by skipping the annual ritual many years in a row?[86]

Carena's two sources for this section, Farinacci and Peña, both argued that failing to confess and receive communion was, as many sources agreed, at the very least a sign of strong suspicion of heresy. But, according to both authors, one could not be called a heretic or a suspect in heresy when the omission only occurred once and when some other factor impeding confession and communion was present.[87] Carena agreed with this restriction; those who were truly suspected heretics would be found to refuse confession and communion over and over, without a legitimate cause.[88] In practice, mid-sixteenth-century inquisitors regularly asked defendants if they had fulfilled the annual duty or not; Peña, Farinacci, and Carena all featured this tactic in their later manuals.

It was Francisco Peña, in his commentary concerning negative heretics, who made it a point to bring up another activity he thought characteristic of philo-Protestantism: iconoclasm. Iconoclasm was not a ritual practice in and of itself, but it served to critique Catholic ritual practice in a publicly sensationalist way. North of the Alps, iconoclastic incidents often preceded implementation of Reform Protestantism.[89] Such a public critique of Catholic ritual practice clearly affected how Peña characterized iconoclasm; for him, it was a completely unambiguous sign of heresy. In his opinion, the act of smashing sacred images and relics could not be interpreted as originating from any possible cause other than heretical belief. While refusing to fulfil the obligation to confess and take communion one or two years in a row could have been motivated plausibly by non-heretical considerations, the act of destroying images, for Peña, could not. In Peña's view, it was 'our reliable custom' that some 'deeds' were so horrible that ignorance of their heretical meaning could not be presumed, or believable, as a defence. As Peña commented to his readers, 'Lutherans' were so well known for desecrating sacred temples and smashing images that no one could claim to be unaware of the act's singular significance as heretical.[90] Farinacci also noted the propensity among all Protestant sects for objecting to sacred images. According to Farinacci, heretics did not venerate images of Christ or the saints, and impudently taught that those images should not be venerated as well.[91]

Cesare Carena, writing in 1636, however, was not quite so unequivocal when it came to interpreting the significance of iconoclasm; his differences with Peña's earlier work, furthermore, might signal a difference between how Catholic authors regarded iconoclasm at the height of the post-Tridentine period and later during the seventeenth century. Concerning those who broke or defiled images for reasons other than heretical belief, Carena thought there was some question as to whether civil courts were the better forum for prosecution. Carena, in his analysis, was perhaps acknowledging that Catholics might destroy sacred images for other reasons; in that, he may have had a perspective more similar to pre-Reformation Europe. As Richard Trexler had noted, for example, Catholics sometimes smashed images of saints because the saints in question had not performed any aid when requested.[92] Carena dealt with this issue in a chapter in which he assessed which forms of blasphemy could be considered heretical or not.[93] In the mid- and late sixteenth century, however, Peña thought that smashing an image was indicative of at least a strong suspicion of heresy almost unequivocally. Everyone knew that act's significance, and smashing sacred images could be assumed to be motivated solely by heretical belief.

In addition, there was one other Catholic tradition that all Protestant sects criticized, as explicated by both Carena and Farinacci: they refused to fast during Lent and other holy days of the liturgical year. As Carena explained to his readers, it was an 'ancient' heresy, but it also stood out in his own time. 'Lutherans' were of the opinion that the custom of abstaining from meat, eggs, milk, and other dairy products was not necessary.[94] After citing the councils that established the necessity of fasting, most notably the Council of Trent (1545–1563), Carena 'briefly' stated that eating these foods on prohibited days was definitely suspicious. His citations proving the point were anything but brief, however;

he listed about fifteen different works as precedent, including the *Repertorium Inquisitorum,* Farinacci, Ugolini, and Peña, among others. But the greatest author of this conclusion was Gregory the Great, who had called it a pagan sin. Carena pointed out just how useful it could be to keep an eye on eating habits, since all types of heretical sects in his time agreed that fasting was not necessary to salvation. But Carena had one important caveat. People who had a valid medical reason or illness, such as a pregnancy, and therefore needed to eat meat during holy fasts could procure a licence to eat those items.[95] Farinacci was more blunt, and strangely did not mention that Catholics could procure a medical licence if necessary. He thought that people who ate meat during Lent, and believed that to do so was not a sin, were heretics and could be punished as such.[96] It is somewhat puzzling that refusing to fast became a sign indicative of philo-Protestant belief in Italian lands, when medical need was clearly recognized as a valid exception. But it is also true that almost all sixteenth-century inquisition tribunals in north-central Italian states saw at least one witness testify that defendants consumed meat and other dairy products in defiance of the tradition.

Eliseo Masini, an inquisitor in Genoa, in his early seventeenth-century manual *Sacro Arsenale,* also discussed what deeds characterized heresy. He abstained from any citation of sources, canon law, church tradition, and scholarly apparatuses, and instead took a conversational narrative tone in explaining the conventions of the inquisition process to his readers.[97] In one of his first chapters, he defined *sospetti d'eresia* for his readers through listing what suspected heretics could be expected to do to reveal themselves. Regarding heretical statements, Masini simply said that they would be statements that 'offended the ears of the listeners.' His list of heretical actions, however, was much more extensive. It included those who engaged in iconoclasm; those who ostensibly lived as Catholics, but did not confess or go to communion once a year; those who ate meat without a legitimate excuse; those who did not go to Mass; those who repeated the sacrament of baptism; and those who went to hear heretical preachers more than once.[98] That Masini was much more detailed concerning actions rather than words perhaps can be attributed to his predecessors' works. But Masini's work is an important example of the end results of this process of adaptation.

There was one other factor pertinent to inquisitorial prosecution regarding evidence: possession of heretical books. Of course, the pertinent question for inquisitors in this situation would be: Could possession of a book be taken to clearly indicate heretical belief?[99] The

Catholic Church had always claimed the right to prohibit the writings of heretics even before the printing press.[100] Eymeric, for example, listed every instance of conciliar or papal authority banning works, which he described according to the heretical ideas contained within.[101] And as Francisco Peña explained toward the end of his commentary, 'now in the Christian republic [are] Indexes,' authorized by the pope and created by good doctors, who damn the doctrines of books, and 'from which nearly no kind of book [is] omitted.[102] Prospero Farinacci, writing over a quarter-century later, saw no need to include the history of damning books; he merely stated that the Index of Prohibited Books, published by Pope Pius IV, was the standard well known to all. Prospero Farinacci, furthermore, noted that juridical experts, such as Martín del Rio, firmly argued that books were a basis from which inquisitors could assume a truly heretical 'state of mind' the same way that ritual practices, or refusal to perform them, could be accurate predictors of heretical mentalities. Therefore, according to Farinacci, those who possessed heretical books should be considered vehemently suspected of some kind of heresy.[103] But according to Cesare Carena, it was also strongly held in 'our common' opinion that those who were caught in possession of heretical books alone, and otherwise had a 'good reputation' as Catholics could not be tortured, meaning that heretical books *alone* could not suffice to indicate true heretical belief. Carena had to admit, however, that there had always been disagreement about that point as well. Finally, Farinacci noted that many authors of inquisitorial manuals did not think an individual's possession of heretical books was enough evidence to punish him or her stringently. In particular, those who printed and sold heretical books solely as a business should be excommunicated; but while the secular arm prescribed cutting off a hand for such a crime, Farinacci did not think inquisitors should spill blood over the printing and selling of heretical books. Instead, they should be punished according to the will of the inquisitor, as *fautores*, or 'favourers' of heresy.[104]

For Peña, Farinacci, Carena, and Eliseo Masini, these 'broad principles' were the theoretical guidelines by which they thought philo-Protestantism could be prosecuted. Their later manuals, and this interpretive point of view, included all potential manifestations of philo-Protestant belief and ritual practice dating from the mid-to-late sixteenth century. As all of these authors stressed repeatedly, from their theoretical persepective these ritual practices were common to all heretical sects in Italian lands, however they defined themselves, and could be taken as more conclusive signs of heretical intent than verbal statements or even possession of heretical books.

In reality, sixteenth-century philo-Protestant conventicles, particularly after 1550, have often been described by historians as 'radical.' The more radical confessions provided a better model for clandestine belief and religious practice and protest, although 'Lutheran' continued to be the all-purpose inquisitorial term for heterodoxy of all kinds. These conventicles were also quite eclectic in their selection of beliefs, and did not necessarily conform to one particular confession of faith in its entirety.[105] In the midst of all of this diversity, Peña's and Farinacci's later refusals to exhaustively categorize each and every permutation of the 'new heresies' makes sense. They, and Carena, emphasized the factors that they thought were common to all the 'sects' drawing on firmly established church law to do so.

It was also an evaluative methodology that recognized the importance of correct ritual practice as a physical expression of correct doctrinal belief, in that the Catholic authors of inquisition manuals, and the post-Tridentine Catholic leadership more generally, were very much like their northern European counterparts, as will be discussed in the next chapter. If philo-Protestants in Italian lands were behaving in all of the above ways from the 1530s and 1540s, it was because they felt it theologically necessary to do so. It was also true that such actions, even if they amounted to the 'mixed signals' of quasi-Nicodemite practice, would be noticeable to the witnesses who came before tribunals to testify, giving inquisitors in north-central Italy evidence with which to begin a prosecution.

Chapter Three

Word and Deed: Indications of Suspicion

According to Pietro Martire (Peter Martyr) Vermigli, God was 'the Lord of heart and body; as he requireth the worship of the heart, even as justly and severely doth he command the outward worship of the body.' Just as the tongue confessed true faith in words, ritual practice confessed true faith in deeds.[1] The former Augustinian canon, who had fled north of the Alps to become the most prominent Italian-born Protestant theologian in mid-sixteenth century Europe, Vermigli decried Nicodemism, or the practice conforming outwardly to Catholicism in all ways while mentally believing otherwise.[2]

For Prospero Farinacci, publishing his manual *Tractatus de haeresi* in 1616, Vermigli's reference to the necessity of practicing religion as well as confessing it verbally would have had particular significance regarding the prosecution of heresy, had he read Vermigli's 1555 work for himself. In the manual, Farinacci answered his own rhetorical question: Could heretical 'deeds' count as proof of suspicion of heresy? Farinacci explained that not only was such a thing possible, but deeds were even 'more apparent' an indication of heresy than spoken words.[3] All of the sources Farinacci consulted to construct his own manual agreed; they all warned that protestations of innocence should not be believed when the suspected heretic's actions indicated otherwise. When someone's heretical 'deeds' had been established legitimately as indicating suspicion of heresy through witness testimony, it was not to the suspect's advantage even to attempt to claim that he or she had no idea that the 'deeds' in question were, in fact, heretical.[4] Heretical-sounding statements, however, did not signal heretical belief quite as clearly, according to Farinacci. Although he pointed out that ambiguous statements, in theory, should be interpreted in a 'good sense,' one of Farinacci's sources, Juan de Rojas, warned that 'Lutherans' would utilize 'obscure and ambiguous words' to deceive 'the souls of Catholics.' When interpreting statements, therefore, both authors instructed their readers to attend closely to the qualities of the person speaking them to make an appropriate judgment.[5]

Authors of inquisitorial manuals in the later sixteenth and early seventeenth centuries aimed to explain the legal standard necessary to establish enough evidence of suspicion of heresy. In the pursuit of such indications of suspicion of heresy, ritual practices, according to manual authors, were an important way of recognizing philo-Protestants and gathering evidence. Absence of ritual practice, or protests against Catholic ones, in and of themselves or coupled with heretical statements strongly indicated suspicion of heresy; heretical-sounding statements alone were much more difficult to judge. Even if philo-Protestants acted against Vermigli's advice and feigned Catholicism, if they were caught participating in heretical conventicles, or discussing Scripture, or attending 'heretical sermons,' as Peña put it, the subterfuge still would not allow them to escape prosecution and punishment. Furthermore 'deeds' could be used as a methodology for contextualizing 'words.' In theory any ambiguous statements, or heretical-sounding propositions, could be weighed against a proven record of Catholic ritual practice, or the opposite, as a frame of reference indicating the appropriate interpretation.

Within a real process, such evidence of heresy would be produced through the testimony of witnesses. Members of the community, whether they came forward voluntarily or were called and required to appear as witnesses, gave testimony; tribunals then decided whether or not there was enough evidence to give rise to suspicion of heresy, cite the person in question before the court, possibly order an arrest, and begin a process. For manual authors, therefore, the theoretical issue of evaluating witness testimony was important to explicate in full. This chapter examines what standards manual authors thought crucial for the evaluation of witnesses and their testimony. Not only did manual authors describe the ideal qualities of good witnesses, but they also tackled the subject of evaluating information that derived from witnesses who were less than ideal, since some invariably would be. Furthermore, the chapter explains the evidentiary standards outlined in these manuals; their authors once again drew on canonical sources and historical precedent to formulate them, and they guided how these authors advised intepreting 'words' and 'deeds.' While matters relating to ritual practice, or 'deeds' could be used to contextualize verbal statements, the reverse was not possible according to these authors.

In practice in the mid-sixteenth century, witnesses in processes gave inquisitors 'points of entry' from which to begin prosecution. What these witnesses noticed, and reported to tribunals oftentimes did have its roots in the works of theologians like Vermigli. For those the inquisition caught were attempting to carry out the principles of their new-found faith through either avoiding or criticizing Catholic ritual practices. Those aspects of ritual practice eventually made their way into later sixteenth- and early seventeenth-century inquisition manuals as examples of evidence to be used in a process, although how exactly that was achieved cannot be traced definitively. The most likely avenues of transmission, however, were process records (to which later manual authors had access) and Catholic polemical literature, which sought to combat Protestant authors. This chapter is concerned with exploring the first likely avenue of transmission; therefore I examine some of the original sources of Protestant thought concerning what those theologians considered to be correct ritual practice and the illegitimacy of Nicodemism. Such an examination illuminates the actions of accused philo-Protestants in Italy, and explains why witnesses saw and heard the things they reported to tribunals. The later manual authors portrayed philo-Protestants as avoiding confession and communion, disparaging images, and eating meat during Lent; and, in many ways, philo-Protestants in Italian states in the mid-sixteenth century were caught doing exactly those things. Therefore, examples of witness testimonies, drawn from processes held during the sixteenth century in Italian states, also are investigated to demonstrate the ways in which daily ritual observance of Catholicism provoked reactions and criticism from philo-Protestants.

The *Inquisitio:* Indications and Proof

The *inquisitio,* or 'questioning,' as a legal system, meant that the judge – the inquisitor – had the power to investigate crimes, call and examine witnesses, and pass judgment. *Inquisitio* also gave greater emphasis to the judge's individual expertise in weighing evidence; it was up to the judge to decide if the evidence was enough, or, as the phrase commonly went, 'clear as the light of day,' to result in a prosecution, and it was hoped a conviction.[6]

However, the authors of inquisition manuals had to acknowledge an earlier system of religious correction, the denunciation, since it had been incorporated into the *inquisitio* and could form an important constituent part of it. According to Richard Fraher, the disadvantage of the *denuntiatio* lay in that it was meant more in the spirit of fraternal correction of sin; therefore the punishments, if the processes were successful, were correspondingly less. Originally the practice, following the Gospel of Mark, required those who denounced someone to give the people they intended to denounce an official warning, and the chance to reform, before proceeding with the denunciation.[7] By the sixteenth century, however, the requirements of *denuntiatio* had been altered to make that system more compatible with *inquisitio,* although not without controversy. Prospero Farinacci made no mention of fraternal correction when discussing the concept, and also explained that beginning a process through denunciation did not preclude proceeding through inquisition. As Tiberio Deciani, a prominent sixteenth-century Italian civil jurist, and Eymeric, among other sources, had explained, on receiving a voluntary denunciation inquisitors should then proceed *ex officio* and continue to investigate, utilizing their powers as inquisitors to call, and require, other witnesses to appear before the tribunal and give testimony. The line between proceeding through denunciation or through inquisition was rather thin, and as Massimo Firpo, among others, has shown, could change over the course of a process; once enough testimony had been gathered to justify beginning a process, testimony from persons summoned by the inquisition as witnesses and required to testify would be rerecorded officially as 'denunciations' as well.[8]

Nicholas Eymeric in the *Directorium Inquisitorum* explained that the *inquisitio* would begin through the public 'fame and clamour' that would reach the ears of an inquisitor, who would then proceed *ex officio* to investigate, although Eymeric did not specify how such indications of suspicion were supposed to reach the inquisitor's ears.[9] Inquisitors, while investigating such public crimes, did have to meet certain benchmarks, or indications, of suspicion of heresy in order to continue the investigation, cite the defendant to appear, perhaps order an arrest, and if the process reached a definitive conclusion, find a defendant guilty. According to Peña, it was finding such indications of heresy that made the *inquisitio* such a laborious process. As Peña explained, a public reputation for heresy had to be proved through preliminary testimony so that the defendant could be surrendered to the court and a process begun. By 'public,' of course, Peña meant 'any words and deeds' viewed and heard by witnesses.[10]

Testimonies and Arrests

The necessary evidentiary standard to be met to initiate a process, uncovered during the *inquisitio,* was ultimately within the control of inquisitors and their tribunals as overseen by the Congregation of Cardinals in Rome in practice. Eymeric, Peña, Farinacci, and Carena, however, struggled to describe the theoretical guidelines outlining what those evidentiary standards should be. Francisco Peña, following Eymeric, initially held that two witness testimonies sufficed to begin a process – that was the general standard. One witness testimony was merely an *indicia,* or 'indication' of heresy. Innocent III (r. 1198–1216), furthermore, had provided the ideal standard concerning what would constitute two valid witness testimonies in inquisition processes; when a witness was asked who among the community had a reputation for heresy, the witness not only should be able to name a prospective suspected heretic, but also explain why that person was suspect.[11] Peña continued to elaborate on this theme by informing his readers that witnesses who could prove suspicion of heresy to tribunals would be able to name specific things that the prospective defendant had said or done. Peña, utilizing a rare illustrative example from the Reformation, since he had claimed to prefer broad principles and had declined to list any new Protestant heresies, posited that witnesses would be able to describe overhearing the prospective defendant asserting that Martin Bucer had instructed people to smash all religious images.[12]

Farinacci, who accounted for every possible disagreement, modification, or nuance in his manual, however, noted that inquisitors often had to deal with less than ideal witnesses. What should one do if two unsuitable witnesses accused a seemingly blameless Catholic? In so doing, he highlighted the role *fama* should play in evaluating all of the participants in inquisition processes, witnesses and defendants alike. *Fama* directly translates as 'fame,' but at this time it was characterized with a broader contextual meaning; 'fame' meant the reputation a person had among his or her community, and it carried legal weight. And although a bad reputation could be earned through committing sins, such as adultery, or crime, when it came to the theoretical principles of inquisitorial prosecution Farinacci firmly grounded his concept of *fama* in ritual practice.

In his discussion of that question, Farinacci also touched on quasi-Nicodemite practices, if only inadvertently. Farinacci specified that a good and honest man should not be convicted by two testimonies alone. If more than two witnesses came forward or were cited, however, the sterling reputation of the person in question, the result of his observed virtue, blameless Catholic life, and correct ritual practice, could only serve to mitigate the punishment he was assigned, not exonerate him completely – the public crime of heresy had to be punished in some way. But ultimately the question of how much punishment, or how much leniency, depended on the strength and number of the testimonies versus the strength of evidence provided by the seemingly blameless *reus* ('criminal').[13] Feigning Catholic practice, therefore, would not exonerate defendants completely if more than two witnesses could testify to words and deeds perpetrated elsewhere outside of the church.[14]

Farinacci also specified certain other limitations to the two-witness rule; for example, two testimonies would not suffice to condemn a defendant if the two witnesses in question were women, and not even three witnesses would suffice if the witnesses were not 'worthy' or 'suitable' ones.[15] As Farinacci summed up the general gist of his entire chapter, in his considered opinion two testimonies might be enough to condemn someone, but 'truly more may be required.' One of the earlier sources on which Farinacci relied was Peña; and Peña emphasized that the inquisitor and the local bishop should agree as to the standard to use as well.[16]

In practice, indications of heresy provided by witness testimony invariably would only become 'proof' through a confession on the part of the suspected heretic, since the confession always had possessed 'the first place' among all types of proof.[17] According to Peña, there was truly no clearer or more effective proof than a confession. In theory, a confession itself was enough proof to condemn someone to ordinary punishment without witness testimony, although such a scenario would mean a defendant coming forward of his or her own volition, confessing to heretical belief, and refusing correction, thereby receiving a sentence of death – all in all, rather unlikely in practice. Peña noted that secular courts only considered that to be true in cases of murder, obliquely referring to one of the differences between secular and canonical procedure.[18]

Worthy and Unworthy Witnesses

Witnesses were crucial because they testified to both the 'words' and 'deeds' of defendants; therefore both kinds of evidence entered the process records through the same medium. Manual authors, in theory, had to express the complex standards by which one could evaluate and weigh the relative value of witness testimony. This was particularly problematic when it came to assessing the relative *fama*, or reputation, of the witnesses. Ideally tribunals should have the sworn testimony of witnesses of stellar reputation; but even in theory manual authors had to admit that witnesses who might be of more dubious reputation still might be capable of giving valuable testimony.

Furthermore, there could be other pitfalls in dealing with witness testimony regardless of the reputations of the people giving it. As Eymeric pointed out in the *Directorium Inquisitorum*, not all witnesses gave the exact same information – and according to Innocent III, the two witness testimonies were supposed to be roughly in agreement as to the details of the crime. So Peña in his commentaries found it necessary to explain what to do with multiple testimonies if none of them agreed as to the particulars of the crime. As Peña postulated hypothetically, one witness in May might have heard the defendant say that Luther did not believe in purgatory, while another witness might have heard the defendant say that Luther denied the power of the pope, but during the month of April (another rare adaptive example in Peña's work).[19] Alternatively, two or more witnesses might have heard approximately the same heretical statements, but in different times and places. For example, one witness, three days previously in the piazza, might have heard the defendant say that Martin Bucer denied the pope as the head of the church, while another had heard the same thing, but had heard it said four days before in the school. Peña candidly admitted that this situation caused grave difficulties.

Peña continued, however, by expressing the opinion that it would be absurd to completely ignore such testimony, since it was entirely possible that the defendant had attempted to proselytize people one at a time, taking each witness aside in a different time and place. If the witnesses' testimony continued to mount against one person in particular, despite differences of time and place in the details, then the inquisitor technically had sufficient indication to employ torture (or, more properly, recommend that the secular arm torture the defendant). But if the defendant did not confess under duress, then the inquisitor could not impose any abjuration or sentence or turn him over to the secular arm for execution.

The two options, therefore, were torture of the defendant based on single testimonies that did not agree – usually not the recommended option – or further investigation until such a time as enough evidence could be gathered that formed a consensus concerning a particular potential heretic. Otherwise, theoretically, there were not enough indications, or at least enough of the right kinds of indications, to justify execution without a confession.[20]

In practice, any testimony concerning either heretical words or deeds had to be investigated properly, duly recorded under oath, and be reasonably credible in order for it to be effective in the course of a process. Since witness testimony was so crucial, in theory all Christians were obligated to testify against those they knew to be heretics on pain of mortal sin and punishment of excommunication. According to Peña, those who refrained from doing so might be suspect of heretical belief themselves because of that refusal.[21] Farinacci pointed out that if the obstinate person in question had suspected family, neighbours, or very close friends reluctance to testify was understandable and therefore would not result in suspicion of heresy. It would, however, still result in punishment of some kind, but only for disobedience, not heresy.[22] Carena cited one minority opinion, ostensibly quoting Simancas, writing that sons and wives, in particular, could not be obligated to testify against fathers and husbands because of their emotional involvement. According to Carena, however, this was not the commonly held opinion among the doctors of the church; family members, although their testimony should be considered more carefully, still could be required to testify.[23]

Some mitigating factors concerning familial power relations were relevant to inquisitorial prosecution. For example, according to Peña, women who neglected to give testimony of heresy were less responsible for their lack of action than men; a wife whose husband ordered her to serve him meat during Lent or other fasts, for example, could be excused for not testifying against him if she had been afraid of what he might do to her if she had.[24] Nevertheless, in theory anyone, family member, friend, or neighbour, could be cited and compelled to give testimony, and punished if he or she refused to present himself or herself to the tribunal.[25]

Family members, or those close physically or emotionally, often made the best witnesses in terms of the quality of information they could provide, but such testimony had to be handled carefully. Eymeric advised that testimony from family members aimed at exonerating the suspected heretic should be assumed to be prejudicial and discounted, since the instinct of spouses and children often was to try to save their relations, either because of affection or because of fears that scandal would taint the family reputation. But family witnesses ideally were to be held to the same Catholic standards as strangers and report heretical relatives to the tribunal for the good of the Catholic community. Cesare Carena, in his early seventeenth-century manual, cited Deuteronomy 13:6 to make this point: 'If thy brother, the son of thy mother, or thy son, or thy daughter, or the wife of thy bosom, or thy friend, which is as thine own soul, entice thee secretly, saying, "Let us go and serve other gods," which thou hast not known, thou, nor thy fathers ... do not yield to such persons.' And according to Augustine himself and other Church Fathers, as Carena explained, those who alienated themselves from the dogma of the church should be called back to it for their own good.[26]

Farinacci reminded his readers that even if a witness made a voluntary denunciation, although this would be welcome and to be encouraged, the case should be investigated nevertheless through the citation of more witnesses. Good denunciations could arise from the conscientious Catholic's fear of sin and death, but when it came to family voluntarily denouncing family, or people voluntarily denouncing others in general, one had to consider other motivations, which might indicate a distinct lack of truthfulness or good faith. For Farinacci money and the possibility of personal animosity were the most obvious possible motivations.[27] Farinacci also recommended that servants or slaves under the authority of the familial household, when asked to testify against their masters should be tortured to ensure the truth of their testimony, a point that originated in Roman civil law. Roman elites apparently had assumed that slaves or servants obviously would testify either on behalf of their masters out of loyalty or lie because of hatred.[28] Finally, Farinacci specified that the testimony of family members, friends, and neighbours could not constitute proof of suspicion of heresy in and of itself. While information from such sources was valuable, there was too great a chance that it might be biased for a case to depend on it alone.[29] Corroborating testimony from those outside the family circle was necessary to fully indicate suspicion in heresy.

Farinacci, when discussing the question of testimony that originated from a person of infamous reputation, usually meaning another person being tried for heresy, pointed out that many times the witnesses had reputations just as flawed as those of the accused. Peña earlier had made the same point his his comments, and both authors were forced to recognize that perjurers, the excommunicated, heretical criminals, the generally infamous, and those 'less worthy' or 'less suitable,' could present the Holy Office with potentially important information. Since such witnesses were of dubious reputation themselves, only two of them would not suffice as full proof, and therefore would not be enough to justify ordinary punishment for negative or relapsed heretics. For Peña and others, in theory, the best test for confirming suspect testimony from the less credible was to torture the witness.[30] According to the authors, however, a process could end in execution if the inquisitor had more than two unworthy sources, unless testimony from more credible sources 'turned aside' the evidence of heresy given by the less than worthy.[31]

Judging the testimony of the unworthy, especially in terms of faith, was not always a clearcut task. Even those who had committed their own crimes could very well be capable of recognizing crimes of heresy. Eymeric was of the opinion that the testimony of 'the infamous,' and other *minus idoneas* ('less worthy' or 'less suitable') people provisionally could be used in the Holy Office's proceedings. Peña, in his commentaries, recognized the sources of this decision: the thirteenth-century councils of Béziers and Narbonne had laid out canons describing the appropriate inquisitorial procedures for investigating Cathars, which were subsequently incorporated into canon law. Peña asserted, supported by the fifteenth-century canon law professor and auditor of the Roman Rota, Felino Sandei, among other sources, that testimony from two such unworthy witnesses was not enough to warrant ordinary punishment (capital punishment), but could be used to assign more mild punishments, such as canonical purgation or penance. As Peña stated, one did not automatically assume that testimony from such unworthy sources was false or perjured.[32] Ideally, however, as the most famous lay law professor in fourteenth-century Bologna, Baldus degli Ubaldi had noted best, according to Peña, the available testimonies would not derive entirely from unworthy sources. More credible witnesses would be found to validate the testimony of the less suitable.

The prospective use of testimony from *socii criminii*, or associates of the heretics who had helped the prospective defendant commit his or her heretical crimes in some way, caused manual authors a few qualms. Peña recommended that the tribunal make further inquiries about these witnesses. For example, he thought it important to discover if the criminal had confessed his or her own crime before he or she was tortured, or to make sure that he or she was not convicted from the testimony of the person against whom he or she now testified. The testimony of these criminal associates was, as Peña wrote, easily disputed, especially if unconfirmed by torture; therefore tribunals would do well to use such evidence very carefully. But Peña acknowledged that secular law disagreed; for example Giulio Claro, a lay legal jurist and expert concerning the uses of torture in civil proceedings, held that testimony from an associate unconfirmed by torture should not be allowed at all as evidence in secular courts.[33] Peña found Simancas's advice to be much more pleasing, since the latter thought that tribunals and inquisitors, after carefully considering the qualities of the person and the nature of the crime, could admit such testimony without torturing the witness.[34] As Farinacci later pointed out in his work , however, Camillo Campeggi, a contemporary of Peña's, in his edition of Ugolini's work had insisted that confirming such testimony through torture was necessary. The Jesuit Martín del Rio, posing yet another divergent opinion in his work concerning witchcraft, thought torture was necessary if only one testimony from a less-than-worthy source was available, but unnecessary if there were two or more testimonies available. The controversy here amounted to one of the conflicts between civil and canon law, since Charles V's criminal law code of 1532, the *Carolina,* was a one of Farinacci's sources alongside legal opinions originating from the works of churchmen.[35]

Farinacci described another debate concerning proof from the less suitable witnesses: Should it only be allowed as evidence during a process if any other evidence was lacking? Simancas and Martín del Rio thought that such evidence should only be allowed in the absence of better. Most legal experts, however, including Giovanni d'Andrea and Umberto Locati, thought that it could help construct a legal case alongside evidence from better sources, as Peña had asserted. Farinacci also took the opportunity to explain, while he was on the subject of the less than worthy, that women definitely could testify during inquisitorial investigations. As he put it, if those associated with heresy could legally testify, then women could as well, since being infamous was, in fact, more of a handicap to credibility than being female.[36]

Finally, it was considered necessary to examine whether or not known perjurers were able to give testimony in inquisitorial proceedings. In particular, Farinacci was referring to witnesses' second testimonies, as opposed to their first. If the second and the first testimonies were not the same, which Farinacci thought would imply that the first testimony was the 'varied and perjured' one, could either of them be employed as evidence? Farinacci thought it was the second testimony that should 'stand,' not the first, supported by a plethora of citations to that effect.[37] The strongest source, however, was canon law and its *Glossa Ordinaria*, which further refined the principle; there had to have been an interval of time between the two depositions, and the second was thought to be more true especially in those cases in which the witness implicated himself or herself in the second one. But if the witness in question implicated others, and still insisted on his or her own innocence or refused to speak, then whichever testimony was variant or perjured was not to be believed.[38] The sole dissenting voice among a variety of canonical sources over the centuries and the traditional gloss of canon law, in this case, was Francisco Peña; he thought that one who revoked his or her first testimony, and only implicated others in the second testimony, but not him- or herself, could be believed.[39] The latter opinions probably concerned those who were both under a suspicion of heresy and expected to give testimony concerning others, but Farinacci emphasized that those who were solely witnesses should be believed should they change their testimonies during a second interview, since good and zealous faith should be presumed as a motivation for any such changes. Peña thought that changed testimony should not be taken at face value, however, unless other presumptions and conjectures indicated that the second testimony was more true. Tiberio Deciani, according to Farinacci, quite logically pointed out that such testimony should be believed when the second testimony was forthcoming, while the first had sought to conceal or protect the suspected heretic in question. This was a reasonable application to all witness testimony of the principle canon law maintained for suspected heretics; if the person in question confessed in the second testimony, after falsely maintaining innocence in the first, then the second was obviously the true testimony.

Apparently some had questioned, however, if the reverse was true: What if the first testimony implicated someone, or the witness, in heresy, but the second exonerated them? Farinacci rather hotly asserted that the second testimony should not be believed and the suspected heretic in question should still be considered vehemently under suspicion, according to canon law. But other authors had argued the contrary, which Farinacci thought was certainly not the true opinion. Simancas had explained the rationale best for Farinacci; in such a grave crime, it was more important to detect heresy than liberate the innocent. Therefore the first testimony should outweigh the second in theory.[40]

In the reality of heresy processes held from the mid-sixteenth century onward on the Italian peninsula, why witnesses testified is as difficult to pin down definitively as it was for later manual authors in theory. The later sixteenth-century and seventeenth-century inquisition manuals, for all their warnings to evaluate witnesses carefully for signs of false testimony, also advised the assumption of zeal for the faith as motivation, unless there was anything specific to indicate otherwise. In the sixteenth-century philo-Protestant heresy cases examined here, most witnesses seem to either have agreed that the defendant deserved to be prosecuted or, at the very least, to have told the truth because the inquisition, as a rather intimidating agent of authority, required it. In the cases in which a full process was the result, few witnesses called before the tribunal refused to answer questions or give any useful information. Witnesses who were discovered to have given false testimony were supposed to be severely punished in theory; while it is possible that informants' testimonies were false or self-serving, the threat of punishment if caught may have kept falsifications to a minimum.[41] Witnesses also could have been giving accurate information, but for their own self-serving reasons. In addition, as Adriano Prosperi and Elena Brambilla have explained, some witnesses testified because their confessors required them to make a 'voluntary' denunciation about others' heterodoxy before receiving absolution for their own sins, or even could require self-denunciation from those who confessed their heretical beliefs to their confessors. Nevertheless, that practice was not uncontested, as Vincenzo Lavenia has explained, since some theologians and jurists were reluctant to allow what they felt to be the secrecy and autonomy of the confessional to be compromised in such a way, although many theologians saw no conflict in the practice.[42] Those of devout faith very well may have testified in order to save their neighbours' immortal souls, and even members of the lower strata of society may have been cognizant of the political and social instability that was thought to come with religious pluralism. And as John Jeffries Martin has recognized, the tribunal was able to establish itself as a viable institution because it gave people a way of working out their religious differences, to the detriment of the unorthodox.[43] These factors probably worked in concert as well as individually in the minds of witnesses as they made the decision to tell the tribunals what they thought they had heard and seen.

Tribunals relied on such testimony, regardless of its origins, and such testimonies usually guided the process from beginning to end.

Testimony provided the particular 'points of entry' the tribunals could use to justify the initiation of a process, and the information witnesses gave tribunals often provided the total basis for questioning defendants as well. Proceeding on the assumption that behaviour reflected doctrine and was an almost certain indicator of philo-Protestantism, witnesses and tribunals both singled out those who removed themselves from, or vehemently and publicly protested, Catholic ritual practices in some way for prosecution. Conversational markers also could serve as indications for witnesses and, by extension, tribunals, since informants reported conversations, in whole or in part, involving statements that could be interpreted as heterodox.

Presumptions, Indications, and Broad Principles of Heterodoxy

Later manual authors, however, theoretically assessed 'words' and 'deeds' differently, in terms of their use as evidence. For Farinacci, the question of whether or not heretical deeds counted as indications of heresy was pertinent to his overall discussion of what counted as sufficient indication of suspicion of heresy to justify a process. Farinacci informed his readers that not only were deeds good proof of suspicion, but also were even 'more apparent' proof than spoken words. Farinacci and those he cited, including Giovanni d'Andrea, the *Repertorium Inquisitorum*, Umberto Locati, Simancas, and Luis de Pàramo, all agreed that heretical deeds demonstrated more than words, since actions 'declare[d] the spirit and will more than words.'[44] Hostiensis and Camillo Campeggi, furthermore, all warned that those who said they were not heretics were not to be believed when their actions indicated otherwise. Juan de Rojas ventured an extreme opinion and insisted that some heretical deeds were so heinous that a confession to heretical intent was even not necessary.[45] When it came to weighing all the indications and suspicions through the medium of witness testimony, manual authors thought that examining ritual practices was an important way of figuring out how to conduct the process as a whole.

But the other doctors of the church Farinacci consulted, including Peña's edition of Eymeric's work, stated that such actions still constituted legal presumptions. Therefore, evidence to the contrary could be admitted as a part of the defence, although such contrary proof would be extremely difficult to present convincingly. Just as deeds could indicate a strong presumption of guilt, deeds also could be used as a means of defence. According to Simancas, as quoted by Farinacci, the strongest defence that one could present was evidence of Catholic ritual observance. True Catholics would pray for the dead or listen to the divine offices – and such behaviour could not be counterfeited quickly or changed to suit an inquisitorial defence. Strong suspicion most definitely could arise, however, from adoring heretics (performing the *melioramentum*, or 'honouring' the perfect), observing heretical ceremonies, refusing to keep religious images in the house, and turning one's hat to the earth instead of raising it at the host's elevation; the last was found in Farinacci's manual as an action common to heretics, and it was common among sixteenth-century philo-Protestants, as we shall see in future chapters.[46]

In another chapter of his manual Farinacci had made clear that he considered the performance of heretical ritual practices an integral part of his preferred definition of heresy, and therefore unable to be excused as anything other than a deliberate act. While he did not provide other examples in this particular chapter, he did scatter references to actions that could be construed as more or less strongly heretical throughout his manual. For Farinacci, as it had been for Peña in the later sixteenth century, iconoclasm was regarded as an act of protest against the fundamental tenets and practices of Catholicism that was unequivocally heretical in meaning. Farinacci also noted those omissions of Catholic ritual practices that would prove significant if such omissions were consistent. Refusing to confess and communicate only once could be attributed to discord in the community, but the more years one neglected to participate the more likely a heretical motivation became. Eating meat during the fasts mandated by the church was the least clear of the three, since licences to do so on account of illness or pregnancy were always possible – but if no other excuse could be provided, heretical intent could then be presumed.[47]

This, of course, was the legal standard Peña had framed and discussed in his late sixteenth-century adaptation of Eymeric's fourteenth-century examination of what truly constituted heretical behaviour. Farinacci presented this standard within the context of how to evaluate what such indications were worth in a process as evidence; he firmly established that evidence of abnormalities in ritual practice was extremely difficult, if not impossible, to explain away – how could anyone participating in heretical rites not be aware of their significance? Conversely, those who had been good and faithful Catholics but also engaged in heretical activities would deserve lesser punishment, perhaps, but still punishment. Quasi-Nicodemite behaviour, coupled with definitive markers of heresy, would not obtain complete exoneration if caught.

In contrast, propositions, or verbal statements, according to Farinacci, could be doubted as to their true meaning. Verbal statements could be more ambiguous in that some statements could be interpreted in more than one way – the statement could sound heretical, but sound Catholic as well. Farinacci briefly advised that such statements really should be interpreted in the best sense possible – the Catholic one – unless there was some reason for the tribunal to think the opposite true. Barring any clear indication that the heretical interpretation was the appropriate one, such as attending heretical conventicles, sermons, or scriptural study groups, a Catholic practitioner should be given the benefit of the doubt and not be presumed to be pulling any sort of 'trick.'[48]

That, however, only held true for those who were otherwise demonstrably good Catholics in terms of their religious behaviour. According to Juan de Rojas, Jews, Moors, and those from 'infected' provinces were not to be allowed any such breaks in how their words should be interpreted, and neither were those who engaged in heretical ritual practices. In Rojas's view, in his own time duplicitous heretics deliberately utilized ambiguous and obscure words to pollute the faith of good Catholics. The only solution to the conundrum of interpretation was to attend closely to the qualities of the person who had spoken in such a way as to indicate the possible presence of heresy.[49] Suspicious-sounding statements coupled with sterling Catholic ritual observance could be given the benefit of the doubt.

Peña, in his commentaries, noted that this same problem might derive from the source of the information; he thought that some witnesses simply would not know enough about Catholic doctrine to be able to definitively state that they had heard something heretical, Peña's confidence in the post-Tridentine Church's preaching true doctrine notwithstanding. Peña pointed out that in this situation, potential suspects probably should be given the benefit of the doubt as well, and the overheard statements interpreted in the best, most 'Catholic,' sense possible.[50] Suspicious-sounding statements coupled with Catholic ritual practice were not necessarily adequate to proceed, or would only provoke the lightest of sentences. Heretical propositions accompanied by lax ritual practice of Catholicism, overt protests against Catholic ritual practices, or, worse, attendance at secret conventicles, were much more definitive in indicating suspicion of heresy.

The Nicodemite Debate

Inquisition manual authors in the late sixteenth and early seventeenth centuries found evidence relating to ritual practice theoretically crucial. Inquisitors prosecuting philo-Protestants in mid-sixteenth century Italian states had found such evidence to be useful as well, because the witnesses who came before the tribunals repeatedly testified to its importance. They often testified as to the defendants' ritual practice, or criticisms of Catholic practices, as we shall see later in this chapter. The inquisitors themselves, or the later authors of manuals, had probably not read the works of Protestant Reformers both north and south of the Alps, which advised their believers to do exactly that; they were probably aware of Reformers' opinions of the Catholic Mass, communion, and confession through Catholic controversial works. But at least some of the philo-Protestants in north Italian areas during the later half of the sixteenth century definitely were reading such works and modifying their behaviour in some ways. Those behaviours, related to ritual practice, most likely influenced how inquisitors at the time came to define what constituted 'Lutheranism' for themselves, and perhaps influenced later manual authors as well.

Although Italian philo-Protestants often behaved in ways that northern Protestant authors and Italian authors in exile expected their followers to, they could be eclectic in which parts of the messages they appropriated. Protestant theologians of all stripes were very clear concerning the necessity of avoiding Catholic ritual practices, emphasized the illegitimacy of adopting Nicodemite or quasi-Nicodemite strategies for survival, and encouraged proselytizing what they thought constituted correct ritual practices to others in the community. Inquisitors from the mid-sixteenth century onward who heard testimony concerning what philo-Protestants said and did probably found more consistency and continuity in the reports of heretical deeds rather than doctrinal statements. It was precisely the consistency of protesting and avoiding Catholic ritual practice that that made such deeds valuable as evidence. Furthermore, a potential defendant's attitude toward Catholic ritual, as revealed through witness testimony, might serve to indicate just how committed the philo-Protestant was to his or her faith; those who completely skipped Catholic Mass, or even attended secret conventicles, could be regarded as more dangerous, from the inquisitorial perspective, than those who discussed a few doctrinal points in casual conversation.

Of Protestants north of the Alps, John Calvin's anti-Nicodemite writings were the most famous condemnation of feigning Catholicism as a means of self-protection. Carlos Eire has discussed Calvin's theological reasons for his condemnation; most notably, it was Calvin's perception of the Catholic Mass as inherently idolatrous that led him to prohibit attending Mass completely for his spiritual followers, regardless of their location. As Eire has explained, Calvin believed that Catholic theology falsely mixed the spiritual and the material in worship. Worship had to be spiritual, as God had set down in Scripture. Deviation from those divine commands had occurred, according to Calvin, because of humanity's fallen condition. Even though men and women were born with the 'seed of religion,' humanity's natural depravity led its practice of religion toward idolatry in worship instead of the Bible, thereby dishonouring God.[51]

Furthermore, for Calvin the spiritual reality of worship was meant to connect the worshipper in this world with God's spiritual world. There was only one divine and superior reality; therefore all religious acts attempted to form a connection between the two. But only the correctly performed act would establish that connection, as when a true Lord's Supper led to mystical and spiritual union with God for the elect. Idolatry, however, not only failed to establish that link to the divine, but also polluted and corrupted the souls of those who attended those ceremonies regardless of their intent. For Calvin, the Catholic Mass was the most important example of idolatry to be avoided by the faithful, but worshipping images and relics of the saints was definitely not good either.[52]

While Calvin's vehement injunctions against Nicodemite behaviour are often considered within the context of France's nascent Calvinist communities, his earliest anti-Nicodemite writings were both the result of his travels to Italy. Having spent about three weeks at the court of Ferrara in 1536 as a guest of Renée of France, wife of Ercole d'Este, Calvin addressed Nicolas Chemin, who remained in Ferrara, in a private letter that Calvin had published along with others in 1537. In these letters he recommended strict separation from the idolatries of Rome, the course of action he also recommended to Renée herself, who nonetheless would take communion at Catholic Mass in 1554 after having been threatened with inquisitorial action. His most clear anti-Nicodemite works, the *Petit Traicté,* concerning the appropriate way in which to conduct the Lord's Supper, and his *Excuse à Messieurs les Nicodemites,* were published in 1543 and 1544, respectively. In the latter, Calvin explained why he did not like the term itself; Nicodemus, after all, had eventually publicly professed Christ. All of Calvin's anti-Nicodemite works were collected into one volume, *De vitandis superstitionibus*, and published in 1549 and 1550, complete with supportive opinions solicited from prominent Reformers including the Lutheran Melanchthon, Vermigli, and Heinrich Bullinger, Zwingli's successor in Zurich. Calvin's anti-Nicodemite works were printed in Italian and circulated in Italian lands from 1555; Geneva, despite Calvin's difficulties with the Italian émigré church, was an important centre for printing Reform works in Italian.

As Eire has explained, Calvin recognized four archetypes of Nicodemite behaviour. There were those who remained in the Catholic priesthood, as he thought, in order to receive income from benefices, but claimed to preach the pure Gospel nevertheless; several preachers in sixteenth-century Italian states had attempted to do just that, such as Bernardino Ochino and Agostino Mainardi, although whether or not they were motivated by the prospect of keeping the income from benefices is debatable. Calvin then condemned those who tried to convert court ladies, but did not take the Gospel or its prescriptions concerning proper worship seriously; that critique was intended for Renée of France's court chaplains. Calvin also derided those who tried to reduce Christianity to a philosophy, rather than believe in and practise a religion (as Carlo Ginzburg and Adriano Prosperi have controversially characterized several early modern Italian intellectuals). Finally, Calvin attacked merchants and common people who feigned Catholicism simply because they were afraid of danger. For Calvin, the solution was not feigning Catholicism – it was to withdraw from the Catholic Church quietly, suffer martyrdom if caught, or flee. For Calvin, the physical body was as much a temple of God as the soul; bodies and souls together must not be profaned and polluted with attendance at Catholic rituals. As Calvin famously put it: 'They are like Master Fifi, who having long practiced the trade of rummage in garbage, no longer smells the foul odor because he has become quite foul-smelling himself, and scorns those who pinch their noses.'[53]

As Peter Matheson has emphasized, the Strasbourg Reformer Martin Bucer in the early 1540s espoused a different view from Calvin's stark choice between withdrawal, flight, or death. Bucer at first authorized attendance at Catholic ritual practices, both as a means of avoiding persecution and as a means of effecting conversions. Bucer thought that following Calvin's advice would, in the short term, abandon those who possibly could become good Christians to the impious and false religion of Catholicism. But even Martin Bucer eventually abandoned this temporary compromise and began to emphasize either risking prosecution or flight as the only legitimate options. Bucer, furthermore, wrote four letters of encouragement to Italian conventicles soon after 1542.[54] But even within that limited period in which Bucer was willing to concede some Nicodemite behaviour, the Strasbourg Reformer also emphasized that proselytizing the unbelievers should continue; he stressed that such Nicodemite behaviour was a temporary compromise until such a time as a significant majority converted to the Reform so that it could be implemented publicly. It is this kind of behaviour that could be termed quasi-Nicodemite, in that proselytizing was still considered necessary.

Pietro Martire Vermigli would come to agree with Calvin but he began his theological activity in Italian lands within the Catholic Church. Therefore his work is instructive, simply because he had experienced the conditions philo-Protestants in Italian lands would face. Vermigli, in fact, had attempted to practice quasi-Nicodemism during one phase of his life, preaching Protestant doctrine while still wearing his Augustinian habit. Originally a Florentine, he had joined the Canons Regular of Augustine in 1514. He was active in the reform-minded circle of the *spirituali*; it was most likely in Naples, as a part of Juan de Valdés's circle, that Vermigli first had read Protestant literature. He also had served Pope Paul III at events such as the Colloquy of Worms (1540); and he had undertaken reform programs in Spoleto, Naples, and Lucca. It was in Lucca that Vermigli organized a theological college at which, according to Girolamo Zanchi, another future exile, Vermigli had his students study Bucer, Melanchthon, Bullinger, and Calvin. But in the summer of 1542 Vermigli experienced his crisis of conscience; he was called before the Augustinian chapter in Genoa to account for himself, and his friends warned him that this was a prelude to being called before the newly reconstituted Inquisition.

Vermigli therefore fled; he subsequently lived in Zurich, Strasbourg, and England, before ending his life once again in Zurich, although some of his colleagues north of the Alps found his theology a bit suspect.[55] Vermigli's perspective concerning Nicodemite behaviour was therefore one born of his own failed attempt, followed by multiple flights seeking the opportunity to teach, preach, and practise openly. Vermigli wrote strongly against Nicodemite behaviour, and advocated that Protestant believers directly proselytize to advance the faith. While lecturing in

Strasbourg in 1554, after leaving England rather than live under Mary Tudor, Vermigli discussed the Book of Judges, which was subsequently published as *Commentary on Judges*. His anti-Nicodemite opinions, drawn from that commentary, were published separately as *A Treatise of the Cohabitacyon of the Faithful with the Unfaithful* in about 1555; that material reappeared in his *Loci communes*, a compilation of his work edited by his friends after his death in 1562. Vermigli was not the only Italian exile to take a hard-line stance concerning Nicodemite behaviour. Pier Paolo Vergerio, the former bishop of Capodistria who had fled in 1549 to avoid his own inquisition process, was the most vituperative concerning the question. In fact, anti-Nicodemite sentiments were prevalent among all prominent Protestant theologians in northern Europe, with the temporary exception of Bucer. The only debate among them seemed to consist of disagreements concerning the state of the soul after abjuring the true faith: Was it eternally damned or not?[56]

Like Ulrich Zwingli, Heinrich Bullinger, and John Calvin, among others, Vermigli emphatically maintained that inward worship of God had to be matched by correct outward worship, as set down by God in Scripture. For Vermigli, God was 'the Lord of heart and body; as he requireth the worship of the heart, even as justly and severely doth he command the outward worship of the body.' Attending Catholic Mass, for the true believer, was an act of idolatry.[57] Those that professed the Gospel, therefore, should not 'pollute themselves in popery, by abjurations and masses.' It was not enough only to have a sincere heart, for God also 'doth require outward actions.' Vermigli, therefore, did not see how dissimulation and lying, either through abjuring the true faith when caught or attending Catholic rituals to avoid prosecution, could be excused. When it came to the sacraments, he argued that those who attended Mass and dissimulated 'so that they may retain their riches, dignity, and estimation' actually offended the weak through their lies. The weak, either insufficiently instructed or insufficiently brave, would be drawn through the example of Nicodemites from 'Christ to Antichrist.'[58] Utilizing correct rituals, or refusing incorrect ones, to proselytize 'weaker brethren' who had yet to understand the true faith was a constant motif in Vermigli's thought, and that of others. Nicodemites, because they pleased themselves instead of God, condemned the salvation of their weaker brethren.

Vermigli, among others, disagreed with Martin Bucer about the status of Nicodemites. Bucer, had temporarily endorsed quasi-Nicodemite behaviour before reversing his opinion, but even before that reversal he had shared some of the same concerns as his colleagues. When he had given some approval to quasi-Nicodemite behaviour, Bucer had emphasized to his followers that they should continue to proselytize as well. How else could what Bucer considered to be the true faith ever be practised openly, if not through seeking converts? But for Vermigli, ritual practice itself was a form of proselytizing – there was no distinction between talking and doing – and thus any Nicodemism was completely illegitimate in any sense.

Vermigli also thought that the Catholic Church's use of images in worship was yet another reason to avoid Catholic ritual practices, as did Ulrich Zwingli of Zurich and John Calvin in Geneva, among others. Martin Luther considered images to be among the *adiaphora,* or practices he thought were not required by God, but that a person could use either well or badly, according to the faith behind the action. But Luther always had been concerned that practices centred on saints' images not slide into an implicit belief in the righteousness of works and abuse; he sometimes expressed the wish that images ideally should be removed from churches, but could be kept as long as those weak or illiterate brethren required them.[59]

Violent iconoclasm – or the smashing of Catholic images and relics – was sensationally common among proponents of the Reformed tradition, although Peña would refer to such violence as 'Lutheran.' As Carlos Eire, Lee Palmer Wandell, Carol Piper Heming, and others have argued, iconoclasm was a central and defining feature of agitation for Reform, particularly in urban areas north of the Alps, despite the efforts of Zwingli, Calvin, and most Reformed theologians to urge caution and the official sanction of authorities before removing images. Zwingli in Zurich, for example, had preached against the use of images, arguing that they inherently encouraged idolatry in those that viewed them, from at least October of 1523, if not earlier. His preaching inspired incidents of iconoclasm before Zurich's city council authorized the removal of images from churches; as Lee Palmer Wandel has pointed out, those that engaged in iconoclasm often justified their actions in terms of instructing their less-enlightened neighbours in the true faith.[60] Vermigli, in his anti-Nicodemite writings, deemed exposure to such images and worship – even if the Christian who participated in such ceremonies was aware that such worship was worthless and availed nothing – inherently dangerous. Informed Christians, because of their sinful natures, would begin to erroneously worship the saints even if they were mindful of not doing so. In this, Vermigli was of a like mind with Zwingli, who had explicitly utilized this danger as the foundation for his own opposition to images.[61]

Luther, Zwingli, Calvin, and Vermigli agreed, however, that fasting during Lent and other times required by canon law and the Catholic Church was in no way integral to the practice of Christianity. In March of 1522 followers of Zwingli, including the printer Froschauer, publicly and prominently ate sausages during Lent, which offended many in Zurich. He also offered some to Zwingli, who declined, but the incident placed Zwingli in the position of having to address the problem. He did so in a sermon he preached in March of 1522, which was published in expanded form the next month.[62]

In the work, Zwingli declared that one could choose to eat or fast; the danger of fasting lay in Christians' viewing it as a good work by which they could earn salvation.[63] Zwingli also thought that the Catholic Church had overstepped its bounds by requiring of men and women that which the Bible itself did not require. But, while true Christians should affirm that fasting during Lent was not necessary to salvation, and demonstrate this to their more dubious neighbours through quoting Scripture out of love for them and concern for their salvation, individual Christians should not necessarily insist on eating meat in the presence of those it would offend.[64]

For Vermigli, breaking the Catholic Church's injunctions to fast during Lent was not a crucial point of church doctrine, either: traditions such as fasting were 'things indifferent.' Agreeing with Zwingli and Luther, Vermigli thought such things might be 'well used' as long as true believers did not think themselves justified by them.[65] Vermigli also thought that Christians might continue utilizing these indifferent practices, in order to avoid offending their weaker brethren. But, like Zwingli, Vermigli asserted that this only could be a temporary compromise. According to Vermigli, the potential offence of weaker brethren was in no way an excuse to participate 'in those things which of themselves are evil and forbidden of God.' For Vermigli, 'meat eating and Mass haunting [were] not like'; therefore a true Christian's attendance at Mass could not be done in order to avoid offending weaker brethren or non-believers.[66]

It is therefore somewhat interesting that, as we shall see in future chapters, eating meat during Lent was popularly interpreted as a sign of 'Lutheranism' in Italian lands and described as such by witnesses before inquisition tribunals. But refusing to fast during Lent, along with refusing to venerate sacred images, refusing to kneel as the consecrated host passed through the streets, and disturbing or denying other Catholic ritual practices, became signs of heresy in the mid-sixteenth century, and were popularly interpreted as such by laypeople, inquisitors, and later manual authors.

From the perspective of those authors in the late sixteenth and early seventeenth centuries, concentrating on ritual practices as a means of identifying and investigating suspected heretics was advantageous because it was a 'broad' adaptation. It is possible that the adaptive principles employed by Peña, Farinacci, and Carena had their origins in mid-sixteenth century inquisitorial practice through a variety of sources, although that is impossible to definitively trace. What can be traced is that a variety of Protestant theologians condemned the Catholic Mass, use of sacred images, and fasting during Lent from a multiplicity of perspectives; and vehemently denouncing Nicodemite and quasi-Nicodemite practices was a common denominator among them all. Philo-Protestants interpreted these messages in certain ways that, they hoped, would offer some protection from prosecution while remaining at least somewhat faithful to their religious principles – many unsuccessfully. Inquisitors, and lay witnesses in mid-sixteenth century communities, often recognized such avoidance of ritual practices, and criticism thereof, for what it was, and acted on it.

Building the Case

Inquisitors required testimony to do so. A case prosecuted in Udine in 1543 had a wealth of witness testimony with which to build a process. But while the Roman Inquisition had been reorganized in 1542, it would not possess an official tribunal in Venice until April of 1547. The Venetian government was concerned that a centralized Holy Office, especially under the aegis of Cardinal Gian Pietro Carafa as inquisitor general, would threaten the integrity of the Venetian secular state. It was in 1547 that the papacy and the Venetian government constituted a tribunal subject to Rome, which nonetheless incorporated the involvement of three Venetian lay officials to protect Venetian interests if need be. But the papal nuncio, Giovanni della Casa, had been charged with prosecuting heresy on behalf of the papacy from 1544; he also had been instrumental in hammering out the 1547 agreement.

Within the Venetian dominion, however, the local church hierarchy, particularly in cathedral towns, acted more quickly with the Venetian's government's tacit consent if not enthusiasm; the Council of

Ten, however, followed the proceedings through diplomatic means. In Udine, it was the patriarch of Aquileia's general vicar, Giovanni Angelo da San Severino, who began prosecuting heretics in June and July of 1543, assisted by a canon, an Augustinian Hermit, and Alberto Pascaleo, the bishop of Chioggia.[67] Pier Paolo Vergerio, the bishop of Capodistria who would flee north rather than attend his own inquisition process in 1549, had proselytized extensively in the Friuli, of which Udine was the capital.[68] At this time in northern Italian areas, what exactly constituted doctrinal orthodoxy and heterodoxy was still fluid for some; the Council of Trent had yet to open and definitively pronounce concerning official doctrine and there was still hope that rapprochement between the different and rapidly multiplying divisions within Christendom would be possible and proselytization necessary to help achieve that goal.[69] Concerning this sect in Udine, which included Francesco Garzotto, Francesco da Milano, Alvise Cavallo, Girolamo (Hieronimo), a shoemaker, and Father Patrizio, witnesses were able to give evidence of the sect's religious orientation by relating to the tribunal the group members' various criticisms of traditional Catholic ritual practice, as will be further discussed in Chapter 6.

Giorgio, a tailor who lived outside of Udine, deposed on 20 July 1543, was fairly specific in his testimony and gave evidence concerning those criticisms undertaken by the philo-Protestant group with which he came in contact. As he explained to the tribunal in Udine, two years previously he had participated in a few conversations with Girolamo, the shoemaker, during which Girolamo had told him not to pray to the saints because they could not intercede for humanity; he had said that Christians were not obligated to fast during the times decreed by the Catholic Church; he had asserted that sacred images were unnecessary and had apparently gotten rid of his; and he had said that it was better to give money to the poor than pay for masses for the dead.[70] Giorgio, however, other than giving a rough time frame, did not necessarily explain the entire context of each conversation.

Francesca, deposed during the same month, was a bit more specific concerning the time and place of the relevant conversations. Francesca described a visit she and her mother had made to Father Patrizio's mother, Caterina (called 'La Centa'). According to Francesca, Patrizio's mother had attempted to excuse her refusal to go to Mass by claiming an illness, but La Centa also had told Francesca that there was not really anything that happened at Mass that she could not do just as well at home. Furthermore, Francesca had heard about other things;

there were two other women who lived in Caterina's district (another Francesca and Tina, Caterina's daughter) who had smashed all of the sacred images in their houses, but Francesca did not know that for certain.[71]

Magister Francesco could not give equally good testimony concerning all members of the group, or every heretically suspect word or deed; a few times he told the tribunal that he did not remember ('*non mi ricordo*'). But concerning those people and conversations he did remember, Francesco could be very specific. Zuane and Francesco Garzotto, for example, had told Francesco, the witness, that they would not stay with him and his friends for the ceremonies at church. When the witness had asked why they would not stay for ceremonies commanded by the Holy Mother Church, Garzotto and Zuane had replied: 'What church?' They thereupon had explained, apparently while still standing in a church, that all the ceremonies were false and that they were leaving.[72]

The group in Udine, therefore, attempted proselytizing in a variety of locations, sacred and lay, public and private. In fact, Father Patrizio had told Magister Niccolò that to pray at home was just as effective religiously and spiritually as praying in a church. The priest had also told Niccolò that it was better to pray the Our Father, since praying the Hail Mary or the Creed would merit him nothing.[73] The group also objected to indulgences, papal power, and interpreting the Eucharist as the literal body and blood of Christ, and had not been at all secretive in Udine about any of this; but the core set of beliefs reported by the witnesses reveals the Udinese group's strategies for proselytizing. Most witnesses reported that they had been present when one of the members of the group critiqued some aspect of Catholic ritual practice, and attempted to get the listeners to believe likewise. Not all witnesses were present for many of those conversations, however; for example, the Augustinian cleric Dominus Francesco had made it a point to visit Father Patrizio when he had been ill. During the visit, Patrizio had told the Augustinian that only God should be worshipped, and therefore only the Pater Noster should be utilized during prayer. The Augustinian admitted that those words had not pleased him very much, but when asked to confirm that Patrizio was a heretic according to his public reputation and community opinion, he declined to do so.[74] Across the forty-six testimonies in question, the tribunal in Udine was able to construct, one testimony at a time, a fairly consistent list of religious topics that the heterodox group in Udine repeatedly had attempted to broach with those they had hoped to convert, as will be discussed further in Chapter 6.

That was also true of the case concerning Pietro Vagnola, prosecuted in Venetian territory in 1547–48, and also discussed in Chapter 6. Vagnola had moved to Grignano in the Polesine to proselytize, so his activities were quite noticeable to witnesses.[75] The process took place in Rovigo under the aegis of Bartolomeo Zerbitano, general vicar for the bishop of Rovigo as well as apostolic protonotary and count Palatine, and Fra Girolamo de Fantis da Lendinara, minor conventual and doctor of theology, appointed inquisitor by the Apostolic See. Vagnola's process, however, also involved the participation of secular authority, in the form of *podestà* Aurelio Michiel.[76] Vagnola's behaviour was incredibly distrubing for both ecclesiastical and lay authorities, since he had proselytized so widely; he had told a certain Giovanni Battista that he would neither view the raising of the host during consecration, nor take off his hat in order to pay reverence to the consecrated host. He had told another witness, Giorgio, not to go to Catholic Mass or other divine offices at all and denied the sacrament of confession. Tommaso, another witness, testified that Vagnola denied all the rites instituted by the Catholic Church. And while Tommaso had never seen Vagnola attend Mass, Vagnola had attended sermons and preaching; nevertheless he had complained to Giorgio that preachers in Grignano did not preach the Gospel. All in all, over six witnesses were able to testify to roughly the same information, including avoidance of, and criticism of, Catholic ritual practices.[77]

That the heterodox revealed themselves through avoiding confession and communion, as well as eating meat during Lent, was a fixture of popular perceptions concerning heresy at the time. Two Venetians utilized that knowledge to falsely accuse. Girolamo Badoer and his brother Alvise, a priest, wanted revenge against Zuane (Giovanni) Finetti, a lawyer who had ensured that Girolamo was thrown in prison for stealing. So, in 1566 the brothers spent over 200 ducats to bribe Finetti's household servants, including his boatman, cook, and maidservant, to claim that their employer had neglected his annual duty of attending confession and communion at Easter, and had served meat on his table during Lent.[78] How Finetti chose to defend himself against these accusations will be discussed in Chapter 5.

Bartolomeo Nelli was a friend and tenant of the Sozzini family, whose descendants would found the Unitarian church in Poland. Nelli had been converted by members of that family with the help of an Italian vernacular Bible while he had rented shop space from them in Siena. Nelli subsequently joined another heretical group after the Sozzini had fled Siena.[79] Nelli's prosecution began toward the end of 1559 because he had quoted St Paul concerning the use of good works while talking about the subject in a spice shop. The conversation had been provoked by a sermon in which the priest, Giovanni Rubiols, had spoken vehemently concerning the necessity of works for salvation. Nelli, in the presence of Ettore d'Andrea, the witness, among others, had asserted that he had read in the Bible that good works were merely a sign that one was among the elect.[80] Despite these conversations, Nelli also would provide evidence of his attendance at Mass and annual confession and communion, which would cause the vicar general for the archbishop, the canon Cesare Campani, and the inquisitor Alessandro del Taia, a conventual Franciscan, no end of confusion, as will be discussed in Chapter 5. In the end, the problem would be solved by Nelli's full confession of heretical belief, unprovoked by torture.[81]

In the processes discussed above, there were no shortage of witnesses able to testify; over forty inhabitants of the Friuli testified against Girolamo (Hieronimo) and his associates, while the other cases involved at least five or six witnesses each. It was also possible, however, to open cases with only two testimonies. It even was possible to open processes, according to the standards spelled out in both fourteenth- and later sixteenth-century manuals, with only single witness testimonies in addition to a more general reputation for irreligiosity or heterodox opinions. Even if philo-Protestants attempted to be subtle and proselytize or practise alternative rituals clandestinely, it still would not take much to be at risk for prosecution – effectively, gossip and one or two people able to testify.

This would be true in Modena, in which a period of more clandestine activity followed more open acts of proselytizing. In Modena, a town subject to the dukes of Ferrara, heresy had been allowed to flourish in the absence of *spirituali* Cardinal Giovanni Morone, if inadvertently. His opposition to the use of force and repression in dealing with heretics created a more open situation for people in Modena who were interested in philo-Protestant ideas. Instead of being confronted with official disapproval, followed by inquisitorial action, Modena's heterodox initially were dealing with an absentee bishop who believed that doctrinal differences could be resolved through mutual discussion and understanding as Christians (and who also believed that a full internal reform of the Church could not take place until a council was called to decide matters of doctrine). In fact, Morone made an extreme effort to prove the basic religious orthodoxy of his diocese's members to forestall inquisitorial action against the *fratelli*, a town-wide group of heterodox believers who had their origins in religious discussions within the town's Accademia. Morone, after spending his early episcopacy dealing with diplomatic obligations on behalf of the papacy north of the Alps, finally had arrived in Modena in May of 1542, and proceeded to spend the summer negotiating with both the city's inhabitants and the ecclesiastical hierarchy for a solution to the spread of heresy. Morone asked for Gasparo Contarini's help in writing a simple catechism, which he hoped would be affirmed by the city's inhabitants. The members of the Accademia, the cultural centre of Modena through which heresy had spread, replied with letters that prevaricated and dissimulated. Grillenzoni and others asserted that accusations of heresy came from 'the ignorant and hypocritical.' Two of the Accademia's members who were consulted concerning the text, Giovanni Bertari and Girolamo Teggia, were displeased that an open and public discussion had not preceded the document's writing and limited their participation to some minor suggestions.[82] But with the promulgation of the papal Bull *Licet ab initio* reorganizing the Roman Inquisition in July of 1542, the situation became more urgent. Two of the most prominent academicians, Francesco da Porto and Valentini, left Modena permanently. Those that stayed made the decision to sign the catechism at the end of the summer. At the beginning of September, the document bore the signatures of forty-four of Modena's most prominent citizens.[83]

By the later 1540s, in a progressively more hostile atmosphere, the *fratelli*, or 'brothers,' as the heretical group called themselves, attempted to keep their religious organization clandestine and out of the public eye. Meeting places in shops and houses were deliberately changed from time to time to put spies and neighbours off the track, for example, and many of the *fratelli* continued to attend Catholic services, attempting to appear as members of the Catholic community. But the presupposed connection between performance and belief meant that many *fratelli* also adopted the practice of walking out of church after the Gospel reading, but before the priest began the ceremonies that led to the consecration toward the end of Mass.[84] This practice became one of the ways in which the congregation could identify the *fratelli* despite their efforts at quiet disobedience.

Proselytizing and religious arguments could take place in some rather interesting locations, leading tribunals to rely on those non-heretical witnesses of dubious reputation. For example, when Alessandro del Fornari came to the attention of the Holy Office, he was already in prison. He had spent June of 1568 in the Modenese city prison, not for religious offences, but because he had hit his wife with a shoemaking tool. While in prison Fornari apparently had attempted to proselytize, or simply argue with, his fellow prisoners by saying that purgatory did not exist. This had offended the other prisoners' ears; one of them, called Florio, had countered that purgatory, in fact, did exist. When Fornari stubbornly persisted in his belief, Florio threatened to report him to Modena's tribunal. Alessandro then insulted Florio by insinuating that he could not support his family, which brought an end to the altercation. Three other witnesses confirmed Florio's testimony; Cristoforo da San Martino made the sign of the cross, because he was illiterate, and the other witnesses, Tomasso and Bartolomeo, did not have surnames. All in all, the witnesses perhaps personified the potential pitfalls of evidence provided by some witnesses perhaps having bad reputations, if for non-religious reasons.[85]

Another witness, who happened to be Diana, Florio's wife, thought that Alessandro's propensity for eating meat on Fridays and Saturdays and blaspheming against the Holy Mother and the saints, even yelling 'God, God, traitor!' at a sacred image of Christ, made it clear that he was a Lutheran.[86] In March of 1568, Florio testified to Fra Niccolò da Finale that he had gone to the cathedral to report that Fornari was a 'Lutheran' to Fra Domenico da Imola because of the argument concerning purgatory while the two were in prison together. But Fornari also had argued about images of saints with Florio while in prison, and after they both were released had come to Florio's house and broken a crucifix while yelling '*Dio traditore!*' (Apparently, their association extended past their prison days.) At the end of his process, Fornari was sentenced as vehemently suspect in heresy and placed under house arrest after performing his public abjuration.[87]

Before the increasing severity of the 1560s, heresy was being brought to the attention of authorities, even under the more benign influence of Bishop Egidio Foscarari, who had arrived in Modena to replace Giovanni Morone in 1550. Claudio da Roteglia, prosecuted in 1555, was brought to the bishop's palace and questioned because he had blasphemed Christ; he had forced his wife to skip Mass, although she had been accustomed to attending all the time; and he had eaten meat during Lent and other vigils of the church.[88] Key witness Jacopo Maria de Crispi called *il rizzo sinistro,* told Fra Angelo Valentini di Modena, the inquisitor, how Claudio spoke badly about images of saints and blasphemed Christ while visiting others' houses.[89] Claudio also, when talking to a Franciscan tertiary, denied the efficacy of Catholic sacraments, blasphemed Christ and the saints (possibly a reference to criticism of images), and had been lax at best concerning his own attendance at Mass and other divine offices.[90] Claudio's case, as will be discussed in the next chapter, would cause a great deal of discussion between the tribunal and Bishop Foscarari; at the centre of the debate was the question of whether or not to employ mercy in Claudio's sentence, due to his rather 'rude' condition, in many senses of the word.

The witnesses' testimony gave inquisition tribunals the points of entry from which they could begin processes. Some processes demonstrate evidence of broad proselytizing on the part of philo-Protestants aimed at building popular support for the implementation of Reform, such as the group of which Girolamo the shoemaker was a part in the Friuli. But even if the behaviour of the prospective defendants was perhaps more subtle and at least quasi-Nicodemite, they still attempted both to engage with others and avoid the Catholic ritual practices they found less than faithful to their religious beliefs. Pietro Vagnola refused to reverence the host, which was, as Farinacci, writing a half-century later would inform his readers, very typical of heretics. All of the testimonies discussed above, in fact, in some way involved the three main ways the three later manual authors examined here – Peña, Farinacci, and Carena – thought heresy could and would manifest in behaviours, including avoiding confession, communion, and Mass, engaging in iconoclasm, and eating meat during Lent. That evidence, among all the other varieties and forms of evidence, would prove crucial during a process.

Chapter Four

The Mercy of the Court

Mercy and punishment were the two poles of the inquisitorial model of prosecution. Thomas Aquinas confirmed that these were the two most important points to consider concerning heresy; mercy, according to him, concerned how to deal with the heretics themselves, while punishment concerned how best to protect the Church as a whole. Unrepentant heretics deserved the punishment of banishment, to be accomplished through both excommunication and the death penalty, in order to ensure the protection of the Catholic faithful. But the Church in principle always had sought the conversion of wanderers for the benefit of their salvation. As Aquinas had interpreted the Apostle Paul, the solution to the conundrum, therefore, lay in the Church only condemning recidivist heretics to death after the second admonition. For Aquinas, the relevant passages came from Titus 3: 9–11: 'After a first and second admonition, have nothing more to do with anyone who causes divisions, since you know that such a person is perverted and sinful, being self-condemned.'[1] For their own benefit penitent heretics were to be given a chance to reform, but if they continued to hold heretical beliefs after having been given that one chance at repentance then the danger presented to the Catholic faithful took precedence and they were to be executed as a result.

In theory, arranging these the two somewhat contrary desires as a coherent prosecutorial system was a bit more complex than Aquinas's straightforward principles. As inquisition manuals reveal, the two principles of mercy and punishment ensured that there was a perennial tension built into the inquisitorial system from its inception. Eymeric's fourteenth-century manual, Peña's late sixteenth-century commentaries, and Farinacci's and Carena's works of the early seventeenth century all encouraged the application of mercy and sharply warned against that virtue's misuse. Inquisitors were supposed to show mercy and leniency, bringing processes to a close by welcoming repentant defendants back to the open arms of the Catholic Church, to utilize a phrase popular both in manuals and in the sentences of processes – but only to those who merited mercy. Misguided mercy, as the manuals warned, would be disastrous for the Catholic community as a whole, since misguided mercy would allow the pestilence of heresy to continue. According to these authors, heretics' abilities to lie, feign penitence, and cheat the true and final punishment they well deserved were incomparable.

During the mid-to-late sixteenth century, the majority of processes for philo-Protestant heresy the Roman Inquisition conducted ended on a more merciful note. Andrea Del Col has attempted to statistically analyse the total number of cases undertaken, despite the difficulties of incomplete documentation. He has estimated that from 1542 until the late eighteenth century, the Roman Inquisition may have opened at least 200,000 processes, and perhaps as many as 300,000, dealing with all forms of heresy, but a significantly lower proportion of opened case files reached the process stage, with perhaps 50,000 to 75,000 resulting in abjurations and sentences. Based on those figures, Del Col estimates that about 1.6 to 2.4 per cent of processes ended with death sentences for the accused. Although the Roman Inquisition's approach to prosecuting cases was demonstrably more severe in the 1550s and 1560s than it was in processes held during the earlier period, on balance most processes ended with confession and reconciliation.[2]

It is difficult, however, to gauge the total number of processes that concerned people who presented themselves voluntarily to tribunals; both Adriano Prosperi and Elena Brambilla have noted the importance of the phenomenon when examining the relationship between confessors and inquisitors in this period. Prosperi has emphasized that, theologically, confession (the internal forum) was ideally a comfort to the penitent spiritually, the result of a good confessor's guidance; the prosecution of a public sin, and therefore public crime (the external forum) was within the inquisitors' realm of authority. Therefore, the construction of religious orthodoxy in early modern Italian states relied on what Prosperi has called 'the rapport between persuasion and punishment.' Brambilla has emphasized that the two forums overlapped, and has referred to the rapport between them as 'the long tradition of double forums,' especially since Dominican friars, specialists in hearing the laity's confessions, also acted as inquisitors. Both posit that inquisitors came closest to acting as confessors when dealing with the voluntarily penitent, even if the penitent 'volunteered' at a confessor's prompting; and Brambilla has emphasized that the the fine distinction between forums most likely would not have been comprehended by most laypeople. During a time of grace (traditionally lasting thirty to forty days) those who came forward voluntarily, confessed their heresies, and submitted to the church's correction were deemed worthy of mercy, in the form of very light punishment.[3] Times of grace and voluntary self-denunciation were certainly important factors, but they were not the only two circumstances that legally could justify the use of judicial mercy.

Inquisition manuals written both before and after the mid-sixteenth century endeavoured to construct reasonable theoretical criteria by which those who were worthy of mercy and therefore lesser punishment could be identified. In particular, their authors emphasized that a number of factors, including the ignorance of the defendant and the speed of his or her confession, could warrant the employment of mercy in all kinds of processes. In this chapter, therefore, I examine both how manual authors conceptualized legally permissible justifications for inquisitors employing mercy when dealing with suspected heretics and how they expected defendants worthy of mercy to behave when asking for it.

In reality, mid-sixteenth century inquisitors had considerable room to manoeuvre when undertaking processes, especially when it came to the particular details of the penance allocated to each convicted suspect at sentencing. What particular prosecutorial tone to strike, in terms of proceeding mercifully or with severity, was often within the judicial purview of the individual inquisitors, but it could also be the result of instructions from the Congregation of Cardinals in Rome. I examine two case studies, both prosecuted in Modena in 1555, in which some members of the tribunal used canon law to justify dealing with defendants mercifully.[4] Although the manuals examined in this chapter were written both before and after these two processes took place – Peña's was closest, published about two decades later – it is notable that members of the tribunal in Modena cited specific points of long-standing canon law to argue for granting mercy to Claudio da Roteglia (Rudilia). Roteglia confessed, but presented himself as an 'ignorant' layperson, whose errors were unintentional and therefore worthy of the tribunal's mercy. To do so, he had to make the argument that he was still a practising Catholic. The tribunals' members were not uniformly persuaded.

While Fra Angelo Valentini, inquisitor general of Ferrara and Modena, argued for a more severe sentence, Egidio Foscarari, Modena's bishop, and the consultor Gasparo Marzolus both argued by letter, largely successfully, that Roteglia should be shown mercy due to his ignorance. Giovanni Terrazzano, by contrast, was literate. He would therefore be unable to argue 'ignorance' as a mitigating factor to Fra Angelo, and thus employed the only available strategy to receive a light sentence – he threw himself on the mercy of the court and confessed.

The outcomes of those two processes in 1555 were largely in accord with Eymeric's fourteenth-century text, as well as the later work of Peña, Farinacci, and Carena. All of the authors identified precise factors they thought, in theory, relevant to making such judgments. At the first of the two extremes, according to the manuals, those most deserving of mercy proved themselves so in two ways: first, they could demonstrate their penitence through the alacrity of their confessions, thereby signalling their willingness to submit themselves to the correction of the Catholic Church. Second, they could prove their 'ignorance' of heresy. Roteglia attempted the second, while Terrazzano resorted to the first. Inquisition manuals extensively discussed what exactly did or did not constitute ignorance – how to decide whether or not the suspected heretic in question had known that what he or she had said or done was in fact heretical. Such condescension towards those further down the hierarchical scale than the manual authors and members of the elites in society in general at the time was quite common. That probably accounts, in part, for the extensive exposition of the subject within the manuals.

As my examination of the manuals demonstrates, however, by the late sixteenth and early seventeenth centuries authors' opinions of the religious knowledge of the laity in general had greatly improved since Eymeric's time – with the effect, at least in theory, of making it more difficult for suspected heretics to claim ignorance as a defence. Francisco Peña, Cesare Carena, and Prospero Farinacci wrote that ignorance of key doctrines was in their day and age nearly impossible, thanks to the post-Tridentine Church's efforts. Nevertheless, suspected heretics brought before tribunals in the mid-sixteenth century did, with regularity, claim such ignorance as a part of their defence strategies, whether they really were 'ignorant' or not, perhaps indicating an awareness of inquisitorial procedure and an attempt to manipulate the elite tribunal members' own condescension to the suspects' benefit. But as the later manual authors make clear, particularly Peña and Farinacci, defendants or those who argued on their behalf only could make credible claims of ignorance or penitence concerning heresy if they had not engaged in any clearly heterodox ritual activity, because such activity would clearly indicate a dangerous level of commitment to, and belief in, heresy. Defendants worthy of mercy should have observed Catholic rites for the most part and proved themselves willing to submit to the correction of the church, thereby demonstrating that they retained at least some attachment to, and belief in, the Catholic Church. Ritual practice was only one element in these processes, but it was an important one that could be used to gauge the level of religious belief and commitment on the part of the defendant.

Systemic Mercy

The best-known feature of inquisitorial mercy was the declaration of a time of grace, usually lasting between thirty and forty days, but the operative principle that guaranteed leniency was the spontaneity of the confessions, made voluntarily and of one's own free will, produced during those times. During the medieval period, when newly appointed inquisitors first arrived at the location of a new tribunal they would require everyone in the community to swear to assist inquisitors in the prosecution of heresy. They also would advise the community that if any heretics came to the tribunal spontaneously and sought to be reconciled to the church of their own volition within the appointed time of grace they would be shown leniency. Such leniency usually consisted of undergoing canonical purgation or abjuration in private, rather than in public, and being given less onerous penances.[5]

Of the sixteenth- and seventeenth-century manuals, Cesare Carena's most clearly expressed how the institution had been adapted to the permanently established tribunals in north-central Italian lands. According to Carena, the pope could declare a time of grace to respond to particular situations. In addition to a newly founded tribunal beginning its activities (a relatively rare event in the seventeenth-century Italian lands), times of grace could be declared when a previous time of grace had been interrupted for some reason, when an entire heretical kingdom had been converted, and when the good Catholics of a given area had been deceived by heretics, for example. But, as Carena thought, Pope Paul IV had declared a time of grace in the third month of his papacy solely because of his authority to do so, rather than as a response to any unusual circumstances.[6] Paul IV's time of grace was perhaps not the most significant in this period from a historian's perspective; Pope Julius III, during the jubilee year of 1550, issued two papal briefs declaring a time of grace. For approximately three months, those who came forward voluntarily to confess ownership of heretical or suspicious books were promised private reconciliation to the Church; they would be referred to a confessor, not an inquisitor, for absolution and they would not have to abjure in public. The second bull promised private abjuration for believers in heresy who voluntarily presented themselves spontaneously to inquisitors, although given the instructions found within inquisitorial manuals, a private abjuration and light punishment could be the result of spontaneous and voluntary presentation in Italian lands if certain preconditions were met. Elena Brambilla, in particular, has argued that the issuance of these two bulls was pivotal in the Catholic Church's battle against philo-Protestant heresy.[7]

The Desire for Correction

Even when there was not a time of grace in effect, people still could spontaneously and willingly present themselves to the Holy Office and expect to be treated more leniently for having done so. Nicholas Eymeric stated in principle that anyone who presented himself or herself for manifest heretical crimes should be punished more gently – if not escape punishment entirely. Peña in his comments specifically noted that this was also true for those who turned themselves in even after the time of grace had ended.[8] The punishment should be mitigated on account of the spontaneity and willingness of the confession, but not dispensed with entirely, since the repentant one had chosen to believe in heresy, at least for a time, and was responsible for that crime. Because Eymeric had not clearly defined what he meant by the term 'gently,' Peña suggested monetary fines or donations to charity as fitting to the circumstances.[9]

Cesare Carena later agreed that people who came to the Holy Office willingly to confess should be dealt with leniently. Carena, as did all of the authors, specified what constituted true spontaneity with legal precision; the tribunal had to be unaware of any indications of heretical crimes, meaning that there had been absolutely no denunciations or incriminating testimony resulting from investigations concerning the individual in question – no *mala fama* ('bad reputation,' or reputation for heresy) had reached the inquisitors' ears in any way. Carena, however, thought there could be a bit more unsavoury a reason for the phenomenon; those who voluntarily presented themselves might do so because they anticipated someone else might denounce them or be called to testify against them, in the near future, and therefore were appealing for leniency while they still could.[10]

Carena, in recognizing this cynical motivation for voluntary appearances before tribunals, once again raised the prospect of quasi-Nicodemism without utilizing the term. While the genuinely penitent were supposed to receive more lenient punishments, Carena affirmed there were authorities who thought that those who only came forward spontaneously out of fear rather than penitence should not be shown such mercy. The danger lay in mistaking one for the other, since those who lied and misrepresented their penitence could potentially continue to spread their heretical beliefs once they were sent back into the community of the faithful. A heretical believer who came forward before anyone else did and then faked penitence to abjure afterwards would be able to continue proselytizing secretly. Authors of inquisitorial manuals sought to express a set of coherent standards by which this pitfall could be avoided.

Almost all of the manuals discussed the difference between sentencing a truly willing and voluntary penitent and sentencing someone who only came forward out of fear, as the authors summed up all other potential motivations. This was such an important distinction that even relapsed heretics who voluntarily came forward and were genuinely penitent could in principle receive a more merciful punishment (especially if their heresies subsequent to the first processes were entirely secret), an important modification to Aquinas's ideas. According to Peña and Carena, this was a very difficult and risky judgment for inquisitors to make concerning relapsed heretics. Therefore Carena, writing in the seventeenth century, advised inquisitors to consult the Congregation of Cardinals before any sentence was pronounced (Peña also had thought such consultation safer). The crux of the problem lay in the fact that relapsed heretics had successfully faked penitence in their first abjurations. They exemplified some other inquisitor's misplaced impulse towards mercy, since he had believed their protestations of sincere confession. As a result some churchmen, such as Simancas, disagreed with Carena and Peña and thought it impossible to believe even voluntary protestations of penitence made by relapsed heretics. Even if relapsed heretics willingly presented themselves to tribunals, they already had destroyed their own credibility.

Peña, however, thought the more lenient sentence the more generally accepted, and quoted Hostiensis as support; no one who had voluntarily turned himself or herself in to a tribunal because of true penitence, including relapsed heretics, could be completely incorrigible, and therefore such people were deserving of at least some mercy. Furthermore, there was a legal technicality to be considered, since the inquisition defined relapsed heretics as those who had been tried and convicted for serious heresy twice (the legal expression of Paul's advice). Since they had voluntarily come forward and confessed the second time, they technically had not been convicted by a full process twice. Peña endorsed the more merciful opinion, citing the decisions of the Council of Béziers (1233) as justification for doing so. Peña thought, and Farinacci later agreed, that relapsed heretics who voluntarily presented themselves to tribunals should be sentenced to perpetual incarceration, obviously a more lenient punishment than execution, in order to safeguard the rest of the Catholic community, although perpetual incarceration rarely lasted for an entire lifetime in practice.[11]

If fear, however, was the primary motivating factor for heretics voluntarily coming forward (whether for the first or second time) rather than true penitence, Carena quoted the Spanish Inquisition's ruling council, the Suprema, as pronouncing that they should not be mercifully received at all; Simancas and Tiberio Deciani, a Spanish and Italian author, respectively, both had promoted that opinion.[12] But according to Peña, no less an authority than Hostiensis had thought that it should be left to each individual judge to decide how much mercy was merited in such cases.[13] Again, the tension lay between the two contradictory impulses of mercy and punishment, the first of which, if misguided, might backfire and and allow heretics the opportunity to continue spreading dangerous heretical lies. The authors examined here, and their sources, did not necessarily agree as to how best to judge such difficult cases.

Cesare Carena, therefore, had two caveats concerning how to tell the difference between the genuinely penitential and the merely fearful when they self-denounced. First, they should be carefully questioned concerning the full extent of their heretical activity. In one of the few occasions he directly addressed how to question defendants, Carena advised his readers to be sure to ask for a full account of the suspected heretics' errors, how long they had persisted in them, what prohibited books they had read, and to name their accomplices in heresy. Carena warned his readers to watch carefully for when the confession was faked – but offered no specific tips as to how to recognize feigned repentance.[14] In fact, many earlier authors, such as Peña, asserted that one could tell whether penitence was feigned or not by the physical behaviour of the defendant in question. At the same time, however, those same authors acknowledged that heretics would lie and employ every possible ruse to feign belief and penitence.[15] In the face of the tension generated between those two principles – that heretics constantly lied, and yet inquisitors should be able to discern lies from truth in deciding who merited mercy – Carena only could advise using good judgment.

The same anxiety about potentially misguided mercy also animated discussions regarding those who were prosecuted because of an investigation for the first time. This discussion revealed past disagreements among canonists as to how to interpret *Ad abolendam*, one of the founding canons of inquisition activities, produced by Lucius III in 1184. Should the canon be interpreted to mean that only those who confessed immediately on their capture and arrest, but before being questioned, should be shown mercy? Carena stated that it was the more common opinion to grant mercy to anyone who confessed before the tribunal moved to pronounce a sentence. As his later passages in this chapter made clear, however, in this particular context the term 'mercy' meant not being executed – if any inquisitions actually had executed all of those who did not confess immediately and in full, before questioning, the percentage of cases that had ended in execution would have risen dramatically. It is notable, however, that such a stringent interpretation of the principles found in *Ad abolendam* existed, if only as a vaguely acknowledged minority and fringe legal opinion.[16]

Carena had a very specific warning for his readers, however, after having established that a confession at any time during a process forestalled use of the death penalty. Carena had to examine just how far that principle could be taken: Could someone be shown mercy for confessing even after he or she already had been sentenced and turned over to the secular arm? Carena thought it was within the rights of inquisitors and bishops to do so. But they should consider whether the already-convicted heretic was suddenly cooperative because he or she feared a very painful death, once again raising the issue of ensuring sincere confessions. To illustrate his reservations concerning this point, Carena referred to a story originally told by Eymeric in the *Directorium Inquisitorum*, indicating that this issue had been a perpetual concern over time. In Catalonia a pertinacious priest, just as he was being drawn up to the stake 'and so the fire having been applied, and thus, from one part having been somewhat scorched, he began to cry out, that he might be let out, because he wanted to abjure .' He thereafter persisted in his heresy for the next forty years, 'infecting' many others.[17] The warning to Carena's readers was clear – misguided mercy could do more harm to the Catholic community than good.

The sincere penitents who voluntarily presented themselves to tribunals and those who gave in and confessed at the last possible moment were, within the pages of manuals, hypothetical cases that represented the full range of theoretical principles involving how to employ mercy and punishment. Those who freely and willingly turned themselves in were to be given the benefit of the doubt and sentenced to light penance in private, if their penitence was genuine. But those who only portrayed themselves as penitent out of fear could only be shown mercy and reincorporated back into the community of the faithful by risking the spiritual health of that very community.

In reality, most of those who came before the Holy Office's mid-sixteenth century tribunals for philo-Protestant heresies neither waited for the last possible moment to confess nor confessed immediately; instead they made their confessions at some stage of their processes. Carena, the seventeenth-century consultant and prosecutor for the Cremonese tribunal, accounted for these more realistic circumstances in his manual, which comprised the bulk of real cases. He reasonably maintained that, when it came to assigning punishment to those judged as suspect in heresy at the end of a process, the relative speed of the confessions should be a factor in deciding on appropriate sentences, whether fear was a factor or not: concerning these punishments, 'one ought to consider the time at which those heretics were converted; for he ought to be punished more gently, who confessed from fear of threatening proof than he who confessed after having been thrown in prison, and he more gently punished than he who confessed after public testimony.' Carena nevetheless thought this principle of sentencing should not be celebrated or widely discussed publicly.[18] Apparently, Carena did not think it prudent to publicize a policy of giving first-time voluntary 'penitents' with less than stellar motivations the benefit of the doubt.

Ignorance of Heresy

There was one last factor that influenced the impulse towards mercy, especially when an immediate confession was forthcoming. All of the authors discussed here made allowances for the truly ignorant – although what constituted true ignorance changed between the fourteenth and the later sixteenth century. Eliseo Masini, in his *Sacro Arsenale* of 1621, stated the long-held general principle: if any people were to fall into heresy because of genuine ignorance, then they should be punished, but not as heretics, provided that they revoked their errors simply and without conditions. Carena, Farinacci, Peña, and Eymeric all had agreed with him in their respective earlier works, but those authors also had defined clearly what they thought did or did not constitute ignorance.[19] In so doing, these authors not only discussed the issue in the terms common to their elite status; they also revealed how the concept of 'ignorance' of religious doctrine and heresy, as a perception, had changed since the late Middle Ages. The post-Tridentine Church's emphasis on the education of the laity had the effect of making the authors of the later sixteenth century dubious about claims of 'ignorance' as a defence.

For Eymeric, and therefore Peña in his commentaries, the issue of defining ignorance came up while providing the answers to twelve questions rhetorically asking what exactly was 'pertaining to observing the faith' for good Catholics.[20] In the process of commenting on Eymeric's text, Peña would establish that in his opinion Eymeric's fourteenth-century recommendations for taking ignorance into account when prosecuting defendants were no longer quite so applicable in the late sixteenth century. In so doing, Peña implicitly recognized the ways in which the printing press had enabled everyone in Europe to have familiarity with the Protestant Reformation as an event.

Eymeric considered the articles of faith as expressed in the *symbolo* (or the Creed) to be the key for establishing an appropriate level of religious knowledge among the laity. For Eymeric, anything that deviated from the Creed could be considered heretical, but that deviation also could be the result of a lack of education. Here again, Eymeric separated religious errors as a general concept from the intent behind them. Some 'ignorant' people, Eymeric implied, merely made mistakes as to what constituted correct Church doctrine, without any real or conscious heretical intent. Those same errors only became heretical when the people who believed in such errors did so because they consciously chose to be heretics – in this sense, the Church placed the onus of defining heresy entirely on the heretics themselves.

Peña, in his commentary, did not discuss the fact that most northern Protestant denominations, particularly the Lutherans, included the ancient creeds in their statements of faith, including the Augsburg Confession of 1530, originally meant by its author, Melanchthon, as an irenic document from which negotiations with Catholic authorities could begin. While the Creed may have proved useful in pursuing Cathars or *conversos*, it was not terribly useful in singling out philo-Protestant suspected heretics, with the exception of antitrinitarians. From the Catholic perspective, northern Protestant heretical sects did not submit themselves to the authority of the one, holy, apostolic, and Catholic Church, but those new Protestant denominations simply redefined 'Catholic' to mean 'universal' or substituted the word 'Christian' in the Creed and continued to use it anyway.[21] But Eymeric and his source Thomas Aquinas, however, had expounded on the Creed at great length; therefore Peña would comment on it as well.

While commenting on Eymeric's text, Peña would adapt the concept by severely limiting the possibility for true ignorance to exist. In his introductory commentary to Eymeric's twelve questions, Peña admitted that Eymeric's principles could reveal the 'single errors' of those who were faithful but ignorant. Nevertheless, he asserted that such 'simple errors' could 'insinuate much,' presumably heretical, to the annoyance of inquisitors. Peña stated that he would refrain from tackling the problem in its entirety because he thought it was more properly the province of theologians. Perhaps this was his way of glossing over his sense that all of this was not terribly applicable to his own time.[22] He had done much the same when praising Eymeric for his restraint in neglecting to spell out every permutation of heretical belief, when Eymeric had quite obviously just done so for many pages of text. Nevertheless, Peña dutifully examined Eymeric's original text, explaining 'therefore this is the sense of the question: Whether any faithful person is obligated to know the articles of faith clearly and openly, and thus so that he should know this to be an article of faith as often as he may have been questioned about this thing?'[23]

The answer, for Eymeric and Thomas Aquinas, had been yes; every Catholic past the age of discernment should know the articles of faith by heart as found in the Creed and should be able to repeat them explicitly from memory as well. But Thomas Aquinas had thought that the uneducated should not be questioned concerning what he called 'the subtleties of faith, except when there is suspicion that they have been corrupted by heretics.' 'The simple' had 'implicit faith' in the faith of their teachers; therefore, if those teachers moved away from the true faith, the simple were not responsible for any heresies their seemingly

Catholic teachers had espoused. All Christians, however, could be expected to know the *symbolo* (the Creed), because by its very nature the Creed was meant to be a public teaching of the crucial elements of faith and belief; therefore it was sung at every Mass.[24] Peña pointed out that this had been the standard among Catholics, without controversy, since the time of Charlemagne, who had instructed priests to repeat the Creed on Sundays so every lay parishioner would learn it by heart.[25]

Eymeric, in his time, had agreed that the members of the laity whom he referred to as 'the simple' should not be fully examined concerning their faith by inquisitors unless there was some clear indication of heretical depravity, as Aquinas had established. For Eymeric, those who were merely ignorant about the more subtle points of doctrine not contained in the Creed would make themselves known by how quickly they gave up their errors when instructed.[26]

It was in response to another of Eymeric's points – the meaning of which Peña found to be completely impenetrable – that Peña hinted at disagreeing with Eymeric's perspective. He stated that the issue was far too complex to untangle within the pages of his commentary. At first, Peña seemed to concede the point, that the ignorant could be excused from being deceived by the learned, as long as they had not been legitimately admonished by the bishop or inquisitor. But Peña had one other caveat concerning the issue, which would become increasingly more important as he commented on Eymeric's twelve questions. Ignorance only could be claimed concerning issues which had not been publicly proclaimed in the Church and therefore were not held to be fully explained.

Peña emphasized that those who were led astray by men masquerading as learned doctors of the church were still in some way responsible for their heretical belief. For Peña, 'for if in this one may stray from the right path of truth, on account of the authority of learned doctors, one will not be entirely excused.' To explain the point, Peña referred to the work of Peter Lombard, who had utilized an analogy concerning heresy to explicate canon laws about marriage. In Peña's view, while the truly ignorant person was not necessarily heretical, especially if led into heresy through lies, that still did not remove the public crime of heresy entirely. Even if led astray by 'some man falsely presenting himself to be some Catholic man while nevertheless he may be a heretic,' Peña insisted that the suspected person still was responsible for the crime at least in part .[27]

Peña seems to have been referring to the phenomenon of Nicodemite preaching. From the 1520s to the late 1540s, a significant number of clerics interested in heterodox ideas, whether those ideas originated north or south of the Alps, preached them to the Catholic faithful in Italian states. Sermons were ideally suited to spreading the message to all levels of society, literate and illiterate, and these preachers did not find subterfuge all that necessary in the first half of the sixteenth century. Giulio della Rovere (da Milano) and Agostino Mainardi, among others, had spread the word of religious reform by mounting pulpits in Catholic churches and preaching while wearing the distinctive clothing of Catholic religious. Many of the preachers came from the Augustinian order and were among the first to adhere to Luther's teachings for that reason. In Giulio della Rovere's sermons given immediately before his arrest in Venice in 1541 (recorded in a book later prohibited), the Augustinian monk exposited the Lutheran ideas of justification by faith and grace alone, alongside exposition of the Gospel as the source of religious truth.[28] By the 1550s and 1560s, these preachers mostly had fled north, been prosecuted, or had begun to toe the Tridentine doctrinal line in their preaching.[29]

During the time in which they had preached heterodox doctrines while wearing the robes of their respective religious orders, however, these men could have been viewed by their listeners as 'learned men' who seemed to be Catholic – because those preachers had presented themselves as Catholic. For Peña, and others at the time, the difficulty lay in accurately reading the attitude of the listeners: Had some of them been in on the joke, so to speak? For Peña, in theory, it was entirely possible for philo-Protestants to attend these sermons precisely because they knew those doctrines being preached were heretical, only to later disingenuously claim to an inquisitorial tribunal that they had obviously assumed anything coming out of the mouth of a man wearing sacral robes was Catholic. It was, however, also theoretically possible that good Catholics had attended an Augustinian's sermons, only to be told later (by other religious, bishops, or inquisitors) about the doctrines' heterodoxy. Peña thought immedite confession was the commonly recognized solution both theologically and legally; that would indicate genuine error and ignorance on the part of good Catholics. But even then, for Peña, a quick confession still did not entirely excuse the listener.

In addition to asserting some responsibility for those who were led astray by others, Peña also severely limited the possibility for true ignorance even to exist in his time. For Peña, the issue arose when commenting on Eymeric's seventh question concerning what the average person could be expected to know about Scripture.[30] According to Eymeric, the ignorant were exceptionally prone to misinterpreting the Bible; in this context, Eymeric really intended to discuss the the 'ignorant' who although literate were not fully qualified to study theology. If someone misinterpreted the scriptural basis for crucial doctrinal beliefs (such as the nature of the Trinity) that was obviously heretical. But if someone misinterpreted or denied something in the Bible that was not essential to the articles of faith, according to Eymeric, that was also heretical, since the erroneous interpreter thereby implied that some part of the Bible was false.

Peña commented surprisingly little about Eymeric's assertion that scriptural misinterpretations were always heretical whether they pertained to essential articles of faith or not. Given the sensationalism of most Protestant sects' insistence on scriptural primacy and the Catholic Church's post-Tridentine restrictions concerning lay access to the Bible, this is a strange omission.[31] In Eymeric's time lay access to the Bible was much more circumscribed by the lack of a printing press and low literacy rates among the population as a whole, although the connection between biblical interpretation and heresy already had been noted nevertheless. Peña here seems to have settled for implying that those who knew how to read and had read the Bible could not possibly be unaware of the Catholic Church's firm claim to a monopoly on biblical interpretation and the possession of the Holy Spirit's guiding influence.[32]

Peña, in his accompanying commentary, admitted that Eymeric's logic concerning which errors concerning Scripture were heretical and which were not 'most clearly' indicated that ignorance could excuse one from Charges of heresy only partially. But for Peña, again, this could only apply to issues that had not been explicated clearly and broadly by the Church.[33] Peña cited over fifteen inquisitorial writings and theologial works to support his point, and claimed that he had omitted many more. He included a set of rules, according to which his readers could navigate their way through the complexities of the late sixteenth-century religious landscape and judge those who the Catholic Church still characterized as ignorant or uneducated defendants and, since they were common people, perhaps only literate in the vernacular.[34] Peña, in his first rule, repeated that those who erred according to the Creed would not be considered heretical unless they refused correction. Peña asserted that he could not see any controversy amongst the doctors of the church about this principle; those who refused correction were pertinacious, a key component of defining heretics, and obviously were aware that their beliefs were heretical.[35]

Peña also described the differing expectations of simple layfolk and theologians, respectively, in terms of what they could be expected to know about faith and doctrine. But it is interesting to note the typical errors he ascribed to each. The uneducated could be expected to deny Christ's crucifixion, death, or resurrection, or deny that prayers for the dead were efficacious, for example. Educated men of the Church could be expected to deny that the Holy Spirit proceeded from the Son, or say that good Christians should not participate in war, or state that bishops were not the superiors of simple priests. Concerning laypeople, Peña implied that those espousing such errors were definitely suspect, even if ignorant, and were most likely heretics, since he instructed his readers that ignorance could only be considered a valid cause only if all other signs of good Catholic faith were clearly present and signs of malicious intent completely absent.[36] If such maliciousness and heretical signs were absent, Peña thought that the most likely source of errors among simple men was their own natural reason. Uneducated people might reasonably decide that God was obviously more powerful than His Son, especially when the Son was in human form, and genuinely believe that the Catholic Church thought the same; their logic was comprehensible, if very mistaken. It was for this very reason that common people fell into error more easily, according to Peña, but again, if they immediately submitted themselves to the correction of inquisitors, they should not be considered heretical, although light punishment was definitely in order.[37]

Peña implied that defendants who showed signs of simply having formed incorrect thoughts would show no signs of owning heterodox vernacular literature, of speaking to heterodox believers, or of attending heretical conventicles. In the reality of a tribunal, defendants often advanced such protestations of unintentional error in the attempt to gain an inquisitor's mercy. Some accused heretics who came before tribunals in the mid-sixteenth century would attempt to defend themselves by stating that their errors came to them through their own logic or thought process, and were not the result of any outside influences; inquisitors in those cases would push hard to discover heretical books or accomplices in heresy, or would gather evidence from witnesses to prove otherwise.[38]

Then Peña again expressed his views concerning the average layperson's responsibility for understanding correct Catholic doctrine when he dealt with the issue of *invincibilis ignorantia*, or ignorance that a person simply could not overcome. Peña described these 'ignorants' as those who had diligently investigated and searched for the truth but were unable to find it, presumably because they lacked the resources to do so. Peña confidently asserted that in his time, fortunately, the Christian religion had been so openly preached, and councils held to determine and promulgate proper faith that such a person could hardly be found.[39] This was a particularly optimistic view of another aspect of the post-Tridentine era; effectively Peña thought that even common people could no longer claim invincible ignorance as a defence during inquisitorial processes. [40]

Peña therefore re-emphasized that claims of ignorance could only apply to those doctrinal issues that were not broadly and publicly explained by the Church as a whole. This, of course, was exactly the problem for much of the first half of the sixteenth century; for many of those concerned with the ongoing splintering of Christendom, the only legitimate vehicle for defining correct Catholic doctrine was a council, and the Council of Trent did not begin until 1545. Yet Peña, writing less than twenty years after the council's conclusion in 1563, applied a stringent standard in his own day and refused to acknowledge the ambiguities of the recent past. Peña seems to have assumed that a heretical preacher in the recent past, even if he had presented himself in the guise of a Catholic, should not be, and would not be, the common person's only source of religious instruction at that time. Those who attended sermons of individual wandering preachers falsely clothed as Catholic clerics should have been able to recognize discrepancies between what that preacher said and what other religious authority figures, such as parish priests, taught every Sunday in their parish churches. Therefore, lay Catholics could be held accountable for repeating what they had heard from the wolves in sheep's clothing – they should have known better. In this, Peña perhaps more accurately assessed the religious knowledge of the laity in his time than Eymeric had in his.

Cesare Carena, echoing Peña in his early seventeenth-century work, also thought the truly ignorant were so rare they could hardly be found anymore.[41] But Carena specified who was responsible for proving that the person in question was in fact ignorant. Usually, it was the procurator fiscal's burden to investigate claims of ignorance. But if the person was a 'notorious' public heretic, established through testimony, then the burden of proof lay with the accused.[42]

Propsero Farinacci added one final caveat for his readers, but, as he put it, he spoke more generally of schismatics, not all heretics.[43] Schismatics separated themselves from the unity of the Church through attending services led by those who denied the authority of the pope. It would be difficult for anyone to argue they had been completely unaware of the religious affiliation of the church or secret conventicle they had attended.[44] Farinacci also advised that torture could be utilized to discover whether or not any given simple person really had thought that their ideas and actions were Catholic, not heterodox. But he also advised that torture should not be utilized in all cases as a general policy, merely against those who had a public reputation (or 'notorious' reputation) for being heretics.[45]

By the late sixteenth and early seventeenth centuries, in theory, the burden of proving ignorance clearly lay with the suspected heretics. Laypeople who had truly sought out Catholic truth, only to be stymied in that pursuit by a lack of resources, qualified as those who could not overcome their religious ignorance. But such ignorant people were declared to be few and far between since, according to Peña, Farinacci, and Carena, the Catholic Church had declared publicly Catholic beliefs through conciliar decisions and promulgations. Furthermore, the only way claims of ignorance could be a credible defence was if those claims were made immediately, preferrably on arrest or during the first questioning. The authors of these manuals acknowledged that even immediate claims of penitence and submission to Catholic dogma and authority could be counterfeit; there was, when prosecuting anyone for the first time, always at least some risk of recidivism after the abjuration. Manual authors, however, seem to have regarded that risk as minimal when dealing with those who confessed immediately and in full, while believing the likelihood of that risk to grow exponentially the longer any given process dragged on.

As the two processes of Claudio da Roteglia and Giovanni Terrazzano demonstrate, lay suspected heretics, when brought before inquisitorial courts in the mid-sixteenth century, often discussed their alleged heretical crimes from those very perspectives. They attempted to portray themselves as cooperative, willing to submit themselves to the authority of the Church from their first questioning sessions. Both men also endeavoured to explain their heretical beliefs and actions within the context of being led astray through the evil actions of others, describing those others as more powerful or inherently more authoritative than themselves. In so doing, they may have been consciously attempting to exploit the clerical elite's attitudes towards lay society to their own advantage. But such a defence, and the accompanying appeal for leniency or mercy, could only work if the suspected heretics in question had not engaged in recognizably unorthodox ritual practices or serious protests against Catholic ritual practice. As Farinacci reminded his readers when he published his work in 1616, schismatics could not possibly claim ignorance of their actions. Whether or not one practised as a Catholic, according to manual authors, theoretically could give inquisitors a barometer by which to measure the other evidence brought before the tribunal.

Rash Ignorance in Modena

How inquisitors in reality distinguished between the ignorant and the heretical depended to a great extent on how they defined and categorized truly heretical activity, which could change according to different circumstances and contexts. The heterodox group in Modena, known as the *fratelli*, or 'brothers,' in many ways exemplified all of the factors described above, including a variety of activities tribunals could consider to be heretical and schismatic. The 'brothers' engaged in convsersations concerning religious doctrine, circulated books ultimately deemed heretical, and held meetings of like-minded Modenese of all socioeconomic strata and educational levels, where Scripture was discussed in a quasi-sacral manner. Modena was also one of the towns in mid-sixteeenth century northern Italy that saw its fair share of preachers wearing the habits of Catholic religious orders who in the 1540s were deemed to be spreading heresy.

That heterodoxy flourished, relative to other towns in Italy, was in no small part due to the irenic approach of the town's bishop, Cardinal Giovanni Morone. Morone was an absentee bishop; because of his importance as a well respected cleric in the 1530s he was sent north of the Alps as a papal legate and initially spent very little time in Modena. His vicar, Domenico Sigibaldi, kept him informed of the goings-on in Modena, however; in a letter to Alessandro Farnese Morone was forced to admit that there were as many heretics in Modena as in Prague. But the bishop was genuinely devout, in favour of reform, and has often been labelled one of the *spirituali* because he approached heterodoxy with a spirit of irenicism and compromise.[46] Morone's personal beliefs and his opposition to the use of force and repression in dealing with heretics allowed for open discussion of philo-Protestant ideas in Modena in the 1520s and 1530s, even more than elsewhere in north-central Italy. The Accademia, a group of upper-class citizens, began meeting to discuss 'poetry and philosophy' at the home of Giovanni Grillenzoni, a doctor, and at his brother's pharmacy. As with other groups of young men in Europe at this time, serious discussion of ancient languages and original sources turned the discussion from philosophical matters to religious ones.[47] The Accademia's members made contact with other heterodox groups in Italy, and surreptitiously circulated letters from Martin Bucer, the Strasbourg Reformer. They were regarded as dangerous by many because of their successful attempts to proselytize ordinary citizens outside the Accademia's elite.[48]

Morone, in response to this group, and others, made an effort to prove the basic religious orthodoxy of his diocese's members to forestall inquisitorial action in the early 1540s. He arrived in Modena in May of 1542; his close friend, Gasparo Contarini, had already helped Morone to write a simple catechism, in the hopes of proving the basic orthodoxy of everyone in the town to the Holy Office.[49] The members of the Accademia replied to Morone's efforts by stalling. Giovanni Bertari and Girolamo Teggia intimated that an open and public discussion of the document should have been held.[50] After the reorganization of the Roman Inquisition in 1542, prominent members of the Accademia began to flee Modena, and those who stayed signed the catechism at the end of the summer. By September, forty-four of Modena's most prominent citizens had done so.[51] But Morone's attempts at compromise merely led to more discretion on the part of the Academicians and other people in Modena interested in heterodox ideas.

Nevertheless, Bartolomeo della Pergola, a Minorite friar, began preaching heterodox ideas publicly in 1544 – exactly the kind of Nicodemite preaching Peña and Farinacci later would recognize as dangerous, since he was preaching philo-Protestant doctrines while dressed in Catholic religious attire. [52] His preaching emphasized justification by faith alone, but in a positive and nonpolemical way (as had been enshrined in the *Beneficio di Cristo*, first printed in Venice in 1543).[53] While preaching to large crowds, he simply explained to his listeners that salvation came from Christ because he had died on the cross to pay for their sins. The Academicians were in favour of his preaching, but, as Domenico Sigibaldi was forced to note, Bartolomeo's preaching did not please everyone.[54]

According to some sources, Bartolomeo's express negation of the merit of good works in earning salvation angered Morone, but even Morone's own inquisitorial proceeding could not settle the question of whether or not he was fully aware of Bartolomeo's preaching of Reform ideas.[55] Bartolomeo della Pergola, during Morone's process beginning in 1557, testified that he had met Morone in Rome in 1543 and discussed 'Lutheran' opinions with him, particularly those concerning justification. But Pergola's testimony was given in a court determined to convict Morone under the instructions of Pope Paul IV, the former general inquisitor appointed by Pope Paul III in 1542. Furthermore, Pergola was referring to these opinions as 'Lutheran' after the relatively free period of religious thought that had existed in Italy from the 1520s to the early 1540s. His assertions, therefore, that Morone had considered his preaching to be 'Lutheran' and had approved cannot necessarily be taken at face value.

After his Lenten preaching in Modena, Pergola went to Bologna, but the Dominicans initiated an inquisitorial proceeding against him almost immediately. Morone later was accused of protecting Pergola from being sent to Rome to be prosecuted by the main tribunal there, but the preacher, after two depositions to the inquisitor in Bologna, returned to Modena and publicly retracted his errors on 15 and 16 June of 1544. In his first retraction, he demonstrated his turbulent state of mind by neglecting to definitively retract all twenty-nine of the articles on the list the Inquisition drew up concerning his errors; he therefore had to repeat his retraction the next day. In the defence phase of his trial, Morone would emphasize his collaboration in bringing off the event.[56]

Pergola's preaching initiated a significant amount of heterodox activity in Modena, particularly among artisans and urban laborers. As processes held in the 1560s demonstrate, Pergola's preaching was the origin of many workshop conventicles where labourers, managers, and shop owners would read heretical books in the vernacular out loud and discuss philo-Protestant doctrines, which became the third factor that spread heresy in Modena.[57] Two books in particular, later deemed heretical, the *Beneficio di Cristo* (printed first in Venice in 1543) and the *Sommario della Sacra Scrittura* (1535) were often read and discussed.[58] Books such as these, along with the stimulus of Bartolomeo's preaching, allowed heterodox ideas and discussions to flourish outside the Accademia in the town's workshops and stores and made them accessible to artisans, workers, and women as well as Modena's educated elite. The *fratelli*, though their reading and discussion, developed into an eclectic, although radical, sect; Zwinglian, Calvinist, and for some, Anabaptist doctrines were combined in ways that could vary from individual to individual.[59]

All of these factors created an environment in which few could claim to be unaware of religious or doctrinal controversies, even after Giovanni Morone renounced his bishopric in 1550 in favour of Egidio Foscarari, who soon took up residence in the town.[60] Foscarari became known for his moderate investigations of heresy and inclination towards the most conciliatory forms of punishment, and was he willing to allow the most permissive doctrinal formulations possible when encouraging convicted suspects to abjure.[61] The process against Claudio da Roteglia (Rudilia), prosecuted in Modena in 1555, is representative of how perceptions of ignorance and penitence could be applied and manipulated within the particular religious milieu of Modena to attempt to create religious homogeneity in a more gentle or conciliatory manner, a process in which Foscarari would play a definitive role. The bishop regularly participated in processes; as John Tedeschi has noted, he or his designated vicar had to agree concerning the use of torture or the convicted suspect's final abjuration and sentence. The bishop or his vicar was therefore a part of any tribunal.

Three witnesses proved key when they testified about Claudio's heretical actions and statements before Fra Angelo Valentini, the inquisitor general of Ferrara and Modena, assisted by Alberto Foschieri da Carpi and Pietro Martire da Lugano. A certain Gasparo, called *il zopo* (*sic.*, 'the lame'), was able to testify to Claudio's reputation in the community: 'It is said he's a Lutheran.' Claudio, according to Gasparo, had eaten meat during last year's vigil of All Saints' and he had blasphemed Christ, saying that 'Christ was a rogue, for that he was crucified.' While his wife used to attend Mass, she had now missed two Masses in a row, which Gasparo attributed to her husband's influence. Claudio, finally, seemed to have dubious personal connections with other suspicious people.[62] The next day, Jacopo Maria de Crispi, called *il rizzo sinistro*, gave his testimony. He had known Claudio for years and he had to admit that most people thought Claudio was a Lutheran because he spoke about religious ideas all the time. In particular, he spoke badly about saints' images and blasphemed Christ while visiting other's houses.[63] Another witness, however, a baker named Geminiano, in whose shop some of these conversations were supposed to have taken place, claimed the contrary. When directly asked whether or not he knew Claudio to be a 'Lutheran,' Geminano replied that 'he did not intend [to be].'[64]

Suor Paola, a Franciscan tertiary, and wife of Battista Marano, came before the tribunal on 1 February 1555 to testify against Claudio da Roteglia's case as her confessor had required, since the confessor had witheld absolution until she did so. She had heard Claudio blaspheme Christ, calling the Saviour 'an ass' in addition to 'a rogue.' And when she had asked him why he did not attend Mass or vespers, Claudio reportedly had said: 'What, it's Mass, what, it's vespers.' Paola also had seen him eat meat on St Peter's day, St Paul's Day, and All Saints'. She described how Claudio would discuss these subjects with apparently anyone and everyone; and Paola had heard Claudio say that there was neither a purgatory nor a heaven as well. She had listened to him deny baptism and all the other sacraments, and had heard of his telling others that clerics ought to be allowed to take wives.[65]

At this point, there was a strong indication that Claudio was suspect, but none of the witnesses told exactly the same story concerning ritual practice. Paola thought that it was Claudio who avoided Mass, Gasparo his wife (although due to Claudio's influence, which would imply that Claudio didn't go, either). Claudio also ate meat at proscribed times, but all the other evidence against him was verbal in nature and inconsistent – while Claudio and his wife avoided Mass, it is doubtful that even inquisitors would have thought Luther in favour of calling Christ an 'ass' and a 'rogue.' One witness even testified on Claudio's behalf – and tried to downplay the heretical conversations that had taken place in his shop.

Because three witnesses had given evidence of heretical words and deeds, however, by 4 February 1555 Claudio found himself brought before the tribunal for his first questioning session. Claudio denied many of the accusations against him, including that he had said anything bad about baptism or the other sacraments – anything but an immediate confession of wrongdoing. He excused his comments concerning purgatory saying 'I said that in anger, saying that there is no other purgatory than in this world.' He affirmed he did believe it existed, and also affirmed that he had participated in sacramental confession in the past year at Sant'Augustino with a monk whose name he did not recall. And while he admitted he had said that monks and priests should be allowed to take wives, because they were men of 'meat and of skin, just like [him],' he denied that he had blasphemed saints' images, but neither did he have them 'in the house.' He confessed he had been wrong, but proferred excuses as to why he really had not meant most of what he said, and offered to produce confirmation of his status as a good practising Catholic.[66]

When Claudio was interrogated again on 6 February, he tried to cooperate and was more forthcoming. For example, he was able to name one or two people he thought were Lutherans, but he strongly suspected that Sebastiano, one of the two, was only joking. Concerning his reported statements in Geminiano's bakery Claudio's answers were vague, although he acknowledged that he 'had spoken [at] the oven with him and others of these Lutheran things one time.' But he also tried to excuse his statements concerning purgatory. Claudio had doubted whether or not purgatory existed because in conversations on the subject, 'some say "yes" and some say "no."' Filipo Valentini, who at one time also had been investigated for heresy, had been present. But Claudio insisted he adored the saints appropriately and had not blasphemed sacred images. He had to admit, however, that he had blasphemed Christ, saying 'whore of Christ' and 'spurned by Christ,' for which he begged the court's pardon, although he claimed he had not called Christ a 'rogue' or said that Christ 'was crucified without cause.'[67]

Because possessing mere 'doubts,' but not heretical belief, was a common excuse proffered by defendants, it is worth further examination, alongside Claudio's assertion that it was the conversations of others that caused his doubts. For the authors of later inquisition manuals, the problem of religious doubt was deceptively straightforward, and could be traced to the first canons concerning heresy. The *Liber Extra* (collected by Raymond of Peñafort and published in 1234), in the first decretal concerning heresy, stated that those who experienced religious doubt were unfaithful – which, in Peña's late sixteenth-century opinion, meant heretical. But Peña further refined this statement by contending that this was only the case if the person in doubt was fully conscious that such doubts were against the Catholic faith.[68] If the person in question suffered from sudden, and secret, temptations, which he or she voluntarily confessed, and was otherwise a faithful practicing Catholic, then such a tormented Catholic was not heretical – participation in Catholic ritual practices was once again the barometer by which to judge.[69] Those who performed the divine offices inadequately, or neglected the sacraments were definitely suspect.[70] Genuine doubters, who suffered occasional torments of conscience, would utilize Catholic ritual practices, especially the sacraments, to nourish their faith and overcome doubt.

While Peña would not write those passages until twenty years later, Claudio, in 1555, attempted to emphasize his standing as a practicing Catholic. On 8 February he effectively stated his 'implicit faith' in the tribunal's right to determine correct doctrine. Claudio admitted that he had made errors concerning the faith, but argued that he was not a full 'Lutheran' heretic. He 'did not hold bad opinions in his heart or his soul,' but had merely spoken carelessly. Claudio invited the tribunal to speak to his confessor, who would be able to vouch for Claudio's lack of heretical intent and status as a practitioner of Catholicism. Claudio also disputed the testimony of those who said he ate meat during Lent, the one act that could be construed as heretical, although not conclusively.[71] On 10 February the tribunal interviewed Claudio's wife, who claimed that her husband had been ill when he ate meat during vigils, and had already confessed the sin and received absolution. Other than that, she largely confirmed the initial testimony, which described blasphemous utterances but not much else. When asked if she spoke from love or hate, she claimed that she testified truthfully for the good of her soul.[72]

On 12 February 1555 the Modenese tribunal discussed how to proceed with Claudio's case: Should he be placed in prison and tortured to discover whether he was heretical in his intent, or not? According to the summary of the meeting recorded by the notary, Nicodemo, Foscarari's vicar, Giovanni, questioned whether or not Claudio should even be put in prison but agreed to abide by the decision of the other consultants. The prior of the Dominican convent, Pietro Martire da Lugano (who had assisted in the interrogations) thought he should be arrested and questioned. Pietro de Fuscheri, a legal consultant, thought he should be questioned without incarceration, unless he did not confess; then with incarceration but without torture, unless he did not confess; and then finally tortured until he did confess, if necessary. Gasparo Marzolus, another consultant, agreed to follow the common recommendation. Nicodemo did not record which recommendation won out. The issue here was how to best secure a confession of heretical intent. Claudio refused to confess to any heretical intent concerning those crimes which the testimony had established as fact, mainly verbal insults concerning Catholic ritual practice.[73] Torture, as Farinacci would write later, was one way to prove whether or not there had been any heretical intent; if there had not been any, the suspected heretic would be capable of continuing to deny it under torture.

In the next interrogation, it became clear that Claudio was definitely not going to be tortured at this stage (whether or not he was still incarcerated remains unclear). But Fra Angelo was most interested in the source of Claudio's religious errors. Fra Angelo asked Claudio if he believed that the consecrated host became the true body and blood of Christ; Claudio said that he believed it, but had heard from others (whom he declined to name) that it did not. Fra Angelo also asked Claudio if he had read religious books, but Claudio denied keeping any books in his house. Claudio admitted that he had thought it was not necessary to keep feast days for saints, even working on such days, because he thought it was only necessary to adore God and not the saints; once again, he declined to name the people who had told him such things. Claudio confessed he had eaten meat because Francesco de Lion (Lyon) had told him all days were equal when it came to the food one ate. Concerning all of his other blasphemies, especially those he made against baptism, the sacraments, and Christ's crucifix, he was willing to leave all to the determination of the church – in other words, submit himelf to the Catholic Church's judgment that those ideas were wrong. He admitted he had doubted the existence of purgatory because, according to Claudio, 'the major part [of people] say that "no" [purgatory does not exist], so [he] doubted it.'[74]

On 19 February 1555, the tribunal drew up a summary of Claudio's process thus far. Claudio, according to the tribunal, had said some things concerning the faith and had held some doubts about certain doctrines, but not definitively so. After sketching out the details of the case, the tribunal stated that, based on the presumptions found in the testimonies, there was not enough evidence to prove that Claudio was a manifest heretic, since there were no clear words or signs that Claudio had intentionally held heretical beliefs in his heart. Furthermore, Claudio was willing to say 'that he believes in all those things that the holy mother Roman church may believe, and in his words he asks pardon,' and claimed that while he had said the words he had not believed what those words signified. Therefore Fra Angelo and the rest of the tribunal thought that Claudio should be sentenced as vehemently suspect in heresy, and therefore ought to abjure publicly and be given salutary penance according to the will of the judge. But, if his reverence Bishop Foscarari preferred that Claudio be sentenced as a heretic, he should let the tribunal know.[75]

Foscarari, in a letter copied into the process records, communicated that he preferred the exact opposite. In his response, he expressed the opinion that Claudio was definitely not a heretic. In fact, 'he was not denounced [for having taught] these things, nor specifically [having defended them], nor [that] he had bad books, nor conversations with other learned heretics or suspects'; therefore, Foscarari thought that there was not even enough evidence to warrant a judgment of vehemently suspect in heresy.[76] Foscarari insisted that Claudio was neither an heresiarch nor teacher of heresy, nor was he pertinacious. Claudio also was not learned himself, and had not talked with those who were. From the beginning of the document, Foscarari was attempting to 'fit' Claudio into a specific type defined in canon law and both Eymeric's and later inquisition manuals – that of the unlearned who had made a few mental errors, but did not meet the textbook definition of heresiaerch or heretic.

Foscarari had spent twenty years learning and teaching in the convent of San Domenico from the age of 12 (1524), and his uncle, Stefano Foscarari, had been the inquisitor general of Bologna. Foscarari was also Master of the Sacred Palace during the pontificate of Paul III, and participated in the drafting a papal Index of Prohibited Books; it was finished after Foscarari's departure in 1552, and was briefly promulgated in 1554. While on occasion Foscarari recognized the Roman Inquisition's right of jurisdiction, in his dealings with individual suspected heretics in Modena after he became bishop in 1550 he earned a reputation for leniency. Filippo Valentini and Giovanni Rangoni, both prominent *fratelli*, were allowed to abjure privately and extraducicially; Foscarari, along with Ercole II d'Este of Ferrara, even allowed Ludovico Castelvestro to flee to Bologna to escape prosecution.

During the pontificate of Paul IV, however, Foscarai would come under suspicion for heresy himself because of his associations with Morone and other *spirituali*, and quite possibly his sympathy for their religious ideas. Michele Ghislieri called Foscarari to Bologna in October of 1558 to answer questions related to Cardinal Morone's prosecution; Foscarari then was sent to Rome in November 1558. Arrested and imprisoned in the Castel Sant'Angelo in January of 1559, he would be absolved of all suspicion after that pope's death in August of 1559. Foscarari ended his life as a respected bishop of Modena. He attended the final phase of the Council of Trent (1562–1563) and was involved in revising Paul IV's Index of Prohibited Books, but he also edited the works of his fellow *spirituali* Reginald Pole. Foscarari in 1555 was not quite in trouble yet, but already he was known for proceeding more gently than some. In addition, as the bishop of Modena it was his responsibility to agree with the inquisitor as to arrest, torture, or punishment, or for his vicar to attend the proceedings in his stead. It was his vicar, Giovanni, who would attend Claudio's eventual sentencing.[77]

Foscarari, in his letter, made his points about the relative merits of Claudio's case by citing canon law; this portion of his correspondence consisted of phrases and quotations, mostly from the *Liber Extra*, followed by citation abbreviations. His writing, here, resembled a commentary concerning canon law rather than a letter composed of complete sentences. He began by pointing out that the case had not been fully proved; furthermore, he suggested, Claudio might simply have spoken rashly or because he was drunk. Claudio also, in Foscarari's view, only had confessed to having some doubts about the Catholic faith and had subordinated himself to the Church's judgment concerning doctrine. His sentence, therefore, should be a light one and he should be allowed to kneel privately before the inquisitor and his notary and abjure his errors. Concerning all of these points, Foscarari cited canon law, in particular the decretals *Ad abolendam* and *Ego Berengarius*.[78] Foscarari additionally reminded Fra Angelo that in such cases it was up to the inquisitor to determine the appropriate punishment; if the person in question was willing to stop having these malignant conversations, then he could be abjured more leniently if Fra Angelo wished it. If Claudio was caught again by the Holy Office, he could be sentenced as a relapsed heretic then (although Foscarari did not mention the danger of Claudio's continued opportunities to spread heretical beliefs in such a situation). Finally, Foscarari quoted Chrysostom, who had preached a sermon concerning Matthew 23 and in it had recommended leniency to those who erred little, especially due to 'crudity.' Foscarari regularly participated in inquisitorial activity, and his recommendation of leniency in this case was not surprising.[79] But his recommendations rested on citing the parts of canon law that emphasized the merciful handling of heresy cases and included some other factors that could mitigate culpability, such as ignorance, doubt, extreme anger, or even drunkenness.[80]

Foscarari probably considered issues of ignorance, anger, and drunkenness as one class of mitigating factors that should influence an inquisitor to be more lenient. Gasparo Marzolus, one of the tribunal's consultants whose communication also was included in the process records, agreed with Foscarari and attributed Claudio's lack of responsibility more specifically to his ignorance. Claudio had admitted to some doubts, according to Marzolus, but had been willing to submit himself to the Church. Mere doubts did not automatically make Claudio unfaithful or a heretic, especially since he did not hold those doubts pertinaciously – and Marzolus made his points largely through partial quotation and citation abbreviations of the appropriate canons.[81] Marzolus referred to selections from the *Liber Extra* and the *Constitutiones Clementinae.* Simple doubt may arise in the soul, but if the person holding those simple doubts does not resist affirming the Catholic faith, then he or she should not be considered heretical. Marzolus also cited the *Glossa Ordinaria* of Giovanni d'Andrea, and, most likely, Panormitanus, both of whom advised that those who could not be proven heretical could not be abjured as heretical.[82] While words may be signs of the soul, they might not be, Marzolus implied, because of extenuating circumstances. Marzolus also simply thought there was not enough evidence to warrant abjuring Claudio more gravely as vehemently suspect in heresy, and recommended a more merciful judgment of him as lightly suspect in heresy. Marzolus thought that Claudio should be admonished canonically to desist from his religious errors and be assigned an appropriate penance.[83]

It appears that the Modenese tribunal decided to split the difference. Claudio made a full abjuration of all of his religious errors. Furthermore, the tribunal, in the record of the sentence, told him that he had merited a judgment of being suspect in heresy. The tribunal informed Claudio that they had asked for advice concerning his case. Fra Angelo and the others warned Claudio to give up his errors, but they also noted Claudio's willingness to submit himself to the Holy Mother Church – exactly the dilemma expressed in Eymeric's manual and later ones. Although the document did not state it specifically, Claudio had not confessed immediately and had resisted submitting himself to the judgment of the Church at first. But Foscarari and Marzolus had argued effectively for regarding Claudio as an ignorant, rash person who was not a serious heretical threat and assumed that the inquisitorial court would be able to follow their legal reasoning and canonical style of citation. Fra Angelo, when he had recommended an abjuration *de vehementi* for Claudio, was interpreting Claudio's case in a more severe light, rather than mercifully, but both interpretations were possible. The tribunal as a whole, and in Foscarari's physical absence, decided on a compromise. They sentenced him to effective penance, which involved attending Mass regularly at San Domenico (home of the tribunal) and presenting himself to the inquisitor or his vicars after Mass. He had to read his abjuration and promise to never speak of such religious errors again. According to the judgment Claudio had to read his abjuration in the sacristy of Santo Domenico *coram multis* ('before many') on 27 February 1555, but he did not have to wear the *abitello*, or yellow habit worn publicly over the defendant's usual clothing at all times, usually required of the vehemently suspect.[84]

Mercy in Good Time

In the case of Giovanni Terrazzano, also called Giovanni da Milano, prosecuted for heresy later that same year, there would be no need for a compromise despite Bishop Foscarari's presence at the sentencing. In September of 1555, Terrazzano was brought before Fra Angelo Valentini, this time assisted by Fra Cherubino della Mirandola and Fra Michele da Brescia, and questioned about a broad variety of heretical ideas. In that first interrogation, he denied having said anything heretical. According to Giovanni, he had never said that the worship of saints' images was idolatrous; or that the pope was the Antichrist; or that priests and friars should take wives; or that he had slandered the Eucharist; or that he had said suffrages for the dead were useless; or that there was no purgatory; or that bishops were not the superior of other ministers; or that pilgrimages were not necessary. Finally, he denied ever having spoken about heretical ideas with others, including Paolo da Campo Gaiano, from whom the tribunal probably learned of Giovanni. In fact, the notary recorded Terrazzano's lack of answers to these questions as 'nunquam dixit,' or 'he never said it.'[85] Terrazzano, however, admitted that he had thought 'all [men] could be priests in their own houses, and give good examples outside of the house too' (the notary Lorenzo recorded the more extensive answers in this questioning session in Italian). He also had thought God was better worshipped in one's heart than on paper, probably a reference to the false use of sacred images or indulgences.[86]

Giovanni later would admit to owning a vernacular New Testament and the *Beneficio di Cristo*, and in his abjuration his literacy was duly noted in full. Claims of complete ignorance of heresy would not have been a terribly effective defence. But he was well aware that a quick confession could speed one's way through in the inquisitorial process. As he was being led from the interrogation room to imprisonment, he told the tribunal that he 'was not satisfied in [his] responses.' They told him that he would be interviewed again in three days time; Giovanni did not answer and left the room.

Giovanni, at the last possible moment during his first interrogation, had indicated his willingness to confess, but only after having gained an idea of what kinds of evidence was in the tribunal's possession through its questioning. During his second interrogation, held on 27 September 1555, he did confess and professed himself willing to return to the 'arms of the Holy Mother Church.' (In this session, the replies were recorded in Latin despite use of the vernacular in many tribunals.) In this interrogation, Giovanni confessed, for example, that he had not believed in worshipping the saints, nor believed in their miracles, since he had thought any miracles should be attributed to God's grace alone. Terrazzano denied that he thought images of Christ were idolatrous, although he admitted that 'the friar Ludovico da Tridento said that they should wish to hold Christ in the heart and not in the picture.' Nevertheless, Giovanni claimed not to have any objections to images of Christ and that he had always possessed them. Giovanni also admitted to denying papal authority and doubting purgatory. Finally, he had 'held and read' the *Beneficio di Cristo*.[87]

Giovanni was held for one more interrogation, which took place on 2 October 1555; it proved to be the most complete and extensive of Terrazzano's questioning sessions. In this interrogation the notary, Fra Domenico, recorded summaries of his first two answers to every question before recording his third, and current, answer. Fra Domenico consistently recorded all three answers to sixteen questions, although some of those questions were intended to clarify previous answers. Clearly, the tribunal was attempting to ensure as full a confession of wrongdoing as possible, while keeping an eye on possible lies, dissimulations, and inconsistencies. Despite Terrazzano's last-second declaration of wanting to tell the truth, the tribunal was quite well aware that, most likely, he had held back or glossed over the full truth in his second questioning session as well.

The first two questions related to Terrazzano's beliefs concerning sacred images. After carefully noting his denials on 23 and 27 September, Fra Domenico recorded his third answer, in which he finally admitted that he thought many of the ignorant erroneously adored images in an idolatrous manner. Terrazzano was then asked about his denial of clerical celibacy. Fra Domenico recorded a simple 'No' for the first interrogation and a simple 'Yes' for the second, before he recorded that 'he believed celibacy in itself to be good' but only a few could observe it successfully Religious should marry, therefore, in order to remain good men, the classic Protestant position concerning matrimony and the priesthood since Martin Luther. Fourth, after two denials, Terrazzano had to admit that 'it was possible that he had said the pope was the antichrist,' but he really did not remember for certain.[88]

Concerning the other heretical points, Terrazzano admitted that he thought men were priests in their own houses; that the saints did not intercede for petitioners; and that the use of their images in worship was often idolatrous. Most tellingly, Terrazzano admitted to having believed that 'there was no purgatory unless in the blood and receiving of Christ,' and that the Mass 'was a commemoration of Christ's death and of his body's sacrifice.'[89] Terrazzano was literate, had read heretical books like the *Beneficio di Cristo*, and some of his heretical statements made in conversation display his knowledge and comprehension of heretical doctrine. But nothing in his process indicated that he was accused of neglecting the sacraments or Catholic ritual practice; in fact, his process only revealed heretical conversations with Paolo da Campo Gaiano. And by this interrogation, his third, Giovanni was the very model of a cooperative defendant.

In the offical record of his heretical crimes, the tribunal only attributed five heretical ideas to Giovanni himself; the others were interpreted as being the result of the bad influence of others. His doubts concerning the existence of purgatory, his opinions concerning the worship and adoration of saints, his anti-papal statements, and his belief that anything not found in Scripture was not obligatory for the Christian were the only beliefs that the tribunal thought were Giovanni's sole responsibility, and he confessed he had believed so for eight years.

The other crimes were carefully noted as attributable to others – those that had led Giovanni astray, including an ostensibly Catholic friar.[90] In his sentencing, therefore, Egidio Foscarari and Fra Angelo agreed that Giovanni was vehemently suspect of heresy, and repeated Giovanni's heretical errors. The court sentenced Giovanni to incarceration and salutary penance, but his prison was 'the whole of the city of Modena.'[91] Giovanni was too well educated to receive a sentence of being lightly suspect for which Marzolus and Foscarari had lobbied on Claudio's behalf. Despite his more severe condemnation, however, his protestations of having been led astray by Fra Ludovico and Paolo da Campo Gaiano were taken at face value, and he was not incarcerated as a result.

Weighing Cases on Their Relative Merits

All of the factors described above, therefore, could affect the outcome of inquisitorial processes, especially in terms of how quickly defendants were processed through the tribunal and the sentences they ultimately received. But those factors – ignorance, drunkenness, anger, time to confession, and willingness to submit – only had an effect if all parties were willing to cooperate and attach value and weight to them. Most importantly, the defendants themselves had to confess, and quickly. The other factors, often brought up as a defence by the accused, but sometimes advanced by mercifully minded bishops or even inquisitors, were only relevant if the first precondition of submission was present. Furthermore, the defendants who successfully employed ignorance or other extenuating circumstances more often than not had to fit the tribunals' own preconceived ideas and cultural assumptions concerning specific socioeconomic, gender, or educational statuses that could make such claims credible.

Finally, neither of the two defendants discussed above would have been able to claim ignorance of heresy if they had engaged in actions that, according later manual authors such as Peña and Farinacci, clearly indicated knowledge of and consent to participation in heretical rites. Claudio da Roteglia's heresies had begun and ended with statements, made rashly in front of others, that Egidio Foscarari was able to characterize as the vague ramblings of an uncouth person. His one action – eating meat during Lent – could also be ascribed to non-heretical causes. Giovanni Terrazzano was literate, and owner of heretical books; claiming complete ignorance, therefore, was not an option in his defence, but the alacrity of his confession and willingness to submit himself to correction eventually had an effect on Modena's tribunal and Foscarari. Terrazzano was abjured as vehemently suspect in heresy concerning his sixteen heretical and erroneous statements, but his sentence specified that he was to remain perpetually incarcerated within the entire city of Modena. Of those sixteen heretical statements, however, only five were attributed to Terrazzano himself. The other eleven were the result of Terrazzano's interactions with other people, particularly an ostensibly Catholic friar. Foscarari and the Modenese tribunal chose to perceive Terrazzano as a layperson who could be led astray by others, especially those 'wolves in sheep's clothing' who abused their superior religious authority to spread heresy, despite the fact that he was a literate layperson who read heretical books in the vernacular. There was precedent for such a point of view in both inquisitorial manuals and canon law, but it seems likely that judgments like these were the reason why Peña, writing thirty years later, protested that, given the notoriety of the religious issues of his day, even laypeople could no longer be considered too ignorant to recognize heresy, even when it came out of the mouths of those wearing Catholic religious habits.

Chapter Five

Confession and Defence: Aggressive Tactics

The Right to a Defence

According to Nicholas Eymeric, allowing accused heretics to defend themselves was at times necessary, but at other times superfluous.[1] Francisco Peña in his later commentaries asserted that Eymeric's legal opinion was fundamentally accurate. For suspected heretics who confessed to all the allegations against them during any of three requisite warnings (interrogations), a legal defence was superfluous indeed; many in fact waived their right to legal advice. Nevertheless, Peña very much affirmed suspected heretics' right to contest the evidence against them if they so chose: 'Because a lawful defence is according to the law of nature, and therefore in no way can be, or ought to be, denied.' This was a long-held opinion in canon law and also was the common opinion among all doctors of the church.[2] Therefore any suspect who asked for the services of a lawyer, trained in both canon and civil law, should be allowed access to one even if that suspect was willing to confess. But Peña specified that those lawyers should not be heretics, or suspect in faith in their own right; heretics, or non-heretical lawyers, could not be allowed to help heretical defendants to walk free.[3]

For the Roman Inquisition, unlike contemporaneous secular legal systems, a confession was absolutely required because, as Peña put it, 'the crime of heresy is devised in the mind and lies hidden in the spirit; commonly it cannot be proved otherwise than through the criminal's own confession.' Confession as full proof had been a principle of inquisitorial prosecution since its inception in the Middle Ages. A speedy confession assured the accused of a quick process and more lenient sentencing. This was precisely because an immediate confession did not only demonstrate penitence and a willingness to submit to the church; a confession made to an inquisitorial tribunal did not require any corroborating evidence, which was not the case in secular courts.[4]

The use of aggressive tactics to mount a defence before the tribunal, and especially the role advocates, or lawyers, could play in this process, has received little attention in its own right. This is, at least in part, because many defendants did not request legal advice; of those who did, their interactions with their lawyers often took place 'off the page,' so much of the interactions between lawyer and client would not be recorded and included in the dossiers' documentation.[5] But the case studies examined in this chapter, those of Zuane (Giovanni) Finetti, tried in Venice in 1566–1567, and Bartolomeo Nelli, prosecuted in Siena in 1559–1560, provide more documentation than most process records, since Finetti, himself a lawyer, and Nelli's lawyer, Lattanzio Lucarini, both used proactive defence strategies. In both cases, furthermore, the advocates' strongest tactic lay in proving the Catholicity of the accused through documentation of proper participation in traditional Catholic 'rites and ceremonies.' Finetti, furthermore, was found to have been falsely accused of failing to perform the annual confession and communion and eating meat during Lent. For Finetti, ritual practice was both the means of false accusation and the means of defence, despite his having some rather dubious personal associations.

This chapter also examines the ways in which the inquisitors during the 1560s and 1570s could utilize equally agresssive tactics in the pursuit of confessions, if appeals to conscience and promises of leniency had fallen on deaf ears. In the cases of Prospero (*capeler*), and Battista Amai della Bambine, an enamel painter, both tried in 1572, Venetian inquisitors literally forced a standoff in the courtroom in hopes of eliciting a confession. While the right to a defence was a 'natural' one, according to Peña writing six years later, allowing a heretic to walk free and continue to endanger the Catholic community through spreading false doctrines was a perversion of justice. Inquisitorial procedure as a whole was an exercise in preserving a legal balance between defendants' rights and enforcing appropriate justice for the protection of the community. The confession satisfied the legal requirements of prosecuting heresy, but it also signified, ideally, the reincorporation of heretical sheep into the Catholic fold. The longer a defendant insisted on innocence or avoided confession, however, the more likely the possibility of heresy hidden 'in the spirit' of the defendant became. That tension – between confession and defence – could lead to heightened aggression on the part of all parties involved in the process.

Advocate or Defender? The Role of the Lawyer

In the inquisition manuals, in theory, there was always a certain amount of apprehension about the use of laywers, plausible explanation to justify seemingly heretical actions, and witnesses for the defence. As Farinacci put it in his 1616 *Tractatus*, the tension existed 'because advocates of heretics can be called their defenders.' Medieval inquisitions, when dealing with Cathar heresy had prosecuted the associates of heretics, who were called favourers, patrons, receivers, and, most importantly here, *defensores* ('defenders') of heretics for the aid and comfort they gave the enemy. The last category, in particular, had been defined in such a way as to include those who verbally supported or gave counsel to heretics. Those defenders, and those willing to fight for heretics militarily, most definitely aided in the spread of heresy. As a result, as Farinacci explained, many of his sources examined the question of how to structure the appropriate participation of legal counsel in processes. A legal defence was a natural right, but advocates could not be allowed to become 'defenders' by aiding a heretic to escape justice and continue to spread heresy in the community. That clearly was prohibited in canon law and a prosecutable offence.[6]

Therefore, for Farinacci and other late sixteenth- and seventeenth-century manual authors, the question became one of explaining how defence lawyers could be legitimately incorporated into the process without violating the precedent of canon law and past exhortations to prosecute protectors and defenders of heretics.[7] As Farinacci stressed, this reconciliation could achieved by making sure that lawyers were not suspect in faith or in any other crime; the source for this regulation was, once again, Francisco Peña's commentaries in the *Directorium Inquisitorum*. Furthermore, Farinacci explained, lawyers who thought they had just cause to defend their clients' innocence should not be assumed to be heretics themselves, even if their clients ultimately were sentenced as suspect in heresy. According to Farinacci, a lawyer could not be called a defender of heretics, if he 'has defended a heretic, believing him to have just cause'; they should be ignorant of the fact that their clients were heretics.[8] In theory, lawyers could defend their clients as long as they were convinced of their clients' innocence, but lawyers could not be allowed to knowingly aid a heretic in avoiding due justice at the expense of the Catholic community.

However, the question of whether or not lawyers (*advocati*, or advocates) might cross that line from helping the genuinely innocent to becoming defenders (*defensores*) of heretics in the sense of protecting them from inquisitorial justice was a point of theoretical tension for manual authors. Cesare Carena even entitled one of the chapters in his seventeenth-century *Tractatus* 'Concerning defenders and lawyers [*advocatis*] of heretics.' Carena for the most part cited Farinacci's earlier manual as his source, but included one piece of information that Farinacci had not. Any inquisitor who wanted to prosecute a defence lawyer for heresy or aiding heretics to escape due inquisitorial justice was advised to ask the permission of his superiors, the Congregation of Cardinals in Rome, according to the terms of the papal bull *Coenae Domini*.[9]

Manual authors enumerated extensive instructions as to what defence lawyers could and could not do to 'advocate' for their clients and avoid becoming 'defenders' of heretics. In his chapter entitled 'What protestations might excuse heresy' Farinacci made the standard of advocacy, applicable to both lawyers and defendants, quite clear. He explained that excuses, or explanations meant to influence the tribunal favourably, could only be believed of those who submitted themselves to the judgment of the Holy Mother Church. It was Simancas in the late sixteenth century, according to Farinacci, who had accused all those who proferred excuses without explicitly submitting to the authority of the Catholic Church of pertinacity, the key component of the definition of heresy itself.[10]

Farinacci's next point began promisingly for at least some people; he admitted that, theoretically, there could be blameless, erroneously accused people who would come before the tribunal and testify that they had always been good Catholics and wished only to live and die in the true faith, a sentiment he deemed 'valid and useful.'[11] But several limits should be kept in mind when listening to such protestations of Catholicity. First and foremost, such protestations could not help those who so obviously behaved differently than their words would seem to indicate, as the doctors of the church long had agreed. Jews who still kept the Sabbath, for example, could not be believed when they said they had faith in the Catholic Church or in the Mass.[12] In theory, only one set of actions could correspond to one set of beliefs. Multiple religious identities, or unclear boundaries between orthodox belief and unorthodox behaviour, or vice versa, theoretically did not exist in inquisition manuals. The effort to extirpate all heresies and heretics lay behind this – Farinacci repeatedly warned to make sure that suspected heretics were not given the opportunity to lie and cheat their way to absolution, with or without legal help. The solution was to refuse to believe any protestations of innocence if Catholic ritual practice was not evident. For manual authors, ritual practice was a benchmark by which other forms of evidence or testimony could be gauged for veracity.

In addition to affirming good Catholic ritual practice, lawyers had one other legitimate option in their advocacy for clients – proving the testimony of credible witnesses to be false. Inquisitors had to admit the possibility of false testimony – that it was the seemingly credible witnesses who had lied and the accused insisting on their orthodoxy who were telling the truth. All manual authors agreed that the penalties for suborning testimony or lying to inquisitors should be severe. But the controversy among many authors, canonists, and legal experts lay in debating whether or not retaliatory, or putative, punishment (*talionis*) should be used, especially when the falsely accused already had been executed.[13]

Carena suggested the phrase 'retaliatory,' following Farinacci and Peña, meant that the exact level of punishment should be tied to when the subterfuge was discovered. If falsely accused defendants had been put to death, then the false witnesses also should be put to death or at the very least sentenced to the galleys. If the process had not yet concluded, or had concluded with a lesser sentence, then extraordinary punishment, such as penance, not putative punishment like whippings, should be imposed.[14] This opinion was once again a compromise between two different and conflicting schools of thought about the subject. But, according to Peña, a letter from Pope Leo X to the Spanish Inquisition, dated 14 December 1518, had settled the issue in favour of matching the severity of the punshment to the effects of the lie on the falsely accused.[15]

Farinacci recommended the galleys or perpetual incarceration as extraordinary sentences for those who were caught in their lies before the victim had been sentenced. If the false witness voluntarily confessed to lying, instead of being discovered some other way, then leniency in assigning punishment also was recommended. Witnesses who lied in order to defend suspected heretics, not accuse them, were also to be given lesser punishments. Ultimately, however, Farinacci agreed that if the victim of such lies had already been sentenced and executed, then the false witnesses could be 'surrendered to the secular arm' after the inquisitor had sought the permission of the Congregation of Cardinals in Rome. [16]

Finally, all the manual authors recognized the most common motivation that generated false testimony and encouraged perjury: enmity. Peña, in his comments about the defence to be allowed to criminals, focused primarily on this issue. He defined *inimicitia* ('enmity') as witness testimony given to the tribunal not 'from zeal for justice' but because of personal grudges. *Inimicitia capitali*, or 'capital enmity,' however, was to be distinguished from 'small enmity,' or the mere fact that the witness was 'infamous.'[17] For the conflict to achieve the level of capital enmity, the level of hatred between the two had to be akin to wishing one another dead, and perhaps even attempting to make that so. In such extreme cases, the entirety of the testimony could be discounted.But, according to Peña, 'truly other crimes, although they may weaken, do not repel' testimony. Peña asserted that all prudent judges should investigate credible accusations of enmity made by defendants to determine if capital enmity could be proven in full. He thought it was within each judge's authority to exercise good judgment when deciding whether to investigate or not, or when establishing a standard by which to prove capital enmity.[18] Eliseo Masini, in his *Sacro Arsenale* of 1621, was more straightforward in explaining how inquisitors could consider capital enmity sufficiently proven. The witnesses to such enmity could not be relatives or domestic servants. Unbiased witnesses should be willing to state that they knew the denunciatory witnesses 'had sought many times to kill him,' the defendant.[19] Farinacci, for his part, applied the same standard of proof to suspicion of capital enmity that he applied to heresy – at least two credible witnesses. Farinacci thought it was the general (but not unanimous) opinion to allow such testimony if the presiding inquisitor felt it was useful in judging the case. Manual authors therefore advised asking witnesses if they possessed any ulterior motives while giving testimony, as a precautionary measure.[20]

Bearing False Witness

The instructions in the manuals discussed above were theoretical, and addressed four distinct questions, all of which would apply to the case involving Zuane (Giovanni) Finetti in 1566–1567. Were lawyers who had associated with heretics to be more carefully watched for signs of heresy? Were those who had associated with other heretics inherently more suspect themselves, lawyers or not? What should be the punishment for those found guilty of giving false testimony? How severe did enmity between witness and accused have to be before testimony could be discounted as useless? In the end, the case of Zuane Finetti demonstrates how lawyers, especially those trained in both canon and civil law, could defend suspected heretics successfully, including themselves.[21]

Finetti's case of 1566–1567 also demonstrates how inquisitorial procedure, clear in theory, could be modified in practice. The punishment inflicted on Girolamo and Alvise Badoer, when it was established to the tribunal's satisfaction that they had lied, was not exactly severe. Fortunately for Zuane Finetti, the tribunal decided that he had been falsely accused well before the possibility of him being falsely sentenced occurred. While the tribunal gave Finetti ample time to prove his innocence of the false accusations of Girolamo and Alvise Badoer, there is little doubt that the two Badoer brothers thought an accusation of heresy could be successful.

Unfortunately for Finetti, the fact that he was, as his accusers stated, a known defender of heretics – perhaps both as a lawyer and as a friend of well-known heretics – rendered him more vulnerable to false accusations. The lawyer had moved in the same social circles as a nobleman from Vicenza, Alessandro Trissino, publicly known in Venice as less than orthodox long before 1566. Finetti had attended dinners with a close circle of friends, including Trissino, which A. Olivieri has described as forums for discussing Calvinist and other heterodox ideas, although the group seems to have discussed non-religious subjects as well. When the Pellizzari brothers' letters were seized by officials, leading to Trissino's process in March of 1563, eventually he fled despite the 1,000 ducat surety put up by his family. Trissino went to Chiavenna where he became pastor of the Reformed congregation there. At first he sent letters back to his old friends, including one to Finetti. But by 1570 Trissino was complaining vehemently in his work that old friends had cut off contact with him and even had participated in inquisition processes. Trissino also vehemently denounced Nicodemite behaviour, despite the fact that at his own process in 1563 he had proffered his chuch attendance at San Lio and participation in communion as evidence of his Catholic orthodoxy – which he maintained even while tortured.[22]

It is notable that the two Badoer had to resort to bribery to initiate Finetti's process despite the lawyer's associations with Trissino and his circle. Nevertheless, the two Badoer had bribed no less than eight people to testify against Finetti. The plot had been hatched in prison, where Girolamo and his accomplices had wound up after robbing Finetti. There they met Bartolo, a servant in 'ca Badoer a San Paolo,' according to one witness. Melchior Patavo, a 'pruner,' was a fellow prisoner who overheard the plan as it was hatched; Giovanni Battista della Pace also knew that the plot had originated with Bartolo talking with Girolamo. Bartolo, when interviewed, revealed that he had been a servant in Finetti's household as well, and admitted that Finetti had eaten meat during Lent while on a trip to Padua or Treviso a few years previously (due to illness, in Bartolo's opinion). From that beginning, Girolamo had decided to set up the lawyer.[23]

As Finetti explained in his manuscript offered to Giulio Contarini as his defence against the charges, Girolamo Badoer reportedly had bribed the witnesses in Finetti's case, aided by Alvise Badoer, his brother, who also happened to be a priest. Alvise Badoer, according to Finetti, used his good name for evil intent; for example he promised one man, Melchior, 'friendship and favour of a Badoer' in return for false testimony.[24] The other witnesses – including Finetti's cook Santa, Niccolò Salamon, the maidservant Corona, and Domenico Barzotto – were bought with money and promises of favours as well. It was apparently a family effort; in addition to Girolamo and Alvise, one other relative was involved, Federico.

Finetti, in another document prepared for his defence, described the full extent of Girolamo Badoer's betrayal. Finetti had taken in Badoer as his servant and, effectively, his majordomo, after he had found him in a poor state because of a quarrel with the College of Venice. Furthermore, when Finetti sought to have Badoer arrested for stealing from him, the lawyer approached the *censori*, or state censors, who regulated contracts between masters and servants, the *avogadori del comun*, the state prosecuting attorneys, and the *singori di notte*, the state body responsible for dealing with crimes such as theft. Finetti insisted that he had treated Girolamo with honour and instructed the other servants referred to him as 'Messer,' only to have Girolamo turn traitor and embezzle funds while Finetti had been ill.[25]

At first Finetti handled the incident by approaching Girolamo's uncle, Federico, who agreed to repay the money to Finetti; in return, the lawyer would allow Girolamo to leave town quietly. Federico Badoer, according to a witness interviewed later in the process, had reneged on the deal. Thus, Finetti would refer to Federico as the source of his torment, because Federico apparently had publicly slandered

Finetti through circulation of a *polizza*, or letter. But it was Girolamo and Alvise who had done the bribing, and they were the only two Badoer prosecuted.[26]

As a household insider, Girolamo had first-hand knowledge of what evidence to manufacture, or knowledge he could exploit, which might prove plausible to an investigating inquisition tribunal. The bought testimony of servants, a cook, and Alvise, a priest, initiated the investigation in which Finetti was accused of revealing his inner philo-Protestant nature through three acts: eating meat during Lent, skipping the annual confession and communion at Easter that year, and failure to provide Madonna Beatrice with last rites, which philo-Protestants denied as a sacrament. Two of those acts appear consistently in later sixteenth and seventeenth-century manuals as 'textbook' philo-Protestant behaviour, so to speak.

Finetti, however, in his own defence, announced to the tribunal that he had twenty-one witnesses who were willing to testify to his 'customs' as well as his faith, and that in deeds and in words Finetti had always lived as a Catholic. And, as Finetti told the tribunal, if two testimonies could legally establish suspicion 'I believe that twenty testimonies are enough to conserve the honor of a claimant and castigate a slanderer.'[27] His legal defence demonstrated an intimate knowledge of how courts weighed testimony as evidence.

Finetti repeated the main points of his defence several times in the document he submitted to the tribunal. According to Finetti: 'I have always confessed and gone to communion, [and] all of mine have confessed and gone to communion; I hear, and they hear, Mass; I had given, by my order, the sacraments of the Church to the Signora Beatrice Cossazza, my relation; I have always reviled the heretics and hunted suspects.'[28]

The suspected heretic Finetti had 'hunted' was Fra Francesco Spinola. A native of Como and former client of the Visconti in Milan, Spinola had led a heterodox conventicle while living in Venice and working as a tutor. He had worked for Zuane Finetti for a short time before the friar's arrest and prosecution in 1564, tutoring the lawyer's children – yet another instance of Finetti having relationships with known suspects. Given Trissino's later complaints about former friends going to the inquisition, it would be tempting to speculate that Finetti, aware of the danger of having known both Trissino and Spinola, had begun helping the inquisition to make sure his name and reputation remained pristine.[29]

When Finetti's case first began Spinola was in prison nearing the end of his process, the records of which unfortunately have not survived. Another suspect with whom Spinola associated, Andrea dei Ugoni, was prosecuted and abjured. Ugoni reported to the tribunal that Spinola had led a philo-Protestant Lord's Supper in Finetti's house; that accusation would be repeated by Girolamo Badoer during his own process for false testimony. Spinola, however, was tortured for the names of his accomplices and had named several, including Ugoni. Although no documentation exists, it is tempting to speculate that the Venetian tribunal was willing to believe Finetti simply because Spinola, mere months away from his own execution on 31 January 1567, had confirmed that Finetti had known nothing of the Lord's Supper held in his house.[30]

Therefore Spinola was still alive, in prison, and cooperating with the tribunal when Finetti reminded them that the tutor had lived in his house for one month only, and 'I [Finetti] suspected his conscience, I threw him out of the house, and with that act I reproved him and accused him as a heretic.'[31] To end his document sent to Giulio Contarini, Finetti asserted that the witnesses were lying and he could prove it. Regarding the charge of eating meat during Lent, for example, levied by his boatman, Niccolò, Finetti asserted:

> 'One of my boatmen, should he maintain [that he wished to leave] my house because I may have eaten meat on prohibited days; if because of this he was affected [in his] conscience . . . the wicked slanderer bought eight *marcei* [unit of money] of fish both Fridays and Saturdays.'[32]

Finetti also explained that he had been in Padua on Holy Saturday with his wife and family visiting Agostin Barbarico, his godfather (*compare*), the *capitano* in Padua. The 'traitor' Girolamo Badoer had accompanied the family on the trip. They had stayed through Easter Sunday before returning to Venice. Finetti claimed that he would introduce testimony proving he had confessed and gone to communion that weekend, and other evidence of his many 'Catholic actions proper to a Christian.'[33]

Finetti's supporters began their testimony in his favour in November of 1566 in front of the papal nuncio, Giovanni Antonio Fachinetti, the Venetian patriarch, Giovanni Trevisan (both of whom had the right to send delegates), the Father Inquisitor Rocco Cataneo, and the three laymen allowed to sit in consultation in Venice. Those three laymen happened to include Giulio Contarini, procurator of Saint Mark, and addressee of one of Finetti's defensive diatribes.[34] By January of 1567 the Venetian tribunal felt it had enough information about the false nature of the charges to arrest Girolamo and Alvise Badoer. The testimony in favour of Finetti continued until at least April of 1567 when the tribunal apparently felt that enough evidence had been gathered to completely dispel all three charges.

The false evidence of Madonna Beatrice's death without last rites proved the easiest to counter. In April of 1567 Madonna Lucrezia, her daughter, cleared up the third of Girolamo Badoer's accusations. The Capuchins who had heard Madonna Beatrice's final confession briefly confirmed Lucrezia's testimony. Lucrezia also gave extensive testimony about the entire incident and sequence of events. In particular, she testified that when her mother had died Messer Zuane had called for the sacristan of San Benedetto, who had given her mother the holy oil. He had called the Capuchin friars to attend her mother as well. As she explicitly told the court: 'I believe that it was Girolamo who went to call them because he did everything, and he knew that she was given the holy oil by them.'[35] Lucrezia also could speculate as to why Girolamo thought the tribunal would find the accusations of heresy plausible:

> 'I know that Messer Zuane chased Spinola from the house, because he was had for suspicion of heresy and that also this Girolamo could know about it, because he heard it in the house. [Prompted] I don't believe that Girolamo was in the house in that time that Spinola was, but I know he heard it said in the house when they spoke of Spinola.'[36]

In addition, Niccolò Papilioni, a presbyter at San Benedetto, confirmed sending holy oil with his sacristan for Madonna Beatrice. In March of 1567 Giuseppe de Bonghi also confirmed that the two Capuchins and the sacristan of San Benedetto had arrived at the Finetti house before Madonna Beatrice's death.[37] But two of those originally bribed to denounce Finetti, the maidservant Corona and the boatman Niccolò, were a bit more equivocal in their new testimonies. Corona confirmed that the Capuchins had been called when Madonna Beatrice lay dying but claimed she could not confirm whether or not last rites were performed because she had been running errands for the household. Niccolò also refused to confirm that last rites had been performed. He admitted that he had seen the two Capuchins come to see Beatrice, but also said: 'I don't know if she confessed [. . .] I don't know to tell you other than that she spoke for awhile.'[38] Corona and Niccolò had testified in April of 1567 and December of 1566, respectively, before Beatrice's daughter appeared to testify; thus, the tribunal had continued interviewing witnesses until Madonna Lucrezia and the two Capuchins provided definitive testimony.

The other two accusations – eating meat during sacred vigils and participation in Catholic ritual practices, especially confession and communion – would be more difficult to dispel without a doubt. In fact, it appears that Finetti may have eaten meat during Lent, while ill, at least once or twice. But several witnesses attempted to cover up for that fact during their testimony, before one witness finally admitted that there had been meat on Finetti's table. The witness, however, claimed that the meat had been for him due to his illness – Finetti had simply been a considerate host.

When it came to tribunals' dealing with consumption of prohibited foods, part of the problem lay in a lack of clarity in policy. The ritual practice was not one of the sacraments, nor considered crucial before the Protestant Reformation. In the wake of believers making it a point to eat meat publicly during Lent, it had become popularly perceived of as an emblematic sign of philo-Protestant heresy in Italian lands. The popular interpretation of eating meat as definitively philo-Protestant may have had its origins in Zwingli's emphasis concerning the role disobeying that tradition, or talking to others about doing so, could have in the proselytizing the 'weaker brethren'; inquisitors often acted on such evidence as if it were definitive proof, perhaps because of the act being mentioned so much in witness testimony.

Yet it always had been the Catholic tradition to allow the sick and injured to eat meat during holy vigils if medically necessary. Exactly how to establish medical necessity beyond a doubt, however, remained unclear even in seventeenth-century manuals. Cesare Carena, for example, in the *Tractatus* of 1636, listed no less than four ways in which an inquisitor theoretically might be convinced that meat really had been eaten because of illness, not all of which included procuring a license. In fact, Carena thought that the inquisitor visibly confirming that the defendant in question looked ill would be proof enough.[39] Therefore eating meat during a Church fast was only an indication of heresy if coupled with other heretical crimes; by itself it was not sufficient evidence of heresy, since it could be done for legitimate reasons.[40]

Much of the testimony in this process, however, was devoted to establishing whether or not Finetti ate meat during Lent, in addition to examining Finetti's other habits of Catholic ritual practice. The tribunal asked witnesses about it, even if the witnesses themselves did not bring it up. Father Papilioni, for example, had to explain to the tribunal that he did not know if Finetti had eaten meat during Lent simply because he never dined at Finetti's house. And although Papilioni asserted that 'I have never heard anything [. . .] said about him' that was not Catholic, he was often busy attending to the governance of the church and could not confirm that Finetti attended Mass often.[41] Santa, the cook, was no more definite in describing what was served on the table during Lent; in her second testimony of November of 1566 the bribed cook changed her testimony and stated that Finetti had definitely not eaten meat during Lent – but if he had, it might have been on Finetti's table because either he or the women of the house were ill.[42] Niccolò, the bribed boatman, was equally unsure about Finetti's eating habits the second time he was questioned; he claimed that in that particular year he had not stayed at Finetti's house for the Lenten season. Niccolò stated that he assumed Finetti went to Mass consistently as well, but had never accompanied him there. Corona, the bribed maidservant, testifying again as late as April of 1567 was even more equivocal: 'Messer Zuane ate meat at the time; so what if he [did]; to the contrary he had much more fish than meat; and I never saw him [Finetti] eat meat during prohibited days.'[43]

Zuane Pietro, a blacksmith, was more definite during his testimony of December of 1566. He had eaten at Finetti's table at Lent and pronounced Finetti a good Christian, without the presence of meat. And while he did not go to Mass regularly with Finetti, the blacksmith said:

> 'Because I went with him a few times to the palazzo on feast days, and we passed through the Church of San Marco, and when it happened, that the sacred host was raised in the Church of San Marco, I saw that the said Messer Zuane Finetti made reverence, raised his hat, and knelt, and beat his chest before the sacred host, but otherwise, I haven't gone to Mass with him as I said above.'[44]

Public ritual practice gave Finetti the opportunity to demonstrate his Catholic orthodoxy through physical reverence. Given his position in society, Finetti must have been expected to participate in the many public rituals – at once sacred and secular – common in Venice. Refusing to perform such reverence became known as a sign of heretical belief, as Farinacci would note in his manual fifty years later.

Santa, Corona, and Zuane Pietro had all been bribed to make their first depositions and then reversed their testimonies; and there is some evidence that Finetti physically threatened some of the bribed witnesses. But it also was true that more highly placed witnesses began to testify concering Finetti's public ritual practice. The tribunal, therefore, had to have wondered which of the two testimonies from the bribed witnesses they really could believe. Prospero Farinacci, for example, publishing in 1616, thought it was the second testimony that could not be believed, and the person in question should remain gravely suspect in heresy. Other writers from a variety of times had disagreed, however, and thought the second testimony more credible than the first.[45]

It certainly could not have helped that Niccolò continued to be truculent in his testimony, although that may have been due to getting caught in perjury, threats, or both. When asked by the tribunal to describe Finetti's religious behaviour, the boatman replied that he was 'a gallant gentleman, and for this as good a Christian as another.'[46] Niccolò, through sticking to what he could or could not personally affirm, left room for doubt and did not sing Finetti's praises as a Catholic, exactly. The boatman also claimed to have known Finetti for over thirty years; presumably he would have delivered his employer to the banquets he had attended from 1558 to 1561 with Trissino and his circle.

Corona, however, was more forthcoming about Finetti's attendance at ritual practices; she stated that Badoer knew full well that Finetti attended Mass at Santa Maria delle Grazie and San Benedetto. Girolamo had waited in the boat with Corona on those occasions for about half the Mass, and for the other half himself had stood in the doorway watching the Mass. Finetti also encouraged his servants to go to Mass, whether they accompanied him or not.[47]

Finetti's friends, testifying in his favour, generally were much more supportive, but also were concerned to explain away the presence of meat on Finetti's table during Lent. Rugoni, a doctor testifying in March of 1567, had seen both meat and fish, but did not know for certain if the lawyer had eaten it. The doctor believed not, since he always had known Finetti to be 'a gentleman fearful of God's majesty, and an observer of the precepts of the Holy Roman Church.' Rugoni also told the tribunal how he had seen Finetti, three or four times at least, in Sant'Angelo and Santo Stefano where he had listened to Mass 'in company.'[48] By April of 1567, the tribunal had a definitive explanation as to why meat had been present, but Finetti had not eaten any. In fact, according to Valerio Chiericati: 'Finding myself sick one time in the house of the said Finetti, [that] it could have been a year ago; they fetched some chicks only on my account, and the others ate fish, that Girolamo had presented. And also, on other prohibited days, the said Girolamo bought the fish, because he was the "spender."' Finally, Chiericati asserted that he had always known Finetti to be a good Catholic and strongly implied that Badoer had to have known that as well. That same day, the doctor Pigafetta, named by Girolamo as one of the people who had seen Finetti eat meat, said the same thing – it had never happened, and Girolamo had been present and knew that, too. Both Pigafetta and Chiericati were from Vicenza, the hometown of Alessandro Trissino, but there is no definitive proof as yet that they were a part of Trissino's Calvinist circle there.[49]

Establishing the fact that Finetti participated in the annual confession and communion rites consistently required of all Catholics also took several different testimonies across the course of the process. Father Papilioni, testifying early in the process in 1566, claimed to have given Finetti communion with his own hands but admitted that he could not remember the year. In addition, Papilioni was unable to confirm that Finetti had confessed that year; he had reconciled the family women, but not Finetti himself. [50] Giovanni Battista Fagnano of San Cassiano and the musician Tommaso Scocienso also attempted to prove Finetti's attendance at confession. Fagnano, testifying in April of 1567, had accompanied Finetti to San Francesco della Vigna two or three years an a row. Also accompanying the men to do their Easter duty was Antonio Tiepolo, who could not testify because at the time of the process he was the Venetian ambassador to Spain. The musician Tommaso, testifying a month later, asserted that Finetti had gone to confession and communion the past Easter at San Benedetto; but the presbyter Papilioni had only been able to confirm communion, not confession.[51]

It was Luca, another boatman in Finetti's employ, who provided definitive testimony regarding Finetti's confession that year. On 3 April 1567, he testified about the family's trip to Padua and confirmed that Girolamo had accompanied them. Luca testified that Finetti had confessed at the monastery of San Francesco while on the way to Padua. The inquisitors even asked Luca to identify the monastery by the clothes the monks wore. On further questioning by the tribunal, however, Luca had to admit that he had not watched Finetti confess: 'I did not see him, because I remained at the bottom, and he went on to that effect.' Luca also admitted that he could not confirm Finetti's attendance at Mass on that day, since he waited below with the boat, but insisted that he had taken the lawyer to Mass at Sant'Elena and Santo Spirito at other times.[52]

Finally, many of the witnesses described exactly how Girolamo and Alvise Badoer had set up Finetti in the first place. In March of 1567, the first witnesss to testify after the arrest and imprisonment of the two Badoer, Giovanni (or Zuane) Battista della Pace, identified as a captain, confirmed that he had heard Finetti discussing testimony with Niccolò Capadoccio. Della Pace had been staying with Finetti at his house in Venice when he had taken a walk with the lawyer. Finetti then had explained that his enemies had gotten him in trouble with the inquisition. Finetti's conversation with Niccolò, whom the witness described as a former servant of Finetti's (most likely the boatman), was quite interesting. Niccolò admitted that Finetti obviously had come to talk about the brothers. Finetti, according to della Pace, had simply admonished Niccolò to tell the truth, since he had not the first time. Niccolò then described how the two brothers had bribed him and promised to tell the truth. And, according to della Pace, Finetti had eaten fish during his visit.[53]

Other witnesses testified to having been present when the false testimony had been arranged. According to Giuseppe, Badoer was upset that Finetti had gotten him thrown in prison (along with three friends, another Badoer, a Mantegna, and a Contarini), so he intended to arrange for the lawyer's inquisition prosecution in revenge. In fact, Giuseppe Bonghi claimed to have been present when Girolamo Badoer had discussed how to set up Finetti with Niccolò the boatman and Battista Fauro. On hearing Badoer's plan to implicate Finetti in heresy, Battista reportedly replied: 'What do I know? What, I know nothing of heresy.'[54] Bonghi had also witnessed Finetti's confrontation with Niccolò; the boatman had stood a bit above Finetti, and admitted 'It is true that Girolamo came to me, and said to me that I should be examined, saying "I want to [start] a quarrel; I want you to say that he [Finetti] ate meat during prohibited days,"' promising they would give him favour. According to Bonghi, Finetti also was looking for Girolamo, too.[55] On 19 April 1567, the lawyer produced Francesco Maresio, who claimed to know all about the plot against Finetti and implicated Alvise as well as Girolamo.[56]

Despite all of this testimony, Girolamo Badoer remained recalcitrant for much of the process. First questioned after his arrest in February of 1567, Badoer continued to insist on Finetti's guilt and clearly thought his accusations were still plausible. He swore that all of the accusations were true and that Finetti had eaten meat during Lent publicly with the doctor Pigafetta (before Pigafetta testified). Badoer also completely denied the bribery charges. Finally, Badoer asserted that 'he [Finetti] had me put in prison, so that I would not be able to talk to anyone else and he would be able to talk to the witnesses in his way.'[57] He attempted to use the quarrel between himself and Finetti to his own advantage and insinuated that the lawyer was suborning testimony to cover his own tracks. He also accused Finetti of bribing the witnesses to give testimony of his orthodoxy. When the tribunal asked Badoer how that had occurred, since the lawyer should not have known their identites, Badoer asserted that Finetti knew the witnesses' identities because their names had been listed in an investigation at the office of the censors.[58]

In June and July of 1567, Girolamo Badoer tried to produce witnesses of his own. Both he and his brother Alvise were given copies of Finetti's defence testimony and access to lawyers to prepare their own defence against the accusations of bearing false witness. By August Alvise and Girolamo Badoer found themselves being brought from the *liona* prison to the tribunal to answer to charges of suborning testimony. Eymeric, Peña, Farinacci, and Carena, despite the years between their respective works, all consistently had the same recommendation. Both should have been severely punished, if not so severely as being given the death penalty or sent to the galleys, since the deception had been discovered in time and Finetti had not been sentenced harshly. But all of the authors also had acknowledged the right of tribunals to use their discretion when assigning punishment in such cases in reality. Given his history as a decent priest and his instantaneous confession, the Venetian tribunal sentenced Alvise to exile on the island of Veglia for seven years in August of 1567 (now Krk, Croatia). Girolamo, however, still continued to insist that he had seen Finetti eat meat, and therefore obviously was a 'Lutheran.'

In fact, in September of 1567 Girolamo claimed he knew of two witnesses who could testify that Spinola had officiated at a communion ceremony 'in the way of Germany' in Finetti's house. No further evidence of this materialized, however, and Girolamo's attempts to appeal directly to Pius V in Rome also failed. In May of 1570, Girolamo was brought forth from prison, confessed, and also was exiled to Veglia as punishment. Finetti, apparently, was present for the confession and was so moved by Girolamo's contrition that he spontaneously forgave him for the entire incident.[59] The Venetian tribunal acted rather discreetly and mercifully in doling out punishments to the two men; Alvise, in fact, was absolved for his good behaviour in Veglia a year later.[60]

Finetti, with his reputation theoretically restored as a result of his innocence, was magnanimous enough to write a letter to the tribunal forgiving the former servant and the priest for their smear campaign against him. But the effort to defend himself had taken almost a year and probably no small expense.[61] Whether the Venetian community accepted his innocence as fact cannot be definitively known, but in Finetti's statement of defence he complained of the injury done to his honour and his family. Without his reputation, how would he make a living to support his wife and eight children, to say nothing of how he would be remembered in perpetuity?[62] His reputation might not have been damaged by his contact with other heretics and this process, as long as the community saw the process's outcome as his vindication and proof of being a good Catholic. But in the wake of having been accused of heresy, even if eventually vindicated, his public reputation may never have completely recovered.

The Badoer brothers, since Finetti was a lawyer known to the tribunal and known to have contact with others suspect in heresy, might have thought him more vulnerable to false accusations in the first place. But Finetti's skills as a lawyer familiar with court systems, and the ways in which he could prove his Catholicity, were also quite useful as well, as were the number of Venetians willing to testify on his behalf. He knew exactly what to do in order to prove his innocence, and he proved that innocence by producing people who could testify that he followed Catholic ritual practices and traditions faithfully.

Contested Meanings

The case of Bartolomeo Nelli, prosecuted in 1559–1560 in Siena, demonstrates how inquisitors could utilize ritual practice as a means to gauge and interpret verbal statements – and the pitfalls of doing so. It is possible that Nelli genuinely thought Catholic ritual practice and belief in justification by faith alone to be compatible, thereby embracing a hybrid religious identity, the existence of which inquisitors simply refused to recognize. It is also possible that Nelli was a very successful quasi-Nicodemite – attending Church while his heretical conversations took place in shops among friends. Regardless, his lawyer, Lattanzio Lucarini, in fact exploited the ambiguity to utilize very aggressive defence tactics. Lucarini attempted to stretch the boundaries of orthodoxy around the inherent ambiguity of verbal statements to Nelli's benefit. If Nelli had not confessed his heretical thoughts, and briefly attempted to stand firm in his faith by refusing the tribunal's correction, Lucarini might have been successful in gaining his client a light and private sentence.

Lucarini constructed his defence around two theological principles. First, he argued that Nelli's beliefs had been viewed positively at one time by at least some in the Catholic Church. Second, Lucarini attempted to argue that his client, as an 'uneducated' layman (and not a professional theologian) had merely got confused and mixed up some key words when he had expressed that legimitately Catholic view of justification. Both tactics proved Lucarini a very astute lawyer, who understood both legal principle and the contemporary religious controversies within the Catholic Church very well indeed.

Regarding the second point of Lucarini's defence, both Eymeric and the later manual authors did make allowances, in theory, for the truly ignorant. If such ignorance was genuine, and coupled with a sincere desire to submit oneself to the church, it could merit the suspect a lesser sentence; the later authors, however, especially Peña, who published twenty years after Nelli's trial took place, thought true ignorance much harder to prove in his time. Farinacci, writing even later, thought such protestations of unintentional error could not be contrary to the facts of the case, as described by witnessess. But if the suspect in question had a record of good Catholic ritual practice, and was willing to submit to the authority of the church, in principle such protestations could move an inquisitor toward showing a defendant leniency. Any and all of these excuses should be diligently investigated, however, since heretics were prone to lying and obfuscation.[63] Therefore, any suspect attempting to defend himself or herself theologically should be able to confirm theological confusion by producing a record of consistent ritual practice.

Farinacci implied in his work of 1616, however, that there might be one other situation in which an excuse of unintentional heresy might be plausible. In that same chapter, he explained that suspected heretics, when accused of heresy about a particular point of doctrine, might try to excuse themselves by claiming that, to their knowledge, the Catholic Church had yet to clearly define the doctrine in question. Therefore, by definition, they could not be accused for believing incorrectly concerning the said doctrine, since there was no clear, orthodox statement of it in the first place. The context of the full sentence makes it clear that Farinacci thought this was likely to happen when the Catholic Church had only formally stated a correct point of doctrine recently. In terms of how to judge such protestations and excuses,

Farinacci merely reiterated that those explanations could only sway the inquisitor if the suspects had not engaged in some clearly heretical behaviour.[64]

Farinacci, in this brief passage, could well have been referring to a situation that had existed in the mid-sixteenth century, and one that Lattanzio Lucarini would attempt to manipulate in 1559–1560. Catholic doctrines defining the most important theological issues central to the Reformation, including justification, were not officially formulated until the Council of Trent. The council's canon on justification was not codified until 13 January 1547; and although the canon circulated in print after 1547, not all of the council's decisions were confirmed by the papacy until 1563 under Pope Pius IV and they were not printed all together until 1564 in Rome.[65] Most likely there was, in this time, some genuine confusion among the general population about the exact beliefs and wording of orthodox Catholic doctrine.

Ritual practice, however, it was thought, could clear up that confusion – and help identify heretical lies. Eymeric and Peña, working two centuries apart, both set the tone when they described the appropriate attitude and techniques to be applied to, as Eymeric put it, the 'fox-like and careful' responses heretics would give to inquisitors' questions. Just as prudent doctors should consider carefully the personal characteristics of their patients, ideally inquisitors should be 'doctor[s] of the soul,' considering the diversity of sects, varieties of errors, and individual characteristics of defendants during questioning, in order to secure a valid confession.[66] One of Eymeric's sources for this opinion was Bernard Gui, the Dominican friar who had served in inquisitorial tribunals for over twenty-five years beginning in 1307. He had probably completed his *Pratica inquisitionis haeretice pravitatis* by 1323–1324. In that manual, Gui even had related a series of possible evasive answers to inquisitors' questions, complete with instructions on how to structure questions in such a way as to be essentially foolproof.[67]

Bartolomeo Nelli, in his process, really did not seem to be lying overtly or attempting verbal 'trickery' and subtleties at first. His record of ritual practice and Lucarini's aggressive tactics almost successfully covered the full extent of his heretical beliefs. Lucarini had been appointed to the case by the Sienese tribunal.[68] It cannot be determined, however, whether or not the lawyer knowingly defended a heretic aggressively. It is possible that Nelli confessed the full range of his beliefs to his lawyer before he confessed them to the tribunal, but it is also possible that the lawyer knew no more than the tribunal at any given time.

Nelli, as his confession would ultimately reveal, had come to his heretical beliefs through the proselytizing of Lelio Sozzini, from whom he rented a shop in Siena. The Sozzini, a family of jurists and law professors, had originated in Siena, although Lelio and Cornelio, sons of the famous Marcantonio, had been raised mostly in Padua where Marcantonio was a law professor. The two brothers spent most of their adult lives in Bologna. Eventually they would move to the Swiss Cantons, particularly Geneva and Zurich; their nephew, Fausto, then would move on to Poland and utilizing his uncle's writings found the Socinian church (later called Unitarianism).[69] In the 1540s and 1550s, however, the Sozzini family represented one current in a general milieu of those interested in philo-Protestantism in Siena. In the 1530s several members of the upper class had begun to explore the ideas of Erasmus and Juan de Valdés, and Bernardino Ochino, general of the Capuchin Order and one of the most popular preachers in Italy, was a Sienese native.[70] The Sozzini were part of a larger heterodox movement in Siena and Tuscany, whose members in the 1540s were attempting to construct an alternative church to that of Rome. Anton Francesco Doni had set up a printing shop with Domenichi in Florence; he subsequently sent the confession of faith of a weaver made shortly before his death in November of 1546 to the barber of Siena's governing magistracy, Basilio Guerrieri, with whom Bartolomeo Nelli was later associated. The confession of faith was predominantly Calvinist, expressing ideas of predestination and a church of the elect. Guerrieri had become interested in philo-Protestant ideas through a letter Bernardino Ochino had written to the Sienese government as he fled north in 1542. In addition, Guerrieri was a member of a group of converts led by Lelio Sozzini, and he proselytized among the members of an artisan confraternity, the Holy Trinity.[71]

By the 1550s, Lelio Sozzini had hoped that Siena's unstable political situation, including a rebellion against the Spanish and absorption into the Medici's Tuscan state, might allow for more religious openness.[72] Lelio even briefly returned from the Swiss cantons to Siena, where he met Nelli, whom he converted to heterodox opinions with a vernacular Bible.[73] Nelli's prosecution began toward the end of 1559 after a witness, Ettore di Andrea, gave testimony about a conversation he had heard in Francesco's spice shop. He, Giulio di Vecchi, Achille Orlandini, Scipione Orlandini, Niccolò Barbiero, and Bartolomeo Nelli were discussing the sermon they all had heard earlier in the day, delivered by Father Girolamo Rubiols. When the conversation turned to good works, the sermon's subject, Nelli argued that good works merited nothing since people were only saved through the glory of Christ. Ettore argued right back that good works could earn one salvation. Nelli, referring to Paul, asserted that 'our works merit nothing.'[74] A few days later, during another conversation in the spice shop, Francesco and Nelli both told Francesco's servant that to believe good works contributed to one's salvation 'was Pelagius's opinion.' Ettore told inquisitors that it was conversations such as these that gave Nelli a reputation (*fama*) for heresy. The next witness provided much the same information to the inquisitor; Nelli, in terms of his reputation in the community, was an infamous 'Lutheran.'[75]

With these two testimonies the inquisitor, Alessandro del Taia, had enough evidence to begin the process. In his testimony, Nelli remembered the conversations in the spice shop a bit differently than those who had given testimony against him. According to Nelli, he had said that the performance of good works was, in fact, good, but one could not gain entrance to paradise through good works *alone* (emphasis mine). He then launched into an explanation of the relationship of good works to faith, the significance of Christ's suffering and death, and how His death related to achieving salvation. This explanation came close to describing the formula of 'double justification' devised at the failed Colloquy of Regensburg in 1541.[76]

Both Nelli and his lawyer Lattanzio Lucarini had to be aware that these ideas were no longer considered the height of orthodox Catholicism. But the fact that they once had been considered licit by at least some members of the Catholic Church's hierarchy, coupled with protestations of ignorance and submission, might have sufficed to receive a relatively light sentence after abjuration.[77] This ambiguity was exactly what Lucarini would try to exploit in Nelli's defence.

The conflict between Nelli's testimony and that of the witnesses' in 1559 exemplified why the authors of later inquisition manuals hoped ritual practice could be utilized to interpret statements contextually. Because Nelli's testimony was substantially different from that of the witnesses', the inquisitor Del Taia left doctrinal discussions behind and began to inquire whether or not Nelli had attended Mass and divine offices recently. Nelli claimed to have gone to San Martino's church on a regular basis and attend Mass at Santo Spirito, a Dominican church, as well. Furthermore, he claimed he took his family with him and even went to church when not required by canon law or custom to do so. He also claimed to have received confession and communion with a

Jesuit priest at Easter, and also with an Augustinian, providing both their names.[78] Either Nelli genuinely saw no conflict between his beliefs about salvation and attending Mass, confessing, and taking communion, or he had taken the trouble to establish a public reputation for attending Catholic ritual practices. But he had discussed his philo-Protestant opinions in front of others in a shop, giving him a public reputation for 'Lutheran' heresy as well – that got him caught.

The inquisitor then asked whether Nelli had any heretical books in his possession, and here Alessandro del Taia was a bit more successful in discovering evidence of heresy. Nelli admitted to having a New Testament in the vernacular (Brucioli's edition), the *Perla di santa chiesa,* a work printed in 1547 which explicated predestination of the saints (the elect), and some of Savonarola's works. The tribunal's staff member dispatched to search Nelli's house found the works he had admitted to owning.[79] Nelli admitted to studying the Gospels in Latin and Italian, but claimed he had not realized that those books were prohibited. He asserted further that he did not utilize the Bible to instruct others: 'I have said my opinion and they theirs.'[80] Heretical books by themselves were not necessarily clear indicators of definitive heretical belief. If Nelli was a good practising Catholic, as he claimed, and had only read a prohibited book or two, then he still might have had a good argument for leniency.

Nelli had made some suspect statements, however, so the inquisitor merely asked how Nelli could claim complete ignorance about which books were proscribed, since the Inquisition had posted a notice of the Index's existence on one of the Cathedral's columns for public edification. Nelli replied that the Index was long, written in Latin, and since he had not known his books were prohibited he had not thought he needed to check.[81] The inquisitor found that argument less than persuasive, and thus the formal charges brought against Nelli contained references to only two heretical crimes: his opinions about good works, which could be construed as slightly unorthodox, and his ownership of heretical books.[82] Alessandro del Taia then gave Nelli ten days to prepare his defence with his lawyer, Lattanzio Lucarini.

Unfortunately, we can only speculate as to why Lucarini was so aggressive in his advocacy of Nelli, since he was appointed to the case by the tribunal. For in Nelli's defence, Lucarini argued in the documents presented to the tribunal that Nelli's crimes were completely unintentional, if grave – intent being one of the defining characteristics of heresy. The lawyer asserted that Nelli had made some unfortunate word choices in expressing his beliefs, but essentially had not meant to be heretical. The lawyer professed Nelli to be willing to submit himself to the determinations of the Catholic Church. Nevertheless, Lucarini had taken the liberty of asking for a a panel of theologians from the Sapienza (the university in Siena) to examine Nelli's opinions and determine their orthodoxy. If Lucarini, at this point, was aware of the fullest extent of Nelli's heterodox beliefs, then he could be characterized as attempting to help his client evade what the inquisition considered appropriate justice; it is just as likely, however, that Lucarini requested the expert panel because Nelli was sticking to his story when dealing with his lawyer as well as the tribunal.

By the time of Nelli's trial, it was quite common for a tribunal to choose to consult experts.[83] But for a defence lawyer to ask for a commission of experts was a very aggressive strategy. Lucarini's theological experts confirmed that Nelli simply had mistaken the correct order of the words in his sentence, thereby emphasizing the role of works less than he should have. In effect, the Sapienza theologians claimed Nelli was *ignorantia*, or an 'ignorant' non-theologian; they maintained that Nelli had understood the concepts involved in justification, but merely expressed them badly because of his lack of theological expertise. Lucarini also arranged for Nelli to be transferred from the archbishop's prison to the Sienese city prison and insisted on repeating all of the witness testimony.[84] The lawyer then intimated that Ettore di Andrea's testimony was the result of personal enmity. Finally, Lucarini pointed out that public opinion knew well that Nelli had confessed and taken communion with the Jesuits that year.[85] Misinterpretation, enmity, and correct performance of Catholic ritual practices were the three pillars of Lucarini's defence.

Alessandro del Taia and the archbishop's vicar, who attended inquisitorial proceedings as the archbishop's representative, consulted two theological experts of their own choosing. The first del Taia consulted was Fra Adeodato da Siena, an Augustinian. He advanced the more severe opinion – Nelli clearly manifested heretical beliefs and behaviour.[86] Gregorio Primaticci, the Dominican chosen by the archbishop's vicar, rendered a less stern opinion; while it appeared that Nelli might be suspect of heresy and bad doctrine, the words Nelli said in his testimony could be interpreted in either a good or bad sense. In that situation, both Eymeric in the fourteenth century and later manual authors recommended giving the suspect the benefit of the doubt and interpreting his or her statements positively, especially if the person in question demonstrated good Catholic ritual practices.[87]

Adeodato da Siena, the more severe consultant, suggested that both consultants be given the chance to interview Nelli face-to-face and ask twelve questions. It was during this interrogation that Nelli, working against Lucarini's efforts to this point, decided to stand firm in his philo-Protestant faith even if it meant his death. Nelli first stated that he had come to his opinions because of his personal readings of the Bible and the illumination of God. He then firmly asserted that people should only have confidence in Christ's glory, not in works, and good works only served as a sign of one's membership in the elect.[88] Nelli, at the end of this interrogation, claimed that he had no other accomplices or co-heretics. Nelli confessed his heterodox opinions and refused to accept the correction of the court. He therefore could be convicted as pertinacious and burned.

Nelli, and his lawyer, had constructed a successful defence, in that if Nelli had continued with it, it is quite likely that he would have received a lenient sentence. But his decision to attempt to stand firm in his faith, finally, after having practised Catholicism publicly while trying to proselytize others in Ettore's shop more 'privately,' changed everything. After that confession, without any accompanying statement of wrongdoing, penitence, or submission to the Church, Lucarini only had one option to save Nelli's life: convincing Nelli to confess to being wrong. It is impossible to know for certain when Lucarini discovered the full extent of Nelli's beliefs, or if it was Lucarini who persuaded Nelli to recant. Nelli, fully aware he was facing torture and then death, could have changed his mind of his own accord; he also could have been hiding as much from his lawyer as from the tribunal up until this questioning session.

The transition, in any case, was rather quick, happening over the course of a few weeks, not months. Although Nelli's process had begun in 1559, only a few weeks elapsed between his admission of heresy and his recantation. It was on 26 February 1560 that Nelli finally admitted the source of his beliefs. Lelio Sozzini had introduced him to heresy, and he had discussed his religious convictions further with Basilio Guerrieri.[89] Nelli, furthermore, finally was willing to admit that he had been wrong to believe and do those things, and confessed he was willing to reconcile with the Catholic Church.

On 8 March 1560, therefore, Bartolomeo Nelli made his final abjuration.[90] The theological discussion initiated by Nelli's defence lawyer had no effect on the abjuration and sentence, but only because Nelli decided not to continue with the strategy he and Lucarini had utilized earlier in the process. Of all the experts consulted, only one, Adeodato da Siena, was unequivocally willing to categorize Nelli as clearly heretical. The other three were willing to make concessions to Nelli's stated ideas. Primaticci clearly thought that Nelli's words were ambiguous and could be taken in either a good or bad sense, and were therefore not conclusive proof. The choice to draw the process out, and attempt to stand firm in his faith, as John Calvin himself, among many others, had counselled, had been Nelli's choice.

Confrontational Tactics

Heresy circulated in Venice and the Serenissima's *terraferma* empire in much the same way as in Modena. The Venetian state's proximity to trade routes leading over the Alps and to areas that had become openly Protestant contributed to Venice's reputation as a hotbed of heretical ideas. The city's status as the most important printing centre in Italy also meant that many heretical books moved through Venetian canals and warehouses.[91] Venice became a destination for exiles from other Italian states, including Pier Paolo Vergerio (before his own flight north), Francesco Stella, Lucio Paolo Rosello, and Alessandro Trissino. Furthermore, that the Venetian government had held off on introducing the reorganized Roman Inquisition until 1547, and insisted on the presence of three lay members of the Venetian government on the tribunal to ensure Venetians were not processed unduly, gave Venice a reputation for moderation and the heterodox some hope of success in Venice long after 1542.[92]

The philo-Protestant movement came to encompass people from all socioeconomic strata in Venice and incorporated a wide variety of doctrinal influences, including Lutheran, Calvinist, and Anabaptist opinions. The heterodox groups' adherents often were seeking ways to deal with the city's increasing social stratification and economic changes across the course of the sixteenth century. According to John Jeffries Martin, open religious discussion in shops had become common, and reading heretical books equally common, among those in the working classes who were literate in the vernacular.[93] Prospero, a hat vendor, and Battista Amai della Bambine, an enamel painter, were both a part of the merchant community of the Rialto, although most decidedly at the lower socioeconomic base of that community and not its height.

By 1572, however, the tribunal in Venice went to great lengths to procure confessions. They employed tactics that more blatantly pressured the accused, even before the use of torture became a factor. As the joint process of these two Venetians demonstrates, tribunals could utilize non-violent and extraordinary tactics to convince defendants that their lies and protestations of innocence would not be believed in order to elicit the all-important confessions. The inquisition's prosecutorial system was flexible, and could be either more lenient or more aggressive according to 'the will of the inquisitor,' as all the manuals put it, or according to the will of those in Rome. Pope Pius V (r. 1566–1572), a former inquisitor general himself, had notably stepped up inquisitorial activity during his papacy. That Pius V would insist on harsher prosecution was immediately understood by Paolo Tiepolo, Venice's ambassador to Rome in 1566, according to John Jeffries Martin, and Pius V soon appointed Giovanni Antonio Facchinetti as the new papal nuncio. Facchinetti gained the cooperation of the Venetian government in increasing prosecutions and making a more public effort to eradicate heresy, including public abjurations.[94]

The joint process began in July of 1572, when Prospero was denounced to the tribunal by Bartolomeo Bressan, a Jesuit priest, accompanied by a Messer Bernardino, a merchant on the Rialto. According to Bartolomeo and Bernardino, Prospero had denied the power of the pope and the authority of priests and friars; had disrespected the Jubilee of 1572, declared on Gregory XIII's papal ascension; had called King Phillip of Spain a tyrant whom God would punish; and, finally, had praised the Huguenots for their victory (which had occurred before the St Bartholomew's Day massacre in August of 1572); and had celebrated the problems King Phillip was having in Flanders (the resurgence of the Calvinist uprising in that year). In addition to his pro-Protestant political opinions, Prospero had forbidden his wife to go to Mass or confession and communion. Bartolomeo also claimed that Prospero had promised to go see an unnamed Catholic theologian with the Jesuit. But even though Prospero had claimed to believe as the Jesuit did, he had backed out. When Bartolomeo Bressan's efforts at more gentle persuasion had failed, he had denounced Prospero to the tribunal consisting of Patriarch Giovanni Trevisan, the nuncio Giovanni Antonio Facchinetti, the inquisitor general Aurelio Schellini da Brescia, and the two laymen Vicente Contarini and Nicola Venier.[95]

The Jesuit and Messer Bernardino named three other potential witnesses – Andrea Centurer, a Messer Domenego, and Messer Fabio

Passamani. In Domenego's questioning session, the tribunal specifically asked the Rialto merchant if he had heard Prospero say anything bad about the pope, priests, or friars and nuns. According to Domenego, he did not know Prospero by name, but he had overheard a certain man have conversations with another merchant during which the man had said that all priests go to whores. The man, presumably Prospero, also had said that 'everyone will be Turks, or Lutherans.' Since Domenego also heard Prospero 'take the part of the Lutherans' in conversation, it seems Prospero would have been quite pleased by a 'Lutheran' takeover of Venice. The prospect of Venice continuously losing ground to the Ottomans in the eastern Mediterranean may have provoked the opposite reaction.[96]

Prospero also had an interesting undertanding of the apostolic succession and papal authority. According to Domenego, while in conversation at the Rialto, when someone had asked if he believed in the power of the pope, Prospero had replied: 'San Piero was a saintly man, and went about barefoot; but these popes are fat, and go about well dressed.' And when the tribunal directly asked Domenego whether Prospero had ever spoken of the Huguenots, Domenego claimed he had overheard Prospero praising them, and added that Prospero had said that the Lutherans in Ljubljana baptized their children in the river. Finally, Domenego had overheard Prospero asking M. Fabio which was better: the religion of the Lutherans or that of the Turks? M. Fabio replied that the Lutherans were better, of course; any Christian denomination superseded Turks, apparently, in terms of which was worse.[97]

Within a few days, however, Domenego came back to the tribunal to make an addendum to his testimony. As he testified, another merchant at the Rialto had asked Prospero and Battista Amai delle Bambine to go to Mass with him one day, but Prospero and Battista had remained outside the church and listened to the Mass from there. That incident also had marked the only time the two had gone to Mass at all, as far as the community at the Rialto was aware.[98]

The next witness, Andrea Centurer, another Rialto merchant, testified that Prospero had defended Lutherans and spoken against the Church for at least two years. In addition to making statements similar to those of Domenego, Centurer testified that Prospero evidently thought freedom of conscience existed in Lutheran countries: 'In the lands of the Lutherans everyone does in his own way.' (That statement was a rather inaccurate estimation of the potential for freedom of conscience in many Protestant states.) Furthermore, Centurer also was interviewed for a second time. He then told the tribunal that Prospero had not been to confession and communion for six years and had not allowed his wife to go to Mass at all.[99] It appears that there was disagreement among the merchants at the Rialto as to whether or not giving testimony and dealing with the Venetian tribunal was a good idea. Bernardo and Vincente, both Rialto merchants who were called to testify, had heard Battista Amai della Bambine and a certain Alvise tell Bernardo that discussing Prospero's beliefs was 'badly done.'[100]

Nevertheless, Prospero was arrested on 2 August, and his first interrogation took place on 4 August 1572. In this interrogation, Prospero refused to admit the charges and in fact went on the offensive. As Prospero announced to the tribunal: 'These are my enemies: Bernardino *padovano*, who sells at the Rialto bridge; Andrea dalle Centurer, who sells at the Rialto; and Messer Biasio who sells in the piazza; and the other Messer Domenego "the big," who sells at the Rialto bridge.' Prospero could guess the identities of three witnesses – but then again, it had been common gossip at the Rialto. When the tribunal began asking very specific questions about the political statements he allegedly made about King Phillip and other princes, Prospero initially claimed not to remember any such thing. He had discussed Geneva once or twice, however. According to Prospero it was Battista Amai della Bambine (whom Centurer also identified as a heretic) who had brought up the subject of Geneva, because he wanted to go live there since everything in Geneva went 'so well.' But Battista apparently could not bear to leave his family behind. Messer Battista had called the pope the true Antichrist, and said that all princes were tyrants and that indugences were worthless. He had discussed all of these things for at least three years, when Battista also had invited Prospero to the baptism of one of his children.[101]

Prospero, however, despite his socializing with this Battista, claimed to be Catholic. When asked whether he had read any books with Battista, Prospero insisted that he had not since he could read little, and the only book he owned was an Office of the Virgin. Prospero also asserted that he had known what was being said about him at the Rialto, but voluntarily presented himself to the tribunal to 'defend [his] honour.' When officials had come to arrest him, he had not been home but had come forward anyway. Finally, he acknowledged that he had not confessed or gone to communion in three years, but swore to the inquisitors that he had intended to do so the very week he had been arrested![102]

In later interrogations, Prospero finally confessed to his philo-Protestant beliefs and actions but he refused to say anything else of significance about Battista, except to assert that Battista thought that people in Geneva performed good works and that indulgences were fables for the damned.[103] The tribunal also wanted to know who had been coming to visit Prospero in prison. Prospero alleged that his only visitor had been his wife, even when warned that he would suffer torture if he did not tell the truth. In his next interrogation, on 18 September, Prospero finally admitted that Battista Amai della Bambine had come to visit him in prison with three companions, Messer Francesco, Zuane Spagnoletto, and Bezzeto. They had demanded to know why he was in prison, but Prospero claimed to have lied and told them it was on account of his debts – a position he maintained through his next two interrogations. But even when the tribunal interviewed him in his prison cell, possibly with torture as a threat, Prospero could only think of one or two more names, including a certain Ambrogio Milanese, to identify as accomplices in heresy.[104] Prospero was interrogated for the fifth time, not because he refused to admit to his heresy, but because the Venetian tribunal thought he was holding back the names of other heretics.

Before his final sentencing, in October of 1572, Prospero would escape from prison for a period of eight days. Prospero turned himself back in to the holy tribunal and professed he was ready to completely submit himself to the tribunal and the Church. While this may seem an unwise choice, unless Prospero wanted to give up his family and his job, and leave Venice altogether, he really had no other option than to accept whatever punishment the tribunal assigned. If he stayed at large, and then were caught, he would be at risk for execution. The tribunal warned Prospero nevertheless that he might be considered as a relapsed heretic – which meant being subject to execution as a punishment – despite turning himself in.[105]

Whether or not a suspect who baulked, changed his or her story or confession, or escaped from prison, should be considered a relapsed heretic was a debatable point with no fixed answer, according to inquisition manuals over the centuries. Authors often argued that a true relapsed heretic had to have formally abjured once before; those who confessed during a process, but changed their minds before having performed the formal, public abjuration were pertinacious, but not relapsed. Heretics who escaped and remained free for one year were declared pertinacious, and excommunicated. According to Farinacci in the early seventeenth century, for example, some Spanish manual authors thought it the common practice to guard those of higher social status more closely and beat the lower-class escapees before reimprisonment. Juan de Rojas thought that those of higher social stations, such as nobles, also should be punished harshly.[106] Farinacci admitted to his readers that Pope Pius V had promulgated a bull in April of 1569 that mandated the use of the death penalty for escaped heretics, but Farinacci did not explicitly endorse that opinion as correct.[107] Peña, who published his edition of the *Directorium Inquisitorum* a mere seven years after Pius V's death, claimed he was contradicting the opinions contained in Camillo Campeggi's contemporaneous edition of Ugolini, and many others, who had endorsed using the death penalty to punish suspected heretics who fled before they were convicted of heresy, without naming Pius V as the source of the legal opinion.[108] Peña quoted Simancas as having written that there was no such thing as a 'common' sentence in these circumstances, a point Ugolini had conceded even when recommending the most severe punishment. Furthermore, he quoted Rojas as writing that the far more likely motivations for fleeing prison were fear of false testimony, the tediousness of incarceration, or the cruelty of torture, and not the determination to commit more heretical acts. Therefore, the escaped suspects could not be considered relapsed in the strictest sense, since they had committed no new heresies.[109] Peña, like Farinacci a few decades later, recommended that those who escaped from perpetual incarceration, assigned as a punishment at the end of a process, should not automatically be considered relapsed and executed if they produced a legitimate excuse for their flight. Other authors in the past had recommended assuming escaped convicts to have feigned penitence during their processes, and therefore also recommended they be executed as pertinacious, impenitent, and relapsed heretics. Again, the issue hinged on how much one wanted to assume concerning belief and motivation based on the mere fact of an escape from prison. As long as credible excuses which had nothing to do with a determination to continue in heresy were theoretically possible, Peña advised caution and further investigation instead of draconian punishments.[110]

In 1572, in reality, the Venetian tribunal employed a more lenient approach. Although the Venetian tribunal threatened to consider him a relapsed heretic, Prospero was not executed; in fact, there is no record of any harsh punishments or floggings related to the prison escape, either. Prospero, after all, had turned himself back in to the tribunal, having thought the better of escaping, and declared himself willing to submit to the authority of the Church.[111]

Prospero still had been in prison when the Venetian tribunal arrested and began the prosecution of Battista Amai della Bambine, whose first interrogation began on 20 September 1572. Battista had been found in Padua and he very well might have been there on business as he later claimed. But his trip to Padua had occurred suspiciously soon after his visit to Prospero in prison. Furthermore, in answer to the tribunal's second question, it just so happened that Battista had gone to confession during the Jubilee in Padua, with a friar, and had gone to communion at Santa Caterina. In all likelihood, he was trying to procure proof of being a good Catholic in anticipation of his impending process. But as the tribunal pressed him to admit, his ritual practices in more recent years were not in evidence; he had not gone to confession or communion but claimed an argument with another person as an excuse. When warned to tell the truth, Battista pleaded: 'I don't know anybody; I have seven children for [whom] to shop and I am poor, like Job.' He denied all of the allegations and claimed he believed as the Holy Church believed. He admitted to being a friend of Prospero, who had been present for the baptism of his 'creature' at San Zulian's.[112]

Battista, however, claimed he had not talked with Prospero for months since Prospero had been locked up in the *liona* prison. But when pressed, he admitted he had seen Prospero in prison, at which point the tribunal accused Battista of telling lies – and they were right. Battista responded that Prospero had told him the real reason for his imprisonment, Lutheran heresy, but that Battista had not believed it. Battista denied everything, and he also hinted that Camillo, who sold candles on the Rialto, might be the true Lutheran the tribunal should be interested in interrogating.[113] In short, Battista was attempting the same tactics that Prospero had tried at first: refuse to confess anything, blame it all on someone else, and profess what he hoped was proof of good Catholic ritual practice. But, as Farinacci would point out five decades later, consistent religious practice was difficult to counterfeit – one year could be pulled off in a hurry, but the contrast to previous years would only stand out all the more.

At this point in his first questioning on 20 September, the tribunal decided to pursue Battista's confession more aggressively but in a fairly unusual way. As the records read: 'Then, [Prospero *capellaro*] was introduced into the Holy Tribunal, in the presence of the said Battista, and he was asked the following.' Battista was confronted in person, face-to-face, with the man who had provided the tribunal with most of their information regarding Battista's heterodoxy. Prospero stood in the courtroom and repeated all of the incriminating evidence against Battista.[114] It had taken at least five separate interrogations to compel Prospero's full confession. The Venetian tribunal hoped that by presenting Battista with the evidence against him in the form of the witness, his friend, he would realize the futility of continuing to deny the allegations and confess immediately

Eliseo Masini, in his early seventeenth-century *Sacro Arsenale*, would describe exactly such a procedure. Masini implied a personal confrontation could take place either between two *rei*, or criminals, implicated in the same crime, or between a criminal and a witness who was not an accomplice in heresy.[115] Describing this procedure, Masini thought that the witnesses, 'if they will come in his face one by one,' could personally confront the suspect with their testimony, the more efficiently expose the suspect's lies.[116] Masini's phrasing could imply that non-heretical witnesses could go through this procedure, but given that tribunals were usually instructed to hide the identity of witnesses from defendants that seems highly unlikely.

When the two people in question were both suspected heretics, however, secrecy apparently was not an issue.[117] Both Peña and Farinacci more briefly mention this procedure in their respective earlier works as well and, unlike Masini, they both made it clear that the two people involved were not only suspect in heresy but of lesser socioeconomic status. Peña also recommended that the inquisitor general in Rome be consulted before attempting such a confrontation since, according to Peña, it was an inherently risky tactic for the cooperative suspect.[118] Masini, probably for that reason, acknowledged in his later manual that either of the two *rei* subjected to this procedure might prove hesitant to speak in front of the other. If the criminal who had already confessed became reluctant to testify to the information he or she had given, then the inquisitors should ask increasingly specific questions to extract the necessary information.[119] Masini also advised that inquisitors could attempt to play the two reluctant criminals off each other, haranguing them until both of them realized that there was no point to holding back any information.[120] Of the three authors, Masini decribed the process of forcing a confrontation between them the most thoroughly. It is possible that Masini, who published his manual in 1621, described the process in such great detail because because he had a great deal of personal experience on the job.

Despite the Venetian tribunal's attempts at playing Battista and Prospero off each other to elicit confessions, only one of them proved cooperative on that day (athough Prospero broke out of prison soon after). Prospero repeated all the information for which the tribunal asked, fully implicating Battista. Battista still denied culpability, if somewhat incoherently on occasion: 'No, what, no, I did not teach them, I don't know that for myself, to want that I teach it to others?'[121] Apparently, Battista was trying to get across that he could not teach what he did not know. The court warned Battista that he would be tortured if he did not tell the truth and returned him to prison; Battista would remain in prison, and be taken into the torture chamber, over the next year, and his process did not end until 1573.

On 23 September 1572, the tribunal interviewed more witnesses from the Rialto. Messer Niccolò, referred to the tribunal by Bernardo, another witness, added new incriminating testimony. When Battista's sister had gone to the image of the Madonna at San Samuele to pray for a miracle, Battista had refused to accompany her. He then blasphemed the whole concept of the Madonna's intervention: 'He told me that it was very thick-headed to believe that a picture of wood could make miracles.' Andrea Centurer, who was brought back in to testify about Battista yet another time, was even more incriminating. He claimed months after his original testimony that Battista was publicly known as a Lutheran: 'Since I have known him, which [has been] for about eleven or twelve years, I have never seen him in church, nor at Mass, nor at confession.' Finally, a string-maker named Francesco related how Battista even disparaged the preachers at San Paolo.[122] Battista's avoidance of Catholic ritual practices and criticism of what he considered to be idolatry was proving to be extensive, indeed.

Armed with this new spate of information, the tribunal called Battista again from prison to be interrogated on 27 September 1572. Battista, somewhat incoherently and ingratiatingly maintained his innocence: 'I have told, I have told, I have told the truth; and I myself imagine that Prospero may have accused me to get him[self] out of prison.' Prospero had been threatened with torture for refusing to name enough heretical accomplices to satisfy the Venetian tribunal, but Battista's had been one of the names he volunteered before torture. Battista said he went to Mass alone early in the morning in order to explain why none of his compatriots at the Rialto had seen him go. He also claimed he had confessed to a friar at San Zuane e Polo, and had been reconciled and taken communion at San Zulian in previous years. Most recently, in

1572, he had gone to communion at San Polo and Santa Caterina, or so he said.[123]

Battista continued his denials into October of 1572, during Prospero's prison break; in that same month, the tribunal finally called Father Honore, the sacristan and subdeacon of San Zulian, before the tribunal to verify Battista's testimony. He swore that Battista had taken communion and was a good Christian. Furthermore, he said, Battista was a very poor man who received charity from the parish in order to feed his family. But Honore recalled these events as having happened about two years previously. When the tribunal questioned him directly, Honore had to admit that Battista had only taken communion once, at the altar of San Giacomo, probably at Easter, and Honore simply did not remember the exact year. Honore, in fact, was forced to admit that he was repeating information provided by another cleric for the most part. Honore further testified that he had seen Battista's wife coming to communion only once. Furthermore, she had not confessed at San Zulian, and neither had any of her children with Battista (but only one of them had reached the age at which children traditionally began to participate in confession and communion).[124] Other than this witness, no other cleric came forward to testify regarding Battista's record of performing and attending Catholic ritual practices.

In April of 1573, months later, Battista was still insisting on his innocence while remaining in prison. Battista's wife appeared before the tribunal to plead for its mercy; this record never gives her name, much less records any questions being asked of her, even though Battista supposedly never let her attend Mass, confession, or communion. She pled with the tribunal to allow her husband to be transferred from prison to house arrest. Given that Battista had trouble supporting his family even when not in prison, her claim that she and her children were starving and in need her husband's financial support was probably true. In August of 1573, Battista was still denying his heretical beliefs and relying on his low social status to make his argument to the tribunal: 'I am a crass person; I don't know neither [how] to read or to write and I believe that they [the saints] pray for us.'[125]

Battista finally confessed in 1573 and told the full story of his heretical beliefs and actions from the beginning. He had been indoctrinated by Antonio Milanese, the preacher Fregoso, and another preacher at San Francesco. He had been taught that there was no purgatory and that the pope was the Antichrist. Battista had taught these things, and that confession to a priest was not necessary, to Prospero, along with other ideas. Battista had believed all of this for at least fifteen or twenty years.

When asked for even more by the tribunal, Battista admitted that he adored the Eucharist only 'in spirit' and believed it to be a commemoration of Christ's death. He had not believed that the host and wine was really the literal body and blood of Christ. The tribunal then asked: 'If in this time he was taking communion?' Battista's response displayed the evolution of some heterodox believers in north-central Italy in the later sixteenth century. Battista simply claimed: 'In some years yes, and in some years no.' But the tribunal clearly was interested in discering whether or not Battista had consciously been aware of being a quasi-Nicodemite – receiving Catholic communion while believing it to simply be a memorial and engaging in heresy elsewhere. Battista's evasive answer probably was not quite the sought response, but the tribunal let the issue go. Concerning his attendance at Catholic ritual practices, particularly the Mass, Battista had avoided them more recently as much as he was able, but in previous years he had gone to Mass, confession, and communion. Battista's philo-Protestant faith most likely had grown stronger over time, to the point of shunning the idolatry of the Mass and openly proselytizing at the Rialto. Another part of his confession confirms that Battista, as he progressed in his heterodox beliefs, took Protestant theologians' injunctions against idolatry seriously. Battista, once he had decided not to believe in the invocation of the saints, had given up making sculptures of them even though this had been his profession at one point in his life.[126] Throughout his process, Battista had pointed to his attendance at Catholic ritual practices to prove his orthodoxy, but the Venetian tribunal had recognized that those events had not taken place recently, while the incriminating information provided by the witnesses and Prospero had been more up to date.

All in all, Battista confessed to much more than the information contained in the testimonies provided by Prospero and other witnesses. He also was expected to provide the names of all of his accomplices, and he was threatened with torture to that end, after his full and complete confession. Despite their efforts over the course of a year, Battista and Prospero ended their inquisition processes in the same way. They confessed and then Biasio da Valvason brought them out of prison in yellow penitential habits to make their public abjurations at San Marco's door, one standing on one side and one on the other. They stood there for more than two hours so that many people would get to know their faces before they were returned to prison. Both men, however, were allowed to stay in Venice and perform salutary penance as punishment because of the extreme poverty of their families.[127] In terms of eliciting their confessions, the time they spent in prison in between their interrogations proved much more effective than the risky confrontational tactics.

The case proves how far tribunals of the Roman Inquisition were willing to go to elicit confessions before employing torture as a last resort. A variety of methods, including more creative options such as face-to-face confrontations, could be utilized over a long period of time, usually months, to draw out confessions of wrongdoing and the appropriate expressions of penitence. Propero and Battista, when they appeared before San Marco in their penitential habits, not only made excellent warnings to other Venetians about the ramifications of engaging in heresy, but also embodied the Catholic Church's ability to save souls and successfully steer the deluded heretics to the true and clear path to salvation.

Confession was the ultimate goal of inquisitorial processes, and the flexible prosecutorial system the Roman Inquisition employed allowed tribunals a great deal of latitutde in eliciting that confession. In the case of Prospero and Battista, the Venetian tribunal acted quite aggressively indeed. But suspected heretics were given ample time to formulate a defence and access to expert legal advice. The cases of Zuane Finetti and Bartolomeo Nelli demonstrate that at least some lawyers could advocate aggressively for their clients and even be successful doing so. Finetti, simultaneously lawyer and suspect, convinced the tribunal that he was falsely accused, and was vindicated. In the case of Bartolomeo Nelli, he almost convinced the tribunal, and perhaps even his lawyer, that he was essentially Catholic if slightly misguided in his conversational habits. His lawyer Lucarini successfully abetted that defence, whether he knew he was protecting a heretic by doing so or not. Nelli attempted to stand firm for his faith towards the end of his trial, but that choice was his, not his lawyer's. In the end, he received a more severe judgment than he would have had he perhaps more fully embraced Lucarini's advice, but ultimately the decision of whether or not to confess, and exactly to what, lay with Nelli alone.

Finally, all of those accused had to account for their religious actions to tribunals in the hopes of utilizing that evidence to overturn denials of heresy. But each of these tribunals had to consider the possiblity of Nicodemism as well. Nelli's attempted defence was credible because he could provide proof of confession, communion, and attendance at Mass and divine offices. Participation in Catholic ritual practices was the barometer by which all other forms of evidence was measured, and unless a suspect could produce abundant proof of correct observation of ritual practice, and had not been seen to avoid Catholic 'rites and ceremonies,' then the suspect really had no other option other than a full confession. But if such evidence could be proferred – as it was by Finetti and Nelli – then the inquisitors had few other options.

Chapter Six

Full Confessions of Faith: Ritual Practice and Intent

Torture became a part of inquisitorial practice early in its development when Innocent IV issued the papal Bull *Ad extirpanda* on 15 May 1252; none of the authors examined here doubted the right of inquisition tribunals to it. Across three centuries, they agreed with the medieval pope's reason for allowing the use of torture: If it was appropriate to utilize torture in cases that involved mere theft, or crimes against a temporal lord, then how could it be inappropriate to utilize it involving crimes against God? From this perspective, no less an authority than Augustine was regarded to have affirmed that since God had made use of physical punishment to lead people to salvation (Saul on the road to Damascus being the stellar example), then the church might do so as well, as a parent might chastise a child for his or her own good. The principle of punishment of some kind had been established in Gratian's *Decretum* of the late twelfth century.[1]

During the Roman Inquisition's prosecution of philo-Protestants from the mid-sixteenth century onwards, the tribunals resorted to torture sparingly; medieval and Spanish inquisition tribunals also utilized torture only in a minority of cases. While inquisition tribunals of necessity relied on the secular arm to arrest and imprison and, if defendants remained pertinacious, torture and execute, tribunals also employed several safeguards intended to monitor the process and avoid extreme cruelty. For example, as John Tedeschi has recognized, defendants could be declared physically incapable of withstanding torture through medical consultation. Furthermore, individual inquisitors did not have to make the decision to employ torture by themselves. In reality inquisitors could consult with legal and theological experts and, increasingly over the later half of the sixteenth century, with the Congregation of

Cardinals in Rome. While inquisitors were not required to abide by consultants' opinions, by the end of the sixteenth century in north-central Italy it became accepted practice for the Congregation of Cardinals to issue the order to torture individual defendants. The congregation was vigilant in monitoring the use of torture, and did not hesitate to correct perceived abuses and violations of procedure. Much was done administratively to ensure that torture was utilized with what was, for the time, comparative restraint.[2]

Despite the moderation with which it was used, and the relatively few cases in which it was employed, torture was an integral part of inquisitorial procedure as a whole. In theory, torture could be resorted to to resolve contradictory evidence. When the witness testimonies, or a partial confession on the part of the defendant, indicated the presence of heresy in 'word or deed,' but the suspected heretic in question denied any heretical intent, torture could be utilized to solve the conflict.[3] If a suspect had engaged in heterodox ritual practices, or avoided Catholic ones, or critiqued Catholic practices through actions such as iconoclasm, as the manual authors all clearly stated the theory, a suspect's claim to lack any heretical intent was implausible indeed. Therefore torture could be used to produce a confession regarding that intent. Those who avoided Catholic ritual practices or attended alternative ones were the most serious suspects, and most likely to be committed philo-Protestant believers. Furthermore, when a suspect affirmed Catholic ritual practice, but had been heard publicly discussing heresies – in other words, seemed quasi-Nicodemite – then torture could be utilized in hopes of discovering the truth. But all the manual authors were aware that attempting to evaluate evidence and reach the truth in reality would not be a process 'as clear as the light of day,' to use of the manuals' ubiquitous phrase. Therefore, this chapter discusses the parameters within which inquisitorial tribunals utilized torture in reality, and examines three mid-to-late sixteenth-century case studies in which tribunals employed torture in an attempt to reconcile conflicts of meaning between 'word and deed.'

When applying torture, eliciting a confession of some kind was the central issue for all of the above reasons. Torture was always present as a threat that could be applied to those who refused to confess, even if it was not carried out. When defendants denied that they had said or done anything heretical, or admitted to 'words and deeds' but denied any heretical intent in speaking or performing them, torture was the option of last resort. A full and complete confession, to both the 'words and deeds' and the heretical intent behind them, coupled with penitence and pleas for the court's mercy, almost certainly would ensure that torture would not be employed. Pertinacity and refusal to answer questions repeatedly, including a refusal to name accomplices in heresy, however, would lead to the employment of torture. Torture also tended to be employed after the defendant had endured a long prison stay. In all probability, those circumstances explain exactly why torture was used so infrequently.

Pertinacity and Procedure

Above all, the most important defining aspect of heresy itself was pertinacity, or the refusal to confess or admit wrongdoing. Nicholas Eymeric, in the fourteenth-century *Directorium Inquisitorum,* defined heretics as those who believed in false doctrines and adhered to them even when instructed otherwise, thereby creating divisions within the unity of the Church.[4] The perfect heretic, according to Eymeric, erred in mind or intellect and held those errors voluntarily and with pertinacity – refusing correction.[5] Torture, therefore, was the final phase in which inquisitors could encourage pertinacious defendants to accept correction and turn back to the Catholic faith.

Eliseo Masini's manual *Sacro Arsenale* (1621) contained a straightforward explanation about the procedural rules of employing torture in inquisitorial tribunals. He instructed that suspected heretics tried in inquisitorial courts, if they refused to confess, could be put to torture two or three times. He explained that torturing the defendant twice was appropriate if the criminal had been 'tortured enough,' and if 'the indications are not very urgent: but otherwise one will come to the third torture.' But if the defendant could undergo those two or three rounds of torture without having confessed to anything, then that defendant could be let go.[6]

Eymeric had written the same thing, and Peña, in his late sixteenth-century commentaries, further elucidated the procedure to be utilized to his readers. He explained that 'it ought to be said clearly' that when indications of a crime from witness testimony had not been turned aside during the defence process, it was not possible to simply absolve him or her.[7] Peña thought that inquisitors could use torture in such situations, both to gain a confession and to make sure that greater heretical crimes had not been committed. Peña recommended that the method of inflicting torture should be geared toward matching the levels of suspicions and conjectures involved, citing the ruling of the Spanish Madrileña court of 1561 as his source.[8] Peña advised his readers that such a use of torture was additionally beneficial when the evidence against a suspected heretic was very grave, to the point that tribunals might think the suspect to be in danger of relapsing after abjuration if the full truth were not discovered (leaving an unreconstructed heretic loose in the Catholic community). In such cases, as Peña implied here, the available proof was enough to justify the use of torture, especially if other factors such as the defendant's general reputation for heresy (*mala fama*) indicated that the defendant was even more seriously heretical than witness testimony indicated. Even one denunciation coupled with a widely held reputation for heresy might be enough to recommend torturing the person in question (although those circumstances could not end in a sentence of capital punishment if the defendant refused to confess).[9]

Peña then continued to explain to his readers Eymeric's pronouncement that if a defendant had been subjected to torture properly and had not confessed, then the inquisitor should repeat the torture. As Peña noted, this meant that the tribunal should begin with 'light' torture on the first day of questioning. But, according to Peña, 'concerning [him] although he may have been tortured sufficiently one time for that turn, nevertheless it remains the law to be tortured a second time.' If the suspected heretic underwent two sessions of torture (of no more than an hour each) without confessing to either word, deed, or intent, and the witnesses' testimonies were insufficient to warrant any form of punishment, then he or she could be said to have overcome the evidence and let go.[10] Further elucidating this point a bit later in the commentary, Peña warned his readers that this entire process would require 'prudent [and] considered' judgment to gauge whether or not the initial evidence had been sufficiently matched by the rigour of the torture.[11]

As Eymeric and Peña both noted, however, the goal of torture was to produce sincere confessions, so both advised that in order to be sure that confessions were true, and not just the result of fear or pain, defendants had to ratify their confessions outside the torture chamber. Eymeric recommended at least a twenty-four hour lapse between torture-induced confessions and their ratification and Peña two or three days. Defendants had the right to revoke their confessions and claim they had confessed only out of fear or pain. But, as Peña explained, if defendants revoked their first confessions, they could be tortured again. Those who confessed and then revoked their confessions had produced new evidence that seemed to indicate potential heresy – the confession itself, even if it was not ratified. The question then became, according to Peña, what to do with those who were tortured twice, confessed under torture twice, and then revoked their confessions twice. Were they to be tortured a third time?

According to Peña, and his source Simancas, the answer was no: 'Therefore it is more kind and safe that he not be tortured a third time on account of a confession having been revoked: because while this is not stipulated as contrary to any law, still it seems exceedingly cruel and inhuman.' Peña had to acknowledge that there was no definitive pronouncement against the practice. Giulio Claro, Boërius, and Paolo Grillandi, among others, thought that torture could be applied a third time, and Masini evidently later agreed with them.[12] Of the three legal experts who thought torture could be applied a third time, two were experts in civil and criminal law (Giulio Claro and Boërius). That inquisitorial authors made more of lay sources describing torture makes sense, since according to John Tedeschi church courts had brought in the practice from lay courts in the thirteenth century.[13] It seems that lay judicial procedures and writings about torture continued to be taken into account long past the thirteenth century.

When specifying exactly what should happen to the defendant after he or she had undergone torture twice without confessing, Peña was forced to deal with another controversial point of inquisitorial procedure: How exactly should Innocent III's bull *Inter sollicitudines* be interpreted? At one point in the text the bull can be read to recommend that a suspected heretic be forced to abjure if the presence of *mala fama* still existed despite the lack of specific evidence or confession, because the defendants in question were publicly friendly with known heretics. Peña's contemporary Camillo Campeggi, inquisitor of Pavia from 1554 and of Ferrara from 1563 to 1568, approved of that interpretation in his edition of Zanchino Ugolini's work. Peña decried the opinion of Campeggi, among 'certain others,' all of whom recommended that inquisitors have more latitude in forcing abjurations. As Peña put it, 'it always seemed more proper to me ... that if he may confess nothing, his canonical purgation is indicated,' which would involve requiring the defendant to formally swear innocence, with the help of *compurgatores*, or 'purifiers,' willing to guarantee continued good behaviour.[14]

It was Cesare Carena in the early seventeenth century who produced a summary of the issue. If it was judged that the defendant had been tortured enough to overcome the witness testimony, then the defendant could be absolved. But Carena also clearly thought it possible that, after the two torture sessions of increasing severity, the defendant might not have overcome all of the evidence against him or her. In such cases, an abjuration, as either lightly or vehemently suspect (*de levi* or *de vehementi*) could be imposed. Carena also specified that the latter circumstances most likely would occur when the defendant had confessed to committing the crime but denied any heretical intent in committing it. In theory, the crime itself deserved punishment and an abjuration, even if there had been no heretical intent in committing it.[15]

Finally, Peña also addressed the issue of using torture in those cases in which only light suspicion of heresy was present. He advised that in those cases torture really ought not be applied, although he fully acknowledged that, in theory, it was technically permissible to do so. Regarding this issue, Farinacci was a bit more equivocal than his predecessor Peña, although he asserted that his opinion agreed with Peña's. Farinacci noted Campeggi's opinion that when the evidence only indicated light suspicion of heresy, the person in question could be tortured to produce that confession. But Farinacci claimed to quote Peña, asserting that Peña had recommended leaving such a decision up to the considered opinion of the judge. Regarding this issue the inquisitor Campeggi was far more stringent in his interpretation of the permissible boundaries of inquisitorial procedure than the curialist Peña. Farinacci neglected to mention that Peña had disapproved; while he thought that torture occurred according to the will of the judge, it should not occur 'according to rashness,' and that the indications of heresy ought to 'be approved by law.'[16]

Peña and other authors, including Simancas, agreed that while one could torture those for whom the available indications and suspicions of heresy were few, it really should not be done. But other authors thought that it was perfectly legitimate, including Carena and Masini in the early seventeenth century. Farinacci noted such a division of opinion concerning the issue but he remained undecided and left each reader to make up his own mind. Carena and Masini were more severe concerning the issue, along with Camillo Campeggi – and all three worked in tribunals as inquisitors, procurators fiscal, or consultors, which perhaps accounts for the differences of opinion.[17]

In the discussions above, the authors debated whether or not light suspicion was enough to warrant torture by evaluating two factors: evidence and intent. For Peña and other authors, in theory, deeds, or heretical actions relating to ritual practice, were clear indicators of strong suspicion and therefore worthy of torture. As Peña put it, some heretical deeds – such as iconoclasm – were so heinous that there could be no other possible intent for such an act than belief in 'Lutheran' heresy.[18] Once what had happened had been established by the testimony of two credible witnesses, denials of what happened would not be believed and neither would denials of heretical intent. Who, Peña had rhetorically asked, could smash an image and not be a philo-Protestant in his day and age?

Cesare Carena, in his *Tractatus*, elucidated the matter even further. If there was no other possible intent for some actions, then there was no need to torture defendants who denied all charges, or who confessed to the action, but not the intent behind it – they were obviously lying and torture was not needed to establish the truth. Carena cited Farinacci to give his readers examples of acts that could have no possible connotation other than the presence of heresy, which included adoring Mohammad or circumcising one's sons. In that last situation, Carena referred, if obliquely, to apostates. He seems to imply that the purely physical evidence of circumcision on a man who claimed to be Christian, and to have been born so, was undeniable to the point that torture and confession were not necessary. Carena noted one dissenting voice, the Spanish Franciscan Alfonso de Castro, who thought that intellectual error was not so easy to presume but, as Carena announced to his readers, he proceeded in the first way not the second. Both Farinacci and Carena emphasized that such a situation could lead to sentencing a defendant as a 'negative' heretic – one who the proof indicated to be heretical but who denied the charges and heretical intent. Circumcision, according to Carena and Farinacci, in theory, was physical and self-evident proof – no confession necessary. But Farinacci warned that even to consider proceeding in such a way would require close consultation with the Congregation of Cardinals in Rome.[19]

According to the manual authors the goal of torture was to discern the *ulteriorem veritatem*, or 'ultimate truth,' through a valid confession. Yet all of these authors were aware that torture was not foolproof. Eymeric stated quite clearly that there were those who could withstand torture without confessing even though guilty and that those who were not guilty might confess to avoid it. Thus, all manuals cautioned that the preliminary evidence, as given in witness testimony, had to be weighty and the case constructed carefully. But those testimonies, as established originally in Roman law and therefore inherited by both the inquisitorial and the secular justice systems, were circumstantial evidence that (most of the time) had to be confirmed by a confession – the 'queen of proof.'[20] Torture was therefore an inescapable part of the intellectual theory of both the inquisitorial and the secular systems. Furthermore, as the authors opined, when the evidence related to ritual practice, in theory, the gist of the evidence should have been clear. If a confession was not forthcoming, then torture was the last resort to elicit one.

As Peña noted in his commentaries, and the mid-sixteenth century case studies examined in this chapter demonstrate, however, the reality of employing such prosecutorial principles might be more complex. According to Peña, it was possible that a defendant would admit to words and deeds, but deny heretical intent.[21] If, after being tortured, the defendant still denied any heretical intent regarding acts not clearly heretical then he or she should be declared lacking in 'heretical depravity' and abjured as vehemently suspect in heresy. If the defendant admitted heretical intent under torture to an act that was clearly heretical, then the defendant should be abjured, but as guilty of formal heresy. As Peña explained, suspicion of heresy could arise from certain acts; the intent behind those acts, when dealing with affirmative heretics, was confirmed or denied through proof, if necessary provided by torture.[22] Thus, torture in theory could be utilized in tribunals to clarify the defendants' state of mind and belief as well as to elicit confessions as to what had been said and done. It could also be employed, relative to ritual practice, to resolve seemingly contradictory evidence.

Constructing Religious Identity

The Modenese tribunal processed Pietro Curioni in 1568, utilizing torture to determine what they thought was the 'ultimate truth' about evidence they considered to be contradictory and conflicting. Initially, from the 1540s, first the irenic Cardinal Giovanni Morone and then Bishop Egidio Foscarari both had treated the broadly heterodox sect in Modena more gently, the former by emphasizing consensus and common ground when developing an irenic confession of faith for Modena in 1542. Foscarari, Morone's successor, employed inquisitorial standards mildly through his role as a member of the local tribunal. By the 1560s, however, the Modenese tribunal, as the Roman Inquisition as a whole, had moved toward more forceful and assertive prosecutions of philo-Protestants; the vicars for Modena, Niccolò da Finale and Angelo Morabini, both of whom participated in conducting this process, worked under the direction of the inquisitor general of Ferrara and Modena, none other than Camillo Campeggi. By this time, the *fratelli* had constituted themselves as a secret, underground heterodox church complete with alternative religious services, including the Eucharist.[23]

Curioni's process, therefore, represents how the flexible system of inquisitorial prosecution could be guided in the direction of greater severity in this era, largely because of the policies of Pope Pius V. But it also demonstrates why Pius V and others in the Church hierarchy felt such an intensification to be necessary. By the time Pietro Curioni, a pharmacist and surgeon, was prosecuted, sympathetic irenicism was no longer the policy of Modenese religious authorities. Curioni himself continued to espouse it, believing in a combination of Catholic and philo-Protestant ritual practices and doctrines. It was the tribunal's goal, however, to impose a single religious identity on Curioni and, in particular, discover whether he was hoping to cover his heretical conversations by appearing to comply with Catholic ritual practice. In Curioni's process, torture was utilized to confirm Curioni's own assertions about the extent of his heretical beliefs and the religious intent behind his participation in Catholic ritual practices.

Natale Gioioso, while walking past Pietro Curioni's pharmacy, had heard a very unusual conversation going on within. A few men passing time in the shop were joking about the execution of a heretic named Magnavacca. Curioni reproved their merriment, saying 'he went straight to heaven just like the thief on the cross.' Hearing such utterances in Curioni's shop was not an unusual occurrence because it was one of the gathering places in which *fratelli* from all social classes met to talk and probably, in some sense, worship.[24] This auricular evidence of a potentially heterodox conversation provided the point from which the Modenese tribunal initiated Curioni's process.

His questioning commenced on 24 March and, at first, Curioni attempted to hide the full extent of his philo-Protestant activity from Niccolò da Finale. Curioni admitted to having participated in heretical conversations in his shop until 1566 or so. But he claimed that for the previous eighteen or twenty months he had spoken about such things only with Giovanni Torrigiano and one or two others. He stressed that he had gone to confession twice a year and communion once a year and as well that he had never had spoken about the Eucharist in his shop.[25] In this questioning session Curioni characterized himself as politely passive – he asserted that Torrigiano had done most of the talking in their conversation while Curioni had merely listened to a former co-believer the pharmacist had not been able to cut off. According to Curioni while Torrigiano and others spoke of their heretical ideas he had paid them no mind: 'And still they said that the pope is the Antichrist and not the vicar of the Church but I never said it, nor did I believe it; again, I believe he is the vicar of Christ.' The other men in the shop also advocated eating meat during Lent.[26] Curioni essentially presented himself in this interrogation as self-correcting, and thought that his correct ritual practice was the reason why the Modenese tribunal should believe that he was not an active participant in philo-Protestantism anymore.

In this same interrogation, however, Curioni had to admit knowing several other heterodox, including one who had read the Scriptures in his shop and Pietro Antonio da Cervia, later tortured and executed in Bologna. Curioni told the tribunal that he had ended his association with Cervia – by throwing him out and never seeing him again – once the surgeon had realized that he was '*cattiva,*' a step he was apparently unwilling to take with Torrigiano. Furthermore, Curioni denied that he had read any heretical books other than a Bible in the vernacular.[27]

Curioni claimed that he remained Catholic despite a few heterodox friends and possession of one illegal book. After this interrogation ended, Curioni fled Modena temporarily. On his return, he once again was brought before the Holy Office's tribunal. During this interrogation, Curioni admitted that he had fled out of fear but he had returned 'to the arms of the Holy Mother Church, and live in a Christian way.'[28] On 29 March, Curioni began to confess to Niccolò da Finale, Fra Angelo Morabini, and Fra Cornelio. Curioni admitted that he had believed that the pope was the Antichrist; that it was all right to eat meat during Lent and neglect to follow other Church laws; and neither indulgences nor prayers for the dead were of any value, since there was no purgatory. Finally Curioni asserted that one should 'neither reverence nor adore [the saints], and that one ought not to invoke the saints to intervene for us, close to God, but only Jesus Christ.'[29] Curioni affirmed that he had read two heretical books, Bernardino Ochino's sermons and the vernacular Bible, and then named his accomplices in heresy.[30]

In subsequent interrogations, at Fra Angelo's and Fra Niccolò's prompting (Fra Angelo on 29 and 31 March; Fra Niccolò during other questioning sessions), Curioni explained that always he had believed in the necessity of sacramental confession to a priest and went to confession during the times determined by the church (Easter). Moreover, regarding the Eucharist, Curioni responded that: 'I am absolutely convinced and have believed that the body of Christ is truly in the consecrated host.'[31] While Curioni's phrasing could be interpreted to support a Lutheran interpretation of the Eucharist, his support of auricular confession as a sacrament could not be so interpreted. The tribunal, in any case, interpreted Curioni's statement to mean that he affirmed transubstantiation. In this confession, Curioni admitted that he adhered to several characteristic philo-Protestant positions common to Lutheran, Reformed, and even Anabaptist believers, and his opposition to sacred images was characteristic of Reformed belief. But for inquisitors, it was the rejection of Catholic doctrines that was important, not the exact origins of that rejection. Curioni nevertheless emphasized that he was a Catholic when it came to complying with the Church's most important ritual practices.

At this point, the inquisitors allowed Curioni to languish in prison for almost a month. His case presented them with no small amount of consternation. The Modenese tribunal had to decide if they were willing to accept the idea that Curioni had fallen into some errors, but not others, essentially constructing his own personal, idiosyncratic system of belief and religious practice. Curioni's case exemplified the reasons why, as Peña would describe in his commentaries a decade or so later, it was hoped that torture could discover the full truth when tribunals suspected that a defendant was more heretical than the evidence seemed to indicate. Was Curioni genuine in his attendance at confession, communion, and Mass, or was he a quasi-Nicodemite? Eleven years previously, Bishop Egidio Foscarari might have been able to point to Curioni's ritual observance as an argument for leniency and more gentle correction of a few doctrinal errors.

In 1568 Curioni would not be shown that consideration. The Modenese tribunal's reluctance to believe that Curioni continued to attend Mass, including the consecration of the host and wine, and go to confession and communion is logical. The tribunal probably was aware of the heretical *cene*, or Lord's Suppers, held by *fratelli* as an alternative to

Catholic Mass.[32] Finally, given that Curioni had contacts and friendships among Modena's philo-Protestant community and participated in conversations with them in his shop, how could the tribunal be expected to accept assertions of Curioni's Catholicism at face value? During an interrogation on 22 April, Curioni again was asked about his beliefs concerning the Eucharist and confession, and asked to name all of his accomplices in heresy. Because this interrogation yielded no new information, the tribunal warned Curioni that he would be questioned again, this time with the aid of torture; the tribunal informed both the vicar of Bishop Giovanni Morone and Inquisitor of Ferrara and Modena Camillo Campeggi of their intent, recorded in the trial dossier on 21 April.[33]

On 24 April, he was brought into the examination room and asked one last time if he had any additional information about other *fratelli.* Despite Curioni's protests that he had already told inquisitors everything about both his heretical beliefs and his fellow philo-Protestants, he was put to the *ligatus*, or 'rope,' which consisted of the defendant's wrists being tied together behind his or her back, attached to a rope, and slowly drawn up into the air. Under that duress, Curioni gave the same testimony. He did not know of any accomplices in heresy other than those he had already named in earlier interrogations. The tribunal also specifically asked about Curioni's Eucharistic and confessional practices. During torture, Curioni was able to maintain that he had always believed 'that the consecrated host truly [is] the body of Jesus Christ,' while also 'he began to yell: "Oh God, Oh God . . ." 'as the notary dutifully recorded.[34]

On the same day (24 April 1568), the inquisitors drew up the final document enumerating all of Curioni's heresies, identical to the list prepared before he was tortured but for the fact that Curioni admitted to being heretical for eighteen years.[35] They therefore ultimately accepted that Curioni continued to go to confession and communion because of genuine belief after torture verified his assertions. Curioni benefitted from consistently maintaining his orthodoxy in terms of ritual practice while being put to the question. Inquisitors believed that, at least in the sense of attending Mass and performing the most important ritual practices, Curioni was still demonstrably Catholic. But Curioni also was forced to condemn his heretical errors and abjure, conforming to the official definition of orthodoxy and, at least outwardly, giving up his own idiosyncratic amalgamation of preferred religious doctrines.

'I don't know the heart of people'

Zuanbattista Sambeni, a dyer, street musician, and general day labourer from Brescia who was tried, tortured, and executed for heresy in Venice in 1568–1569, came from a similar demographic as Prospero and Battista Amai della Bambine and also was often in need of charity. In terms of his doctrinal orientation, he was one of those John Jeffries Martin has described as an eclectic Anabaptist and quite determinedly so – he maintained those beliefs even under the stress of torture. His case also demonstrates why a variety of inquisitorial authors across centuries in theory, and tribunals in reality, could find oral evidence of heretical crimes frustratingly ambiguous and imprecise. Sambeni proved to have a talent for constructing replies that the tribunal found exasperatingly difficult to pin down as to their meaning and intent.

Sambeni was first denounced by Odorico Grison, a member of an Anabaptist group in Venice who had journeyed to Padua to participate in what he considered to be pure ceremonies of baptism and the Lord's Supper during a recent Christmas.[36] Odorico, who had been in prison and interrogated several times for over a month at the instigation of his brother Piero, named Sambeni as an accomplice in heresy on 13 March 1567. According to Odorico, Zuanbattista was not present at the ceremonies at Christmas; he was merely an acquaintance who accompanied Odorico to visit Valerio Perosin, a flour merchant, to discuss the Gospels. Odorico admitted that Sambeni knew the Gospels well but did not know if Zuanbattista held any of the 'new opinions' or not.[37] Another witness, Vittorio, a Venetian native, mentioned talking with a Brescian who had read the Gospels and what were most likely Paul's Epistles. Vittorio also stated that Zuanbattista worked as a *tintore*, or dyer. But Vittorio did not know the man's name and he could not state without a doubt whether or not the man held heretical opinions.[38]

The evidence against Sambeni was quite thin at this stage; one witness who could name him, one who could not. Both agreed that Sambeni had read the Gospels and clearly knew them well, but could not or would not say much else. The Venetian tribunal at first seemed willing to acknowledge Sambeni as, at most, a peripheral acquaintance of the Anabaptist group. In his first two interrogations, held on 13 and 16 September 1568, respectively, Zuanbattista only admitted to buying and reading the vernacular Gospels, which had caused him to doubt purgatory's existence and the intercession of the saints. He had talked about those things with Valerio over the course of a month or two when he worked in a barber shop Valerio patronized. But Valerio had not taught him those errors – he had come to them through his own reading of the Gospels. And when asked who had told Sambeni to buy and read the Gospels, he responded that the idea had come 'in my mind.' Sambeni attempted to distance himself from all of his heretical associates, although perhaps as much for their protection as his. He claimed to have talked to Odorico only three or four times ever and refused to inform on the Anabaptist group. While he acknowledged that he was aware of what constituted Anabaptism, he maintained: 'I never heard them mention or say that anybody was rebaptized.' Regarding his ritual practice, he asserted that he had taken communion in a church in Asolo and had confessed with the vice-curate there, Father Troilo. The good father also had absolved Sambeni for his religious doubts. In Venice, he had confessed to an Augustinian who preached publicly.[39]

By Zuanbattista's third interrogation held on 23 September, however, the tone had taken a distinct turn for the worse; the tribunal's notary recorded that Sambeni 'Was warned and admonished to tell the truth clearly, that otherwise the Holy Office' would not fail to put him through 'the rigorous ends of justice.' Sambeni nevertheless stuck to his story and insisted he had met Odorico only three or four times – in the street outside the church of the Madonna dell'Orologio, for example.[40] Gradually, Sambeni grew willing to admit to a few more minor points. For example in his testimony of 26 October Zuanbattista denied ever having accompanied Odorico or Valerio to Vittorio's shop to get flour, but by 5 November he was willing to confess that the visit had happened. Finally, the tribunal also wanted to know where Sambeni had travelled. Zuanbattista admitted having been in Turin and Milan but vehemently denied having visited Calvinist Geneva or the Valtellina, the latter of which would turn out to be a lie.[41]

The Venetian tribunal already had received notice that Sambeni had been in the Valtellina and much else besides. He had been prosecuted for heresy by in Brescia seven or eight years previously and had abjured. The tribunal therefore was aware that they were dealing with a relapsed heretic and not a primarily Catholic person who attended the appropriate ritual practices but still retained a few religious errors or doubts. The Venetian tribunal made that fact clear to Sambeni and included in Sambeni's current Venetian dossier copies of some parts of his previous process. His cousin Francesco and Filippo, another witness, both had testified in 1562 that they had seen Sambeni refuse to raise his hat when the consecrated host was elevated and make other

Catholic reverences appropriate in church (behaviour that Farinacci would point out to his readers fifty years later as being characteristic of heretics).[42]

In another document, the Venetian tribunal made a record of the crimes of which Sambeni had been convicted in 1562. He had believed that the pope was not the true vicar of Christ; that indulgences had no spiritual value; that auricular confession was not necessary; and that transubstantiation was wrong. Even worse, when Zuanbattista had fled Brescia and gone to Chiavenna, in the Valtellina, he had begun attending *cene*, or the Lord's Supper, with the Protestant religious community there.[43] In Brescia and Chiavenna, Sambeni had practised his religion rather openly. In Venice he had been far more circumspect, to the point of going to Catholic confession and communion, quite possibly to construct a quasi-Nicodemite cover for his beliefs. But the Venetian tribunal knew not to take Sambeni's assertions that he had confessed and taken communion with Catholic priests at face value. As Farinacci would put it best later in his manual, such information was not to be believed when the defendant in question had attended schismatic rituals – and that Sambeni definitely had done before arriving in Venice.[44]

The interrogations that took place on 19 April incorporated all the elements of the first process and the subsequent information from Brescia. The tribunal focused on asking who Zuanbattista had known in Venice and with whom he had spoken elsewhere. Sambeni resolutely refused to give an inch. He claimed enmity with key witnesses in his previous process, he refused to admit to reading clearly heretical books, and he claimed he merely doubted purgatory's existence because of certain passages in the Gospel of Mark. Zuanbattista apparently thought admitting to doubt was not the same as admitting to heretical errors, as had Claudio (much more successfully) in Modena in 1555.[45]

Since the tribunal knew full well that Sambeni was relapsed, they decided to expedite Sambeni's case and moved him to the public prison in San Giovanni in Bragora. Nevertheless, Sambeni claimed ignorance and a lack of maliciousness, and told the tribunal that: 'I am a good Christian, and I want to live and die like all good Christians do and be obedient to the Holy Mother Church in all that she commands.' The tribunal duly noted that he genuflected deeply before the tribunal as he made his promises of good Catholic faith, although, given his relapsed status, such protestations presumably were not received well.[46]

On 19 July the Venetian tribunal began to employ torture as a means of discovering the ultimate truth of the case. Zuanbattista was taken 'to the usual torture location' and informed that he had already confessed to two heretical errors: doubting the existence of purgatory and the ability of saints to intervene for supplicants. Fra Eliseo, the commissar, the tribunal's vicar, and two of the three laymen who sat on the tribunal, Federico Barbadico and Andrea Badoer, wanted to know if 'you [Sambeni] have had other errors, and bigger [ones] than these, and which [ones], and your companions and accomplices in similar matters.'[47] The tribunal clearly was not accepting Zuanbattista's characterization of his thoughts about purgatory and the saints as mere doubts or, at worst, errors of ignorance.

Over the course of two interrogations involving torture, Sambeni stuck firmly to his beliefs. He was relapsed and therefore would be executed; that he refused to characterize his beliefs as 'errors' for which he was penitent perhaps was unsurprising, if brave. According to later manuals, Sambeni could reconcile himself to the Church and be strangled before his body was burned, or maintain his heterodox beliefs until the end, and die unmercifully – although in Venice heretics were drowned in the lagoon. But death it would be; Farinacci, in his seventeenth-century work, noted that in the distant past inquisitors had recommended perpetual incarceration instead of execution if the relapsed heretic was sufficiently penitent and if it did not cause scandal in the community; in fact Eymeric had mentioned just such a possibility in his fourteenth-century work. In Peña's opinion, however, published a decade after this trial, that practice had been discontinued.[48] Given all the factors, of which Sambeni most likely was aware, his refusal to penitently confess mental error makes sense, since there was no longer any advantage to be gained by doing so.

More surprising was Sambeni's consistent employment of modes of expression including terms such as 'Catholic,' 'Mass,' and 'Church.' He used them in such a way as to simultaneously claim and define those terms as his own and yet imply concurrence with the later sixteenth-century Catholic Church. It is doubtful that Sambeni was attempting to fool the tribunal into believing him to be Catholic. Nevertheless, such an effort was extraordinarily similar to the examples Bernard Gui had given to illustrate his warnings about heretics' trickery and lies in his thirteenth-century manual. For example, in Gui's work, the hypothetical Waldensian would claim to believe what 'the Holy Church teaches us to believe and hold,' and when asked to define the Holy Church, would reply 'Sir, what you say and believe to be the Holy Church.'[49] Sambeni's exchanges were equally frustrating for the inquisitorial staff present at the torture sessions in Venice:

IT HAS BEEN SAID TO HIM: Through the harshness of the process one may know that you have believed other than [what] you have confessed.
HE [SAMBENI] HAS RESPONDED: I believe that which the Creed confesses and [what] the Creed says.
HAVING BEEN ASKED: Beyond the Creed, do you not believe also in the Church?
HE HAS RESPONDED: I believe in the Holy Church.
HAVING BEEN ASKED: What you do intend for this church?
HE HAS RESPONDED: I say to the most excellent sirs, the union of faithful Christians.
HAVING BEEN ASKED: Which [one], this union of Christians?
HE HAS RESPONDED: I believe that this Holy Church and these faithful Christians that you ask me are those who have placed their hope in Jesus Christ, living son of God.
IT HAS BEEN SAID TO HIM: Those are words that all the heretics say; but you ought to say the true distinction of the faithful Christians from heretics.[50]

As the questioning continued, those present clearly got frustrated and attempted to formulate an airtight question: Did Sambeni believe that 'in the Council of Trent' it was determined that all Catholics were those 'who believe that which the Holy Roman and Apostolic Church believes, and that all others contrary to this faith are damned, and held for heretics?' Zuanbattista merely repeated that all those who believed in the living son of God would be saved. While Sambeni consistently vowed that 'I cannot judge this, because I do not know the heart of people and I cannot make that judgment,' regarding who should be considered a heretic, he also implicitly denied the tribunal's right to do so as well.[51]

A strategy of carefully phrased responses had long been portrayed as a defensive 'trick' in inquisitorial manuals. In addition to Gui, who wrote in the early fourteenth century, Eymeric thought that all heretics would use verbal 'tricks' to seem less culpable. Juan de Rojas (or Royas), as quoted by Farinacci, accused duplicitous heretics of using vague and ambiguous words.[52] This was such a consistent point of agreement among inquisitorial authors across the centuries that Sambeni's evasive answers most likely only had the effect of signalling heretical belief and duplicity to the Venetian tribunal. But Sambeni consistently utilized irenic terminology, whatever his motivation – repeatedly he pointed out that he believed in the Creed, for example. And he would not let go of one core idea: all those who believed in Christ would be saved as the Holy Gospels preached. Sambeni claimed God gave him the grace to say such a thing and refused to confirm that the pope and councils had a monopoly on the inspiration of the Holy Spirit. He implied that he was actually in possession of the Holy Spirit as he formulated his religious beliefs. It was Sambeni's refusal to accept the correction and instruction of the Church that ultimately made him a recalcitrant heretic.[53]

Sambeni's second interrogation involving torture was held on 2 August 1569, and during the session Sambeni declined to change any of his previous answers. But he also claimed that he believed 'that which the Holy Catholic and Apostolic Church [believes], as it is said in the Creed in the Holy Mass.' Sambeni clarified during the interrogation, when the tribunal insisted he do so, that he really meant those articles that conformed to Scripture. When asked if he thought that all the articles considered necessary by the Catholic Church conformed to the Holy Gospels, Zuanbattista replied that he did not know, since he was 'the least worm.' The tribunal also recognized what else was missing from these declarations and therefore specifically asked whether or not he believed in papal authority. Sambeni replied: 'In what I have read; I haven't found it,' meaning he had found nothing about papal authority in the Gospels.[54] During this, his second interrogation by torture, Sambeni implied that he approved of the Ancient Church and even more subtly tried to imply that the contemporary Catholic Church and his church were, or ought be, the same. But he refused to affirm papal primacy when pushed to give a definitive answer. The members of the tribunal not only were attempting to construct airtight questions, but also employing the recommendations that would be highlighted by both Peña within a decade and later Farinacci. The tribunal proceeded according to 'general principles' and asked him to confirm Catholicism.[55] Sambeni, therefore, was incriminating himself as much through what he *would not* say as through affirming any definitively heretical beliefs.

So, to determine his sentence, the Venetian tribunal consulted a panel of jurists and two of its lay members, Federigo Valaresso and Andrea Badoer. When Sambeni next came before the Venetian tribunal, he was sentenced to death as an unrepentant and relapsed heretic. That sentence was carried out in September of 1569; he was taken by boat out of the lagoon and drowned in the sea.[56]

Willingness to Confess: Some or All?

Girolamo (Hieronimo), a shoemaker in Udine, was a part of a well-known philo-Protestant sect prosecuted in 1543–1544. Since this group was caught and prosecuted after a decade or two of rather open religious discussion on the Italian peninsula there would be no shortage of people who could testify against the group. Girolamo's associates had been quite open about their religious ideas and opinions. In spite of the group's unguarded religious behaviour, however, Girolamo's case would turn out to be anything but straightforward. The difficulty lay in deciding what constituted a valid confession and how much a defendant's willingness to confess should affect the process's outcome.

Udine lay in the patriarchate of Aquileia, in which the patriarch maintained a residence effectively rendering him bishop of the city. Politically, Udine lay within the boundaries of Venice's empire on the mainland in the province of the Friuli. In that province eventually there would be two inquisitorial tribunals: one in Udine, since it was both political capital and seat of the patriarch, and the other in Concordia and Portogruaro, which held jurisdiction over the diocese of Concordia. The two courts in both locations would be led by inquisitors after the reconstituted Roman Inquisition was introduced in Venetian territory in 1547 (with the bishop or his vicar participating in key phases of the process, including arrest, the decision to employ torture, and sentencing). But in 1544 in Venice, there was still an inquisitor, because the position had existed since the medieval period; Fra Marino Venier, at this point in Venice working with the support of the papal nuncio (but without the support of the Venetian government), would be drawn into this case on appeal. On the *terraferma* before 1547, local bishops or their representatives could prosecute heretics utilizing the *inquisitio* procedure, as had been true since the Middle Ages. Therefore it was the patriarch of Aquileia's vicar, Giovanni Angelo da San Severino (also an episcopal ordinary and apostolic protonotary), assisted by the Augustinian Hermit Agostino da Carlenari, educated in canon law, Paolo da Caporiaco, a professor of theology, and Alberto Pascaleo, the Dominican bishop of Chioggia, who would conduct Girolamo's process.[57]

The presence of heterodox in Udine was not secret or clandestine; Pier Paolo Vergerio and others had proselytized extensively in the area. Other members of the sect included Francesco Garzotto, Francesco da Milano, Alvise Cavallo, and Father Patrizio of Udine, all of whom had been actively proselytizing in recent years. No fewer than forty-six deponents gave evidence against the accused heretics, testifying on successive days in July of 1543.[58]

Of all the members of the heterodox group in Udine, however, witnesses reported the least concerning Girolamo. While the witnesses could give particularly detailed descriptions of the beliefs and actions of the Franciscan Francesco Garzotto, many of them describing the same incidents, few of the forty-six deponents discussed Girolamo extensively. The priest Piero Bucinus, who served in Udine's major church, for example, said that Girolamo was reputed publicly to be a heretic and had fled Venice to take up residence in Udine because of it. Bucinus had not seen Girolamo at Mass, but he also had not heard or personally seen anything particularly incriminating about the shoemaker.[59] Florian Garzotto, another witness, told the tribunal that the group had met at Girolamo's shoe shop where they would talk while Girolamo worked. But, according to Florian, Francesco Garzotto had done most of the talking – it was Francesco who had told people in the shop that indulgences were of no spiritual value and the pope had no right to sell them. Francesco Garzotto also had led the attack on Santa Maria delle Grazie in which the crowd had smashed all of the images in the church, including a statue of the Madonna reputed to perform miracles. Peña, of course, would describe iconoclasm thirty years later as sensationally and unequivocally heretical. Francesco, finally, publicly decried transubstantiation.[60] Florian could name Girolamo's shop as a meeting point but did not attribute any heretical statements or actions to Girolamo definitively.

Master Giorgio, a tailor living just outside Udine, was one of the witnesses who could testify about Girolamo in detail. He maintained that Girolamo had told him one should not pray to the saints because they had no intercessionary power and therefore revering their images was useless; in addition, he had said that eating meat during Lent was not a sin and that people could not perform good actions of their own free will, only bad ones. Giorgio had heard both Francesco Garzotto and Girolamo dispute the papal succession after St Peter and encourage people to pray only to God.[61] Another tailor, Leonardo, gave information solely concerning Girolamo. He had heard Girolamo disparage the body of Christ and sacred images, and assert that money was better spent by donating to the poor rather than purchasing indulgences during Jubilees. Finally, according to Leonardo, 'when the sacrament passed through before his shop he did not kneel, but he did raise his hat properly.'[62]

Giovanni Garzotto, who lived in the Borgo Santa Lucia in Udine, testified that both Francesco Garzotto and Girolamo had discussed a Latin New Testament in public. Girolamo had discussed the smashing of images and the justification for it as he had found in the book *Pasqualino in estasi* by Celio Secondo Curione. The book was an Erasmian satire considered important to philo-Protestant circles in Italian states because of its critique of the Catholic Church's ecclesiastical hierarchy and advocacy of each person's right to read Scripture. Girolamo, inspired by Curione, had declared the worship of sacred images to be instituted by the Devil. But Giovanni Garzotto had not seen Girolamo in Santa Maria delle Grazie during the attack on the Virgin's image.[63]

Thus, only a minority of the forty-six witnesses had specific information concerning Girolamo's heretical beliefs and activities. Those witnesses offered information that did not precisely agree as to specific times, places, and conversations, and therefore could be considered 'single' testimonies. As Peña would note thirty years later, this was not the strongest base of evidence from which to proceed, but Eymeric had stated the principle strongly as well.[64]

In Girolamo's first interrogation, held on 16 July 1543, the patriarch's vicar Giovanni Angelo first discussed Girolamo's lack of reverence for the consecrated host. Girolamo admitted: 'It's true that I didn't kneel, but I did raise my hat properly and I didn't laugh at anyone that accompanied the sacrament of the body of Christ.' He claimed that one 'reveres the host and God with faith, and for that I didn't realize that I may not have made due reverence [to it].'[65] The tribunal recorded that he confessed to the error.

Other than that Girolamo denied having said most of the heretical propositions ascribed to him, with some qualifications. He claimed to believe in purgatory and papal authority to issue indulgences outright. Girolamo denied thinking it was not a mortal sin to eat meat during those times when it was prohibited by the church. He also maintained that he believed in the Mass, appealing to saints for intervention, and that good works were holy, worthy, and necessary to salvation. Girolamo also claimed to think that auricular confession was a necessary sacrament; in some years, he insisted, he had confessed two or three times, not just the once required at Easter. He neither was asked to provide, nor did he provide, the name or names of his confessors.

Some of Girolamo's statements during this interrogation were more problematic, however. He claimed that his advocacy of the Our Father had nothing to do with disparaging other traditional prayers. He simply thought the Our Father was the best because it was directly biblical. And when asked to state what he believed concerning the Holy Roman Church, Girolamo insisted that the Holy Church was comprised of all faithful Christians. When asked whether he thought the pope was the head of this church, Girolamo replied that Jesus Christ had ordained the pope as his vicar. Giovanni Angelo then redirected his question: Did Girolamo think that the Roman Church was the union of faithful Christians, with the pope as its head? Girolamo replied: 'I say and respond much what I said above,' that the Church is guided by the Holy Spirit, 'and that for that this church cannot err. [Saying after some time] That [I hold it], the Roman church as the head of this union of Christians.'[66]

Concerning his accomplices in heresy, Girolamo admitted that Cecho Garzotto, Francesco Garzotto, Angelo the painter, Pasqualino, and a few others had been in his shop. But they had been discussing religious ideas, Girolamo claimed, because they had been trying to convert a Jew, Moses, whose cousin Marco also had been present.[67] Girolamo therefore presented himself as a good Catholic who only admitted to having refused to kneel to a passing consecrated host since he had been so moved by the sight internally. That the vicar, Giovanni Angelo, had to drag forth an affirmation of papal primacy and the validity of the Roman Church, produced after a rather long pause, was more troubling.

In Girolamo's second interrogation, held on 2 August 1543, Alberto Pascaleo, bishop of Chioggia, and Agostino, an Augustinian Hermit, also participated. Pascaleo was a Dominican trained in theology and he had been born in Udine, which perhaps explains his presence at the questioning session. During the questioning, Girolamo reaffirmed his belief in transubstantiation, papal authority, and the intercession of the saints. He denied having said that he followed the Gospel alone; Girolamo claimed to have said that he followed Christ and his servants but did not specify who he thought these to be. Girolamo also slightly changed his views concerning some of the articles of faith discussed in this interrogation. Regarding the role of good works he said: 'I said this, that we cannot do good works without the grace of Christ,' which could be interpreted as Catholic if the tribunal so chose. He also denied blaspheming indulgences and other suffrages for the dead, but admitted that he had said donations to the poor were better and asserted that the salvific results of such charitable giving should be left to God. But overall, Girolamo claimed to behave as a good Catholic. He not only went to Mass but brought his children and workers along with him, he maintained. He also denied having read any heretical books, such as *Tre Mure*.[68]

Francesco Garzotto, however, in his interrogation held on the same day, confessed. He had denied the intercession of the saints and asserted that all good works were performed with the grace of Christ, who had given his life to save all Christians, a more unambiguous statement of justification by faith alone. And when asked to name his accomplices he was quite expansive. He alleged that there were over four hundred believers in Aquileia and he named Girolamo among them. It was the most damning proof against Girolamo thus far, and the strongest proof that Girolamo's denials could not be taken at face value. The other two defendants interrogated, Alvise Cavallo and the priest Patricio, also gave full confessions of their heretical 'words and deeds.[69]

On 6 August 1543 Girolamo, along with Francesco Garzotto, was taken to the torture chamber to discover the complete truth. Garzotto was threatened torture so he could reveal more names of accomplices, even though he had given many already. The notary recorded, in a summary paragraph, what transpired and the evidence gained from it.[70] Girolamo, according to another summary, also was interrogated concerning his accomplices in the torture chamber. He named at least one potential heretic, Signor Vardate, but claimed that he did not know if Vardate held opinions that were definitively Lutheran. The tribunal was fairly restrained in the session, but Girolamo had to have found the situation threatening at the very least. After the session, but before Girolamo's confession, the tribunal interviewed two more witnesses concerning Girolamo, and they did not contribute any new evidence.[71]

On 7 August 1543, Giovanni Angelo, the vicar, drew up a list of Girolamo's heretical 'words and deeds.' The notary recorded whether Girolamo affirmed or denied the accusations, as he had for the other defendants. Girolamo was accused of neglecting to genuflect and lift his hat when the Eucharist passed his shop in procession; Girolamo confessed that he had lifted his hat, but had not genuflected. Girolamo also admitted that he had criticized the Church for offering the laity bread without wine during communion; he had criticized the cult of the saints; he had called the pope the Antichrist and denied apostolic succession; he had denied free will; he had said that to eat meat during Lent was not a sin; he had blasphemed indulgences; he had said that suffrages for the dead were of no value; he had asserted that all Christians were priests and equals; and he had not gone to Mass. But Girolamo maintained that he was falsely accused of saying that the pope and cardinals persecuted evangelists.[72] On 9 August he and his fellow penitents were sentenced as a group. The sentence itself described the progress of the process from the beginning until this point and confirmed that of the group, Girolamo had been the most intractable, but had confessed after torture.[73]

Given his confession, Girolamo should have publicly abjured in Udine's cathedral and become a public example – instead, he made himself a public scandal. Encouraged by Pietro di Percotto, Girolamo stood in front of the church congregation, as Andrea Del Col has described, and explained why most of the accusations against him were not accurate. He announced that his confession 'was not free, but compelled by fear of torture.'[74] In addition to his objections to the tribunal's procedure, Girolamo explained exactly why his beliefs were not 'heretical.' But the religious explanations and rationalizations Girolamo shared with those citizens of Udine who were present may have seemed quite alarming, despite Girolamo's protestations of loyalty to the Catholic Church. For example, when speaking of the seventh accusation against him – that Girolamo denied it was a sin to eat meat during the times prohibited by the church – his explanation of what he meant really was almost identical to Ulrich Zwingli's sermon concerning the subject. According to Girolamo, the Gospels said that men were not saved by what they ate, but if the custom was observed by everyone then it should be observed. Girolamo also qualified some of his statements by asserting that if he had said it, hypothetically that would have been 'bad.' The implication was that no one could prove he had said such a thing.[75]

In October of 1543, Girolamo submitted a defence document that utilized both religious and legal arguments. It had been written with the help of Pietro di Percotto, who would later be prosecuted himself for his role in encouraging Girolamo's scandalous abjuration.[76] The religious arguments in this document were quite similar to those of that abjuration. Girolamo, in the document, attempted to explain how his actions and beliefs could be considered Catholic theologically. The tribunal, however, interpreted them as a clear sign that he was not willing to submit to their judgment as to what was, or was not, correct doctrine. For example, Girolamo still acknowledged that he had not knelt when the Eucharist passed his shop, but he insisted that 'Paul everywhere said he served God in spirit' and also quoted Anselm's commentary on Corinthians to support his opinion.[77] Girolamo also submitted a list of his good Catholic ritual practices. Among others, he pointed out that he kept images of the Virgin Mary in his house for devotional purposes and argued that he and his three children were models of Catholic behaviour, attending divine offices. Girolamo reminded the tribunal that the religious conversations in which he participated were aimed at the successful conversion of a Jew.[78]

The document also made relevant arguments concerning the nature of the evidence and procedural rules. Most likely Piero contributed the technical legal points, although the document was signed by Girolamo. The manifesto maintained that most of the evidence against Girolamo came from single testimonies. As Percotto put it in his rather officious Latin, 'singlular' testimonies were worth 'nothing.'[79] While a single accusation did not constitute full proof, it was enough to allow the use of torture as both Eymeric and Peña had maintained, the first long before this process took place and the latter not long after. In this case torture had produced a confession, considered the ultimate full proof. But at the end of the document, Girolamo attempted to retract that very confession once again by claiming that he had not freely confessed but only had done so due to the coercion of torture. He asked the tribunal in Udine to vacate the earlier decision and declare him innocent of the charges. He signed the document 'Girolamo, a good, honest, Catholic and Christian-living man.'[80]

In the wake of the public scandal and the submission of a defence document, the tribunal in Udine was then faced with figuring out what do to about all of this. In principle, defendants could retract confessions produced under torture when asked to ratify them at least twenty-four hours after the torture itself. Retraction of a confession after sentencing was another question entirely. Girolamo was assigned to house arrest on his own recognizance while the tribunal deliberated.

Throughout January of 1544 the tribunal considered whether it was possible to revoke a confession after sentence, or if Girolamo's attempts to do so constituted relapsing into heresy after one valid process had concluded.[81] According to Farinacci's later advice on the subject, a defendant who refused to abjure at all was pertinacious and therefore should be handed over to the secular arm, eventually. As his source, Farinacci pointed to the apostolic letter of Martin V in 1418 that dealt with the processes, convictions, and executions of Jan Hus and Jerome of Prague. Hus had refused to confess and abjure and was executed;

Jerome of Prague initially had recanted, but then took back his recantation and was executed. It is possible that the Augustinian Hermit and legal consultant, Agostino, was aware of the legal principle involved, if not necessarily Jerome of Prague's case, since pertinacity was one of the defining characteristics of heresy in general. In these cases, however, both men had refused to abjure before the formal condemnation and sentencing; Girolamo had done so afterwards. Therefore the situation here was a bit different, but Farinacci, Peña, and Carena all later would suggest a solution for these circumstances (perhaps precisely because they had come up in the course of processes in the mid-sixteenth century). Carena, summarizing his two earlier colleagues in his seventeenth-century work, stated those who revoked their confessions after their sentences were impenitent. But the appropriate course of action was to re-imprison the person who revoked the confession and make an effort to convince him or her to confess again. Only if such a confession was not forthcoming should the impenitent one be turned over to the secular arm to be burned alive.[82]

In April of 1544, the tribunal was apparently still undecided; they questioned Girolamo concerning the details of the abjuration and the defence document's genesis. By May of 1544 the tribunal had decided – Girolamo was sentenced as a relapsed heretic. Girolamo had confessed and reconciled to the Catholic Church, only to fall into heresy again. The abjuration in the pulpit therefore constituted a separate incident of heresy and not a mere continuation of one process. Given the alarming and public nature, and theological specificity, of the explanations Girolamo had given to justify revoking his confession, apparently the tribunal found his protestations of fear and ignorance less than credible.[83] Girolamo therefore signed another confession, encompassing the fourteen errors that the tribunal had thought to be his full list of heretical crimes. In addition, he admitted that Piero had tricked him into reading the scandalous abjuration. Such a characterization of a shoemaker being led further astray by someone apparently more educated fit the common inquisitorial perspective.[84]

In June of 1544, however, Victor Barbadico, the *podestà*, or Venetian-appointed governor of Udine, wrote to Venice for advice; it appears that Girolamo and his friends prompted the *podestà*'s intervention, believing that the Venetian tribunal might be able to help overturn Girolamo's sentence. While he had been briefed concerning the secular arm's relationship to inquisitorial tribunals when he had been governor of Brescia, Barbadico could not remember ever hearing of a case like this one. He had to ask the vicar for dossier excerpts to figure out why Girolamo was condemned to death, since he had not been involved in the case personally until this point. When the vicar and the *podestà* later met, 'on the third day he [the vicar] thought me [Barbadico] completely confused.' Therefore Barbadico refused to move forward with the execution until such a time as the situation was clarified for him.[85]

Barbadico and the Udinese tribunal received a response from Father Inquisitor Fra Marino Venier *il zotto* ('the lame') in Venice, who would later become known for his leniency to some defendants and prosecuted for it.[86] In his letter, the inquisitor argued against considering Girolamo a relapsed heretic from a legal standpoint. To clarify the matter, Fra Marino referred the tribunal to the technical definition of a relapsed heretic codified in the *Liber Sextus* of Boniface VIII in 1298 and the bull *Ad abolendam*. Fra Marino quoted the exact language of the first verbatim: a relapsed heretic was one who after the abjuration of errors or after being properly purged before a priest was caught again in the same heresy he had abjured. Such a relapsed heretic should be turned over to the secular arm for punishment.[87]

Fra Marino also quoted Chapter 9 of Bernard of Parma's *Glossa Ordinaria* concerning *Ad abolendam*. He reminded the tribunal in Udine that the secular arm was responsible for punishing heretics, but only, according to the bull, if the defendant was not repentant.[88] For Fra Marino, Girolamo could not be counted as a relapsed heretic. First, he had not completed the abjuration at all and therefore his process had not come to an official end. Second, Girolamo claimed repentance regarding the two crimes to which he was willing to confess – and, incidentally, the only two crimes about which there was some proof in the form of witness testimony. Finally, Fra Marino noted that Girolamo was a mere artisan. As Egidio Foscarari had done with Claudio da Roteglia, Fra Marino argued that a simple layman should be dealt with more leniently. 'Ignorant' people were not to be excused totally of responsibility for their religious errors but they should be treated more gently. Fra Marino placed most of the blame for the errant abjuration at the feet of Pietro, as had the tribunal. Therefore Girolamo, in Fra Marino's opinion, should not have been sentenced as a relapsed heretic.[89]

Girolamo had made another appeal concerning his case on 1 February 1544, through his new lawyer, Giuseppe Belgrado. The appeal was addressed to Cardinal Marino Grimani, patriarch of Aquileia, but was heard by his canon, Federico Belgrado. It questioned the sentence of death on the grounds that the vicar Giovanni Angelo and his tribunal had not allowed Girolamo to defend himself against the charges during the first process. Belgrado and Girolamo claimed the shoemaker had not been given copies of the testimony in order to prepare his defence, which was required in inquisitorial procedure. The sentence deemed Girolamo to be a publicly known and notorious heretic; the lawyer, Belgrado, countered that Girolamo had not been allowed to reject that assertion with testimony to the contrary that would have proved his innocence, also permissible in inquisitorial procedure. Finally, the lawyer argued, 'Because he cannot be called impenitent, for whom repenting without sinning is unjust,' and therefore the sentence should be vacated.[90]

Finally, the parties agreed to sort the case out once and for all. Girolamo was assigned a new procurator, Fra Marco Antonio; the governor Barbadico remained involved in the case to ensure that all proceeded appropriately; and Gherardo Busdrago was called in to judge the case. Busdrago was the auditor for Giovanni della Casa, the papal nuncio to Venice, who was directing heresy prosecutions there.[91] Ultimately, Busdrago decided to overturn the verdict of Giovanni Angelo, the patriarch's vicar, because of another point of inquisitorial law. According to Busdrago, Giovanni Angelo had acted contrary to the constitutions of Clement V, as promulgated at the Council of Vienne (1311–1312).[92] To prevent abuse, inquisitors were not able to imprison, torture, or pass sentences of harsh punishment without notifying the bishop first, and vice-versa.[93] Giovanni Angelo had acted alone during Girolamo's process, sentencing, and subsequent condemnation as a relapsed heretic. It does seem that Girolamo was instructed to abjure the crimes to which he had confessed before torture during the first process, and not those he later retracted.[94]

Busdrago, therefore, did not follow either Fra Marino's logic in overturning the case or the grounds that Girolamo himself had claimed – he had not been allowed a proper defence or the chance to retract his confession, as Eymeric had affirmed was the right of defendants in the fourtheenth century.[95] Instead, Busdrago overturned it on another technicality; the vicar had acted alone. Most likely Busdrago was saving face for all parties concerned, since Giovanni Angelo had to have acted with the permission of all the relevant authorities at the time. The ruling did not question Giovanni Angelo's competence directly, which could have angered the patriarch. But it is also true, based on what one can tell from the records, that Giovanni Angelo perhaps had not acted according to traditional *inquisitio* procedure concerning torture, confirmation of confessions produced by torture, and the right to a defence.

Girolamo had confessed to one or two key crimes, particularly his refusal to pay due reverence to the consecrated host. That confession, coupled with the testimonies, was enough evidence to indicate suspicion of deeper heretical beliefs and crimes. That justified the trip to the torture chamber to bring about confession of those crimes, even though witness testimony could be construed as 'single' in nature. But Girolamo had not revoked his confession at the appropriate time, although it seems he might not have been given the chance to do so. Nor had Girolamo been given the chance to prepare a defence, according to his own assertion. The session was only recorded as a summary, so it is difficult to say with certainty if Girolamo was asked to either confirm or deny the confession at least twenty-four hours later. Nevertheless, even if Girolamo had been allowed to present a defence before being put to the question, he probably still would have been tortured.

The ideas Girolamo eventually utilized during his appeal simply served to indicate suspicion of heresy even more strongly to the tribunal, since his theologically based defences firmly asserted his right to judge correct doctrine for himself according to his reading of Scripture. But if he had been tortured about the twelve articles he denied, and either refused to confess during both sessions or retracted his confession after both sessions, it is possible that his process would have ended the same way it did after Busdrago's intervention. Girolamo was most definitely not innocent, but he confessed to, and abjured, the two heretical beliefs to which he had been willing to confess all along.

Pure and Simple Answers

Not much is known of Pietro Vagnola before he arrived in Grignano, a small town near Rovigo in the Venetian mainland empire. He was a jurist from Siena and an enthusiast of Lutheran beliefs. Vagnola was quite open about his enthusiasm – he had moved to the area specifically in order to proselytize the peasants there.[96] According to a letter dated 8 March 1547, Vagnola, working as a manager for Jacopo Fogiola, was an active proselytizer, 'to be sowing Lutheran heresy with his poisonous words and false suggestions at the said estate and among very many simple rural people and seducing those same ignorant ones' away from the Catholic faith. Vagnola also had quite a few Lutheran books from which he proselytized the illiterate. For the tribunal this was clearly a case of a literate heretic leading the more ignorant astray.[97] As a corrupter of others Vagnola, in the opinion of religious officials near Rovigo, needed to be brought under control.

Since Vagnola had proselytized so widely and openly there was no shortage of witnesses capable of relating Vagnola's ideas to the tribunal. Because the compromise which lead to the Roman Inquisition's introduction to Venetian territory was being finalized at this point in 1547, the tribunal consisted of Asciano da Ferrara, vicar for the bishop of Adria; Leonardo Maggio, who held degrees in canon and civil law; the apostolic protonotary Bartolomeo Zerbitano; Fra Antonio Francesco Auximano of the Friars Minor; Fra Francesco Montepulciano, a Servite; and the Venetian *podestà* in Rovigo, Aurelio Michiel. As Giorgio, son of Antonio and originally from Padua, testified to the vicar of the bishop (whose episcopal seat was in Rovigo), Pietro had spoken to him three times about matters of faith. In the first conversation, he had told Giorgio not to go to Mass because the priests neither preached the Gospel to the people nor did they have the authority to consecrate the host. Vagnola also denied the validity of praying to saints, indulgences, and suffrages for the dead, and taught that working on a feast day was not a sin. Finally, according to Pietro, 'one should not confess or say his sins neither to friars nor to priests, but that one should confess with the mouth to God with the mind or the heart.' [98]

Giovanni Battista, another witness, added that Pietro did not go to Mass and decried the elevation of the host. On those presumably few occasions Vagnola did attend Mass, 'he did not move his hat, nor make any other reverence' when the consecrated host was raised.[99] Tommaso Barberio, a labourer, also said that he never saw Pietro attend Mass, but that he frequented preaching in the local churches. According to Tommaso, Pietro had complained that 'a priest with a concubine or rogue cannot consecrate the host during Mass.' Pietro also denied indulgences and the authority of the pope.[100] Although there were some differences between the different testimonies, at least six of the deponents agreed as to Pietro's specific beliefs and actions.

Yet the local tribunal would engage in a great deal of correspondence with the Venetian tribunal about Pietro Vagnola's case. Aurelio Michiel, Asciano da Ferrara, and other personages involved in the process would find themselves in need of clarification – but not about proof of heresy, since that was clear enough. What they needed to know was how properly to utilize torture and how much of a confession was necessary as a prelude to punishment. Despite Vagnola's protestations that he and the tribunal really should agree religiously, once it became clear that the tribunal thought him in the wrong he was still quite reluctant to let go of his Lutheran and Erasmian ideas.

Pietro was arrested and imprisoned on the same day as the above testimonies were taken, 8 March 1547. In his first interrogation on 9 March, Vagnola, now rather famously, declared that his beliefs were in accord with those of the tribunal, and 'according to the laws of justice, [the tribunal] will judge me and liberate me as innocent.'[101] First, the tribunal wanted to know about Vagnola's educational background; it learned that Pietro had studied natural philosophy and for eight years had studied law in Venice. There he had met Giacomo Fogiola at the Rialto and had moved to Fogiola's estate to study Scripture. While Vagnola asserted his attendance at preaching and vespers, and wanted to discuss how he had told the workers that their good works would be useless without faith and a sincere appreciation for Christ's sacrifice, the tribunal wanted to know: 'Do [you] go to Mass every morning? To feasts?' While Pietro might have been able to verbally reconcile his beliefs with the tribunal's, his refusal to attend Mass clearly stood out as unambiguous. Pietro attempted to explain that he had done so because of certain scruples in his conscience; he objected to 'evil priests who administer [Mass] many times for greed and profit.'[102]

On 10 March, Pietro clarified his position. The priest in Grignano kept a concubine, and Vagnola had heard from Antonio Falasco that priests should not consecrate the host the morning after having had a woman. Vagnola also admitted that it had been more than a year since he had taken communion at San Polo and confessed to a priest at San Lio, both in Venice. He denied thinking that sacerdotal confession was unnecessary. Vagnola thought people should mentally confess to God, then go to the priest for the sacrament and absolution, a formulation that came startlingly close to describing an individual's full examination of conscience before seeing a priest, which would be encouraged of Catholic faithful by good confessors after the Council of Trent.[103]

Vagnola also claimed to uphold papal authority, but he was accused of criticizing indulgences. He admitted that 'it is true, several times that I saw the sale of indulgences I murmured [about] them and they scandalized me.' He also explained his evolving belief in purgatory. According to Pietro, initially he could not find evidence of purgatory in Scripture, a fact he had passed along in conversation. But since that time, happily, he had found such evidence in Paul.[104] Much of his testimony proceeded in this way; Vagnolo gave answers that apparently he believed were acceptable to the tribunal as orthodox.

For example, when he had spoken of the invocation of the saints, Vagnolo admitted he had said that the saints did not go to Christ on behalf of their postulants. He had said, however, 'that the saints are members of Christ' and that one should not consider them to be 'spirits in the sky separate from the body of Christ;' therefore they did not 'go' to intercede with Christ in a physical sense.[105] This was not so much of a declaration of clear philo-Protestant doctrine as more of an educated perspective of the nature of souls after death and their relationship to Christ. The tribunal even might have agreed that he had a point, but there was one key difference between themselves and Pietro. Vagnolo was an educated person seeking to make his own religious decisions and interpretations utilizing his reading of the Gospel and he also avoided Mass and the sacraments performed by a priest he considered to be unworthy. Although he acknowledged the Church's right to require fasting during Lent and promote suffrages for the dead, he also claimed the right to read Scripture and form his own religious judgment. In his interrogations he attempted to speak to the tribunal as an equal.

While in prison, most likely unsolicited, Vagnola sent the tribunal document after document he thought attested to his genuinely Catholic belief. By 3 April 1547, the local tribunal was willing to let Vagnola out of prison as long as he paid three hundred gold ducats as a surety.[106] Asciano of Ferrara and the rest of the tribunal also acknowledged that they were in something of a stalemate with Vagnola, since he was refusing to confess that he was wrong and not Catholic.

To instruct the tribunal in Rovigo about the situation, once again Gherardo Busdrago, auditor to the nuncio Giovanni della Casa, was consulted; after reading the dossier thus far, he told Asciano and his staff in Rovigo that they had proceeded incorrectly. Vagnola, according to Busdrago, clearly was infected with heresy and 'perverse fantasies.' If Vagnola did not wish 'to confess his error fully,' which could be found in the testimonies of witnesses, he should be taken to 'rigorous examination.' He therefore should be warned that in a day or two he would be put to the question if he did not 'purely and simply' confess the truth. The local tribunal should be present for the examination, and the notary should record all things diligently. Neither the governor, nor any representative of the secular arm, should be present, since they had no official place in the proceedings due to lack of jurisdictional competence. On 22 April 1547, the Roman Inquisition agreed to allow the papal nuncio, the patriarch or his designated vicar, and three Venetian laymen from the secular government sit on the inquisitorial tribunal. But under the medieval structure, laymen did not have the right to sit in the tribunal; since Busdrago's letter was dated 1 April 1547, his assertion that the *podestà* should not have been in attendance was technically still true, although he had not objected to the same situation in Udine in 1544.[107]

When the local tribunal sent its functionaries to cite Vagnola and order him to present himself before the tribunal, they found that he had fled; as Bartholomeo Zerbitanus (Bartholomew the Serbian), one of the religious consultants, helpfully wrote in the dossier records in October of 1547, this made Vagnola suspect of heresy, contumacious, and excommunicated from the church. By November, Vagnola had returned to the tribunal's custody, and again there was a great deal of subsequent discussion as to how to proceed. Busdrago sent another missive to Rovigo and advised that if the tribunal could proceed 'in the way of the sacred canons' and avoid previous errors, then 'good and customary justice with the satisfaction of everyone and the praise of omnipotent God' would be achieved.[108] Other consultants weighed in advising how to proceed, including Jacopo Facino of Feltre, Francesco Campagnella, and Fabio Bonifacio.

Therefore, in November and December the witnesses were called to the tribunal to repeat their testimony. Much of the questioning, however, concerned events that may have occurred after Vagnola was released on bail. While many of the witnesses repeated their testimony about what Pietro had said and done before he was arrested, Giovanni Battista maintained that after Vagnola had been released once again he had failed to lift his hat and perform due reverence when passing an image of the Virgin Mary, even though Giacomo and other companions had done so. In Giovanni Battista's opinion, this had to have been a deliberate omission. Jacopo Zagus, testifying on the same day, reported that Vagnola had not lifted his hat in due reverence to the Virgin when passing an image of her painted on the side of a certain Raul's house. During a Mass said more recently, Pietro had stood near the baptismal font but almost no one who was there and interviewed by the tribunal in Rovigo saw him clearly enough to know whether or not he lifted his hat during the elevation of the host. Jacopo Zagus also reported that Vagnola's friends had attempted to sway testimony a few days before the process began again; Zuane Barbiero had wanted Zagus to say he had lied in his first interrogation. Other than Zagus and Giovanni Battista no one could say they had seen Pietro definitively acting like a 'Lutheran' during Mass.[109] But it is possible that Pietro strategically placed himself next to the baptismal font at Mass so as not to be seen. It is also possible that Pietro's friends had done their work well and the town's population was a bit too intimidated to testify fully about the incident.

Therefore on 13 January 1548, the tribunal in Rovigo turned their attention to questioning Vagnola himself again. They told Pietro that he had been put back in prison not as punishment but simply to keep him in custody during the new process. He also was warned to answer all of the questions put to him 'purely and simply,' echoing the phrase Busdrago had used when advising the tribunal as to how to proceed in April of 1547. Vagnola was presented with fifteen points that were a summary of his heretical statements and actions from the first phase of his process; then they added that after he had left prison he had not been seen making reverence to the host at Mass. Pietro also was warned that unless he confessed 'purely and simply' he would be tortured. By 18 January 1548, Pietro had written another missive to the tribunal attempting to explain himself. In this document, for the first time, he expressed penitence and remorse and confessed that 'I know my greatest error [that I made] was having talked of these things with rustic and ignorant persons.' But regarding the accusations of neglecting due reverence, Pietro asserted – unconvincingly – that he had merely forgotten.[110]

The next day, the tribunal in Rovigo brought Pietro into the bishop's palace to question him in person. For most of the accusations, the notary simply recorded a one-word affirmative response next to the appropriate number – very much a pure and simple answer. Regarding the new charge Pietro simply said that he did not remember whether or not he had lifted his hat when passing images of the Madonna or during Mass. When admonished to tell the truth again 'purely and simply,' Pietro admitted that he had not performed the traditional reverence but that 'I have venerated it with the heart.' Admonished again, Pietro simply said that he had done so inconsiderately and not contemptuously.[111]

In the interrogation held on 20 January, the tribunal was even more draconian in their admonitions to answer 'purely and simply.' The formerly effusive Vagnola, who had written page after page explaining how his ideas were essentially Catholic and in agreement with the tribunal's, was reduced to answers of four or five words: an affirmation, a denial, or a claim of forgetfulness. Anytime Pietro seemed as if he were about to launch into a long explanation or excuse, the tribunal stopped him and admonished him to produce 'pure and simple' answers. For example, when Vagnola claimed, 'I don't remember if I raised my hat to the image of the Madonna because I don't remember seeing any images of the Madonna,' the tribunal once again 'admonished that he should respond purely and simply.'[112]

The Rovigo tribunal took Gherardo Busdrago's advice so seriously that they effectively shut down Vagnola's rhetoric completely. And when brought to the torture room, Pietro confessed to preaching that priests did not have the authority to consecrate the host and that it was not legitimate to venerate images of saints, two accusations he had denied up to this point. He also finally admitted he had not venerated the host or the image of Mary after he had been let go the first time. Afterwards, Vagnola genuflected and begged the inquisitor, 'as [his] pastor,' to show mercy, although it does seem that the tribunal considered the possibility of execution due to pertinacity.[113]

Vagnola, as the correspondence of Giovanni Andrea Ferraro, chaplain and curator of the church in Grignano (who made no mention of having a mistress) informed Busdrago, made his abjuration in the church after preaching, to assuage the scandalized population in attendance.[114] The ultimate truth was achieved by the tribunal's implementation of Busdrago's instructions to make Vagnola answer 'simply and purely' instead of continuing to give Vagnola a platform on which to explain how his beliefs were Catholic and in accordance with their own. In the end, however, Vagnola's true penitence was achieved after a visit to the torture chamber – whether or not his religious ideas were Catholic was not his decision to make, but the tribunal's, and his repeated refusals to perform ritual practices with reverence clearly marked him as heretical.

Confession: The Nature of Religious Truth

The Roman Inquisition utilized torture to elicit confessions – ideally confessions in which the inquisitors' right to judge religious orthodoxy was fully acknowledged. Those who confessed to believing in heresy for the first time, and confessed that the church was right to judge those beliefs as heretical, could expect to be reconciled, even if torture had been employed to produce that confession. As Francisco Peña explained to his audience, since the confession was the 'queen of proof,' it was the tribunal's job to make sure that the confession was as accurate and complete as possible. Torture not only could be useful in eliciting confessions; it also could also be utilized to make sure that greater heretical crimes had not been committed, especially if relapse seemed likely.

The contrast between mercy and punishment, then, animated this phase of the process as well. Torture to gain as full and complete a confession as possible was meant both to protect the Catholic community and ensure the spiritual health of the defendant in question. Inquisition manual authors and inquisitors, however, were aware that physical pain was not necessarily a foolproof guarantee of truth. But the only possible solution to that problem in the inquisitorial system lay in making sure of the quality of the evidence from witnesses, and in attempting to control the use of torture carefully. If a first-time defendant was tortured on two separate occasions without confessing to the accusations uncovered during the investigation, then those accusations could be considered overcome.

That also could be true for single accusations as well – which highlights the complexities of applying torture in specific cases. In two of the processes discussed above, tribunals used torture to reconcile what they considered to be conflicting evidence. Pietro Curioni was willing to admit that he had not believed in purgatory, or the intervention of the saints, or the efficacy of indulgences, but he insisted that he had always gone to confession, communion, and Mass. Given the Modena tribunal's full knowledge of heterodox Lord's Supper ceremonies in the town, the tribunal was not willing to take those assertions at face value; they used torture to confirm that Curioni had not committed greater crimes. For Girolamo, the shoemaker in Udine, the outcome was eventually the same. He only had been willing to confess to two heresies, but the tribunal was convinced that, as an associate of open iconoclasts, his list of heresies had to be longer. Torture and fear induced a fourteen-point confession on Girolamo's part, but that confession was not allowed to stand. In the end, both Curioni and Girolamo only abjured those errors to which they were willing to confess.

Admitting some wrongdoing and demonstrating at least some willingness of correction was key, however. Pietro Vagnola and Zuanbattista Sambeni caused the tribunals in Venice and Rovigo no end of problems because both insisted that they had as much a right to judge religious truth as the inquisitors. Vagnola, prosecuted for the first time, finally expressed repentance and culpability when brought to the torture room and abjured as a penitent heretic submissive to the tribunal and Church.

Sambeni, prosecuted for the second time, was relapsed; therefore only the state of his soul was at stake. The Venetian tribunal was unable to reconcile the unrepentant Sambeni despite two rounds of torture.

Vagnola's and Sambeni's processes both contained elements of ritual practice as well. Vagnola was known in his community for attending preaching but avoiding Mass, and even when out on bail while the tribunal debated what to do about his lack of confession was unable to resist publicly refusing to reverence the consecrated host and Virgin Mary. Sambeni, although he insisted he had confessed and communed in Venice, was also known to have attended services at the Protestant church in Chiavenna. In this he differed from Curioni, whose process turned up no evidence of alternative religious practices. But Sambeni's process was also emblematic of manual authors' and tribunals' worst fears – a false abjurer who attempted to cover his heretical conversations with a confession or two. It was that kind of quasi-Nicodemite behaviour that worried tribunals, and led to manual authors decrying the duplicitous natures of lying heretics.

Chapter Seven

Mind and Body: The Opportunity for Redemption

When a process was brought to a successful conclusion, the inquisitorial tribunal rendered judgment and assigned a fitting punishment. Because the inquisitorial justice system only executed completely impenitent and relapsed heretics, most of the time tribunals were confronted with the dilemma of reintegrating repentant defendants back into the Catholic Church. In a sense, it was the prospect of sentencing and reintegrating the penitent who recanted heresy that guided the process from the first questioning and made eliciting as full and complete a confession as possible a necessity. The duality between mercy and punishment, or between religious conversion and legal punishment, concerned manual authors because it was in developing theoretical guidelines of what should constitute appropriate sentences that the tension between those ideals came to the fore. Legally, defendants who confessed and were convicted of the public crime of heresy ought to be publicly punished for it, manual authors agreed. Religiously, the penitent deserved to be welcomed back into the arms of the Catholic Church mercifully (sometimes even to the point of sparing the penitent public punishment). But what was simultaneously punishment and penitence had to be structured in such a way as to give contrite defendants their chance at redemption without endangering the wider Catholic community. In the reality of sixteenth-century processes, tribunals in north-central Italy availed themselves of ritual practice to accomplish both punishment and, it was hoped, rehabilitation.

The ways in which manuals in theory, and tribunals in reality, categorized repentant defendants initially had developed in the medival period, as had much of inquisition procedure. In late sixteenth and early seventeenth-century manuals, it was generally accepted that first-time penitents could be classified according to three or four different levels of severity: lightly suspect in heresy (*suspectus de levi*), vehemently suspect in heresy (*suspectus de vehementi*), and formal heresy (*haeresis formali*) were the three most commonly used in practice. The fourth, violently suspect in heresy (*suspectus de violentia*) was included in many manuals. That terminology, however, reflected a slight modification of medieval terms; furthermore, post-Tridentine manual authors updated definitions of what constituted each level of severity to include philo-Protestant 'words and deeds.' And for each level of severity there was a corresponding range of punishments. These were meant to be exemplary to the larger Catholic community, as has often been discussed, and therefore a clear warning to everyone not to engage in heresy or discuss heretical doctrines. For this same reason, those who were convicted as vehemently suspect in heresy, or of formal heresy, were required to decry their heresies in public, in the form of an abjuration. The lightly suspect, according to Francisco Peña among others, could abjure in the bishop's palace or the tribunal's seat if his or her crimes had not been committed publicly. But public offences required public admissions of wrongdoing.[1]

Often these public statements of guilt and repentance were made during *autos da fé* in which the multitude, both clerical and lay, would observe the spectacle of groups of people judged suspect in heresy ritually expiating the scandal of their public heresies through abjurations while wearing a yellow penitential habit called an *abitello*. Convicted defendants left at large in the community also, in theory, were expected to continue wearing their penitential habits over their clothing for a certain number of years, thereby serving as a continuous warning to the Catholic community, although the Congregation of Cardinals in Rome was known to waive or forgive the requirement for a variety of reasons.[2] Such heightened scrutiny, additionally, could have been meant as a kind of collective surveillance by the community for its own benefit, since inquisitors and other clergy simply could not watch every convicted suspect in heresy on a daily basis, especially in urban areas. Given that witnesses in the community testified to provide evidence of heresy in the first place, the yellow penitential habit, if worn, and the public abjuration served the purpose of drawing the attention of the community of the faithful, who could collectively ensure that such violations, if not the heretical thoughts behind them, did not happen again.

It was in proposing guidelines for sentencing that late sixteenth- and seventeenth-century manual authors stressed Catholic ritual practice as a key component – the more serious the ritual violations, the more elaborate the penance (although manuals listed a number of options concerning appropriate punishment, including fines as well). In the mid-sixteenth century tribunals opted to assign punishments firmly grounded in Catholic ritual practice; in that sense, the manuals might well reflect what had become established practice and technique since the Middle Ages. In fact most of the punishments assigned to the guilty and repentant involved the performance of Catholic ritual practices for several years past the conviction, regularly supervised by priests of whom the tribunal approved, and sometimes by the tribunal itself. What was both punishment and salutary penance, therefore, also was an attempt at continued surveillance, it was hoped, carried out by a conscientious confessor.

It was in assigning these salutary penances that inquisitors and confessors, ideally, collaborated to protect the community, although daily clerical surveillance was most likely a practical impossibility. Although the internal forum (*foro interno*) of the confessional and the external forum (*foro externo*) of inquisitorial justice were in theory separate areas of jurisdiction, in practice there was a relationship between the two, although the extent and nature of that relationship has been the subject of much historical debate, as will be discussed more extensively below. But inquisitors were authorized to dispense absolution in both forums (*in utroque foro*) to convicted heretical suspects when ending the process.[3] The punishments, and oftentimes what constituted clerical oversight of them, provided another point of convergence between the internal and external forums. Heresy, as defined theoretically within inquisition manuals, contained an inherent element of mental error joined to certain characteristic behaviours and outward expression. And while manual authors fully acknowledged that punishment was intended to be both a public example to others and an expiation of public sin, the assignment of ritual penance also indicated that mid-sixteenth century tribunals were concerned with offering at least the *opportunity* of spiritual rehabilitation, which derived from a long-held principle of Catholic theology. The salutary penances assigned as punishment thus were multivalent and simultaneously served a variety of purposes.

'Heretics ought to be gathered and compelled'

Although the forms of penance in the later sixteenth century followed distinctive patterns and adaptations, they were grounded in long-standing Catholic tradition. The rationale for the use of corrective force had become a part of Catholic theology through Augustine's writings against the Donatists, particularly his Letters 93 and 185. The Donatists, as Peter Brown has explained, thought that sin could have no part in the Christian Church. According to the Donatists, bishops who had collaborated with Roman officials during the last persecution, that of Diocletian in 303–305, by handing over Scripture to be burnt were no longer worthy of possessing any spiritual authority. The Donatists therefore replaced the collaborator bishop of Carthage, Caecilian, with a 'pure' candidate, who was soon succeeded by Donatus. The sect also believed that sacraments, such as baptism, when performed by unworthy clergy were invalid and needed to be repeated by a worthy priest or bishop if the unworthy state of the first officiator was discovered later. Thus, for inquisition manual authors in the late sixteenth and early seventeenth centuries, the Donatists were the precursors of the Anabaptists, who were obviously, according to the polemical arguments in the manuals, reviving an old heresy dealt with long ago. This was also the template example that laid out the theoretical logic pertaining to how such convicted suspects should be punished and given the opportunity to reach salvation, which Augustine had formulated over a thousand years previously.

The Christian Church in Africa was in a state of schism until Augustine's time and, in fact, the Donatist Church was numerically superior to Augustine's orthodox Catholic Church, approved of by Rome.[4] To solve the problems of schism and heresy Augustine had approved of the use of force to compel Donatists to attend orthodox Catholic services; punishments included taking away legal rights, confiscating church property, exiling Donatist leaders, and physically beating slaves and peasants. Augustine justified such force through his interpretation of Luke 14:6–24, which described the parable of the great supper and for which the Latin Vulgate utilizes the phrase *compelle intrare* ('compel [them] to come in'). But, as Frederick J. Russell has argued, in Letters 93 and 185 Augustine utilized the Vetus Latina, the pre-Jerome Latin translation of the Bible, and consequently the phrase *cogo intrare*, which can mean 'collect' or 'gather' as well as 'force.' Through discipline (*disciplina*), according to Augustine, people could be led to correct doctrine and belief; by gathering heretics and schismatics in the church, even if forcibly, they might be led to thinking about (*cogito*) and internalizing the doctrines (*doctrina*) of the orthodox Catholic Church. Through force, the Donatists and other heretics could be given the opportunity to absorb and believe correct doctrine – in other words, to experience conversion.[5] This entire line of reasoning would be used to justify the use of torture, salutary penances, and even the death penalty by inquisitions in later centuries.

The Roman Inquisition's specific historical and cultural circumstances were a bit different than those in Augustine's time. Augustine had to confront a Donatist population larger than that of his own orthodox congregation brought unwillingly to his church by imperial law and hope for their subsequent conversion. All inquisitions since the thirteenth century, including the Roman Inquisition, dispensed punishments to those who professed to have experienced conversion already during their processes. Yet Prospero Farinacci, writing twelve hundred years after Augustine, utilized the same terminology to describe the punishment to be meted out to heretical offenders: 'heretics ought to be gathered and compelled [*cogendi et compellendi sunt*], so that they may be returned to the faith, even if having been instilled in them by fear of death.' Farinacci's source for this was the papal bull *Ad abolendam*, the founding bull of medieval inquisitions promulgated by Lucius III in 1184 and, as Farinacci asserted, commonly accepted by all doctors of the church.[6]

It was Konrad Braun, however, whose work both Peña and Farinacci utilized as a source, who fully explained his interpretation of the historical context of Augustine's methods concerning the Donatists and the appropriate application of those methods, with a few modifications, to his own day. His two works, *Libri sex de haereticis in genere* and *Breve introductione de haeretici*, were printed in the late 1540s and addressed the question of why those who were heretically suspect should be compelled back into the church. Braun addressed why he thought Augustine's ideas were theologically sound even though the apostles had not recommended forced church attendance (in the overtly worded sense) in the New Testament. According to Braun, even if inspired by fear of pain or death the stated desire to repent and (re)convert to orthodox Catholicism was deserving of the inquisition's mercy. Therefore the punishments the tribunals assigned to such defendants were meant to encourage the continuation of that conversion.[7]

Augustine, as Russell has discussed, saw forced attendance in orthodox churches as a means of encouraging internal conversions through sustained 'external pressure' or 'behavioural modification.' Imperial law kept the Donatists from the temptations of continued sin and error, so that Scripture, preaching, the sacraments, and ritual practice could give them the *opportunity* to come to the truth.[8] During inquisition processes beginning in the mid-sixteenth century, tribunals assigned punishments which functioned in much the same way. Convicted suspects assigned salutary penance would be kept from the temptation to engage in heresy again through the mandatory use of orthodox ritual practices. And with the more seriously heretical marked publicly and ritually through the abjuration it was possible that the wider Catholic community could join in the process of behavioural modification through external pressure. Both the clergy and the laity should monitor closely the rehabilitative process, while the repentant heretics performed the public punishment/penance that corresponded to their public sins.

Manual authors, however, even if only theoretically, had to acknowledge that even with salutary penance encouraging orthodox faith such conversions might not have occurred. Relapsed heretics, or those who had confessed and abjured at the end of one process only to be caught in heresy again, obviously had managed to feign penitence once before. It was theoretically possible that anyone who had been subjected to an inquisitorial investigation, whether they were judged lightly or more seriously heretical in that first process, could turn out to be relapsed at a later date; the issue was one of probability. Those who were absolved because there was not enough evidence to prove the case, for example, presented little danger of relapse, while the vehemently suspect presented a greater danger of relapse. Absolution was almost entirely merciful, as was canonical purgation, because a lack of evidence warranted an abundance of mercy. But as the charges, crimes, and resulting salutary penances grew more serious what constituted mercy for such defendants was proportionally less. The balance shifted from religious mercy to legal punishment, but neither mercy nor rehabilitation were entirely forgotten.

The judgments that were most clear and least troubling to manual authors, therefore, were those at the extremes of the system. Impenitent heretics and relapsed heretics were to be turned over to the secular arm to be burned alive, as was commonly held by all canonists, inquisitorial authors, and theologians.[9] Innocence was possible, according to Eymeric, but should be rare; the more common sentence should be absolution. It was the appropriate end to a process when there had been no confession or conviction because no legitimate testimony, nor facts in evidence, had proved the case, and no other suspicion of heresy or public reputation for heresy remained. Thus, Eymeric declared, the defendant was 'totally immune' regarding the crime.[10] But 'immune,' and the consequent absolution, was meant to declare that nothing was proved regarding the case, which was not quite the same as completely innocent. The defendant was let go without any further penalties, but if he or she was tried again for the same heresies because new proof had come to light, then a prior judgment of absolution could not obstruct a new verdict of condemnation. Inquisition verdicts of nothing being proven and absolution, therefore, could not constitute double jeopardy – being tried for the exact same set of crimes twice.[11] As Prospero Farinacci put it succinctly in his early seventeenth-century manual, 'because in the crime of heresy, no one ought to be absolved as innocent [. . .].[12] Even when it came to dealing with those whose cases had not produced much if any proof of heresy, inquisitorial authors included a 'fail-safe' measure to guard against the possibility that the defendant in question was, in fact, heretically suspect. Either full proof just had not existed at the time of that process, or that suspect had committed the same crimes again after leaving the courtroom. Either way, the inquisitorial system accounted for the fact that a lack of evidence did not mean, necessarily, a lack of danger to the Catholic community in the future.

As Peña explained to his readers in his late sixteenth-century commentary concerning Eymeric's text, the 'fail-safe' explicitly was intended to overcome the legal opinion of many, including Juan de Rojas and Simancas, who believed sentences never could 'cross over' in judicial proceedings – the authors' expression for double jeopardy. Peña did not name who was in favour of double jeopardy, but the discussion had been brought to a close by Pius V (former inquisitor general Michele Ghislieri) in a papal rescript entitled *Inter multiplices curas*, which declared that sentences from one process in inquisitorial courts could not be carried over to another.[13] Farinacci also emphasized that the case would be considered 'unproved' if the defendant in question did not confess under torture but even those circumstances did not prevent any future processes from leading to a condemnation.[14] He brought up the one exception to the rule: false witness. Anyone who was the victim of false denunciation or false testimony could truly be declared 'innocent' in every sense of the word (as Zuane Finetti was declared innocent in Venice in 1566–1567).[15]

Inquisitors had another option for absolving those against whom the case had not been fully proved: canonical purgation. All the same conditions as described above applied except that the defendant, for whatever reason, had a public reputation for heresy in the community, although there were no firm indications of suspicion of heresy. Again, this sentence was not one of complete innocence, but absolution, and the defendant in question had to swear solemnly that he or she had not engaged in heresy, supported by *compurgatores*, or 'purifiers,' willing to guarantee his or her behaviour.[16] And according to Peña's commentaries, a public reputation for heresy could exist at two levels of severity: lightly and vehemently. Those who were purged of a vehement public reputation for heresy could, if they were caught again in exactly the same kind of heresy (not the exact same crime) for which they first had been tried unsuccessfully, be tried again as relapsed heretics. Peña was careful to instruct his readers that this was only true if the kind of heresy was exactly the same; if caught committing a different heresy, the person who had been canonically purged, even vehemently, was not considered relapsed. In addition, those who had been purged of a light public reputation for heresy would not be considered relapsed but tried again for continuing heretical belief.[17] Peña, past a certain point, thought that those who had generated suspicion publicly were too inherently dangerous to absolve because the case remained at that time unproven. He recommended a sentence that would allow more severe sanctions if it turned out that the defendant in question had been heretical after all.

Farinacci, furthermore, specified that those who refused to purge themselves of the public infamy for heresy in the Catholic community, or who could not find 'purifiers' willing to swear on their behalf, could be punished instead. That judgment and penance should only take place after the defendant in question had been excommunicated for over a year, as specified in Innocent IV's 1254 edict *Noverit universitas* and Nicholas IV's restatement of the same principle in 1281. If the defendant in question who had refused to purge himself or herself still refused to do so after a year of excommunication then he or she would be condemned as a heretic, and an impenitent one at that.[18] But whether that meant executing such obstinate defendants was another question, and a rather controversial one. The *Repertorium Inquisitorum* and Hostensis presented arguments against it, since 'this is presumptive proof and not true [proof].'[19] Just as many other authors, if not more, however, held a refusal to undergo purgation as grounds for death, and even those who argued against it acknowledged that it was possible. According to Farinacci, in theory inquisitors could resort to sentencing the defendant who neglected to undergo purgation to perpetual incarceration (in reality, often only a few years).[20] Finally, if the defendant responded to these options by producing a confession, then he or she should not be turned over to the secular arm but abjured and assigned a salutary penance instead.[21]

Even those who were to be canonically purged in theory could be executed or imprisoned if they denied the need to 'purge' the public shame of the stain of heresy or could not find supporters to uphold their reputations as Catholics. In all likelihood the threat of such punishments was probably intended to produce a confession instead, assuming that scruples of conscience lay behind the refusal to undergo purgation. Similarly, Farinacci thought that those who underwent purgation could be considered relapsed heretics in certain circumstances but sharply discouraged use of the death penalty as punishment then as well.[22] Noncompliance, after all, only indicated the presence of some error or heresy through an absence of cooperation, not the firm proof of a confession. But the inquisitorial system had a few safeguards in place if those they absolved or canonically purged turned out to be much more heretical than the available proof had indicated at the time of the first process.

Conversely, manual authors theoretically recommended mercy, in some form, to those condemned to death if they were penitent, although this too was controversial. Could penitent relapsed heretics have their sentences of death commuted to 'perpetual' incarceration?[23] Peña thought such a commutation appropriate when the relapsed heretic in question had come forward of his or her own volition.[24] There was also some disagreement among manual authors as to what really constituted 'relapsed' status. But Farinacci and Carena thought it generally accepted that only those who had been abjured for formal heresy at the conclusion of their first processes, and were at least vehemently suspect of heresy in their second processes, or vice versa, would be considered fully relapsed.[25] As Carena summarized, if the defendant had been abjured of formal heresy once and subsequently was convicted of being vehemently suspect in heresy, then deeming him or her a relapsed heretic was something of a 'legal fiction.' The official verdict had been 'suspect in heresy,' not 'heretic.'[26] But that legal fiction existed for the better protection of the Catholic community. Some manual authors were more severe and asserted that if the previously abjured person was caught associating with other heretics again, usually considered a light indication, tribunals still should pursue judgment as a relapsed heretic, for example.[27] They argued that the defendant in question was clearly signalling his or her intent to continue in heresy, willingly, despite having been given the opportunity to reform. Most manual authors, however, did not consider the lightly suspect eligible to be sentenced as relapsed heretics, although Carena admonished his readers to punish such light multiple offenders 'more gravely.'[28]

As Carena conveyed to his readers penitent relapsed heretics should be deserving of small mercies even though they had successfully deceived the church once before.[29] Farinacci reminded his readers that it was customary to execute even penitent relapsed heretics since their penitence had no bearing on temporal punishment; the effects of the defendant's penitence were considered to be purely spiritual. Mercy, for both Carena and Farinacci, would consist of allowing the penitent relapsed to receive the sacraments of confession and the Eucharist before execution and a death by strangulation before burning. In theory, tribunals had a responsibility to see to the disposition of the heretic's soul after death.[30] Eymeric, writing two and a half centuries before Farinacci, had expressed the same idea. Furthermore, even the impenitent should be given every chance to embrace that spiritual mercy. Execution, according to Peña's commentaries, should be delayed for a few days in order to give the impenitent one last chance to turn back from the eternal damnation that would surely follow execution.[31]

At the extreme ends of manual authors' theoretical reasoning concerning punishment, the need to be both merciful and protect the community affected how they constructed models of ideal sentences and procedures for execution, abjuration, canonical purgation, and absolution. Which principle was most in evidence was determined by their perceptions of the danger each defendant presented to the Catholic community. Most cases that came before the Roman Inquisition's tribunals in the later sixteenth century in reality did not warrant judgments at either end of the spectrum. The most commonly processed cases ended in defendants being judged as either lightly or vehemently suspect in heresy, or of formal heresy, in which penitence, punishment, rehabilitation, and the protection of the wider Catholic community were all fairly balanced as relevant factors at the end of the process.

It was Farinacci who noted to his readers that tribunals should be careful not to call these defendants heretics either in the written sentences or verbally during the abjuration process. Heretics were pertinacious – they refused to recant – and these defendants had confessed their errors and were assumed to be penitent.[32] Peña, updating Eymeric's definitions in his commentaries, described light suspicion to mean that the person in question had only committed acts or said words that gave rise to suspicion of heresy rarely instead of frequently.[33] Peña also thought that only those whose crimes had been 'secret' should be abjured lightly and therefore in the bishop's palace or the seat of the tribunal.[34] One who was lightly suspect did not need to be made an example of publicly, nor subjected to close public scrutiny; the implication of both Eymeric's and Peña's definitions was that the lightly suspect had little real contact with or commitment to heretical belief.

Eymeric described the differences between abjurations as vehemently or violently suspect, but Peña updated the categorizations and gave examples of what had come to constitute each level by his own time. Eymeric described what he felt constituted the vehemently suspect – those who favoured heretics, or impeded their apprehension, or received them, or defended them, could be considered vehemently suspect of heresy.[35] In another chapter of his manual, Eymeric described at length the activities in which those who supported heretics engaged. In short, Eymeric was describing the distinction between Cathar perfect or Waldensian *barbes* and those that supported them materially.[36] Heretical clergy, or those who genuinely believed in the perfect or *barbes* (*credentes*), were characterized as violently suspect. Eymeric thought that those violently suspect of heresy would engage in the *consolamentum*, or 'consolation,' and reverence heretics. In fact, for Eymeric, anything 'that pertains to their rites' should be adjucated as violently suspect.[37]

Peña once again consulted other sources to explain Eymeric's meaning in his commentaries and then added a few examples of his own. For Peña, those who were vehemently suspect engaged in heretical words or deeds frequently as opposed to rarely, a concept for which Peña cited Jean Gerson (who had written in the early fifteenth century). In so doing, Peña gave an example of an action that, if repeated frequently without an appropriate explanation, would indicate vehement suspicion of heresy: eating meat on prohibited days.[38] Violent suspicion of heresy, as defined by Peña in consultation with Gerson's writings, remained the same. Those who attended or employed the rites of heretics or other religions, but who were willing to confess and reform, were violently suspect in heresy. Peña utilized the example of 'he who crosses over or returns to the rites of Jews' to illustrate his point.[39]

Peña's explanations provided something of a history of heresies encountered by inquisitions. The binary division between perfect and followers, characteristic of medieval Catholic descriptions of Catharism and Waldensianism, had served as one example, as had the phenomenon of converted Jews or Muslims committing apostasy. Regarding philo-Protestantism, Peña singled out violating the canonical norms for fasting as pertinent and relevant. Over time, the standard for judging culpability had been adapted to combine frequency with severity; and severity was defined according to the standard of ritual practice. As for Eymeric's descriptions concerning exactly how to punish defenders, receivers, and favourers, Peña rather testily claimed that Eymeric could not be expected to describe every possible set of circumstances that could come up in inquisitorial processes – therefore Peña himself would refrain from attempting to do so as well.[40]

Eliseo Masini represented the fullest expression of that adaptation when he explained all three levels of abjuration in his work, *Sacro Arsenale* (1621). Masini addressed the question of exactly what practices and statements constituted each level of suspected guilt more thoroughly than his fellow late sixteenth- and early seventeenth-century authors, in that he gave his readers comprehensive lists of crimes for each category rather than one or two examples, perhaps a manifestation of his practical experience as an inquisitor. Concerning those to be lightly abjured Masini simply, as an exemplar form of a sentence and abjuration, asserted that those who said heretical words, but denied believing them in their hearts, qualified as 'lightly suspect.' In fact, those who had said such things probably had only done so for a 'joke,' which other authors also advised could be taken under consideration as a mitigating circumstance.[41]

The list of actions and words that constituted vehement suspicion of heresy, however, was much longer and no laughing matter. Those who blasphemed God or the Virgin Mary; those who did not hear Mass on feast days as commanded by the Church; those who said that the Mass did not conform to the precepts of the Holy Mother Church; those who avoided sacramental confession; those who ate meat during times in which it was prohibited by the Church; those who did not make reverence to sacred images; and those who denied purgatory were all to be considered vehemently suspect. All of those crimes related to Catholic ritual practice.[42]

Those who were violently suspect of heresy, according to Masini, were people who had committed actions that were even more injurious to the true faith, or who had explicitly confessed themselves to be followers of a particular heretic or sect. Even Masini, briefly, explained to his readers that violent suspects of heresy not only talked to heretics but also venerated them and asked them for the 'consolation,' although he did not explain any of these terms or their original frame of reference.[43] More appropriate to Masini's time were his explanations that those who were violently suspect in heresy would smash sacred images; refuse to believe in transubstantiation; dissuade people from performing good works, saying they were not necessary for salvation; or would 'have with the heart renounced the holy Christian and Catholic faith and adhered to the impious sect of Luther, or Calvin.'[44]

It was when Masini gave his readers a sample abjuration appropriate for those guilty of formal heresy that ritual practices became even more of a predominant defining factor. Those who avoided confession and communion, or argued against ritual fasting, or spoke against the cult of the saints, or criticized others for going to Mass and refused to go to Mass themselves, and, finally, confessed that they thought the impious and 'diabolical' sect of Calvin was the true Church of Christ, and that the 'Catholic and Apostolic Roman Church [was] the synagogue of Satan and the whore of Babylon, mother of all fornication and abomination, and spiritual sodomy, regarding the doctrine that it holds and teaches' were guilty of formal heresy. [45] The defining aspect of both vehement and violent suspicion of heresy were actions and criticisms related to Catholic ritual practice – but in theory the violently suspect would make a statement of loyalty to a particular heretical sect.

Formal heresy was exemplified by those who not only had believed in heresies, but had attempted to teach them to others, according to Eymeric. Such formal heresies could be repented by heresiarchs, as Eymeric called them elsewhere, but those who actively hid and attempted to spread their heresies and convert others were obviously too dangerous to be allowed to live at large in the Catholic community. Suspects in formal heresy, Eymeric advised, should be assigned the punishment of perpetual incarceration as a result and subsequent manual authors followed suit. The authors additionally warned to observe these people carefully for signs of feigning their penitence; those guilty of formal heresy were the most dangerous convicted suspects and the most likely to be faking their penitence to escape the death penalty.[46] Many defendants, as we have seen in previous chapters, insisted to tribunals that they neither learned their heresies from others, nor taught them others, and small wonder. If they had admitted that their criticisms of Catholic ritual practice or conversations were active attempts at proselytizing, they very well might have received the most serious punishment short of death.

In his commentaries concerning formal heresy, Peña saw fit to explain both the origin of the heresies and the source of the recommendation to assign salutary penance as well as perpetual incarceration as punishment: Augustine. Even when isolated from the larger Catholic community for its own good, the individual penitent should be given a chance at redemption. Later in the same commentary Peña reiterated that inquisitors should be examining those convicted of formal heresy for their penitence, or 'converted condition,' and humility in order to prevent any false protestations of penitence.[47]

When it came to describing sentences appropriate for each of these levels, Farinacci explained that the matter of extraordinary punishment was left up to each inquisitor's discretion. (Ordinary, or capital, punishment, was a mandatory sentence for the impenitent, and relapsed heretics.) First, as Farinacci pointed out, penitent heretical suspects could not be absolved of their suspected heresies unless they were assigned punishment of some kind. The inquisitor, however, should carefully consider the particular qualities of each defendant before assigning that punishment, 'so that the punishment to be imposed' may be 'medicine' rather than 'venom and such that the penitent can carry out.' The punishment should be appropriate to each penitent's circumstances and crimes and help reform the suspect (*corrigatur*). [48] For salutary penance, Farinacci very briefly, quoting Eymeric, prescribed either pilgrimages, prayers, periods of fasting, or charity.[49] And as Carena noted, while the medieval and Spanish inquisitions provided strong precedent for the confiscation of convicts' goods, in Italy it was the general custom to allow the penitent and their families to recover their goods as an act of mercy on the part of Italian tribunals.[50]

Farinacci was much more expansive in describing the factor that should affect the punishment: the speed of the confession.[51] Farinacci duly noted two other adaptations that had taken place in earlier years; he observed that while the category of violently suspect had been common in the Middle Ages, more recently the vehemently and violently suspect generally were considered to be the same category.[52] He also noted that by his day the punishment of perpetual incarceration (during which penance should be performed) had been replaced by a sentence of at least three years in the galleys. His sources for this were Campeggi and Rojas.[53] As we shall see below, the obligation to perform salutary penance also followed convicts to the triremes.

Of all the authors of manuals examined here, Masini, since he structured his manual to provide ideal templates of forms, provided the clearest example of the salutary penance inquisitors should assign to penitent convicted suspects. According to Masini, it was appropriate to have penitents fast 'simply' one Friday a month, and on bread and water every Friday during March, and on Holy Friday, for the rest of their lives. On one day per week, they also should say the seven penitential psalms, with the litanies, and then the Corona of the Virgin Mary. Every Sunday they should say the Our Father and Hail Mary five times each, and the Creed once, all while kneeling in front of a sacred image. Finally, four times a year, they had to confess and commune with a priest deputized to do so by the Holy Office; Masini suggested Christmas, Easter, Pentecost, and All Saints' as significant times in which to do so.[54] These all were traditional penances assigned to penitents at confession for centuries; in the later sixteenth century they served as the tribunals' rehabilitative punishment as well.

Confession and Penance

The inquisitors' assignment of a confessor approved by the tribunal to those who were convicted of being suspect in heresy was the point at which the external sin of heresy and the internal sin of conscience could coincide. As scholars have noted, while the internal forum of conscience and external forum of public crime (against God and government) were defined as jurisdictionally separate canonically, the two forums possessed similarities and points of contact. Confession and communion had been required of every Catholic since the edict of Lateran IV in 1215; the council had intended it as an anti-Cathar measure, although discerning the means and frequency of enforcement in the Middle Ages and early modern period has proved problematic.[55]

Sacramental and inquisitorial confession were conceptualized in similar terms historically, and the Council of Trent affirmed those similarities by upholding the Church's traditions in metaphorically describing confession as a judicial process (although viewing the sacrament as penitents embracing a 'new life' remained common in practice as well). Carlo Borromeo, the bishop of Milan whose implementation of Tridentine reforms became exemplary in late sixteenth-century Europe, instructed the confessors in his diocese to treat the sacrament as if it were a proceeding, for example. Confession consisted of verifying the penitent's disposition and the investigation of the 'case,' followed by the confessor's sentence and the assignation of a just punishment. For Carlo Borromeo, that punishment/penance should be public if the sin committed was 'scandalous' to the community. In fact, according to Wietse de Boer, assigning public penance to the penitent became increasingly more common during the Counter-Reformation.[56]

Confession remained distinct from inquisitorial proceedings, however, because the process was initiated by self-accusation: the penitent was both accuser and accused. Furthermore, the sacrament lacked the threat of torture; it excluded forms of additional evidence or any investigation; and it should result in absolution, not condemnation. But, as Adriano Prosperi has emphasized, in their fight against heresy some inquisitors and authorities in the Church hierarchy argued for the necessity of having access to information divulged in the confessional, however indirectly.[57] Confessors, according to Prosperi, dealt solely with the *foro interno*, or internal forum of conscience. Heresy was not within confessors' abilities to absolve, since it pertained to the *foro externo*, or external forum of public crime. Therefore the Church made it a point to instruct confessors to whom a layperson made an admission of heretical belief to refuse absolution and refer the person to a tribunal for prosecution. Furthermore, confessors were instructed to ask those who confessed if they knew of anyone in the community who engaged in heresy; confessors were also expected to instruct those who knew suspected heretics to denounce them. Even more hotly debated at the time was the prospect of confessors revealing the confessions of those who did not go to inquisition tribunals when instructed to do so; there were those in the Catholic hierarchy who argued that to do so did not violate the secrecy of the confessional. Prosperi has characterized these developments as distinctively new in the sixteenth century and a response to emergency conditions brought about by the Protestant Reformation.[58] The use of confessors as informants for the Roman Inquisition, however, Elena Brambilla has contended, was not necessarily an abuse of confessional secrecy invented by the post-1542 Roman Inquisition but rather a development of long duration. She has characterized the relationship between the internal and external forums as overlapping in significant ways, such as the ability of mendicant friars, and the pope through the Apostolic Penitentiary, to absolve penitents of the punishments assigned by bishops in episcopal courts for public crimes such as adultery. She also has pointed out that many laypeople might not have been aware of the theological and legal distinctions between the two forums; for them, a confession was a confession. But both Prosperi and Brambilla have recognized that many laypeople came before the inquisition as self-denunciators only in the most technical sense, since their confessors had required their cooperation.[59]

Thus, Easter communion for all of the laity, only proceeding after confession, became the foundation for the potential cooperation between inquisitors and priests and their bishops, in the effort to maintain social order and control. Enforcement, however, was another matter. Wietse de Boer has found that in Counter-Reformation Milan, Carlo Borromeo for the most part succeeded in constructing the confessional sacrament as an instrument of social control; a Milanese diocesan visitation demonstrated that most adults were going to confession and communion every year.[60] Both Prosperi and Brambilla have characterized the cooperation between inquisitors and confessors as an ecclesiastical corps that regulated social life through rites of passage that coincided with the sacraments of confession and communion. In Milan the activist reforming bishop made every effort to accomplish social discipline through confession and communion.[61]

This system, however, which may have been intended to function as a net to catch social deviance, was not without its problems in practice. As De Boer notes concerning Milan, before Borromeo's reforms many confessors were badly trained or failed to perform their duties adequately.[62] Other areas in Italy attempted reforms of parish clergy along the lines of Borromeo's, but it is unclear if they were equally successful. Giovanni Romeo has found that Naples in the late sixteenth century had approximately 1,800 confessors to serve a population of about 250,000 inhabitants. He has estimated that in different areas in Italy at the time of the Council of Trent's conclusion only 10 per cent to 60 per cent of penitents confessed once a year.[63] De Boer also points out that the expansion of the Roman Inquisition's power did not automatically render confessors agents of the inquisition. Bishops were supposed to be a key part of an inquisition tribunal, but bishops such as Borromeo could choose to be competitors instead, claiming authority and attempting to prosecute blasphemy (which could be considered heretical in certain circumstances), magic, and philo-Protestant heresy without the involvement of inquisitors.[64] Many jurisdictional disagreements and individual confessors' ideas concerning their duty to the secrecy of confessions interfered with the close cooperation of inquisitors and confessors. That laypeople could choose to confess to a member of the monastic orders rather than their parish priest also complicated parochial surveillance. Finally, confessors ultimately lacked any method of enforcement other than excommunication, especially to ensure that they received a full and honest confession from their penitents. Confessors had to rely on their powers of persuasion and the penitents' spiritual sincerity to elicit a full confession.[65] Inquisitors used persuasion as an important part of their techniques for extracting confessions of heresy, but they also had the threat of torture at their disposal if the subjects of their investigations chose to lie or omit information (regardless of how seldom that technique was utilized in practice).

Confessors, and the entire sacrament of penance, were a potential source of information concerning heretical suspects for inquisitors, although an imperfect one. But, as authors of inquisition manuals made clear, confessors theroretically should be involved in the continued penitence, rehabilitation, and surveillance of convicted defendants – their involvement was just as important, if not more so, at the conclusion of a process as it could be in initiating one. Confessors chosen or approved of by tribunals would utilize confession and communion four times a year to monitor those convicted of suspicion of heresy. The confessor, it was hoped, would oversee 'behaviour modification' to ensure continued reform. That the community became involved in such surveillance as well, and the very existence of relapsed heretics as a judicial category, indicates that clerical surveillance often was not implemented perfectly.

Ritual Practice and Prayer

The prayer cycles – the penitential psalms, the litanies, the Corona, the Lord's Prayer, the Hail Mary, and the Creed – were traditional penances assigned to those who voluntarily went to confession and communion once a year and, for many Catholics, constituted a part of their private religious devotion whether allocated by a confessor or not. But there were several constituent parts of these penances with which philo-Protestants might have had significant qualms of conscience were they inclined to continue in their heterodox beliefs. In particular, Masini stipulated that ritual fasting should be an integral part of these penances, as was performing all of the weekly necessary prayers in front of a sacred image. Together with regular attendance at Mass (which manual authors probably assumed as a matter of course) and enforced confession and communion, inquisitorial penances required philo-Protestants to perform ritual practices that almost all Protestant theologians decried as idolatrous, and which the Roman Inquisition recognized as being the doctrinal source of the most typical 'Lutheran' ritual practices and criticisms of Catholic ones. Tradition provided the solution to new sixteenth-century heresies and a means of rehabilitating convicted suspects.

The records of abjurations and sentences at Trinity College, Dublin, highlight the important role that tribunals and Church hoped rehabilitative punishment could play in inquisitorial prosecution in a very real sense. The abjuration and sentencing records were excerpted from processes held during the 1560s and 1580s and prosecuted either by the central tribunal in Rome or by the branch tribunals in towns such as Cremona or Faenza. Of the cases prosecuted in Rome, many had been transferred to the central tribunal's jurisdiction, usually because of the notoriety or danger presented by the suspects; the final stages of the process would be administered by four cardinals from the Congregation of Cardinals. The abjurations, sentences, and punishments allocated therefore tend to be more severe than average. In many of the sentences, furthermore, the convicted suspects in heresy were required to abjure not only in Rome but also in the towns that were the points of origin for the cases, so their public abjurations could be instructive and illuminating for the Catholic community there. It is possible that the extraction of the sentences from the full records was for the purposes of correspondence, to inform the local tribunals what was to be expected of these convicted suspects when they returned. The abjurations and sentences from the regional tribunals also might have been extracted for the purposes of correspondence to keep Rome apprised of the processes being conducted in those localities.[66] Examining these sentences as an aggregate group is useful because it allows comparison of sentences and salutary penances from variety of inquisitors and tribunals from differing locations and across time. Given all of the variable factors to be considered at the end of a process, collectively the tribunals were remarkably consistent in their sentencing techniques.

The most severe punishments were reserved for the most dangerous convicts and involved physical isolation from the Catholic community. But even those who were sentenced to row in the galleys, an experience John Tedeschi has described as a 'living hell,' were expected to demonstrate their repentance.[67] The sentences pronounced in Rome in the 1560s utilized the option relatively frequently; the tribunal at this time was operating much more severely, in part due to the influence and direction of Pope Pius V (1566–1572), who had been the inquisitor general Michele Ghislieri beginning in 1558. In 1564, for example, a certain Damiano was instructed to abjure his heretical crimes in Santa Maria Sopra Minerva while wearing the yellow penitential habit affixed with the sign of the cross. Damiano had learned his religious errors in Geneva and returned to Naples to proselytize; he had been arrested and his process had been begun in Naples before its transfer to Rome. Among other errors, Damiano believed that it was not a sin to eat meat during Lent and other days; that pilgrimages were idolatrous, as was venerating the images and relics of saints, because they could not intercede with God; that good works could not earn one salvation; that God had predestined everyone for salvation or damnation before the creation; and that all Masses and ceremonies of the Catholic Church were invented by men, not God or Jesus. For these errors and about ten others Damiano was sentenced to the galleys for five years. Cardinal Giovanni Michele Saraceni, however, specified that Damiano was required to repeat five Ave Marias and five Pater Nosters every day as he rowed as a part of the penance to be paid for his public crimes. The cardinal ended the sentence by expressing that he reserved the right to moderate or commute the above punishment and penance out of mercy.[68]

Don Francesco de Stanghi, a cleric initially tried in Faenza, received an even more elaborate penance in Rome in 1567. The four cardinals (Luigi Pisani; Marc Antonio Colonna; Alessandro Crivelli; Gianfrancesco Gambara) stated that he had been brought to Rome because the tribunal at Faenza thought he had not made a full confession. Don Francesco was instructed to abjure several errors in Santa Maria Sopra Minerva while wearing the penitential habit, including that he had denied transubstantiation, the necessity of auricular confession, and the ability of good works to help one reach salvation. He also admitted to contact with other heretics. Because, as a cleric he was held to a higher standard, he received a more severe sentence than many laypeople would have for similar lists of crimes. He was sentenced to row in the galleys for seven years, during which he was to pray the Pater Noster and Ave Maria five times each day. Should he survive rowing for seven years, he had still more penance to complete. For another seven years following the galleys, Don Francesco should, on every *festa,* fast, and in the mornings go before the cross at a church and say the seven penitential psalms along with the litany and the offices of the dead. Every Saturday he was to say the Corona of the Virgin, and he was required to confess and commune four times per year. Finally, he was to come before the inquisitorial tribunal once a month to demonstrate his lack of heretical backsliding.[69]

Don Francesco, according to the tribunal, had been reluctant to confess to his errors fully. Another defendant from Faenza, whose process ended in July of 1567, also received a sentence of galley service for five years, during which he was instructed to pray, and a subsequent penitential sentence should he survive. The list of heresies that comprised his abjuration actually was much shorter than that of Don Francesco; among the seven errors, this defendant's objections to suffrages for the dead and votives dedicated to saints and their images figured most prominently. For seven years after his galley service, he was instructed to fast and hear Mass while praying the Corona of the Virgin Mary, and say the seven penitential psalms in front of a crucifix in church every morning, in addition to going to confession and communion four times a year and presenting himself once a month to the local tribunal's ordinary in order to ensure continued rehabilitation and surveillance. The severe sentence, according to the records, was the result of this defendant's reluctance to confess, and not the frequency or long list of crimes to which he eventually confessed.[70]

In the sentences concerning galley service, not every defendant was assigned further penance to perform should he survive. But even with the most brutal of sentences, inquisitors and the cardinals sitting on the central tribunal in Rome were careful to include at least a token manifestation of care for the defendant's soul in the form of instructing penitent oarsmen to pray the Our Father and the Hail Mary, the latter of which many philo-Protestants in Italian states believed was not a legitimate prayer. Even when dealing with the most dangerous, obstinate, or blatantly sacrilegious convicted suspects, tribunals held out the opportunity to experience a conversion of some kind, although the galley sentence itself would seem to indicate that tribunals assigning such a punishment thought complete rehabilitation of faith unlikely.

Efforts at saving the soul through continued pastoral care and perpetual incarceration, both of which doubled as continued surveillance, was still current practice as late at the 1580s. In 1580, for example, Marco Gonzaga, bishop of Mantua, and the inquisitor Giulio Doffi instructed Camillo da Bozzolo to abjure to no less than twenty-two heresies. In many locations and to great public scandal, Camillo had preached predestination, denied the necessity of confession or fasting, and held that 'wicked priests' could not absolve sin, that transubstantiation did not exist, and that there was no more difference between Catholics and Lutherans than between Guelfs and Ghibellines, among other heresies. Camillo was condemned to perpetual incarceration – the sentence specified that it should last for his entire life. But the inquisitor and bishop also specified that Camillo had to wear the penitential habit and could not leave his prison without permission. Therefore, most likely, he could continue to work, see his family, and have his incarceration commuted at a later date, despite the sentencing instructions. Finally, Camillo had to fast on bread and water every Sunday, go to confession and communion four times a year, and say the third part of the rosary every day. While he was physically restricted for the time being, and therefore incapable of spreading his heresies (in theory), Camillo was assigned salutary penance to be completed during his incarceration.[71]

Concerning Mario Galeota, the tribunal in Rome in June of 1567 was even more specific as to the duration of 'perpetual' incarceration, at long last. Son of the lord of Monasterace, Galeota was both a humanist and military expert; in 1539 he led infantry troops into Calabria to defend against Turkish incursions, for example. Galeota was an ardent follower of Juan de Valdés for much of his adult life; he had translated two of Juan de Valdés's works into Italian and was a key member of the *spirituali* in Naples. He was the subject of two investigations, the first at the behest of the viceroy of Naples in 1548 and the second conducted by the archbishop of Naples at the request of the Roman Inquisition in 1552. Pope Paul IV ordered his arrest and transferral to Rome in late 1555; Galeota spent the years 1556 to 1559 in prison in Rome. Just before Paul IV's death in 1559, Galeota had been allowed to reside outside of prison. In response to Paul IV's death, the Roman populace had decided to express their feelings concerning his papacy by attacking and sacking inquisitorial buildings and burning records. Because his process dossier had gone up in smoke, the new pope, Pius IV was able to absolve Galeota, when he voluntarily presented himself to the congregation after 'escaping,' on which Galeota returned to Naples. He came under suspicion again, however, in 1564, and by 1565 would find himself imprisoned in Rome again. This was the process that finally ended with his conviction and abjuration, after having spent two years in prison undergoing multiple interrogations, including being tortured. The abjuration of 1567 asserted that he had escaped from prison and listed a set of crimes about which he had never expressed remorse in the past. And while Galeota had been absolved in 1560, he had not been declared 'innocent.' Galeota's sentence seemed quite harsh at the time. It specified that he would be held in perpetual incarceration for five years, and that both during and after his incarceration he should never live again in Naples, where he had provoked so much public scandal. Yet by 1571 Galeota had moved back to Naples and once again held government positions until his death.[72]

According to inquisitorial manuals, convicted suspects in heresy ought to be sentenced according to their age, station, and quality;

although Galeota was prosecuted and initially sentenced to perpetual incarceration, he was not sent to the galleys.[73] A group of gentlemen from Bologna were sentenced according to their station in some ways, and at the end of their processes, their sentences involved rather hefty financial penalties. Their status also affected how the inquisitor of Bologna, Antonio Balducci, and the archbishop, Gabriele Paleotti, proceeded; while initiating the case in Bologna, they questioned the suspects more informally and after briefly arresting them released them on bail. One of the group's central figures, Girolamo Vittori, was able to flee because the investigation moved slowly and cautiously. Balducci, however, made it a point to communicate his actions with the congregation's general commissary, Umberto Locati, every step of the way. Since the case was so sensitive, the noblemen and others associated with the group were moved to Rome for prosecution in 1567. There they remained in the Holy Office's prison, and a few of them were tortured before confessing.[74] Each of the defendants abjured at least twenty heretical 'words and deeds,' including articles concerning the idolatry of the Mass, the illegitimacy of venerating saints and images, and denying the need to fast during Lent and at other times of the year. The first convicted suspect to abjure, Giovanni Francesco, was assigned perpetual incarceration. But Giovanni Francesco, according to the records, had confessed easily and liberally as well. He was also told to spend at least a thousand *scudi* constructing an appropriate location for his and his fellow convicted suspects' incarceration and rehabilitation.[75] In fact, even though some of them had been tortured to bring about a legitimate confession, they all were given exactly the same sentence.[76] In comparison, a shoemaker named Giovanni Zerbino ('the Serbian'), who had emigrated from Geneva and had lived in Rome for many years, practising his trade and proselytizing, was given a galley sentence of five years for a much shorter list of crimes than those of the Bolognese gentlemen, although Giovanni had been equally reluctant to confess.[77]

Other stations and qualities could modify sentencing, punishment, and salutary penance, usually in a more merciful direction, including those of age and gender. Caterina de Bartolo of Novara, who had objected to the idolatry of the Mass, decried the Catholic Church's use of sacred images, and called the consecrated host a 'little bit of pasta,' was sentenced to perpetual incarceration accompanied by salutary penance.[78] But according to both Peña and Farinacci, especially in the case of women, in theory a sentence of incarceration could be modified as a mercy to her family. As they pointed out, the term 'perpetual' was a formality only, and in the case of married women the sentence could be commuted to house arrest, most likely because their household and childcare work could not be easily replaced by most families. Peña mentioned no other sources for this opinion (and acknowledged that the Council of Béziers seemed to prohibit it); he recommended consulting the Congregation of Cardinals in Rome before employing such a mercy.[79] So few women were prosecuted for philo-Protestant heresy, however, that it is difficult to generalize as to whether the Roman Inquisition employed house arrest consistently as an appropriate punishment, and there was no mention of a merciful modification in Caterina de Bartolo's sentence.[80]

Those whose actions were not quite as publicly dangerous, and therefore abjured as lightly suspect and in private, received similar salutary penances without the perpetual incarceration. Vehement abjurations, such as those for whom the sentence was perpetual incarceration or the galleys, took place in public and could involve 'perpetual' incarceration, but not always. In fact, if the case had been transferred to Rome those convicted suspects often were required to return to their points of origin to abjure publicly again before undertaking their required sentences. The vehemently suspect were the most visible of the didactic examples the Roman Inquisition hoped would deter others from falling into heresy, since they continued to move through the community, either immediately or once their sentences of 'perpetual' incarceration had been commuted. In public they were constant reminders of the dangers of heresy; the tribunals that sent them back to their communities had to make sure that there was less of a chance of recidivism or proselytization *because* they would still be allowed some freedom of movement.

Niccolò of Bologna, a layman who lived near the abbey of San'Andrea, was sentenced as vehemently suspect of heresy in 1580. He apparently had great familiarity with heretics, which might have been why the tribunal thought it necessary to single him out for heightened scrutiny. After his abjuration, while dressed in his habit, for one year Niccolò was to confess and commune at Christmas, Easter, and Pentecost. He also to say the seven penitential psalms on six feast days during that year and every Saturday pray the Corona of the Virgin. Finally, on three Sundays in a row he was to spend the day kneeling before the major altar at his parish church with a candle in his hand and listening to Mass.[81] Giovanni Battista, abjured in Rome in 1567, had been a great friend of Giovanni Francesco de Aloisio (Alois), who had been executed as an impenitent heretic in Naples in 1564. Aloisio had been yet another aristocratic disciple of Juan de Valdés, and had managed to protect both himself and others until the 1560s. His execution, conducted after having informed on a good many of his compatriots during his process in Rome, triggered a riot in Naples. Giovanni Battista, during his own process conducted in the wake of Aloisio's, had admitted that he believed five errors for the duration of seven years: that good works could not merit salvation; that indulgences were a joke and invented by the papacy to raise money; that there was no purgatory; that faith in Christ alone was salvific; and that the predestined were the true members of the Christian Church. After making his abjuration in Santa Maria Sopra Minerva, for the space of five years Giovanni Battista had to listen to Mass every morning, say the seven penitential psalms every Sunday before Mass, fast on bread and water every Saturday, and say the Corona in church before the holy crucifix. For seven years, furthermore, Giovanni Battista had to make offerings for the souls of the dead in purgatory, and confess and commune four times a year at Christmas, Easter, Pentecost, and the Assumption. Finally, before Giovanni Battista left Rome, he had to visit the seven churches of the pilgrimage route by which penitent pilgrim visitors could earn an indulgence: St Peter's Basilica, St John Lateran, St Mary Major, St Paul Outside the Walls, St Sebastian, the Church of the Holy Cross, and St Lawrence.[82]

These penances, given Giovanni Battista's list of heretical errors, seem to be tailored to exactly those practices and beliefs he had rejected when he had been a heterodox believer – for his seven years of heretical beliefs he would do seven years of salutary penance, which involved the ritual practices associated with speeding souls through purgatory by the performance of good works, particularly pilgrimage and indulgences. The same was true of the sentence assigned to Francesco Vinta, who was initially prosecuted in Volterra before finding his case transferred to Rome in 1567. He was instructed to abjure sixteen heretical errors, a quarter of which concerned the cult of the saints. As a part of his salutary penance, therefore, he was instructed to pray to religious images that he was required to procure and keep in his own private room. Francesco also was abjured lightly, not vehemently; given his long list of heresies, and the rather large number of heretical books he possessed, he must have come forward and confessed either voluntarily or soon after his arrest. But as lightly suspect, his prayers to images could be offered in the privacy of his own home and not publicly in a church.[83] Scipione Cremona, abjured as lightly suspect in 1580, definitely had come forward spontaneously and voluntarily. Scipione had not believed in the cult of the saints, or sacramental confession, or the pope's authority to issue or sell indulgences. Scipione therefore was required, for a period of ten years, to fast every Friday and say an office for the souls of the dead once a week. He also had to confess and take communion from a tribunal-approved priest four times a year. Finally, he had to check in with the Holy Office once a month and keep the tribunal appraised of his activities.[84] Having doubted the existence of purgatory and the pope's authority to issue indulgences on behalf of those in it, and having denied the efficacy of sacramental confession, Scipione performed acts of worship concerning those very theological points as his salutary penance.

A bookseller from Ferrara, in much the same way, was made to stay away from the objects that had provided the basis for his heretical beliefs. Originally prosecuted in Bologna, Antonio Saveri had admitted to the tribunal that he not only sold heretical books but also believed their contents as well. Antonio was sentenced to salutary penance as vehemently suspect in heresy (*de vehementi*); he could not leave either Rome or Bologna without the permission of the Holy Office's commissary in Rome or the ordinary in Bologna and he could no longer keep or sell books to make his living. He only could work as a bookbinder, presumably in a reliably Catholic bookman's shop.[85] In this case, salutary penance was accompanied by physical and professional restrictions to minimize Antonio's potential for both recidivism and opportunities to spread heresy to others.

Bolio, a layman from Ancona, also received a sentence customized to suit his heretical crimes. Sent to the inquisition to denounce himself 'voluntarily' by his confessor in 1580, Bolio had not believed in the efficacy of pilgrimages, among two or three other heresies. He was instructed in his sentence to make a pilgrimage to the church of the Madonna in the countryside outside Ancona and procure a plenary indulgence. He also was instructed to confess and commune four times a year and to say five Our Fathers and five Hail Marys every feast day.[86] The pilgrimage was a short one in terms of distance, but according to the manuals inquisitors and bishops in theory should not assign penances that the convicted suspect in heresy would be unable to perform. It is possible that Bolio was not capable of performing a longer pilgrimage financially. It also is possible that Bolio, since his list of heretical beliefs was comparatively short, and because he had 'voluntarily' come forward with the encouragement of his confessor, was given a penance that was as light as the crime. Whatever the 'lightness' of the salutary penance, however, it was spiritually significant.

Matching appropriate salutary penances with the theological contents of the heretical crimes – those who had protested the idolatry of the cult of the saints being sentenced to pray to sacred images, and the like – was all the more significant in light of the attitudes of many Protestant Reformers toward particular Catholic ritual practices. John Calvin, of course, was the strongest proponent of this perspective; since Calvin rejected any possibility of separating body and spirit during the act of worship, he most strenuously prohibited Reformed believers from attending Catholic ritual practices. According to Calvin, the Mass, the cult of the saints, veneration of holy relics, and the like were all idolatrous rituals that would pollute the faith of any Reformed believer who engaged in their practice.[87]

Pietro Martire Vermigli and Pier Paolo Vergerio, among other Italian exiles, also roundly condemned feigning Catholicism as a means of survival. In particular, Vermigli condemned Nicodemite behavior in his *A Treatise on the Cohabitacyon of the Faithful with the Unfaithful*, saying that true believers ought not to 'pollute themselves in popery, by abjurations and masses,' for God 'doth require outward actions.'[88] Pollution would begin, extrapolating theoretically, when a Reformed believer agreed to abjure in the first place, and continued through the performance of salutary penance – and Vermigli, the former Augustinian canon who had fled rather than face inquisitorial prosecution, perhaps knew what was at stake better than any other theologian north of the Alps. Ulrich Zwingli, while he did not consider Catholic fasting practices harmful to faith so long as they were not utilized idolatrously, thought no such compromise possible concerning the cult of the saints.[89] Even the Reformers who had been, in the 1530s and 1540s, more inclined to view quasi-Nicodemite behaviour as a kindly, if temporary, accommodation had begun to adopt a more hard-line stance as confessionalization in Western Europe advanced.[90] Almost all Catholic ritual practices – sacramental, liturgical, and para-liturgical alike – if practised would only (according to these theologians) serve to pollute the pure and true faith of the Reformed believer. It would seem that the tribunals of the Roman Inquisition, in their sentencing practices, agreed and hoped to utilize that perspective to their advantage. But what the Reformers termed pollution, the Roman Inquisition characterized as the salutary penance that they hoped could begin to inculcate Catholic orthodox faith, even if the abjuration had been produced by fear of martyrdom. Augustinian concepts of the conversion and renewal (*renovatio*) that could occur if the unfaithful were compelled to enter the church physically, even through force, was a common intellectual theme among all of the magisterial theologians of the later sixteenth century in Europe, and one church's pollution was another church's hope for renewal.

Thus, the inquisitorial system was set up to ensure that those who were sincere in their confessions and desire to return 'to the arms of the Catholic Church' received ample instruction and guidance pastorally, but inquisitors, clergy, and the larger Catholic community simultaneously kept a close watch on those that might have just been 'playing along' to save their own lives or avoid the galleys. Inquisitors may have believed, as did many theologians in early modern Europe, that where the body was forced to go the mind might follow. There is no doubt that the mind did not, in fact, always follow; there is ample evidence that those brought before inquisitorial tribunals dissimulated when making their confessions and abjurations, and inquisitors saved their most severe treatment for relapsed heretics.[91] From the perspective of inquisitorial authors, and tribunals in reality, heretical beliefs continuing to be held purely in mind were not a matter for their jurisdiction.[92] But any outward expression of those beliefs, whether in word or in deed, went beyond the realm of thought and was actionable. Words and conversations constituted unauthorized religious discussion, and deeds comprised the proselytization or practice of heterodox religion; and both were very much subject to inquisitorial proceedings, with the latter considered more dangerous than the former. When it came to the rehabilitation of such public sinners, even Augustine knew that compelling, or gathering, the heterodox within the arms of the Holy Mother Church did not guarantee religious conversion but simply provided a long-term, structured opportunity for it.[93] Fortunately for inquisitors their sentencing practices provided for the continued surveillance of convicted suspects of heresy, should their confessions turn out to have been dissimulations, and their heterodox opinions be once again acted on publicly. But it was through the practice of religion – religious ritual – that the tribunals of the Roman Inquisition hoped to lead penitential heretics back among the faithful so recidivism might be avoided. Punishment was concurrently penance, opportunity to reform, warning to the community, and surveillance by the community should the opportunity to reform fail.

Conclusion

The Boundaries of Orthodoxy

Inquisition manuals explained the intricacies of inquisitorial procedure, but beginning with Francisco Peña's edition of Eymeric's *Directorium Inquisitorum,* they also reflected the principles of Counter-Reformation confessionalization. And the process records from the mid-sixteenth century onward demonstrate how legal traditions and practices utilized by the Roman Inquisition attempted to achieve those principles. But the eventual success of confessionalization and the parameters of what became orthodox Catholicism beginning in the middle part of the sixteenth century perhaps were not a foregone conclusion. In the first years after Martin Luther's initial protest in the 1520s and 1530s it had not been at all clear exactly where those confessional lines would be drawn. Melanchthon's attempt to formulate a compromise confession of faith at the Diet of Augsburg in 1530; the Colloquy of Ratisbon in 1541, during which Catholic and Protestant prelates agreed on a formula of justification, only to disagree concerning the meaning and form of the Eucharist; Charles V's attempted compromises during the Augsburg Interim of 1547–1548, which allowed for the marriage of priests, communion in both kinds, and the freedom to preach justification by faith alone; all were attempts at compromise of some kind.

All of those attempts, however, and the idea of restructuring the Catholic Church as an umbrella organization under which a variance of doctrinal positions or interpretations could be accommodated, did not work out. In the case of the Augsburg Interim, for example, it was because, despite the concessions described above, many people still objected to the fully Catholic Mass Charles V commanded to be performed. Melanchthon, always more irenically inclined than Luther

(d. 1546), officially gave his approval to the Interim arguing both that church ritual largely encompassed 'indifferent things' and that one had to obey the lawful secular power of Charles V. Nevertheless the compromises of the interim proved unpopular and caused a split among Lutheran theologians. Matthias Flacius Illyricus, for example, criticized Melanchthon for his willingness to compromise and denounced the idea of attending Catholic ritual practices on the grounds that it compromised religious freedom. Thus, even some interpretations of Lutheranism came to object to Catholic ritual practices and the Mass in principle. In the words of one scholar, this split prevented the growth of Lutheranism in central Europe in the second half of the sixteenth century, leaving the field for growth clear for the Reformed tradition. Begun by Ulrich Zwingli and continued by Heinrich Bullinger and John Calvin, the Reformed position completely decried Catholic ritual practices as idolatrous, polluting, and dangerous.[1] While even as late as the 1560s some would still hope for compromise, the process of confessionalization and church-building also was well underway. Protestant state churches sought to distinguish themselves from each other as well as from Catholicism, and the Anabaptists sought to withdraw from official state churches entirely to construct what they considered to be pure, and voluntary, communities of the elect.

While there had been those in the Catholic hierarchy who had been open to religious compromise with nascent Protestant churches north of the Alps, including the *spirituali,* the more conservative evaluations of, and attitudes towards, Luther's ideas and subsequent iterations of Protestant denominations had existed in those years as well. During the first two or three years after Luther's actions in Wittenberg many in the Catholic Church's hierarchy simply characterized Luther as a jealous monk. But with the papal Bull *Exsurge Domine* in 1520 the Church's leadership offered a serious reaction in terms that would not only make its way into polemical literature but also into the legal analysis of inquisition manuals.[2] Master of the Sacred Palace, Sylvester Prierias, had written the bull on behalf of Pope Leo X (thus it refers to Leo X as the author). While the bull's criticisms were based directly on Luther's objections to some Catholic beliefs and practices, the points selected as important or emphatically objectionable reflected how the Church, theologically, accepted a reciprocal relationship between doctrine and practice. The order of topics in the bull mirrored that of Luther's *Ninety-Five Theses,* which began by disputing penance, sacramental confession, and indulgences before moving on to issues concerning the nature of faith. In the *Ninety-Five Theses*, Luther initially took issue not only with a group of Catholic beliefs but also the ritual practices associated with them, and the Catholic Church responded on those terms.[3]

The document opened by appealing to God and Peter to judge (the unnamed Luther) and protect their Church. The bull then proceeded to quote Jerome, who compared heretics to those 'whose last defense . . . is to start spewing out a serpent's venom with their tongue when they see that their causes are about to be condemned, and spring to insults when they see they are vanquished.'[4] The document also refers to the Apostle Paul's injunction that 'there have to be factions among you.'[5] While Luther's evaluation of Paul's writings led to his criticisms of Catholicism, Catholic authors often referred to this quotation from Paul when discussing any type of heresy.[6]

Furthermore, the document specifically presented many of Luther's errors as originating among the Greeks and Bohemians, expressing sorrow that these pernicious errors were being revived in Germany.[7] Prierias may have been acknowledging Luther's original contributions to 'heresy' by referring to 'other errors' that were 'either heretical, false, scandalous, or offensive to pious ears, [and] seductive of simple minds, originating with false exponents of the faith who in their proud curiosity yearn for the world's glory.' But the introductory statements end by comparing the current errors (Luther's name still had not been mentioned at this point) to those of the Hussites and Wycliffites, and Jerome of Prague, already condemned at the Council of Constance (1414–1418). That council also was offered as evidence of the Germans' traditional opposition to heresy and all Germans, especially political leaders, were enjoined to expel or exterminate all heretics from Germany.[8]

This more conservative evaluation of Luther's ideas and objections to several important Catholic ritual practices existed alongside more irenic attempts at compromise (in fact, many thought Prierias had mishandled the situtation quite badly). Other options and possibilities, among many, did exist; Cardinal Pole had come within four votes of the papacy, after all.[9] But Prierias's work was grounded in Thomistic theology, traditional definitions of what constituted heresy, and firmly embraced the idea, rooted in Augustine, that there were no 'new' heresies, only revivals of previous ones. Those sources also were utilized to construct canon law, particularly its instructions for the prosecution of heresy; but canon law was not a static unchanging code. Inquisitorial manuals developed alongside the full corpus of canon law over the same period and often expressed further adaptations and procedures parallel to the Church's law. In composing these manuals, their authors relied upon their own experiences with heresy, often derived from activity as inquisitors, and the entire body of Catholic literature, both legal and theological, which had dealt with heresy from the Church Fathers onward.[10]

None of these manuals was the one standard, however, and each author had his own particular recommendations and parameters of appropriate techniques. This was still true in the early 1540s when the Roman Inquisition was reconstituted to deal with all varieties of mid-sixteenth century heterodoxy. The manuals produced in the later sixteenth century were, in many cases, revived and re-edited manuals from the fourteenth century. As such, they tended to expose these disparities in practice. In the case of Francisco Peña, these divergences were revealed when he decried what he considered to be the ill-considered recommendations of other authors and assert what he thought to be the better way of proceeding – and in some cases that ill-considered opinion was Nicholas Eymeric's. Prospero Farinacci, in his seventeenth-century manual, perhaps more objectively and more judiciously, sought to record every possible legal permutation before providing his own particular judgment on whatever issue was at hand. But sometimes he was content to recommend that each tribunal should utilize its own, hopefully informed, judgment.

Both Cesare Carena and Eliseo Masini, writing a bit later than Farinacci, produced manuals that largely began to weed out the plethora of voices that had contributed to the theoretical underpinnings of inquisitorial practice. Carena's two major sources were Peña and Farinacci, although he did include some others, and his manual was still in Latin. Masini's was composed mostly in Italian and cited no sources at all. Yet both of their respective works still bore the traces of the process achieved in the mid-to-later part of the sixteenth century – the adaptation of past inquisitorial usage to a new religious landscape.

It was apparent, furthermore, in Francisco Peña's commentaries concerning Eymeric's text, which parts of those legal and theological traditions would be kept and which would be left behind. Peña thought that general principles were far more effective for inquisitors when faced with a veritable flood of heretical errors to prosecute. Other learned doctors of the Church had already attempted the task of cataloguing every known form of heresy, which Peña characterized as perhaps even impossible to achieve. Therefore he would not be repeating Eymeric's seventy-plus page attempt at that very task.[11] Instead Peña focused his editorial efforts on explicating the broader theological and canonical traditions of defining heresy and prosecuting it.

Given the contents of Eymeric's fourteenth-century manual, however, it also was readily apparent that some parts of the work would require a process of contextual and theoretical adaptation nonetheless. Therefore Peña dutifully affirmed Eymeric's definition of a perfect heretic: one who held serious religious error in the mind and held onto that error with pertinacity, despite the church's attempts at correction. The definition derived from Thomas Aquinas's *Summa* as did the general standard by which inquisitors could judge particular beliefs heretical – anything that disagreed with the articles of faith, sacred Scripture, or anything the Church determined to be necessary to the faith.[12] But other definitions of heresy and heretics, quoted by Peña to expand upon Eymeric's text, made it clear that those very broad principles were inextricably attached to the particular context and heresy from which they had been developed, and the educational background and perspective of each author.[13] Prospero Farinacci, writing about thirty years after Peña, cited sources that were indicative of the particular context of the later sixteenth and early seventeenth centuries. He also declined to attempt to catalogue every known form of heresy, clearly influenced by Peña.[14] Heresy, even in its very definition, despite Catholic controversialists' claims to the contrary, was not a static concept and continuously was adapted to different contexts and from different perspectives.

The principles of inquisitorial prosecution initially had developed within a particular context – that of prosecuting the Cathars and then the Waldensians in the thirteenth century – so the chapters of Eymeric's fourteenth-century manual still bore the signs of that legacy. Peña, writing even later, had to adapt those early principles to his own time. To do so, Peña had to do some fairly extensive research in the Biblioteca Apostolica, finding no less than three manuscript sources to help both himself and his readers figure out the terminology and what thirteenth- and fourteenth-century Catholic controversialists had thought were the fundamental principles of those heresies.[15] The distinctions between *credentes* (believers in heretics), *fautores* (those who favoured and helped heretics), *receptores* (those who received heretics in their houses), and *defensores* (defenders of heretics) were specific to the Cathar religious structure. But they also were the original source of defining who did, and who did not, believe in heresy. Of those four categories, only the first, *credentes*, could be considered heretical in all cases; the latter three could be, or not, depending upon intent.

It was during his explanations of what exactly constituted *credentes* that Peña strongly emphasized the importance of ritual practices, or 'deeds,' in prosecuting heretical believers and once again reflected how those principles had been adapted to his own time. Taking heretics into one's house and supporting them were actions that might have occurred because of beliefs, but they could also have happened because of familial loyalty, other obligations, or, in the case of tavern owners and innkeepers, because of profit. Attending heretical sermons, though, especially more than once or twice, indicated commitment to a heretical belief system.

In a like vein the *consolamentum*, the *melioramentum*, and, later, Waldensian confessionary, Eucharistic, and prayer practices, all indicated the suspicion of heretical belief without a truly public word having to be spoken. Even if attempting clandestine belief and avoidance of public religious debate, the need to practise a communal religion, and the steps one took to do so, theoretically also provided the best way to prove heretical suspicion and begin a process. Eymeric had cited the parable of two sons in Matthew 21:28 to prove his point, which Peña interpreted for his readers at length. Two sons were instructed to go work in the vineyard; one son initially refused to obey his father and work in the vineyards, but changed his mind and went to work later, while the other son told he father he would go, and then did not. Actions, therefore, clearly were superior to words in indicating one's true intent. It was in this commentary that Peña expressed confidence that the prosecutorial principle at work could be adapted readily to his own day.[16] That adaptation happened, which perhaps explains why Prospero Farinacci, and even Cesare Carena and Eliseo Masini, still made references to Cathar belief structures, ritual practices, and the terminology Catholic theologians, lawyers, and inquisitors had used to describe them, more than three centuries after the religion's decline in Western Europe.

To adapt the general principle in question, Peña essentially proceeded to ask: What actions could have no possible motivation other than belief in heresy? For Peña, the answer lay in iconoclasm, since the smashing of Catholic ritual objects and images was such a sensationalist, public, and notorious critique of Catholic doctrine and ritual practice, it could have no other motivation. Since the 'Lutherans' were so well known for it, who could possibly claim to be unaware of the act's singular significance as heretical?[17] In this one adaptation, Peña expressed simultaneously the core of confessionalization, the principles Counter-Reformation Catholicism, and the legal proof well suited to inquisitorial prosecution. For Peña, ideally, the earth-shaking events of the Protestant Reformation, including its most sensationalized aspect, were so well known and publicized that quite literally no one could claim to be ignorant of them or unaware of their significance. The Catholic Church, furthermore, during the Counter-Reformation, engaging in its own process of confessionlization, emphasized traditional Catholic ritual practices as a means of solidifying and maintaining community religious cohesion and Catholicity. For Peña, this was also a way to measure and prosecute heresy.

Cesare Carena and Eliseo Masini, writing in the early seventeenth century, both presented their assessment of ritual practices, and critiques of Catholicism, in a much more streamlined form. For Carena, in particular, avoiding Mass, and refusing to confess or go to communion repeatedly were the most characteristic actions of philo-Protestants. These general principles of prosecution, furthermore, had the advantage of being firmly grounded in church traditions; the latter, that of the laity's required confession and communion at Easter, had been instituted in 1215 at the Fourth Lateran Council specifically as an anti-heresy measure.[18] Counter- Reformation Catholic prelates, such as Carlo Borromeo, attempted to enforce the measure even more strongly than it had been in the past for that very reason. The other action that came to be popularly definitive of philo-Protestant intent, if not quite so firmly in theory, was the eating of certain foods during times prohibited by the church, originally declared a heresy typical of former pagans in the early church. There were other, non-heretical reasons why one could procure a license to do so, but within in the wider Catholic community in Italian lands it came to be considered a definitive sign of heresy.

All of these acts' significance as heretical to Catholic authors also had been promoted as constituting the 'true faith' within the pages of Protestant theological and polemical works during the Reformation. From indifference, to sarcastic quips concerning misuse and abuse, to accusations of idolatry, pollution, and corruption, the Catholic Mass and the Church's ritual practices were continuously under fire for much of the sixteenth century. The major Protestant controversialists, furthermore, saw participation in those ritual practices (even Luther, if the rituals were performed incorrectly or with an imperfect understanding of their significance) as idolatrous and harmful to the soul. Zwingli, Vermigli, Calvin, Bullinger, and many, many others not only objected to performance of those ritual practices on the grounds that they harmed the individual who engaged in them; they also objected on the grounds that to do so would prevent the enlightenment of the 'weaker brethren' who had yet to learn about or experience what each of those theologians defined as the true faith as well. How could people still mired in the idolatrous muck of Catholic rites be brought to the true faith, if those who already knew better did not model that true faith for them visibly as well as verbally? Thus, even eating meat during Lent, although not essential to salvation according to Zwingli, could provide an opportunity for explanation, witness, and proselytizing those, in his view, desperately in need of the truth.

Prospero Farinacci later closely analysed the significance of those ritual practices, or 'deeds,' within his seventeenth-century manual regarding their value as legal proof. For Farinacci, actions 'may declare the spirit and will more than words' and, characteristic of his methodology, he cited every available source to support his point.[19] In particular, he pointed out that Hostiensis, Antonio de Butrio, and Camillo Campeggi thought action more valuable because they could uncover lies and false assertions – anyone who had performed heretical ritual practices could not credibly claim Catholic belief or lack of heretical intent during a process. Hostiensis and Antonio de Butrio were scholars active in the thirteenth and fourteenth centuries respectively; Camillo Campeggi, in addition to editing a fourteenth-century inquisition manual, was the inquisitor general, first in Pavia, then Ferrara and Modena, for over a decade. For scholars and inquisitors writing manuals, defendants could mount a defence and attempt to provide reasons, rationalizations and justifications for committing those 'deeds.' But given that those same authors, and Juan de Rojas, thought evidence of Catholic ritual practice the best means of defence for an accused suspect, excuses for having performed heretical rituals were quite difficult to present persuasively. For Farinacci thought that even protestations of drunkenness or extreme anger would be worthless if the person claiming such in his or her defence had performed heretical rites. If tribunals were to allow such excuses to work, 'certainly all heretics might escape unpunished, because they all might speak thus,' making a mockery of the very idea of inquisitorial prosecution and protection of the faith.[20]

In fact, what one did in terms of ritual practice was thought to be a good standard by which to measure the more ambiguous realm of verbal statements and other forms of evidence. Farinacci quoted Juan de Rojas to explain exactly what those reasons could be; according to Rojas, Jews, Moors, and those from provinces infected with heresy definitely should not be given the benefit of the doubt concerning what they said. Rojas maintained that events in his own time had cast up heretical liars everywhere, ready to lead people from what he considered to be the true faith through false, duplicitous, and ambiguous words. For Farinacci, and Rojas, false claims regarding Catholic beliefs made by deceitful heretics could be recognized for the lies they really were by closely examining the overall qualities of religiosity of such defendants. That principle was also quite compatible with the late sixteenth- and early seventeenth-century authors' stated goal of generating 'broad principles' by which to prosecute rather than engaging in detailed analysis of all known heretical beliefs. Whatever was said, 'deeds' would point the way toward a correct judgment on the tribunals' part.

For Farinacci, this discussion was bound up inextricably with two other important aspects of inquisitorial prosecution: proof and witnesses. The ideal proof, and the ideal witnesses that produced it during the *inquisitio*, were two of the most contentious theoratical topics examined within the pages of inquisitorial manuals, and for good reason. Witnesses were the medium of proof – it was their testimony that provided the 'points of entry' to begin processes. In reality, it was the tribunal's job to discern whether or not enough witness testimony existed to justify the opening of a process, and especially whether or not the proof was serious enough to warrant an arrest and custodial incarceration.

Therefore the rule that a process could begin based upon the sworn testimony of two worthy witnesses was deceptively simple. Many authors and authorities disagreed with the two-witness standard; some thought three or more necessary to condemn a defendant if those witnesses had less than ideal reputations themselves. It was possible to consider one witness testimony, in addition to other, more general evidence of a public reputation for heresy, enough to arrest, and begin a process. More general evidence of *infamia*, according to the manuals, consisted of single testimonies – testimonies that went uncorroborated by other witnesses. For the two worthy witnesses to provide a secure basis from which to open a process, their testimony had to be in rough agreement concerning the time, place, and events in question.

As the depositions from a variety of locations in mid-to-late sixteenth-century northern Italian states demonstrate, in reality many witnesses gave evidence that focused on ritual practice. When proselytizing was relatively open, finding enough witnesses to open a process was not necessarily difficult. And those witnesses (who in some cases, numbered over forty people) reported to tribunals that they had heard criticism of, or attacks upon, the cult of the saints, religious images, and the sacrifice of the Mass. Eating meat during the fasts prescribed by the Church was probably the most common accusation. But even in those processes in which only two or three witnesses could be found, due to more subtle attempts at quasi-Nicodemite behaviour, ritual practice remained a common point in witness testimonies.

Once the trial began, inquisitorial tribunals examined the defendant to procure a confession. Theoretically, in manuals ranging from the fourteenth to the early seventeenth centuries, there was a constant tension between the need to show mercy to the penitent and protect the larger Catholic community from heresy's stain. Because of that dichotomy, the speed of a defendant's confession came to be considered one good measure of sincere penitence and a sign that mercy was warranted. The quickest confessions came from those who presented themselves to the Holy Office, whether 'encouraged' by their confessors or not. But those who confessed within the first or second questioning sessions could also be assured of some leniency when it came to sentencing, if the tribunal was so inclined, as was the case with Giovanni Terrazzano. He was sentenced more leniently, since his place of perpetual incarceration, the technical punishment for his level of heretical belief, was the entire city of Modena.

The other factor manual authors traditionally found to be legitimate grounds for mercy was a defendant's religious ignorance. According to no less an authority than Thomas Aquinas, explicit faith, or a full explanation of doctrine, was only required of those with the education necessary to comprehend it. The ignorant were not expected to make such an explicit statement of understanding and were less responsible for heresy, especially if led astray by their betters. But Peña thought that by his time, ignorance of the core religious issues of the Protestant Reformation was much more difficult to maintain convincingly. In particular, Peña thought the entire event so notorious that no one could claim ignorance of it. But Egidio Foscarari, one of the more irenically inclined prelates in the mid-sixteenth century, sucessfully utilized ignorance to ensure a more 'gentle' verdict for Claudio da Roteglia, whose process was held twenty years before Peña published his more rigorous opinions concerning the subject.

All manual authors affirmed the right to present a defence; the Roman Inquisition even assigned lawyers to those who could not afford them. That principle had caused manual authors to rectify a potential conflict in inquisitorial terminology. *Defensores*, or defenders of heretics, and the lawyers who helped suspected heretics present their defence before the tribunal were not the same thing. To ensure that the distinction always remained, lawyers' activities on behalf of their clients were limited carefully. Lawyers only could defend their clients if they genuinely thought those clients were innocent. If they were not innocent, it was the lawyers' job to advise their clients to confess and throw themselves on the mercy of the court. Everyone had the right to contest the charges against them but, in theory, not in such a way as to allow heretics to walk free (that, after all, was the definition of a *defensor*).

The restrictions on the tactics defendants could use during their processes also effectively made it impossible to argue one's innocence on doctrinal grounds. Protesting that one knew Catholic doctrine better than a tribunal, after all, more likely would be interpreted as a sign of pertinacity, not doctrinal sophistication. One's best bet was to prove something amiss with the witness testimony that formed the foundation of the case, as the falsely accused lawyer Zuane (Giovanni) Finetti was able to do. Prospero, the *capeler*, and Battista Amai della Bambine were not so fortunate; they did not have very many licit arguments to make. Both Prospero and Battista, in addition to the rather interesting political and religious opinions they advanced on the Rialto, tended to avoid Mass, and both had not performed the required confession and communion in quite some time. To bring an end to what the Venetian tribunal was convinced were false protestations of Catholicism, they used confrontational tactics – they made Prospero and Battista confront each other as well as the tribunal. That incident did not have the desired effect, but apparently the rather long prison stays each was subjected to did, a circumstance Peña would note as sometimes more effective in producing confessions than torture only a few years later.

Prospero's and Battista's protestations of innocence were not convincing because they never went near Catholic Mass or confession; Bartolomeo Nelli, prosecuted in Siena, for the most part actually had. He was almost able to successfully pull of his quasi-Nicodemitism, with the help of his unusually aggressive lawyer. Both Nelli and his lawyer Lucarini engaged in the kind of verbal manipulation and obfuscating tactics manual authors, both Eymeric and later ones, warned their readers against repeatedly. If Nelli had not decided, at one point, apparently to embrace martyrdom, it might have worked completely; he might have been convicted and penanced even more gently. When he changed his mind about dying for the true faith and confessed, he took a large risk, perhaps intentionally.

Zuanbattista Sambeni, prosecuted in Venice, also engaged in verbal manipulation and repeated refusals to confess. Unlike Nelli, however, Sambeni had not constructed a plausible quasi-Nicodemite cover. In fact, he had been prosecuted once before, in Brescia, and in between his time in Brescia and Venice, had joined a heretical church. Nevertheless, Sambeni utilized, from the tribunal's perspective, maddeningly vague statements as a defence. He refused to confess his irenic beliefs in any form clearly definable as a particular heretical creed and was obstructionist in his answers, refusing to confirm his belief in Catholicism as defined by the tribunal even when tortured. But his lack of ritual practice of Catholicism certainly did not indicate full commitment to orthodoxy. Above all, he refused to admit he was wrong – since he was a relapsed heretic, he was destined to be executed whether he remained pertinacious and unrepentant or not.

Torture, although it occurred in an extremely small minority of cases, was a useful tool for the tribunals in a variety of ways. The only sure way for a defendant to avoid being tortured was to confess, perhaps exactly the reason why it was used only in a minority of cases. In the case of Pietro Curioni, it allowed the Modenese tribunal to reconcile some of his admitted heresies with his consistent claim that he had continued to attend Mass including the consecration of the host and wine, which many *fratelli* avoided as a matter of conscience. The tribunal probably was unwilling to believe that Curioni continued to attend the most important Catholic ritual practices because his apothecary shop was a known meeting point for philo-Protestants in Modena. Curioni managed to continue his assertions of Catholic ritual practice under torture, which is why the tribunal ultimately had no choice but to believe him.

The case of Girolamo (Hieronimo) involved the exact opposite problem. That tribunal in Udine was led by the patriarch of Aquileia's vicar, since the Roman Inquisition would not be introduced to Venetian territories until 1547. Prosecuted in 1543–1544, Girolamo was associated with a group of heterodox who objected to the idolatry of images so much that they engaged in iconoclasm and openly proselytized among the people there. But when Girolamo, after having been tried and minimally tortured, ascended the pulpit to make his abjuration, he instead made a full statement of faith that he claimed to be essentially Catholic, but which the tribunal in Aquileia clearly thought heretical. The problem, however, lay in Girolamo's later assertions that he had only confessed to fourteen heretical errors from fear of the torture. The case, from the legal perspective, was difficult for the local tribunal to deal with because Girolamo's claims and the way his trial had proceeded fell into a something of a lacuna in canon law and inquisitorial procedure. He could not be declared relapsed because he had not committed his heresies twice even though he had baulked at his abjuration. Later inquisition manuals, including Peña's, would recommended that the subject who refused to abjure be returned to prison and convinced to confess to all the charges, perhaps precisely because such problems had arisen in the 1540s.

Ultimately Girolamo was given a new trial, on the pretext that the vicar in charge, Giovanni Angelo da San Severino, had proceeded alone. But it is possible that Girolamo had been improperly prosecuted – the documentation relating to his torture is a mere paragraph in the trial records and he signed his abjuration the same day, not at least twenty-four hours later, as the inquisitorial manuals advised was standard procedure. The new trial, led by Gherardo Busdrago, who would also be involved in the case against Pietro Vagnola, ended in Girolamo's abjuration of the two heresies to which he was willing to confess. The procedural violations might have been the cause of the leniency shown to Girolamo, although it is true that in general inquisitorial activity, whether under the aegis of the Roman Inquisition or conducted out of bishops' palaces, tended to be more lenient in the 1540s and 1550s.

While the distinction between the internal forum of sin, dealt with by confessors, and external forum of public heresy had been made since the Middle Ages, both manual authors, and tribunals, were concerned with expiation and rehabilitation. In theory, for those convicted of crimes of lesser severity, the original principle established by Augustine still held: *cogo intrare*. Penances – expiations of public sin, public warning, public punishment (for those convicted at least as severely as *de vehementi suspecti*), and continued public surveillance – were also opportunities for spiritual rehabilitation and the inculcation of Catholic belief. As originally theorized by Augustine, repeated engagement with the ritual practices of the church, and participation in the community of faith, even if forced, might bring souls back to true belief. Both Peña and Farinacci quoted Augustine as the original source of this theory of behavioural modification, and quoted his language in expressing the theory behind such ritual punishment. In reality, it is doubtful that repentant convicted suspects could be monitored on a daily basis; even a sentence of perpetual incarceration usually resulted in release a few years later. While every attempt was made to involve the entire Catholic community, clerical and lay, in continuing to watch convicted suspects for further signs of heresy, the implementation most likely remained imperfect due to a sheer lack of resources. Heresy was an incorrect individual choice of belief, held with pertinacity, but it was also a crime against the community of the Church and communal religious practice. The origins of the problem, and the means of prosecuting it, was also perceived to be the best attempt at a solution.

Notes

Introduction

1 John Calvin, 'Short Treatise on the Supper of Our Lord, Jesus Christ,' in J.K.S. Reid, trans. and ed., *Calvin: Theological Treatises* (The Library of Christian Classics, Volume 22) (Philadelphia, PA: The Westminster Press, 1954), p. 162. 'Ainsi nou voyons qu'une telle multitude de ceremonies en la Messe est un forme de Iuifverie, plainement contraire à la Chrestienté. Ie n'entens pas de reprouver les ceremonies, lesquelles servent à honnesteté et ordre publique, et augmentent la reverence du Sacrement, moyennant qu'elles feussent sobres et convenables.' (John Calvin, 'Petit Traicté de la Saincte Cene de N.S. Iesus Christ,' in *Corpus Reformatorum,* Vol. 33, *Ioannis Calvini Opera Quae Supersunt Omnia,* Vol. 5, ed. G. Baum, E. Cunitz, and E. Reuss [Brunswick and Berlin: C.A. Schwetschke and Son, 1866], p. 455.) The above quotation was among Calvin's more restrained criticisms of Catholic rites and ceremonies.

2 The term 'Protestant' is somewhat anachronistic when applied to this period; yet it does remain useful as a catch-all term for the developing denominations north of the Alps. Many non-Catholic believers in Italian lands in this time, however, did not completely embrace only one variety of northern European Protestantism exclusively, and were also influenced by Italian reform currents; therefore they can defy being categorized according to the more specific terms of, for example, 'Calvinist' or 'Zwinglian.' When referring to the subjects prosecuted by the Roman Inquisition, the terms 'philo-Protestant' and 'heterodox' are useful in that they identify a certain nexus of beliefs, issues, and practices, and can indicate a variety of confessional stances, and more individual, and eclectic, beliefs. The authors of the inquisitorial texts examined in this work utilized the term 'Lutheran'

to describe all new varieties of Christianity that developed during the Reformation; the term's very inaccuracy renders it useless to the modern scholar.

3 Ritual theory has been a subject of much discussion among scholars; according to David Kertzer, it can be narrowly defined as a specifically religious action or broadly defined as any standardized human activity (David Kertzer, *Ritual, Politics, and Power* [New Haven: Yale University Press, 1988], p. 8). While my work discusses ritual practices in specifically the religious sense, I do not limit my definition of ritual practice to liturgical actions and celebrations that take place solely within sacred locations in the presence of clergy. Instead, I utilize a broader sense of ritual practice in much the same way as Robert Scribner in *Popular Culture and Popular Movements in Reformation Germany* (London: The Hambeldon Press, 1997), which incorporates ritual practices that, while often encouraged by the clergy, often took place outside their direct supervision either singly or in groups, such as private devotions to saints or pilgrimages. I do not, however, include the wide variety of folk magical practices, which Scribner terms 'private conjurations,' since during the Reformation and Counter-Reformation both Protestant and Catholic churches held these practices in increasing amounts of disapproval. See Scribner, *Popular Culture*, pp. 17–48. The recent literature concerning the role of ritual, both religious and secular, in early modern society is extensive; important works include Edward Muir, *Ritual in Early Modern Europe* (New York: Cambridge University Press, 1997); Susan C. Karant-Nunn, *The Reformation of Ritual: An Interpretation of Early Modern Germany* (New York: Routledge, 1997); and Calros M.N. Eire, *War against the Idols: The Reformation of Worship from Erasmus to Calvin* (New York: Cambridge University Press, 1986), among many others.

4 Wolfgang Reinhard, 'Reformation, Counter-Reformation, and the Early Modern State: A Reassessment,' *The Catholic Historical Review* 72 (1989): 393. Reinhard has asserted that, 'social control by senior members of your own community probably is more effective than that of an outside authority, even when that authority possessed its own police force or, as in the case of the Catholic Church, such a formidable organization as the Spanish or Roman Inquisition.' I argue that the Roman Inquisition was successful because it enlisted the aid and support not only of local elites but also people from all levels of society. This study addresses the issues raised by Thomas A. Brady Jr. in 'Confessionalization – The Career of a Concept,' in John M. Headley, Hans J. Hillerbrand, and Anthony J. Papalas, eds., *Confessionalization in Europe, 1555–1700: Essays in Honor and Memory of Bodo*

Nischan (Burlington, VT: Ashgate, 2004), pp. 1–20, by examining confessionalization from the perspective of broader ritual practice in order to adress how different strata of early modern Catholic societies approached heterodox ideas and participated in their success or repression, and to place religion and religious practice at the forefront of the confessionalizing process. While this study does not explicitly examine the question of state-building or modernization, it is worth noting that inquisitorial tribunals had to make use of secular resources to carry out their prosecutions, since the secular arm was needed to arrest and, sometimes, jail suspects. If necessary, it was also the secular state that provided for torture and execution as well.

5 Adriano Prosperi, *Tribunali della coscienza: Inquisitori, confessori, missionari* (Turin: Einaudi, 1996), pp. 234–43; Prosperi has recognized that, although the internal forum of conscience (confession) and the external forum of public punishment and justice (inquisition) were, in theory, jurisdictionally separate, inquisitors often came close to acting as confessors when dealing with the voluntarily penitent. I argue that inquisitors, while concerned with public punishment, also were concerned with the salvation of even the most obdurate, ideally.

6 Francisco Peña, *Directorium Inquisitorum* (Venice: Apud Marcum Antonium Zalterium, 1595), p. 447: '[. . .] in crimine haeresis, ex sola reorum confessione ad condemnationem procedi potest; quia cum haeresis crimen mente concipiatur et in animo lateat, plerumque non potest aliter probari, quam per propriam confessionem reorum [. . .].' See also Christopher F. Black, *The Italian Inquisition* (New Haven: Yale University Press, 2009), p. 69. Inquisition manuals recognized different subcategories of heresy. I explore what manual authors would have called 'heretical sects': varieties of Christianity and some forms of apostasy. Witchcraft, false sanctity, and other forms of heresy prosecuted by tribunals received separate treatments in manuals, and the techniques and post-Reformation perspectives discussed in this book do not necessarily apply to them.

7 Francisco Bethencourt, 'Les rites de l'Inquisition: Réflexions autour d'un projet de recherche,' in Heinz Mohnhaupt and Dieter Simon, eds., *Vorträge zur Justizforschung: Geschichte un Theorie*, Volume 1 (Frankfurt am Main: Vittorio Klostermann, 1992), pp. 135–52, esp. p. 136; Bethencourt, *The Inquisition: A Global History, 1478–1835* (New York: Cambridge University Press, 2009), especially his explanation of the importance of inquisition 'rites and etiquette,' pp. 27–34. It is unclear, however, how much the Italian tribunals mirrored the patterns of Spanish Inquisition tribunals regarding certain aspects of Iberian practice, such as the ritual entry made by newly appointed inquisitors.

8 Malcolm Lambert, *The Cathars* (Malden MA: Blackwell, 1998), pp. 116–30; Edward Peters, *Inquisition* (New York: The Free Press, 1988), pp. 12–17; Andrea Del Col, *L'Inquisizione in Italia: Dal XII al XXI secolo* (Milan: Oscar Mondadori, 2006), pp. 63–109 for the elimination of Cathar heresy in France and Italy, and pp. 120–7 concerning the *inquisitio* and process procedure. In the medieval period, while individual tribunals and inquisitors often wrote each other, and the papal Curia, to keep everyone apprised of inquisitorial activities, there was no clearly defined central organization. Each tribunal's staff, including the inquisitor, was initially appointed on an ad hoc basis, even if some of the tribunals later became permanently established. See also Black, *Italian Inquisition*, pp. 57–9, concerning secrecy, and pp. 1–18 about medieval and Spanish precedent.

9 James B. Given, *The Inquisition and Medieval Society: Power and Discipline in Languedoc* (Ithaca: Cornell University Press, 1997), pp. 14–15; Peters, *Inquisition*, pp. 44–53. Until the Roman Inquisition's reorganization, the appointment of inquisitors was often made by conventual votes in inquisitorial provinces or, in Lombardy and the Kingdom of Naples, by the vice-general of the Dominican order, and subsequently confirmed by the pope, according to the procedures laid out in Innocent IV's bull of 1254, *Cum super inquisitione*. That bull also approved the same procedures for the nomination of Franciscan inquisitors in Treviso, the Romagna, Tuscany, the Marches, Umbria, and Lazio. The provinces initially remained the same, geographically, when Pope Paul III reorganized the hierarchical administrative structure in 1542. See Michael Tavuzzi, *Renaissance Inquisitors: Dominican Inquisitors and Inquisitorial Districts in Northern Italy, 1474–1527* (Boston: Brill, 2007), pp. 1–45, 79–109; Andrea Del Col, *L'Inquisizione in Italia*, pp. 91–3. In Spanish territory, by 1484, it was administered by the Suprema, the council of legal and theological experts led by Spain's inquisitor general, which coordinated activity and monitored prosecutorial standards; the Suprema reported mostly to the Catholic monarchs. Henry Kamen, *The Spanish Inquisition: An Historical Revision* (New Haven: Yale University Press, 1997), pp. 44–50, 138–42.

10 John Tedeschi, 'The Organization and Procedures of the Roman Inquisition: A Sketch,' in Tedeschi, ed. *The Prosecution of Heresy: Collected Studies on the Inquisition in Early Modern Italy* (Binghamton, NY: Medieval and Renaissance Texts and Studies, 1991), pp. 127–9. Tedeschi also points out that most Italian inquisitors had backgrounds in theology. Andrea Errera, *'Processus in causa fidei': L'evoluzione dei manuali inquisitoriali nei secoli XVI–XVIII e il manuale inedito di un inquisitore perugino* (Bologna: Monduzzi, 2000), pp. 4–6. Andrea Del Col, *L'Inquisizione in Italia*,

pp. 292–3, 396. Del Col also has asserted that even after 1542, bishops, nuncios, and commissaires given papal briefs to prosecute heresy remained incredibly important, and the Roman Inquisition did not become the dominant force against heresy until the 1550s; see Del Col, 'I rapporti tra i giudici di fede in Italia dal medioevo all'età contemporanea,' in Susanna Peyronel Rambaldi, ed., *I Tribunali della fede: Continuità e discontinuità dal medioevo all'età moderna; Atti del XLV Convegno di studi sulla Riforma e sui movimenti religiosi in Italia, Torre Pellice, 3–4 settembre 2005* (Turin: Claudiana, 2007), pp. 105–6.

11 Prosperi, *Tribunai della coscienza*, pp. 65–75; Black, *Italian Inquisition*, pp. 19–54, esp. pp. 22–6 concerning divergent agendas between pope and the congregation in Rome and pp. 38–9 and 41–5 concerning the political and religious situation in Milan and Naples. Lucca operated its own tribunal, with the cooperation of the local bishop, from 1545, rather than accept the appointment of an inquisitor from Rome despite pressure to do so. See Black, pp. 40–1. For a more general explanation of the political situation, especially the Italian Wars in which Spain and France fought for political predominance on the Italian Peninsula, see Gregory Hanlon, *Early Modern Italy, 1550–1800* (New York: St. Martin's Press, 2000), pp. 62–75.

12 Errera, '*Processus in causa fidei*,' pp. 85–8. The manuals circulating in the first decades after 1542, both printed books and manuscripts, were originally written in the medieval period or the fifteenth and early sixteenth centuries in Spain, and reflected the influence of each of those particular contexts. Also see Del Col, *L'Inquisizione in Italia*, p. 118.

13 James B. Given, *Inquisition and Medieval Society*, p. 45; the structure, form, and content of these manuals could vary, including formularies for documents, sample questioning sessions, and descriptions of heresies.

14 William Hamilton Bryson, *Dictionary of Sigla and Abbreviations to and in Law Books before 1607* (Charlottesville, VA: University of Virginia Press, 1975), pp. 10–13; James A. Brundage, *Medieval Canon Law* (New York: Longman, 1995), pp. 44–69; Andrea Del Col, *L'Inquisizione in Italia*, pp. 66, 127. Canon law consisted of Gratian's *Decretum* (c. 1140), the *Liber Extra* of Pope Gregory IX (1234), the *Liber Sextus*, produced under the aegis of Boniface VIII (1298), and the *Clementinae*, the collection of Clement V (1317). The glosses, in succession, were those of Karolus de Tocco (1215); Johannes Teutonicus (about 1216); Accursius (1228); Jacobus Columbi (about 1240); Bernard of Parma (c. 1245); Bartholomew of Brescia (d. 1258); and Giovanni d'Andrea (about 1300).

15 Given, *Inquisition and Medieval Society*, p. 50. Given discusses the issue of safely destroying heretical works while leaving inquisitors sources of

information concerning heresy in the manuscript manuals of the medieval period.

16 Antoine Dondaine, 'Le manuel de l'inquisiteur,' *Archivium Fratrum Praedicatorum,* Vol. 17 (1947): 89; Edward M. Peters, 'Editing Inquisitors' Manuals in the Sixteenth Century: Francisco Peña and the *Directorium Inquisitorum* of Nicholas Eymeric,' *The Library Chronicle* 40 (1974): 95–107; Andrea Errera, 'Manuali per inquisitori,' in *Dizionario storico dell'Inquisizione,* Vol. 2, ed. Adriano Prosperi, assisted by Vincenzo Lavenia and John Tedeschi (Pisa: Scuola Normale Superiore Pisa, 2010), pp. 975–81, esp. pp. 975–6.

17 Tedeschi, 'Organization and Procedures,' esp. pp. 130–9; Tedeschi, 'Inquisitorial Sources and Their Uses,' in *The Prosecution of Heresy,* p. 53 concerning the presence of manuals among tribunals' collections of books. See also Del Col, *L'Inquisizione in Italia,* pp. 118–19; Adriano Prosperi, 'L'Arsenale degli inquisitori: Saggio introduttivo al catalogo della Mostra della Biblioteca Casanatense' in Angelo Valentini Claudiana ed., *Inquisizione e Indice nei secoli XVI–XVIII: Controversie teologiche dalle raccolte casanatensi* (Vigevano: Diakronia 1998), pp. 6–12; Black, *Italian Inquisition,* pp. 68–71; and concerning tribunals' funding, pp. 102–4. According to Black, in Ferrara and Modena Jewish communities were pressed to donate funds, and the Bolognese tribunal was dependent upon a stipend from the archbishop.

18 Many historians have noted the Catholic Church's tendency, at the time, to utilize 'Lutheranism' as a generic term meant to denote all new Protestant confessions. Silvana Seidel Menchi has reasoned that perhaps they kept the term simply because Luther was the first, and therefore had the most psychological impact, but notes that the lack of differentiation between the rapidly developing Protestant denominations was very much present in inquisitorial *processi*. I argue that this lack of differentiation both was a product of the Church's past encounters with heresies and served a particular propagandistic purpose in the sixteenth century. See Silvana Seidel Menchi, *Erasmo in Italia, 1520–1580* (Turin: Bollati Boringhieri, 1987), p. 42.

19 The association of Anabaptists with Donatists would have been particularly fruitful from polemical and inquisitorial perspectives, since it was Augustine who had first rationalized utilizing the secular state to enforce church uniformity and attendance during the Donatist controversy. See Frederick H. Russell, 'Persuading Donatists: Augustine's Coercion by Words,' in William E. Klingshirn and Mark Vessey, eds., *The Limits of Ancient Christianity: Essays on Late Antique Culture and Thought in Honor of R.A. Markus* (Ann Arbor: University of Michigan Press, 1999), pp. 115–30. Manual authors utilized arguments similar to those of many Catholic

polemicists, particularly when it came to defending Catholic ritual practices as well as doctrines. As Ralph Keen as argued, for many Catholic polemicists the cultural practice of religion was inseperable from doctrinal questions. Polemicists utilized the Ancient Fathers, both as authoritative sources of Catholic traditions equal to that of Scripture, and as sources that authoritatively established certain beliefs and practices as heretical. See Ralph Keen, 'The Fathers in Counter-Reformation Theology in the Pre-Tridentine Period,' in Irena Backus, ed., *The Reception of the Church Fathers in the West*, Vol. 2 (New York: Brill, 1997), pp. 705–18.

20 For Melanchthon, see Salvatore Caponetto, ed., *I principii della teologia* (Rome: Istituto storico italiano per l'età moderna e contemporanea, 1992), p. 41: 'Con minor fatica si possono tuor via i vecchi pelagiani che i nuovi pelagiani de' nostri tempi, i quali, benché non nieghino essere del peccato originali, che tutte le opere degli uomini, tutte le forze umane siano peccati, perciò un poco più copiosamente diremo della forza e compito del peccato origionale.' Concerning Pelagius, Augustine, and original sin, see Peter Brown, *Augustine of Hippo* (Berkeley and Los Angeles: University of California Press, 1967), pp. 340–52. Concerning Martin Luther's use of the term 'Pelagian' as applied to the Catholic Church, see Manfred Schulze, 'Martin Luther and the Church Fathers,' *Church Fathers in the West*, Vol. 2, pp. 579–97; for John Calvin's, Johannes van Oort, 'John Calvin and the Church Fathers,' ibid., pp. 672–3.

21 For example, Cesare Carena in his *Tractatus de de Officio Sanctissimae Inquisitionis* (Cremona: Apud Marc'Antonium Belpierum, 1636), p. 334: 'Attamen, existimo ego dictum illud procedere posse, ubi opus quod sit, magis communiter ab Haereticis laudaretur, et probetur, et de illo essent plurimae spetialies Haereses, pro ut adsunt in casu nostro, in quo omnes fere nostri temporis Haeretici convenient in reprobando ciborum delectu in Ieiuniis.' This will be discussed extensively in Chapter 3.

22 Peters, 'Editing Inquisitors' Manuals,' p. 96; Agostino Borromeo, 'Eymeric, Nicolau,' in *Dizionario storico dell'Inquisizione*, Vol. 2, pp. 568–70.

23 Peters, 'Editing Inquisitors Manuals,' pp. 97–102; Agostino Borromeo, 'A proposito del *Directorium Inquisitorum* di Nicolas Eymerich e delle sue edizioni cinquecentesche,' *Critica Storica* No. 4 (1983): 499–547, esp. 502–20; Vincenzo Lavenia, 'Peña, Francisco,' in *Dizionario storico dell'Inquisizione*, Vol. 3, pp. 1186–9. In this work, I employ one of the 1595 reprints of the 1587 edition because it is the definitive one. When the Spanish requested that Peña be elevated to the cardinalate, Pope Clement VIII refused because Peña had disagreed stridently and publicly with the decision to

absolve Henry IV of France of heresy and acknowledge his conversion to Catholicism. Peña later declined the bishopric of Tortosa or Albarracín to stay in Rome.

24 Niccolò Del Re, 'Prospero Farinacci giureconsulto romano (1544–1618),' *Archivio della società romana di storia patria* 98 (1975): 135–220, esp. pp. 174–5; Laurie Nussdorfer, 'Lost Faith: A Roman Prosecutor Reflects on Notaries' Crimes,' in *Beyond Florence: The Contours of Medieval and Early Modern Italy*, Paula Findlen, Michelle M. Fontaine, and Duane J. Osheim, eds. (Stanford: Stanford University Press, 2003), pp. 101–14; A. Mazzacane, 'Farinacci, Prospero,' in *Dizionario Biografico degli Italiani* 45 (Rome: Istituto della Enciclopedia Italiana, 1995), pp. 1–5; S. Feci, 'Farinacci, Prospero,' in *Dizionario storico dell'Inquisizione*, Vol. 2, p. 579.

25 See H.C. Lea, *Materials Toward a History of Witchcraft*, Vol. 2 (New York: T. Yoseloff, 1959), pp. 942–3; Tedeschi, 'Inquisitorial Sources,' p. 55; Agostino Borromeo, 'Carena, Cesare,' in *Dizionario storico dell'Inquisizione*, Vol. 1, pp. 272–3. Both Carena's and Masini's manuals resemble Vincenzo Castrucci's manuscript manual, described by Andrea Errera in his work, '*Processus in causa fidei*' esp. p. 249 and following. Errera has recognized, furthermore, Masini's and Carena's manuals concerning procedure as the two most dominant from 1621 until the 1730s. See Errera, 'Manuali per inquisitori,' pp. 980–1.

26 Black, *Italian Inquisition*, pp. 104–9. Masini's correspondence with the bishop of Ancona, Cardinal Carlo Conti, is an especially illuminating example of a good relationship between bishops and inquisitors and the everyday tasks of inquisitors. See also Tedeschi, pp. 52–3; P. Fontana, 'Masini, Eliseo,' in *Dizionario storico dell'Inquisizione*, Vol. 2, pp. 1006–7.

27 Eliseo Masini, *Sacro Arsenale; Overo Prattica dell'officio della S. Inquisizione*, ed. Tommaso Menghini (Rome: 1693; StaatsBibliothek Digitalisat 4 J.can.p.5504), pp. 228–9 : 'Ma il Reo durerà negando nella seconda tortura, egli purga la prima confessione e deve lasciarsi andare, quando però sia stato bastevolmente tormentato e gl'indizi non siano molto urgenti: che altrimenti si potria venire alla terza tortura.'

28 For example, see Silvana Seidel Menchi, 'The Inquisitor as Mediator,' in Ronald K. Delph, Michelle M. Fontaine, and John Jeffries Martin, eds., *Heresy, Culture, and Religion in Early Modern Italy* (Kirksville, MO: Truman State University Press, 2006), pp. 173–92, esp. pp. 189–90; Andrea Del Col, *L'Inquisizione in Italia*, pp. 119–20. In general, Adriano Prosperi views the dichotomy between conciliation and repression as represented by confessors and inquisitors, respectively (*Tribunali della coscienza*, pp. 11–15; pp. 223–5), but has recognized that inquisitors could act gently or mildly

(pp. 221–2). I am interested in exploring the legal criteria for employing either a harsh or more lenient approach.

29 Black, *Italian Inquisition*, pp. 64–7, 208–9; Carlo Ginzburg, 'The Inquisitor as Anthropologist,' in Ginzburg, ed., *Clues, Myths, and the Historical Method* (Baltimore: Johns Hopkins University Press, 1989); Prosperi, *Tribunali della coscienza*, pp. 203–4.

30 Andrea Del Col, *Inquisizione in Italia*, p. 125.

1. Philo-Protestantism in Italian Lands: Beliefs and Practices

1 ASMo, *Inquisizione*, Busta 5, fasc. 20, 1568, *Contra Alessandrum Fornarium*, fols. 1r–v: 'Allesandro dove avete così ben studiate voi che il Purgatorio non sia, et detto Allesandro disse a Florio dove trovate voi che la sia et esso Florio disse la Santa Madre Chiesa me lo comanda. Et detto Allessandro rispose così tre volte la Santa Madre Chiesa te lo comanda et Florio disse siate testimoni se gli frati di San Domenico sappessero questo te meriteranno anzi meriti il fuoco.' Concerning the issue of proselytization in prison, and prison conditions in sixteenth-century Italian states in general, see Marion Leathers Kuntz, 'Voices from a Venetian Prison in the Cinquecento: Francesco Spinola and Dionisio Gallo,' *Studi veneziani*, n.s. 27 (1994): 79–126.

2 ASMo, *Contra Alessandrum Fornarium*, fol. unpg.

3 ASMo, *Contra Alessandrum Fornarium*, fol. unpg. Fra Niccolò da Finale was appointed inquisitorial vicar of Modena in 1566, since at the time Modena was a part of the inquisitorial region of Ferrara, Modena, and Reggio. Fra Niccolò reported to Camillo Campeggi, the Dominican inquisitor of the province from c. 1567 to c. 1568. Campeggi was very active in his duties; he vigorously applied himself to his post in Ferrara, and admired the Spanish Inquisition's more stringent approach, lamenting what he perceived of as his compatriots' leniency. His enthusiasm caused conficts with the secular government (the d'Este ducal family) and local religious officials which Carlo Borromeo was dispatched to sort out from February–March of 1568. By 1568, in Modena, Fra Niccolò was alternating with the bishop of Modena, Cardinal Giovanni Morone, in conducting processes; Morone's own tangled dealings with the Roman Inquisition will be discussed later in this chapter. Campeggi, during his tenure as inquisitor, also participated in the third session of the Council of Trent in 1562–1563. He also found the time to re-edit and expand Zanchino Ugolini's medieval manual *De haereticis tractatus aureus*, which was then printed in Rome in 1568.

See Giuseppe Trenti, *I processi del tribunale dell'Inquisizione di Modena: Inventario generale analitico, 1489–1874* (Modena: Aedes Muratoriana, 2003), pp. 311–13 concerning Niccolò da Finale and his interaction with Cardinal Morone. For Camillo Campeggi, see Valerio Marchetti, 'Campeggi, Camillo,' in *Dizionario biografico degli Italiani,* Vol. 17 (Rome: Istituto della Enciclopedia Italiana, 1974), pp. 439–40; Adriano Prosperi, 'Campeggi, Camillo,' in *Dizionario storico dell'Inquisizione,* Vol. 1, ed. Adriano Prosperi with Vincenzo Lavenia and John Tedeschi (Pisa: Scuola Normale Superiore Pisa, 2010), pp. 252–3.

4 ASMo, *Contra Alessandrum Fornarium,* fol. unpg.; Fornari was tortured before producing this confession. See also Cesare Bianco, 'Bartolomeo della Pergola e la sua predicazione eterodossa a Modena nel 1544,' *Bollettino della Società di Studi Valdesi* no. 151 (July 1982): 10.

5 The starting point and duration of early modern Catholic reform has been described in a variety of ways, but most scholars agree that the perceived need for church reform predated Luther's protest, perhaps as early as the mid-fifteenth century. See Robert Bireley 'Early Modern Catholicism,' in *Reformation and Early Modern Europe: A Guide to Research,* ed. David M. Whitford (Kirksville, MO: Truman State University Press, 2008), pp. 575–62 and Bireley, *The Refashioning of Catholicism 1400–1750: A Reassessment of the Counter Reformation* (Washington, DC: The Catholic University of America Press, 1999), esp. pp. 25–44 concerning religious orders; Michael Mullet, *The Counter-Reformation and Catholic Reformation in Early Modern Europe* (London: Routledge, 1999); John O'Malley, *Trent and All That: Renaming Catholicism in the Early Modern Era* (Cambridge, MA: Harvard University Press, 2000); Nelson H. Minnich, 'The Last Two Councils of the Catholic Reformation: The Influence of Lateran V on Trent,' in *Early Modern Catholicism: Essays in Honour of John W. O'Malley SJ,* ed. Kathleen M. Comerford and Hilmar M. Pabel (Toronto: University of Toronto Press, 2001), pp. 3–25. For the continued importance of Savonarola in the sixteenth century, see Donald Weinstein, *Savonarola and Florence: Prophecy and Patriotism in the Renaissance* (Princeton: Princeton University Press, 1970) and Lauro Martines, *Fire in the City: Savonarola and the Struggle for Renaissance Florence* (New York: Oxford University Press, 2006); for Protestant appropriations of Savonarola as a forerunner of the Reformation, see Bruce Gordon, '"This Worthy Witness of Christ": Protestant Uses of Savonarola in the Sixteenth Century,' in *Protestant History and Identity in Sixteenth-Century Europe,* Vol. 1, *The Medieval Inheritance,* ed. Bruce Gordon (Aldershot, UK: Scolar Press, 1996), pp. 93–107.

6 William V. Hudon, 'Religion and Society in Early Modern Italy – Old Questions, New Insights,' *American Historical Review* 101, no. 3 (June 1996): 795; see also Hudon, *Marcello Cervini and Ecclesiastical Government in Tridentine Italy* (De Kalb: Northern Illinois University Press, 1992), esp. pp. 12–17. Hudon, in both works, proposes the term 'Tridentine Catholicism' to refer to this time in Catholic religious history ('Religion and Society,' p. 803), but parts of this book deals with the Roman Inquisition's activities before the Council of Trent took place beginning in 1545. Eric Cochrane also noted the thematic emphasis on returning to past states of devotion in his discussion of religious revival among religious orders and confraternities beginning in the late Renaissance See Eric Cochrane, *Italy 1530–1630*, ed. Julius Kirshner (New York: Longman, 1988), pp. 106–18.

7 See, for example, Wietse de Boer, *The Conquest of the Soul: Confession, Discipline, and Public Order in Counter-Reformation Milan* (Boston: Brill, 2001), pp. 7–11.

8 See, for example, Federico Chabod, *Lo Stato e la vità religiosa nell'epoca di Carlo V* (Turin: Einaudi, 1934); Delio Cantimori, *Eretici italiani del cinquecento* (Florence: G.S. Sansoni, 1939), with a new edition published by Einaudi in 1992.

9 Eric W. Cochrane, 'Counter Reformation or Tridentine Reformation? Italy in the Age of Carlo Borromeo,' in *San Carlo Borromeo: Catholic Reform and Ecclesiastical Politics in the Second Half of the Sixteenth Century*, ed. John M. Headley and John B. Tomaro (Cranbury, NJ: Associated University Presses, 1988), esp. p. 37; see also Anne Jacobson Schutte, 'Periodization of Sixteenth-Century Italian Religious History: The Post-Cantimori Paradigm Shift,' *Journal of Modern History* 61 (1989): 269–84; and Hudon, 'Religion and Society,' pp. 784–7.

10 Hudon, 'Religion and Society,' p. 794; Anne Jacobsen Schutte, 'Periodization,' pp. 269–70.

11 For Contarini, see Elisabeth Gleason, *Gasparo Contarini: Venice, Rome, and Reform* (Berkeley and Los Angeles: University of California Press, 1993), pp. 11–25; pp. 202–3; and pp. 226–56. Concerning the de-emphasis of 1541–1542 as a sharp break in both church policy and the hopes of some of the laity, see Anne Jacobson. Schutte, 'Periodization,' pp. 269–84. For other analyses of Ratisbon (Regensburg), see Dermot Fenlon, *Heresy and Obedience in Tridentine Italy: Cardinal Pole and the Counter Reformation* (Cambridge: Cambridge University Press, 1972), pp. 45–61; Peter Matheson, *Cardinal Contarini at Regensburg* (Oxford: Clarendon Press, 1972), pp. 97–144. For a different interpetation of the council's end, see

Daniel A. Crews, *Twilight of the Renaissance: The Life of Juan deValdés*, esp. pp. 135–59, who contends that the colloquy was surprisingly successful, given the lack of expectations; Paul III and the more conservative Italian cardinals, according to Crews, ensured its failure due to disapproval of the colloquy's formula of justification.

12 Heiko Oberman, *Luther: Man between God and the Devil*, trans. Eileen Walliser-Schwarzbart (New Haven: Yale University Press, 2006), pp. 188–90.

13 Oberman, *Luther*, pp. 192–7.

14 Oberman, *Luther*, pp. 226–45. Luther agreed with the Catholic Church, and later Reformers such as Ulrich Zwingli and John Calvin, that baptism should be administered to infants, although each interpreted the significance of the sacrament at least a bit differently. All of those denominations, however, would have to defend performing the sacrament in infancy against the Anabaptists, who reserved baptism for adults because they thought only those who had reached the age of reason could comprehend fully the concepts of sin and Christ's message of salvation through faith.

15 Eva Maria Jung, 'On the Nature of Evangelism in Sixteenth-Century Italy,' *Journal of the History of Ideas* 14 (1953): 511–27; José Nieto, *Juan de Valdés and the Origins of the Spanish and Italian Reformation* (Geneva: Libraire Droz, 1970). While this group, and the beliefs associated with it, are often referred to as 'Valdesian,' I will employ the term 'followers of Valdés' simply to avoid confusion between them and the Waldensians, followers of Waldo of Lyon, of the twelfth and thirteenth centuries discussed in Chapter 2.

16 For explanations concerning the core group of more irenic churchmen, and noblewomen's role in organizing and maintaining it, see Diana Robin, *Publishing Women: Salons, Presses, and the Counter-Reformation in Sixteenth-Century Italy* (Chicago: University of Chicago Press, 2007); Massimo Firpo, 'Juan de Valdés e l'evangelismo italiano: Appunti e problemi di una ricerca in corso,' in *Tra Alumbrados e 'spirituali': Studi su Juan de Valdés e il valdesianismo nella crisi religiosa del' 500 italiano*, ed. Massimo Firpo (Florence: Olschki, 1990)

17 Regarding Morone's trial, see Massimo Firpo, ed., *Il processo inquisitoriale del cardinale Giovanni Morone: Edizione critica*, 7 vols. (Rome: Istituto storico italiano per l'età moderna, 1981–1985); for Carnesecchi's, see *I processi inquisitoriali di Pietro Carnesecchi (1557–1567): Edizione Critica*, ed. Massimo Firpo and Dario Marcatto, 2 vols., vol. 2 in 3 parts (Vatican City: Archivio segreto vaticano, 1998–2000). See also Camilla

Russell, *Giulia Gonzaga and the Religious Controversies of the Sixteenth Century* (Turnhout: Brepols, 2006), pp. 79–80, 166–7, 190–208; C. Donadelli, 'Galeota, Mario,' in *Dizionario storico dell'Inquisizione,* Vol. 2, pp. 634–5.

18 Daniel A. Crews, *Juan de Valdés,* quotation pp. 105–6, and also pp. 35–46.

19 For the influence of Erasmus on Spanish intellectuals, including Valdés, see Crews, pp. 27–35. For Erasmus's impact on the Italian peninsula, see especially Silvana Seidel Menchi, *Erasmo in Italia* (Turin: Bollati Boringhieri, 1987). See also James D. Tracy, *Erasmus of the Low Countries* (Berkeley and Los Angeles: University of California Press, 1996), pp. 90–3, pp. 110–12. For example (quoted in Tracy, p. 112, originally from *Ratio Verae Theologiae*), Erasmus explained the parable of Jesus cursing a fig tree that bore no fruit as 'indicating that no kind of man is more hateful than those who are impious under the pretext of piety and live irreligiously while professing religion by their title and dress.'

20 Seidel Menchi, *Erasmo in Italia,* pp. 41–8, 307–21.

21 Tracy, *Erasmus,* p. 117.

22 Camilla Russell, *Giulia Gonzaga,* pp. 43–51.

23 Cochrane, *Italy,* 123–34.

24 Paul V. Murphy, *Ruling Peacefully: Cardinal Ercole Gonzaga and Patrician Reform in Sixteenth-Century Italy* (Washington, DC: Catholic University of America Press, 2007), pp. 75–108.

25 Hudon, *Marcello Cervini,* pp. 110–28;

26 Silvana Seidel Menchi, 'Inquisizione come repressione o inquisizione come mediazione? Una proposta di periodizzazione,' in *Annuario dell'Istituto storico italiano per l'età moderna e contemporanea* 35–6 (1983–84): 53–77; Siedel Menchi, 'Inquisitor as Mediator,' in *Heresy, Culture, and Religion in Early Modern Italy: Contexts and Contestations,* ed. Ronald K. Delph, Michelle M. Fontaine, and John Jeffries Martin (Kirksville, MO: Truman State University Press, 2006), pp. 173–92.

27 Hudon, 'Religion and Society,' pp. 797–8; Edward Peters, *Inquisition,* pp. 296–315.

28 Silvana Seidel Menchi, 'Le traduzione di Lutero nella prima metà del Cinquecento,' *Rinascimento,* ser. II, 17 (1977): 31–109.

29 Salvatore Caponetto, 'Due tradotte opere di Melantone da Ludovico Castelvetro: "I Principii de la Theologia di Ippofilo da Terra Negra," e "Dell'autorità della Chiesa e degli scritti degli antichi,"' *Nuova Rivista Storica* 70 (1986): 253–74. Melanchthon, a humanist

educated in rhetoric and classical languages, converted to Luther's cause sometime before 1519 and was one of Luther's most valuable supporters. His humanist writing skills appealed to those also educated in humanism as much as his doctrines.

30 Melantone, *I principii della teologia*, ed. Salvatore Caponetto (Rome: Istituto storico italiano per l'età moderna e contemporanea, 1992), pp. 41–60. Melanchthon also contrasted the assertions of pagan philosophers with evidence from Genesis to make his point, an apparent attempt to appeal to his more educated readers. For Augustine's arguments against Pelagius, see Peter Brown, *Augustine of Hippo* (Berkeley and Los Angeles: University of California Press, 1967), pp. 342–75.

31 See, for example, Salvatore Caponetto, *The Protestant Reformation in Sixteenth-Century Italy*, trans. Anne C. Tedeschi and John Tedeschi (Kirksville, MO.: Thomas Jefferson University Press, 1999), pp. 119–41; pp. 190–220.

32 Salvatore Caponetto, *Protestant Reformation*, p. 25; Paul Grendler, *The Roman Inquisition and the Venetian Press, 1540–1605* (Princeton: Princeton University Press, 1978), pp. 63–127, 182–200. Although many localities in north-central Italy generated their own indexes of prohibited books, the Roman Inquisition did not produce its own until 1559. Nevertheless, inquisitors often mention 'prohibited books' in trials that took place before 1559, meaning books listed in the local indexes and guides.

33 The *Dottrina Vecchia e Dottrona Nuova* was an anonymous translation of Urbanus Reghius's 1525 work, *Novae doctrinae ad veterem Collatio*. The work refrained from overtly criticizing the Catholic Church, but advocated justification by faith alone, and disparaged the efficacy of good works performed without faith. See Caponetto, *Protestant Reformation*, pp. 26–7. The *Sommario della Sacra Scrittura*, also anonymous, first appeared in 1534, and was also a translation of a work originally written in Dutch in 1523. It also promoted justification by faith alone without engaging in polemical arguments or mentioning Luther by name; Susanna Peyronel Rambaldi, *Dai Paesi Bassi all'Italia: 'Il Sommario della Sacra Scrittura': Un libro proibito nella società italiana del Cinquecento* (Florence: L.S. Olschki, 1997).

34 See Ruth Prelowski, 'The "Beneficio di Cristo,"' introduction and translation, in *Reformation Studies in Honor of Laelius Socinus*, ed. John Tedeschi (Florence: Felice le Monnier), 1965, pp. 23–102. For an explanation of the sources of religious thought in the work, see Carlo Ginzburg and Adriano Prosperi, *Giochi di Pazienza: Un seminario sul 'Beneficio di Cristo'* (Turin: Giulio Einaudi, 1975).

35 Tommaso Bozza, *La Riforma cattolica: Il Beneficio di Cristo* (Rome: Libreria Tombolini, 1972).
36 Prelowski, trans., 'The "Beneficio di Christo,"' p. 67.
37 Elisabeth Gleason, *Reform Thought in Sixteenth-Century Italy* (Chico, CA: Scholars Press, 1981), pp. 104–5.
38 Caponetto, *Protestant Reformation*, pp. 28–9.
39 At this point in Venice, the papal nuncio Girolamo Aleandro was heavily involved in directing the local inquisitor to prosecute the heterodox despite the fact that the Roman Inquisition had yet to be reorganized. John Jeffries Martin, *Venice's Hidden Enemies: Italian Heretics in a Renaissance City* (Berkeley and Los Angeles: University of California Press, 1993), pp. 27, 54–5, 102.
40 George H. Williams, 'The Two Social Strands in Italian Anabaptism, ca. 1526–ca. 1565,' in *The Social History of the Reformation*, ed. Lawrence P. Buck and Jonathan W. Zophy (Columbus, OH: Ohio State University Press, 1972), pp. 156–207, esp. pp. 168–74, 180–7. Pier Paolo Vergerio, as a proponent of the magisterial Reform church, had to fight for control of churches in Rhaetia against Renato and his followers; see Caponetto, *Protestant Reformation*, pp. 148–50, 254–6; Martin, *Venice's Hidden Enemies*, pp. 99–111.
41 Williams, 'Two Social Strands in Italian Anabaptism,' pp. 175–80, 184; Daniel A. Crews, *Juan de Valdés*, pp. 9–15
42 Martin, *Venice's Hidden Enemies*, pp. 111–22; John Jeffries Martin, *Myths of Renaissance Individualism* (New York: Palgrave Macmillan, 2004), pp. 41–7; Andrea Del Col, 'Shifting Attitudes in the Social Environment toward Heretics: The Inquisition in the Friuli in the Sixteenth Century,' in *Ketzerverfolgung im 16. und frühen 17. Jahrhundert: Vorträge gehalten anlässlich eines Arbeitsgesprächs vom 1. bis 5. Oktober 1989 in der Herzog August Bibliothek Wolfenbüttel*, ed. Hans Rudolf Guggisberg, Bernd Moeller, and Silvana Seidel Menchi (Wiesbaden: Harrassowitz, 1992), pp. 65–86, esp. p. 70. Del Col points out that a group of heterodox in the Friuli read and discussed Melanchthon, Zwingli, Bucer, and Calvin, even though 'these tenets, theologically not always strictly compatible, [and] were merged by people who felt the overwhelming necessity of criticizing and overturning traditional Catholic doctrines and practices.'
43 Ugo Rozzo, 'Le "Prediche" veneziane di Giulio da Milano,' *Bolletino della Società di Studi Valdesi* 152 (1983): 3–30.
44 Caponetto, *Protestant Reformation*, p. 19.

45 Guido dall'Olio, *Eretici e inquisitori nella Bologna del Cinquecento* (Bologna: Istituto per la storia di Bologna, 1999), p. 81.
46 Guido dall'Olio, *Bologna*, p. 82.
47 B. Fontana, 'Documenti Vaticani contro l'eresia luterana in Italia,' *Archivio della Società romana di storia patria* XV (1892): 132.
48 Aldo Stella, 'La lettera del cardinale Contarini sulla predestinazione,' *Rivista di storia della Chiesa in Italia,* XV (1961): 437; and especially Elisabeth Gleason, *Gasparo Contarini*, pp. 261–76.
49 Caponetto, *Protestant Reformation*, pp. 30–1. Concerning the Roman Inquisition's role in the process of confessionalization, see Paolo Simoncelli, 'Inquisizione Romana e Riforma in Italia,' *Rivista Storica Italiana* 100 (1988): 1–125.
50 Richard Trexler, *Public Life in Renaissance* Florence (New York: Academic Press, 1980), pp. xix–xxii. Trexler mainly was concerned with dispelling the idea of Renaissance humanism, and the Renaissance in general, as a non-religious or even 'neo-pagan' movement. For a particularly good discussion of Trexler and the historiography of religion in Renaissance towns, see David M. D'Andrea, *Civic Christianity in Renaissance Italy: The Hospital of Treviso, 1400–1530* (Rochester, NY: University of Rochester Press, 2007), pp. 1–12.
51 Trexler, *Public Life*, pp. 47–73, and 247. Trexler has asserted, as well, that Renaissance Florentines had a sense of idolatry – it occurred when worshipping the image in question did not work.
52 Trexler, *Public Life*, pp. 100–2.
53 Richard Trexler, 'Florentine Religious Experience: The Sacred Image,' *Studies in the Renaissance* 19 (1972): 25; 34.
54 David Gentilcore, *From Bishop to Witch: The System of the Sacred in Early Modern Terra d'Otranto* (Manchester: Manchester University Press, 1992), p. 37; pp. 94–127. For a similar study concerning Spain, see especially William Christian, *Local Religion in Sixteenth-Century Spain* (Princeton, NJ: Princeton University Press, 1981).
55 D'Andrea, *Hospital of Treviso*, pp. 1–38, esp. pp. 4 and 27; see also John Henderson, *Piety and Charity in Late Medieval Florence* (Oxford: Clarendon Press, 1994); Brian Pullan, *Rich and Poor in Renaissance Venice: The Social Institutions of a Catholic State, to 1620*, (Cambridge, MA: Harvard University Press, 1971); Nicholas Terpstra, *Lay Confraternities and Civic Religion in Renaissance Bologna* (Cambridge: Cambridge University Press, 1995).
56 Michelle M. Fontaine, 'The Compagnia de Santa Maria dei Battuti in Modena on the Eve of Catholic Reform,' in *Confraternities and Catholic*

Reform in Italy, France, and Spain, ed. John Patrick Donnelly, SJ and Michael W. Maher, SJ, (Kirksville, MO: Truman State University Press, 1999), pp. 55–6, 69–73.

57 Edward Muir, 'The Virgin on the Street Corner: The Place of the Sacred in Italian Cities,' in *Religion and Culture in the Renaissance and Reformation*, ed. Steven Ozment (Kirksville, MO: Sixteenth Century Journal Publishers, 1989), pp. 25–30. For the count of 406, see pp. 19, 30.

58 Muir, 'Virgin on the Street Corner,' p. 39.

59 Edward Muir, *Civic Ritual in Renaissance Venice* (Princeton, NJ: Princeton University Press, 1981), pp. 5–8, 16–17.

60 Muir, *Civic Ritual*, pp. 224–5.

61 Muir, *Civic Ritual*, pp. 74–102, 212–13, 243–4.

62 Muir, *Ritual in Early Modern Europe*, pp. 7–8. Both Muir and Scribner describe the yearly liturgical calendar; Muir, *Ritual in Early Modern Europe*, pp. 55–80, esp. p. 59 and Scribner, *Popular Culture*, pp. 17–48.

63 Natalie Zemon Davis, 'The Sacred and the Body Social in Sixteenth-Century Lyon,' *Past and Present* 90 (Feb. 1981): 56–62.

64 Carlos M. N. Eire, *War against the Idols: The Reformation of Worship from Erasmus to Calvin* (New York: Cambridge University Press, 1986), pp. 67–8.

65 Bodo Nischan, 'Becoming Protestants: Lutheran Altars or Reformed Communion Tables?' in *Worship in Medieval and Early Modern Europe: Change and Continuity in Religious Practice*, ed. Karin Maag and John D. Witvliet (Notre Dame, IN: University of Notre Dame Press, 2004), pp. 84–111, esp. pp. 96–8.

66 Eire, *War against the Idols*, pp. 62–73; Susan C. Karant-Nunn, *Reformation of Ritual: An Interpretation of Early Modern Germany* (London: Routledge, 1997), pp. 130–7.

67 Eire, *War against the Idols*, pp. 77–86.

68 Oberman, *Luther*, pp. 237–40. Duke Phillip of Hesse, in the effort to maintain a united Protestant front against any religious or military intervention on the part of Holy Roman Emperor, and staunch Catholic, Charles V, sponsored the Colloquy of Marburg in 1529, at which Luther and Zwingli attempted to come to some agreement concerning the doctrinal significance of the Eucharist. The effort utterly failed; Zwingli, although perhaps of better temper in the negotiations, was just as irrevocably attached to his interpretation as Luther was to his own.

69 Eire, *War against the Idols*, pp. 212–20. Lutherans continued to argue against this interpretation of idolatry and the dangers of backsliding; Lutheran theologians insisted that idolatry only existed in the heart of one

whose understanding was imperfect. See Nischan, 'Becoming Protestants,' pp. 101–3.

70 Eire, *War against the Idols*, pp. 256–59.

71 George Hunston Williams, *The Radical Reformation* (Philadelphia, PA: The Westminster Press, 1962), pp. 118–27, 299–306. Anabaptism developed, to a certain extent independently, in multiple locations in Europe during the Reformation. In Zurich, former allies of Zwingli, Conrad Grebel, Felix Mantz, and Georg Blaurock among them, first argued for adult baptism in 1524; in Augsburg and southern Germany, Anabaptist theology can also be traced to Johann Denck. While all Anabaptist groups and underground churches engaged in missionary work and proselytizing, the lack of any defining central organization meant that there could be a fairly wide divergence between the doctrinal formulations of different Anabaptist conventicles past the one common element of embracing the believers' baptism.

72 John Jeffries Martin, *Venice's Hidden Enemies*, pp. 89–96, 99–122. In northern Europe in the 1550s, Lutheran, Calvinist, and other Reformed churches began utilizing ritual as a means of consolidating church organization and attempting to form separate confessional identities among their parishioners, although as Bodo Nischan has argued, this was often a contentious process, particularly when rulers, who had personally converted from Lutheranism to Calvinism, attempted to 'Calvinize' their Lutheran state churches. See Bodo Nischan, 'Ritual and Protestant Identity in Late Reformation Germany,' in *Protestant History and Identity in Sixteenth-Century Europe*, Vol. 2, *The Later Reformation*, ed. Bruce Gordon (Aldershot, UK: Scolar Press, 1996), pp. 144–58. See also Paolo Simoncelli, 'Inquisizione Romana e Riforma in Italia,' concerning Martin Bucer's role as an arbiter between heterodox believers' disagreements concerning the correct interpretation of the Eucharist and predestination through four letters sent in the 1540s; among those causing the discussion was Camillo Renato (pp. 38–54).

73 Caponetto, *Protestant Reformation*, p. xviii. Much of the historiography concerning the Roman Inquisition focuses on this aspect of using the responses given during trials to place conventicles within a particular denominational affiliation, be it Calvinist, Anabaptist, or other. The questions inquisitors asked to elicit this information are more rarely considered.

74 Hudon, 'Religion and Society,' pp. 790–1; quotation, p. 802.

75 John Frymire, '*Demonstrationes catholicae*: Defining Communities through Counter-Reformation Rituals,' in *Defining Community in Early Modern Europe*, ed. Michael J. Halvorson and Karen E. Spierling (Burlington, VT: Ashgate, 2008), pp. 163–4.

76 Ronald K. Delph, 'Polishing the Papal Image in the Counter-Reformation: The Case of Agostino Steuco,' *Sixteenth Century Journal* 23, no. 1 (Spring 1992): 38–40.
77 Michelle M. Fontaine, 'For the Good of the City: The Bishop and the Ruling Elite in Tridentine Modena,' *Sixteenth Century Journal* 28, no. 1 (Spring 1997): 34–8.
78 Michelle M. Fontaine, 'Making Heresy Marginal in Modena,' in *Heresy, Culture, and Religion in Early Modern Italy: Contexts and Contestations*, ed. Ronald K. Delph, Michelle M. Fontaine, and John Jeffries Martin (Kirksville, MO: Truman State University Press, 2006), pp. 41–4.

2. 'He may be a patron and receiver of heretics': Adapting the Principles of Prosecution

1 ASVe, Busta 7, fasc. 17, *Contra Riccardum Pictorem Conegliano*, 13r: 'Contra supradicta Ricardum Pictorem habent multa et praecipue quod sit fautor et receptator hereticorum, et in specie cuiusdam Alexii Augustini de Bellenzono, qui aliquis abiuravit in hoc Santo Officio et penitentia sibi ... fugit ad hereticos Anabaptistas Moravae.' A significant number of Anabaptists from the Friuli and Istria emigrated to Moravia; see, for example, Giovanna Paolin, 'I contadini anabattisti di Cinto,' *Il Noncello* 50 (1980): 91–124.
2 ASVe *Contra Riccardum Pictorem Conegliano*, fol. 8v: 'e specialmente contra uno che in Conegliano aveva disseminato e distribu[ito] alcuni libri di pessima e pestifera dottrina per contaminare e infettare le povere e innocente anime degli fanciulli di quello loco, et contra un Maestro Riccardo pittore del medesimo luogo eretico notorio e incorrigibile e contra tutti gli complici di loro.' Lionello Puppi has argued that Inquisitor Faenzi essentially framed Riccardo, since it was he who informed the tribunal in Conegliano of Riccardo's supposed activities, and the source of the inquisitor's information remains unclear. Lionello Puppi, *Un trono di fuoco: Arte e martirio di un pittore eretico del Cinquecento* (Rome: Donzelli Editore, 1995), pp. 99–104.
3 ASVe *Contra Riccardum Pictorem Conegliano*, fols. 2r–v: 'che venire alla loro sententia [*sic;* sentenza] definitiva rilassando questo Reo, come relapso [*sic;* rilasso] e impenitente al braccio secolare del prefetto Magnifico Podestà, il quale né abbia poi di fare quella debita essecutione, che si conviene secondo la disposizione de[gli] sacri canoni.'
4 *Vergentis in senium*, see X5.7.10; and X5.7.15 (*Corpus iuris canonici*, Vol. 2, ed. Emil Friedberg and Aemilius Ludwig Richter [Leipzig: Bernard Tauchnitz, 1881], cols. 782–7) for Gregory IX's application of the death

penalty to believers. For the 1582 revised version of canon law, which Francisco Peña edited in committee, see *Corpus juris canonici emendatum et notis illustratum*. Gregorii XIII. pont. max. iussu editum. (Rome : In aedibus Populi Romani, 1582), *Decretales d. Gregorii papae IX*, cols. 1675–6 for *Vergentis in senium*, and col. 1686 for *Excommunicamus* of Gregory IX and regulations concerning punishment. The gloss for the latter states that those who learn, but do not teach, heresy and those who support heretics although they may not yet believe, should be punished as heretics because they further the cause of heresy.

5 Regarding Peña's edition of Eymeric's text, see Edward M. Peters, 'Editing Inquisitors' Manuals in the Sixteenth Century: Francisco Peña and the Directorum Inquisitorum of Nicolas Eymeric,' *The Library Chronicle* 40 (1979): 95–107; Agostino Borromeo, 'A proposito del *Directorium Inquisitorum* di Nicolas Eymerich e delle sue edizioni conquecentesche,' in *Critica Storica* 4 (1983): 499–547, esp. pp. 502–20. Peña, of course, having worked for the Curia in a variety of capacities, including serving on the committee that revised canon law for publication in 1582, was well equipped to undertake his role as editor of Eymeric's work.

6 Edward M. Peters, *Inquisition* (New York: The Free Press, 1988), pp. 265–8.

7 For Gratian's status as a normative text, see Michael H. Hoeflich and Jasonne M. Grabher, 'The Establishment of Normative Legal Texts: The Beginnings of the *Ius commune*,' in *The History of Medieval Canon Law in the Classical Period, 1140–1234: From Gratian to the Decretals of Pope Gregory IX*, ed. Wilfried Hartmann and Kenneth Pennington (Washington, DC: The Catholic University Press of America, 2008), pp. 1–21; Peter Landau, 'Gratian and the *Decretum Gratiani*,' ibid.; for Gratian's *Decretum* as a 'rule of life,' see Mario Bellomo, *The Common Legal Past of Europe, 1000–1800*, trans. Lydia G. Cochrane (Washington, DC: The Catholic University of America Press, 1995), pp. 66–7. For Gratian's assertion that legal justice, even for the Church, only applied to external acts, see Bellomo, ibid., p. 163; James A. Brundage, *Medieval Canon Law* (New York: Longman, 1995), pp. 44–8, 59–62; R.H. Helmholz, *The Spirit of Classical Canon Law* (Athens, GA: University of Georgia Press, 1996), pp. 17–19. Adriano Prosperi has argued that the relationship between confessors, responsible for the internal forum of sin, and inquisitors' control of external justice was crucial in constructing religious conformity in the Counter-Reformation; see *Tribunali della coscienza: Inquisitori, confessori, missionari* (Turin: Einaudi, 1996), pp. xiii–xxi. Vincenzo Lavenia, however, has examined the ways in which theologians and jurists in the medieval and early modern period argued for the autonomy of the confessional from the inquisitorial

process. In particular, some theologians and jurists, such as Jean Gerson, thought that a secret heretic who had not caused public infamy and scandal through openly proselytizing could be reconciled in the confessional without recourse to inquisitorial denunciation; in the Reformation period, Tommaso da Vio (Cajetan) agreed in theory, although he thought the number of secret heretics willing to be corrected in the privacy of the confessional to be very small, since heretics were known for their pertincaty. See Lavenia, *L'infamia e il perdono: Tributi, pene e confessione nella teologia morale della prima età moderna* (Bologna: Il Mulino, 2004), pp. 51–7, 101–29.

8 William Hamilton Bryson, *Dictionary of Sigla and Abbreviations to and in Law Books before 1607* (Charlottesville, VA: University of Virginia Press, 1975), pp. 10–13; James A. Brundage, *Medieval Canon Law*, pp. 49–56; R.H. Helmholz, *Spirit*, pp. 4–32; Bellomo, *Common Legal Past*, pp. 71–4, 167–77. For Peña's career at the papal Curia under Gregory XIII, see Edward M. Peters, 'Editing Inquisitors' Manuals,' pp. 95–107. According to Brundage, after c. 1375, most new legal judgments and principles concerning Church law generally came from the decisions of the Rota, the highest papal court. Those decisions were compiled and circulated in manuscript until 1500, and thereafter printed.

9 James B. Given, *Inquisition in Medieval Society Power, Discipline and Resistance in Languedoc* (Ithaca: Cornell University Press, 1997), p. 45; A. Dondaine, 'Le manuel de l'inquisiteur,' *Archivum fratrum praedicatorum* 17 (1947): 89.

10 Given, *Inquisition in Medieval Society*, pp. 13–14; Malcolm Lambert, *Medieval Heresy: Popular Movements from the Gregorian Reform to the Reformation*, 3rd ed. (Cambridge, MA: Blackwell, 2002), pp. 99–114; cit. n.4.

11 Nicholas Eymeric, *Directorium Inquisitorum* (Venice: Apud Marcum Antonium Zalterium, 1595), pp. 230–1; Peña, p. 231. For Peña's technique in his commentaries, see also Agostino Borromeo, 'A proposito del *Directorium Inquisitorum*,' p. 522. Borromeo has argued that in so doing, Peña was more concerned with procedure and less with theological distinctions. For the propensity of legal scholars to ascertain the collective 'common opinion' of canonists, see R.H. Helmholz, *Spirit*, p. 23.

12 Peña, *Directorium Inquisitorum*, p. 232; Prospero Farinacci made it clear that Alfonso de Castro's opinion was singular: 'Ubi ex Alphonso a Castro, quem allegat, de iusta haereticorum punitione, lib. 1. cap. 7 dixit haereticum esse eum " [Q]ui postquam verum Baptismum suscepit, et fuit instructus sufficienter in fide catholica, pertinaciter errat contra id, quod scit ab Ecclesia catholica pro fide teneri, sive oppositum veritatis asserens, sive de ipsa veritate

dubitans"[. . .].' (Prospero Farinacci, *Tractatus de haeresi* [Cremona: Apud Marc'Antonium Belpierum, 1636], p. 3).

13 Guido Terrena was also the author of a *Summa de haeresibus* (Francisco Bertelloni, 'Guido Terrena,' in *A Companion to Philosophy in the Middle Ages*, ed. Jorge J.E. Gracia [Malden, MA: Blackwell, 2003], p. 291.) The scholarship concerning Tomás de Torquemada is voluminous; the most recent biographical study is John Edwards, *Torquemada and the Inquisitors* (Stroud, UK: Tempus, 2005), esp. pp. 11–19 for biographical information, but Torquemada has been discussed in the literature concerning the Spanish Inquisition. For Torquemada, and the Spanish Inquisition more generally, see Henry Kamen, *The Spanish Inquisition: A Historical Revision* [New Haven: Yale University Press, 1997]. Alfonso de Castro was also an official theologian, accompanying Cardinal Grennis at the Council of Trent, and professor of theology at Salamanca (*The Catholic Encyclopedia*, Volume III, 1909, 'Alfonso de Castro'). Konrad Braun served as a legal expert concerning heresy cases in Bayern (Maria Barbara Rößner, *Konrad Braun (ca. 1495–1563) – ein katholischer Jurist, Politiker, Kontroverstheologe und Kirchenreformer im konfessionellen Zeitalter* [Münster: Aschendorff, 1991]). Albert Pighius's most prominent work was entitled *Ten Books on Human Free Choice*, published in 1542, to which John Calvin wrote a refutation. See John Calvin, *The Bondage and Liberation of the Will: A Defence of the Orthodox Doctrine of Human Choice against Pighius*, trans. G.I. Davies and ed. N.S. Lane (Grand Rapids, MI: BakerBooks, 1996), esp. pp. xiii–xvii.

14 Eymeric, *Directorium Inquisitorum*, p. 236; Peña, pp. 237–8: 'Earum sit mentio in concilio Constantiensi, sessio 15 tit. de sententia contra Ioannem Huss et in Bulla Martini quinti approbatoria condemnationis Ioannis Wycliff et Ioannis Huss, quae habetur in ultima sessione eius concilii et in Bullario litterarum Apostolicarum pro officio sanctissimae Inquisitionis quae in fine huius voluminis referuntur.' John Wyclif's official condemnation occurred during Session 8 of the Council of Constance (4 May 1415) and Session 15 (6 July 1415); the latter session also condemned Jan Hus. See Norman P. Tanner, SJ, ed., *Decrees of the Ecumenical Councils*, Vol. 1, *Nicaea I to Lateran V* (Washington, DC: Georgetown University Press, 1990), pp. 403–51, esp. p. 427. Peña included the apostolic letter of Martin V that condemned Wyclif, Hus, and Jerome of Prague, and the canons condemning their beliefs in an appendix to the *Directorium Inquisitorum* entitled 'Litterae Apostolicae pro Officio Sanctissimae Inquisitionis,' pp. 68–76.

15 Peña, *Directorium Inquisitorum*, p. 233: 'Prudentissime autem Eymericus per regulas generales investigat, quot modis aliqua propositio haereticae dici possit, ne sit opus singula haeretica dogmata commemorare, quae pertinaciter asserta haereticum constituant: quod fecerunt nonulli doctores, ut alibi diximus.'

16 Eymeric, p. 319: 'ubi enim haec duae concurrunt, haereticum perfecte faciunt.' Thomas Aquinas, *Summa Theologiae*, 2a2ae II, I; 2a2ae II, 2,Vol. XXXI, ed. T.C. O'Brien (New York: McGraw Hill, 1964–), esp. pp. 83–7.

17 Eymeric, *Directorium Inquisitorum*, pp. 319–20.

18 Eymeric, ibid., p. 321: 'Haeretici vero secreti per oppositum dicendi sunt, qui eorum, quae sunt fidei habent errorem in mente et proponunt habere pertinaciam in voluntate: sed tamen verbo vel facto exterius non ostendunt.' Concerning this form of Nicodemism, see Carlo Ginzburg, *Il nicodemismo: Simulazione e dissimulazione religiosa nell'Europa del '500* (Turin: Giulio Einaudi, 1970), pp. 159–81, esp. p. 179; Adriano Prosperi, *L'eresia del Libro Grande: Storia di Giorgio Siculo e della sua setta* (Milan: Feltrinelli, 2000), pp. 322–37; John Jeffries Martin, *Myths of Renaissance Individualism* (New York: Palgrave Macmillan, 2004), pp. 21–61. Carlos Eire has interpred Nicodemism as a response to fear of persecution rather than a theological doctrine. See Eire, *War against the Idols: The Reformation of Worship from Erasmus to Calvin* (New York: Cambridge University Press, 1986), pp. 234–75; Carlos M.N. Eire, 'Calvin and Nicodemism: A Reapprisal,' *Sixteenth Century Journal* 10, no. 1 (Spring 1979): 45–69. Vincenzo Lavenia has examined the rather controversial history of Catholic theologians' and jurists' opinions concerning the prosecution of secret heretics; but, realistically, this situation occurred when secret heretics revealed their heretical opinions to their confessors. As Lavenia has explained, some theologians and jurists, most notably Alfonso del Castro, maintained that secret heretics were obligated to go through a process and make restitution for their crime, although that meant subjecting themselves to public infamy and property confiscation. Others, most notably Jean Gerson and Domingo de Soto, thought that fraternal correction, or the confessor correcting the penitent within the secrecy of the confessional without forwarding him or her to the inquisition for prosecution, was an appropriate response to secret heresies. See Lavenia, *L'infamia e il perdono*, pp. 51–9; 183–217. Peña thought secret heretics should be constrained to seek out tribunals by their confessors, but also recommended lesser punishment, as Lavenia has emphasized. See Peña, pp. 121–2.

19 Peña, *Directorium Inquisitorum*, p. 321: 'De haereticis manifestis agunt Hostiensis, Zabarella, Panormitanus, Antonius de Butrio, et

communiter Canonistae in c. super quibusdam extra de verborum significatione, Bernardus Lutzemburgus in catalogo haereticorum, liber 1 c. 12'; 'Nec indiget longa disputatione tractatio huc de manifestis haereticis, qui scilicet manifesti dicantur, cum Romanus Pontifex id aperte definierit in d. cap. super quibusdam de verborum significatione quod adducit hic Ermericus: Et summa est quinque vel sex modis dici posse aliquem haereticum manifestum.' *Corpus iuris canonici*, Vol. 2, cols. 923–4 (X 5.40.26).

20 Eymeric, *Directorium Inquisitorum*, p. 322: 'Ad hanc respondemus, quod haeretici affirmativi dicti sunt, qui habent eorum quae sunt fidei errorem in mente: et verbo vel facto ostendunt, se modis praedictis habere pertinaciam in voluntate.' See also Richard M. Fraher, 'Preventing Crime in the High Middle Ages: The Medieval Lawyers' Search for Deterrence,' in *Popes, Teachers, and Canon Law in the Middle Ages*, ed. James Ross Sweeney and Stanley Chodorow (Ithaca: Cornell University Press, 1989), pp. 224–7.

21 A process held in Spain came to such an end; see 'Trial of Marina González, 1494,' in *The Spanish Inquisition, 1478–1614: An Anthology of Sources*, ed. and trans. Lu Ann Homza (Indianapolis, IN: Hackett Publishing Company, 2006), pp. 27–49. The issue will be further discussed in Chapter 3.

22 Some sixteenth-century theologians, such as Albertus Pighius, postulated that truly secret heresy, contained completely in the mind with no outward revelation, was impossible; see Lavenia, *L'infamia e il perdono*, p. 289, and p. 39ff.

23 Peña, *Directorium Inquisitorum*, p. 322: 'Multum sunt notanda haec verba: et verbo, vel facto, quibus non obscure videtur indicare Eymericus affirmativos haereticos dici posse, non modo ex verbis, verum etiam ex factis, quasi facta interiorem animi credulitatem et intentionem prae se ferant.'

24 Peña, ibid., p. 322: 'Ac primum quidem plurimum referi intelligere, an quis sponte, vel coacte facta haereticalia commiserit. Si per coactionem et metum fecit, quid sit sentiendum copiose docui supra par. 1 super q. 9 quod non est hic iterum inutiliter repetendum'; 'Si vero sponte quis facta haereticalia committat, ut intelligatur, quando in eum velut in haereticum sit procedendum, facta distinguenda sunt.'

25 Peña, ibid., pp. 322–3: 'Quadam enim sunt facta ex quibus violentae oriuntur suspiciones, ut cum quis de haeresi infamatus, aut suspectus tempore mortis petit consolationem ab haereticis iuxta consuetudinum eorum, et similia de quibus diximus infra par. 3 tit. de signis quibus diversarum sectarum haeretici cognosci possint. Atque haec si quis committat praesumptione iuris et de iure contra quam non admittitur regulariter probatio, censetur

haereticus, et habere praesumitur pertinaciam in voluntate, de quibus potest vere hic locus accipi.'

26 Peña, ibid., p. 323: 'His factis proxima sunt illa, in quibus errore exprimitur manifeste, quae nullo modo possunt in bonam partem accipi, ut daemones adorare, idolis gennua flectere, reverentiam haereticis suo more exhibere, communionem ab eis iuxta ritum suum accipere, se more Iudaeorum circumcidere, Mahometo divinum cultum praestare et similia.'

27 Peña, ibid., p. 323: 'Iam hoc est diligentissima observandum, quod quamvis ex his factis fictione iuris praesumatur haeresis vel apostasia, nihilominus tamen cum ea praesumptio solum sit praesumptio iuris, adversus eam probatio in contrarium admitti poterit [. . .] nam qui daemones adoravit, aut ob amorem, aut ob cupiditatem habendi thesaros, se fecisse dicere poterit: et qui caeteros ritus infidelitatis patravit, ab commeda temporalia id fecisse dicere poterit absque ulla mentis errore: quamvis, ut verum fatear, difficulter haec possunt persuaderi, nec iudices debent huiusmodi excusationes admittere nisi cum exquisitissima consideratione: quis enim facile credat a volente et non coacto haec absque errore mentis fuisse perpetrata?' I will discuss intent and torture extensively in Chapter 6.

28 Peña, ibid., p. 323: '[Q]uamvis ex illis suspicio haeresis oriatur, attamen nec haeresis, nec haeresos credentia inde nascitur, et ob id in eos, qui talia facta committunt, non poterit procedi tanquam contra haereticos, aut haereticorum credentes, sed solum tanquam contra suspectos; cum facta interdum patrentur ex affectione carnali, interdum praecibus amicorum, interdum vero pecunia interveniente, ut optime docuit Guido Fulcodius [. . .].'

29 Concerning *conversos* prosecuted in Italian lands, Christian-Jewish relations (particularly in Venice), and the importance of circumcision as proof of apostasy, see Christopher F. Black, *The Italian Inquisition* (New Haven: Yale University Press, 2009), pp. 141–7, 217–19. There were also cases of children being circumcised by parents in mixed families, or families who had ostensibly converted to Christianity; see Christopher F. Black, *Early Modern Italy: A Social History* (New York: Routledge, 2001), pp. 202–3.

30 See Umberto Locati, *Opus quod iudiciale inquisitorum* (Rome: Antonii Bladii Impressores Camerales, 1570), p. 119: 'Unde et Philosophi qui quasdam positiones habebant praeter communem opinionem et sententiam aliorum, sectas et haereses constituebant.' Born near Piacenza, Locati entered the Dominican order in 1520 at San Giovanni in Canale. He earned degrees in canon law and theology, possibly at Bologna, before becoming inquisitor of Pavia in 1558. By 1560, Locati had returned to San Giovanni in Canale

both as prior and as inquisitor of Piacenza. By 1566 he was called to Rome to act as the general commissary for the Congregation of Cardinals. He enjoyed a particularly close relationship with Pope Pius V, former inquisitor general Michele Ghislieri, to whom he dedicated his *Opus* in 1568; the work was printed again in 1570 and 1583. Locati divided the *Opus* into four parts, including an analysis of processes he had conducted, summaries of communications to Rome and other tribunals, and a formulary for edicts and the like. Bishop of Bagnorea by 1568, Locati had to retire from first his duties as commissary, in 1571, and then his duties as bishop in 1581 due to declining health; he died in Piacenza in 1587. See S. Ragagli, 'Locati, Umberto,' *Dizionario storico dell'Inquisizione*, Vol. 2, ed. Adriano Prosperi with Vincenzo Lavenia and John Tedeschi (Pisa: Scuola Normale Superiore Pisa, 2010), pp. 929–30.

31 Prospero Farinacci, *Tractatus*, p. 2: '[. . .] quod dixit Albertius Pighius, *Campen*. L. 4 c. 8 dum describendo haeresim dixit, haeresim esse: "Non morum, non confessionis, sed fidei vitium, quo quis singulare aliquid a communi Ecclesiae catholicae fide, et sententia eligit et proinde se ipsum ab Ecclesia separat, quae se rectius sentire, credereque praesumit et ob id haeresis, hoc est, electio haud insignificanter appellatur." Refert eum Pegna in additionibus ad Eymericum, d. quaset. 1. comment. 26. fol. mihi 246. col. 2. in fine.'

32 Farinacci, ibid., p. 2: 'Haec autem diffinitio, quod sit bona non, cum non convertatur cum suo diffinito, pluribus probat idem Albertin. in d. rubr. de Haeret. q. 1. n. 7 et seqq.' Luis de Pàramo also wrote *On the Origin and Development of the Office of the Holy Inquisition, and on its Dignity and Fruitfullness*, published in two books in Madrid in 1598. He situated the inquisition within the entirety of a larger Church history that began with the fall of Adam; he argued, more pertinently from the modern perspective, that bishops had lost the task of investigating heresy because they had failed the Church through their own negligence and vigorously reaffirmed the Spanish monarchy's control of Spanish Inquisition tribunals. His work also, given its perspective, favoured the Catholic view that all heresy in the sixteenth century was simply the latest version of 'old' heresies (Edward Peters, *Inquisition*, pp. 265–8).

33 Farinacci, *Tractatus*, p. 3: 'Et quibus quidem diffinitionibus, haeresim pluribus modis committi, errorumque plures esse species dubitandum non est [. . .].'

34 Farinacci, ibid., p. 3: 'Sic et plures haereticorum sectas reperiri, nec etiam dubitandum, quas si hic referre et explicare voluissem, lectori nimis essem taediosus, sufficiat partier illum remittere ad Extravagan. Ioan. XXII edi-

tam de anno 1318 [. . .].'; 'Ad quos omnes lectorem remitto, cum nostri instituti non sit omnes haereticorum sectas, aut species enumerare, sed tantum de eorum inquisitione et punitione tractare.' *Corpus iuris canonici* Vol. 2, cols. 1213–14 (Extrav. Jo. XXII 7.1) or *Extravagantium viginti d. Joannis papae XXII tum communes*, Vol. 4, *Corpus iuris canonici*, cols. 70–5.

35 Farinacci, *Tractatus*, p. 4: '[. . .] ubi quod Haeresiarcha dicitur ille, "Qui gignit errorem": item, "Qui docet errorem, quem ipse gignit, vel sequitur": item, "Qui publice defendit errorem." ' Farinacci was quoting the *Repertorium Inquisitorum*.

36 Farinacci, ibid., p. 5: 'Affirmativus haereticus est ille, qui errorem, quem habet in mente, aut verbo, aut factis ostendit et fatetur.' For Arnaldo Albertini, see Nadia Zeldes, *'The Former Jews of This Kingdom': Sicilian Converts after the Expulsion, 1492–1516* (Boston: Brill, 2003), pp. 223–5.

37 Farinacci, *Tractatus*, p. 9: 'Et Ioannis de Anan. numero nonno, et est textus, qui tamen loquitur in non credente articulum fidei, quod Christus esset verus homo, in capite Cum Christus et ibi glossa et communiter omnes Canonistae, extra eodem, et de male sentientibus, vel male docentibus circa Sacramenta est expressus in capite *Ad Abolendam Universos. Extra eodem.* ubi dicitur, 'Universos, qui de Sacramento Corporis, et Sanguinis Domini Nostri Jesu Christi, vel de Baptismate, seu peccatorum Confessione, Matrimonio, vel reliquis ecclesiasticis Sacramentis aliter sentire, aut docero non metuunt, quam sacrosancta Romana Ecclesia praedicat et observant, haereticos credendos esse [. . .].' The significance of *Ad abolendam* has received wide attention in many scholars' work; therefore the following citations are not comprehensive. Edward Peters, *Inquisition*, pp. 47–8; James B. Given, *Inquisition and Medieval Society*, pp. 13–22; R.H. Helmholz, *Spirit*, pp. 338–65. The original text of *Ad abolendam* is available in *Corpus iuris canonici*, col. 780 (X 5.7.9). The text of *Ad abolendam* contained references to the perfect, as well as believers, defenders, and supporters of heretics; it was intended to deal with both Cathar and Waldensian heresy, among others. Raymond of Peñafort included *Ad abolendam* when he compiled and edited the *Liber Extra* on behalf of Gregory IX. See Walter Wakefield and Austin P. Evans, 'Introduction: A Historical Sketch of the Medieval Popular Heresies,' in *Heresies of the High Middle Ages*, ed. Wakefield and Evans (New York: Columbia University Press, 1969), pp. 33–4.

38 Farinacci, *Tractatus*, p. 10: 'ubi propterea subdit Scripturae divinae intelligentiam, et interpretationem sumendam esse ab Ecclesiae catholicae, quae veritatem praedicat, nec fallere, neque falli potest. Concordat Concilium Tridentinam sessionem 4 ibi per eum allegatum prohibens

sacram Scripturam in alium sensum trahi debere, quam solet catholica Ecclesia interpretari.' Farinacci was quoting Simancas. The Council of Trent dedicated a canon to the issue, especially in conjunction with apostolic tradition, which was produced during the council's fourth session (8 April 1546). See Tanner, ed., *Ecumenical Councils*, Vol. 2, pp. 663–5.

39 Farinacci, *Tractatus*, p. 9: 'Et licet nonulli Doctores dixerint non credentes articulos fidei non esse proprie haereticos; sed largo modo, nisi etiam eorum pravitatem contra fidem alios doceant [. . .].'

40 Wakefield and Evans, 'Heresy in the Thirteenth and Early Fourteenth Centuries, 1216–1325,' in *Heresies of the High Middle Ages*, p. 265. The editors, in the introduction to translations of excerpts taken from works written in Italy in the early thirteenth century, by Salvo Burci and probably Peter of Verona respectively, note that both authors considered Cathars 'the greatest enemy of the Orthodox church,' although both described other heretical beliefs as well.

41 Malcolm Lambert, *The Cathars* (Malden, MA: Blackwell Publishers, 1998), p. 20, for medieval scholars' use of Augustine as a source; in the second edition of his work *Medieval Heresy*, after considering the research of R.I. Moore, Jeffrey Russell, and Brian Stock, among others, Lambert stated that he no longer believed that there had been any contact between Bogomils and Cathars in southern France. Daniel Callahan and Bernard Hamilton, among others, however, have recently argued that there was some contact between the Bulgarian dualist sects and those in Western Europe. Daniel Callahan (in 'Ademar of Chabannes and the Bogomils,' in *Heresy and the Persecuting Society in the Middle Ages: Essays on the Work of R.I. Moore*, ed. Michael Frassetto [Boston: Brill, 2006], pp. 31–41) has argued that a mid-eleventh century letter from Heribert concerning the appearance of heretics at Périgord (discovered by G. Lobrichon), together with Ademar's sermons concerning Cathar heresy (examined by Michael Frassetto as well), indicate a link between the two areas. Bernard Hamilton (in 'Bogomil Influences on Western Heresy,' in *Essays on the Work of R.I. Moore*, pp. 93–114), has argued that the French often described Cathars as 'Bulgarians,' and has described how the more contentious sects of northern Italy consciously described themselves as belonging to the Bulgarian *ordo*, or not. Concerning the Council of Rheims, see Wakefield and Evans, 'Introduction,' pp. 38–9.

42 See Arthur Siegel, 'Italian Society and the Origins of Eleventh-Century Western Heresy,' in *Essays on the Work of R.I. Moore*, ed. Michael Frassetto, pp. 43–72.

43 Andrea Del Col, *L'Inquisizione in Italia: Dal XII al XXI secolo* (Milan: Oscar Mondadori, 2006), pp. 75–7, 81–109; R.H. Helmholz, *Spirit*, pp. 339–65.

44 Lambert, *Cathars*, pp. 21–3; see also Callahan, 'Ademar of Chabannes and the Bogomils,' *Essays on the Work of R.I. Moore*, pp. 36–8. In addition to those core beliefs, which Callahan compares to those of the Bogomils, Cathar sects in France, according to the polemical literature, objected to Catholic baptism, and found the Mass and the Eucharist insignificant. Susan Taylor Snyder has found, however, that Italian Cathars in Bologna around 1300 participated in Catholic rituals (Susan Taylor Snyder, 'Cathars, Confraternities, and Civic Religion: The Blurry Border between Heresy and Orthodoxy,' in *Essays on the Work of R.I. Moore*, pp. 241–51), particularly their participation in a flagellant confraternity, without, as Taylor Snyder argues, recognizing Catholic flagellation and Cathar beliefs as antithetical.

45 For sixteenth-century references to Cathar believers adoring heretics, see Eymeric's original text and Peña's commentaries concerning the subject in the *Directorium Inquisitorum*, pp. 201, 367.

46 Lambert, *Cathars*, pp. 153–4, for networks of support; pp. 141–2 for a description of the *melioramentum* (or 'adoration' of the Cathar perfect). For sixteenth-century references to Cathar believers adoring heretics, see Eymeric's original text and Peña's commentaries concerning the subject in the *Directorium Inquisitorum*, pp. 201, 367.

47 Lambert, *Cathars*, pp. 92–3. For text of *Vergentis in senium*, see X5.7.10 (*Corpus iuris canonici*, Vol. 2, cols. 782–3). Innocent III incorporated legal principles against heretics into the law of the Church through the promulgations of canons at Lateran IV; see Anne J. Duggan, 'Conciliar Law 1123–1215: The Legislation of the Four Lateran Councils,' in *History of Medieval Canon Law in the Classical Period*, ed. Wilfried Hartmann and Kenneth Pennington. The canons promulgated at Lateran IV were quickly received into the canonical tradition, and applied legally; see A. García y García, 'The Fourth Lateran Council and the Canonists,' ibid., pp. 367–78, particularly concerning the canons' incorporation into the *Liber Extra*.

48 Jean Duvernoy, ed. and trans., *Le register d'Inquisition de Jacques Fournier (Évêque de Pamiers): 1318–1325* (Paris: Mouton Editeur, 1978). For example, see p. 116, 'qu'il les avait amendés et corrigés et d'avoir à abjurer toute hérésie s'élevant contre la sainte Eglise romaine, mere et maîtresse de toutes les Eglises, et à denoncer les croyants, fauteurs, receleurs, et tous autres de sa secte, lui significant que faute par lui de le faire incontinent, il serait procédé contre lui selon le droit et les sanctions canoniques, comme contre un hérétique obstiné et impenitent.'

49 John H. Arnold, *Inquisition and Power: Catharism and the Confessing Subject in Medieval Languedoc* (Philadelphia: University of Pennsylvania Press, 2001), pp. 42–3. See also Wakefield and Evans, 'Introduction,' p. 50: 'In both groups, in allusion to the habit of wearing special sandals, terms such as "Sandal-wearers" were applied to their preachers, who also became known as the "perfect."' For an explanation of speculation concerning *sabot/Insabbatati* see Lambert, *Medieval Heresy*, pp. 80–1.

50 Lambert, *Medieval Heresy*, pp. 70–80; K. Utz Tremp, 'Valdo e valdeismo medievale,' in *Dizionairio storico dell'Inquisizione*, Vol. 3, pp. 1634–6.

51 F. Valls Taberner, ed., 'El diplomatari de San Ramón de Penyafort,' in *Analecta sacra Tarraconensia: Revista de ciencias histórico-eclesiásticas* 5 (1929): 254–61, 255: 'Credentes vero dictis haeresibus, similiter haeretici sunt dicendi.' For Ramón de Peñafort, see James A. Brundage, *Medieval Canon Law*, pp. 222–3.

52 Taberner, ed., 'Penyafort,' p. 255: 'Defensores dicimus qui scienter defendant haereticos vel Inzabbatatos, verbo vel facto vel quocumque ingenio, terris suis vel alibi, quominus Ecclesia posit exercere suum officium ad extirpandam haereticam pravitatem.' Peñafort also described *celatores*, or 'hiders,' and *occultatores*, or 'concealers,' or those who had promised not to reveal anything about heretics to inquisitors. Those two categories came to be subsumed under 'receivers' and 'favourers' (*receptores* and *fautores*). See also Arnold, *Inquisition and Power*, p. 43.

53 Taberner, ed., 'Penyafort,' p. 256: 'proviso tamen quod perfecti haeretici, vel dogmatizantes eorum errores, vel credentes relapsi in credentiam post abiuratam haeresim vel renunciatam, in perpetuo carcere intrudantur, haeresi penitus abiurata et absolutione habita excommunicationis, ut ibi salvent animas suas et alios de caetero non corrumpant.'

54 Bernard Gui was born in Limousin in 1261 or 1262. He probably came from the minor nobility and took the Dominican habit in 1279. He studied logic, and then theology until 1290. He was prior at several Dominican convents for the next seventeen years until his appointment as Inquisitor of Toulouse in 1307. During his service there, he wrote his other work dealing with the Inquisition, the *Liber sententiarum inquisitionis Tholosanae ab anno Christi MCCCVII ad annum MCCCXXIII*, a collection of sentences pronounced during his years at Toulouse. He was appointed bishop of Tuy in 1323, but seems never to have taken up residence there. In 1324, he was transferred to the see of Lodève, where he died on 31 December 1331. Wakefield and Evans, 'Bernard Gui's *Practica*,' in *Heresies of the High Middle Ages*, pp. 373–4, 381.

55 Lambert, *Medieval Heresy*, pp. 80–5; K. Utz Tremp, 'Valdo,' pp. 1634–6.

56 Andrea Del Col, *L'Inquisizione in Italia,* pp. 408–16; Lambert, *Medieval Heresy,* pp. 383–92, 411–14.

57 Eymeric, *Directorium Inquisitorum,* p. 366: 'Factis autem, ut si haereticos adoraverint (eorum verbis utendo) reverentiam eis suo more exhibuerint: consolationem vel communionem ab eis receperint, seu similia, quae ad ritum eorum pertinent, perpetraverint: sermones eorum et praedicationes non tantum semel, vel bis, sed frequentius audierint et similia egerint, per quae eorum animus quae credant eorum erroribus, apud iudicem per exteriora probabiliter convincatur.'

58 Eymeric, ibid., p. 366.

59 Peña, ibid., p. 367. Petrus de Palud (d. 1342; Pierre de la Palu; Pierre de la Palud) wrote the *Liber bellorum Domini pro tempore Nove Legis* before 1329; the work was a compilation of chronicles from the Christian era, including the crusades to the East as well as the Albigensian crusades. Fragments of the work still exist in the Vatican archives (MS Regina Christiana 547), Paris, and the University of Pennsylvania (MS Lea 45). See Jean Dunbain, *A Hound of God: Pierre de la Palud and the Fourteenth-Century Church* (New York: Clarendon Press, 1991), pp. 127–8.

60 Peña, *Directorium Inquisitorum,* pp. 367–8.

61 Peña, ibid., p. 367: 'Haec ibi, quae tametsi eius saeculi haereticis competant, facile possunt caeteris accommodari, spectatis singulorum haereticorum conditione, ritu, et ceremoniis.' There were two councils of Narbonne, held in 1227 and 1235 respectively, which condemned Cathars and those that protected them from Church and secular authority. See Edward H. Landon, ed., *A Manual of the Councils of the Holy Catholic Church,* Vol. 1 (Edinburgh: John Grant, 1909), pp. 64–5, 391–2. *HarperCollins Study Bible,* p. 2301 (2 John 7–11): 'Many deceivers have gone out into the world, those who do not confess that Jesus Christ has come in the flesh; any such person is the deceiver and the antichrist! Be on your guard, so that you do not lose what we have worked for, but may receive a full reward. Everyone who does not abide in the teaching of Christ but goes beyond it does not have God; whoever abides in the teaching has both the Father and the Son. Do not receive into the house or welcome anyone who comes to you and does not bring this teaching; for to welcome is to participate in the evil deeds of such a person.' Regarding the councils of Narbonne and Béziers, see Dondaine, 'Le Manuel de l'inquisiteur,' pp. 90–1, p. 97.

62 Peña, *Directorium Inquisitorum,* p. 367: 'Multo facilius est cognoscere credentes haereticorum ex verbis, quam ex factis.'

63 Peña, ibid., p. 368. Zanchino Ugolini, a Bologna-trained lawyer wrote his manuscript, later called the *Tractatus super materia haereticorum,* at the

request of Fra Donato da Sant'Agata, inquisitor for the Romagna, around 1330. According to Ugolini, most inquisitors lacked legal training, not theological, so the work dealt with procedure almost exclusively. By the mid-sixteenth century in Italian lands, however, this was not the case; most inquisitors, especially Dominicans, were probably trained in both theology and law. The work was reprinted in Rome in 1568 at the behest of Pope Pius V (Michele Ghislieri, a former inquisitor); Camillo Campeggi edited the work in much the same way that Peña edited Eymeric's. Peña, in fact, included Campeggi's commentaries and Ugolini's original text, along with corrections made by Diego di Simancas, in the compilation *Tractatus universi iuris*, which included other inquisitorial manuals as well, first printed in the late 1580s. See Peter Diehl, 'An Inquisitor in Manuscript and in Print: The *Tractatus super materia hereticorum* of Zanchino Ugolini,' in *The Book Unbound: Editing and Reading Medieval Manuscripts and Texts*, ed. Siân Echard and Stephen Partridge (Toronto: University of Toronto Press, 2004), pp. 58–77, esp. pp. 55–60. For Camillo Campeggi, see Valerio Marchetti, 'Campeggi, Camillo,' in the *Dizionario biografico degli Italiani*, Vol. 17 (Rome: Istituto della Enciclopedia Italiana, 1974), pp. 439–40; Campeggi served as inquisitor of Pavia from 1554, and also of Ferrara (in 1557), together with Modena (from 1563), ending his tenure as inquisitor general of all three in 1567–68. See also Adriano Prosperi, 'Campeggi, Camillo,' in the *Dizionario storico dell'Inquisizione*, Vol. 1, pp. 252–3.

64 Concerning philo-Protestant conventicles, especially after 1550, see Cesare Bianco, 'La comunità di "fratelli" nel movimento ereticale modenese del '500,' *Rivista Storica Italiana* 92 (1980): 644; Susanna Peyronel Rambaldi, *Speranze e crisi nel Cinquecento modenese: Tensioni religiose e vita cittadina in tempi di Giovanni Morone* (Milan: Franco Angeli, 1979), pp. 246–63; Salvatore Caponetto, *The Protestant Reformation in Sixteenth-Century Italy*, trans. Anne C. and John Tedeschi (Kirksville, MO: Thomas Jefferson University Press, 1991), pp. 30–1; John Jeffries Martin, *Venice's Hidden Enemies: Italian Heretics in a Renaissance City* (Berkeley and Los Angeles: University of California Press, 1993), pp. 89–122.

65 Eymeric, *Directorium Inquisitorum*, p. 366: 'Nuper nec refert etiam, an quis voluntatem suam verbis exprimat, aut factis [. . .] Quem progentiores immo plus est facto quam verbo aliquid facere. argu. De appella. Dilecti. Magis enim est standum factis quam verbis, ut docet Christus Matth. 21.'

66 *HarperCollins Study Bible* (New York: HarperCollins Press, 1989), pp. 1896–7. Umberto Locati, Peña's contemporary and commissary general for the Roman Inquisition beginning in 1566, agreed. He cited Antonio de Butrio and Ioannes de Imola, two other inquisition manual authors, as his

sources, but he clearly expressed the idea that deeds could indicate more than words ('Quinimo plus est factis aliquid demonstrare [. . .]') and, in fact, words were not necessary as proof of heresy if evidence of deeds had been found: '[. . .] ubi ponatur certi casus per quos quis incidit in haeresim facto et opere, licit nihil asserat, et per consequens manifeste haereticus dici potest, in quantum sunt in eo signa infidelitatis.' See Locati, *Opus quod iudicale*, pp. 127–8.

67 Peña, *Directorium Inquisitorum*, p. 368: 'Verissima est haec Eymerici sententia, ut scilicet adversus huiusmodi credentes, quos ultimo loco numeravit, procedatur velut contra suspectos, qui compellantur vel abiurare, vel se purgare, aut tormentis subiiciantur [. . .].'

68 Eymeric, ibid., p. 368–9.

69 Peña, ibid., p. 369: 'Haec tamen sententia non procederet, quoties haereticus esset publice denuntiatus et notorius: tunc enim scientia praesumeretur in receptante, non ignorantia [. . .].' Receivers were not accused and processed because of their beliefs; therefore, the number of times they received heretics was not an issue. Proving knowledge of the guests' status as heretics was necessary, but proving heretical beliefs on the part of the receivers was not. Jews and other infidels theoretically could be prosecuted as receivers of heretics.

70 Eymeric, ibid., p. 370: 'Quidam alii sunt, qui non defendunt errorem, sed personam errantem: utpote illi, qui resistunt viribus et potentia ne haeretici ad manus iudicis fidei veniant examinandi, vel puniendi et similia: et tales sunt excommunicati, iuxta c. allegatum, excommunicamus 1. § credentes.'

71 Peña, ibid., p. 371: 'Et sub his generalibus verbis comprehenduntur omnes defendendi modi, qui in hac causa possunt contingere: nam et cum armis et sine armis potest quis defendere haereticum: potest et clamoribus monendo illum ut fugiat: potest defendere illum in iudicio: item extra iudicium: denique, ut ullo verbo dicam, quicunque officium Inquisitionis quacunque ratione impediunt, haereticorum defensores per consequentiam dici possunt.' Whether or not lawyers working for heretical clients could be considered 'defenders' of heretics will be examined in Chapter 5.

72 Farinacci, *Tractatus*, p. 90: 'Et ex omnibus praedictis differentiis inter haereticos et credentes, nulla mihi magis placet, quam ea, quam posuit Cardin. Tolen. in loco praeallegato: illae enim aliae differentiae, quibus dicitur, haereticum esse proprie eum, qui errorem gignit; credentem autem qui eius errorem sequitur, constituunt differentiam potius inter Haeresiarcham et credentem quam inter credentem et haereticum.'; 'Tertio, si sciens et videns aliquem ut haereticum, ab Ecclesia damnatum,

contendat illum fuisse, vel esse virum bonum et laudabilem; per hoc enim credit bonam illius fuisse vitam, bonamque doctrinam et per consequens credens haereticorum est, credensque haereticorum erroribus, licet implicite.'

73 Farinacci, ibid., p. 91.

74 Farinacci, ibid., p. 74: 'Bartolom. Ugol. In tractatu de censuris Pontifici reservatis, in Glossa, Fautores, in princip. num. 1 ubi dixit fautorem esse illum 'Qui vel ne ob illud crimen oppugnentur, ipsis opem feri; vel animarum dat; quod in illo crimine perseverent; vel, ubi eos ab haeresi avocare, castigare ve potest, ipsos tolerat, aut alimenta, sumptusve praestat; vel de habitatione eos accomodat' folio mihi 76 col. 1.'

75 Peña, *Directorium Inquisitorum*, p. 374: 'Iam ut nihil desideretur eorum quae utilia sunt ad cognoscendam perfecte hanc fautorem tractationem, libet hic addere quibus indiciis et signis potissimum cognoscantur, ergo in summa illa fratris Ivoneti, cuius fragmentum extat in saepe citato codice membraneo bibliothecae Vaticanae [. . .].'; 'Hactenus Ivonetus, quae quamvis incondito et insuavi stylo sint dicta, non tamen propterea sunt aspernenda: nam quod bonum est, non ex verbis, quibus dicitur sed ex natura sua, quocunque modo dicatur, pensandum est.' Ivonetus was a Dominican monk who wrote a *Summa contra Catharos et Valdenses* in the early thirteenth century. In reality the work was a badly done transcription of a manuscript authored by Moneta da Cremona. See C. Longo, 'Ivonetus,' in *Dictionnaire d'histoire et de géographie ecclésiastique*, ed. R. Aubert, Vol. 26 (Paris: Letouzey et Ané, 1997), p. 473.

76 Farinacci, *Tractatus*, p. 74: 'Quartum, quando quid amaro vultu, torvisque oculis aspicit persequutores haereticorum.'

77 Farinacci, ibid., pp. 95–6: 'Limita II eandem III ampliationem: quia receptans consanguineum haereticum, non excusatur a tota poena receptationis haereticorum, sed mitius punitur, [. . .].'

78 Farinacci, ibid., pp. 95–6: 'Verius tamen est receptatores haereticorum puniendos esse arbitraria et extraordinaria poena.' For Tiberio Deciani (1509–1582), see Marco Cavina, ed., *Tiberio Deciani (1509–1582): Alle origini del pensiero giuridico moderno; Atti del Convegno internazionale di studi storici e giuridici, Udine, 12–13 Aprile 2002* (Udine: Editrice Universitaria Udinese, 2004).

79 Cesare Carena, *Tractatus de Officio Sanctissimae Inquisitionis* (Cremona: Apud Marc'Antonium Belpierum, 1636), pp. 83–4: '[. . .] quod licet, ut quis incidat in excommunicatinem bullae requiratur, quod receptet haereticum, ut haereticus est, attamen non requiritur formalis intentio favendi haeresi, sed sufficit indirecta et putativa, alias inquit et bene vix posset

reperiri receptator et fautor, qui etiam non esset Haereticus et ibi reprobat Sanch. loco supra citato.'; 'Controversia tamen est [. . .].'; 'Dicendum secundo, in impositione istius mitioris poenae, habenda est ratio graduum consanguinitatis, ut mitius puniantur qui gradu proximi sunt receptato Haeretico, quam remotiores, ita Pegna ubi supra [. . .].'; Peña, *Directorium Inquisitorum*, p. 382: 'Rursus, consanguineorum, seu coniunctorum ratio habenda erit: nam filius receptans patrem haereticum, uxor virum, frater fratrem levis puniendi sunt, quam si remotiores, sive alios non usque adeo coniunctos receptassent, aut defendissent.' Agostino Borromeo, 'Carena, Cesare,' in *Dizionario storico dell'Inquisizione*, Vol. 1, pp. 272–3.

80 Peña, *Directorium Inquisitorum*, p. 367.

81 Both of those practices also had been condemned as heretical when performed outside the Catholic Church in the past. According to the authors of inquisitorial manuals, it was the Waldensians who held alternate communion services as described above; but it was the Donatists who would rebaptize adults because their previous baptisms were considered to be invalid. Inquisitorial manuals discussed *rebaptizati*, but usually in the context of Augustine's anti-heretical works concerning Donatists, and the medieval edicts concerning valid baptism. For example, in Peña's commentary he discussed the subject in relation to Alexander III's edict concerning those who were not sure whether or not they had been baptized. See Peña, *Directorium Inquisitorum*, pp. 36–7.

82 Robert A. Pierce, *Pier Paolo Vergerio: The Propagandist* (Rome: Edizioni di Storia e Letteratura, 2003), pp. 166–98.

83 Alfonso de Castro, *Adversus omnes haereses*, fol. 46r: 'Donatistae siquidem (prout Augustinus in libro de haeresibus refert) rebaptizant eos, qui ab Ecclesia catholica ad eos veniunt'; 'Hic nostro tempore scripsit Ioannes Faber volumen grande contra Anabaptistas.' The book to which de Castro referred was probably Johann Faber's, *Adversus Doctorem Balthasarum Pacimontanum: Anabaptistarum Nostri Saeculi primum authorem, orthodoxae fidei Catholica defensio* (1528).

84 See, for example, John M. Frymire, '*Demonstrationes catholicae*: Defining Communities through Counter-Reformation Rituals,' in *Defining Community in Early Modern Europe*, ed. Michael J. Halvorson and Karen E. Spierling (Burlington, VT: Ashgate, 2008), pp. 163–82; Michelle Fontaine, 'Making Heresy Marginal in Modena,' in *Heresy, Culture, and Religion in Early Modern Italy: Contexts and Contestations*, ed. Ronald K. Delph, Michelle M. Fontaine, and John Jeffries Martin (Kirksville, MO: Truman State University Press, 2006), pp. 41–4.

85 For the importance of the Fourth Lateran Council, and the doctrine of transubstantiation, as a means of combating Cathar heresy, see Malcolm Lambert, *The Cathars*, pp. 108–11 and James B. Given, *Inquisition and Medieval Society*, pp. 44–5. Adriano Prosperi, in particular, has viewed the relationship between confessors and inquisitors as capable of controlling the orthodoxy of dioceses and territorial states; see Adriano Prosperi, *Tribunali della coscienza* esp. pp. 279–300, 316–32. Prosperi has characterized the relationship between inquisitors and confessors as one in which confession became subordinate to inquisitorial goals in response to the sixteenth-century crisis in religion (pp. 257–60); but Elena Brambilla has argued that the distinction between the internal and external forums (confession and inquisition, respectively) overlapped in significant ways. See Elena Brambilla, *Alle origini del Sant' Uffizio: Penitenza, confessione e giustizia spirituale dal Medioevo al XVI secolo* (Bologna: Il Mulino, 2000), pp. 347–59. She therefore argues that confessors referring penitents to inquisition tribinals to 'self-denounce' was not necessarily a violation of the secrecy of the confessional but a long-standing canonical procedure; see 'Il segreto e il sigillo: Denunce e comparizioni spontanee nei processi inquisitoriali,' in *I Tribunali della fede: Continuità e discontinuità dal medioevo all'età moderna; Atti del XLV Convegno di studi sulla Riforma e sui movimenti religiosi in Italia, Torre Pellice, 3–4 settembre 2005*, ed. Susanna Peyronel Rambaldi (Turin: Claudiana 2007), esp. pp. 150, 159–61. Concerning the enforcement of the annual requirement, see Wietse De Boer, *Conquest of the Soul: Confession, Discipline, and Public Order in Counter-Reformation Milan* (Boston: Brill, 2001) pp. 194–5, who has found that the energetic reforming bishop of Milan, Carlo Borromeo, enforced the requirement. But Giovanni Romeo, in *Ricerche su confessione confessione dei peccati e Inquisizione nell'Italia del Cinquecento* (Naples: Città del sole, 1997), pp. 85–7, has found that in other bishoprics lacking such reform, such as Naples, enforcement was quite lax, as it had been in many areas of Europe before the Counter-Reformation. Eric Cochrane also has asserted that over 5,000 avoided the annual requirement even after the reforms of Gian Matteo Giberti in Verona (1524–1543); see Cochrane, *Early Modern Italy 1530–1630*, ed. Julius Kirshner (New York: Longman, 1988), p. 146.

86 Carena, *Tractatus*, p. 351.

87 Farinacci, *Tractatus*, p. 15: '[. . .] ubi de haeresi suspectos esse affirmat eos, qui fidelium consortium evitarent, poenitentiam nunquam assumerent, divina Officia nunquam audirent, ecclesiastica Sacramenta nunquam perciperent, non ieiunarent et his similia; posse que contra eos Inquisitores procedere. Ex quibus cum appareat rem valde dubiam reddi, firmari potest

conclusio, Non dici haereticum, nec de haeresi suspectum Christianum ex eo solo, quod quolibet anno iuxta praeceptum Ecclesiae non communicet, cum ex aliquo interveniente impedimento hoc facere non potuerit.'

88 Carena, *Tractatus*, p. 351: 'Si tamen versaremur in persona, alias de haeresi suspecta agereturque de dicta omissione per plurimos annos, sine ulla legitima, vel colorata causa et de obstinata voluntate non communicandi, tunc posset talis ommitens inquiri et puniri, uti suspectus de Haeresi, stante maxime disp. Concilii Tridentii Sess. 13 de Sacramento Eucharist. Can. 9.'; Farinacci, *Tractatus* p. 15: 'Amplia XIII ut de haeresi suspectus sit etiam ille [. . .] si invenerint illum comedere carnes in diebus prohibitis ab Ecclesia, credentem non esse peccatum, poterunt tanquam haereticum punire.' For a discussion of how enmity between two members of the community could cause abstention from the Eucharist, and the problems this caused, particularly in terms of disrupting religious unity, although in a Lutheran setting, see David Warren Sabean, *Power in the Blood: Popular Culture and Village Discourse in Early Modern Germany* (New York: Cambridge University Press, 1984), pp. 37–60.

89 See, for example, Carlos M.N. Eire, *War against the Idols*, pp. 78–87; Carol Piper Heming, *Protestants and the Cult of the Saints in German-Speaking Europe* (Kirksville, MO: Truman State University Press, 2003), esp. chapters 3 and 4; Lee Palmer Wandel, *Voracious Idols and Violent Hands: Iconoclasm and Reformation in Zurich, Strasbourg, and Basel* (New York: Cambridge University Press, 1995). The importance of iconoclasm to Reformers north of the Alps will be discussed more extensively in Chapter 3.

90 Peña, *Directorium Inquisitorum*, p. 324: 'In his ergo breviter more nostro certiora tradentes, primum statuendum est, in arduis et horrendis factis non esse praesumendam oblivionem: nam ut Plinius affirmat, in rebus arduis non laeditur, aut alteratur memoria . . . idest in factis gravibus et insignibus in quibus non praesumitur oblivio, quamobrem si quis Lutheranorum more templa sacra dirvisset, aut delevisset imagines Sanctorum aut hereticas propositiones ex proposito praedicasset, aut scripsisset, tametsi longum tempus post haec facinora transivisset [. . .].'

91 Farinacci, *Tractatus*, p. 11: 'Squillacen. *de fide catholic. cap. 59* ubi quod imagines Ecclesiae frangens aliasque iniurias illis faciens non dicitur Haereticus, nisi esset defamatus, quod talia faceret, existimans eas non esse venerandas, et multo magis, si pertinaciter asseveraret, esse peccatum adorare id, quod repraesentatur per imagines.'

92 Richard Trexler, 'Florentine Religious Experience: The Sacred Image,' *Studies in the Renaissance* 19 (1972): 20–2.

93 Carena, *Tractatus* pp. 163–9.

94 Carena, ibid., p. 332: 'Praemittendum est hoc loco Antiquam extare haeresim nostris temporibus, renovaam a Sectariis quibusdam, improbantem in Ieiuniis delectum ciborum, quam late (ut alios omittam) reprobavit Greg. Valentia [. . .].'

95 Carena, ibid., p. 334: 'Attamen, existimo ego dictum illud procedere posse, ubi opus quod sit, magis communiter ab Haereticis laudaretur et probaretur, et de illo essent plurimae spetiales Haereses, pro ut adsunt in casu nostro, in quo omnes fere nostri temporis Haeretici conveniunt in reprobando ciborum delectu in Ieiuniis [. . .].' On Friday and Saturday during Lent, but also at other religiously significant times, the Catholic Church instructed that only one meal should be eaten per day, and that the meal should not include any products of animals, including meat, milk, butter, cheese, or eggs. Veronica Franco defended herself against the accusation by explaining she only ate meat during Church feasts due to her pregnancies; see Margaret F. Rosenthal, *The Honest Courtesan: Veronica Franco, Citizen and Writer in Sixteenth-Century Venice* (Chicago: University of Chicago Press, 1992), esp. pp. 172–3. Defendants before the tribunals often claimed illness as an excuse, as will be discussed in future chapters.

96 Farinacci, *Tractatus*, p. 15.

97 John Tedeschi, 'Inquisitorial Sources and Their Uses,' in *The Prosecution of Heresy: Collected Studies on the Inquisition in Early Modern Italy*, ed. Tedeschi (Binghamton, NY: Medieval and Renaissance Texts and Studies, 1991), p. 52–3.

98 Eliseo Masini, *Sacro Arsenale; Overo Prattica dell'officio della S. Inquisizione*, ed. Tommaso Menghini (Rome: 1693; StaatsBibliothek Digitalisat 4 J.can.p.5504), pp. 6–7: 'le quali offendoni l'orecchio degl'uditori e non le diaciarono [. . .].'

99 See Paul Grendler, *The Roman Inquisition and the Venetian Press, 1540–1605* (Princeton: Princeton University Press, 1978); according to Grendler, during the Renaissance and early years of the Reformation, while no one argued that the Church should allow the reading of clearly heretical books, there were a significant number of humanists who argued that readers could be trusted to interpret what was good in a work and leave behind the rest of the content, as with pagan classical sources, humanist, or scientific titles written by Protestants; see pp. 63–70. The first papal index was produced during the pontificate of Paul IV in 1559, but soon after his death his successor Pope Pius IV began revising the index due to the general outcry that it was too severe (Grendler, pp. 115–27).

100 Eymeric, *Directorium Inquisitorum*, pp. 89- 90.
101 Eymeric, ibid., pp. 308–18.
102 Peña, ibid., p. 310: 'Illud hic tandem monebo, huic Decreto Gelasii prohibitorum librorum, respondere nunc etiam in respublica Christiana Indices, quibus damnatae doctrinae libri adnotantur, quos Romani Pontificis auctoritate viri docti Romae consciunt, nullum fere librorum genus omittentes, quorum dogmata non expendant.'
103 Farinacci, *Tractatus*, pp. 44–6: 'retinentes penes se libros haereticorum, mento praesumandos haereticos, cum hoc perspicet et tradant pontificae Cosntitutiones.' Paul Grendler has described how many bookmen, who might also have been convinced Protestants, but showed no other visible sings of their beliefs, were treated lightly or let go without further investigation, and argues that the Venetian Inquisition in the 1560s might have been too overworked to investigate them properly. Given that bookmen with no heretical connections were also treated lightly, being given penances and ordered to pay fines as punishment, it is tempting to think that bookmen, unless there were other clear indications of personal heretical belief, were assumed to be primarily businessmen stocking a product for sale because the inquisition did not consider possession of books alone sufficient proof of heresy at that time.
104 Carena, *Tractatus*, p. 213: 'At verius est hoc esse Iudici arbitrarium consideratis omnibus circumstantiis et qualitatibus nam.'; p. 215: 'Disputant DD an sola retentio libri prohibiti, sit sufficiens inditium ad torquendum retentorem in qua re. Communis nostrorum traditio fuit, ut sola retention in homine bonae famae non faciat contra ipsum inditium ad torturam, ita Farin. qui alios allegat d. qaest. 180 n. 48 [. . .].'
105 John Martin, *Venice's Hidden Enemies*, pp. 111–22; Andrea del Col, 'Shifting Attitudes in the Social Environment toward Heretics: The Inquisition in the Friuli in the Sixteenth Century,' in *Ketzerverfolgung im 16. und frühen 17. Jahrhundert: Vorträge gehalten anlässlich eines Arbeitsgesprächs vom 1. bis 5. Oktober 1989 in der Herzog August Bibliothek Wolfenbüttel*, ed. Hans Rudolf Guggisberg, Bernd Moeller, and Silvana Seidel Menchi (Wiesbaden: Harrassowitz, 1992), p. 70.

3. Word and Deed: Indications of Suspicion

1 Pietro Martire Vermigli, *A treatise of the cohabitacyon of the faithfull with the unfaithfull* (Strasbourg, 1555), fol. 23r: 'The tongue doth confess the thing that lyeth in the heart by words; so doings do give a confession thereof in deed.'

2 John Patrick Donnelly, SJ, 'Social and Ethical Thought of Peter Martyr Vermigli,' *in Peter Martyr Vermigli and Italian Reform,* ed. Joseph C. McLelland (Waterloo, ON.: Wilfrid Laurier University Press, 1977), pp. 107–19, esp. p. 110. For the question of risking martyrdom in particular, see Peter Matheson, 'Martyrdom or Mission?A Protestant Debate,' *Archiv für Reformationsgeschichte* 80 (1989): 154–72.

3 Prospero Farinacci, *Tractatus de haeresi* (Cremona: Apud Marc'Antonium Belpierum, 1636), p. 188: 'Dic. Quod haeresis probatur, non solum ex ore ipsius haeretici sed etiam ex factis haereticalibus, evidentiorque est probatio illa, quae ex factis oritur, quam quae ex verbis, cum facta magis hominu mentem animum et voluntatem declarent, quam verba, quout haec, et similia scripserunt [. . .].'

4 Farinacci, ibid., p. 189: 'Quod, quando aliquis convincitur de factis haereticalibus, illi non prodest allegare, quod non mala intentione haec egerit, quin ut haereticus condemnari debeat: ex plene deductis supra q. 179 n. 54 et seq. [. . .].'

5 Farinacci, ibid., p. 188: 'Quia verba dubia tunc demum interpretanda sunt in bonum sensum quando fuerint prolata sine dolo; secus si cum dolo secundum Menoch. Cons. 82 nu. 53 vers. 1 ubi tamen subdit, in dubio dolum non praesumi.'; 'Rojas, in tr. De haereticis par. Prima n. 205 et seqq. Praesertim, ut ipse inquit hac nostra tempestate in haereticis et Lutheranis, qui verba obscura et ambigua passim decipiendos et inquinandos Catholicorum animos, proferre solent et nu. 379 et seqq. Ubi pariter et generaliter pluribus probat, hac in re esse attendendam qualitatem personarum, quae haereticalia verba proferunt, an scillicet sint rustici, et grossi ingenii et his similia [. . .].'

6 See Richard M. Fraher, 'Preventing Crime in the High Middle Ages: The Medieval Lawyers' Search for Deterrence,' in *Popes, Teachers, and Canon Law in the Middle Ages,* ed. James Ross Sweeney and Stanley Chodorow (Ithaca, NY: Cornell University Press, 1989), pp. 226–8; Fraher, 'IV Lateran's Revolution in Criminal Procedure: The Birth of the *Inquisitio,* the End of Ordeals, and Innocent III's Vision of Ecclesiastical Politics,' in *Studia in Honorem Eminentissimi Cardinalis Alphonsi M. Stickler,* ed. Rosalio Iosepho Card. Castillo Lara (Rome: LAS, 1992), pp. 107–11; Andrea Del Col, *L'Inquisizione in Italia: Dal XII al XXI secolo* (Milan: Oscar Mondadori, 2006), pp. 81–109, 120–7.

7 Fraher, 'IV Lateran's Revolution,' pp. 102–3. Vincenzo Lavenia has examined how the tradition of fraternal correction remained relevant to theologians seeking a way to reincorporate penitent secret heretics without resorting to inquisitorial denunciation, which in Spain included property

confiscation as a punishment of restitution once an inquisition process had been initiated. For much of the medeival and early modern period, however, many prominent theologians and jurists argued that confessors should push even secret heretics toward denouncing themselves to the inquisition as an obligation, or even thought confessors obligated to denounce them. See Lavenia, *L'infamia e il perdono: Tributi, pene e confessione nella teologia morale della prima età moderna* (Bologna: Il Mulino, 2004), pp. 101–29.

8 Farinacci, *Tractatus*, p. 140; see also Cesare Carena, *Tractatus de Officio Sanctissimae Inquisitionis* (Cremona: Apud Marc'Antonium Belpierum, 1636), p. 196, concerning fraternal correction. Massimo Firpo, ed., *Il processo inquisitoriale del cardinale Giovanni Morone: Edizione critica*, 7 vols. (Rome: Istituto storico italiano per l'età moderna, 1981–1985).

9 Eymeric, *Directorium Inquisitorum* (Venice: Apud Marcum Antonium Zalterium, 1595), p. 417: '[. . .] et est quando non est aliquis accusator, nec denunciator, sed fama laborat in aliqua civitate vel loco, quod aliquis dixit vel fecit aliqua contra fidem, et clamor ad aures Inquisitoris pervenit pluries publica fama deferente, et clamosa insinuatione producente: Et tunc Inquisitor inquirat non ad instantiam partis, sed ex officio.'

10 Peña, ibid., p. 424.

11 Peña, ibid., p. 424: '"Hic potes colligere qualiter probetur infamia; debet enim dicere testis, eum de quo agitur, de tali crimine diffamatum: et si quaeretur ab eo, apud quos est infamatus; debet respondere, apud tales: et nisi eos assignet, non videtur bonam reddere causam dicti sui. Praeterea quia non potest sciri, an sint graves, vel malevoli." Haec Innocentius.' The Roman Inquisition often began to interview witnesses by asking them if they knew of anyone heretical or scandalous in their community. But if a witness was called to testify concerning a specific person, and failed to name that person in response, the tribunals sometimes simply asked the witness about the specific person in question by name.

12 Peña, ibid., p. 425: '[. . .] publice dicit, Bucerum verbi gratia imagines sanctorum delevisse, hoc est publica voce dici a populo [. . .].'

13 Farinacci, *Tractatus*, p. 206: '[. . .] idem Franciscus Pegna [. . .] ubi propterea dixit, quod, quando reus est spectatae virtutis et probitatis, integrae famae et incorruptae vitae, tunc iuxta Eymerici sententiam non erit incongruum, aut mitius punire, aut sententiam differre, donec forte aliae superveniant coniecturae.' Peña's edition of Eymeric's *Directorium Inquisitorum* was Farinacci's source for the opinion. Concerning the legal uses of *fama* see, for example, Thomas Kuehn, '*Fama* as Legal Status in Renaissance Florence,' in *Fama: The Politics of Talk and Reputation in Medieval*

Europe, ed. Thelma Fenster and Daniel Lord Smail (Ithaca, NY: Cornell University Press, 2003), pp. 27–46, and Jeffrey A. Bowman, 'Infamy and Proof in Medieval Spain,' ibid., pp. 95–117; Christopher F. Black, *The Italian Inquisition* (New Haven: Yale University Press, 2009), pp. 224–30.

14 Farinacci, *Tractatus*, p. 206: 'testatus fuerit contrarium opinionem esse commune, apud eum tamen servari affirmat saltem tres testes require ad convincendum aliquem de haeresi [. . .].'

15 Farinacci, ibid., p. 206: '[. . .] ubi propterea infert ad effectus condemnandi haereticum in poenam ordinariam, non sufficere depositionem duarum mulierum'; '[. . .] ubi quod nec etiam haereisis probatur per tres testes, quando non sunt idonei.' Farinacci's sources here included Calderini, Albertino, Simancas, Rojas, and Eymeric.

16 Farinacci, ibid., p. 206: 'Quia, an in crimine haeresis, ad convincendum aliquem duo testes sufficient, an vero plures requirantur, Iudicis arbitrio remissum videtur ex Hostiensis Cardinale, Philippo Franco, et Gundisalvo in locus relates per Conrad in pract. Rubr. de haereticis numer. 10 (sed an isti Doctores tale quid dicant per te ipsum videas.).'; Peña, *Directorium Inquisitorum*, p. 425.

17 Peña, *Directorium Inquisitorum*, p. 445, 'Et ratio est, quoniam inter omnia probationum genera, reorum confessio obtinet primum locum de quo vide quae dico statim in commentario sequenti.'

18 Peña, ibid., p. 447: '[. . .] quia cum haeresis crimen in mente concipiatur et in animo lateat, plerumque non postest aliter probari, quam per propriam confessionem reorum.'

19 Peña, ibid., p. 617: 'Primo, cum duo vel plures deponunt de diversis haeresibus; item diversis locis atque temporibus; ut cum, verbi gratia, unus dicit se audisse Lutherum negantem Purgatorium mense Maio: alius vero dicit se audisse eundem Lutherum negantem potestatem summi Pontificis mense Aprilis.'

20 Peña, ibid., p. 619: 'Quia vero ex dictis talium testium probatorum quidem et idoneorum magna et urgentia nascuntur indicia adversus illum, quae unam et eandem aut plures et easdem haereses diversis locis et temporibus dicitur repetivisse, torquendus erit: quod si nihil fateatur (quia hoc cause non videtur sufficienter superasse indicia in tortura, eaque dilvisse, seu, ut melius loquar, purgasse) non crederem iniquum ut abiurare quoque compellatur de vehementi, eique aliae salutares poenitentia iniungantur; at nullo modo tam quam negativus tradendus est curiae saeculari [. . .].'

21 Peña, ibid., pp. 373–4; see also Carena, *Tractatus*, p. 193, who attributed the principle to Gregory IX in *Excommunicamus* and Innocent IV in *Noverit*,

both of which could be read in the section of the *Directorium Inquisitorum* which reprinted all of the papal bulls relevant to inquisitorial prosecution.

22 Farinacci, *Tractatus*, p. 198: '[. . .] ubi tamen declarat, nisi quis citaretur ad testificandum contra affines, vel consanguineos, vel etiam amicissimos: tunc enim licet propter inobedientiam puniri possit, non tamen de haeresi suspectus habendus est.'

23 Carena, *Tractatus*, pp. 194–5.

24 Peña, *Directorium Inquisitorum*, p. 374.

25 Peña, ibid., pp. 600–1.

26 The full quotation is: 'If anyone secretly entices you – even if it is your brother, your father's son or your mother's son, or your own son or daughter, or the wife you embrace, or your most intimate friend – saying, "Let us go worship other gods," whom neither you nor your ancestors have known, any of the gods of the people around you, whether near you or far away from you, from one end of the earth to the other, you must not yield to or heed such persons. Show them no pity, or compassion and do not shield them.' Deuteronomy 13:6–8 (*HarperCollins Study Bible*, ed. Wayne A. Meeks et al. [New York: HarperCollins, 1993], p. 290); Carena, *Tractatus*, p. 192.

27 Farinacci, *Tractatus*, pp. 198–9.

28 Farinacci, ibid., p. 217: 'Amplia I hanc regulam: quia quamvis regulariter servus contra Dominum testis esse non possit [. . .] hoc tamen fallit in crimine haeresis, in quo et contra Dominos testimonium perhibere coguntur et etiam torquere Simanchas [. . .] ubi quod servi contra Dominos admittuntur, sed cum tormentiis: quia sic etiam admittuntur in crimine Laese Maiestatis.' *Servus* can mean either servant or slave; it was common practice in Roman law to torture any slave giving testimony against his or her master in capital cases. It was assumed that their testimony was inherently biased, and that the infliction of pain was necessary to gain truthful testimony. See Edward Peters, *Inquisition* (New York: The Free Press, 1988), pp. 16–17; Peters, *Torture* (New York: Basil Blackwell, 1985), pp. 11–39.

29 Farinacci, *Tractatus*, p. 217: 'Amplia III ut non solum domestici et familiares et etiam consanguinei et affines contra consanguineos et propinquos in crimine haereisis deponere possint et faciant plenam probationem [. . .].'

30 Peña, *Directorium Inquisitorum*, p. 603: 'Sensus est, praedictos testis periuros, vel excommunicatos, vel socios criminis, vel infames, aut denique alias minus idoneas, in crimine quidem haereses, seu in criminibus exceptis admitti: ceterum duo ex ipsis non sufficere ad plenam probationem faciendam, vel ad poenam delicti ordinariam imponendam, sed ad

praesumptionem vel aliqualem probationem faciendam, vel indicium ad torturam, vel poenam extraordinariam imponendam.'

31 Peña, ibid., pp. 603–4: ' Sit secunda axioma: Plures quam duo testes inhabiles et minus idonei in hoc crimine tunc facient plenam probationem et ad condemnationem, seu poenam criminis ordinariam imponendam sufficient [. . .].'; 'Quamvis in multis causis testis valde dignus et alius testis infamis, seu minus idoneus coniugantur ad faciendam plenam probationem, quia integra et superabundans fides unius supplet defectum alterius [. . .].'

32 Peña, ibid., p. 603: '[. . .] si ex coniecturis aliquibus non praesumantur falsae dicere; tunc tales plures quam duo, additis aliis coniecturis de veritate criminis sufficient ad condemnationem.' For Felino Sandei, see G. Arrighi, *Felino Sandei (1444–1503): Canonista e umanista* (Lucca: Accademia a Lucchese di scienze, lettore e arti, 1987).

33 Peña, *Directorium Inquisitorum*, p. 604: 'Illa est etiam in hac quaestione praecipuae dubitatio, An huiusmodi testes suspecti et minus idonei cum admittuntur, torqueri debeant an potius dictis ipsorum sine tortura sit standum et glossa 15 q. 6 in summa, torquendos autumat, sive sint servi, sive viles personae, vel etiam si sint liberi homines, dummodo sint criminosi et infames, vel obscuri vel ignoti [. . .].'

34 Peña, ibid., p. 604: 'Sed magis mihi placet sententia Iacobi Simancae de cathol. Instit. tit. 64 num. 38 asserentis, socium criminis absque tormentis indicium facere maius aut minus pro personarum qualitate et criminum et aliarum circumstantiis. Verum est causa torqueri etiam postest, ut proxime dictum est.'

35 Farinacci, *Tractatus*, p. 208: '[. . .] ubi simplicter dixit, depositionem socii criminis non afficere, nisi fuerit in tortura confirmata, reprobatio Simancha contrarium tenente ex constitutione Carolina, quae in Imperio solum servanda erit, subditque hanc torturam socio criminis esse inferendam specialiter pro confirmatione suae depositionis [. . .].' Farinacci was quoting Simancas through Martín del Rio's text *De disquisitionis magicae*.

36 Farinacci, ibid., p. 209: 'Amplia IV etiam in mulieribus, quae, quod in crimine haeresis admittantur, nulla est dubitatio: si enim admittuntur infames, utique multo magis admitti debent mulieres: maior enim est exceptio, infamia, quam sexus: sed quando hoc verum sit [. . .].'

37 Farinacci, ibid., p. 211: 'Et isto casu, quando testis, qui in crimine haeresis deposuit, est varius et periurus, statur secundo dicto, et non primo [. . .].'

38 Farinacci, ibid., p. 211: 'Limita I propsitam regulam, ut tunc demum testis varii, et periuri credatur secundo dicto, quando deponit non solum contra

alios, sed etiam contra se; secus si de aliis fateretur, et de se negaret, aut nihil diceret, sic enim probare videtur text. in cap. Accusatus § Licet de haereticis in 6 in illis verbis in principio: '"Iurantes tam de se quam de aliis super facto haeresis dicere veritatem," et iterum "infra Stare debet tam contra se, quam contra reliquo."'

39 Farinacci, ibid., p. 211: 'Contrarium, quod testi periuro credatur revocando primum dictum, etiam quod non deponat contra se, sed solum simpliciter deponat contra alios, defendit Francisc. Pegn. in additionibus ad Eymeric in Direct. Inquisit. par. 3 quaest. 65 commentar. 114 versic. rursus haec sententia et seq. fol. mihi 655 col. 2.'

40 Farinacci, ibid., p. 212: 'Limita V ut in crimine haeresis testis secundo dicto potius stetur, quam primo, dummodo in primo negaverit, in secundo fateatur alias secus [. . .].'; 'Contrarium, quod scilicet non sit vera opinio eorum qui putant non aliter posteriori testimonio fidem, cum testis prius testimonium corrigit contra haereticos in favorem fidei catholicae aliter secus plene defendit Simanchas [. . .].' Simancas was one of the most important Spanish jurists and inquisitors of the sixteenth century. Educated at the College of Santa Cruz, he became inquisitor of Valladolid in 1545 and was appointed to the *Suprema* in 1559. At the request of Philip II, Simancas oversaw the process of Bartolomé de Carranza, archbishop of Toledo, accused of heterodox beliefs similar to those of the *spirituali* in Italian lands. Simancas followed the case to Rome on its transfer, and lived there from 1567 to 1576 until the case concluded. Carranza then died a few days later. It was during this time that Simancas published a revamped edition of his manual (originally published in Spain in 1552 as *Institutiones Catholicae*). Entitled *De catholicis institutionibus* in 1575 in Rome, Simancas took account of the differences between Roman and Spanish procedure, often to the detriment of the Italians, in Simancas' opinion, since he stated that he wanted to instruct inexpert Italian inquisitors. But his work, especially his smaller and more easily consulted *Enchiridion* (1568), was highly regarded nevertheless. See S. Pastore, 'Simancas, Diego de,' '*Dizionario storico dell'Inquisizione*, Vol. 3, ed. Adriano Prosperi with Vincenzo Lavenia and John Tedeschi (Pisa: Scuola Normale Superiore Pisa, 2010), pp. 1430–1; A. Errera, 'Manuali per inquisitori,' ibid., Vol. 2, pp. 978–9.

41 John Tedeschi, 'Preliminary Observations on Writing a History of the Roman Inquisition,' in *The Prosecution of Heresy: Collected Studies on the Inquisition in Early Modern Italy* ed. Tedeschi (Binghamton, NY: Medieval and Renaissance Texts and Studies, 1991), pp. 3–29; false testimony, and the punishments incurred, will be fully examined in Chapter 5.

42 Adriano Prosperi, in particular, has viewed the relationship between confessors and inquisitors as capable of controlling the orthodoxy of dioceses and territorial states; see Adriano Prosperi, *Tribunali della coscienza: Inquisitori, confessori, missionari* (Turin: Einaudi, 1996), esp. pp. 279–300, 316–32. Prosperi has characterized the relationship between inquisitors and confessors as one in which confession became subordinate to inquisitorial goals in response to the sixteenth-century crisis in religion (pp. 257–60); but Elena Brambilla has argued that the internal and external forums dated to the high middle ages, and overlapped; see Elena Brambilla, *Alle origini del Sant' Uffizio: Penitenza, confessione e giustizia spirituale dal Medioevo al XVI secolo* (Bologna: Il Mulino, 2000), pp. 347–59. Lavenia has emphasized how property confiscation of convicted heretics, particularly in Spain, complicated the issue for jurists and theologians; see Lavenia, *L'infamia e il perdono*, pp. 101–29. How witnesses became aware of what constituted heresy is difficult to establish definitively, since oral conversations most likely played an important role. Francisco Bethencourt has pointed out the role of inquisitors reading edicts aloud to congregations in churches, in which inquisitors would describe what was considered heresy. Most of the edicts Bethencourt has studied were created in the late sixteenth or seventeenth centuries; but the contents of those edicts correlates with inquisitors' manuals in how heresy was described. The tribunals' familiars, or lay staff, and confraternities dedicated to supporting the tribunals most likely also played a role. See Francisco Bethencourt, *The Inquisition: A Global History, 1478–1834* (New York: Cambridge University Press, 2009), pp. 171–2; 206–10; Christopher F. Black, *Italian Inquisition*, pp. 71–5 for witnesses and denunciations and pp. 119–22 for confraternities.

43 John Jeffries Martin, *Venice's Hidden Enemies: Italian Heretics in a Renaissance City* (Berkeley and Los Angeles: University of California Press, 1993), p. 21.

44 Farinacci, *Tractatus*, p. 188: 'non solum ex ore ipsius haeretici sed etiam ex factis haereticalibus, evidentiorque est probation illa, quae ex factis oritur, quam quae ex verbis, cum facta magis hominum mentem animem et voluntatem declarent, quam verba [. . .].'

45 Farinacci, ibid., p. 189: 'Quod, quando aliquis convincitur de factis haereticalibus, illi non prodest allegare, quod non mala intentione haec egerit, quin ut haereticus condemnari debeat: ex plene deductis supra q. 179 n. 54 et seqq.'

46 Farinacci, ibid., p. 189: '[. . .] et sic inquisiti innocentia probatur ex actis, dictisque contrariis haeresi, utputa, si probetur, reum quotidie rem divinam audire, pro animis defunctorum orare, aliaque huiusmodi facere,

quae facere solent boni et catholici Christiani: non enim potest quisquam subito fingi nec repente mutari, aut natura converti [. . .].'; p. 190: 'ubi de eo qui domi suae nullas Sanctorum imagines tenebat.'

47 Farinacci, ibid., pp. 188–9.

48 Farinacci, ibid., p. 188: 'Quia verba dubia tunc demum interpretanda sunt in bonum sensum quando fuerint prolata sine dolo; secus si cum dolo secundum Menoch. Cons. 82 nu. 53 vers. 1 ubi tamen subdit, in dubio dolum non praesumi.'

49 Farinacci, ibid., p. 188: 'Rojas, in tr. De haereticis par. Prima n. 205 et seqq. Praesertim, ut ipse inquit hac nostra tempestate in haereticis et Lutheranis, qui verba obscura et ambigua passim decipiendos et inquinandos Catholicorum animos, proferre solent et nu. 379 et seqq. Ubi pariter et generaliter pluribus probat, hac in re esse attendendam qualitatem personarum, quae haereticalia verba proferunt, an scillicet sint rustici, et grossi ingenii et his similia [. . .].'

50 Peña, *Directorium Inquisitorum*, p. 601: '[. . .] quod in primis contingit testibus imperitits, qui nesciunt veritates catholicas ab erroribus secernere et separare; et propterea in hac causa, omnino est vitanda in testium dictis vel obscuritas vel ambiguitas.'

51 Carlo Ginzburg and Adriano Prosperi have argued that Nicodemism contituted a formal theology of Christian belief, but largely define Nicodemism as existing completely in the mind. See Carlo Ginzburg, *Il nicodemismo: Simulazione e dissimulazione religiosa nell'Europa del '500* (Turin: Einaudi, 1970), pp. 159–81, esp. p. 179; Adriano Prosperi, *L'eresia del Libro Grande: Storia di Giorgio Siculo e della sua setta* (Milan: Feltrinelli, 2000), pp. 322–37. In contrast, John Jeffries Martin, *Myths of Renaissance. Individualism* (New York: Palgrave Macmillan, 2004), pp. 21–61. Carlos Eire has interpreted Nicodemism as a response to fear of persecution rather than a coherent theological doctrine. See Eire, *War against the Idols: The Reformation of Worship from Erasmus to Calvin* (New York: Cambridge University Press, 1986), pp. 202–5, 234–75; Carlos M.N. Eire, 'Calvin and Nicodemism: A Reapprisal,' *Sixteenth Century Journal* 10, no. 1 (Spring 1979): 45–69; Eire points out the contradictions in Ginzburg's sources.

52 Eire, *War against the Idols*, pp. 212–14, 225–6. Zwingli, while not quite as severe in his Eucharistic theology and sharp warnings against pollution, believed that the meaning of the Eucharist and some presence of Christ at the ceremony were dependent on the faith of those participating in it as well. See W. P. Stephens, *Zwingli: An Introduction to His Thought* (Oxford:

Clarendon Press, 1992), pp. 105–6. The importance of avoiding idolatry, in the form of images and relics, will be discussed below.

53 Eire, *War against the* Idols, pp. 241–7; see also 'Answer of John Calvin to the Nicodemite Gentlemen Concerning Their Compaint that He is too Severe (1544),' in *Come Out From Among Them: 'Anti-Nicodemite' Writings of John Calvin,* ed. and trans. Seth Skolnitsky (Dallas, TX: Protestant Heritage Press, 2001), pp. 99–131, esp. p. 101.

54 Even the more irenic Protestants (such as the Lutheran Melanchthon, who negotiated with Catholic imperial authorities on several occasions), while willing to compromise concerning some *adiaphora,* were not willing to make doctrinal concessions (see Euan Cameron, 'The Possibilities and Limits of Conciliation: Philipp Melanchthon and Inter-Confessional Dialogue in the Sixteenth Century,' in *Conciliation and Confession: The Struggle for Unity in the Age of Reform, 1415–1648,* ed. Howard P. Louthan and Randall C. Zachman [Notre Dame, IN: University of Notre Dame Press, 2004], pp. 77–81). Peter Matheson, 'Martyrdom or Mission?' pp. 163–4; Matheson, 'Martin Bucer and the Old Church,' in *Martin Bucer: Reforming Church and Community,* ed. D.F. Wright (New York: Cambridge University Press, 1994), pp. 11–13. Concerning Martin Bucer's letters to Italian conventicles, see Salvatore Caponetto, *The Protestant Reformation in Sixteenth-Century Italy,* trans. Anne C. Tedeschi and John Tedeschi (Kirksville, MO: Thomas Jefferson University Press, 1999), pp. 55–6. For preachers in Italian lands expositing Protestant doctrines while still in holy orders, see Ugo Rozzo, 'Le "Prediche" veneziane di Giulio da Milano,' *Bolletino della Società di Studi Valdesi* 152 (1983): 3–30; Caponetto, *Protestant Reformation,* p. 19; see also Chapter 1.

55 Caponetto, *Protestant Reformation,* pp. 277–80, pp. 327–31. In particular, a significant number of citizens would flee Lucca and emigrate to Calvin's Geneva in order to continue practising what they saw as the true faith. See also Frank A. James III, 'Introduction,' in *Peter Martyr Vermigli and the European Reformations: Semper Reformanda,* ed. James (Boston: Brill, 2004), pp. xiv–xviii; see also Philip McNair, *Peter Martyr in Italy: An Anatomy of Apostasy* (New York and Oxford: Clarendon Press, 1967); James, 'Introduction,' pp. xix–xxi. Luther's consubstantiation, which preserved a direct sense of Christ in the Eucharist, differed from Reformed opinion, all branches of which interpreted the sacrament to be a more mystical or spiritual connection with Christ, grounded in the faith of the congregation. For explanations concerning the differences between Vermigli, Bullinger, and Bibliander concerning predestination, see J. Wayne Baker, *Heinrich Bullinger and the Covenant: The Other Reformed Tradition* (Athens, OH: Ohio

University Press, 1980), pp. 27–54. Vermigli advocated strong double predestination, as did Calvin: God predestined some for salvation, and others for damnation. Bullinger preferred a position that resembled single predestination, which in his opinion preserved God's essential goodness; while he rejected unrestricted free will, and thought that all who believed in Christ would be saved through God's gift of grace, man sinned and was damned through choice, the first such choice having been Adam's. God's foreknowledge that Adam would sin did not necessarily imply God compelling Adam to sin, as Calvin and Vermigli believed. Bibliander emphasized man's choices even more than Bullinger – according to Bibliander, all men were adopted sons of God unless their choices to sin determined otherwise. In Roman Inquisition trials, this was often expressed colloquially as 'man has free will to do evil, but not good.'

56 Concerning Vergerio's polemics, see M.A. Overell, 'Vergerio's Anti-Nicodemite Propaganda and England, 1547–1558,' *Journal of Ecclesiastical History* 51, no. 2 (April 2000): 296–318, esp. pp. 297–8; John Patrick Donnelly, SJ, 'The Social and Ethical Thought of Peter Martyr Vermigli,' in *Peter Martyr Vermigli and Italian Reform*, ed. Joseph C. McLelland (Waterloo ON: Wilfrid Laurier University Press, 1977); pp. 107–19, esp. p. 110. For the question of risking martyrdom in particular, see Peter Matheson, 'Martyrdom or Mission,' pp. 154–72. Concerning Vergerio's development, career as a Catholic prelate, and flight north, see Anne Jacobson Schutte, *Pier Paolo Vergerio: The Making of an Italian Reformer* (Geneva: Librairie Droz, 1977), especially Chapter 9 concerning Vergerio's anti-Nicodemite message to his followers after his flight.

57 Vermigli, *Cohabitacyon*, fol. 23r: 'The tongue doth confess the thing that lyeth in the heart by words; so doings do give a confession thereof in deed.' See also fols. 26r–27r concerning Vermigli's evaluation of Catholic Mass.

58 Vermigli, *Common places*, trans. Anthony Marten (London: Henry Denham and Henry Middleton, 1583), p. 540. See also, concerning Protestant defences of this behaviour, Beat Hodler, 'Protestant Self-Perception and the Problem of *Scandalum*: A Sketch,' in *Protestant History and Identity in Sixteenth-Century Europe*, Vol. 1, *The Medieval Inheritance*, ed. Bruce Gordon (Aldershot, UK: Scolar Press, 1996), pp. 23–30.

59 Carol Piper Heming, *Protestants and the Cult of the Saints in German-Speaking Europe* (Kirksville, MO: Truman State University Press, 2003), pp. 60–1.

60 Eire, *War against the Idols*, pp. 78–87; Carol Piper Heming has recently characterized iconoclasm (if ideally more orderly and controlled) as

incredibly important to northern Reformers because the use of images in Catholic worship represented the nexus in which several concerns, both doctrinal and ecclesiastical, met, including works, righteousness, monasticism, purgatory and indulgences, and financial abuses. See Carol Piper Heming, *Protestants and the Cult of the Saints*, esp. chapters 3 and 4; Lee Palmer Wandel, *Voracious Idols and Violent Hands: Iconoclasm and Reformation in Zurich, Strasbourg, and Basel* (New York: Cambridge University Press, 1995). Iconoclasm also loomed large in anti-Protestant polemical literature; see, for example, Christopher S. Wood, 'In Defense of Images: Two Local Rejoinders to the Zwinglian Iconoclasm,' *Sixteenth Century Journal* 19, no. 1 (Spring 1988): 25–44.

61 Vermigli, *Common places*, p. 346: 'God must be worshipped in spirit and in truth, and no man is so ignorant not to recognize that images are neither'; p. 334, 'The matter of images is not all one: for sometimes they be made of stone, of wood, metall, plaister, claie and such other like.'

62 Bruce Gordon, *The Swiss Reformation* (New York: Manchester University Press, 2002), pp. 52–3. Zwingli (1483–1531) was born in Wildhaus in the Swiss cantons; he attended the University of Vienna and attained an MA by 1506; he then became a parish priest in Glarus until 1516. But the two decisive influences on his theology were Erasmus and, to a certain extent, Luther, although it appears Luther's ideas, once they became public after 1517, confirmed much of what Zwingli already thought was true. Inspired by Erasmus's humanism and critique of empty ritualistic ceremonies, Zwingli developed his ideas concerning the primacy of Biblicism and a dichotomy between inward faith and outward worship. Zwingli oversaw the implementation of his Reform theology in Zurich; the sermon concerning food was soon followed by a request that the town council approve clerical marriage in July 1522. During the disputation concerning these issues held before the town council and spectators from the town in January 1523, he emphasized the authority of Scripture to determine doctrine and worship, rather than the Catholic Church's authority and tradition. Zwingli, however, let the town council set the pace of the reform. Thus while the council agreed with Zwingli that images and the Mass were inventions of the Catholic Church and required reform in 1523, images were not removed until 1524, and the Mass was not reformed until 1525. W. P. Stephens, *Zwingli: An Introduction to His Thought* (New York: Clarendon Press, 1992), pp. 12–21.

63 Ulrich Zwingli, 'Concerning Choice and Liberty Respecting Food,' trans. Lawrence A. McLouth, in *The Correspondence of Huldreich Zwingli, Together*

with Selections from His German Works, ed. Samuel Macauley Jackson (New York: G.P. Putnam's Sons, 1912), pp. 73–6.

64 Zwingli, 'Choice and Liberty Respecting Food,' p. 94.

65 Vermigli, *Cohabitacyon,* fol. 35r: 'They were thinges indifferent and as such things might be well used'; 'Those things might therefore be kept and observed for a time so that men did not use them with that mind (as I said) to be justified by them.'

66 Vermigli, *Cohabitacyon,* fol. 36v: 'To abstain or not abstain from meats was then a thing indifferent. In such things the stronger must bear with the infirmity of the weaker; but meat eating and Mass hauntings are not like, for this is no thing indifferent but manifestly evil as it is sufficiently proves and therefore it is not to be done in respect of bearing with any man that is weak.'

67 Andrea Del Col, 'Organizzazione, composizione e giurisdizione dei tribunali dell'Inquisizione romana rella repubblica di Venezia (1500–1550)' *Critica Storica* 25 (1988): 244–94, esp. pp. 264–9 concerning Giovanni della Casa and his interactions with the Venetian government, pp. 278–92 concerning the way in which local vicars, bishops, and rectors acted as inquisitors on the Venetian *terraferma,* and esp. p. 282 for the constitution of the tribunal there. See also Martin, *Venice's Hidden Enemies,* pp. 51–6.

68 Andrea Del Col, 'Shifting Attitudes in the Social Environment toward Heretics: The Inquisition in the Friuli in the Sixteenth Century,' in *Ketzerverfolgung im 16. und frühen 17. Jahrhundert: Vorträge gehalten anlässlich eines Arbeitsgesprächs vom 1. bis 5. Oktober 1989 in der Herzog August Bibliothek Wolfenbüttel,* ed. Hans Rudolf Guggisberg, Bernd Moeller, and Silvana Seidel Menchi (Wiesbaden: Harrassowitz, 1992), p. 69; Del Col describes heresy has having 'several hundred adherents.' Udine was also proselytized intensively by Pier Paolo Vergerio; his sister, Coletta, was a nun in the Clarist convent of San Francesco. She and some of her fellow nuns were converted to Lutheranism, as others in the town would be. A certain Nicola of Treviso would later proselytize Anabaptist beliefs in the area. See Caponetto, *Protestant Reformation,* p. 193. Concerning Vergerio's flight north, see Anne Jacobson Schutte, *Pier Paolo Vergerio: The Making of an Italian Reformer* (Geneva: Librairie Droz, 1977), especially chapter 9 concerning Vergerio's anti-Nicodemite message to his followers after his flight.

69 Andrea Del Col, 'Shifting Attitudes,' pp. 66–7; Del Col also notes that the records of all the the processes undertaken by the general vicar were sent to Venice 'for some reason'; Girolamo, the shoemaker, however, appealed

to the Venetian tribunal to overturn his sentence (pp. 70–2); Del Col, 'L'abiura trasformata in propaganda ereticale nel duomo di Udine (15 Aprile 1544),' *Metodi e ricerche* 2 (1981): 57–72.

70 ASVe, *Sant'Uffizio*, Busta 1, Fasc. 2, *Contra Geronimo calleger*, fols. 23v–24v.

71 ASVe, *Contra Calegaro Girolamo*, fols. 8v–9r: 'Io ho preso da una Francesca e una Tina che stanno in detto borgo che detta Centa abbia straziato le figure dei crucifixi et altri santi aveva in casa ma non lo so da vera.'

72 ASVe, *Contra Calegaro Girolamo*, fols. 8r: 'Io gli risposi voglio stare in quello che comanda la Santa Madre Chiesa e lui disse "Qual chiesa?"'

73 ASVe, *Contra Calegaro Girolamo*, fol. 8v: 'e che si meritava tanto a dire una oratione á laudo per Dio in casa quanto a dirlà in una chiesa e che non si merita mené Credo né Ave Maria ma solo la Pater Noster.'

74 ASVe, *Contra Calegaro Girolamo*, fol. 13r. Some members of the group did engage publicly in iconoclasm; see Del Col, 'L'abiura trasformata', pp. 57–72.

75 Silvana Seidel Menchi, 'Italy,' trans. Anne Jacobsen Schutte, in *The Reformation in National Context*, ed. Bob Scribner, Roy Porter, and Mikuláš Teich (New York: Cambridge University Press, 1994), pp. 181–201, esp. pp. 190–1; Menchi, 'The Inquisitor as Mediator,' in *Heresy, Culture and Religion in Early Modern Italy: Contexts and Contestations*, ed. Ronald K. Delph, Michelle M. Fontaine, and John Jeffries Martin (Kirksville, MO: Truman State University Press, 2006), p. 177; Ugo Rozzo and Silvana Seidel Menchi, 'The Book and the Reformation in Italy,' trans. Karin Maag in *The Reformation and the Book*, ed. Jean-François Gilmont and Karin Maag (Brookfield, VT: Ashgate, 1998), p. 361.

76 Del Col, 'Organizzazione,' pp. 283–4.

77 ASVe, *Sant'Uffizio*, Busta 6, fasc. 15, *Contra Vagnola Pietro*, fols. 1r–3v: 'E non si deve confessare o dire gli suoi peccati né a fratte né a prette, ma che si deve confessare a bocca a Dio con la mente o cuore.'

78 ASVe, *Sant'Uffizio*, Busta 21 Fasc. 2, *Contra Gerolamo e Alvise Badoer, e Giovanni Fineti*, unp. The tribunal in Venice at this time consisted of the papal nuncio Giovanni Antonio Facchinetti, the Patriarch Giovanni Trevisan, and the Dominican inquisitor Valerio Faenzi. In addition, four laymen served as the Venetian government's representatives – Paolo Cornelio, Marco Moresini, Giulio Contarini, and Girolamo Grimani. When inquisitor Faenzi was ill he was assisted by Rocco Cataneo, an auditor. See also Nicholas Davidson, 'The Inquisition in Venice and Its Documents: Some Problems of Method and Analysis,' in *L'Inquisizione romana in Italia nell'età moderna: Archivi, problemi di metodo e nuove richerche; Atti del seminario internazionale Trieste, 18–20 maggio 1988*, ed. Andrea Del Col and

Giovanni Paolin (Rome: Ministero per i beni culturali e ambientali/Ufficio centrale per i beni archivistici, 1991), p. 126.

79 The Sozzini, a family of jurists and law professors, had originated in Siena. Lelio and Cornelio, sons of the famous Marcantanio Sozzini, jurist and professor of canon law at the University of Padua, had been raised mostly in Padua and spent most of their adult lives at Bologna. Along with their nephew Fausto, they developed highly idiosyncratic beliefs, and Fausto would go on to found the Socinian church (Unitarianism) in Poland; but in the 1550s they were part of a larger religious milieu in Siena that explored heterodox ideas. In Poland, Fausto Sozzini developed a systematic theology that included rejecting all ideas of original sin, the idea of a immortal soul separate from God (all human beings contained a divine spark that returned to its origins after death), Christ's divinity, and any concept of hell or purgatory (since Christ's death opened the possibility of immortality for believers). In addition, Sozzini stressed free will and reason and rejected any concept of grace and believed that the Eucharist was the only sacrament (completely disavowing baptism). Czesław Miłosz, *The History of Polish Literature*, 2nd ed. (Berkeley and Los Angeles: University of California Press, 1983), pp. 34–5. See also Caponetto, *Protestant Reformation*, p. 301; Valerio Marchetti, *Gruppi ereticali senesi nel Cinquecento* (Florence: La nuova italia, 1975), pp. 143–64.

80 ASS, *Notarile antecosimiano* 2776, *Processus et inquisitio contra magistrum Bartholomeum olim magistri Iohannis de Nellis fabrum ferrarium ac abiuratio*(hereafter *Processo contro Bartolomeo Nelli*), fol. 1r: 'nella bottega di Francesco speziale dove era ancora Niccolò Barbiero, Scipione Orlandini, M[esser] Achille Orlandini, Giulia di Vecchi speziale e così ragionamento della predicazione fatta il giorno dal padre Girolamo. Messer Giulio e da quella seguitando ragionamento ... e la quale opinione contraposse Bartolomeo con dire l'opere nostre non meritavano niente e allegava si non perché ma che noi siamo salv[ato] per Christo e non per bene opere [sic].'

81 ASS, *Processo contro Bartolomeo Nelli*, fol. 8r–v; fols. 35r–36v.

82 Massimo Firpo, 'Gli "spirituali," l'Accademia di Modena, e il formulario di fede del 1542: Controllo del dissenso religiose e nicodemismo,' *Rivista di storia e letteratura religiosa* 20 (1984): 77–8; now reprinted in *Inquisizione romana e Controriforma: studi sul cardinal Giovanni Morone (1509–1580) e il suo processo d'eresia*, rev. ed. (Brescia: Morcelliana, 2005), pp. 35–129.

83 Massimo Firpo, 'L'Accademia di Modena,' pp. 88, 102–4. Many of the Academicians prevaricated over the course of the summer, but the insti-

tution of an inquisition and the flight of several important clerics with reform ideas convinced them that they did not have much of a choice.

84 Susanna Peyronel Rambaldi, *Speranze e crisi nel Cinquecento modenese: Tensioni religiose e vita cittadina in tempi di Giovanni Morone* (Milan: Franco Angeli, 1979), Chapter 2; Massimo Firpo, 'L'Accademia di Modena,' pp. 58–64. Morone himself, while a cardinal, would be prosecuted as a heretic in 1557, during the papacy of the zealous former inquisitor Paul IV. After Paul IV's death, he was released from prison, his reputation rehabilitated, and he would go on to preside over the Council of Trent's closing sessions in 1562. Massimo Firpo edition of the process records is truly comprehensive.

85 ASMo, *Inquisizione*, Busta 5, fasc. 20, 1568, *Contra Alessandrum Fornarium*, fol. 1r–v; Fra Niccolò da Finale was appointed inquisitorial vicar of Modena in 1566, since at the time Modena was a part of the inquisitorial region of Ferrara, Modena, and Reggio. Fra Niccolò reported to Camillo Campeggi, the Dominican inquisitor of the province from c. 1567 to c. 1568. Alessandro Fornari was convicted of being vehemently suspect in heresy and assigned to house arrest on April 27, 1568.

86 ASMo, *Contra Alessandrum Fornarium*, fol. unpg.

87 ASMo, *Contra Alessandrum Fornarium*, fol. unpg.

88 ASMo, *Inquisizione*, Busta 3, no. 13, *Processi 1555–1568, Contra Claudium Rudiliam*, testimony of Gasparo, 27 January 1555, fol. 159r: 'Se dice che l'è luterano.' The interviews took place in the bishop's palace. Silvana Seidel Menchi also has mentioned that he was not alone in saying such things in Modena; see *Erasmo in Italia*, pp. 93–4.

89 ASMo, *Contra Claudium Rudiliam*, testimony of Jacobus Maria de Crispis *detto il rizzo sinistra*, 28 January 1555, fol. 161r. For Egidio Foscarari, see Michelle Fontaine, 'For the Good of the City: The Bishop and the Ruling Elite in Tridentine Modena,' *Sixteenth Century Journal* 28, no. 1 (Spring 1997): 29–43, esp. 29, ff. 1.

90 ASMo, *Processi 1555–1568, Contra Claudium Rudiliam*, Testimony of Paula, 1 February 1555, fol. unpg. Fra Alberto Foschieri and Fra Paolo da Modena also participated in the process; some of the interrogations took place in the tribunal's seat, the convent of San Domenico.

4. The Mercy of the Court

1 Thomas Aquinas, *Summa Theologiae*, 2a2ae. II, 3 Vol. XXXI, ed. T.C. O'Brien (New York: McGraw Hill, 1964–); Titus 3:9–11: 'But avoid stupid controversies, genealogies, dissensions, and quarrels about the law, for they are unprofitable and worthless. After a first and second admonition, have

nothing more to do with anyone who causes divisions, since you know that such a person is perverted and sinful, being self-condemned.' (*HarperCollins Study Bible*, p. 2246.)

2 See Andrea Del Col, *L'Inquisizione in Italia: Dal XII al XXI Secolo* (Milan: Mondadori, 2006), pp. 772–84; Christopher F. Black, *The Italian Inquisition* (New Haven: Yale University Press, 2009), pp. 134–6. For earlier statistical estimates concerning the percentage of suspects reconciled to the Church, see John Tedeschi, 'The Organization and Procedures of the Roman Inquisition: A Sketch,' in *The Prosecution of Heresy: Collected Studies on the Inquisition in Early Modern Italy* (Binghamton, NY: Medieval and Renaissance Texts and Studies, 1991), p. 152; Tedeschi with William Monter, 'Toward a Statistical Profile of the Italian Inquisitions, Sixteenth to Eighteenth Centuries,' ibid., pp. 89–126. The Roman Inquisition's activities noticeably intensified during the papacies of Paul IV (Gian Pietro Carafa, pope 1555–1559) and Pius V (Michele Ghislieri, pope 1566–1572), as compared with earlier papacies, which Andrea Del Col has characterized as a period of relative caution. See Agostino Borromeo, 'Paul IV,' and Nicole Lemaitre, 'Pius V,' in *The Papacy: An Encyclopedia*, Vol. 2, gen. ed. Philippe Levillain (New York: Routledge, 2002), pp. 1127–9 and 1176–8; Del Col, *Inquisizione in Italia*, pp. 309–19, 395–441; Silvana Seidel Menchi, 'The Inquisitor as Mediator,' in *Heresy, Culture, and Religion in Early Modern Italy: Contexts and Contestations*, ed. Ronald K. Delph, Michelle M. Fontaine, and John Jeffries Martin (Kirksville, MO: Truman State University Press, 2006), pp. 173–92, esp. pp. 189–90.

3 Adriano Prosperi, *Tribunali della coscienza: Inquisitori, confessori, missionari* (Turin: Einaudi, 1996), p. xv; Elena Brambilla, *Alle origini del Sant'Uffizio: Penitenza, confessione e giustizia spirituale dal Medioevo al XVI secolo* (Bologna: Il Mulino, 2000), pp. 347–59; Brambilla, 'Il segreto e il sigillo: Denunce e comparizioni spontanee nei processi inquisitoriali,' in *I Tribunali della fede: Continuità e discontinuità dal medioevo all'età moderna; Atti del XLV Convegno di studi sulla Riforma e sui movimenti religiosi in Italia, Torre Pellice, 3–4 settembre 2005*, ed. Susanna Peyronel Rambaldi (Turin: Claudiana, 2007), p. 150.

4 The Dominican Fra Angelo Valentini interrogated both defendants in person; Claudio da Roteglia's process took place in late January and early February, and Giovanni Terrazzano's in July and August. For Roteglia's process, Fra Angelo was assisted by Fra Alberto Foschieri da Carpi, Modena's vicar general, and Fra Pietro Martire da Lugano, both Dominicans. It seems that Egidio Foscarari was not physically present for Roteglia's process but he was present for Terrazzano's sentencing at the very least; Fra Angelo was also assisted in Terrazzano's process by Fra Cherubino da Mirandola and Fra Michele da Brescia.

5 Nicholas Eymeric, *Directorium Inquisitorum* (Venice: Apud Marcum Antonium Zalterium. 1595), pp. 409–11, and Peña, ibid., pp. 409–11. See also Henry Kamen, *The Spanish Inquisition: An Historical Revision,* rev. ed. (New Haven: Yale University Press, 1998), pp. 174–6; Malcolm Lambert, *The Cathars* (Malden, MA: Blackwell Publishers, 1998), pp. 127–8; John Tedeschi, 'Organization and Procedures,' pp. 133–4; Christopher F. Black, *Italian Inquisition*, pp. 60–3.

6 Carena, *Tractatus de Officio Sanctissimae Inquisitionis,* (Cremona: Apud Marc'Antonium Belpierum, 1636), p. 377. Concerning an entire kingdom being converted, Carena probably meant situations like that of Queen Mary in England, who declared Catholicism the official religion again after years of Protestant rule. Those who reconverted to Catholicism individually after practising and believing in another Christian sect, according to standard inquisitorial practice, had to abjure their errors and recant during a process, even if the conversion was voluntary.

7 Andrea Del Col, *L'Inquisizione in Italia*, p. 337. Prosperi, *Tribunali della coscienza*, pp. 221–3 and Brambilla, *Alle Origini del Sant'Uffizio*, pp. 103–10 and 437–68, and 'Il segreto e il sigillo,' pp. 122–5. Vincenzo Lavenia has pointed out that it was precisely because the Roman Inquisition generally did not confiscate the property of voluntarily penitent secret heretics that the Italian institution enjoyed a reputation of being more merciful as compared to its Spanish counterpart. See Lavenia, *L'Infamia e il perdono: Tributi, pene e confessione nella teologia morale della prima età moderna* (Bologna: Il Mulino, 2004), pp. 286–99.

8 Eymeric, *Directorium Inquisitorum*, p. 410, Peña, ibid., p. 412.

9 Peña, ibid., p. 411.

10 Carena, *Tractatus*, p. 373: 'Primus casus est, de eo, qui scit vel suspicatur se praeventum, et sic metu probationum in Santo Officio comparvit, et confessus est, et in hoc casu, licet mitius iste comparens sit tractandus, Locat[us] post Iudit[io] Inquisit[or] inter casus decisos Placentiae Casu. 7. ubi quae tales mitius sunt tractandi et cum eis mitiori est agendum Abiuratione attamen non debet gaudere beneficio sponte comparentium colligitur hoc ex supra alleg. doct. nam, et est praeventus, et scit, vel suspicatur se praeventum, Farin[acci] ubi supra n. 37.'

11 Peña, *Directorium Inquisitorum*, p. 412: 'Contrarium videtur tenere Simancas de catholicae institutionis tit. 57 no. 21 et seq. sed nostra sententia benignior est, illud certe verum est, huic homini acriorem poenitentiam esse in ungendam.' Peña advised that voluntarily penitent relapsed heretics be sentenced to perpetual incarceration. Concerning 'perpetual' incarceration, see John Tedeschi, 'Organization and Procedures,' pp. 147–8;

for leniency shown to those who voluntarily came forward, pp. 133–4. According to Vincenzo Lavenia, Simancas and Peña disagreed concerning several issues; for example, Simancas (reversing his opinion in his earlier work, *Institutiones Catholicae* of 1552) took the Roman Inquisition to task for refraining from confiscating the property of voluntary penitents in his *Enchiridion judicium violatae religiones* (1568); see Lavenia, *L'Infamia e il perdono*, pp. 286–99.

12 Carena, *Tractatus*, p. 375: 'Quamvis in hac re, tutissimum sit supremum tribunal consulere, ut Animadvertit Symanch. in Enchirid. tit. 60 n. 6 et Pegna loco alleg. vers. quia tamen. Haec tamen intelligenda sunt, ubi relapsus, vere esse sponte comparens, et secus dicendum ubi metu probationum in Sancta Officio comparvisset, ut quia scivit V.G. quod aliquis se praeparabat ad eum accusandum, vel quia rumor erat, quod erat accusandus, nam tunc nullo modo talis relapsus est ad Misericordiam recipiendus [. . .].'

13 Prospero Farinacci, *Tractatus de haeresi* (Cremona: Apud Marc'Antonium Belpierum, 1636), p. 293: 'Vide tamen Constitutionem Frederici Imperatoris incip[it] "Commissi" relata per Pegna inter litteras apostolicum, in Directorium Inquisitorum fol. mihi 16 ubi expresse caveri videtur in § "Si quia vero," territos metu mortis redire volentes ad fidei unitatem iuxta canonicas sanctiones ad agendum poenitentiam in perpetuum carcerem dettuendos esse. Et propterea poenitentes et redeuntes ad fidem, etiam metu mortis perterriti, recipientur in supremo urbis totiusque Christianae Reipublicae sanctae, et generalis Inquisitionis generali Tribunali.'; Peña, *Directorium Inquisitorum*, p. 412.

14 Carena, *Tractatus*, p. 374: 'Moneri etiam debent ad dicendam integram veritatem, alias quod habebuntur, uti diminuti confitentes et ficte conversi.'

15 John Jeffries Martin makes this point as well; see Martin, *Myths of Renaissance Individualism* (New York: Palgrave Macmillan, 2004), pp. 21–33. The exact techniques employed by both inquisitors and defendants will be discussed in Chapter 6. See also James B. Given, *Inquisition in Medieval Society: Power, Discipline, and Resistance in Languedoc* (Ithaca: Cornell University Press, 1997), p. 47; Eymeric, *Directorium Inquisitorum*, pp. 430–5, and Peña's commentaries, also pp. 430–5.

16 *Tractatus*, p. 376; *Corpus iuris canonici*, Vol. 2, ed. Emil Friedberg and Aemilius Ludwig Richter (Leipzig: Bernard Tauchnitz, 1879–81), cols. 779–80 (X 5.7.9): 'Laicus autem, quem aliqua praedictarum pestium notoria vel privata culpa resperserit, nisi, prout dictum est, abiurata haeresi et satisfactione exhibita confestim ad fidem confugerit orthodoxam, saecularis iudicis arbitrio relinquatur, debitam recepturus pro qualitate facinoris ultionem.' Carena named some sources, which interpreted *Ad*

abolendam to mean that any investigated suspect should be considered automatically pertinacious for not coming forward voluntarily – but acknowledged that as an extreme minority opinion.

17 Carena, *Tractatus*, pp. 40–1: '[. . .] et ita etiam nos experientia docuit et exemplum refert Eymericus in Direct[orium] p. 3 in 10 modo terminandi processum, n. 204 vers. et de facto de quodam Sacerdote, qui uti impoenitens non relapsus, in civitate Barchinon[ensis] in Cathalonia, fuerat traditus brachio saeculari, et igni applicatus et etiam ex una parte, aliqualiter adustus, coepit clamare, quod educeretur, quia volebat abiurare, et sic factum fuit, sed post quatuordecim annos, inventus fuit permanisse continue in haeresi, ac multos infecisse, unus uti impoenitens relapsus fuit combustus[. . .].'

18 Carena, ibid., p. 41: 'In harum tamen poenarum Impositione maxima ratio habenda est ad tempus, quo haeretici isti convertuntur, nam mitius puniendus est, qui metu imminentium probationum confitetur, quam, qui in carceres coniectus confitetur, et mitius punitur hic, quam qui post publicatas attestationes confiteretur [. . .].'; p. 373. During this discussion, Carena brought up the issue of punishing even those who confessed by confiscating their property; Carena noted that in north-central Italy it was the general practice to return those goods to those that had confessed. Earlier in the chapter, Carena also specified that those who were willing to confess quickly should be processed equally quickly by tribunals, so that the penitent did not have remain imprisoned too long (p. 35).

19 Masini, *Sacro Arsenale; Overo Prattica dell'officio della S. Inquisizione*, ed. Tommaso Menghini (Rome: 1693; StaatsBibliothek Digitalisat 4 J.can.p.5504) , p. 345. Ignorance was considered a mitigating factor that limited culpability in a variety of contexts; Gratian, in the decretals, explained that ignorance deriving from inability to learn mitigated responsibility for sinfulness or ethical mistakes. Those that remained in ignorance because they could learn, and could have sought out the appropriate knowledge, but chose not to, were responsible for their own ethical violations. The inquisitorial authors explored in this chapter retained those distinctions in assessing types of ignorance, and applied them to heresy in much the same way. See Marcia Colish, *Peter Lombard*, Vol. 2 (New York: Brill, 1994), pp. 479–80.

20 Eymeric, *Directorium Inquisitorum*, p. 58: 'In quaestiones duodecim; De pertinentibus ad fidem observatio.'

21 Eymeric included the text of the Apostles' and Nicene Creeds on pp. 45–6 of the first part of his manual, and Peña noted the Creeds' origins in the Greek

schism, and their usefulness in combatting Arian and Pelagian hereises, among others, in the Church's past, on p. 46. See also Mark A. Noll, ed., 'The Augsburg Confession (1530),' in *Confessions and Catechisms of the Reformation* (Vancouver, BC: Regent College Publishing, 1991), pp. 84–121, esp. the introduction and bibliography, pp. 81–4; Peter Martyr Vermigli, 'The Apostles' Creed: A Plain Exposition of the Twelve Articles of the Christian Faith,' trans. Mariano Di Gangi, in *The Peter Martyr Library*, Vol. 1, *Early Writings: Creed, Scripture, Church*, ed. Joseph C. McLelland (Kirksville, MO: Sixteenth Century Essays and Studies, 1994), pp. 27–79, esp. p. 62; 'The Church that today wants to be called *the* Catholic Church has divided and fragmented its catholicity more than any other. Had it been content to follow the religion and worship taught to us in the Scriptures, these many divisions would not have happened. But she has never ceased manufacturing these innovations. And to dominate others, she has inisisted that everyone be compelled to accept them.' For the Catholic Church, and the magisterial Protestant churches (primarily Lutheran, Zwinglian, and Calvinist), emphasizing the Creed, complete with its statement of the Trinity, drew attention to the 'heresies' of antitrinitarians and Socinians, which the magisterial churches, Catholic and Protestant alike, found horrifying.

22 Peña, *Directorium Inquisitorum*, p. 58: 'Hactenus Eymericus ex variis Conciliorum, summorum Pontificum Romanorum, et sanctorum, Patrum locis multa fidei dogmata collegit, quae ad institutum huius primae partis spectabant, in quibus de suo nihil apponens, sola recitatione contentus fuit. Nunc duodecim quaestionibus complectitur multae, quae ad fidem ipsam, et fidei obligationem pertinentex, quorum ignoratione fideles in singulares errores facile incidere possint: insinuans etiam multae, quae iam proximus ad negotium Inquisitorum spectant. In his nos omissis multis, quae Theologorum propria sunt, ea tantum adnotabimus, quae insigniora sunt, quaeque magis ad suspectum iustitutum attinent.'

23 Peña, ibid., p. 59: ' Sensus ergo quaestionis hic est: An quilibet fidelis obligetur clare et aperte scire fidei articulos, ita ut sciat hunc esse articulum fidei, quoties de ea re fuerit interrogatus.'

24 Peña, ibid., pp. 59–60: ' Et in summa concludit hic Eymericus ex Sancto Thoma, quemlibet obligari ad credendum explicite fidei articulos, reliqua vero, quae in sacris litteris continentur, explicite credere non est ad salutem necessarium, quae quomodo sint accipienda, in sequentibus declarat manifestus.' Thomas Aquinas thought that the uneducated should not be questioned concerning what he called 'the subtleties of faith, except when there is suspicion that they have been corrupted by heretics.' 'The simple'

had 'implicit faith' in the faith of their teachers; therefore, if those teachers moved away from the true faith, the simple were not responsible for any heresies their seemingly Catholic teachers had espoused (2a2æ. 2, 7 and 2a2æ. 1,9).

25 Peña, ibid., p. 60: 'Hac ibi, et in synodo Rhemensi sub Carolo Magno anno domini 813 celebrata cap. 2 ita scriptum legitur: 'Ut orationem, quam Dominus noster Iesus Christus discipulos suos orare docuit, verbis discerent, et sensu bene intelligerent: qua illam ignorare nulli Christiano licet'.'

26 Eymeric, ibid., p. 61: 'Simplices enim non sunt examinandi de subtilitatibus fidei, nisi quando habetur suspicio, quae sint ab haereticis depravati: quia in his, quae ad subtiliatem fidei pertinent, solent fidem simplicium depravare. Sed cum inveniuntur non pertinacieter perversae doctrinae adhaerere, si in talibus ex simplicate deficiant, non eis imputatur.'

27 Peña, ibid., p. 61: 'Omissis verbo hoc loco multis et p[l]ene inextricabilibus difficultatibus, quae horum occasione verborum disceptari potuissent, in praesenti difficultate ita mihi videtur dicendum: tamdiu idiota a viro docto deceptus in fide excusabitur in humano iudicio, quamdiu non fuerit legitime admonitus per Episcopum, vel Inquisitorem, aut alium cui legitime admonendi ius competit sed hoc intellegendum videtur cum deceptus est in his, quae non sunt in Ecclesia ita evulgata et quae explicite credere non tenebatur: nam si in his deviet a recto veritatis tramite, propter viri docti auctoritatem non omnino excusabitur. Quid autem sit sentiendum de eo, qui credidit aliqui viro fingenti se esse aliquem virum catholicum cum tamen sit haereticus, vide Magistrum lib. 4 sent. distinct. 30 cap. 1 et ibi S. Bonaventuram in verbo si quid haereticus dubio 2 de quo dicam super q. 7 huius partis.' The reference is to Peter Lombard's *distinctio* 30 concerning marriage; Lombard thought that, like some who had thought they were learning Catholic doctrine because the heretic had lied and called himself Catholic, a man who married a woman who had lied about her identity was not married at all. *Sent.* 4. d. 30. c. 1.

28 Ugo Rozzo, 'Le 'Prediche' veneziane di Giulio da Milano,' *Bolletino della Società di Studi Valdesi* 152 (1983): 3–30.

29 Salvatore Caponetto, *The Protestant Reformation in Sixteenth-Century Italy,* trans. Anne C. and John Tedeschi (Kirksville, MO: Thomas Jefferson University Press, 1999), p. 19.

30 Eymeric, *Directorium Inquisitorum,* p. 62: 'An teneatur unusquisque explicitam fidem habere de contentis in sacra scriptura.'

31 Eymeric, ibid., pp. 62–3, and Peña, ibid., pp. 63–4.

32 The two indexes relevant to this time period were the more severe Index of 1559, created under Paul IV's papacy, and the 1564, or Tridentine, Index,

created after the protests from some of the Council of Trent's participants, which was ostensibly less severe than the Pauline one. See, for example, Christopher Black, *Church, Religion, and Society in Early Modern Italy* (New York: Palgrave Macmillan, 2004), pp. 182–3 for an overview; for more extensive studies see especially Paul Grendler, *The Roman Inquisition and the Venetian Press, 1540–1605* (Princeton: Princeton University Press, 1978) and the essays in Gigliola Fragnito, ed., *Church, Censorship, and Culture in Early Modern Italy* (New York: Cambridge University Press, 2001). In particular, the Council of Trent ruled that textual Scripture and tradition, including the Catholic Church's traditional stances concerning how to interpret Scripture, were equally valid sources of authority, with the Holy Spirit guiding both. Access to the Bible in the vernacular, however, was not formally banned until the Index of 1596. See Gigliola Fragnito, *La Bibbia al rogo: La censura ecclesiastica e i volgarizzamenti della Scrittura (1471–1605)* (Bologna: Il Mulino, 1997).

33 Peña, *Directorium Inquisitorum*, p. 63: '[Quoting Eymeric, p. 62] 'Circa huiusmodi ergo absque; periculo haeresis aliquis falsum potest opinari, antequam consideretur, vel determinatum sit, et cetera.' Nam his verbis apertissime indicatur ignorantiam ab haeresi excusare et per consequens a poenis in haereticos latis; neque vero haec est solius Thomae aut Eymerici sententiae his locis [. . .].'

34 Peña, ibid., p. 63: '[. . .] et alii quos prudens omitto. Nos partim ex his, partim aliunde sequentes regulas ad huius loci illustrationem collegimus, quibus in foro exteriori sit locus quoties is casus occurrat; occurrit autem saepe.'

35 Peña, ibid., p. 63: 'De hac regula video ullam controversam inter Doctores. Haec tamen in sequentibus amplius declarabitur. Si quis ergo in his deficeret, non posset iustam ignorantiae causam allegare, cum ex instituto et praecepto legis Christianae haec scire obligetur, et nescire nullatenus praesumatur.'

36 Peña, ibid., p. 64: '[. . .] quod vix est credibile nescire Theologos ad Ecclesiae communem fidem pertinere: si quis inquam ita per ignorantiam errare se dicat, haereticus praesumendus est, ac velut talis iudicandus in foro exteriori, nisi forte tam esse stupidus, imperitus, et rusticus, ut iudicibus fidei per spicuum fiat eum omni prorsus malitia caruisse: talis erat ille, qui dicebat Patrem et Filium et Spiritum Sanctum simul incarnatos fuisse, quia legerat illud: 'Qui natus est de virgine, cum Patre, et sancto Sprirtu.' Hic n. in grammatica potius quam in fide deprehensus fuit errare.'

37 Peña, ibid., p. 64: 'Ut si quis rusticus motus quadam ratione naturali dixisset, quod in divinis Pater est maior Filio, quoniam in humanis maior est,

creditque Ecclesiam ita tenere; revera hic haereticus non est, nisi admonitus in errore persistat.'

38 Zuanbattista Sambeni, discussed in Chapter 6, told the Venetian tribunal that his religious errors were of his own invention. ASVe, *Sant'Uffizio*, Busta 22, fasc. 2, *Contra Odoricum Grisonium et complices*, fols. 29v–32r, esp. 30v: 'Io ho imparato errori interpretando la scrittua secondo la mia fantasia.'; John Jeffries Martin, *Venice's Hidden Enemies: Italian Heretics in a Renaissance City* (Berkeley and Los Angeles: University of California Press, 1993), p. 144.

39 Peña, *Directorium Inquisitorum*, p. 64: 'Voco autem invincibilem seu insuperabilem ignorantiam, eam quam homo superare non potuit, postquam diligentem adhibuit solicitudinem in veritate investiganda. Sed ut ingenue fatear quod sentio. Hodie post tam apertam Christianae religionis notitiam, et tam late patentem Evangelii promulgationem, et tot Conciliorum et sacrorum Doctorum lucem, vix in his, quae fidei sunt, ignorantia invincibilis, seu insuperabilis esse potest.'

40 Raising the level of education among both parish clergy (none of the inquisitorial manuals admit to the existence of clergy who were perhaps less educated than the ideal) and the laity was a priority during the years after the Protestant Reformation, but efforts to do so were generally less than universally successful and took a great deal of time to implement. See Black, *Church, Religion, and Society*, Chapter 5, 'Priests and Parishoners' and Chapter 6, 'Religious Education' for an overview of Counter-Reformation educational movements.

41 Carena, *Tractatus*, p. 14: 'His praemissis, loquendo de ignorantia invincibili, (quae tamen in praxi vix dari potest) ac etiam de ignorantia probabili, clarum est, quod hae excusant ab haeresi [. . .].'

42 Carena, ibid., p. 14: 'Quo vero ad ignorantiam crassam Magis, communis opinionis est D.D. quod illa a peccato haeresis excuset, quem taliter ignorans si est paratus corrigi, non potest dici habere pertinatiam, quae est ad haeresim necessaria [. . .].' Concerning the burden of proving or disproving ignorance, see Carena, p. 85.

43 Farinacci, *Tractatus*, p. 30: 'Simplicitas an, et quando excusat ab haeresi, et illius poena.'; 'Contrarium, quod simplicitas non excuset, per text. in cap. Schisma, 24 quaest. 1 et ibi Closta in verbo, "Magis" et in verbo "Ignorantia," voluit Arnald[us] Albertin[us] in repetitione rubr. de haereticis, in 6 quaest. 13 num. 13 et 23. Sed textus ille non loquitur in omni haeresi, sed in schismate, de quo infra dicam; ultra quod etiam loquitur de haereticis non paratis se corrigere: prout advertit Angelica in Summa, in verbo, "Fides," num. 8 vers. "Nihil facit ad materiam," quod et idem

dixit in Repert[orium] Inquisitorum in verbo "Fides" sub. vers. "Utrum simplices".'

44 Farinacci, ibid., p. 31: 'Et propterea simplicitatem non excusare in crimine schismatis: quis quilibet tenetur scire, quod divisio ab Ecclesia Romana magnum est crimen.'

45 Farinacci, ibid., pp. 29–31: 'Credulitas praedicta excuset errantem, non in articulis fides, qui continentur in Symbolo, quos quis explicite scire tenetur sed in aliis fidei credibilibus extra dictos articulos.' Another criteria inquisitors could use to determine the difference between light and vehement suspects was the number of crimes in total, or number of times heretical crimes had been committed. See Farinacci, p. 192: '[. . .] quod vehemens suspicio sumitur ex signis exterioribus operum aut verborum ex quibus capitur argumentum concludens frequenter et ut in pluribus, quod talia dicens, vel faciens est haereticus [. . .].'

46 Susanna Peyronel Rambaldi, *Speranze e crisi nel Cinquecento modenese: Tensioni religiose e vita cittadina ai tempi di Giovanni Morone* (Milan: Franco Angeli, 1979), pp. 70–2. Domenico Sigibaldi, his vicar, oversaw the day-to-day operations of the bishopric. While Morone and Sigibaldi faithfully corresponded and Morone was always well apprised of the religious situation in his bishopric, there was little he could do from such a distance, and Sigibaldi did not have the same authority as a resident bishop.

47 Grillenzoni welcomed anyone interested in discussing philosophical, and eventually religious, matters and made little effort to keep his meetings, and the topics discussed during them, clandestine. His meetings therefore welcomed people from all social classes and grew quite large. Concomitant with Bartolomeo della Pergola's heretical preaching in the town, it encouraged the discussion of Protestant ideas. For a fuller description of Grillenzoni's meetings, see Peyronel Rambaldi, *Speranze e crisi*, pp. 230–1.

48 Martin Bucer, the leading Reformer of Strasbourg, wrote letters to Italian conventicles, particularly with a humanist audience in mind. The most irenic of the Reformers, in these letters he emphasized the message's most integral components: justification by faith alone, Christ's establishment of only two sacraments, and love of one's neighbour. He continued corresponding with groups in Modena and other north Italian cities until about 1544. His letters written in 1541 and 1542, during the Colloquy of Ratisbon, occupy a particular importance; in his letters dated 17 August, 19 September, and 23 December he acknowledged the failure of the hoped-for reconciliation and continued to expound on the more sensitive points of doctrine that John Calvin's writings had brought into question,

predestination and the meaning of the Eucharist. See Caponetto, *Protestant Reformation*, pp. 52–5; A. Al Kalak, 'Modena, Accademia,' in *Dizionario storico dell'Inquisizione*, Vol. 2, ed. Adriano Prosperi with Vincenzo Lavenia and John Tedeschi (Pisa: Scuola Normale Superiore Pisa, 2010), pp. 1055–6.

49 Massimo Firpo, 'Gli "spirituali," l'Accademia di Modena, e il formulario di fede del 1542: Controllo del dissenso religiose e nicodemismo,' *Rivista di storia e letteratura religiosa* 20 (1984): 58–64. It was during this summer that Morone was elevated as a cardinal; he received his red hat from Contarini in nearby Bologna, where the latter had been sent as papal governor after the failure at Ratisbon. Firpo, p. 66.

50 Massimo Firpo, 'L'Accademia di Modena,' pp. 77–8.

51 Ibid., pp. 88, 102–4. Many of the Academicians prevaricated over the course of the summer, but the institution of an inquisition and the flight of several important clerics convinced them that they did not have much of a choice.

52 Morone, for his part, claimed that Bartolomeo was recommended to him as a good preacher and that he was not aware of Bartolomeo della Pergola's dangerous ideas. For more on Morone's relationship with Bartolomeo, see Massimo Firpo, 'L'Accademia di Modena,' pp. 44–6.

53 Lancellotti (Tommasino de' Bianchi), a Modenese chronicler, explained this in his *Cronaca*, vol. VIII, p. lxiv: 'Il detto frate predica se non l'evangelo, né mai nomina né santi, né dottori della chiesa, né dice di quaresima, né di digiuno et molte altre cose che vanno a gusto degli accademici. Io ho notato questo discorso per vedere alla fine delle sue prediche quello che seguirà, perché molti credono andare in paradiso in calze solate, perché dice che Christo ha pagato per noi.' Cit. Cesare Bianco, 'Bartolomeo della Pergola e la sua predicazione eterodossa a Modena nel 1544,' *Bollettino della Società di Studi Valdesi* no. 151 (July 1982): 10; concerning the *Beneficio di Cristo*, see Adriano Prosperi, '*Beneficio di Cristo*,' in *Dizionario storico dell'Inquisizione*, Vol. 1, pp. 178–9.

54 Domenico Morando, during his testimony for Morone's inquisitorial process, quoted Sigibaldi as saying of the preaching of Bartolomeo della Pergola: 'a una parte della città satisfacessi, a l'altra no.' Massimo Firpo, ed., *Il processo inquisitoriale del cardinale Giovanni Morone: Edizione Critica*, Vol. 1 (Rome: Istituto storico italiano per l'età moderna, 1981–85), pp. 275–6.

55 Cesare Bianco, 'Bartolomeo della Pergola,' pp. 12–13. Most likely, Morone's non-dogmatic stance and own beliefs meant that he thought Bartolomeo was emphasizing faith but not necessarily preaching Protestant heresy.

56 Bianco, 'Bartolomeo della Pergola,' pp. 14–15, 20, 26. Bianco's source for della Pergola's retractions, at the prompting of Bolognese inquisitors,

Modenese Dominicans, and with the agreement of Morone, was the correspondence of Sigisbaldi and Lancelotti's chronicle.

57 Cesare Bianco has used these processes to attempt a reconstruction of the contents of Bartolomeo della Pergola's sermons, but the twenty-year gap between the time of the sermons and the processes meant that the suspects in these cases probably had contact with other heterodox ideas beyond those of Bartolomeo's. Since Bartolomeo was attempting to preach to a large audience in public and simultaneously maintain his status as a Catholic cleric, he probably concentrated on certain important points, such as faith, without overtly disparaging others. Bianco, 'Bartolomeo della Pergola,' esp. p. 28. The workshop conventicles were often scheduled for Sundays and feast days as conscious alternatives to attending Catholic Mass, and were imbued with a sacramental quality; see Cesare Bianco, 'La comunità di "fratelli" nel movimento ereticale modenese del '500,' *Rivista Storica Italiana* 92 (1980): 644 and Peyronel Rambaldi, *Speranze e crisi*, pp. 246–63.

58 Benedetto da Mantova, *Il Beneficio di Cristo*, cited in Bianco, 'Bartolomeo della Pergola,' p. 29.

59 A. Al Kalak, 'Modena, Accademia,' pp. 1055–6.

60 Michelle M. Fontaine, 'For the Good of the City: Bishop and Elite in Tridentine Modena,' *Sixteenth Century Journal* 28, no. 1 (Spring 1997): 29–43, esp. p. 29, ff. 1.

61 Cesare Bianco, 'La comunità,' p. 621; Susanna Peyronel Rambaldi, *Dai Paesi Bassi all'Italia: "Il Sommario della Sacra Scrittura"; Un libro proibito nella società italiana del Cinquecento* (Florence: Leo S. Olschiki, 1997), pp. 247–8; John Tedeschi, 'The Status of the Defendant before the Roman Inquisition,' in *Ketzerverfolgung im 16. Und frühen 17. Jahrhundert*, ed. Hans Rudolf Guggisberg, Bernd Moeller, and Silvana Seidel Menchi (Wiesbaden: Otto Harrassowitz, 1992), pp. 125–46, esp. p. 142. For other instances of bishops intervening in processes, even appealing to Rome, see Black, *Italian Inquisition*, p. 51, for example.

62 ASMo, *Inquisizione*, Busta 3, par. II, 1554–1555, Libro VI, fasc. 13, *Contra Claudium Rudiliam*, testimony of Gasparo, 27 January 1555, fol. 159r: 'Si dice che l'è luterano.'; 'che lo predetto Claudio dice che Cristo è stato un ribaldo, per questo è stato crucifixo.' The interviews took place in the bishop's palace, and the notary tended to record the testimony of the participants in the third person, rather than the first, as he should have done.

63 ASMo, *Contra Claudium Rudiliam*, testimony of Jacobus Maria de Crispis *detto il rizzo sinistra*, 28 January 1555, fol. 161r.

64 ASMo, *Contra Claudium Rudiliam*, testimony of 2 February 1555, fol. unpg.: 'Respondit: Che non so; non intend[e].'

65 ASMo, *Contra Claudium Rudiliam,* Testimony of Paula, 1 February 1555, fol. unpg.: 'Dixit che Cristo è un ribaldo, un asino [. . .]'; 'Et quando v[a]nno dalla messa, o che la vede andare o a vespero [sic] e il dice "cosa, è messa, cosa, è vespero" [. . .]'; 'Et che il dice che non è purgatorio né paradisio.'

66 ASMo, *Contra Claudium Rudiliam,* Testimony of Claudio, 4 February 1555: 'Respondit: Che la detto che sono così di carne et di pelle com'è lui.'; 'Respondit: Che so la detto che la detto [sic] in collera dicendo che non è altro purgatorio che in questo mondo.'; 'Respondit: Che non ha beste[mmiato] delg'imagine et che non ha in casa.' Fra Angelo's questions were recorded in Latin; for example, 'An credat esse purgatorium in alia vita?'

67 ASMo, *Contra Claudium Rudiliam,* Testimony of Claudio, 6 February 1555, fols. 163v–164r: 'An faciat professione de huiusmodi rebus interrogatis et maxime in forno germiniani fornarii loquat de huius? Respondit: Che l'è vero che il parla et che l'ha parlato in quel forno per lui et per gli altri de queste cose lutherane una volta.'; '[. . .] che alcuni dicono di "si" et alcuni di "no," qualche volte ho dubit[at]o et per questo che penso qualche volte di avere detto che non è.'; 'Que non dixit che Christo ribaldo che potro fu stai in paradiso adorne suo tempo et fu non sei stato crucifixo sensa causa. Ma altramente l'ho bestemmiato come a dire "al disprezzo di Christo" e "puta di Christo" et simile altre bestemmie et di questo il domando perdonanza.'

68 Peña attributed further elaborations to the papal letters, and mentioned Burchard of Worms' argument that the decretal should be attributed to either Pope Sixtus or Julius, not Stephen. According to Peña, the text of the papal decrees created confusion among canonists, who thought that the text really discussed the issue of whether or not non-Christians could testify before inquisitorial tribunals. Peña reasonably pointed out that if that had been the case, the decretal would have included the information in the *causa* concerning testimony, not heresy, and stated unequivocally that the decretal should be taken to mean that those who doubted the true faith were to be judged heretical, in principle. See Peña, *Directorium Inquisitorum,* p. 81: 'Quare cum hoc fragmentum ponatur sub titulo de haereticis, non autem sub titulo de testibus, verius videtur, si dicatur, velle hic Romanum Pontificem definire, eos qui de fide Catholicam dubitant, haereticos esse indicandos.' Peña also pointed out that the term 'infideles' could be translated as unfaithful as well as infidel. See also X5.7.1, col. 778.

69 Peña, ibid., p. 82: 'Et de hoc dubitationis genere sit haec prima conslusio: dubitatio circa credibilia, proveniens ex subitanea seu subrepitita ten-

tatione, nec haereticum facit, nec sapit haeresim; quia frequenter contra voluntatem accidit, immo qui se bene confirmat in fide, et talibus motibus resistit, meretur, sicut ille qui resistit stimulis carnis, aut aliis pravis cogitationibus.' Given that no less a Church Father than Augustine famously had battled with both lust and doubt, such an accomodation to conscientious Catholics would be obvious to Peña.

70 Peña, ibid., pp. 83–4: 'At si peccatores huiusmodi consortium fidelium evitarent, nunquam assumerent poenitentiam numquam audirent divina officia; numquam ecclesiastica reciperent sacramenta; vel aliqua Ecclesiae mandata suo tempore non observarent: non ieiunarent debito tempore absque legitimo impedimento, et non abstinerent ab esu carnium sicut praecepit Ecclesia, aut alia his similia negligerent aut facerent, cum ex his indiciis suspicio haereisis oriatur maior vel minor pro qualitate peccatis et aliarum circumstantiarum. Tunc inquisitor posset procedere contra tales cap. excommunicamus d. 1 § adiicimus, de haeretic. cap. inter sollicitudines de purgatione canon. Et tradit Zanchinus praecitato loco et dixi plene par. 3 titu. et signis et indiciis, quibus diversarum sectarum haeretici cognosci possint.'

71 ASMo, *Contra Claudium Rudiliam,* Testimony of Claudio, 8 February 1555, fol. 164v: 'Respondit que vere non est lutheranus nec habet malas opiniones in anima et in corde sed si locutus est aliquando ex incuria et loquacitate et de omnibus petit veriam paratus corrigi in futurum et invenire confessore quae possit testificari de eo in conscientia et quae ex hoc videbit quae non est lutheranus.' See, for example, Carena, p. 332: 'Praemittendum est hoc loco Antiquam extare haeresim nostris temporibus, renovaam a Sectariis quibusdam, improbantem in Ieiuniis delectum ciborum, quam late (ut alios omittam) reprobavit Greg. Valentia tom. 3 in Summ D Tho. disp. 9. q. 2 punct. 2. vers. 2.'

72 ASMo, *Contra Claudium Rudiliam,* Testimony of Stradea, wife of Claudio, 10 February 1555, fol. 165r: 'An bono animo vel an odio vel amore haec dicat?'

73 ASMo, *Contra Claudium Rudiliam,* 12 February 1555, fol. 165v: 'Tertia Magistrus Doctorus Petrus Fuscherius Conclusit quae primo debeat examinari sine carceretis et etiam haec si non confitetur quidpiam debet in carcerari et sine tormentis examinari si non confitetur tormentari.' In addition to communicating with each other, tribunals also communicated reasonably frequently with the Congregation of Cardinals in Rome; Francisco Bethencourt has estimated at least once a month for the more remote tribunal of Udine; and Grazia Biondi once every two or thee weeks in Modena (see Bethencourt, *The Inquisition: A Global History, 1478–1834* (New York: Cambridge University Press, 2009), pp. 55–7.

74 ASMo, *Contra Claudium Rudiliam*, Testimony of Claudio, 13 February 1555, fols. 166v–167r. 'Respondit: Quae propterea [sic] che la maggior parte disse che "non," che l'ha dubitato.'

75 ASMo, *Contra Claudium Rudiliam*, Correspondence 19 February 1555, fol. 168r: '[. . .] ma che lui crede in tutte queste cose quello che creda la santa madre chiesa Romana in delle sue parole né domanda perdonanza talmente che confessa le parole ma dice che non ha creduto quello che significano le parole [. . .].';'Et se pur le piace come heretico condannarlo, dica il suo giuridico et l'havero caroza [avrò carrozza] VS mi raccomando.'

76 ASMo, *Contra Claudium Rudiliam*, undated correspondence, fols. 168r–v: 'Et pro inforamtione della cosa dico che lui non è denuntiato de abbia insegnare queste cose né defendere propriamente, né che abbia libri cattivi né conversatione con alcuni dotti heretici o sospetti, si che si porro giudicare che non apparendo l'animo suo.'

77 See Fontaine, 'For the Good of the City,' p. 35; Paul Grendler, *The Roman Inquisition and the Venetian Press*, p. 94; S. Feci, 'Foscarari, Egidio,' in *Dizionario storico dell'Inquisizione*, Vol. 2, p. 615.

78 ASMo, *Contra Claudium Rudiliam*, undated correspondence, fols. 168r–v. For *Ad abolendam*, see X5.7.9 (*Corpus iuris canonici*, Vol. 2, cols. 780–782); for *Ego Berengarius*, see D. 2 de cons. c. 42 (ibid., Vol. 1, cols. 1328–1329). Foscarari also quoted C. 1 q. 7 c. 14 (*Corpus iuris canonici*, Vol. 1, col. 433): 'Quociens a populis aut a turba peccatur, quia in omnes propter multitudinem vindicari non potest, inultum solet transire. Priora ergo dimittenda dico Dei iudicio, et de reliquo maxima sollicitudine precauenda.' and C. 24 q. 3 c. 7 (ibid. col. 992). Concerning Berengar and the Eucharistic controversy, see Charles M. Radding and Francis Newton, *Theology, Rhetoric, and Politics in the Eucharistic Controversy, 1078–79* (New York: Columbia University Press, 2003), pp. 1–31 for a brief overview.

79 ASMo, *Contra Claudium Rudiliam*, undated correspondence, fols. 168r–v: 'Cum talis delatus non, nisi suspectas habebat, ideirco non ab re fuerit immo per utile ac necessarium. Ut coram D. Inquisitore pronuntibus testibus, atque notaro, private delatus humilior genibus flexis promissos qualem eisdem aliquando termeri confexerit abiunt errores.' Foscarari probably referred to Chrysostom's 23rd homily concerning Matt 7:1 ('Judge not, lest ye be judged'), in particular, 'You see, we ought not to upbraid nor trample upon them, but to admonish; not to revile, but to advise; not to assail with pride, but to correct with tenderness. Not for him, but thyself, dost thou give over to extreme vengence by not sparing him, when it may be needful to give sentence on offenses' (*A Select Library of the Nicene and Post-Nicene Fathers of the Christian Church*, Vol. 10, *Saint*

Chrysostom: Homilies on the Gospel of Matthew, ed. Philip Schaff [New York: Charles Scribner's Sons, 1888], p. 158). See also Fontaine, 'For the Good of the City,' pp. 36–43, concerning Foscarari's use of public ritual to revive Catholicism, civic identity, and maintain good and peaceful relationships among the civic elites. In particular, the public rituals Fontaine describes could often force signs of heretical belief from Modena's remaining heterodox, such as refusing to perform the appropriate reverences for consecrated hosts and saints' images, either in church or as such objects passed in the streets.

80 See, for example, Carena, *Tractatus*, p. 15: '[. . .] proferentem verba haeretica, ioco, lubrico linguae, ex magna ira, vel ob magnam animi comotionem et corporis dolorem vel etiam recitative, recitando sl. aliorum haereses non esse uti haereticum puniendum, sed alia poena extraordinaria et maxime pecuniaria [. . .].'

81 Peña, *Directorium Inquisitorum*, p. 63: 'et in Ecclesia vulgati, ac solemnizati, haereticus est, si pertinacia adiungatur: nunquam enim est haeresis sine pertinacia, ita docet Eymericus nu. 2 et S. Thomas hic ab Eymerico citatus.'

82 ASMo, *Inquisizione*, Busta 3, par. II, 1554–1555, Libro VI, fasc. 13, Correspondence of Gaspar Marzolus, 27 February 1555, fols. 170r–v. See also X1.2.2 (*Corpus iuris canonici*, Vol. 2, col. 8) :'Contrarium sententies ut haeretici sunt censendi, nisi ab errore respiciant, et correctioni apostolicae sedis se supponant. Abb. Siculis.' See also Clem. 5.10.1 (ibid. Vol. 2, col. 1191): 'Porro hanc sanctionem ad pendentia trahimus, non obstantibus privilegiis, conventionibus, statutis et consuetudinibus quislibet, quae contra praemissa seu aliquod praemissorum religiosis ipsis in nullo volumus suffagari.' Marzolus also referred to Giovanni d'Andrea's and Panormitanus's commentaries concerning *Ad abolendam* (X5.7.9); printed versions of the *Glossa Ordinaria* for the *Liber Extra*, which was written primarily by Bernard of Parma, often included *Additiones* written by d'Andrea and Panormitanus, along with Hostiensis's contributions as well (James Brundage, *Medieval Canon Law* [New York: Longman, 1995], p. 209). Finally, Marzolus additionally referred to C.24 q.1 c.14 (*Corpus iuris canonici*, Vol. 1, col. 970): 'Sancta Romana ecclesia, quae semper immaculata permansit, Domino providente et B. apostolo Petro opem ferente in futuro manebit, sine ulla hereticorum insultatione atque firma et immobilis omni tempore persistet.' Giovanni d'Andrea (Ioannis Andreae, d. 1348) was a celebrated canonist, who taught at Bologna for most of his career, as one of the few lay canon law experts in the Middle Ages. He served the city as a diplomat, travelling to wait on Pope John XXII among others. He produced several published works and *consilia*, or written consultations on behalf of

clients; in addition to his *Additiones* he wrote the accepted *Glossa Ordinaria* for the *Liber Sextus* and *Clementine constitutions,* a commentary concerning the *Liber extra* (which he entitled *Novella,* in honor of both his mother and daughter of that name), and a *Summa* concerning marriage (Brundage, *Medieval Canon Law,* pp. 216–17).

83 Ippolito Marsili (b. 1450), studied law at Bologna, and subsequently taught the subject at Padua and Ferrara; from 1465 to 1474 he held the canon law chair at Ferrara and Pisa. He also taught civil law at Bologna beginning in 1482. Marsili was active politically as well, serving as governor for Genoese territories and as the captain of Valle de Lugano. (See L. Pallotti, 'Marsili, Ippolito,' *Dizionario biografico degli italiani,* Vol. 70 [Rome: Istituto della Enciclopedia Italiana, 2008], pp. 764–7). Alessandro Tartagni (1424–1477) was a noted lay specialist, whose consultations (*consilia*), of which he produced about fifty a year across a twenty-five year career, were highly regarded (Trevor Dean, *Crime and Justice in Late Medieval Italy* [New York: Cambridge University Press, 2007], p. 97).

84 ASMo, *Inquisizione,* Busta 3, par. II, 1554–1555, Libro VI, fasc. 13, Sentence of Claudio de Roteglia, 27 February 1555, fol. 171, and abjuration, 27 February 1555, unp.

85 ASMo, *Inquisizione,* Busta 3, par. II, 1554–1555, Libro VI, fasc. 14, *Contra Ioannis Terrazanus,* Interrogation of 23 September 1555, fols. 120r–v. It appears that a different notary, Lorenzo da Castro Goffredo, recorded Giovanni Terrazzano's process than had recorded Claudio da Roteglia's, which was done by Nicodemo da Modena. Lorenzo da Castro Goffredo wrote in Latin on occasion instead of the vernacular and recorded answers in the third person rather than the first.

86 ASMo, *Contra Ioannis Terrazanus,* Interrogation of 23 September 1555, fols. 120r–v: 'Che non ha detto questo cosa ma che crede bene che ogni sia sacerdote in casa sua, e anche fuora di casa danda buoni esempi.' Giovanni Terrazzano was a part of a Lutheran discussion group that included the also-prosecuted Paolo da Campo Gaiano and Pietro Curioni (discussed in Chapter 6). Peyronel Rambaldi, *Dai Paesi Bassi,* pp. 234–9 and *Speranze e crisi,* p. 261. Given Terrazzano's vernacular literacy, and membership in a group that discussed heterodox ideas, it is remarkable that the tribunal and Foscarari were willing to allow Terrazzano to portray himself as 'led astray' by others.

87 ASMo, *Contra Ioannis Terrazanus,* Testimony of 27 September 1555, fols. 126r–v: '[. . .] dixit ut asservit quod non esse satisfactus in responsionibus [*sic.*; 'responsis'] [. . .]'; '[. . .] non obstantibus responsi[is] supra scriptis dictis in altro constituto quae vult redire ad gremium sancte matris ecclesiae et reconciliari illi qua propter.'; '[D]ixisse Fra Ludovico de Tridento

quae vellant habere Christum in cordem et non in picturam non tamen credidit imaginem Christum esse malam quam semper se habuit.'; 'Dicat habuisse et legisse librorum intitolato Beneficium di Christi[. . .].'

88 ASMo, *Contra Ioannis Terrazanus*, Testimony of 2 October 1555, fol. 127r: 'Respondit: 23 Sept. quod Non; 29 Aio; Respondit: Quod dixit et credidit quod celibatus sunt eam multis et malorum eo quod non observans si a paucibus et quod bonum esset si habent uxorum credidit tamen celibatum in se esse bonum iuxta consilium [. . .].'; 'Respondit: Quod potest esse quae dixerit papam esse Antichristum non tamen negando quod si vicarius Christi et quod non recordare.' Martin Luther felt that God rarely gave the gift of maintaining true celibacy; therefore priests, monks, and nuns were condemned to imperfectly maintain an impossible standard, breaking their vows of chastity and committing fornication. See Heiko A. Oberman, *Luther: Man between God and the Devil*, trans. Eileen Walliser-Schwarzbart (New Haven: Yale University Press, 1989), pp. 272–83, for a discussion of Luther's attitudes towards marriage.

89 ASMo, *Contra Ioannis Terrazanus*, Testimony of 2 October 1555, fol. 127v: 'Dixit quod Missa esse commemoratione mortis Christi et sacrificium corporis [. . .].'; 'Dixit non esse purgatorium nisi in sanguine et latus Christi intendens quod passionis [. . .].'

90 *Contra Ioannis Terrazanus*, undated and unpaginated.

91 ASMo, *Contra Ioannis Terrazanus*, Sentence, undated and unpaginated; 'Pro carcere assignamus tibi totam civitatem Mutinae.'

5. Confession and Defence: Aggressive Tactics

1 Nicholas Eymeric, *Directorium Inquisitorum* (Venice: Apud Marcum Antonium Zalterium, 1595), p. 446: 'Secundum quod prorogat et dilatat Inquisitoris iudicium, sententiam et processum est defensionum concessio: et haec interdum est superflua, interdum necessaria.'; Francisco Peña, ibid., p. 447: 'Dandus est autem advocatus cum reus negat obiecta crimina: nam si fateatur, nullo advocato indiget: idque postquam tres monitiones factae fuerint reo, ut libere veritatem fateatur.' The activities of defence lawyers in Spanish Inquisition courtrooms is noted in Henry Charles Lea, *A History of the Inquisition in Spain*, Vol. 3 (New York: Macmillan Company, 1922), pp. 42–50. For the Roman Inquisition's employment of defence lawyers, see John Tedeschi, 'The Organization and Procedures of the Roman Inquisition: A Sketch,' in *The Prosecution of Heresy: Collected Studies on the Inquisition in Early Modern Italy* (Binghamton, NY: Medieval and Renaissance Texts and Studies, 1991), pp. 135–9. As Tedeschi has described, if the suspect wished to confess and not contest the charges

after three admonitions to confess then no lawyer would be procured or assigned to the case. See also Christopher F. Black, *The Italian Inquisition* (New Haven: Yale University Press, 2009), pp. 78–81.

2 Francisco Peña, *Directorium Inquisitorum*, p. 447: 'Quoniam iusta defensio est de iure naturae, et propterea nullo modo potest, aut debet denegari, l. ut vim et ibi communiter Doctores [. . .].'

3 Eymeric, ibid., p. 446: 'Et sic concedentur sibi advocatus, probus tamen et de legalitate non suspectus, vir utriusque iuris peritus et fidei zelator [. . .].' Peña, in his commentaries, noted that the defence lawyers should be given copies of the testimony of witnesses, in order to prepare a defence, but instructed that the witness' names should be removed from those copies in order to preserve the secrecy of witness testimony (Peña, p. 447).

4 Peña, ibid., p. 447: '[. . .] in crimine haeresis, ex sola reorum confessione ad condemnationem procedi potest; quia cum haeresis crimen mente concipiatur et in animo lateat, plerumque non potest aliter probari, quam per propriam confessionem reorum [. . .].' See also Andrea Del Col, *L'Inquisizione in Italia: Dal XII al XXI secolo* (Milan: Oscar Mondadori, 2006), pp. 120–6. John Langbein has dealt with the way in which confession was utilized in the secular judicial system extensively. If there were two witnesses willing to swear to the guilt of the accused, through the direct observation of the crime (not hearsay or circumstantial evidence of crime), then the accused could be condemned without a confession. If there were *indicia*, or half-proofs that indicated guilt, but the sum total of the evidence fell short of the direct observation of two witnesses, then a confession was required for condemnation, acquired through torture if necessary (John H. Langbein, *Torture and the Law of Proof: Europe and England in the Ancien Régime*, rev. ed. [Chicago: University of Chicago Press, 2006], pp. 4–5). Inquisitions functioned differently in that a confession to the facts of the case, accompanied by an admission of wrongdoing and willingness to repent, would suffice to save the suspect's life and result in abjuration and penance, if it was the suspect's first process for heresy.

5 In high-profile cases, such as Cardinal Giovanni Morone's prosecution, the official documentation is voluminous and Morone's correspondence has also survived. But Morone was a prince of the Church who, though undergoing prosecution for heresy, had access to resources and allies on a level unmatched by most of the tribunals' defendants, especially the 'everymen.' In average or typical cases, evidence of interactions between lawyers and clients is more sparse. See Massimo Firpo, ed., *Il processo inquisitoriale del cardinal Giovanni Morone: Edizione critica*, Vol. 3, *I documenti difensivi* (Rome:

Istituto storico italiano per l'età moderna, 1981–1985), esp. pp. 15–26 in the introduction concerning Morone's resources and Vol. 4, *Il processo divensive bolognese e la sentenza,* ibid., pp. 13–31 regarding the natural right to a legal defence.

6 Farinacci, *Tractatus de haeresi* (Cremona: Apud Marc'Antonium Belpierum, 1636), p. 340: 'Amplia I. Quia Advocati haereticorum dici possunt eorum defensores: secundum Anchar[num] [. . .] ubi pluribus exornat, quod advocando et procurando quis dicitur praestare auxilium et favorem delinquenti.' See also the discussion in Chapter 2 concerning *Ad abolendam* and other canonical decrees, which provided for the prosecution of *defensores,* or 'defenders' of heresy.

7 Farinacci, ibid., p. 340: 'Amplia VII ut pro haeretico non solum advocare prohibitum sit, sed etiam supplicare, et pro eo supplicans et orans dicitur proprie favere [. . .].'

8 Farinacci, ibid., pp. 341–2: 'Vide tamen Angelicam in summa in verbo Haereticus, numer. 25 vers. Nota tamen, ubi dixit, quod non dicitur haeretici defensor, qui haeretico patrocinatur, credens eum habere iustam causam, etiam quod postea appareat, quod non erat iusta causa [. . .].'; 'Amplia X ut Advocatus haeretico consilium, auxilium, favorem, et patrocinum praestare non debeat, non solum in iudicialibus sed nec etiam in extraiudicialibus [. . .]'; 'Limita I propositam regulam, ut non incurrat aliquam poenam Advocatus, qui pro haeretico patrocinatur, ignorans illum esse haereticum Decian[us] in tract. crim. l. 5 ca 51 num. 4.'

9 Cesare Carena, *Tractatus de Officio Sanctissimae Inquisitionis* (Cremona: Apud Marc'Antonium Belpierum, 1636), pp. 92–3: '[. . .] ubi quod nullo modo Advocatus, potest accusatio de haeresi praebere suum patrocinium, nisi de licentia superiorum et quod ita iudicavit Supremum Mechlinense Consilium Freitas ad Roder. de confes. solicit. q. 23 n. 28 ubi quod praebens consilium inquisito, etiam iustum inscio Inquisitore arbitrarie puniri debet, et ita practicatum in Santo Officio attestatur [. . .].' Carena also quoted the papal bull *Coenae Domini* (Book 2, canon 1, question 32, number 9) and inquisitorial instructions pertaining to a particular case. The lack of citations from other manuals, coupled with *Coenae Domini*'s annual publication and the instructions from the tribunal in Rome, would seem to indicate that this was a relatively recent innovation in Carena's time.

10 Farinacci, *Tractatus,* p. 27: 'Regula sit, quod protestatio excuset protestantem, et ideo quando quis aliquid haereticale assereret dubitans in fide errare, si protestatur, quod non intendit a fide recedere, sed quod corri-

gere separatum exhibet et iudicio sanctae Matris Eclesiae submittit; tunc talis protestatio ipsum excusat et praeservat ab omni haeresis crimine.' Farinacci quoted Simancas's *Enchiridion*, title fifty, number two, which was entitled *De protestatione*.

11 Farinacci, ibid., pp. 27–8: 'Amplia II ut protestatio eo magis bona et utilis sit facta ab eo, qui laborat in extremis et qui aliquando fuerit de haeresi inculpatus, ut scilicet dicat et asserat se fuisse et esse Catholicam, tenuisse et tenere fidem catholicam quam tenet et praedicat Romana Ecclesia et cum eadem fide vixisse et mori velle. Hanc enim protestationem validam et utilem esse pluribus probat Alberic [. . .].'

12 Farinacci, ibid., p. 28: '[. . .] vel in specie dicat se credere Messiam iam venisse aut caetera huiusmodi mysteria; et tamen iuxta ritum Iudaeorum pascalem Agnum occidat, et manducet Sabbathum colat, vel similia perpetret; is, inquam, protestatione non iuvabitur, ut ibi per eum.'

13 Peña, *Directorium Inquisitorum*, p. 623: 'Sed iam qua poena affici debeat testis falsus in hos tribunali doceamus. Ac primun videtur dicendum eos non esse plectendos talionis peona, nec tradendi in aliquo casu curiae saecular, prima quia nullo iure veteri nominatim cautam inventio in hac causa, ut testes hac poena plectantur.' Peña would decide, after two pages of opinions, that Leo X had settled the question in favour of retaliatory punishment; see below.

14 Carena, *Tractatus*, p. 369 and following; Farinacci, *Tractatus*, p. 204; Peña, *Directorium Inquisitorum*, p. 625: 'Caeterum observandum est ex verbis superioris rescripti non quemlibet falsum testem in hoc tribunali delinquentem, curae saeculari relinqui posse, sed illum tantum qui graviter seu notabiliter nocuit ei, contra quem deposuit: tunc autem exempli gratiae notabiliter nocere intelligitur, cum de vera et formali haeresi deposuit adversus aliquem. Illi vero maxime nocuerunt et propterea eis nullo pacto parcendum putarem, cum ille contra quem deposuerant, velut negativus et impoentitens ob eorum depositiones et testificationes traditus fuit curiae saeculari et ultimo supplicio affectus. Nam hoc casu eos gravissime nocuisse, plusquam manifestum est, id quod ex illis rescripti verbis aperte colligitur, videlicet: sicque huiusmodi diabolicae artis ministerio plerumque damnatur insontes.'

15 Peña, ibid., p. 624: 'Postremo Leonis Papae decimi diploma extat directum Adriano Cardinali generali Inquisitoris Hispaniae, Datum Romae apud Sanctum Petrum die 14 Decembris anno MDXVIII. Pontificatus sui anno sexto, quo Inquisitoribus Hispaniae conceditur, ut possint falsum testem curiae saeculari relinquere irregularitatis securi.'

16 Farinacci, *Tractatus*, pp. 203–5, esp. p. 204: 'Amplia VII ut multo magis poena talionis immo et traditionis curiae saeculari locum habeat in testis falsum deponente quando ex falso testimonio quis fuit condemnatus: sic enim colligitur ex verbis Diplomat. Leonis X relati per Franciscus Pegnam [. . .].'

17 Peña, *Directorium Inquisitorum*, p. 448: '"Illis tantum exceptionibus fidem testium evacuantibus in totum, quae non ex zelo iustitiae, sed de malignitatis fomite procedere videantur: ut sunt conspirationes et inimicitiae capitales: alia vero crimina etsi debilitent, non repellunt, maxime ubi testes de crimine fuerint emendari." Haec ibi: "In Narbonensi quoque c. 24 et 25 ita. Quamvis in huiusmodi crimine, propter ipsius enormitatem, omnes criminosi et infames et criminis etiam participes, ad accusationem, vel testimonium admittantur."' See also Tedeschi, 'Organization and Procedures,' p. 140.

18 Peña, *Directorium Inquisitorum*, p. 449: 'Aliorum vero inimicorum et criminosorum dicta quantum debilitentur, aut quantum sit illis detrahendum propter inimicitiam aliam praeter capitalem, aut propter alia crimina, arbitrio iudicantis relinquitur id investigare et iudicare, quod facile fortassis poterit deprehendere vir prudens ex personarum et negotii qualitate [. . .].'

19 Eliseo Masini, *Sacro Arsenale;Overo Prattica dell'officio della S. Inquisizione*, ed. Tommaso Menghini (Rome: 1693; StaatsBibliothek Digitalisat 4 J.can.p.5504), pp. 190–4: 'Item qualiter descripti in calce articulorum sunt infentissimi inimici et capitalissimi hostes dictic N. eo, quod pluries voluerunt illum occidere, nec unquam destiterunt, insidias illi tendere.'

20 Farinacci, *Tractatus*, p. 213: '[. . .] quod testis inimicus non admittitur in crimine haeresis, semper praesupponit capitalem inimicitiam, secus utique sentiens, si non fuerit capitalis [. . .].'

21 Concerning Zuane Finetti's legal education, including his training in both forms of law, see Gino Benzoni, 'Un Ulpiano mancato: Giovanni Finetti,' *Studi veneziani* n.s. 25 (1994): 35–71, esp. 48–50 for Finetti's education and career as a Venetian *cittadino* in government service. See also Nicholas Davidson, 'The Inquisition in Venice and Its Documents: Some Problems of Method and Analysis,' in *L'Inquisizione Romana in Italia nell'età moderna: Archivi, problemi di metodo e nuove ricerche; Atti del seminario internazionale Trieste, 18–20 maggio 1988*, ed. Andrea Del Col and Giovanna Paolin (Rome: Ministerio per i beni culturali e ambientali; Ufficio centrale per i beni archivistici, 1991), p. 126; see also Black, *Italian Inquisition*, pp. 71–2.

22 See, for example, Achille Olivieri, 'Alessandro Trissino e il movimento calvinista vicentino del Cinquecento,' in *Rivista di Storia della Chiesa in Italia* 21 (Gennaio-Giugno, 1967): 54–117, esp. pp. 58–9, 68.

23 ASVe, *Sant'Uffizio*, Busta 21, Fasc. 2, *Contra Girolamo e Alvise Badoer, e Giovanni Fineti*, fol. 44r: 'E quando essere 15 giorni, venne un Bortholo [sic], il qual credo che l[ui] serve in ca Badoer a San Paolo, al quale disse Hieronymo ... che in villa non so, se [lui] fu a Padova overo Treviso che [lui] mangiare luganega.' (See also fols. 41r; 45r–v). *Luganega* was a Venetian dialect term for 'sausage.'

24 ASVe, *Contra Girolamo e Alvise Badoer, e Giovanni Fineti*, unp.: '[...] ma mal usando il Badoer quel nome incontaminato com'egli usa malamente quelli di questo Papà santissimo [...].'; 'Melchioro [sic] poi fa ampl[i] a fede che [es]sendo sollecitato alla falsità da quel prete lo fu promessa d'un Badoer l'amicizia e favore.' John Tedeschi has discussed how expert legal knowledge was probably a requirement for being able to mount any kind of defence in inquisitorial courts ('Organization and Procedures,' p. 137). Fra Marino, *il zotto*, the extremely irenic and accommodating inquisitor of Silvana Seidel Menchi's 'The Inquisitor as Mediator,' in *Heresy, Culture, and Religion in Early Modern Italy: Contexts and Contestations*, ed. Ronald K. Delph, Michelle M. Fontaine, and John Jeffries Martin (Kirksville, MO: Truman State University Press, 2006), pp. 173–92, was later prosecuted for heresy himself. His defence also consisted of attempting to prove a major conflict between himself and the new inquisitor pursuing the case, and giving evidence of his good behaviour as a priest, including saying Mass. ASVe, *Sant'Uffizio*, Busta 12, *Contra Padre Marin da Venezia*, July, 1551. The archivist who organized the inquisition records translated 'Hieronymo' as 'Girolamo'; for consistency's sake, I will also refer to him as Girolamo Badoer, although 'Geronimo' is also a possible translation from the Latin.

25 ASVe, *Contra Girolamo e Alvise Badoer, e Giovanni Fineti*, unp. For a description of the relationship between Finetti and his servant, Girolamo Badoer, see Dennis Romano, *Housecraft and Statecraft: Domestic Service in Renaissance Venice, 1400–1600* (Baltimore: Johns Hopkins University Press, 1996), pp. 224–5; for the state bodies regulating servants and crime, see Romano, *Housecraft and Statecraft*, pp. 41–74, and Romano, 'The Regulation of Domestic Service in Renaissance Venice,' *Sixteenth Century Journal* 22, no. 4 (1991): 661–77, esp. 668; for the structure of the Venetian government, see Robert Finlay, *Politics in Renaissance Venice* (New Brunswick, NJ: Rutgers University Press, 1980), esp. pp. 39–40 regarding the Collegio's role in the Venetian state as the committee that controlled the Senate's legislative agenda; it consisted of the Doge, his six ducal councillors (which would include Giulio Contarini, the recipient of Finetti's defence document), and sixteen other ministers.

26 ASVe, *Contra Girolamo e Alvise Badoer, e Giovanni Fineti,* unp.: 'Questi testimoni, che sono al nostro di 21 tutti uniforme, tutti concordia danno conti dei miei costumi e fanno fede, che in atti, e in parole sia vi[ss]uto innocente.'; 'Fu adunque la scritture Messer Federico l'autore del mio tormento, lo fa sospetto il mio lamento perciò che nissuna ragione persuade, che non avendone ci parte inappagliarsi alla menarmene fuori d'ogni proposito a capital[e] nemi[co] concitandolo lo d[icevano] le parole che [. . .].'

27 ASVe, *Contra Girolamo e Alvise Badoer, e Giovanni Fineti,* unp.: '[. . .] e se du[i] testimoni legitimi fanno fede della colpa d'un reo, e sono atti a tor[nar]gli la vita, credo che bastano venti a conserv[a]r[e] l'honore d'un attore e castigar[e] uno calunniatore, massimamente quando che oltre i testimoni, la cui fede in danno [e] tentano gl'avversari di far[e] sospetta.'

28 ASVe, *Contra Girolamo e Alvise Badoer, e Giovanni Fineti,* unp.: 'Ora sono stato adunque falsamente imputato, poiché mi sono sempre confessato e communicato, si sono confessati e communicati tutti i miei, ho ascoltato e hanno ascoltata la messa, sono stati dati d'ordine mio i sacramenti della chiesa alla Signora Beatrice Cossazza mia parente, ho vituperato gli eretici, e cacciati i s[o]spetti, né insomma ho tralasciato nissuno ufficio dovuto a me come Catholico, e Christiano, e come un padre e di famiglia e de[gli] figliuoli a quali oltre una diligente istituzione mi sono affaticato che la mia vita serva per vivace maestra de suoi futuri costumi.'

29 Marion Leathers Kuntz, *The Anointment of Dionisio: Prophecy and Politics in Renaissance Italy* (University Park, PA: Pennsylvania State University Press, 2001), pp. 177–9; A. Olivieri, 'Alessandro Trissino,' pp. 73–4.

30 Marion Leathers Kuntz, 'Voices from a Venetian Prison in the Cinquecento Francesco Spinola and Dionisio Gallo,' *Studi veneziani,* n.s. 27 (1994): 98–9, 105. According to Kuntz, some details of Spinola's process and activities in prison are available through other processes, especially Ugoni's and that of Dionisio Gallo (who shared a cell with Spinola) and the papal nuncio, Cardinal Alessandro Fachinetti's, correspondence concerning the case.

31 ASVe, *Contra Girolamo e Alvise Badoer, e Giovanni Fineti,* unp.: 'È stato il Spinola meco un mese all'istituzione de[gli] miei figliuoli, ebbi sospetta la sua coscienza, et lo spinsi di casa, e sono di quello atto rimproverato e per eretico accusato, che die fare di se stesso[. . .]'

32 ASVe, *Sant'Uffizio, Contra Girolamo e Alvise Badoer, e Giovanni Fineti,* unp.: '[. . .] che un mio barcarolo affermasse volere partire di casa mia perché io mangiassi carne i giorni proibiti si perché questa è troppo affettata coscienza, si perché lo istituto della mia casa e provato e (sic) dal Signore Chieregato, dal magnifico Stagnano, dalla magnifico Vitturi, da Marietta e Corona, dall' eccellente Brusco da Domenico Barzotto testimonio

dell'avversario, che fa fede con giuramento, che lo scelerato calunniatore comprava otto marcei di pesce e gli venerdi e i sabbati.'

33 ASVe, *Contra Girolamo e Alvise Badoer, e Giovanni Fineti*, unp.: 'pure a Padova mi confessai et lo seppe Hieronymo come dalla mag[nifi]ca Vitturi viene affermato . . . che potesser [potere] far[e] fede ch'io mi sia confessato, ch'io mi sia communicato, che habbi [abbia] cacciato il Spinola, e vituperate gli eretici, e di molte altre mie attioni cattolica debite a cristiano, e a innocente.'

34 For the composition of the Venetian tribunal, negotiated by the papacy and Venetian state government in 1547, five years after the Roman Inquisition's reorganization, see John Jeffries Martin, *Venice's Hidden Enemies: Italian Heretics in a Renaissance City* (Berkeley and Los Angeles: University of California Press, 1993), pp. 51–6. Before 1547, the Venetian tribunal, originating in the medieval period, had operated in Venice and the Veneto under the direction of the papal nuncio, but there were conflicts between it and the Venetian state. See also Andrea Del Col, 'Organizzazione, composizione e giurisdictione de tribunali dell'Inquisizione Romana nella repubblica di Venezia (1500–1550),' *Critica storica* 25 (1988): 244–94.

35 ASVe, *Contra Girolamo e Alvise Badoer, e Giovanni Fineti*, fol. 22v: 'Quando mia madre Madonna Beatrice mori esso M[esser] Zuane mandò a chiamar[e] il sacrista di San Benedetto che li venisse[ro] a dato l'olio santo e credo che fu Hieronymo che l'andasse a chiamar[e] perché il faceva ogni cosa, et lui sapeva che se li dava l'olio santo.' For Lorenzo's brief testimony, see fol. 30r.

36 *Contra Girolamo e Alvise Badoer, e Giovanni Fineti*, fol. 22v: 'Io so che Messer Zuane caccia di casa il Spinola, perché lo aveva per sospetto di eresia et questo lo può sapere anche Hieronymo perché lui lo ha inteso in casa. Subdens: Non credo che Hieronymo fu in casa in quel tempo che era il Spinola, ma so che lui lo ha inteso dire in casa quando si parlava del Spinola.'

37 *Contra Girolamo e Alvise Badoer, e Giovanni Fineti*, fol. 2r for Papilioni's testimony.

38 ASVe, *Contra Girolamo e Alvise Badoer, e Giovanni Fineti*, fol. 20r for Corona's testimony; for Niccolò's, fols. 5r–6r: 'Io l'ho per così galante gentilhuomo et per così buon Cristiano quanto un'altro.'; '[. . .] che vene certi frati di Capuccini a confessarla, che se diceva che l'era sua confessore non so se la si confessasse, l'[andate] ben in camera da lei ma non vi so dire altro a quello che si diceva percorsa [. . .].'

39 Carena, *Tractatus*, pp. 339–40: ' Primo igitur infirmitas probatur per attestationem medicorum [. . .].'; 'Quarto probatur per aspectum corporis

aegroti, ita Actius d. Rubr. 37 n. 28 ut VG si facies sit extenuata tristis et c. et generaliter, de variis aliis modis probandi infirmitatem, vide Odd[ofredus] [. . .].' One could produce a doctor to prove the veracity of the illness; one could produce the testimony of his domestics (including, one presumes, his cook); one could produce an oath of illness; or the inquisitor himself could take a good, hard look at the person and see if he or she was visibly sick.

40 Ulrich Zwingli, 'Concerning Choice and Liberty Respecting Food,' trans. Lawrence A. McLouth, in *The Correspondence of Huldreich Zwingli, Together with Selections from His German Works* ed. Samuel Macauley Jackson (New York: G.P. Putnam's Sons, 1912), pp. 73–6. John Tedeschi, 'Organization and Procedures,' p. 154, in addition to Carena, above. Tedeschi has noted that the central tribunal in Rome had to keep emphasizing that it was not definitive proof in and of itself.

41 ASVe, *Contra Girolamo e Alvise Badoer, e Giovanni Fineti,* fol 1v–2r: 'Io non ho mai sentito a dire da alcuno cosa Cattolica da lui per cinto di Religione.'; 'Mi non ho visto, non so de lo vien[e] a[lla] messa altramente perché non dago [sic] a mente e attendo al governo della chiesa.'

42 ASVe, *Contra Girolamo e Alvise Badoer, e Giovanni Fineti,* fol. 3r: 'Io non l'ho mai visto a mangiar[e] carne nei detti giorni proibiti, eccetto quando [lui] si am[m]alava e anche le donne.'

43 ASVe, *Contra Girolamo e Alvise Badoer, e Giovanni Fineti,* for Corona's testimony, fol 20r: 'Respondit: Messer Zuane mangia carne al tempo; che se né può mangiare; anzi l'ha più grado il pesce, che la carne; et mai l'ho veduto mangiare carne nei giorni proibiti.'; for Niccolò's testimony, fols. 5r–6r.

44 ASVe, *Contra Girolamo e Alvise Badoer, e Giovanni Fineti,* fols. 4r–v: 'Mi non sono stato mai a messa con lui, ma perché andava qualche volte con lui in palazzo gli giorni feriali, et passavamo per Chiesa di San Marco et quando occorreva, che si doveva levare il Sacramento nella Chiesa di San Marco vedeva che il detto M Zuane faceva riverentia, si levava la baretta, et si ingenocchiava et si batteva il petto dinanzi al Sacramento che altramente non sono andato a Messa con lui come ho detto di sopra.' See my discussion of Venetian public ritual in Chapter 1, and Farinacci's opinion that failing to raise one's hat was a sure sign of heretical intent in Chapter 3.

45 Farinacci, *Tractatus,* p. 212.

46 ASVe, *Contra Girolamo e Alvise Badoer, e Giovanni Fineti,* fols. 5r–6r: 'Io l'ho per così galante gentilhuomo et per così buon Cristiano quanto un'altro.'

47 ASVe, *Contra Girolamo e Alvise Badoer, e Giovanni Fineti,* fol. 20r.

48 ASVe, *Contra Girolamo e Alvise Badoer, e Giovanni Fineti,* fol. 17v: 'E abbiamo udito messa in compagnia'; 'Perché l'ho sempre conosciuto per gentiluomo

temoroso della Maestà di Dio, et osservator[e] degli precetti della Santa Romana Chiesa.'

49 ASVe, *Contra Girolamo e Alvise Badoer, e Giovanni Fineti*, fol. 24r–v: 'Ritrovandomi una volta amalato in casa del detto Fineti che che (sic) può essere un'anno erano portati qualche pollastra solamente per conto mio, et gl'altri mangiavano pesce, che Hieronymo era presente; et anche negli altri giorni proibiti il detto Hieronymo comprava del pesce perché era spenditore.' Chiericati and Pigafetta were the family names of men associated with Trissino's Calvinist cirlce in his native Vicenza; see Achille Olivieri, *Riforma ed ereisa a Vicenza nel Cinquecento* (Rome: Herder Editrice, 1992), esp. pp. 324–46 and Salvatore Caponetto, *The Protestant Reformation in Sixteenth-Century Italy*, trans. Anne C. Tedeschi and John Tedeschi (Kirksville, MO: Thomas Jefferson University Press, 1999), p. 36. However, none of those Olivieri has discussed were named Valerio Chiericati or Antonio Francesco Pigafetta. An Antonio Pigafetta, a doctor, however, was living north of the Alps and in contact with other Italian exiles by 1572. See S. Ragagli, 'Simoni, Simone,' in *Dizionario storico dell'Inquisizione*, Vol. 3, ed. Adriano Prosperi with Vincenzo Lavenia and John Tedeschi (Pisa: Scuola Normale Superiore Pisa, 2010), pp. 1432–3.

50 ASVe, *Contra Girolamo e Alvise Badoer, e Giovanni Fineti*, fol 2r.: 'Questo non so, né manco l'ho inteso a dire, perché io non gli pratica in casa.'

51 ASVe, *Contra Girolamo e Alvise Badoer, e Giovanni Fineti*, fol. 29r; fol. 43r: 'Io et tutta la casa e anche Messer Zuane si avevamo confessato et communicato insieme queste Pasqua prossime passata nella chiesa di San Benedetto.'

52 ASVe, *Contra Girolamo e Alvise Badoer, e Giovanni Fineti*, fol. 19v:'Fuit sibi dictum. De che colore vanno vestiti detti monace.'; 'Io non [lo] vidi, perché restai da basso et lui andò su a quell'effetto. Io non vidi il frate che lui confessava, ma il stette un gran pezzo. Io vogavo in mezzo, e io aspettavo gl'aspettandolo in barca, ma io non so che l'era anda[to] a messa, l'era però ora di andar[e] a messa, et andavamo qualche volte a Santa Lena, e al Spirito Santo, nelli quali [luogi] ho mena[t]o detto M[esser] Zuane [al] la festa ad ora delle messe.' *Vogare*, in Venetian dialect, meant to push the boat.

53 ASVe, *Contra Girolamo e Alvise Badoer, e Giovanni Fineti*, fols. 9v–10v.

54 ASVe, *Contra Girolamo e Alvise Badoer, e Giovanni Fineti*, fol. 11r: 'E lui disse perché M[esser] Zuane mi ha imputato, che io ho fatto polizze doppi[o] et mi v[u]ol[e] far[e] metter[e] in pr[i]gion[e]; E Dio. Mantegna a M[esser] Federico Badoer, e uno da ca Contarini che non lo so il nome, e lui Hieronymo disse "Io voglio dar[e] una querela ad esso Fineti alla

eresia." '; 'Et lui disse "io voglio dare una querela ad esso Fineti alla eresia." ' Et respondendo Battista disse "Che so mi! Che non so niente di eresia." Et Hieronymo disse "Volgio che tu sii essaminato et che ti me servi, et ti voglio fare essaminare che l'ha mangiato carne gli giorni proibiti." Et Battista disse "Non lo posso dire." Bonghi's testimony concerning this meeting, and Giovanni Battista della Pace's, come closest to portraying Finetti as threatening despite the fact that they testified on his behalf.

55 ASVe, *Contra Girolamo e Alvise Badoer, e Giovanni Fineti*, fols. 11v–12v: 'E esso Niccolò stett[e] così un poco sopra di se talmente, che M[esser] Zuane hebbe [abbia] fatica[to] di farli dir[e] quel che lui disse, "Perché [il] minacciava?"'; 'L'è vero che Hieronymo è stato da mi, et ha detto che lui mi vuole fare essaminare, dicenda "voglio dargli una querela, Voglio che tu dichi che l'ha mangiato carne negli giorni proibiti, promettendogli de fargli di piaceri [. . .]."'

56 ASVe, *Contra Girolamo e Alvise Badoer, e Giovanni Fineti*, fol. 47v.

57 ASVe, *Contra Girolamo e Alvise Badoer, e Giovanni Fineti*, fols. 7v–9v: '[. . .] esso mi ha fatto in pr[i]gione, acciocchè non potessi parlare ad alcuno et fra tanto ha potuto fare dire ai testimoni a suo modo [. . .].'

58 ASVe, *Contra Girolamo e Alvise Badoer, e Giovanni Fineti*, fol. 8v: 'Esso seppe gli testimoni, che dovevano essere essaminati perché erano nominati anche al Officio SS. Censorii [. . .].'

59 ASVe, *Contra Girolamo e Alvise Badoer, e Giovanni Fineti*, 59r; 64r: 'Io posso dire che ho alcuni che proveranno che in casa del Fineti è stava fatta la cena al modo di Germania, cioè io [ho] dui testim[oni] . . . che il Spinola ha detto che haveva fatto la cena al modo di Germania in casa del Fineti [. . .].'; for Girolamo's confession, see fols. 69r–70r. Henry Charles Lea has noted that in Spain, despite the Suprema's repeated insistence to punish false witness and suborning of testimony severely, those found guilty of either crime were often assigned lenient punishments. See Lea, *A History of the Inquisition in Spain*, Vol. II, pp. 554–8. But this was not the case with all the punishments assigned to those convicted of false witness; the central tribunal in Rome, which consisted of four of the members of the Congregation of Cardinals that oversaw the Roman Inquisition's operations, found a group of men guilty of organizing a conspiracy to falsely accuse someone of heresy in 1566, and the men were sentenced to be publicly whipped. See TCD MS 1224, *Sentences*, Vol. 2, fols. 73r–74v.

60 ASVe, *Contra Girolamo e Alvise Badoer, e Giovanni Fineti*, fols. 67r–v.

61 According to Eliseo Masini, the Holy Office was obligated to help poor defendants with their expenses, both by assigning lawyers to help them

in their defence, and by paying for the travel of exculpatory witnesses when necessary; see Masini, *Sacro Arsenale*, p. 335; Tedeschi, 'Organization and Procedures,' p. 136. Finetti, however, was quite rich (see Benzoni, 'Un Ulpino mancato,' p. 37), and therefore most likely paid his own expenses.

62 ASVe, *Contra Girolamo e Alvise Badoer, e Giovanni Fineti*, unp.

63 Farinacci, *Tractatus*, p. 28

64 Farinacci, ibid., p. 28: 'Limita V ut protestatio excuset in non definitis per Ecclesiam, vel in dubiis, secus autem in iam definitis: tunc enim protestatio, tanquam facto contraria non excusat. Quae enim per Ecclesiam iam matura deliberatione sunt determinata, non debent ulterius in quaestionem deduci [. . .].'

65 *Canons and Decrees of the Council of Trent*, ed. Rev. H.J. Schroeder, OP (Rockford, IL: Tan Books and Publishers, 1978), pp. 29–46.

66 Eymeric, *Directorium Inquisitorum*, p. 428: 'Tertium est: quomodo et qualiter responsibus vulpinis et cautelosis haereticorum obviabit.'

67 Walter Wakefield and Austin P. Evans, 'Bernard Gui's Description of Heresies,' in *Heresies of the High Middle Ages*, ed. and trans. Wakefield and Evans (New York: Columbia University Press, 1969), pp. 373–4. Wakefield and Evans, in their introduction to the work, describe the genesis of Gui's manual; the first four books contained formula for conduct, sentencing, and amelioration of penalties. The first three books were based on Gui's own experiences and sentences drawn from his twenty-five years as an inquisitor, but the fourth book, a collection of papal bulls, canons of councils, and other instructions for inquisitors, drew on an older, anonymous Italian work probably written in about 1280–1292. The fifth book also utilized other authors' work (unattributed, unlike later manual authors), including David of Augsburg, the Cathar heretic Peter Autier's confession, and Stephen of Bourbon. Concerning Gui's advice about the proper way to structure questions in order to eliminate evasive answers, the issue will be explored more fully in Chapter 6.

68 Valerio Marchetti, *Gruppi ereticali senesi nel Cinquecento* (Florence: La nuova italia, 1975), p. 193.

69 In Poland, Fausto Sozzini developed a systematic theology that included rejecting all ideas of original sin, the idea of a immortal soul separate from God (all human beings contained a divine spark that returned to its origins after death, Christ's divinity), and any concept of hell or purgatory (since Christ's death opened the possibility of immortality for believers). In addition, Sozzini stressed free will and reason, rejected any concept of grace, and believed that the Eucharist was the only sacrament (completely disavowing baptism). Czesław Miłosz, *The History of Polish Literature*,

2nd ed. (Berkeley and Los Angeles: University of California Press, 1983), pp. 34–5.

70 See Bernardino Ochino, *Seven Dialogues*, ed. and trans. Rita Belladonna (Ottawa: Dovehouse Editions, 1988), and her introduction, pp. vii–xxxi.

71 See Salvatore Caponetto, *Protestant Reformation*, p. 300; Marchetti, *Gruppi ereticali senesi*, pp. 260–3.

72 Siena in the 1550s and 1560s found itself recovering from political and religious tumult. The Tuscan city had quartered troops for Holy Roman Emperor Charles V who, since the sack of Rome in 1527, had established his military presence on the peninsula, which included the construction of a citadel in Siena. That city's citizens, however, objected to the continuous presence of Spanish troops and rebelled in 1552 and subsequently suffered brutal repression. In 1529, Charles V had laid siege to Florence and re-established the Medici as rulers under that city's first unofficial duke, Alessandro. In 1555, Alessandro's successor, Cosimo I, attacked Siena in order to complete Florentine domination of the Tuscan region. The city held out for a year before capitulating because of hunger, and Siena came under Florentine administration by 1559. See Gregory Hanlon, *Early Modern Italy, 1550–1800* (New York: St. Martin's Press, 2000), pp. 53–4.

73 Caponetto, *Protestant Reformation*, pp. 304–5.

74 ASS, *Notarile antecosimiano* 2776, *Processus et inquisitio contra magistrum Bartholomeum olim magistri Iohannis de Nellis fabrum ferrarium ac abiuratio* (hereafter *Processo contro Bartolomeo Nelli)*, fol. 1r: 'nella b[o]ttega di Francesco spe[z]iale dove era ancora Niccolò Barbiero, Scipione Orlandini, M[esser] Achille Orlandini, Giulio di Vecchi spe[z]iale e così ragionamento della predica[z]ione fatta il giorno dal padre Girolamo. Messer Giulio e da quella seguitando ragionamento ... e la quale opinione contraposse Bartolomeo con dire l'opere nostro non meritavano niente e allegava si non perché ma che [sic] noi [si]amo salvi per Christo e non per bene opere.'

75 ASS, *Processo contro Bartolomeo Nelli*, fol. 1v–2r: ' Civi nenné il detto Bartolomeo gli dissi ch'è meritato; detto che lui andava dicendo che l'opinione allegategli lascere avanti era di Pelagio'; fol. 3r–v: 'Quid vanno[eunt] sermones ad invice habuerum super Deo operibus o [vel] qui predetto Bartolomeo auderet de piis operibus?' Both Protestant and Catholic polemicists utilized terminology drawn from the Ancient Church's dealings with heresies. See Manfred Schulze, 'Martin Luther and the Church Fathers,' in *The Reception of the Church Fathers in the West*, Vol. 2, ed. Irena Backus (New York: Brill, 1997), pp. 579–97; Johannes van Oort, 'John Calvin and the Church Fathers,' in ibid., pp. 672–3; and concerning Pelagius, Augustine, and original sin, see Peter Brown, *Augustine of Hippo*

(Berkeley and Los Angeles: University of California Press, 1967), esp. pp. 340–52 and W.H.C. Frend, *The Rise of Christianity* (Philadelphia: Fortress Press, 1984), pp. 673–80, and the introduction, p. 11, ff. 15.

76 Peter Matheson, *Cardinal Contarini at Regensburg* (Oxford: Clarendon Press, 1972), pp. 97–144. Nelli's legal counsel, Lucarini, tried to defend Nelli's statements by shifting the emphasis back to the validity of works, thereby bringing Nelli within the outer reaches of Catholic theology.

77 *Canons and Decrees of the Council of Trent*, pp. 29–46.

78 ASS, *Processo contro Bartolomeo Nelli*, fol. 8r–v: 'An ipse sit solus andare missa et alia divina offitia?'; 'An ipse sit solitus confiteri quali per anno peccata sua et sacramentum eucaristie accipter?'; 'Io so solito confessarmi e communicarmi così io come tutta la mia famiglia. E questo anno mi sono confessato e communicato dal padre Chretius della Compagnia di Jesù e de fra Giberto augustino di Santo Martino.'

79 ASS, *Processo contro Bartolomeo Nelli*, fol. 8v; Marchetti, *Gruppi ereticali*, pp. 188–9. Paul IV's Index of Prohibited Books placed over sixty editions of vernacular Bibles on the Index (see Paul Grendler, *The Roman Inquisition and the Venetian Press, 1540–1605* [Princeton: Princeton University Press, 1977], pp. 115–17). Nelli may have owned a Latin version that was not placed on the Index, but, in spirit, the Index was meant to keep laypeople from interpreting the Bible for themselves, as Nelli was clearly doing here.

80 ASS, *Processo contro Bartolomeo Nelli*, fol. 13r: 'Io ho detto l'opinione mia e loro la loro.' Nelli claimed he had studied the Bible to better instruct his family, and had received his copy from a Dominican friar. For the last two books found in his house, Nelli chose not to explain himself beyond identifying the source; the *Perla di santa chiesa* he had bought in the marketplace about a month previously, whereas he had been given Brucioli's dialogues by Francesca di Cristoforo Cristofani, a Sienese noblewoman, about a year before; *Processo contro Bartolomeo Nelli*, fol. 15v; Marchetti, *Gruppi ereticali*, p. 189.

81 ASS, *Processo contro Bartolomeo Nelli*, fol. 15r. While Luther, rather famously at the time, utilized his principle of the priesthood of all believers to support the male head of a household's role as the domestic religious leader, Catholic theologians also had been known to perceive of male household headship in a similar light. Therefore Nelli's excuse was not necessarily explicitly Protestant, although inquisitors could choose to interpret it as such.

82 ASS, *Processo contro Bartolomeo Nelli*, fols. 19v–20r.

83 Later inquisition manuals continue to emphasize the necessity of consulting experts; see, for example, Farinacci, in the *Tractatus*, who utilized Peña

as his source, pp. 153–4: '[. . .] ubi quod periti convocandi erunt Theologi, Canonistae, et Legistae, et ibi Francisc. Pegna in addition comm. 116 vers. Caeterum, ubi praesertim quod quando Inquisitores sunt iurisperiti (ut in Hispania) debent in consultores, Theologos convocare, folio mihi 681 col. 3.' Farinacci also noted that such experts should not expect to be paid for giving their expert counsel, and also could expect for their identities to be protected if their opinions were passed in writing to the defence. See also John Tedeschi, 'Organization and Procedures,' p. 137, for the suggestion that some lawyers were appointed as a matter of patronage, and Christopher F. Black concering the consultation of experts (*Italian Inquisition*, p. 59).

84 ASS, *Processo contro Bartolomeo Nelli*, fol. 21r–v. Marchetti, *Gruppi ereticali*, pp. 193–4. 'Opera nostra "tamquam nostram" discriminandole da quelle fatte come frutto della grazia di Dio, che meritano e "quae sunt necessaria" alla nostra salute.'

85 ASS, *Processo contro Bartolomeo Nelli*, fols. 28r–v, 29v, 30r–v; Marchetti, *Gruppi ereticali*, pp. 196–7.

86 ASS, *Processo contro Bartolomeo Nelli*, fols. 25r–26r (parere di Adeodato da Siena [9 February 1560]). 'Haeresis est manifesta.'

87 ASS, *Processo contro Bartolomeo Nelli*, fol. 33r (parere di Gregorio Primaticci [9 February 1560]).

88 ASS, *Processo contro Bartolomeo Nelli*, fols. 35r–36v:'confidare in Gesù Christo e non né l'opere ... segno della gratia e dell'elettione.'

89 Marchetti, *Gruppi ereticali*, p. 198: 'I have believed and held that the good works we perform do not have that efficacy of works performed by the grace of Jesus Christ.'

90 Marchetti, *Gruppi ereticali*, pp. 267–8.

91 Grendler, *The Roman Inquisition and the Venetian Press*, pp. 182–200; John Jeffries Martin, *Venice's Hidden Enemies: Italian Heretics in a Renaissance City* (Berkeley and Los Angeles: University of California Press, 1993), pp. 34–48, 51–7.

92 Caponetto, *Protestant Reformation*, pp. 191–92; Martin, *Venice's Hidden Enemies*, pp. 71–96; Ugo Rozzo and Silvana Seidel Menchi, 'The Book and the Reformation in Italy,' trans. Karin Maag in *The Reformation and the Book*, ed. Jean-François Gilmont and Karin Maag (Brookfield, VT: Ashgate, 1998), pp. 341–3.

93 Martin, *Venice's Hidden Enemies*, Chapter 6, esp. pp. 168–9.

94 Martin, *Venice's Hidden Enemies*, pp. 182–3.

95 ASVe, *Sant'Uffizio*, Busta 8, *Contra Prosperum Capellarum et Battista dale Bambine, 1572–73*, fol. 1r: 'Proibisce [la] sua mog[l]ie che non vada a[lla]

messa e per quanto ho inteso [la] sua mog[l]ie dice che lui non si confessa né si communica e io volendolo lev[a]r[e] delle sue male opinione, che ha dell'authorità del papà l'ho invi[t]ato a venir[e] con mi da qualche Padre Theologo e benché mi promettesse di voler[e] venire, niente di manco si pensi, et non voler[e] venire secondo l'ordine che avevamo insieme: ma mi disse "Credo, come credere voi. Non voglio venire altramente."' Either the notary, or a later copyist, did not see fit to include the names of the Patriarch, nuncio, or inquisitor along with their titles; only Vicente Contarini and Nicolas Venier were mentioned by name. The Jesuit did not get in trouble for attempting fraternal correction first, although it would be the opinion of most tribunals in Italian lands that confessors should forward heretics to the tribunals for prosecution; see, for example, the *Directorium Inquisitorum*, pp. 121–2 and Vincenzo Lavenia, *L'Infamia e il perdono: Tributi, pene e confessione nella teologia morale della prima età moderna* (Bologna: Il Mulino, 2004), pp. 286–99. In 1572, the Calvinist cause and the Dutch Revolt were reignited with the seizure of the port towns of Brill and Vlissingen and William of Orange's return to the provinces with an army sponsored by French Huguenots (see Andrew Pettegree, 'Religion and the Revolt,' in *The Origins and Development of the Dutch Revolt*, ed. Graham Darby [New York: Routledge, 2001], esp. pp. 78–80). The 'victory of the Huguenots,' a month before St Bartholomew's Day Massacre, was probably a reference to the Peace of St Germain, concluded in 1570, which halted the third civil war, and led to Catherine de Medici's attempts to arrange the marriage between Marguerite de Valois and Henry of Navarre (see Mack P. Holt, *The French Wars of Religion, 1562–1629* [New York: Cambridge University Press, 1995], pp. 76–8). Gregory XIII (pope 1572–1585) declared jubilee indulgences several times throughout his papacy; the first, on his ascension in 1572, excepted heretics, but his subsequent declaration in 1578 included heretics in the declaration of indulgence (see Lea, *A History of the Inquisition of Spain*, Vol. 2 [London: Macmillan, 1922], p. 26).

96 ASVe, *Contra Prospero Capellarum et Battista dale Bambine*, fol. 1v: Et quod [i.e. E perché] diceva tenendo la parte de[gli] Luterani.' According to John Martin's characterization of the political situation in the Mediterranean during the early 1570s, by 1573 the Venetian state, after the initial success of the Battle of Lepanto in 1572, had been forced to reach an embarrassing separate peace with the Ottoman Turks. Martin, *Venice's Hidden Enemies*, pp. 199–200.

97 ASVe, *Contra Prospero Capellarum et Battista dale Bambine*, fol. 2r: 'San Piero era un santo huomo, et andava descalzo; et questi papi sonno grassi, et vanno ben vestiti [. . .].'

98 ASVe, *Contra Prospero Capellarum et Battista dale Bambine,* fol. 2v. Martin has described how many at the Rialto, accustomed to foreign religious customs, thought that Prospero and Battista should not have been brought before the tribunal, and criticized the witnesses willing to provide information; see *Venice's Hidden Enemies,* pp. 210–11.

99 ASVe, *Contra Prospero Capellarum et Battista dale Bambine,* fol. 3r: 'Et dice che "In terre de Luterani, ogn'uno fa a suo modo."'

100 ASVe, *Contra Prospero Capellarum et Battista dale Bambine,* fol. 3v; Martin, *Venice's Hidden Enemies,* pp. 210–11.

101 ASVe, *Contra Prospero Capellarum et Battista dale Bambine,* fol. 5r: 'Sono mei inimici: Bernardin[o] padovano che vende sul ponte da Rialto; Andrea dalle Centurer, che vende per Rialto; e Messer Biasio che vende per piazza; l'altro Messer Domenego grande che vende sul ponte da Rialto.'; fols. Fv-5r: 'Il qual mi diceva che nella Città di Ginevra, si faceva tanto bene, e mi diceva che il Papà era un vero Antichristo.'

102 ASVe, *Contra Prospero Capellarum et Battista dale Bambine,* fol 5v: 'Io sapev[o] ben[e] di questa cosa, et volev[o] presentarmi per defendere il mio honore'; 'Sono tre anni che non mi son[o] confessato né communicato, et mi voleva confessare questa settimana passata.' Martin, *Venice's Hidden Enemies,* pp. 210–11.

103 ASVe, *Contra Prospero Capellarum et Battista dale Bambine,* fols. 7v–8v.

104 ASVe, *Contra Prospero Capellarum et Battista dale Bambine,* fol. 9r.

105 ASVe, *Contra Prospero Capellarum et Battista dale Bambine,* fol. 21v for the escape; fols. 19v–21v for Piero Orbe's testimony. This issue will be discussed more broadly in Chapter 6.

106 Farinacci, *Tractatus,* p. 310: 'Vide tamen in hic Simanch[as] catholicar. institution. titul. 15 rubr. de custodia reorum, num. 23, ubi dixit, moribus receptum esse, quod si inquisitus haereticus ex carcere aufugiat, aut aufugere tentaverit, si honestior sit, diligentius custodiatur; si vilior, fustibus caedatur, causa iterum tractetur, nec propterea pro confesso habeatur [. . .].'

107 Farinacci, ibid., p. 310: 'Et rursus vide Bullam Pii V Si de protegendis, et c. in versicul. Quive, carcerem, et c. ubi frangenti carcerem, seu custodiam publicam, aut privatam, laesae Maiestatis criminis poenam imponit [. . .].' Concerning those who fled perpetual incarceration, a punishment meted out to the most serious, but penitent, abjured suspects in heresy, Farinacci also presented the full range of opinions amongst inquisitorial authors and canonists. According to Farinacci, Giovanni d'Anania, Archidiaconus, Giovanni d'Andrea, and Calderini all recommended execution as punishment of a relapsed heretic. Umberto Locati thought there was violent presumption of the person in question being relapsed, but no absolute proof. Many authors

thought that the person was impenitent, but not relapsed (Farinacci, p. 309). Juan de Rojas, inquisitor of Valencia, published his *De haereticis una cum quinquaginta analyticis assertionibus et privilegiis Inquisitorum* in Valencia in 1572 (Lea, *A History of the Inquisition of Spain,* Vol. 2, p. 476).

108 Peña, *Directorium Inquisitorum,* p. 468: 'Insignis est hic Eymerici locus et vera doctrina contra Zanchinum tract. de haeret. c. 10 num. 4 et Campegium ibidem versi, fregit carcerem et quosdam alios asserentes, eum qui fuit in carcerem coniectus ad custodiam pro crimine haeresis, si fugiat pro convicto habendum et tanquam haereticum esse danmandum.'

109 Peña, ibid., p. 468: 'In crimine tamen haeresis locum non habet haec communis sententia, ut vere scripsit Simancas de catho. instit. tit. 16 nu. 23 et in tractatu adnotationum ad Zanchinum c. 8 quem sequitur Ioannes Rojas in dicto tract. de haeret. par. 2 assertio 15 quibus omnino censeo subscribendum: nam effractio carceris, seu fuga nihil habet commune cum haeresi et potius praesumendum est carceris taedio, aut metu falsorum testium, aut ob saevitiam tormentorum aufugisse, quam quod errore intellectus id fecerit.'

110 Peña, ibid., p. 468: 'Ad haec, nullo iure haec tam saeva Zanchini opinio comprobatur, nec videtur rationi consonum solam fugam, aut carceris effractionem, violentam generare haeresis suspicionem, ex qua fugiens aut fugeret at tentans debeat ut haereticus condemnari. Quanto igitur rectius scripserit hic Eymericus, ostendunt aperte quae proxime diximus, fuga itaque praecedenti suspicioni aliquid addit, ut docet hic auctor: id vero quantum sit, et quale ex delicti et persona qualitate et indiciis criminis prudens Inquisitor iudicabit.' See also Peña, p. 644.

111 *Contra Prospero Capellarum et Battista dale Bambine,* fol. 22r.

112 ASVe, *Contra Prospero Capellarum et Battista dale Bambine,* fols. 11r–v: 'Mi non conosco niuno; ho sette figlioli da fare a spesa et sono poveretto come Iobbe.'; 'Si l'è mio compare, e lo mi ha battizato una creattura a S. Zuliano.' 'Creature' was a term often used to describe a child who was not expected to live.

113 ASVe, *Contra Prospero Capellarum et Battista dale Bambine,* fols. 12v–13v. Camillo would also be brought into the tribunal and interrogated, but he mostly provided evidence concerning Prospero and Battista, and was not asked about his own activities, probably due to a lack of evidence other than Battista's vague references (see fols. 25v–26v).

114 ASVe, *Contra Prospero Capellarum et Battista dale Bambine,* fols. 13v–14r: 'Allora fu introd[ot]to nel Santa Tribunale et alla presen[za] del d[e]tto Battista Prospero Capellaro. E le fu domandato ut infra.' Battista, on 6

Oct. 1573, would be conducted to the torture chamber, a year after these confrontational tactics had not worked (fol. 41v).

115 Tedeschi, 'Organization and Procedures,' p. 132; for confrontation, p. 139.

116 Masini, *Sacro Arsenale*, p. 142: 'Lette adunque giudizialmente al Reo negativo le deposizioni de' testimoni nel modo che già s'è detto, si faranno venire in faccia di lui ad uno ad uno separatamente; e dato a ciascuno di essi il giuramento alla presenza d'esso Reo e anco al medesimo Reo, e riconosciutisi il Reo e i testimoni vicendevolmente, dovranno i testimoni in faccia al detto Reo ratificare e confermare le cose che l'altra volta contro di lui deposero, nella forma che segue: [. . .].'

117 Masini, ibid., p. 139: 'Et sibi dicto, quod haec sunt subterfugia et frivole excusationes quibus se tegere inaniter conatur. Et quid dicet, si aderunt aliqui, qui affirmabunt in eius faciem, quod talia et talia, tali tempore et loco dixerit ac fecerit respective?'

118 Peña, *Directorium Inquisitorum*, p. 526: '[. . .] maiores Inquisitores consulant certe in supremo senatu Sacrosanctae et generalis Inquisitionis Romanae nunquam fiunt huiusmodi confrontationes, nisi re cognita et decreto interposito per Illustrimos cardinales in tota Christiana repub. Inquisitores generalies; ut vel hinc caeteri intelligant quam caute in re tam periculosa sit progrediendum.'; Farinacci, *Tractatus*, pp. 201–2. Farinacci also included another technique to use in the tribunal when the deponent did not know the criminal by name – a line-up, with the witness hidden, to identify the correct suspect, a process which Masini also described (although this procedure must not have been employed at all regularly in practice.)

119 Masini, *Sacro Arsenale*, p. 140: 'E negando egli tuttavia, si esorti a dir la verità così: Et sibi dicto, quod bene advertat dicere veritatem et caveat a mendaciis, quoniam aderunt, qui contrarium omnino in eius faciem deponent.'

120 Masini, ibid., p. 139: 'E se pure starà saldo nella sua ostinazione, gli si farà nuova istanza in questa foggia: Et denuo sibi dicto, quod omissis huiusmodi ambagibus et subterfugiis, velit se resolvere vritatem dicere, si praemissa omnia et singula (ut supra) dixerit et fecerit.'

121 ASVe, *Sant'Uffizio*, Busta 8, *Contra Prospero Capellarum et Battista dale Bambine, 1572–73*, fol. 14r: 'Non che non gli ho insegnato, non la so per me, volere che l'insegno ad altr[i]?'

122 ASVe, *Sant'Uffizio*, Busta 8, *Contra Prospero Capellarum et Battista dale Bambine, 1572–73*, fols. 15v–17r: 'Lui mi ripose che l'era gran pava de tonto a credere che una pittura de legno facesse miracoli.'; 'Dapoì che

l'cognosco, che sono circa xi o xii anni non l'ho mai visto né in giesa né a messa né a perdoni.'

123 ASVe, *Sant'Uffizio*, Busta 8, *Contra Prospero Capellarum et Battista dale Bambine, 1572–73*, fols. 19v–20r: 'Qual che ho detto, ho detto, ho detto [sic] la verità et mi sono imaginato che Prospero mi abbia accusato per uscire lui di prigione.'

124 *Contra Prospero Capellarum et Battista dale Bambine, 1572–73*, fol. 24v–25r. While Wietse de Boer has found that confession before communion in Carlo Borromeo's Counter-Reformation Milan was almost universal during this time period, other scholars have noted that clergy in other cities and provinces in Italy were not so comprehensive in its implementation. See Wietse de Boer, *Conquest of the Soul: Confession, Discipline, and Public Order in Counter-Reformation Milan* (Boston: Brill, 2001), pp. 5–42, 193–4. See also Giovanni Romeo, *Ricerche su confessione dei peccati e Inquisizione nell'Italia del Cinquecento* (Naples: Città del Sole, 1997), pp. 85–7. Romeo has estimated that in various areas of the Italian peninsula, anywhere from 10 per cent to 60 per cent of penitents confessed once a year.

125 ASVe, *Contra Prospero Capellarum et Battista dale Bambine, 1572–73*, fols. 30r–31r: 'Sono persona crassa non so né leggere né scrivere et credo che gli preghino per noi.'

126 ASVe, *Contra Prospero Capellarum et Battista dale Bambine, 1572–73*, fols. 37v–38r: 'Ei dictum, Se in questo tempo lui si communicava? Respondit: Qualche anno si, et qualche anno no.'

127 ASVe, *Contra Prospero Capellarum et Battista dale Bambine, 1572–73*, fols. 44r–v: '[. . .] sono stati due ore continue su detta porta con il concorso di molto populo.'

6. Full Confessions of Faith: Ritual Practice and Intent

1 John Tedeschi, 'The Organization and Procedures of the Roman Inquisition: A Sketch,' in *The Prosecution of Heresy: Collected Studies on the Inquisition in Early Modern Italy* (Binghamton, NY: Medieval and Renaissance Texts and Studies, 1991), p. 141; R.H. Helmholz, *The Spirit of Classical Canon Law* (Athens, GA: University of Georgia Press, 1996), pp. 346–7; see also C. 23 q. 1 c. 2; C. 23 q. 5 c. 10; and C. 23 q. 4 c. 20. C. 23 q. 1 c. 7 which provided for the confiscation of heretics' goods as punishment. See *Corpus iuris canonici*, Vol. 1, ed. Emil Friedberg and Aemilius Ludwig Richter (Leipzig: Bernhard Tauchnitz, 1879), cols. 891; 934–5; 906. For God's afflicition of Paul (Saul) with blindness on the road to Damascus, after which he converted, see Acts 9.1–19 (*HarperCollins Study*

Bible, Wayne A. Meeks, gen. ed. [New York: HarperCollins Publishers, 1989], pp. 2074–5).

2 John Tedeschi, 'Organization and Procedures,' p. 141–5; Christopher F. Black, *The Italian Inquisition* (New Haven: Yale University Press, 2009), pp. 81–8. The secondary literature Tedeschi cites is exhaustive, including Edwin Peters, *Torture* (New York: Blackwell, 1985; 2d ed. Philadelphia: University of Pennsylvania Press, 1996) and John Langbein, *Torture and the Law of Proof: Europe and England in the Ancien Régime*, rev. ed. (Chicago: University of Chicago Press, 2006). Tedeschi maintains that torture first appeared in a lay legal manual, the *Liber iuris civilis* of Verona in 1228 and was brought into the inquisitorial process thirty years later (Tedeschi, 'The Status of the Defendant before the Roman Inquisition,' in *Ketzerverfolgung im 16. und frühen 17. Jahrhundert*, ed. Hans Rudolf Guggisberg, Bernd Moeller, and Silvana Seidel Menchi [Wiesbaden: Otto Harrassowitz, 1992], p. 139); John Langbein has emphasized torture as a response to the abolishment of the use of ordeals in ecclesiastical courts at the Fourth Lateran Council of 1215 (*Torture and the Law of Proof*, pp. 5–7). R.H. Helmholz has described the legal underpinnings of the relationship between ecclesiastical courts and the secular arm; according to Helmholz, the Gregorian interpretation, in which the secular arm was thought to hold its authority from God, but through the delegation of the Church, led to conclusion that the secular arm should simply enforce the judgment of ecclesiastical courts; see Helmholz, *Spirit of Classical Canon Law*, pp. 352–5; pp. 360–4.

3 Francisco Peña, alone of all the sources consulted here, expressed the opposite opinion; he thought that torture should only be utilized to produce a confession from the suspect, and not to reconcile conflicting facts. See Peña, *Directorium Inquisitorum* (Venice: Apud Marcum Antonium Zalterium. 1595), p. 593.

4 Eymeric, *Directorium Inquisitorum*, pp. 230–1.

5 Eymeric, ibid., p. 319: '[. . .] ubi enim haec duae concurrunt, haereticum perfecte faciunt.' Eymeric attributed this definition to Thomas Aquinas in his *Summa*.

6 Eliseo Masini, *Sacro Arsenale; Overo Prattica dell'officio della S. Inquisizione*, ed. Tommaso Menghini (Rome: 1693; StaatsBibliothek Digitalisat 4 J.can.p.5504), pp. 228–9: 'Ma se il Reo durerà negando nella seconda tortura, egli purga la prima confessione e deve lasciarsi andare, quando però sia stato bastevolmente tormentato e gl'inditii non siano molto urgenti: che altrimenti si potria venire alla terza tortura.' As John Langbein has described, in secular courts of law, not only could a defendant be tortured more than two or three times, but also a confession would result in

condemnation and execution, not reconciliation and rehabilitation. See Langbein, *Torture and the Law of Proof*, pp. 12–16. Of the small percentage of those cases that utilized torture during the proceedings, it is probable that only a handful resulted in defendants who were let go because they refused to confess to any heretical crimes or intent whatsoever. John Tedeschi has cited three cases in which the defendants overcame torture and were let go, two of which occurred in 1626 and one in 1567; see Tedeschi, 'Organization and Procedures,' p. 186, ff. 117.

7 Peña, *Directorium Inquisitorum*, p. 482: 'Quare hoc articulo ita clarius est dicendum: cum delictum est semiplene probatum, vel sunt talia indicia adversus reum, ut non posit simpliciter absolvi ab instantia seu accusatione; tunc ad dilvendum delicti suspicionem tria sunt in hoc tribunali prodita remedia: purgatio canonica, de qua egit auctor in superiori modo processum fidei terminandi: abiuratio de vehementi, seu levi, de qua agit in sequentibus: et tormentum, de quo nunc differit.' Also see John Tedeschi, 'Organization and Procedures,' p. 144; Andrea Errera, '*Processus in causa fide': L'evoluzione dei manuali inquisitoriali nei secoli XVI-XVIII e il manuale inedito di un inquisitore perugino* (Bologna: Monduzzi, 2000), p. 39; and Andrea Del Col, *L'Inquisizione in Italia: Dal XII al XXI secolo* (Milan: Oscar Mondadori, 2006), p. 122.

8 Peña, *Directorium Inquisitorum*, p. 482, 'Itaque hoc remedium per torturam non differt praecipue ab aliis penes indicia aut suspiciones, ut hic videtur simpliciter velle Eymericus, ita ut quae non sufficiunt ad abiurationem, sufficiant ad torturam: quia generaliter id falsum videtur: sed differt quo ad modum infligendi, quamvis easdem ubique contingat adesse suspiciones et coniecturas. Atque haec est vera et solida doctrina, comprobata etiam per Madrilianam instructionem anno Domini MDXLXI c. 46. 47. et 48. quae suis locis retulimus.'

9 Peña, ibid., p. 482, '[. . .] ut talia indicia concurrant contra reum, ex quibus non possit tuto imponi abiuratio de vehementi, aut alia gravior, cum ea sit gravissima poenae ob periculum relabendi: ea tamen indicia sufficientia indicabuntur ad torturam infligendam, quae non est adeo periculosa, ut per eam indagetur veritas [. . .].'

10 Peña, ibid., p. 483, 'Non ergo loquitur de eo, qui iuxta qualitatem indiciorum omnia iam tormenta superavit, sed de illo qui licet semel fuerit pro illa vice sufficienter tortus, adhuc tamen secundum iura remanet torquendus, quod indiciant apertissime illa verba: "Ad continuandum tormenta, non ad iterandum".' Eliseo Masini, in his manual, described differing methods of torture extensively; he described the *tormento del fuoco*, or torment by fire, the application of screws to the ankles, and beat-

ings with sticks, in order to torture those who were not strong enough to undergo 'the cord,' the usual method of torture. Masini, *Sacro Arsenale*, pp. 216–19.

11 Peña, *Directorium Inquisitorum*, p. 485, 'Tunc autem dicitur reus tortus sufficienter, quando ita rigida inflicta est sibi tortura, ut iudicio prudentum considerata indiciorum qualitate ea ipsa indicia purgaverit et nihil fuit confessus, sed in tortura semper mansit in negative. Ut ergo intelligatur quando per torturam indicia sint purgata, commensuranda est qualitas rigiditatis inflictae torturae, cum qualitate gravitati indiciorum.' See also Tedeschi, 'Organization and Procedures,' p. 144.

12 Peña, *Directorium Inquisitorum*, p. 485: '[. . .] quod cum reus bis tortus, bis confitetur et revocat, tertio possit torqueri, et de integro quaestio haberi. Caeterum haec sentntiae multis videtur nimis crudelis, ac multis rationibus refelli potest. Primum, quia nulla lege certae miti cur rursus, quia confessio secunda facta in tormentis non generat novum indicium, cum sit eadem cum prima confessione tandem, quoniam qua ratione per torquetur, posset et pluries torqueri, cum nulla diversitatis ratio commoda assignari possit. Quare benignius et securis est, ne quis ob revocatam confessionem tertio torqueatur: nam hoc praeterquam quod nulla certa lege cavetur, crudele etiam nimis, et inhumanum videtur.'

13 Tedeschi, 'Organization and Procedures,' pp. 141–3; Giulio Claro wrote the *Decisiones criminals super quaestionibus de indiciis et tortura*, saying that his manual did not examine theory or doctrine, but was expressly devoted to practice (quoted in Niccolò Del Re, 'Prospero Farinacci giureconsulto romano (1544–1618),' in *Archivio della Società romana di Storia patria* 97 [1975]: 135–200, esp. p. 171). Boërius, or Nicolas de Bohier (or Boyer, 1469–1539) published three works in the sixteenth century: *Tractatus de officio et potestate legati a latere in regno Françiœ* (1509); *Tractatus de seditiosis* (1515); *Concilia seu responsa juris* (1554). See R. Naz, 'Bohier, Nicolas (ou Boyer),' in the *Dictionnaire de droit canonique*, Vol. 2, ed. R. Naz (Paris: Librairie Letouzey et Ané, 1937), p. 930.

14 Peña, *Directorium Inquisitorum*, p. 485, p. 115: 'Atque ex hac interpretatione, quae semper mihi verior visa est, refellitur sententia Cardinalis in Clemen. I de usuris § sane q. 22 nume. 12 et Francisci Squillacensis tracta. de fide catho. cap. 31 num. 1 et quorundam aliorum asserentium, reum vehementer suspectum prius torquendum: quod si nihil confiteatur, purgationem ei esse indicendam, et si fuerit expurgatus tandem ut abiurare quoque compellatur: nam haec sententia nimis est saeva, et cum unaquaeque; harum poenarum sit efficax ad tollendam suspicionem, plane iniquum est reum tot poenis subiicere. ita Simancas de cathol. Instit. tit. 56 num. 18 et seq.'

In the bull *Inter sollicitudines*, the original passage read '[. . .] donec scandalum sopiatur, ita tamen ut publice familiaritatem haereticourm abiuret' (X 5.34.10)

15 Cesare Carena, *Tractatus de Officio Sanctissimae Inquisitionis* (Cremona: Apud Marc'Antonium Belpierum, 1636), p. 23: 'Quod si ob aliquam rationem et causam visum fuerit consideratis praedictis qualitatibus tormentum non fuisse inflictum, cum debito rigore, tunc imponere ei poterunt abiurationem de levi, vel de vehementi, aut aliquam poenam pecuniariam.'

16 Prospero Farinacci, *Tractatus de haeresi* (Cremona: Apud Marc'Antonium Belpierum, 1636), p. 149: 'Dic arbitrio Iudicis relinqui, quae sint indicia sufficientia ad torquendum in crimine haeresis: ut in specie per Campeggius [. . .] Francisco Pegna in additionibus ad Eymeric. in Direct[orium] Inquis[orum] par. 2 comment. 39 littera D fol. mihi 518 col. 2, ubi dixit quod licet indicia ad torturam sint Iudici arbitraria non tamen proinde temerie, et in qualibet causa sunt adhibenda tormenta, nec ex quilibet indiciis, nisi illis, quae de iure subsistant et approbentur.' Farinacci also referred his readers to Campeggi's edition of Ugolini, and Juan de Rojas.

17 Carena, *Tractatus*, p. 171; Masini, *Sacro Arsenale*, pp. 209–10, 214–15; Farinacci, *Tractatus*, p. 149.

18 Peña, *Directorium Inquisitorum*, p. 324: 'In his ergo breviter more nostro certiora tradentes, primum statuendum est, in arduis et horrendis factis non esse praesumendam oblivionem: nam ut Plinius affirmat, in rebus arduis non laeditur, aut altaretur memoria.'

19 Carena, *Tractatus*, p. 21: 'Haec tamen Farinatii Doctrina non est ita indistincte accipienda, sed duo factorum genera sunt distinguenda, Alia namque sunt clara et manifeste haeresim significant, ut quia cum ad ea natura proni minime simus, non ob aliud gesta intelligunt, quam ob errorem intellectus cui sunt Adoratio Mahumetis, re iudaizatio circumcisio et simila.'; Farinacci, *Tractatus*, p. 5: 'Et quidem in supremo et generali Christianae Reipublicae Inquisitionis Romanae Tribunali, in quo summa cum pietate, et misericordia procedi solet, magna cum circumspectione proceditur; nec ita de facili ille, qui prima facie apud aliquos negativus haberetur, ab ipso supremo Tribunali, uti talis punitetur.'

20 Tedeschi, 'Organization and Procedures,' pp. 143–4.

21 See Carena, *Tractatus*, pp. 340–1 concerning permissible excuses for eating meat during Lent. Despite the manuals' warnings against interpreting the practice as a clear indicator of heresy, as John Tedeschi notes, in 1574 Fra Paolo da Ferrara, on the staff of the Roman Congregation of Cardinals, had to write to the inquisitor of Bologna and inform him that the imprisonment

and torture of a defendant only accused of eating meat during Lent, who was willing to confess and proferred the excuse of simple forgetfulness, was badly done on the inquisitor's part. This is, most likely, what the manual authors thought would constitute a small amount of evidence indicating suspicion. See Tedeschi, 'Organization and Procedures,' pp. 153–4.

22 Peña, *Directorium Inquisitorum*, p. 323: 'Et si post torturam legitime adhibitam in negativa persistunt, dicentes se non habuisse pravam intentionem, tunc similiter abiurat ut vehementer suspecti.'

23 See Susanna Peyronel Rambaldi, *Dai Paesi Bassi all'Italia: 'Il Sommario della Sacra Scrittura': un libro proibito nella società italiana del Cinquecento* (Florence: L.S. Olschki, 1997), pp. 233, 238–9; Susanna Peyronel Rambaldi, *Speranze e crisi nel Cinquecento modenese: Tensioni religiose e vita cittadina ai tempi di Giovanni Morone* (Milan: F. Agnelli, 1979), p. 261; Michelle M. Fontaine, 'For the Good of the City: The Bishop and the Ruling Elite in Tridentine Modena,' *Sixteenth Century Journal* 28, no. 1 (Spring 1997): 34–8. Curioni's name had come up during what appears to be a voluntary reconciliation, which took place at the bishop's palace and was recorded by Foscarari's vicar in June of 1555, but the information concerning Curioni was not specific (Busta 3, par. II, 1554–1555, Libro VI, fasc. 14). Records of that process were included with the records from Curioni's process of 1568. Giovanni Terrazzano was also interrogated concerning Pietro Curioni and Paolo da Campo Gaiano in 1555 during his own process, but he denied any knowledge of Curioni's activities. Since Curioni was not accused of being a relapsed heretic, it is doubtful he was sentenced formally in 1555.

24 Salvatore Caponetto, *The Protestant Reformation in Sixteenth-Century Italy*, trans. Anne C. Tedeschi and John Tedeschi (Kirksville, MO: Thomas Jefferson University Press, 1999), p. 259; Cesare Bianco, 'La comunità di "fratelli" nel movimento ereticale modenese del '500,' *Rivista Storica Italiana* 92 (1980), pp. 671–2. This fact came out in Natale Gioioso's own inquisitorial proceeding. ASMo, *Inquisizione*, Busta 5, 1568, *Contra Natale Gioioso*, constituted 17 March 1568. Almost nothing is known of Magnavacca himself, since he was not a native of Modena.

25 ASMo, *Inquisizione*, Busta 5, *Processi 1555–1568*, *Contra Petrum Curionem*, 24 May 1568, fols 1r–v: ' Et io mi confesso due volte l'anno et mi communico due volte l'anno. Non però io è parlato (sic) del sacramento dell'Eucharistia in detta mia b[o]ttega.'

26 ASMo, *Contra Petrum Curionem*, 24 May 1568, fols. 1v–2r: 'Gli predetto dicano nella mia b[o]ttega che si può mangiare carne ogni giorni indifferenza senza peccato. Et dicevano ancora che il papà è Antichristo è non

vicario della chiesa ma io non lo dissi mai né lo cred[u]t[o] mai ancora ho creduto che sia Vicario de Christo.'

27 ASMo, *Contra Petrum Curionem*, 24 May 1568, fol. 2v: '[. . .] detto Cervia io ebbi sospetto che fosse cattivo e però io mi avrò che l'ebbi lo gettai via per non vederlo anch'io mai più.' See also Christopher F. Black, *Italian Inquisition*, pp. 84, 222.

28 ASMo, *Contra Petrum Curionem*, fol. 4v: 'Io sono tornato per venire a giustificare che quello ch'io ho fatto fugendo l'ho fatto per fall[ato] et timore et per tornare al grembo della Santa Madre Chiesa, e vivere Christianamente.'

29 ASMo, *Contra Petrum Curionem*, fols. 4v–5r: 'Et dico ch'io ho creduto et tenuto che le Indulgentie papali non siano di alcuno valore et che il Papà non fosse Vicario di Christo in terra, et che [gli] su[i] leggi non fossero da tale osservate. Et che nell'altra vita non sia il purgatorio et conseguentemente i suffragi de bene non giovano a[gli] Morti, ondé lo fatto dell'ellemosine per amor di Dio. Et che le immagin[e] de Dio e de[gli] santi non si debbano riverire né adorare, et che gli santi non si debbano invocare per interventari per noi, appresso Dio, ma solo Giesù Christo.'

30 ASMo, *Contra Petrum Curionem*, fol. 5v.

31 ASMo, *Contra Petrum Curionem*, fol. 6v–7r: 'Io sempre creduto che la confessione sacramentale sia necessario al Christiano et che possa che absolutione de[gli] suoi peccat[i] dal sacerdote et sempre mi sono confessato ne[gli] tempi determinati dalla Chiesa.'; 'Respondit: Si assolumente convinco et avere creduto che il corpo di Giesù Christo realmente sia nell'ostia consecrate.'

32 See, for example, the evidence presented concerning the *fratelli*'s Suppers by Pietro Antonio da Cervia during the course of his process held in Bologna. John A. Tedeschi and Josephine von Henneberg, eds. and trans., 'Contra Petrum Antonium a Cervia Relapsum et Bononiae Concrematum,' in *Italian Reformation Studies in Honor of Laelius Socinus*, ed. John A. Tedeschi (Florence: Felice Le Monnier, 1965), pp. 245–6.

33 ASMo, *Contra Petrum Curionem*, fols. 7v–8v.

34 ASMo, *Contra Petrum Curionem*, fol. 9v: 'Et sit ellevatus et sit clamare dicens "O Padre, abbia misercordia . . . io non so che dice prego Iddio che mi avrà cascare quale sudette s'io so altro, et se conosco altri complici o eretici et se né havesse conosciuto né me gli riccordo."'; 'che la confessione de[gli] peccati al sacerdote è necessaria per ottenere l'absolutione da lui et che nell'ostia sacra sia realmente il corpo di Giesù Christo.'; 'Instituit ipsum unus oritum torqueri qui tortus esse coepit clamare dicens "O Dio, Dio, io non so pigliano, io non so pigliano!"'

35 ASMo, *Contra Petrum Curionem*, fol. 10r–v.

36 John Jeffries Martin, *Venice's Hidden Enemies: Italian Heretics in a Renaissance City* (Berkeley and Los Angeles: University of California Press, 1993), pp. 144–6.

37 ASVe, *Sant'Uffizio*, Busta 22, fasc. 2, *Contra Odoricum Grisonium et complices*, fol. 21r: 'Io non so fermamente che lui tenesse di queste opinione nuove.'

38 ASVe, *Contra Odoricum Grisonium et complices*, fol. 25r-fol. 26r: 'Et dicto [sic] se vi fosse detto il nome di questo bresciano ve ne ricordarle? Respondit: No, perché non l'ho mai sapevuto.'

39 ASVe, *Contra Odoricum Grisonium et complices*, fols. 29v–32r, esp. 30v: 'Chi fu quello che persuasse esso constituto a comprare la scrittura? Respondit: Nel mio cervello.'; 'Et se gli ho mai sentito nominare o dire che alcuni se rebatt[ez]za[va]no.' Martin, *Venice's Hidden Enemies*, p. 144. Father Troilo, according to Sambeni, thought it appropriate to absolve 'secret' religious doubts in the confessional without referring Sambeni to a tribunal to self-denounce; concerning the controversy about that practice, see Lavenia, *L'Infamia e il perdono: Tributi, pene e confessione nella teologia morale della prima età moderna* (Bologna: Il Mulino, 2004), pp. 286–99.

40 ASVe, *Contra Odoricum Grisonium et complices*, fols. 33r–v: 'Fu avvertito et ammonito a dire la verità, de plano che altramente il Santo Offitio non potrà mancare di volerlo per gli termini rigorosi della giusti[z]ia.'

41 ASVe, *Contra Odoricum Grisonium et complices*, fols. 34v–35r.

42 ASVe, *Contra Odoricum Grisonium et complices*, unpg.; Farinacci, *Tractatus*, pp. 189–90: '[. . .] eo qui sanctissimo Sacramento dum elevaretur, tecto capite oculisque ad terram fixis, nullam praestitit reverentiam et his simila et n. 21 ubi de eo qui domi suae nullas Sanctorum imagines tenebat.'

43 ASVe, *Contra Odoricum Grisonium et complices*, fols. 43v–44v; Martin, *Venice's Hidden Enemies*, p. 199. Valtellina and Chiavenna were well known as locations, beyond Venetian jurisdiction, with Italian-speaking Protestant churches; Pier Paolo Vergerio and Agostino Mainardi were among the formerly Catholic who led congregations there. See Silvano Cavazza, 'Pier Paolo Vergerio nei Grigioni e in Valtellina (1549–1553): Attività editoriale e polemica religiosa,' in *Riforma e società nei Grigioni: Valtellina e Valchiavenna tra '500 e '600*, ed. Alessandro Pastore (Milan: Franco Agnelli, 1991): 33–62.

44 Farinacci, *Tractatus*, p. 30.

45 ASVe, *Contra Odoricum Grisonium et complices*, fols. 36r–37r.

46 ASVe, *Contra Odoricum Grisonium et complices*, fols. 38r–v: 'Non ma solo prego [gli] Signori Vostri che mi abbia pietà et che non voglia riguardare alla mia ignoran[za]; non avendo fallato per malititia [malignità] perché sono buon Christiano et volgio vivere et morire come fanno gli buoni

Christiani et essere obediente alla Santa Madre Chiesa in tutto quello che la comanda. Et di eis non habere aliquid aliud dicere pro defensione sua. Et cum maxima submissione genu flexis.'

47 ASVe, *Contra Odoricum Grisonium et complices*, fol. 39r: 'Constitutus ad locum solitum tortura coram Reverendis Vicario et Padre Fra Eliseo commisario cum assistentia Excellentissimi D. Federico Barbadico et D. Andrae Baduario Baptista tintor [. . .] se tu avevi altri errori et maggiore di questi, et quali et gli tuoi compagni et complici in simile materia et con quelli che tu hai conferito le tue opinione.' Federico Valaresso, a layman, was also involved in the case; as were the Patriarch Giovanni Trevisan, the nuncio Giovanni Antonio Facchinetti, and the general inquisitor.

48 Farinacci, *Tractatus*, p. 294; Eymeric, *Directorium Inquisitorum*, p. 524, Peña, p. 525. The Venetian government wished to avoid the potential civil unrest that could be caused by public executions; see Martin, *Venice's Hidden Enemies*, pp. 68–9.

49 Walter Wakefield and Austin P. Evans, 'Bernard Gui's Description of Heresies,' in *Heresies of the High Middle Ages*, ed. and trans. Wakefield and Evans (New York: Columbia University Press, 1969), pp. 397–8; also excerpted in James B. Given, *Inquisition and Medieval Society: Power, Discipline, and Resistance in Languedoc* (Ithaca: Cornell University Press, 1997), pp. 46–7.

50 ASVe, *Contra Odoricum Grisonium et complices*, fol. 39v: 'Fuit sibi dictum: Per rigor del processo si conosca che tu hai creduto altro di quello hai confessato. Respondit: Mi credo quello che confessa il Credo, et quello che dice il Credo. Interrogatus: Oltre il credo non credes (sic) tu anche nella Chiesa? Respondit: Mi credo nella Santa Chiesa. Interrogatus: Che intendes tu per questa chiesa? Respondit: Dico alle excellissimus Signori la unione de[gli] fideli cristiani. Interrogatus: Quale questa unione de Cristiani? Respondit: Credo che questa Santa Chiesa et questi fideli Cristiani che voi mi domand[at]e sono quelli che hanno posta la sua speranza in Giesù figliuolo di Dio vivo. Fuit sibi dictum: Queste sono parole che dicono tutti gli eretici; però debbi dire la distintione vera degli fedeli Cristiani da[gli] eretici.' These beliefs were expressed by other heterodox in Venice and elsewhere during their processes; while it was a nondogmatic formulation of church membership, probably intended to embrace as wide a variety of Protestant opinions as possible, it also provided defendants with evasive language to utilize during inquisition processes. The notary, in this exchange, 'Latinized' a few of the verbs.

51 ASVe, *Contra Odoricum Grisonium et complices*, fol. 39v–40r: 'Anzi qualmente et sempre et ultimamente nel Concilio di Trento è stato determinato

et si crede da tutti gli Cattolici di Christo quelli soli esser[e] salvi, che credono quello crede la Santa Romana et Apostolica Chiesa et tutti gli altri contrari a questa fede sono dannati, et tenuti per eretici?'; 'Non so, non posso giudicare questo, che non so il cuore delle persone et non posso fare questo giudi[z]io.'

52 Farinacci, *Tractatus*, p. 188: 'Limita II Quia verba dubia tunc demum interpretanda sunt in bonum sensum quando fuerint prolata sine dolo; secus si cum dolo secundum Menoch. [. . .] ubi tamen subdit, in dubio dolum non praesumi.'; 'Rojas, in tr. De haereticis par. Prima n. 205 et seqq. Praesertim, ut ipse inquit hac nostra tempestate in haereticis et Lutheranis, qui verba obscura et ambigua passim decipiendos et inquinandos Catholicorum animos, proferre solent et nu. 379 et seqq.' Juan de Rojas, educated in canon and civil law at Salamanca, was inquisitor of Valenica, among other positions, before becoming bishop of Agrigento and inquisitor of Sicily in 1577 (shortly before his death in 1578). His work, *De haereticis*, was part of a longer work he had published in Spain in 1566. It was published in Venice for the first time in 1583, and reprinted by Peña in 1584 in Rome. Peña cited Rojas extensively beginning in his 1587 commentaries concerning the *Directorium Inquisitorum*. See John Tedeschi, 'Royas, Juan de,' in *Dizionario storico dell'Inquisizione*, Vol. 3, ed. Adriano Prosperi with Vincenzo Lavenia and John Tedeschi (Pisa: Scuola Normale Superiore Pisa, 2010), p. 1337.

53 ASVe, *Contra Odoricum Grisonium et complices*, fols. 40v–41r.

54 ASVe, *Contra Odoricum Grisonium et complices*, fol. 41v: 'Io confesso Clarissimi Signori che credo che quello che crede la Santa Chiesa Cattolica et Apostolica, come si dice nel credo nella Santa Messa'; 'Respondit: Di questo non so giudicare, e non so giudice perché sono un minimo vermo.'; 'Ei dicto domanda se lo Santo Evangelio dice che il Papà sia vicario di Christo o no? Respondit: In quel che ho letto non l'ho trovato.' Protestant theologians often endorsed the formulas of faith produced by early Church councils, and the legitimacy of those councils; see, for example, Pietro Martire Vermigli's 'Whether Evangelicals Are Schismatics for Having Separated from the Papists,' trans. Mariano di Gagni and Joseph C. McLelland, in *The Peter Martyr Library*, Vol. 1, *Early Writings: Creed, Scripture, Church*, ed. Joseph C. McLelland (Kirksville, MO: Sixteenth Century Essays and Studies, 1994), pp. 171–224; and 'The Apostles' Creed: A Plain Exposition of the Twelve Articles of the Christian Faith,' trans. Mariano di Gagni, in *Early Writings*, Vol. 1, pp. 27–79.

55 Peña, *Directorium Inquisitorum*, p. 23; Farinacci, *Tractatus*, p. 9; both authors discussed the use of Church councils' articles and canons to more generally confirm the faith of the defendant.

56 ASVe, *Contra Odoricum Grisonium et complices*, fols. 43v–44v; Martin, *Venice's Hidden Enemies*, p. 199.

57 See John Tedeschi, 'Organization and Procedures,' p. 128. Inquisitorial manuals produced in the sixteenth and seventeenth centuries describe the jurisdictional issues involved; see, for example, Cesare Carena, p. 434. In addition, the diocesan bishop participated in inquisitorial processes even when there was an inquisitor in the diocese; as John Tedeschi has noted, the bishop, or his designated vicar, had to be present, and agree, concerning the use of torture or the defendant's final abjuration and sentence. See John Tedeschi, 'The Status of the Defendant before the Roman Inquisition,' in *Ketzerverfolgung im 16. und frühen 17. Jahrhundert: Vorträge gehalten anlässlich eines Arbeitsgesprächs vom 1. bis 5. Oktober 1989 in der Herzog August Bibliothek Wolfenbüttel*, ed. Hans Rudolf Guggisberg, Silvana Seidel Menchi, and Bernd Moeller, pp. 125–46, esp. p. 142. Andrea Del Col has described the jurisdictional arrangements for the Friuli extensively; see 'Shifting Attitudes in the Social Environment toward Heretics: The Inquisition in the Friuli in the Sixteenth Century,' in *Ketzerverfolgung im 16. und frühen 17. Jahrhundert*, esp. pp. 66–7; Del Col, *L'Inquisizione nel Patriarcato e diocesi di Aquileia, 1557–59* (Trieste: Edizioni Università di Trieste; Centro studi storici Menocchio, 1998), pp. xxii–ccxxiii. Venice had some resident inquisitors beginning in the medieval period until 1547; in the 1530s, the Holy See began to utilize nuncios (papal ambassadors) to Venice to supervise relations between inquisitors and the Venetian government since the Council of Ten, responsible for criminal justice, had attempted to interfere in several high-profile cases. See Andrea Del Col, 'Organizzazione, composizione e giurisdictione de tribunali dell'Inquisizione Romana nella republica di Venezia (1500–1550),' *Critica storica* 25 (1988): 247–8, 259–70. Del Col also has pointed out that from 1542 until the 1550s, local bishops, nuncios, and commissaries were just as important, if not more so, than inquisition tribunals in prosecuting heresy; see 'I rapporti tra i giudicci di fede in Italia d dal medioevo all'età contemporanea,' in *I Tribunali della fede: Continuità e discontinuità dal medioevo all'età moderna; Atti del XLV Convegno di studi sulla Riforma e sui movimenti religiosi in Italia, Torre Pellice, 3–4 settembre 2005*, ed. Susanna Peyronel Rambaldi (Turin: Claudiana, 2007), pp. 93–9,

58 Andrea Del Col, 'Inquisition in the Friuli,' p. 69; Del Col describes heresy has having 'several hundred adherents.' Udine was also proselytized intensively by Pier Paolo Vergerio; his sister, Coletta, was a nun in the Clarist convent of San Francesco. She and some of her fellow nuns were converted to Lutheranism, as would others in the town. A certain Nicola

of Treviso would later proselytize Anabaptist beliefs in the area. See Caponetto, *Protestant Reformation*, p. 193.

59 Andrea Del Col, 'L'abiura trasformata in propaganda ereticale nel duomo di Udine (15 Aprile 1544),' *Metodi e ricerche* 2 (1981): 57–72. ASVe, *Sant'Uffizio*, Busta 1, Fasc. 2, *Contra Calegaro Girolamo, Francesco Garzoso, Francesco da Milano, Cavallo Alvise, Venier Girolamo, Percotto Pietro, e Patrizio (prete) Udine*), fol. 13v: 'Che ha[nno] tutto a dire de Maestro Hieronymo caleger che l'è eretico e che fin in Vene[z]ia era da questa sorte e che sia publico eretico e che niun lo potrà vedere e che esso Hieronymo può dire con verità che mai ha visto esso Maestro Hieronymo a missa.' Although Andrea Del Col has referred to Girolamo as 'Hieronymo,' an archivist rendered the name as 'Girolamo' when listing the trial records; for the sake of consistency, so have I.

60 ASVe, Fasc. 2, *Contra Calegaro Girolamo*, fols. 15r–v.

61 ASVe, Fasc. 2, *Contra Calegaro Girolamo*, fols. 23v–24v.

62 ASVe, Fasc. 2, *Contra Calegaro Girolamo*, fols. 25v–26r: '[. . .] et quando passa il sacramento per innanzi la sua bottega non se ha inginocchiato ma ben il faceva la baretta [il berretto].'

63 ASVe, Fasc. 2, *Contra Calegaro Girolamo*, fols. 26v–27r; Del Col, 'L'abiura trasformata,' pp. 57–61. See also Caponetto, *Protestant Reformation*, pp. 32–4. Curione was a humanist-trained schoolteacher; he fled north and took refuge in Lausanne and Basel.

64 Peña, *Directorium Inquisitorum*, p. 617–19; Eymeric, pp. 615–16.

65 ASVe, Fasc. 2 *Contra Calegaro Girolamo*, fols. 36r–37v: 'Il è vero, che non mi ho inginocchiato ma ben mi ho cavata la berretta et non mi ho fatto riso d'alcuno che accompagni il Sacramento del corpo di Christo.'; ' Che con la fede si riverisce il sacramento et Iddio, et per questo non ho realizzato che non gli abbia avuto la debita riveren[za].'

66 ASVe, Fasc. 2, *Contra Calegaro Girolamo*, fols. 36r–37v: 'Respondit: Io dico et respondo quanto ho detto di sopra e credo che la sia recta dal spirito santo questa chiesa santa (sic), della qual sopra ho detto, e che per questa tal chiesa non può errare. [Dicens tandem] che l'ho [tenuto] la chiesa Romana per capo di questa unioni christiani.' It was the notary who wrote 'recta' in Latin.

67 ASVe, Fasc. 2, *Contra Calegaro Girolamo*, fols. 37v–38r.

68 ASVe, Fasc. 2, *Contra Calegaro Girolamo*, fols. 38v–39r: 'Avere [sic] detto questo che non potremo (sic)fare [l']opera buona senza la grazia di Christo.' *Tre Mure* was an Italian abbreviation for Martin Luther's *An den christlichen Adel deutscher Nation von des christlichen Standes Besserung* ('Address to the German Nobility Concerning Christian Liberty'); the

full Italian title was *Libro della emendazione e correzione dello stato cristiano*. See Silvana Seidel Menchi, 'Le traduzione di Lutero nella prima metà del Cinquecento,' *Rinascimento*, ser. II, 17 (1977): 31–109, esp. 97. Pascaleo had been professor of Thomistic theology at Sant'Agostino in Padua from 1518 to 1531, and again breifly from 1533 to 1535; ironically enough, Pietro Martire Vermigli, the future Reformed theologian, attended his lectures. As bishop of Chioggia, he became known for his reform efforts, and activities to deal with Lutheran heresy, which probably accounts for his involvement in the process. He died in Udine on Christmas Day, 1544. See Philip McNair, *Peter Martyr in Italy: An Anatomy of Apostasy* (Oxford: Clarendon Press, 1967), pp. 104–5.

69 ASVe, Fasc. 2, *Contra Calegaro Girolamo*, fols. 40r–v. Andrea Del Col has found other sources that corroborate Garzotto's perception of numbers; see Del Col, 'L'abiura trasformata,' p. 58. The other two defendants interrogated, Alvise Cavallo and the priest Patricio, also gave full confessions and abjured.

70 ASVe, Fasc. 2, *Contra Calegaro Girolamo*, fol. 52r: '[. . .] et postea ligatus fuit . . . interrogatus de complicibus. Repsondit pro ut supra, et nescire de aliis nisi de primo loco nominatis in eius constitutus.'

71 ASVe, Fasc. 2, *Contra Calegaro Girolamo*, fols. 52r–v; fol. 53r for the additional testimonies. On fol. 59v, in a further summary, the tribunal noted that Girolamo had been minimally tortured due to a physical impediment of some kind.

72 ASVe, Fasc. 2, *Contra Calegaro Girolamo*, fols. 57r–v.

73 ASVe, Fasc. 2, *Contra Calegaro Girolamo*, fols. 59r–61r.

74 Del Col, 'L'abiura trasformata,' pp. 57–72; ASVe, Fasc. 2, *Contra Calegaro Girolamo*, fol. 70v: '[. . .] et asserta confessio et praemisso non fuit libera, sed coacta metu tormentorum'; 'Quae dictus Magister Hieronymus est vir probus, honestus, Catholice, et Christiane vivens.'

75 ASVe, *Sant'Uffizio*, Busta 1, Fasc. 3, *Contra Calegaro Girolamo*, fol. 94v: 'Et perché se dissi altramente, Io dissi male.' 'Per ho creduto che non l'havere (sic) mai detto, et se lo dissi io dissi male.' See also Ulrich Zwingli, 'Choice and Liberty Respecting Food,' p. 94.

76 On 6 May 1544, Pietro made his own abjuration, in which he confessed that he had helped Girolamo write the altered abjuration. Pietro denied having been given any documents from Girolamo's process to read, and in his confession he specified that his only access to the proceedings came from the shoemaker himself; see ASVe, *Sant'Uffizio*, Busta 1, Fasc. 3, *Contra Calegaro Girolamo*, fols. 1–2v. See Peyronel Rambaldi, *Dai Paesi Bassi*, pp. 186–216.

77 ASVe, Fasc. 2, *Contra Calegaro Girolamo,* fol. 66r.

78 ASVe, Fasc. 2, *Contra Calegaro Girolamo,* fols. 70v–71r.

79 ASVe, Fasc. 2, *Contra Calegaro Girolamo,* fol. 66v: 'Opponitur praetera quo ad depositionem quinto testis de 40 dum dicit quae in transitu sacramenti me apot[h]ecam dici inquisiti ipse aufug[e]re intra domum quia ipse testis non probare in unicus et singulis et de audire alieno deponens.'; 'et esse singularis et unicus; et si dictum unius dictum nullis.'

80 ASVe, Fasc. 2, *Contra Calegaro Girolamo,* fol. 70v: '[. . .] et asserta confessio et praemisso non fuit libera, sed coacta metu tormentorum'; 'Quae dictus Magister Hieronymus est vir probus, honestus, Catholice, et Christiane vivens.'

81 ASVe, Fasc. 2, *Contra Calegaro Girolamo,* fols. 77r–79r.

82 As his source, Farinacci read Martin V's apostolic letter in Peña's edition of Eymeric; Farinacci, *Tractatus,* p. 316: 'incipien[s] relata per Francis[us] Pegna, fol. mihi 98 in litteras apostolicis,' and Peña, 'Litterae apostolicae pro Officio Sanctissimae Inquisitionis,' an appendix to the *Directorium Inquisitorum,* pp. 68–76; Carena, *Tractatus,* p. 43: 'Praxis contra hos impoenitentes est, ut diu in carceribus detineantur, saepius moneantur, ut convertantur, quod si noluerint poenitere tradendi sunt curiae seeculari, ut vivi comburantur, ita Pegna p. 2 comm. 65 vers. in his, Farin. d. q. 196 n. 4 et seq. ubi alii allegantur, Non obstantibus iis quae in contrarium ab haereticis alligatur, ex. Matth. 13 vers. 30 finite utraque [. . .].'

83 ASVe, Fasc. 2, *Contra Calegaro Girolamo,* fols. 85v–87v.

84 ASVe, Fasc. 3, *Contra Calegaro Girolamo,* fols. unp.: '[. . .] che sed[ot]to et fraudulamente [i]ngan[n]ato da Pietro per c[a]usa in luo[g]o della vera abiuratione reciti il contrario si come lui confesso et abiuro dove io al presente confesso al mio fallo et abiuro nella forma soprascritta et cerco l'absolu[z]ione dalli prelati della Santa Chiesa et la contegna peniten[za] delli miei errori.' This document was extracted from the full process on 21 February 1544 by Fra Marino *il zotto,* discussed below.

85 ASVe, Fasc. 3, *Contra Calegaro Girolamo,* fol. unp.: '[. . .] detto Magistro calegaro cond[an]nato per il Reverendo vicario patriarchale per imputa[z]ione di eresia al pena capital[e] et dirli tutto quello mi occorresse in questo proposito, onde non posse[de]ndo dare a quelle più particolar[e], et più sincera informa[z]ione che mandarli il processo sopra di ciò formate, Immediate ordini al cancellario che il prefatto Reverendo vicario che devesse estrarre la copia del tutto il processo, il quale mo [ora] terzo giorno me lo ha pensato tutto confuso.' See also Andrea Del Col, 'Shifting Attitudes,' p. 72.

86 Silvana Seidel Menchi, 'The Inquisitor as Mediator,' in *Heresy, Culture, and Religion in Early Modern Italy: Contexts and Contestations,* ed. Ronald

K. Delph, Michelle M. Fontaine, and John Jeffries Martin (Kirksville, MO: Truman State University Press, 2006), pp. 173–92; Seidel Menchi, 'Marino da Venezia,' in *Dizionario storico dell'Inquisizione,* Vol. 2, p. 987. Within the next decade or two, Fra Marino would be the subject of an investigation conducted by his successor as inquisitor of Venice, precisely because of his leniency toward defendants. See also Del Col, 'Organizzazione,' pp. 263–4.

87 ASVe, Fasc. 3, *Contra Calegaro Girolamo,* fol. unpg.: '[. . .] qui post abiurationem errois, vel postquam se proprii antistitis examinatione purgaverint, si deprehensi fuerint in abiurationem haeresim recidisse, saeculari decernuntur iudicio, sine ulla penitus audientia relinquendi.' See also Eymeric's *Directorium Inquisitorum,* p. 105, where Eymeric repeated canonical decretals in full, and X.5.7.9 (*Corpus iuris canonici,* Vol. 2 [Leipzig: Bernhard Tauchnitz, 1881], col. 780).

88 ASVe, Fasc. 3, *Contra Calegaro Girolamo,* fol. unpg.: 'Laicus autem, nisi (prout dictum est) abiurata haeresi et satisfactione exhibita, confestim ad fidem orthodoxam, saecularis iudicis arbitrio relinquatur, debitam recepturus, pro qualitate facinoris ultionem et infra.' Bernard of Parma (d. 1266), a thirteenth-century canonist, taught at Bologna after studying under Tancred. He wrote the *Glossa Ordinaria* for the *Liber Extra* (James Brundage, *Medieval Canon Law* [New York: Longman, 1995], p. 210).

89 ASVe, fasc. 3, *Contra Calegaro Girolamo,* unpg., letter of Fra Marino, dated 12 October 1544. In arguing for Girolamo's ignorance and lesser degree of culpability, Marino was referring to the same aspects of canon law as Egidio Foscarari (in chapter four), who also utilized *Ad abolendam* to argue for the lesser culpability of laypeople. Marino also utilized c. 9 of *De poenitentia.*

90 ASVe, fasc. 3, *Contra Calegaro Girolamo,* unpg., defence document submitted 1 February 1544: 'Quia impoenitens dici non potest, cui poenitentia absque peccato iniusta est, praefuit praefato Messer Hieronimo [. . .].'

91 Busdrago sat in for Giovanni della Casa during processes as his representative, including that of Pier Paolo Vergerio (see Anne Jacobsen Schutte, *Pier Paolo Vergerio: The Making of an Italian Reformer* [Geneva: Libraire Droz, 1977], pp. 219, 248, 251.) Both Busdrago and Fra Marino were present in Venice in 1543–1544, along with the nuncio Della Casa. According to Del Col, Busdrago and Della Casa were more powerful than Fra Marino; see Del Col, 'Organizzazione,' pp. 264–5 and 'Della Casa, Giovanni,' in *Dizionario storico dell'Inquisizione,* Vol. 1, pp. 459–60.

92 Clem. 5.3.1; *Corpus iuris canonici,* Vol. 2, cols. 1181–2; ASVe, fasc. 3, *Contra Calegaro Girolamo,* unpg. letter of Gherardo Busdrago.

93 John Tedeschi has stated that this was intended to prevent abuse; 'Organization and Procedures,' pp. 141–4. See also Peña in his commentaries, *Directorium Inquisitorum*, pp. 577–81.

94 ASVe, Fasc. 3, *Contra Calegaro Girolamo*, unpg., session of 14 January 1545; see also Tedeschi, 'Organization and Procedures,' p. 143.

95 Eymeric, *Directorium Inquisitorum*, pp. 446, 485.

96 Silvana Seidel Menchi, 'Italy,' trans. Anne Jacobsen Schutte, in *The Reformation in National Context*, ed. Bob Scribner, Roy Porter, and Mikuláš Teich (New York: Cambridge University Press, 1994), pp. 181–201, esp. p. 190; Seidel Menchi, 'The Inquisitor as Mediator,' p. 177; Ugo Rozzo and Silvana Seidel Menchi, 'The Book and the Reformation in Italy,' trans. Karin Maag in *The Reformation and the Book*, ed. Jean-François Gilmont and Karin Maag (Brookfield, VT: Ashgate, 1998), p. 361.

97 ASVe, *Sant'Uffizio*, Busta 6, fasc. 15, *Contra Vagnola Pietro*, fol. 1r: [. . .] et seminare verbis suis venenosis ac falsis suggestionibus haeresim Lutheranum in praedicta villa et apud quamplures rurales homines simplices et ignaros ipsos educendo contra dogmati constitutiones [. . .].'

98 ASVe, *Contra Vagnola Pietro*, fols. 1r–1v: 'Et non si deve confessare o dire gli suoi peccati né a frate né a prete, ma che si deve confessare a bocca a Dio con la mente o cuore.' Giovanni Domenico de Cupis was bishop of Adria at this time; illegitimate son of Julius III, he was elevated to cardinal in 1517 and became master of the Sacred College in 1537. The *podestà*, Aurelio Michele, sat with the tribunal from the first questioning.

99 ASVe, *Contra Vagnola Pietro*, fols. 2v–3r: '[. . .] et non si mosse la barretta né ni altro reveren[za] fece [. . .].'

100 ASVe, *Contra Vagnola Pietro*, fols. 3v–4r: 'Io non l'ho visto mai andare a messa ma non so perché se non è stato per il fango [. . .] uno prete concubinato o ribaldo non può consecrare l'ostia nella messa.'

101 ASVe, *Contra Vagnola Pietro*, fol. 5v: '[. . .] ma secondo il diritto della Giusti[zia] mi giudicavano et mi liberavano come innocente.' See also Seidel Menchi, 'Inquisitor as Mediator,' p. 177. Rovigo was the home of a strong, tightly knit Calvinist community in the 1550s, with strong ties to Bernardino Ochino and Peter Martyr Vermigli, but Vagnola does not seem to have been a forerunner of that sect; see Caponetto, *Protestant Reformation*, pp. 203–5. See also Black, *Italian Inquisition*, p. 86.

102 ASVe, *Contra Vagnola Pietro*, fol. 6r: 'Se gli va a messa ogni mattina?'; 'Se gli va alle feste?'; '[. . .] dalli cattivi sacerdoti s'administrava [messa] molte volte per avari[zia] et per guadagno [. . .].'

103 ASVe, *Contra Vagnola Pietro,* fols. 6r–7r.

104 ASVe, *Contra Vagnola Pietro,* fols. 7r–v: 'Io credo di si, e il vero d'alcune volte che io ho visto vendere dalle indulgentie ne ho mormorato et me ne sono scandalizati.'

105 ASVe, *Contra Vagnola Pietro,* fol. 10r: 'Io ho detto che gli santi sono membri di Christo et che non si di vanno [divenivano] considerare in cielo come spiriti separat[i] dal corpo di Christo. E non dalle intentione andare a intercedere ma considerargli uno istesso corpo con Christo dalle quale lui è capo e per consequenemente non potersi andare a loro che non si vadi a Christo.'

106 ASVe, *Contra Vagnola Pietro,* unpg., 3 April 1547: 'D. Petrum Vagnola detentum in carceribus et ipsius relaxationem instantem sive in casu non apprense mandi de solvendo ducatos trecenti auri omne exceptione.'

107 ASVe, *Contra Vagnola Pietro,* unpg. correspondence, 1 April 1547: '[. . .] perché si conosce chiaramente questa persona essere tutta infetta di perversa fantasia e che timore pene si va pa[rl]ando al meglio che sa, a necessario per giusti[z]ia, non volendo de plano confessare l'errori suoi del quale per testes di venire ad rigorosum examen.'; 'nisi infra duos dies pure et simpliciter veritatem confitetur et devenitur ad rigorosum examen.' Martin, *Venice's Hidden Enemies,* p. 51.

108 ASVe, *Contra Vagnola Pietro,* unpg. correspondence 25 October 1547 and 20 November 1547: 'Potranno procedere nella causa de detto incarcerato in quel modo degli sacri canoni dispenenno et espedire detto cause in modo che ogn'uno abbia da riguardarsi d'incorette in simili errori usando pure la sua buona et solita giusti[z]ia con satisfattione d'ogn'uno et laude del omnipotente Dio.'

109 ASVe, *Contra Vagnola Pietro,* unpg. testimony of Giovanni Battista and Iacobus Zagus 23 November 1547: 'Credo che fusse domenica otto giorni se non mi fa[r]lo che venendo da messa Zuane Barbiero si accosto a mi dicendomi M. Pietro si lamenta molto di fatti tuoi [. . .] Io lo dissi che avendo avuto giuramento aveva detto la verità e che la mia depositione sua scritta e che non si poteva fare altro e lui repli[ca]to e disse che per salvare un'uomo non si deve dire tutto quello che si ha suggiendo mi sarai esaminato un'altra volta vedi de smonzare più che tu poi e inter alla lo mi disse che aveva detto nella mia depositione che mi vene fantasia che busarlo fuora per le fenestre.' None of the witnesses interviewed on 23 November or 6 January (at least fifteen people in all) could say whether or not they saw Pietro Vagnola lift his hat and perform reverence to the host during Mass. See also Farinacci, *Tractatus,* pp. 188–9.

110 ASVe, *Contra Vagnola Pietro*, unpg. testimony 13 January 1548, and notations 18 January 1548: 'Ma grandissimo errore conosco avere fatto avendo raggionato di quelle con persone rustiche et ignoran[za] [. . .].'
111 ASVe, *Contra Vagnola Pietro*, unpg. testimony 19 January 1548: 'Iterum admonitus quae respondat pure et semplice dicte assertioni xviii dixit Io non l'avessi venerate con la ber[r]e[t]ta vedendole et considerandole l'avevo venerasse con il cuore. Iterum admonitus quae pure respondeat dixit quomodo contemptum sed per inconsiderationem non veneratus est.'
112 ASVe, *Contra Vagnola Pietro*, unpg. testimony 19 January 1548: 'Non ricordare avessi mai cava la berretta alla immagine della Madonna perché non mi ricordo avere veduto alcuna immagine della Madonna.'
113 ASVe, *Contra Vagnola Pietro*, unpg. testimony 23 January 1548; 'Et post haec genuflexis coram . . . dixit Io prego la SV Reverendissima come pastore mio mi accettai per sua peccorella estimando.' There was a medical doctor present, three questions were asked, and after those three questions Vagnola knelt and cried before those present, but the notary did not record any statement concerning the method of torture or signal that torture had begun, so it appears Vagnola was shown the instruments but not tortured.
114 ASVe, *Contra Vagnola Pietro*, unpg. correspondence, dated 13 March 1548.

7. Mind and Body: The Opportunity for Redemption

1 Francisco Peña, *Directorium Inquisitorum* (Venice: Apud Marcum Antonium Zalterium, 1595), p. 488: 'Praeterea differunt ex quorumdam sententia ratione loci ubi fiunt: quoniam abiuratio de levi sit in domo Episcopi vel Inquisitoris: at abiuratio de vehementi sit in publico in conspectu populi ad hoc convocati, ut voluit Ioannes Rojas [. . .].'
2 See, for example, concerning the Roman Inquisition, John Tedeschi, 'The Organization and Procedures of the Roman Inquisition: A Sketch,' in *The Prosecution of Heresy: Collected Studies on the Inquisition in Early Modern Italy* (Binghamton, NY: Medieval and Renaissance Texts and Studies, 1991), pp. 145–53; Andrea Del Col, *L'Inquisizione in Italia: Dal XII al XXI secolo* (Milan: Oscar Mondadori, 2006), pp. 116–39. Concerning the *auto da fé* in general, see Henry Charles Lea, *The Inquisition of the Middle Ages*, Vol. 1 (New York: Harper Brothers, 1887), pp. 391–3; Francisco Bethencourt, 'The *Auto da Fé*: Ritual and Imagery,' *Journal of the Warburg and Courtauld Institute* 55 (1992): 155–68; Bethencourt, *The Inquisition: A Global History, 1478–1834* (New York: Cambridge University Press, 2009),

pp. 246–315, esp. pp. 310–15 concerning the Roman Inquisition's relatively low-key affairs; Adriano Prosperi, *Tribunali della coscienza:Inquisitori, confessori, missionari* (Turin: Einaudi, 1996), p. 175. For sentencing in addition to abjuration and the congregation's forgiveness of the requirement to wear an *abitello*, see Christopher F. Black, *The Italian Inquisition* (New Haven: Yale University Press, 2009), pp. 88–99.

3 Wietse de Boer has noted the similarities between inquisitorial and confessional manuals in his work; see *The Conquest of the Soul: Confession, Discipline and Public Order in Counter-Reformation Milan* (Leiden: Brill, 2001), pp. 5–42; see also Francisco Bethencourt, 'Les rites de l'Inquisition: Réflexions autour d'un projet de recherche,' in *Vorträge zur Justizforschung: Geschichte un Theorie*, Vol. 1, ed. Heinz Mohnhaupt and Dieter Simon (Frankfurt am Main: Vittorio Klostermann, 1992), pp. 135–52, esp. p. 136. See also Elena Brambilla, *Alle origini del Sant'Uffizio: Penitenza, confessione e giustizia spirituale dal Medioevo al XVI secolo* (Bologna: Il Mulino, 2000), pp. 347–59, in which Brambilla has argued that ecclesiastical reservation of certain sins to inquisitors, bishops, or the papacy had been a long-standing tradition in the Church and overlapped in some ways. For a contrasting interpretation, see Adriano Prosperi, *Tribunali della coscienza*, pp. 234–43, in which he characterizes the relationship as one of clearer separation, linked through the duty of confessors to refuse absolution to people who confessed to heresy, and withhold absolution to those who knew heretics until denunciations were made to tribunals, as a new feature of the Roman Inquisition's relationship with other clergy in the sixteenth century. Thomas N. Tentler has also pointed out how private penance and reconciliation, from the beginning of its development in the medieval period, was concerned with both social discipline and consolation of the sinner. See Tentler, *Sin and Confession on the Eve of the Reformation* (Princeton, NJ: Princeton, University Press, 1977), pp. 12–27, and pp. 301–18 concerning the ecclesiastical reservation of certain sins, including heresy, to authorities higher than the local parish priest.

4 Peter Brown, *Augustine of Hippo* (Berkeley and Los Angeles: University of California Press, 1967), pp. 212–25. Brown also points out that Augustine's vision of the Catholic Church was one that included everyone in the community physically, if not spiritually. Emperor Theodosius made the practice of orthodox Catholicism obligatory with the law *Cunctos populos* in 380 CE; Theodosius also promulgated laws that provided for enforcement of Nicene orthodoxy against Arians, pagans, and other heretics, including the Donatists, by monetarily fining members of the administrative classes and the use of corporal punishment against those lower down on the social scale. (See Bill Leadbetter, 'From Constantine to Theodosius (and Beyond),'

The Early Christian World, Vol. 1, ed. Philip F. Esler [New York: Routledge, 2000], pp. 283–7 and W.H.C. Frend, *The Rise of Christianity* [Philadelphia: Fortress Press, 1984], pp. 668–73.) Augustine supported these efforts, and justified them theologically utilizing Jesus's parable of the wheat and the tares; in any given church, those who were truly faithful Christians would always be surrounded by those who were not. But Augustine justified requiring religious attendance, mandated by the state, because such requirements could be a legitimate impetus that led the faithful 'wheat' to God.

5 Frederick J. Russell, 'Persuading the Donatists: Augustine's Coercion by Words,' in *The Limits of Ancient Christianity: Essays on Late Antique Thought and Culture in Honor of R. A. Markus*, ed. William E. Kingshirn and Mark Vessey (Ann Arbor: University of Michigan Press, 1999), pp. 115–30. Thomas N. Tentler has recognized that in the Ancient Church, among all faithful, penance for serious sin took place in public before the congregation, and could only be performed once during the serious sinner's lifetime. He has traced the development of private confession and penance to the Penitentials developed in early medieval Ireland and Britain. See Tentler, *Sin and Confession*, pp. 4–12.

6 Prospero Farinacci, *Tractatus de haeresi* (Cremona: Apud Marc'Antonium Belpierum, 1636), p. 219: 'Regula sit, quod haeretici cogendi et compellendi sunt, ut ad fidem redeant, etiam illis incusso timore mortis; alioquin ad eam condemnabunt: sic enim communiter receptum esse videre est apud Ant. De Butrio in c. Ad abolendam num. 22 extra de haeretici et ibi etiam Abb. n. 11 vers. In Glossa, in verbo Sponte [. . .].' *Ad abolendam* also called on secular authorities to support the Catholic Church in its pursuit and punishment of heretics, thereby codifying the use of the secular arm to enact executions, although it is unclear whether this was immediately acted on by the Holy Roman Emperor Frederick Barbarossa. See Peter Diehl, '*Ad abolendam* (X 5.7.9) and Imperial Legislation against Heresy,' *Bulletin of Medieval Canon Law* 19 (1989): 1–11.

7 Konrad Braun, *Breve introductione de haeretici* (Victorem Moguntiae per Franciscum Behem Typographum, 1549), Biblioteca Casanatense, Extt. Misc. in 8° volume 705. Unpaginated, in Chapter 2, 'An haeretici et ab eis decepti inviti ad confessionem verae et Catholicae fidei cogi possint ac debeant.'

8 Russell, 'Persuading the Donatists,' pp. 123–6. Sara T. Nalle has found that inquisitors in Tridentine La Mancha attempted to contribute to a broader reform of religious belief in general through their prosecutions in later sixteenth-century Spain, and often assigned penances to that end; but the number of cases involving definitively Protestant beliefs and practices were far fewer than in Italian lands. See Sara T. Nalle, *God in La Mancha: Religious*

Reform and the People of Cuenca, 1500–1650 (Baltimore, MD: Johns Hopkins University Press, 1992), esp. pp. 56–69, 118–29.

9 Farinacci, *Tractatus*, p. 220: 'Amplia III ut haereticus impoenitens non solum morti tradatur, sed etiam comburatur et ista ignis poena approbata est de iure divino, civili, canonico, et consuetudinario ut communiter notant Doctores [. . .].'

10 Eymeric, *Directorium Inquisitorum*, p. 474: '[. . .]reperitur ab obiecto haeresis crimine immunis totaliter, et hoc est, quando delatus non convincitur, nec confessione propria, nec facti evidentia, nec testium productione legitima; nec alias suspectus, nec diffamatus publice de praedicto crimine reperitur.'

11 Eymeric, ibid., p. 474. As R.H. Helmholz has recognized, there was considerable controversy concerning the question of double jeopardy in Church courts in general, and especially concerning the practice of canonical purgation in particular. A decretal in the *Liber Extra* was often interpreted to authorize subsequent prosecution, but later canonists expressed a divergence of opinions concerning the matter, and seem to have tailored their opinions to particular contingencies (R.H. Heimholz, *The Spirit of Classical Canon Law* [Athens, GA: The University of Georgia Press, 1996], pp. 296–7). Inquisitorial manuals very carefully avoided this problem entirely concerning inquisitorial verdicts through using the term 'innocent' very sparingly indeed, and held that those who were canonically purged were eligible to be considered relapsed in certain circumstances, as will be discussed below.

12 Farinacci, *Tractatus*, p. 151: 'Limita III Quia in crimine haeresis nemo absolvendus est tanquam innocens, sed solum ob non probatum crimen [. . .].'

13 Peña, *Directorium Inquisitorum*, p. 475: 'Verum omissis iam antiquis controversiis, novissime Pius V Pont. Max. rescripto quodam incipiente: Inter Multiplices curas. Quod est impressum inter litteras apostolicas pro officio Inquisitionis, in fine huius operis, iustissime cavit, ne sententiae in causa fidei unum quam transiverint aut deinde transeant in rem iudicatam.'

14 Farinacci, *Tractatus*, p. 151: 'Amplia V ut etiam sententia ferenda sit absolutoria ad favorem illius qui de haeresi suspectus torturam sustinuit, dixi supra, haec eadem quaestione, num. 126 et sequentibus; hic non repeto.'

15 Farinacci, ibid., p. 151: 'Sublimita hanc III limitationem, nisi constaret de falsitate testium examinatorum contra inquisitum, per eorum confessionem, utputa, quia poenitentia ducti faterentur se falsum dixisse: hoc enim casu cum constet de manifesta delati innocentia et de aperta testium iniquitate, poterit ipse delatus tanquam innocens absolvi et declarari [. . .].'

16 Eymeric, *Directorium Inquisitorum*, pp. 475–76; Peña, pp. 477–80. See also Richard M. Fraher, 'Preventing Crime in the High Middle Ages: The Medieval Lawyers' Search for Deterrence,' *Popes, Teachers, and Canon Law in the Middle Ages*, ed. James Ross Sweeney and Stanley Chodorow (Ithaca: Cornell University Press, 1989), pp. 224–5.

17 Peña, *Directorium Inquisitorum*, pp. 479–80: '[. . .] qui ut vehementer infamatus se purgavit: nam non censebitur relapsus nisi recidat in eadem haeresim, de qua prius se purgavit: ita docet hic Eymericus, quod videntur apertissime velle iurae paulo antea relata et Hostensis.'

18 Farinacci, *Tractatus*, p. 317: '[. . .] Quo loci pariter cavetur, negligentem se purgare non prius haereticum condemnari posse, nisi prius excommunicatus per annum in excommunicatione perstiterit: quod et idem antea statutum erat in Constitutione Innocenti IV edita de anno 1254 incipien. Noverit Universitas relata per Pegnam ubi supra fol. 21 vers. Qui autem inventi; et vide etiam in idem aliam Constitut. Nicolai IV editam de anno 1281 incip. Noverit Universitas vers. Qui autem relatam, ut supra a fol. mihi 67.

19 Farinacci, ibid., pp. 317–18: '[. . .] ubi dixit, quod licet deficiens in purgatione habeatur pro confessio, vel convicto haec tamen est probatio praesumptiva et non vera, et propter praesumptionem probationem in crimine haeresis nunquam quis traditur curiae saeculari, ut ibi per eum (qui tamen loqui videtur, qui in purgatione deficit poenitens vult eam adimplere et ad fidem redire de quo dixi infra hac eadem quaest. Num 55).' Farinacci, here, was referring to the *Repertorium Inquisitorum*.

20 Farinacci, ibid., p. 318: 'ubi dixit quod licet contentio sit Doctores de poena eius, qui deficit in purgatione, verior tamen et receptior est sententia, ut reus in purgatione deficiens puniendus sit poena ordinaria criminis ac si vere convictus esset iuxta tamen modum et qualitatem iudicii, quo reus coactus fuit se purgare; poena scilicet ordinaria, si contra ipsum processum fuit per accusationem, extraordinaria autem abritrio Iudicis, si professum fuit per denunciationem aut inquisitionem: et deinde concludit, quod cum hodie de crimine haeresis promotor fiscalis semper accuset consequens est, ut qui deficit in purgatione non secus atque consummatus haereticus, poena ordinaria puniri debeat et in Enchiridione.' See also Tedeschi, 'Organization and Procedures,' pp. 147–9 concerning the often temporary nature of 'perpetual' incarceration.

21 Farinacci, ibid., p. 319.

22 Farinacci, ibid., p. 324: 'Licet, nunquid post purgationem sibi iniunctam relapsus in haeresim tradendus in Curiae Saeculari, non videatur bene

resolutum, ideo consulendam esse Sedem apostolicam [. . .].' Farinacci utilized Peña's edition of Eymeric and Campeggi's edition of Ugolini here.

23 Farinacci, ibid., p. 322: 'Etsi olim relapsi haeretici non Curiae Saeculari tradebantur, sed perpetuo carceri mancipabantur [. . .].' Farinacci simply referred his readers to Giovanni Calderini and the *Repertorium Inquisitorum* concerning the issue of minimizing public scandal.

24 Peña, *Directorium Inquisitorum*, p. 413.

25 Farinacci, *Tractatus*, p. 323: 'Limita II eandem sextam ampliationem, ut procedat, prout loquitur, quando scilicet haereticus primo loco abiuravit de vehementi et postea iterum in haeresim incidit, de qua est confessus aut convictus; secus si primo abiuravit de levi: tunc enim non dicitur relapsus, etiam quod post hanc abiurationem haeresim confiteatur, actu de haeresi convictus sit [. . .].' Cesare Carena, *Tractatus de Officio Sanctissimae Inquisitionis* (Cremona: Marc'Antonium Belpierum, 1636), p. 46: 'Ex quibus iuribus colligitur, quod ille iudicari debet relapsus, qui vel primo abiuravit haeresim formalem et postea incidit in vehementem suspitionem, vel qui primo abiuravit de vehementi et postea incidit in haeresim formalem sufficit [. . .].' Peña, concerning how exactly to define a relapsed heretic, was not quite so precise; in his commentaries concerning Eymeric's original text, he simply ruled out the lightly suspect, even if caught again after their abjurations. He also expressed the opinion, however, that favourers, even if caught aiding heretics multiple times, should not be executed as relapsed heretics, even though some past authors had advocated for the practice (see Peña, pp. 387–8).

26 Carena, *Tractatus*, p. 46: 'Secunda conclusio est de eo, qui dicitur relapsus iuris fictione, ut si abiuravit de vehementi articulum de Purgatorio vel de puritate BVM et postea deprehenditur per confessionem vel probationem testium, incidisse in easdem species haeresim formaliter [. . .].'

27 Carena, ibid., p. 47–8: 'Quinta conclusio, si quis prius abiuravit de levi quia non constabat de eius haeresi, vel de vehementi suspitione, et postea inveniatur conversationem habuisse cum haereticis, vel alia fecisse de quibus in d.c. accusatus § ille quoque, si pendente hoc 2 processu, probetur, et constet eum tunc fuisse haereticum, quando abiuravit de levi, habendus est pro Relapso, Ratio est, quia apparet eum in prima abiuratione fuisse impoenitenem, nec voluisse veritatem fateri et caetera [. . .].'

28 Carena, ibid., p. 48: 'Eodem modo, qui abiuravit de levi, si in vehementem, vel levem Haeresis suspitionem incidat, non potest dici relapsus, lz. sit gravius puniendus, Pegn. D. comm. 83 parte 2 sub littera B. Sanctar. Ubi supra, Farin. D. q. 195 n. 22, 23 et 24.'

29 Carena, ibid., p. 48: 'Relapsus absque ulla misericordia, relaxatur bracchio saeculari, nam sufficit tales per falsam conversionem Ecclesiam semel decepisse [. . .].'

30 Farinacci, *Tractatus*, p. 294: 'Veritas est, quod prima opinio procedit quoad poenam temporalem; secunda quoad poenam spiritualem: et sic haereticus relapsus, licet poenitens non evitet poenam corporalem; tamen bene eidem ministrantur Sacramenta Ecclesiae, videlicet poenitentiae et Eucharistiae: ut per D. Tho. 1.1 quaest. 11 art. 4 ubi propterea dixit, etiam relapsos recipi in iudicio Dei [. . .].'

31 Eymeric, *Directorium Inquisitorum*, p. 510: '[. . .] Episcopus et Inquisitor mittent ad dictum delatum relapsum in carcere inclusum, duos vel tres probos viros, et praesertim religiosos, vel clericos fidei zelatores, eidem relapso non suspectos sue ingratos, sed familiares et gratos et isti intrabunt ad eum captata hora competenti, et loquentur sibi de contemptu mundi et miseriis vitae praesentis et gaudiis ac gloria paradisi.' See Peña, p. 519 for the same method applied to impenitent heretics.

32 Farinacci, *Tractatus*, p. 152.

33 Peña, *Directorium Inquisitorum*, p. 379: [. . .] non quidem frequenter, sed raro, seu casu, quod talia dicens vel faciens haereticus sit: quod deducitur levi consequentia [. . .].'

34 Peña, ibid., p. 488: '[. . .] hanc abiurationem de levi non modo secreto, verum etiam publice fieri posse, cum is qui sic abiurat, publice est de haeresi suspectus, item abiurationem de vehementi et publice et secreto ob eandem rantionem fieri posse, docet paulo post Eymericus [. . .].'

35 Eymeric, ibid., p. 377: Utpote, si aliqui comperiantur, qui eos, quos sciunt haereticos forte, occultent, favorem impedant: associent: visitent: munera offerant: recipiant: defensent, et similia exercentes: tales namque vehementer de haeresi sunt suspecti [. . .].'

36 Eymeric, ibid., pp. 380–2.

37 Eymeric, ibid., p. 377: 'Utpote, si aliqui reperiantur, qui haereticos adoraverint: seu eis reverentiam suo more exhibuerint: consolationem vel communionem ab eis reciperint: vel simila, quae ad ritum eorum pertinent [. . .].'

38 Peña, ibid., p. 379: '[. . .] quoniam haec vehemens suspicio su praesumptio sumitur ex signis exterioribus operum aut verborum, ex quibus capitur argumentum concludens frequenter et ut in pluribus, quod qui talia dicit ver facit, est haereticus; ut si quis diebus prohibitis absque necessitate et superioris facultate, carnibus vesceretur [. . .].' Jean Gerson, one of the most famous theologians of the later fourteenth and early fifteenth centuries, first studied at and then became chancellor of the University of Paris

in 1395, and remained in that position until 1415. He was active as an academic, reformer, politician, and conciliarist, particularly at the Council of Constance (1414–1418); he was also an implacable opponent of heresy. He wrote more than five hundred works, including ones devoted to mysticism and lay religious devotion. See Brian Patrick McGuire, ed., *Jean Gerson: Early Works* (New York: Paulist Press, 1998), pp. 1–74.

39 Peña, *Directorium Inquisitorum*, p. 379: 'Haec praesumptio seu suspicio violentia, ut optime scribit Gerson tract. de protestatione, consideratione ultima, nascitur ex signis exterioribus operum aut verborum, ex quibus concludi solet efficaciter et fere semper, quod talia dicens vel faciens est haereticus, ut si quis transit, vel redit ad ritus Iudeorum c. contra Christianos, de haeret. lib. 6 item si quis in causa fidei excommunicatus per annum in excommunicatione anima pertinaci duravit.'

40 Peña, ibid., p. 382: 'Tametsi valde laboriosum sit in qualibet arte casus singulares et individuos praescribere, cum indicandae ab arte repellantur, ut admonet philosophi, nihilominus hic Eymericus, ut absolutam tradat Inquisitoribus eorum, quae ad suum mutius pertinent cognitionem, etiam particulares casus commemorat: non tamen omnes, qui contingere possunt: id enim impossibile esset, sed eos tantum, qui variis iuris locis continentur.' In his comments, Peña provided the rationale and justifications for punishing *fautors, defensors,* and *receptors,* as discussed in Chapter 2.

41 Masini, *Sacro Arsenale, Overo Prattica dell'officio della S. Inquisizione,* ed. Tommaso Menghini (Rome: 1693; StaatsBibliothek Digitalisat 4 J.can.p.5504), p. 257: 'Fosti però d'ordine nostro carcerato in questo Santo Officio, nel quale più volte avanti di noi col tuo giuramento essaminato, confessati esser vero che con la suddetta occassione avevi inconsideratamente, e così per burla, proferito le sopradette parole ereticali, negando d'averle mai col cuore credute in modo alcuno.'

42 Masini, ibid., pp. 260–71.

43 Masini, ibid., p. 272: '[. . .] che [h]avessi non pur conversato più volte con gli [H]eretici, ma [h]avutili in venerazione, accompagnatili, com[m]unicato con esso loro e chiesta da essi la consolazione, &c.'

44 Masini, ibid., pp. 274–5: '[. . .] ti sei reso a questo Santo Officio violentamente sospetto d'[h]aver col cuore ri[n]negata la santa Fede Cristiana e Cattolica e aderito all'empia setta di Lutero, o di Calvino, e tenuto e creduto in particolare [. . .].'

45 Masini, ibid., pp. 277–87, esp. p. 277: '[. . .] approvando l'empie e sacrileghe sette di Giovanni [H]us, di Martino Lutero e di Calvino'; p. 279: '[-] che la sacrosanta, Cattolica e Apostolica Romana Chiesa sia la sinagoga di

Satanasso e la meretrice Babilonica, madre di fornica[t]ioni e abomina[t]ioni, e Sodoma spiritualmente, quanto alla dottrina che tiene e insegna [. . .].'

46 Eymeric, *Directorium Inquisitorum,* p. 503: 'Talis enim esto quod multis annis steterit in haeresi praedicta, ac etiam aliis quibuscumque, illas crediderit, e dogmatizaverit, multosque induxerit in errores; si tandem cum effectu illas haereses consenserit abiurare et satisfactionem congruam ad arbitrium Episcopi et Inquisitoris exhibere non est tradendus brachio saeculari ultimo supplicio feriendus, nec si est clericus degradandus, sed est ad misericordiam admittendus, iuxta cap. Ad abolendam § praesenti. Extra de haeret. et abiurata primis haeretica pravitata est in perpetuum carcerem detuendum, iuxta c. Excommunicamus 2 § si quis et absolutionis beneficio imperito et iniuncto eidem, quod talibus iniungi consuerit iuxta c. Ut officium, provisio tamen sollerter, ne simulata fictione redeat fraudulenter, et Episcopum et Inquisitorem, immo seipsum fallendo, sub ogni specie lupum gerat.'

47 Peña, ibid., p. 508: 'Alterum commendum ostendit hic auctor dum ait: 'Verum etiam ut sic lapsi humiliores deinceps fiant, ac poenitentiae operibus exerceantur.' Sit enim saepe mutlos eorum qui in haereses labuntur et vere convertuntur, ita poenitentia operibus insistere, ac vetera daemonis opera detestari ut et ipsi non modo sibi, verum etiam humilitatis et vera poenitentia exemplo aliis prosint vehementer.' See also Luarent Mayali, 'The Concept of Discretionary Punishment in Medieval Jurisprudence,' in *Studia in honorem eminentissimi cardinalis Alphonsi M. Stickler,* ed. Rosalio Iosepho Card. Catillo Lara (Rome: LAS, 1992), pp. 299–315, esp. 303–5 for the development of the two types of punishment in the *Decretals.*

48 Farinacci, *Tractatus,* p. 301: '[. . .] Tabien. In summa in dicto verbo, Haereticus, num. 23 et 24, ubi dixit quod licet isto casu Inquisitor poenitenti imponere debeat eam poenam, quae magis ab ipso timetur, ut corrigatur; adhuc tamen considerare debet conditionem personae, ut imponenda poena sit magis medicina, quam venenum et talis, ut illam poenitens adimplere possit.' Thomas N. Tentler has noted that confessors' manuals advised priests to consider the exact same two factors when assigning penance to penitents – the appropriate remedy for specific sins, and the penitents' abilities to carry out the penance. See Tentler, *Sin and Confession,* pp. 333–40.

49 Farinacci, *Tractatus,* pp. 301–2: 'Eymeric in Director. Inquisitor. par. 3 quaest. 103 versic. Respondemus, quod sic ubi propterea infert, quod Inquisitor potest imponere peregrinationes, orationes, abstinentias, et eleemosynas [. . .].'

50 Carena, *Tractatus* pp. 41–2. While the Roman Inquisition regularly returned sequestered goods to the penitent, or the heirs of heretics, tribunals often received at least some income from sequestered goods. See Black, *Italian Inquisition*, pp. 102–4.
51 Farinacci, *Tractatus*, p. 302.
52 Farinacci, ibid., p. 194.
53 Farinacci, ibid., p. 301: '[. . .] ubi bene explicate consideranda per Iudicem in arbitrando poenam imponendam ex vehementi suspicione. Repertor. Inquisitorum, in verbo Abiurare vers. Item nota, quod tunc poenare linquitur arbitrio Inquisitoris, et vers. seq. et in verbo Carcer, vers. sed quaeritur utrum Inquisitor ubi propterea quod potest inquisitor poenitenti abiuratio et absoluto, ultra poenam carceris iniungere etiam aliam salutarem poenitentiam.'; p. 302: '[. . .] ubi testatur quod hodie loco perpetui carceris condemnantur ad triremes, saltem per trienium [. . .].' As John Tedeschi has explained, Carena noted the transition from incarceration to service in the galleys in the late sixteenth and early seventeenth centuries. See also Tedeschi, 'Organization and Procedures,' pp. 146–8.
54 Masini, *Sacro Arsenale*, p. 285: 'E acciocché dal benignissimo e clementissimo Dio Padre delle misericordie ottenghi più facilmente la remissione e il perdono de' suddetti tuoi errori ed [h]eresie, per penitenze salutari t'imponiamo: che per tutto il rimanete della vita tua digiuni ogni primo Venerdì ciascun mese semplicemente, tutti li Venerdì di Marzo e anco il Venerdì santo in pane e acqua; che per il detto tempo reciti una volta la settimana i Sette Salmi Peniten[t]iali, con le Litanie e Preci seguenti, e appresso la Corona della Beatissima sempre Vergine Maria, e ogni domenica cinque volte per il *Pater Noster* e l'*Ave Maria* e una volta il *Credo*, inginocchiato avanti qualche sacra Immagine; e finalmente che durante la vita tua, come di sopra, confessi sacramentale quattro volte l'anno i tuoi peccati al Sacerdote, che da noi ti sarà deputato, e di sua licenza ti comunichi nelle quattro principali solennità, cioè della Natività e Resurrezione di N.S. Gesù Cristo, della sacra Pentecoste e di tutti i Santi.'
55 See Adriano Prosperi, *Tribunali della coscienza*, pp. 258–60; he argues that the post-Tridentine church came to be dominated by the inquisitorial use of confession; see also p. 478, in which he argues that confession became subordinated to inquisitorial purposes. Thomas Tentler also has argued for continuity in the Church's use of public penance as a remedy for public sin, tracing the origins of public restitution and punishment to the traditions of the early Church; see Tentler, *Sin and Confession*, pp. 319–40.
56 Wietse de Boer, *Conquest of the Soul*, pp. 54–67.
57 Adriano Prosperi, *Tribunali della coscienza*, pp. 265–76; 291–300; 473–84.
58 Brambilla, *Alle origini del Sant'Uffizio*, pp. 347–9.

59 Brambilla, *Alle origini del Sant'Uffizio*, pp. 146–53; 176–204; 356–9; Brambilla, 'Il segreto e il sigillo: Denunce e comparizioni spontanee nei processi inquisitoriali,' in *I Tribunali della fede: Continuità e discontinuità dal medioevo all'età moderna; ; Atti del XLV Convegno di studi sulla Riforma e sui movimenti religiosi in Italia, Torre Pellice, 3–4 settembre 2005*, ed. Susanna Peyronel Rambaldi (Turin: Claudiana, 2007), pp. 111–61, esp. pp. 124–40, 150, although many of her examples pertain to witchcraft prosecutions in the seventeenth century.

60 De Boer, *Conquest of the Soul*, pp. 194–5. Prosperi, in particular, refers to the two nets – that of inquisitors, and that of bishops – meant to catch heretics, and argues that between the internal and external forums the Church could preserve the orthodoxy of distinct geographic territories; see *Tribunali della coscienza*, pp. 316–32. Christopher F. Black has recently noted that inquisition tribunals did not have enough staff to achieve all stated goals and relied on the help of others, particularly other clerics, paid or unpaid. See Black, *Italian Inquisition*, pp. 99–101.

61 Prosperi, *Tribunali della coscienza*, p. xxi.

62 For a full explanation of confessional improprieties in pre-Tridentine Italy, see De Boer, *Conquest of the Soul*, pp. 5–42.

63 Giovanni Romeo, *Ricerche su confessione confessione dei peccati e Inquisizione nell'Italia del Cinquecento* (Naples: Città del sole, 1997), pp. 85–7; according to Eric Cochrane, even after the reforms of Gian Matteo Giberti in Verona (1524--1543), some 5,000 managed to avoid confessing and taking communion. See Cochrane, *Early Modern Italy 1530–1630*, ed. Julius Kirshner (New York: Longman, 1988), p. 146.

64 De Boer, *Conquest of the Soul*, p. 44.

65 Romeo, *Ricerche su confessione*, p. 80.

66 John Tedeschi has discussed early sevententh-century correspondence between the central tribunal in Rome and its regional subsidiaries, often in his footnotes in 'Organization and Procedures.' See also Andrea Del Col, 'Organizzazione, composizione, e giurisdictionede tribunali dell'Inquisizione Romana nella Republica di Venezia,' *Critica Storica* 25 (1988): 244–94.

67 Tedeschi, 'Organization and Procedures,' p. 149.

68 TCD MS 1224, *Sentences*, Vol. 2, fols. 38r–v. For the nature of the sources, see also John Tedeschi and William Monter, 'Towards a Statistical Profile of the Italian Inquisitions, Sixteenth to Eighteenth Centuries,' in *The Prosecution of Heresy*, pp. 100–4. Consulted in microfilm at the library of Trinity College, Dublin.

69 TCD MS 1224, *Sentences*, Vol. 2, fols. 182r–183r; As Romano Canosa has noted, Don Francesco de Stanghi was tried alongside several other cler-

ics in Faenza, including Don Girolamo dal Pozzo, who was assigned to perpetual incarceration. A greengrocer, Iammone de Mina, was sent to the galleys for five years. See Canosa, *Storia dell'Inquisizione in Italia: Dalla metà del Cinquecento alla fine del Settecento,* Vol. 5, *Napoli e Bologna; la procedura inquisitoriale* (Rome: Sapere, 2000, 1990), pp. 179–83, esp. p. 177.

70 TCD MS 1224, *Sentences,* vol. 2, fols. 184r–185r: '[. . .] et esaminato dopo acluni pergiuri e variationi, perseverasti negando nelli tuoi esamini di essere stato eretico [. . .].'

71 TCD MS 1225, *Sentences,* Vol. 3, fols. 77r–78v; Delio Cantimori also examines some of these sentences in his work, including Camillo da Bozzolo and Scipione Cremona, examined below. See Cantimori, *Umanesimo e religione nel Rinascimento* 2nd ed (Turin: Einaudi, 1975*)*, 28–36.

72 TCD MS 1224, *Sentences,* Vol. 2, fols. 131r–133v: 'Mario Galeatta gentilhuomo [sic] et barone neapolitano delato al Santo Offitio per suspitione de haeresi [sospetto d'eresia . . .] et Mario figliuolo del quondam gentilhuomo[. . .].' See also Salvatore Caponetto, *The Protestant Reformation in Sixteenth-Century Italy,* trans. Anne C. and John Tedeschi (Kirksville, MO: Thomas Jefferson University Press, 1999), pp. 69–70. Camilla Russell, *Giulia Gonzaga,* pp. 79–80, 166–7, 190–208; Black, *Italian Inquisition,* pp. 23–6, 130, 255–7; C. Donadelli, 'Galeota, Mario,' in *Dizionario storico dell'Inquisizione,* Vol. 2, ed. Adriano Prosperi with Vincenzo Lavenia and John Tedeschi (Pisa: Scuola Normale Superiore Pisa, 2010), pp. 634–5.

73 For example, see Farinacci, *Tractatus,* pp. 301–2; and John Tedeschi, 'Organization and Procedures,' pp. 147–50.

74 Guido Dall'Olio, *Eretici e inquisitori nella Bologna del Cinquecento* (Bologna: Istituto per la storia di Bologna, 1999), pp. 316–21; Black, *Italian Inquisition,* 95–6.

75 TCD MS 1224, *Sentences,* Vol. 2, fols. 163r–64r

76 TCD MS 1224, *Sentences,* Vol. 2, fols. 173r–174r: 'vedendo che eri reticente al confessare tutta la verità, fu ordinato che contra dite si procedesse al rigoroso esamine, al quale volendone venire, confessasti liberamente te aver tenuto e creduto gli infrascritti errori e eresie [. . .].'

77 TCD MS 1224, *Sentences,* Vol. 2, fols. 139r–140r.

78 TCD MS 1225, *Sentences,* Vol. 3, fols. 170 r–v: 'che l'ostia sacra levata del sacerdote nella messa o[v]vero posta nel Tabernacolo non sia altro che un poco de pasta o carta [. . .].'

79 Farinacci, *Tractatus,* p. 305; Peña, *Directorium Inquisitorum,* pp. 641–2.

80 Farinacci, *Tractatus,* p. 31.

81 TCD MS 1225, *Sentences,* Vol. 3, fols. 29 r–v.

82 TCD MS 1224, *Sentences*, Vol. 2, fols. 14v–15r; Black, *Italian Inquisition*, pp. 44–5.
83 TCD MS 1224, *Sentences*, Vol. 2, fols. 124r–125r.
84 TCD MS 1225, *Sentences*, Vol. 3, fols. 41r–43r.
85 TCD MS 1224, *Sentences*, Vol. 2, fols. 177r–178v: 'che tu Antonio figlio del quondam Benfioli de Saveri Ferrarese ligature et venditore de libri abitante in Bologna avesti avuto dato et vendato alcuni libri prohibiti et hvesti tanti de tuoi come d'altri [. . .].' Antonio Saveri was caught with books by Valdés, Celio Curione, Pier Paolo Vergerio, John Calvin, Bernardino Ochino, Erasmus, and Alfonso de Valdés, and others that the tribunal 'non sapevi gli nomi.' Concerning bookmen who sold heretical books for profit, but did not necessarily believe in their contents, see Chapter 5.
86 TCD MS 1225, *Sentences*, Vol. 3, fols. 202r–203r.
87 Carlos Eire, *War Against the Idols: The Reformation of Worship from Erasmus to Calvin* (New York: Cambridge University Press, 1986), pp. 212–14, 241–7. See also Chapter 1. Ugo Rozzo and Silvana Seidel Menchi, 'The Book and the Reformation in Italy,' trans. Karin Maag, in *The Reformation and the Book*, ed. Jean-François Gilmont and Karin Maag (Brookfield, VT: Ashgate, 1998), pp. 324–36.
88 Vermigli, *Common places*, trans. Anthony Marten (London: Henry Denham and Henry Middleton, 1583), p. 540. See also, concerning Protestant defences of this behaviour, Beat Hodler, 'Protestant Self-Perception and the Problem of *Scandalum*: A Sketch,' in *Protestant History and Identity in Sixteenth-Century Europe*, ed. Bruce Gordon, Vol. 1, *The Medieval Inheritance* (Aldershot, UK: Scolar Press, 1996), pp. 23–30.
89 Eire, *War against the Idols*, pp. 78–82.
90 Scholars have emphasized that even Bucer and Wolfgang Capito eventually gave up such an opinion and recommended the more demanding positions of Calvin and Vermigli. See Peter Matheson, 'Martin Bucer and the Old Church,' in *Martin Bucer: Reforming Church and Community*, ed. D.F. Wright (New York: Cambridge University Press, 1994), pp. 11–13.
91 See, for example, John Jeffries Martin, *Myths of Renaissance Individualism* (New York: Palgrave Macmillan, 2004), esp. pp. 21–61, in which he sees the choice of many heterodox to prudently refrain from publicly acting on their beliefs, or dissimulate when brought before inquisitors, as evidence of self-awareness of individuality; and both Carlo Ginzburg, *Il nicodemismo: Simulazione e dissimulazione religiosa nell'Europa del '500* (Turin: Giulio Einaudi, 1970), pp. 159–81, esp. p. 179, and Adriano Prosperi, *L'eresia del Libro Grande: Storia di Giorgio Siculo e della sua setta* (Milan: Feltrinelli, 2000), pp. 322–37, for the continued existence of

heretical beliefs mentally even when outward ritualistic conformity was maintained.

92 See, for example, Cesare Carena, *Tractatus*, pp. 50–1: '[. . .] illud ei sufficienter haeresim manifestaret, unde per actus indifferentes manifestans Haeresim, non potest dici haereticus, puta si mente quis assentiretur propositioni huic, Deus non est Trinus, et exterius verba haec tantummodo proferet [. . .].'

93 Frederick H. Russell, 'Persuading the Donatists,' p. 121.

Conclusion: The Boundaries of Orthodoxy

1 See, for example, James D. Tracy, *Europe's Reformations, 1450–1650: Doctrine, Politics, and Community* 2nd ed. (New York: Rowman and Littlefield, 2006), pp. 90–1.

2 Elisabeth Gleason, 'Sixteenth-Century Italian Interpretations of Luther,' *Archiv für Reformationsgeschichte* 60 (1969): 161.

3 John Dillenberger, ed., *Martin Luther: Selections from His Writings* (New York: Doubleday, 1962), xix, 490–500. As Dillenberger explains in his introduction, the immediate cause for Luther's ninety-five theses was the preaching of indulgences in Saxony. He objected to the practice of selling indulgences and the theology that allowed that practice; see also Michael Tavuzzi, who has explained how Prierias's tactics in handling Luther have been criticized from the sixteenth century to the present. Prierias, in immediately pronouncing Luther's disputations in the *Ninety-Five Theses* heretical because they questioned papal power, generally is regarded to have made a serious tactical error; Tavuzzi, *Prierias: The Life and Works of Silvestro Mazzolini da Prierio, 1456–1527* (Durham, NC: Duke University Press, 1997), pp. 104–15.

4 *Exsurge Domine: Bull of Pope Leo X issued June 15, 1520*, www.papalencyclicals.net. Accessed 5 August 2008.

5 1 Cor. 11:18–19: 'For, to begin with, when you come together as a church, I hear that there are divisions among you; and to some extent I believe it. Indeed, there have to be factions among you, for only so will it become clear who among you are genuine' (*HarperCollins Study Bible*).

6 *Exsurge Domine*, 15 June 1520.

7 Augustine, *Contro Cresconio grammatico Donatista* (Testo latino dell' edizione Maurina controntato con il *Corpus Christianorum Latinorum*, ed. and trans. Eugenio Cavallari [Rome: Città Nuova, 2000]). See Book 1 for Augustine's assertions that different heretical sects essentially repeat the same errors over time.

8 *Exsurge Domine*, 15 June 1520; see also Malcom Lambert, *Medieval Heresy: Popular Movements from the Gregorian Reform to the Reformation* (Cambridge, 1992), esp. chaps. 8, 13, and 15.

9 Dermot Fenlon, *Heresy and Obedience in Tridentine Italy: Cardinal Pole and the Counter-Reformation*. (Cambridge: Cambridge University Press, 1972); Thomas F. Mayer, *Reginald Pole: Prince and Prophet* (New York: Cambridge University Press, 2000).

10 James B. Given, *Inquisition and Medieval Society: Power, Discipline, and Resistance in Languedoc* (Ithaca: Cornell University Press, 1997), p. 45.

11 Francisco Peña, *Directorium Inquisitorum* (Venice: Apud Marcum Antonium Zalterium, 1595), p. 233: 'Prudentissime autem Eymericus per regulas generales investigat, quot modis aliqua propositio haereticae dici possit, ne sit opus singulare haeretica dogmata commemorare, quae pertinaciter asserta haereticum constituant: quod fecerunt nonulli doctores, ut alibi diximus.'

12 Eymeric, ibid., p. 319–20: 'ubi enim haec duae concurrunt, haereticum perfecte faciunt.' Thomas Aquinas, *Summa Theologiae*, 2a2ae II, I; 2a2ae II,2.

13 Peña, ibid., p. 232; .

14 Farinacci, *Tractatus de haeresi* (Cremona: Apud Marc'Antonium Belpierum, 1636), pp. 2–3.

15 Peña, *Directorium Inquisitorum*, p. 367.

16 Eymeric, ibid., p. 367; Peña, p. 367.

17 Peña, ibid., p. 324: 'In his ergo breviter more nostro certiora tradentes, primum statuendum est, in arduis et horrendis factis non esse praesumendam oblivionem: nam ut Plinius affirmat, in rebus arduis non laeditur, aut alteratur memoria.'

18 Cesare Carena, *Tractatus de Officio Sanctissimae Inquisitionis* (Cremona: Apud Marc'Antonium Belpierum, 1636), esp. pp. 350–1.

19 Farinacci, *Tractatus*, p. 188: 'non solum ex ore ipsius haeretici sed etiam ex factis haereticalibus, evidentiorque est probatio illa, quae ex factis oritur, quam quae ex verbis, cum facta magis hominu mentem animum et voluntatem declarent, quam verba, quout haec, et similia [. . .].'

20 Farinacci, ibid., pp. 35–7.

Bibliography

Archival Sources

Archivio di Stato di Modena (ASMo), *Inquisizione*
Busta 3, par. II, 1554–1555, Libro VI, fasc. 14, *Contra Ioannis Terrazanus*
Busta 3, par. II, 1554–1555, Libro VI, fasc. 13, *Contra Claudium Rudiliam*
Busta 5, fasc. 20, 1568, *Contra Alessandrum Fornarium*
Busta 5, Processi 1555–1568, *Contra Petrum Curionem*
Archivio di Stato di Siena (ASS)
Notarile antecosimiano 2776: *Processus et inquisitio contra magistrum Bartholomeum olim magistri Iohannis de Nellis fabrum ferrarium ac abiuratio*
Archivio di Stato di Venezia (ASVe), *Sant'Uffizio*
Busta 1, fasc. 2, *Contra Calegaro Girolamo*
Busta 6, fasc. 15, *Contra Vagnola Pietro*
Busta 7, fasc. 17, *Contra Riccardum Pictorem Conegliano*
Busta 8, *Contra Prosperum Capellarum et Battista dale Bambine*
Busta 12, *Contra Padre Marin da Venezia*
Busta 21, Fasc. 2, Fasc. 3 *Contra Girolamo e Alvise Badoer, e Giovanni Fineti*
Busta 22, fasc. 2, *Contra Odoricum Grisonium et complices*
Busta 5, Processo 1555–1568, *Contra Natale Gioioso*
Trinity College, Dublin (TCD)
MS 1224, *Sentences*, Volume 2
MS 1225, *Sentences*, Volume 3

Printed Primary Sources

A Select Library of the Nicene and Post-Nicene Fathers of the Christian Church, Vol. 10, *Saint Chrysostom: Homilies on the Gospel of Matthew*, ed. Philip Schaff, 157–66. New York: Charles Scribner's Sons, 1888.

Aquinas, Thomas. *Summa Theologiae*, Vol. 31, ed. T.C. O'Brien. New York: McGraw Hill, 1964–.

Augustine. *Contra Cresconio grammatico Donatista*, ed. and trans. Eugenio Cavallari. Rome: Città Nuove, 2000.

Braun, Konrad. *Breve introductione de haeretici*. Victorem Moguntiae per Franciscum Behem Typographum, 1549.

Calvin, John. *The Bondage and Liberation of the Will: A Defence of the Orthodox Doctrine of Human Choice against Pighius*, ed. N.S. Lane and trans. G.I. Davies. Grand Rapids, MI: Baker Books, 1996.

– Answer of John Calvin to the Nicodemite Gentlemen Concerning Their Compaint That He Is too Severe (1544).' In *Come Out from among Them: 'Anti-Nicodemite' Writings of John Calvin*, ed. and trans. Seth Skolnitsky, 99–131. Dallas, TX: Protestant Heritage Press, 2001.

– 'Short Treatise on the Lord's Supper.' In *Calvin: Theological Treatises*, trans. J.K.S. Reid, 140–66. Philadephia, PA: The Westminster Press, 1954.

– 'Petit Traicté de la Saincte Cene de N.S. Iesus Christ.' In *Corpus Reformatorum*, Vol. 33, *Ioannis Calvini Opera Quae Supersunt Omnia*, Vol. 5, ed. G. Baum, E. Cunitz, and E. Reuss, 429–60. Brunswick and Berlin: C.A. Schwetschke and Son, 1866.

Carena, Cesare. *Tractatus de Officio Sanctissimae Inquisitionis*. Cremona: Apud Marc'Antonium Belpierum, 1636.

Canons and Decrees of the Council of Trent, ed. Rev. H.J. Schroeder, OP. Rockford, IL: Tan Books and Publishers, Inc., 1978.

Corpus iuris canonici. 2 Vols., ed. Emil Friedberg and Aemilius Ludwig Richter. Leipzig: Bernard Tauchnitz, 1879–1881.

Corpus juris canonici emendatum et notis illustratum. Gregorii XIII, pont. max. iussu editum. Rome: In aedibus Populi Romani, 1582.

De Castro, Alfonso. *Adversus omnes haereses*. Paris, 1560.

Eymeric, Nicholas, and Francisco Peña. *Directorium Inquisitorum*. Venice: Apud Marcum Antonium Zalterium, 1595.

Farinacci, Prospero. *Tractatus de haeresi*. Cremona: Apud Marc'Antonium Belpierum, 1636.

Gui, Bernard. '*Practica*.' In *Heresies of the High Middle Ages*, ed. and trans. Walter L. Wakefield and Austin P. Evans, 373–445. New York: Columbia University Press, 1969.

Locati, Umberto. *Opus quod iudiciale inquisitorum*. Rome: Antonii Bladii Impressores, 1570.

Lombard, Peter. *Sentences*, Vol. 4, ed. Giulio Silano. Toronto: Pontifical Institute of Mediaeval Studies, 2007–2010.

Masini, Eliseo. *Sacro Arsenale; Overo Prattica dell'officio Della S. Inquisizione*, ed. Tommaso Menghini. Rome, 1693. Bayerische StaatsBibliothek Digitalisat, 4 J.can.p.5504.

Melantone [Melancthon]. *I principii della teologia*, ed. Salvatore Caponetto. Rome: Istituto storico italiano per l'età moderna e contemporanea, 1992.

Tedeschi, John, and Josephine von Henneberg, eds and trans. '*Contra Petrum Antonium a Cervia Relapsum et Bononiae Concrematum*.' In *Italian Reformation Studies in Honor of Laelius Socinus*, ed. John Tedeschi, 243–68. Florence: Felice le Monnier, 1965.

Vermigli, Pietro Martire. *Common places*, trans. Anthony Marten. London: Henry Denham and Henry Middleton, 1583.

– *A treatise of the cohabitacyon of the faithfull with the unfaithfull*. Strasbourg, 1555.

– 'The Apostles' Creed: A Plain Exposition of the Twelve Articles of the Christian Faith,' trans. Mariano Di Gagni. In *The Peter Martyr Library*, Vol. 1, *Early Writings: Creed, Scripture, Church*, ed. Joseph C. McLelland, 27–79. Kirksville, MO: Sixteenth Century Essays and Studies, 1994.

– 'Whether Evangelicals Are Schismatics for Having Separated from the Papists,' trans. Mariano Di Gagni and Joseph C. McLelland. In *The Peter Martyr Library*, Vol. 1, *Early Writings: Creed, Scripture, Church*, ed. Joseph C. McLelland, 171–224. Kirksville, MO: Sixteenth Century Essays and Studies, 1994.

Zwingli, Ulrich. 'Concerning Choice and Liberty Respecting Food.' In *The Correspondence of Huldreich Zwingli, Together with Selections from His German Works*, ed. Samuel Macauley Jackson and trans. Lawrence A. McLouth, 70–112. New York: G.P. Putnam's Sons, 1912.

Secondary Works

Adorni-Braccesi, Simonetta. 'Maestri e scuole nelle repubblica di Lucca tra Riforma e Controriforma.' *Società e storia* 33 (1986): 559–94.

Al Kalak, A. 'Modena, Accademia.' In *Dizionario storico dell'Inquisizione*, Vol. 2, ed. Adriano Prosperi with Vincenzo Lavenia and John Tedeschi, 1055–6. Pisa: Scuola Normale Superiore Pisa, 2010.

Arnold, John H. *Inquisition and Power: Catharism and the Confessing Subject in Medieval Languedoc*. Philadelphia: University of Pennsylvania Press, 2001.

Arrighi, G. *Felino Sandei (1444–1503): Canonista e umanista*. Lucca: Accademia Lucchese di scienze, lettore e arti, 1987.

Baker, J. Wayne. *Heinrich Bullinger and the Covenant: The Other Reformed Tradition*. Athens, OH: Ohio University Press, 1980.

Battistella, Antonio. 'Processi d'eresia nel Collegio di Spagna (1553–1554): Episodo della storia della Riforma in Bologna.' *Atti e memorie – Deputazione di storia patria per le provincie di Romagna* 3, no. 19 (1901): 138–87.

Belladonna, Rita. 'Introduction.' In Bernardino Ochino, *Seven Dialogues*, ed. and trans. Rita Belladonna, vii–xxxi. Ottawa: Dovehouse Editions, 1988.

Bellomo, Mario. *The Common Legal Past of Europe, 1000–1800*, trans. Lydia G. Cochrane. Washington, DC: Catholic University of America Press, 1995.

Benzoni, Gino. 'Un Ulpiano mancato: Giovanni Finetti.' *Studi veneziani*, n.s., 25 (1994): 35–71.

Bertelloni, Francisco. 'Guido Terrena.' In *A Companion to Philosophy in the Middle Ages*, ed. Jorge J.E. Garcia, 291. Malden, MA: Blackwell, 2003.

Bethencourt, Francisco. *The Inquisition: A Global History, 1478–1834*. New York: Cambridge University Press, 2009.

– 'The *Auto da Fé*: Ritual and Imagery.' *Journal of the Warburg and Courtauld Institute* 55 (1992): 155–68.

– 'Les rites de l'Inquisition: Réflexions autour d'un projet de recherche.' In *Vorträge zur Justizforschung: Geschichte un Theorie*, Vol. 1, ed. Heinz Mohnhaupt and Dieter Simon, 135–52. Frankfurt am Main: Vittorio Klostermann, 1992.

Bianco, Cesare. 'Bartolomeo della Pergola e la sua predicazione eterodossa a Modena nel 1554.' *Bolletino della Società di Studi Valdesi* 151 (July 1982): 3–49.

– 'La comunità di "fratelli" nel movimento ereticale modenese del' 500.' *Rivista Storica Italiana* 92 (1980): 621–79.

Bireley, Robert. *The Refashioning of Catholicism, 1450–1700: A Reassessment of the Counter-Reformation*. Washington, DC: Catholic University of America Press, 1999.

– 'Early Modern Catholicism.' In *Reformation and Early Modern Europe: A Guide to Research*, ed. David M. Whitford, 57–79. Kirksville, MO: Truman State University Press, 2008.

Black, Christopher. *Church, Religion, and Society in Early Modern Italy*. New York: Palgrave Macmillan, 2004.

– *The Italian Inquisition*. New Haven: Yale University Press, 2009.

– *Early Modern Italy: A Social History*. New York: Routledge, 2001.

Borromeo, Agostino. 'A proposito del *Directorium Inquisitorum* di Nicolas Eymerich e delle sue edizioni cinquecentesche.' *Critica Storica* 4 (1983): 499–547.

– 'Paul IV.' In *The Papacy: An Encyclopedia*, Vol. 2, gen. ed. Philippe Levillain, 1127–9. New York: Routledge, 2002.

– 'Carena, Cesare.' In *Dizionario storico dell'Inquisizione*, Vol. 1, ed. Adriano Prosperi with Vincenzo Lavenia and John Tedeschi, 272–3. Pisa: Scuola Normale Superiore Pisa, 2010.

– 'Eymeric, Nicolau.' In *Dizionario storico dell'Inquisizione*, Vol. 2, ed. Adriano Prosperi with Vincenzo Lavenia and John Tedeschi, 568–70. Pisa: Scuola Normale Superiore Pisa, 2010.

Bowman, Jeffrey A. 'Infamy and Proof in Medieval Spain.' In *Fama: The Politics of Talk and Reputation in Medieval Europe*, ed. Thelma Fenster and Daniel Lord Smail, 95–117. Ithaca, NY: Cornell University Press, 2003.

Bozza, Tommaso. *La riforma cattolica: Il Beneficio de Cristo*. Rome: Libreria Tombolini, 1972.

Brady, Thomas A., Jr. 'Confessionalization – The Career of a Concept.' In *Confessionalization in Europe, 1555–1700: Essays in Honor and Memory of Bodo Nischan*, ed. John M. Headley, Hans J. Hillerbrand, and Anthony J. Papalas. Burlington, VT: Ashgate, 2004.

Brambilla, Elena. *Alle origini del Sant'Uffizio: Penitenza, confessione e giustizia spirituale dal Medioevo al XVI secolo*. Bologna: Il Mulino, 2000.

– 'Il segreto e il sigillo: Denunce e comparizioni spontanee nei processi inquisitoriali.' In *I Tribunali della fede: Continuità e discontinuità dal medioevo all'età moderna; Bollettino della Società di Studi Valdesi*, ed. Susanna Peyronel Rambaldi, 111–61. Turin: Claudiana, 2007.

Brown, Peter. *Augustine of Hippo*. Berkeley and Los Angeles: University of California Press, 1967.

Brundage, James. *Medieval Canon Law*. New York: Longman, 1995.

Bryson, William Hamilton. *Dictionary of Sigla and Abbreviations to and in Law Books before 1607*. Charlottesville, VA: University of Virginia Press, 1975.

Callahan, Daniel. 'Ademar of Chabannes and the Bogomils.' In *Heresy and the Persecuting Society in the Middle Ages: Essays on the Work of R.I. Moore*, ed. Michael Frassetto, 31–41. Boston: Brill, 2006.

Cameron, Euan. 'The Possibilities and Limits of Conciliation: Philipp Melanchthon and Inter-Confessional Dialogue in the Sixteenth Century.' In *Conciliation and Confession: The Struggle for Unity in the Age of Reform*, ed. Howard P. Louthan and Randall C. Zachman, 77–81. Notre Dame: University of Notre Dame Press, 2004.

– *The Reformation of the Heretics: The Waldenses of the Alps, 1480–1580*. New York: Oxford University Press, 1984.

Canosa, Romano. *Storia dell'Inquisizione in Italia: Dalla metà del Cinquecento alla fine del Settecento*, Vol. 1, *Modena*. Rome: Sapere 2000, 1986.

– *Storia dell'Inquisizione in Italia: Dalla metà del Cinquecento alla fine del Settecento*, Vol. 5, *Napoli e Bologna; la procedura inquisitoriale*. Rome: Sapere 2000, 1990.

Cantimori, Delio. *Eretici italiani del Cinquecento: Ricerche storie*. 1937; Rpt. Florence: Sansoni, 1967.

– *Umanesimo e religione nel Rinascimento*. 2nd ed. Turin: Einaudi, 1975.

Caponetto, Salvatore. *Aonio Paleario e la Riforma protestante in Toscana*. Turin: Claudiana, 1979.

– 'Due opere di Melantone tradotta da Ludovico Castelvetro: *I Principii de la Theologia de Ippofiloda Terra Negra* e *Dell'autorità della Chiesa e degli scritti degli antichi*.' *Nuova Rivista Storica* 70 (1986): 253–74.

– *The Protestant Reformation in Sixteenth-Century Italy*, trans. Anne C. Tedeschi and John Tedeschi. Kirksville MO: Thomas Jefferson University Press, 1999.

Cavazza, Silvano. 'Pier Paolo Vergerio nei Grigioni e in Valtellina (1549–1553): Attività editoriale e polemica religiosa.' In *Riforma e società nei Grigioni: Valtellina e Valchiavenna tra '500 e '600*, ed. Alessandro Pastore, 33–62. Milan: Franco Agnelli, 1991.

Cavina, Marco, ed. *Tiberio Deciani (1509–1582): Alle origini del pensiero giuridico moderno; Atti del Convegno internazionale di studi storici e giuridici, Udine, 12–13 Aprile 2002*. Udine: Editrice Universitaria Udinese, 2004.

Cazenave, Annie. 'Aveu et contrition: Manuels des confesseurs et interrogatoires d'inquisition en Languedoc et in Catalogne (XIIIe–XIVe siècles).' In *La piété populaire au moyen âge; Actes du 99e Congrès National des Société Savantes, Besançon, 1974, Philologie et Histoire*, Vol. 1, 333–52. Paris: Bibliothèque Nationale, 1977.

Chabod, Federico. *Opere*, Vol. 3, *Lo Stato e la vita religiosa a Milano nell'epoca di Carlo V*. Turin: Einaudi, 1971.

Christian, William. *Local Religion in Sixteenth-Century Spain*. Princeton: Princeton University Press, 1981.

Cochrane, Eric W. 'Counter Reformation or Tridentine Reformation? Italy in the Age of Carlo Borromeo.' In *San Carlo Borromeo: Catholic Reform and Ecclesiastical Politics in the Second Half of the Sixteenth Century*, ed. John M. Headley and John B. Tomaro. Cranbury, NJ: Associated University Presses, 1988.

– *Italy 1530–1630*, ed. Julius Kirshner. New York: Longman, 1988.

Colish, Marcia. *Peter Lombard*, Vol. 2. New York: Brill, 1994.

Collett, Barry. *Italian Benedictine Scholars and the Reformation: The Congregation of Santa Giustina of Padua*. Oxford: Clarendon Press, 1985.

Crews, Daniel A. *Twilight of the Renaissance: The Life of Juan de Valdés*. Toronto: University of Toronto Press, 2008.

D'Andrea, David. *Civic Christianity in Renaissance Italy: The Hospital of Treviso, 1400–1530*. Rochester, NY: University of Rochester Press, 2007.

Dall'Olio, Guido. *Eretici e inquisitori nella Bologna del Cinquecento*. Bologna: Istituto per la storia di Bologna, 1999.

Davidson, Nicholas. 'The Inquisition in Venice and Its Documents: Some Problems of Method and Analysis.' In *L'Inquisizione romana in Italian nell'età moderna: Archivi, problemi di metodo e nuove richerche; Atti del seminario internazionale Trieste, 18–20 maggio 1988*, ed. Andrea Del Col and Giovanni Paolin, 117–31. Rome: Ministero per i beni culturali e ambientali/Ufficio centrale per i beni archivistici, 1991.

Davis, Natalie Zemon. *Fiction in the Archives: Pardon Tales and Their Tellers in Sixteenth-Century France*. Stanford, CA: Stanford University Press, 1987.

– 'The Sacred and the Body Social in Sixteenth-Century Lyon.' *Past and Present* 90 (February 1981): 40–70.

Dean, Trevor. *Crime and Justice in Late Medieval Italy*. New York: Cambridge University Press, 2007.

De Boer, Wietse. *The Conquest of the Soul: Confession, Discipline, and Public Order in Counter-Reformation Milan*. Leiden: Brill, 2001.

Del Col, Andrea. *L'Inquisizione in Italia: Dal XII al XXI secolo*. Milan: Oscar Mondadori, 2006.

– 'Della Casa, Giovanni.' In *Dizionario storico dell'Inquisizione*, Vol. 1, ed. Adriano Prosperi with Vincenzo Lavenia and John Tedeschi, 459–60. Pisa: Scuola Normale Superiore Pisa, 2010.

– 'Il controllo della stampa a Venezia e A. Brucioli.' *Critica Storia* 17 (1980): 457–510.

– 'Shifting Attitudes in the Social Environment toward Heretics: The Inquisition in the Friuli in the Sixteenth Century.' In *Ketzerverfolgung im 16. und frühen 17. Jahrhundert: Vorträge gehalten anlässlich eines Arbeitsgesprächs vom 1. bis 5. Oktober 1989 in der Herzog August Bibliothek Wolfenbüttel*, ed. Hans Rudolf Guggisberg, Silvana Seidel Menchi, and Bernd Moeller, 65–86. Wiesbaden: Harrassowitz, 1992.

– *L'Inquisizione nel Patriarcato e diocesi di Aquileia, 1557–59*. Trieste: Edizioni Università di Trieste; Centro studi storici Menocchio, 1998.

– 'Organizzazione, composizione e giurisdizione dei tribunali dell'Inquisizione romana rella repubblica di Venezia (1500–1550).' *Critica Storica* 25 (1988): 244–94.

– 'L'abiura trasformata in propaganda ereticale nel duomo di Udine (15 Aprile 1544).' *Metodi e ricerche* 2 (1981): 57–72.

– 'I rapporti tra i giudici di fede in Italia dal medioevo all'età contemporanea.' In *I Tribunali della fede: Continuità e discontinuità dal medioevo all'età moderna; Atti del XLV Convegno di studi sulla Riforma e sui movimenti religiosi in Italia, Torre Pellice, 3–4 settembre 2005*, ed. Susanna Peyronel Rambaldi, 83–110. Turin: Claudiana, 2007.

Delph, Ronald K. 'Polishing the Papal Image in the Counter-Reformation: The Case of Agostino Steuco.' *Sixteenth Century Journal* 23, no. 1 (Spring 1992): 35–47.

Del Re, Niccolò. 'Prospero Farinacci giureconsulto romano (1544–1618).' *Archivio della Società romana di Storia patria* 97 (1975): 135–200

Diehl, Peter. 'An Inquisitor in Manuscript and in Print: The *Tractatus super materia hereticorum* of Zanchino Ugolini.' In *The Book Unbound: Editing and Reading Medieval Manuscripts and Texts*, ed. Siân Echard and Stephen Partridge, 58–77. Toronto: University of Toronto Press, 2004.

– '*Ad abolendam* (X 5.7.9) and Imperial Legislation against Heresy.' *Bulletin of Medieval Canon Law* 19 (1989): 1–11.

Dillinberger, John. 'Introduction.' In *Martin Luther: Selections from His Writings*, i–xxxiii. New York: Doubleday, 1962.

Donadelli, C. 'Galeota, Mario.' In *Dizionario storico dell'Inquisizione*, Vol. 2, ed. Adriano Prosperi with Vincenzo Lavenia and John Tedeschi, 634–5. Pisa: Scuola Normale Superiore Pisa, 2010.

Dondaine, Antoine. 'Le manuel d'inquisiteur.' *Archivium Fratrum Praedicatorum* 17 (1947): 85–194.

Donnelly, John Patrick, SJ. 'The Social and Ethical Thought of Peter Martyr Vermigli.' In *Peter Martyr Vermigli and Italian Reform*, ed. Joseph C. McLelland, 107–20. Waterloo, ON: Wilfrid Laurier University Press, 1977.

Donovan, S. 'Alphonsus de Castro.' In *The Catholic Encyclopedia*, Vol. 3. New York: Robert Appleton Company, 1908. http://www.newadvent.org/cathen/03415a.htm

Duggan, Anne J. 'Conciliar Law 1123–1215: The Legislation of the Four Lateran Councils.' In *The History of Medieval Canon Law in the Classical Period, 1140–1234: From Gratian to the Decretals of Pope Gregory IX*, ed. Wilfried Hartmann and Kenneth Pennington, 318–66. Washington, DC: Catholic University Press of America, 2008.

Dunbain, Jean. *A Hound of God: Pierre de la Palud and the Fourteenth-Century Church*. New York: Clarendon Press, 1991.

Duvernoy, Jean, ed. and trans. *Le register d'Inquisition de Jacques Fournier (Évêque de Pamiers): 1318–1325*. Paris: Mouton Editeur, 1978.

Edwards, John. *Torquemada and the Inquisitors*. Stroud, UK: Tempus, 2005.

Eire, Carlos M.N. 'Calvin and Nicodemism: A Reappraisal.' *The Sixteenth Century Journal* 10, no. 1 (Spring 1979): 45–69.

– *War against the Idols: The Reformation of Worship from Erasmus to Calvin*. New York: Cambridge University Press, 1986.

Errera, Andrea. *'Processus in Causa Fidei': L'evoluzione dei manuali inquisitoriali nei secolo XVI–XVIII e il manuale inedito di un inquisitore perugino*. Bologna: Monduzzi, 2000.

– 'Manuali per inquisitori.' In *Dizionario storico dell' Inquisizione*, Vol. 2, 975–81.

Feci, S. 'Farinacci, Prospero.' In *Dizionario storico dell'Inquisizione*, Vol. 2, ed. Adriano Prosperi with Vincenzo Lavenia and John Tedeschi, 579. Pisa: Scuola Normale Superiore Pisa, 2010.

– 'Foscarari, Egidio.' In *Dizionario storico dell'Inquisizione*, Vol. 2, ed. Adriano Prosperi with Vincenzo Lavenia and John Tedeschi, 615. Pisa: Scuola Normale Superiore Pisa, 2010.

Fenlon, Dermot. *Heresy and Obedience in Tridentine Italy: Cardinal Pole and the Counter-Reformation*. Cambridge: Cambridge University Press, 1972.

Finlay, Robert. *Politics in Renaissance Venice*. New Brunswick, NJ: Rutgers University Press, 1980.

Firpo, Massimo, ed. *Il processo inquisitoriale del cardinale Giovanni Morone: Edizione critica*, 7 vols. Rome: Istituto storico italiano per l'età moderna, 1981–1985.

Firpo, Massimo, and Dario Marcatti, eds. *I processi inquisitoriali di Pietro Carnesecchi (1557–1567): Edizione critica*, 2 vols., vol. 2 in 3 parts. Vatican City: Archivio Segreto vaticano, 1998–2000.

– 'Juan de Valdés e l'evangelismo italiano: Appunti e problemi di una ricerca in corso.' In *Tra Alumbrados e 'spirituali': Studi su Juan de Valdés e il valdesianismo nella crisi religiosa del '500 italiano*, ed. Massimo Firpo. Florence: Olschki, 1990.

– 'Gli 'spirituali,' l'Accademia di Modena, e il formulario di fede del 1542: Controllo del dissenso religiose e nicodemismo.' *Rivista di storia e letteratura religiosa* 20 (1984): 40–111.

Fontaine, Michelle M. 'For the Good of the City: The Bishop and the Ruling Elite in Tridentine Modena.' *Sixteenth Century Journal* 28, no. 1 (Spring 1997): 29–43.

– 'Making Heresy Marginal in Modena.' In *Heresy, Culture, and Religion in Early Modern Italy: Contexts and Contestations*, ed. Ronald K. Delph, Michelle M. Fontaine, and John Jeffries Martin, 37–52. Kirksville, MO: Truman State University Press, 2006.

– 'The Compagnia de Santa Maria dei Battuti in Modena on the Eve of Catholic Reform.' In *Confraternities and Catholic Reform in Italy, France, and Spain*, ed. John Patrick Donnelly, SJ, and Michael W. Maher, SJ, 55–73. Kirksville, MO: Truman State University Press, 1999.

Fontana, Bartolomeo. 'Documenti Vaticani contro l'eresia luterana in Italia.' *Archivio della Società romana di storia patria* 15 (1892): 71–165; 365–474.

Fontana, P. 'Masini, Eliseo.' In *Dizionario storico dell'Inquisizione*, Vol. 2, ed. Adriano Prosperi with Vincenzo Lavenia and John Tedeschi, 1006–1007. Pisa: Scuola Normale Superiore Pisa, 2010.

Fragnito, Gigliola, ed. *Church, Censorship, and Culture in Early Modern Italy*. New York: Cambridge University Press, 2001.

– *La Bibbia al rogo: La censura ecclesiastica e i volgarizzamenti della Scrittura (1471–1605)*. Bologna: Il Mulino, 1997.

Fraher, Richard M. 'Preventing Crime in the High Middle Ages: The Medieval Lawyers' Search for Deterrence.' In *Popes, Teachers, and Canon Law in the Middle Ages*, ed. James Ross Sweeney and Stanley Chodorow, 212–33. Ithaca, NY: Cornell University Press, 1989.

– 'IV Lateran's Revolution in Criminal Procedure: The Birth of the *Inquisitio*, the End of Ordeals, and Innocent III's Vision of Ecclesiastical Politics.' In *Studia in Honorem Eminentissimi Cardinalis Alphonsi M. Stickler*, ed. Rosalio Iosepho Card. Castillo Lara, 97–111. Rome: LAS, 1992.

Frend, W.H.C. *The Rise of Christianity*. Philadelphia: Fortress Press, 1984.

Frymire, John. '*Demonstrationes catholicae*: Defining Communities through Counter-Reformation Rituals.' In *Defining Community in Early Modern Europe*, ed. Michael J. Halvorson and Karen E. Spierling, 163–82. Burlington, VT: Ashgate, 2008.

Garcia y Garcia, A. 'The Fourth Lateran Council and the Canonists.' In *The History of Medieval Canon Law in the Classical Period, 1140–1234: From Gratian to the Decretals of Pope Gregory IX*, ed. Wilfried Hartmann and Kenneth Pennington, 367–78. Washington, DC: Catholic University Press of America, 2008.

Gentilcore, David. *From Bishop to Witch: The System of the Sacred in Early Modern Terra d'Otranto*. Manchester: Manchester University Press, 1992.

Ginzburg, Carlo. 'Due note sul profetismo cinquecentesco.' *Rivista Storica Italiana* (1966): 184–227.

– *Il nicodemismo: Simulazione e dissimulazione religiosa nell'Europa del '500*. Turin: Giulio Einaudi Editore, 1970.

– 'The Inquisitor as Anthropologist.' In *Clues, Myths, and the Historical Method*, ed. Carlo Ginzburg, 156–64. Baltimore: Johns Hopkins University Press, 1989.

Ginzburg, Carlo, and Adriano Prosperi. *Giochi di pazienza: Un seminario sul 'Beneficio di Cristo.'* Turin: Einaudi Editore, 1975.

Given, James B. *Inquisition in Medieval Society: Power, Discipline and Resistance in Languedoc*. Ithaca: Cornell University Press, 1997.

Gleason, Elisabeth. 'Sixteenth-Century Italian Interpretations of Luther.' *Archiv für Reformationsgeschichte* 60 (1969): 160–73.

– *Gasparo Contarini: Venice, Rome, and Reform*. Berkeley and Los Angeles: University of California Press, 1993.

– *Reform Thought in Sixteenth-Century Italy*. Chico, CA: Scholars Press, 1981.

Gordon, Bruce. '"This Worthy Witness of Christ": Protestant Uses of Savonarola in the Sixteenth Century.' In *Protestant History and Identity in Sixteenth-Century Europe*, Vol. 1, *The Medieval Inheritance*, ed. Bruce Gordon, 93–107. Aldershot, UK: Scolar Press, 1996.

– *The Swiss Reformation*. New York: Manchester University Press, 2002.

Gregory, Brad. *Salvation at Stake: Christian Martyrdom in Early Modern Europe*. Cambridge: Harvard University Press, 1999.

Grendler, Paul. *The Roman Inquisition and the Venetian Press, 1540–1605*. Princeton: Princeton University Press, 1978.

Hamilton, Bernard. 'Bogomil Influences on Western Heresy.' In *Heresy and the Persecuting Society in the Middle Ages: Essays on the Work of R.I. Moore*, ed. Michael Frassetto, 93–114. Boston: Brill, 2006.

Hanlon, Gregory. *Early Modern Italy, 1500–1800*. New York: St. Martin's Press, 2000.

Helmholz, R.H. *The Spirit of Classical Canon Law*. Athens, GA: University of Georgia Press, 1996.

Heming, Carol Piper. *Protestants and the Cult of the Saints in German-Speaking Europe*. Kirksville, MO: Truman State University Press, 2003.

Henderson, John. *Piety and Charity in Late Medieval Florence*. Oxford: Clarendon Press, 1994.

Hoeflich, Michael, and Jasonne M. Grabher. 'The Establishment of Normative Legal Texts: The Beginnings of the *Ius commune*.' In *The History of Medieval Canon Law in the Classical Period, 1140–1234: From Gratian to the Decretals of Pope Gregory IX*, ed. Wilfried Hartmann Kenneth Pennington, 1–21. Washington DC: Catholic University Press of America, 2008.

Holder, Beat..'Protestant Self-Perception and the Problem of *Scandalum*: A Sketch.' In *Protestant History and Identity in Sixteenth-Century Europe*, Vol. 1, *The Medieval Inheritance*, ed. Bruce Gordon, 23–30. Aldershot UK: Scolar Press, 1996.

Holt, Mack P. *The French Wars of Religion, 1562–1629*. New York: Cambridge University Press, 1995.

Homza, Lu Ann. *Religious Authority in Sixteenth Century Spain*. Baltimore: Johns Hopkins University Press, 2000.

Hudon, William. 'Religion and Society in Early Modern Italy – Old Questions, New Insights.' *American Historical Review* 101, no. 3 (June 1996): 783–804.

– *Marcello Cervini and Ecclesiastical Government in Tridentine Italy*. De Kalb: Northern Illinois University Press, 1992.

– 'Inquisition Trial of Marina González, 1494.' In *The Spanish Inquisition, 1478–1614: An Anthology of Sources*, ed. and trans. Lu Ann Homza, 27–49. Indianapolis, IN: Hackett Publishing Company, Inc., 2006.

James, Frank A. III, ed. 'Introduction.' In *Peter Martyr Vermigli and the European Reformations: Semper Reformanda*, xii–xxv. Boston: Brill, 2004.

Jedin, Hubert. *A History of the Council of Trent*, 2 vols., trans. Dom Ernest Graf. London: Nelson, 1961.

Jung, Eva Maria. 'On the Nature of Evangelism in Sixteenth-Century Italy.' *Journal of the History of Ideas* 14 (1953): 511–27.

Kamen, Henry. *The Spanish Inquisition: An Historical Revision*. Rev. ed. New Haven: Yale University Press, 1998.

Karant-Nunn, Susan C. *The Reformation of Ritual: An Interpretation of Early Modern Germany*. London: Routledge, 1997.

Kertzer, David. *Ritual, Politics and Power*. New Haven: Yale University Press, 1988.

Kuehn, Thomas. '*Fama* as Legal Status in Renaissance Florence.' In *Fama: The Politics of Talk and Reputation in Medieval Europe*, ed. Thelma Fenster and Daniel Lord Smail, 27–48. Ithaca, NY: Cornell University Press, 2003.

Kuntz, Marion Leathers. 'Voices from a Venetian Prison in the Cinquecento: Francesco Spinola and Dionisio Gallo.' *Studi veneziani*, n.s. 27 (1994): 79–126.

– *The Anointment of Dionisio: Prophecy and Politics in Renaissance Italy*. University Park, PA: Pennsylvania State University Press, 2001.

Lambert, Malcolm. *The Cathars*. Malden, MA: Blackwell Publishers, 1998.

– *Medieval Heresy: Popular Movements from the Gregorian Reform to the Reformation*. 3rd ed. New York: Blackwell, 2002.

Landau, Peter. 'Gratian and the *Decretum Gratiani*.' In *The History of Medieval Canon Law in the Classical Period, 1140–1234: From Gratian to the Decretals of Pope Gregory IX*, ed. Wilfried Hartmann and Kenneth Pennington, 22–54. Washington DC: Catholic University Press of America, 2008.

Landon, Edward H., ed. *A Manual of the Councils of the Holy Church*. Edinburgh: John Grant, 1909.

Langbein, John H. *Torture and the Law of Proof: Europe and England in the Ancien Régime*. Rev. ed. Chicago: University of Chicago Press, 2006.

Lavenia, Vincenzo. *L'Infamia e il perdono: Tributi, pene e confessione nella teologia morale della prima età moderna*. Bologna: Il Mulino, 2004.

– 'Peña, Francisco,' In *Dizionario storico dell'Inquisizione*. Vol. 3, ed. Adriano Prosperi with Vincenzo Lavenia and John Tedeschi, 1186–9. Pisa: Scuola Normale Superiore Pisa, 2010.

Lea, Henry Charles. *A History of the Inquisition in Spain*, Vols. 2 and 3. New York: Macmillan, 1922.

– *Materials toward a History of Witchcraft*, Vol. 2, ed. Arthur C. Howl. Philadelphia: University of Pennsylvania Press, 1939.

– *The Inquisition of the Middle Ages*, Vol. 1. New York: Harper Brothers, 1887.

Leadbetter, Bill. 'From Constantine to Theodosius (and Beyond).' In *The Early Christian World*, Vol. 1, ed. Philip F. Esler, 258–94. New York: Routledge, 2000.

Lemaitre, Nicole. 'Pius V.' In *The Papacy: An Encyclopedia*, Vol. 2, gen. ed. Philippe Levillain, 1176–78. New York: Routledge, 2002.

Longo, C. 'Ivonetus.' In *Dictionnaire d'histoire et de géographie ecclésiastique*, Vol. 26, ed. R. Aubert, 473. Paris: Letouzey et Ané, 1997.

Marchetti, Valerio. *Gruppi ereticali senesi del Cinquecento*. Florence: La nuova italia, 1975.

– 'Campeggi, Camillo.' In *Dizionario biografico degli Italiani*, Vol. 17, 439–40. Rome: Istituto della Enciclopedia Italiana, 1974.

Martin, John Jeffries. *Myths of Renaissance Individualism*. New York: Palgrave Macmillan, 2004.

– *Venice's Hidden Enemies: Italian Heretics in a Renaissance City*. Berkeley and Los Angeles: University of California Press, 1993.

Martines, Lauro. *Fire in the City: Savonarola and the Struggle for Renaissance Florence*. New York: Oxford University Press, 2006.

Matheson, Peter. *Cardinal Contarini at Regensburg*. Oxford: Clarendon Press, 1972.

– 'Martyrdom or Mission? A Protestant Debate.' *Archiv für Reformationsgeschichte* Vol. 80 (1989): 154–72.

– 'Martin Bucer and the Old Church.' In *Martin Bucer: Reforming Church and Community*, ed. D.F. Wright, 5–16. New York: Cambridge University Press, 1994.

Mayali, Laurent. 'The Concept of Discretionary Punishment in Medieval Jurisprudence.' In *Studia in honorem eminentissimi cardinalis Alphonsi M. Stickler*, ed. Rosalio José Castillo Lara, 299–315. Rome: LAS, 1992.

Mayer, Thomas F. *Reginald Pole: Prince and Prophet*. New York: Cambridge University Press, 2000.

Mazzacane, A. 'Farinacci, Prospero.' In *Dizionario Biografico degli Italiani*, Vol. 45, 1–5. Rome: Istituto della Enciclopedia Italiana, 1995.

McGuire, Brian Patrick. 'Introduction.' In *Jean Gerson: Early Works*, ed. McGuire, 1–74. New York: Paulist Press, 1998.

McNair, Peter. *Peter Martyr in Italy: An Anatomy of an Apostasy*. Oxford: Clarendon Press, 1967.

Miłosz, Czesław. *The History of Polish Literature*. 2nd ed. Berkeley and Los Angeles: University of California Press, 1983.

Minnich, Nelson H. 'The Last Two Councils of the Catholic Reformation: The Influence of Lateran V on Trent.' In *Early Modern Catholicism: Essays in Honour of John W. O'Malley S.J.*, ed. Kathleen M. Comerford and Hilmar M. Pabel, 3–25. Toronto: University of Toronto Press, 2001.

Muir, Edward. *Civic Ritual in Renaissance Venice*. Princeton, NJ: Princeton University Press, 1981.

– *Ritual in Early Modern Europe*. New York: Cambridge University Press, 1997.

– 'The Virgin on the Street Corner: The Place of the Sacred in Italian Cities.' In *Religion and Culture in the Renaissance and Reformation*, ed.

Steven Ozment, 25–40. Kirksville, MO: Sixteenth Century Journal Publishers, 1989.

Mullet, Michael. *The Counter-Reformation and Catholic Reformation in Early Modern Europe*. London: Routledge, 1999.

Murphy, Paul V. *Ruling Peacefully: Cardinal Ercole Gonzaga and Patrician Reform in Sixteenth-Century Italy*. Washington, DC: Catholic University of America Press, 2007.

Nalle, Sara T. *God in La Mancha: Religious Reform and the People of Cuenca, 1500–1650*. Baltimore Johns Hopkins University Press, 1992.

Naz, R. 'Bohier, Nicolas (ou Boyer).' In *Dictionnaire de droit canonique*, Vol. 2, ed. R. Naz, 930. Paris: Librairie Letouzey et Ané, 1937.

Nieto, José. *Juan de Valdés and the Origins of the Spanish and Italian Reformation*. Geneva: Libraire Droz, 1970.

Nischan, Bodo. 'Becoming Protestants: Lutheran Altars or Reformed Communion Tables?' In *Worship in Medieval and Early Modern Europe: Change and Continuity in Religious Practice*, ed. Karin Maag and John D. Witvliet, 84–111. Notre Dame, IN: University of Notre Dame Press, 2004.

– 'Ritual and Protestant Identity in Late Reformation Germany.' In *Protestant History and Identity in Sixteenth-Century Europe*, Vol. 2, *The Later Reformation*, ed. Bruce Gordon, 142–58. Aldershot, UK: Scolar Press, 1996.

Noll, Mark A., ed. 'The Augsburg Confession (1530).' In *Confessions and Catechisms of the Reformation*, 84–121. Vancouver: Regent College Publishing.

Nussdorfer, Laurie. 'Lost Faith: A Roman Prosecutor Reflects on Notaries' Crimes.' In *Beyond Florence: The Contours of Medieval and Early Modern Italy*, ed. Paula Findlen, Michelle M. Fontaine, and Duane J. Osheim, 101–14. Stanford: Stanford University Press, 2003.

Oberman, Heiko. *Luther: Man between God and the Devil*, trans. Eileen Walliser-Schwarzbart. New Haven: Yale University Press, 2006.

Olivieri, Achille. 'Alessandro Trissino e il movimento calvanista vicentino del Cinquecento.' *Rivista di Storia della Chiesa in Italia* 21 (Jan.–June, 1967): 54–117.

– *Riforma ed ereisa a Vicenza nel Cinquecento*. Rome: Herder Editrice, 1992.

O'Malley, John. *Trent and All That: Renaming Catholicism in the Early Modern Era*. Cambridge, MA: Harvard University Press, 2000.

Overell, M.A. 'Vergerio's Anti-Nicodemite Propaganda and England, 1547–1558.' *Journal of Ecclesiastical History* 51, no. 2 (April 2000): 296–318.

Pallotti, L. 'Marsili, Ippolito.' In *Dizionario biografico degli italiani*, Vol. 70, 764–7. Rome: Istituto della Enciclopedia Italiana, 2008

Paolin, Giovanna. 'I contadini anabattisti di Cinto.' *Il Noncello* 50 (1980): 91–124.

Pastore, S. 'Simancas, Diego de.' In *Dizionario storico dell'Inquisizione*, Vol. 3, ed. Adriano Prosperi with Vincenzo Lavenia and John Tedeschi, 1430–31. Pisa: Scuola Normale Superiore Pisa, 2010.

Peters, Edward M. 'Editing Inquisitors' Manuals in the Sixteenth Century: Francisco Peña and the *Directorum Inquisitorum* of Nicolas Eymeric.' *The Library Chronicle* 40 (1979): 95–107.

– *Inquisition*. New York: The Free Press, 1988.

– *Torture*. New York: Basil Blackwell, 1985.

Pettegree, Andrew. 'Religion and the Revolt.' In *The Origins and Development of the Dutch Revolt*, ed. Graham Darby, 67–83. New York: Routledge, 2001.

Peyronel Rambaldi, Susanna. *Dai Paesi Bassi all'Italia: 'Il Sommario della Sacra Scrittura': Un libro proibito nella società italiana del Cinquecento*. Florence: L.S. Olschki, 1997.

– *Speranze e crisi nel Cinquecento modenese: Tensioni religiose e vita cittadina in tempi di Giovanni Morone*. Milan: Franco Angeli, 1979.

Pierce, Robert A. *Pier Paolo Vergerio: The Propagandist*. Rome: Edizioni di Storia e Letteratura, 2003.

Po-Chia Hsia, Ronnie. *Social Discipline in the Reformation: Central Europe 1550–1750*. New York: Routledge, 1989.

Prelowski, Ruth, trans. and introduction. 'The "Beneficio di Cristo."' In *Reformation Studies in Honor of Laelius Socinus*, ed. John Tedeschi, 21–102. Florence: Felice le Monnier, 1965.

Prosperi, Adriano. *L'eresia del Libro Grande: Storia di Giorgio Siculo e della sua setta*. Milan: Feltrinelli, 2002.

– *Tra evangelismo e Controriforma: G.M. Giberti, 1495–1543*. Rome: Edizioni di storia e letteratura, 1969.

– *Tribunali della coscienza: Inquisitori, confessori, missionari*. Turin: Einaudi, 1996.

– 'Campeggi, Camillo.' In *Dizionario storico dell'Inquisizione*. Vol. 1, ed. Adriano Prosperi with Vincenzo Lavenia and John Tedeschi, 252–3. Pisa: Scuola Normale Superiore Pisa, 2010.

– *'Beneficio di Cristo.'* In *Dizionario storico dell'Inquisizione*, Vol. 1, ed. Adriano Prosperi with Vincenzo Lavenia and John Tedeschi, 178–9. Pisa: Scuola Normale Superiore Pisa, 2010.

– 'L'Arsenale degli inquisitori: Saggio introduttivo al catalogo della Mostra della Biblioteca Casanatense.' In *Inquisizione e Indice nei secoli XVI–XVIII, Controversie ieologiche dalle raccolie casanatensi*, ed. Angela Adriana Cavarra, 6–12. Viegvano: Diakronia, 1998.

Pullan, Brian. *Rich and Poor in Renaissance Venice: The Social Institutions of a Catholic State, to 1620*. Cambridge, MA: Harvard University Press, 1971.

Puppi, Lionello. *Un trono di fuoco: Arte e martirio di un pittore eretico del Cinquecento*. Rome: Donzelli Editore, 1995.

Radding, Charles M., and Francis Newton. *Theology, Rhetoric, and Politics in the Eucharistic Controversy, 1078–79*. New York: Columbia University Press, 2003.

Ragagli, S. 'Locati, Umberto.' In *Dizionario storico dell'Inquisizione*, Vol. 2, ed. Adriano Prosperi with Vincenzo Lavenia and John Tedeschi, 929–30. Pisa: Scuola Normale Superiore Pisa, 2010.

– 'Simoni, Simone.' In *Dizionario storico dell'Inquisizione*, Vol. 3, ed. Adriano Prosperi with Vincenzo Lavenia and John Tedeschi, 1432–3. Pisa: Scuola Normale Superiore Pisa, 2010.

Reinhard, Wolfgang. 'Reformation, Counter-Reformation, and the Early Modern State: A Reassessment.' *The Catholic Historical Review* 72 (1989): 383–404.

Robin, Diana. *Publishing Women: Salons, Presses, and the Counter-Reformation in Sixteenth-Century Italy*. Chicago: University of Chicago Press, 2007.

Romano, Dennis. *Housecraft and Statecraft: Domestic Service in Renaissance Venice, 1400–1600*. Baltimore: Johns Hopkins University Press, 1996.

– 'The Regulation of Domestic Service in Renaissance Venice.' *The Sixteenth Century Journal* 22, no. 4 (1991): 661–77.

Romeo, Giovanni. *Ricerche su confessione dei peccati e Inquisizione nell'Italia del Cinquecento*. Naples: Città del sole, 1997.

Rosenthal, Margaret F. *The Honest Courtesan: Veronica Franco, Citizen and Writer in Sixteenth-Century Venice*. Chicago: University of Chicago Press, 1992.

Rößner, Maria Barbara. *Konrad Braun (ca. 1495–1563) – ein katholischer Jurist, Politiker, Kontroverstheologe und Kirchenreformer im konfessionellen Zeitalter*. Munich: Aschendorff, 1991.

Rotondò, Antonio. 'Tommaso Bavellino.' *Dizionario biografico degli italiani*, Vol. 7. Rome: Istituto della Enciclopedia Italiana, 1965.

– 'Per la storia dell'eresia a Bologna nel secolo XVI.' *Rinascimento*, 2, no. 2 (1962): 104–54.

Rozzo, Ugo. 'Le 'prediche' veneziane di Giulio da Milano.' *Bolletino della Società di Studi Valdesi* 152 (1983): 3–30.

Rozzo, Ugo, and Silvana Seidel Menchi. 'The Book and the Reformation in Italy,' trans. Karin Maag. In *The Reformation and the Book*, ed. Jean-François Gilmont and Karin Maag, 319–67. Brookfield, VT: Ashgate, 1998.

Russell, Camilla. *Giulia Gonzaga and the Religious Controversies of the Sixteenth Century*. Turnhout: Brepols. 2006.

Russell, Frederick J. 'Persuading the Donatists: Augustine's Coercion by Words.' In *The Limits of Ancient Christianity: Essays on Late Antique Thought and Culture in Honor of R.A. Markus*, ed. William E. Kingshirn and Mark Vessey, 115–30. Ann Arbor: University of Michigan Press, 1999.

Sabean, David. *The Power in the Blood: Popular Culture and Village Discourse in Early Modern Germany*. New York: Cambridge University Press, 1984.

Schulze, Manfred. 'Martin Luther and the Church Fathers.' In *The Reception of the Church Fathers in the West*, Vol. 2, ed. Irena Backus, 573–626. New York: Brill, 1997.

Schutte, Anne Jacobson. 'The *Lettere Volgari* and the Crisis of Evangelism in Italy.' *Renaissance Quarterly* 28 (1975): 639–88.

– 'Periodization of Sixteenth-Century Italian Religious History: The Post-Cantimori Paradigm Shift.' *Journal of Modern History* 61 (1989): 269–84.

– *Pier Paolo Vergerio: The Making of an Italian Reformer*. Geneva: Libraire Droz, 1977.

Scribner, Robert. *Popular Culture and Popular Movements in Reformation Germany*. London: Hambeldon Press, 1987.

Seidel Menchi, Silvana. *Erasmo in Italia, 1520–1580*. Turin: Bollati Boringhieri, 1987.

– 'Inquisizione come repressione o inquisizione come mediazione? Una proposta di periodizzazione.' In *Annuario dell'Istituto storico italiano per l'età moderna e contemporanea* 35–36 (1983–4): 53–77.

– 'The Inquisitor as Mediator.' In *Heresy, Culture, and Religion in Early Modern Italy: Contexts and Contestations*, ed. Ronald K. Delph, Michelle M. Fontaine, and John Jeffries Martin, 173–92. Kirksville, MO: Truman State University Press, 2006.

– 'Le traduzione di Lutero nella prima metà del Cinquecento.' *Rinascimento*, ser. II, 17 (1977): 31–109.

– 'Italy,' trans. Anne Jacobsen Schutte. In *The Reformation in National Context*, ed. Bob Scribner, Roy Porter, and Mikuláš Teich, 181–201. New York: Cambridge University Press, 1994.

– 'Marino da Venezia.' In *Dizionario storico dell'Inquisizione*, Vol. 2, ed. Adriano Prosperi with Vincenzo Lavenia and John Tedeschi, 987. Pisa: Scuola Normale Superiore Pisa, 2010.

Siegel, Arthur. 'Italian Society and the Origins of Eleventh-Century Western Heresy.' In *Heresy and the Persecuting Society in the Middle Ages: Essays on the Work of R.I Moore*, ed. Michael Frassetto, 43–72. Boston: Brill, 2006.

Simoncelli, Paolo. 'Inquisizione Romana e Riforma in Italia.' *Rivista Storica Italiana* 100 (1988): 1–125.

Snyder, Susan Taylor. 'Cathars, Confraternities, and Civic Religion: The Blurry Border between Heresy and Orthodoxy.' In *Heresy and the Persecuting Society in the Middle Ages: Essays on the Work of R.I. Moore*, ed. Michael Frassetto, 241–51. Boston: Brill, 2006.

Stella, Aldo. 'La lettera del cardinale Contarini sulla predestinazione.' *Rivista storia della chiesa in Italia* 15 (1961): 411–41.

Stephens, W. P. *Zwingli: An Introduction to His Thought.* Oxford: Clarendon Press, 1992.

Taberner, F. Valls, ed. 'El diplomatari de San Ramón de Penyafort.' In *Analecta sacra Tarraconensia: Revista de ciencias histórico-eclesiásticas* 5 (1929): 249–304.

Tanner, Norman P., SJ, ed. *Decrees of the Ecumenical Councils,* Vol. 1, *Nicaea I to Lateran V.* Washington, DC: Georgetown University Press, 1990.

Taplin, Mark. *The Italian Reformers and the Zurich Church, c. 1540–1620.* Burlington, VT: Ashgate. 2003.

Tavuzzi, Michael. *Prierias: The Life and Works of Silvestro Mazzolini da Prierio, 1456–1527.* Durham, NC: Duke University Press, 1997.

– *Renaissance Inquisitors: Dominican Inquisitors and Inquisitorial Districts in Northern Italy, 1474–1527.* Boston: Brill, 2007.

Tedeschi, John. 'Florentine Documents for a History of the "Index of Prohibited Books."' In *Renaissance Studies in Honor of Hans Baron,* ed. Anthony Molho and John Tedeschi, 577–605. Florence: C.G. Sansoni, 1971.

– 'Notes toward a Genealogy of the Sozzini Family.' *Reformation Studies in Honor of Laelius Socinus,* ed. John Tedeschi, 275–311. Florence: Le Monnier, 1965.

– 'The Organization and Procedures of the Roman Inquisition: A Sketch.' In *The Prosecution of Heresy: Collected Studies on the Inquisition in Early Modern Italy,* ed. John Tedeschi, 127–203. Binghamton, NY: Medieval and Renaissance Texts and Studies, 1991.

– and William Monter. 'Towards a Statistical Profile of the Italian Inquisitions, Sixteenth to Eighteenth Centuries.' In *The Prosecution of Heresy: Collected Studies on the Inquisition in Early Modern Italy,* ed. John Tedeschi, 89–126. Binghamton, NY: Medieval and Renaissance Texts and Studies, 1991.

– 'Preliminary Observations on Writing a History of the Roman Inquisition.' In *The Prosecution of Heresy: Collected Studies on the Inquisition in Early Modern Italy,* ed. John Tedeschi, 3–29. Binghamton, NY: Medieval and Renaissance Texts and Studies, 1991.

– 'Inquisitorial Sources and Their Uses.' In *The Prosecution of Heresy: Collected Studies on the Inquisition in Early Modern Italy,* ed. John Tedeschi, 47–88. Binghamton, NY: Medieval and Renaissance Texts and Studies, 1991.

– 'The Status of the Defendant before the Roman Inquisition.' In *Ketzerverfolgung im 16. und frühen 17. Jahrhundert,* ed. Hans Rudolf Guggisberg, Sivlana Seidel Menchi, and Bernd Moeller, 125–46. Wiesbaden: Otto Harrassowitz, 1992.

– 'Rojas, Juan de.' In *Dizionario storico dell'Inquisizione,* Vol. 3, ed. Adriano Prosperi with Vincenzo Lavenia and John Tedeschi, 1337. Pisa: Scuola Normale Superiore Pisa, 2010.

Tentler, Thomas N. *Sin and Confession on the Eve of the Reformation.* Princeton NJ: Princeton University Press, 1977.

Terpstra, Nicholas. *Lay Confraternities and Civic Religion in Renaissance Bologna.* Cambridge: Cambridge University Press, 1995.

Tracy, James D. *Erasmus of the Low Countries.* Berkeley and Los Angeles: University of California Press, 1996.

– *Europe's Reformations, 1450–1650: Doctrine, Politics, and Community.* 2nd ed. New York: Rowman and Littlefield, 2006.

Trenti, Giuseppe. *I processi del tribunale dell'Inquisizione di Modena: Inventario generale analitico, 1489–1874.* Modena: Aedes Muratoriana, 2003.

Trexler, Richard. *Public Life in Renaissance Florence.* New York: Academic Press, 1980.

– 'Florentine Religious Experience: The Sacred Image.' *Studies in the Renaissance* 19 (1972): 7–41.

Utz Tremp, K. 'Valdo e valdeismo medievale.' In *Dizionairio storico dell'Inquisizione,* Vol. 3, ed. Adriano Prosperi with Vincenzo Lavenia and John Tedeschi, 1634–36. Pisa: Scuola Normale Superiore Pisa, 2010.

Van Oort, Johannes. 'John Calvin and the Church Fathers.' In *The Reception of the Church Fathers in the West,* Vol. 2, ed. Irena Backus, 661–700. New York: Brill, 1997.

Wakefield, Walter A., and Austin P. Evans, eds. *Heresies of the High Middle Ages.* New York: Columbia University Press, 1969.

Wandel, Lee Palmer. *Voracious Idols and Violent Hands: Iconoclasm and Reformation in Zurich, Strasbourg, and Basel.* New York: Cambridge University Press, 1995.

Weinstein, Donald. *Savonarola and Florence: Prophecy and Patriotism in the Renaissance.* Princeton: Princeton University Press, 1970.

Williams, George Hunston. 'The Two Social Strands in Italian Anabaptism, ca. 1526–ca. 1565.' In *The Social History of the Reformation,* ed. Lawrence P. Buck and Jonathan W. Zophy, 156–207. Columbus: Ohio State University Press, 1972.

– *The Radical Reformation.* Philadelphia: Westminster Press, 1962.

Wood, Christopher S. 'In Defense of Images: Two Local Rejoinders to the Zwinglian Iconoclasm.' *Sixteenth Century Journal* 19, no. 1 (Spring 1998): 25–44.

Zeldes, Nadia. *'The Former Jews of this Kingdom': Sicilian Converts after the Expulsion, 1492–1516.* Boston: Brill, 2003.

Index